The Oxford Dictionary of

Foreign Words and Phrases

Andrew Delahunty is a freelance lexicographer who has authored and contributed to a wide range of dictionaries and reference works, including *The Oxford Dictionary of Allusions* and *Goldenballs and the Iron Lady: A Little Book of Nicknames*.

Oxford Paperback Reference

The most authoritative and up-to-date reference books for both students and the general reader.

ABC of Music
Accounting
Allusions
Animal Behaviour
Archaeology
Architecture and Landscape Architecture
Art and Artists
Art Terms
Arthurian Literature and Legend
Astronomy
Battles
Better Wordpower
Bible
Biology
British History
British Place-Names
Buddhism
Business and Management
Card Games
Century of New Words
Chemistry
Christian Art
Christian Church
Classical Literature
Classical Myth and Religion
Classical World
Computing
Contemporary World History
Countries of the World
Dance
Earth Sciences
Ecology
Economics
Education
Encyclopedia
Engineering*
English Etymology
English Folklore
English Grammar
English Language
English Literature
English Surnames
Environment and Conservation
Euphemisms
Everyday Grammar
Family and Local History
Finance and Banking
First Names
Food and Nutrition
Foreign Words and Phrases
Geography
Humorous Quotations

Idioms
Irish History
Islam
Kings and Queens of Britain
Law
Law Enforcement
Linguistics
Literary Terms
London Place-Names
Mathematics
Medical
Medicinal Drugs
Modern Design
Modern Quotations
Modern Slang
Music
Musical Terms
Musical Works
Nicknames
Nursing
Philosophy
Physics
Plant Sciences
Plays
Pocket Fowler's Modern English Usage
Political Quotations
Politics
Popes
Proverbs
Psychology
Quotations
Quotations by Subject
Rhymes
Rhyming Slang
Saints
Science
Scientific Quotations
Scottish History
Shakespeare
Ships and the Sea
Slang
Sociology
Space Exploration
Statistics
Superstitions
Synonyms and Antonyms
Weather
Word Histories
World History
World Mythology
World Religions
Zoology

forthcoming

The Oxford Dictionary of

Foreign Words and Phrases

SECOND EDITION

Edited by ANDREW DELAHUNTY
First edition by JENNIFER SPEAKE

UNIVERSITY PRESS

OXFORD

UNIVERSITY PRESS

Great Clarendon Street, Oxford OX2 6DP

Oxford University Press is a department of the University of Oxford.
It furthers the University's objective of excellence in research,
scholarship, and education by publishing worldwide in

Oxford New York

Auckland Cape Town Dar es Salaam Hong Kong Karachi
Kuala Lumpur Madrid Melbourne Mexico City Nairobi
New Delhi Shanghai Taipei Toronto

With offices in

Argentina Austria Brazil Chile Czech Republic France Greece
Guatemala Hungary Italy Japan Poland Portugal
Singapore South Korea Switzerland Thailand Turkey Ukraine Vietnam

Oxford is a registered trade mark of Oxford University Press
in the UK and in certain other countries

Published in the United States
by Oxford University Press Inc., New York

First published 1992
First issued as an Oxford University Press paperback 1993
Reissued with new covers 1996
Reissued with new covers and new material 2005
This second edition published 2008
Second edition issued as an Oxford University Press paperback 2010

British Library Cataloguing in Publication Data

Data available

Library of Congress Cataloging in Publication Data

Data available

Typeset by SPI Publisher Services, Pondicherry, India
Printed in Great Britain
on acid-free paper by
Clays Ltd., St Ives plc

ISBN 978-0-19-954368-7

1 3 5 7 9 10 8 6 4 2

Contents

Preface to the Second Edition   vii

Preface to the First Edition   ix

Pronunciation Guide   xiii

Oxford Dictionary of Foreign Words and Phrases   1

Special features
  French   136
  German   142
  Hindi and Urdu   157
  Islam   170
  Italian   171
  Japanese   174
  Latin   194
  Pseudo-foreign words   279
  Spanish   325
  Sport   327
  Winds   375
  Yiddish   379

Appendix   383

Preface

to the Second Edition

E nglish has been described by leading language expert David Crystal as 'a vacuum cleaner... It sucks words in from any language it makes contact with.' And quite a large vacuum-cleaner—English has sucked in words from over 350 languages around the world—working at an ever faster rate.

Of course, words are subject to the people who use them and, once in circulation, expressions from other languages are assimilated into English at different speeds. As an example let us take words from French, a very rich source of imports into English, most notably after the Norman Conquest and at the time of the French Enlightenment. At one end of the scale we might have *affaire de cœur* and *esprit de corps*, still printed in italics to indicate their foreign origin, or *soi-disant* and *au fond*, retaining distinct features of the original pronunciation; at the other, *cafe* and *facade*, which are losing their accents in common written usage, and the fully anglicized *bizarre* and *brunette*.

From Bonbon to Cha-cha, a revised edition of the *Oxford Dictionary of Foreign Words and Phrases* first published in 1997, aims to take account of the increasing globalization of the English language over the last ten years. Certain terms from the first edition, considered fully naturalized, have been omitted to make room for many of the new linguistic migrants which have filled important gaps and enriched our speaking and writing. Accordingly we welcome, among others, *issei* and *reiki, doosra* and *jalfrezi, bruschetta* and *macchiato, jilbab* and *niqab, catenaccio* and *galactico*—and at the same time we are offered an unparalleled insight into our social and cultural history. The information throughout is derived from Oxford's unique dictionary resources and based on analysis of the two-billion-word Oxford Corpus which monitors the English language as it used today.

Preface
to the First Edition

The *Oxford Dictionary of Foreign Words and Phrases* records the influx of words from a variety of other languages into both American and British English, concentrating especially on those introduced during the course of the twentieth century. Older dictionaries in this field tend to have a preponderance of French and Latin expressions; many of these are indeed still current and are represented in the present work by 1990s citations, but the English language is now open to new words on a worldwide basis. Many recent introductions reflect an unprecedented cultural eclecticism, particularly in what might be called 'lifestyle' words—those dealing with areas such as fashion, cuisine, ethnic music, and recreation.

There is nothing new about sources for foreign words being indicative of historical or cultural events. The influx of French military terms in the early eighteenth century, for instance, can be linked to the Continental campaigns of the Duke of Marlborough. More recently, the British Raj in India spawned a large number of Anglo-Indian terms for the various functionaries and institutions necessary to keep the wheels of empire turning. However, neither of these two categories is heavily represented in late twentieth-century speech, *nouvelle cuisine* being more fashionable than fortification and *karma* having a higher profile than imperial administration.

The criteria for currency that have been applied in the selection of entries mean that there is a bias in favour of words first introduced during this century. An exception to this is the large category of words, particularly from the classical languages, that are recent introductions or revivals with exclusively scientific senses; these are excluded on the grounds that they do not fulfil the other criterion of currency, namely that the word may be encountered in non-specialist literature. However, many other words have both technical and more general senses, and in such cases the technical senses are generally included or mentioned in the entry, as the evolution of the various senses once they have entered the language is often interesting in itself. For instance, *flèche*, which occurs in Middle English with its basic French meaning of 'arrow', soon became obsolete after its first introduction (most probably because it duplicated an already established word); reintroduced from Modern French with a variety of special applications, it has fared better. Terms that have been introduced purely as terms of art in particular sports or other fields of activity and have remained so (or have not had time to move beyond their restricted area) have been excluded; admitting terms for bullfighting passes or judo throws would have considerably increased the proportion of, respectively, Spanish and Japanese entries.

Introduced expressions have met with varying fortunes in English, but certain patterns can be seen. On the whole, phrases tend to be more resistant to naturalization than single words. At one end of the scale of naturalization, many words, especially those from Old French and Latin, have become totally assimilated in spelling, pronunciation, and plural form, and are thus no longer thought of as foreign in any sense other than the purely etymological. Others (such as *restaurant*) are nearing the end of this process of assimilation, with only some slight variation in standard pronunciation as a gesture towards an alien origin. Others, particularly Latin and French phrases, have remained obstinately 'foreign' over several centuries.

Italicization is a helpful but not infallible clue to the extent of assimilation, the rule of thumb being that the more 'foreign' a word is felt to be the more likely it is to be distinguished in this way. However, italics are generally retained in practice even for well-established words where there might be any possibility of confusion with an English word, as between *pace* (Latin ablative singular of *pax* used as a preposition) and 'pace' English noun and verb. Practice regarding italics however varies between British and American English and between publisher and publisher. For this reason, and to avoid the appearance of prescription, no attempt has been made to distinguish between italic and non-italic in the headwords in this dictionary.

Retention of accents is another indicator of awareness of the foreign origin of a word, since the native English writer has a strong tendency to drop them. In this respect the spelling *detour*, to take a common example, is well down the route to total assimilation, but the pronunciation still has a faint echo of the original *détour*.

How far spelling can move away from the original before a word can be said to be wholly Anglicized is not only a matter of the dropping or retention of accents. Various words from the Romance languages have doubled or single consonants in the original and the opposite in the usual English spelling: examples are *concessionnaire* in French, but 'concessionaire' in English, *improvvisatore* in Italian, but 'improvisatore' in English; on the other hand it is 'commando' in English but *comando* in Portuguese. Some variation in unstressed vowels also appears (*imprimitura* in Italian, but predominantly 'imprimatura' in English). However, in none of these cases does the fluctuation in spelling seriously affect the perception of the word as 'foreign'.

More latitude has been allowed in the case of words transcribed from non-Roman alphabets, and significant variants have been noted. For instance, Greek *kappa*, formerly often transcribed as *c*, is now more frequently rendered *k*, particularly in specialist contexts. Variation between *s* and *sh* and between *c* and *ch* occurs in transliterations from various languages of the Indian subcontinent. Attempts by users to make transliterations conform to English spelling norms have not disqualified words, since they generally do not disguise the alien origin of the word itself.

To keep the dictionary within reasonable bounds, several whole categories of words have been excluded, unless there is some strong reason to make an exception for a particular member of the class. If a word has a transferred meaning in English or is sufficiently at home to be used figuratively, it is generally included; thus, made-up words, even those with impeccable classical Greek or Latin elements such as *homophobia*, *megalomania*, are usually not admitted, but *utopia* is included. A very few other words such as *braggadocio* that are not genuine foreign words at all have been allowed in on the basis of their being so easily mistaken for a genuine borrowing. Also in are Latin phrases such as *infra dig.* that are seldom or never given their full form in English usage. Currencies, obsolete coins, weights and measures, and scientific units are excluded, but exceptions are made for *shekel* and *sou* on account of their metaphorical uses. Plant and animal names do not have entries unless they are also the names of a commodity that is widely traded or used; thus *jojoba* and *vicuña* are both in.

Evidence for use in the latter part of the twentieth century almost always guarantees inclusion, although some items which duplicate good English expressions and which are therefore unlikely to move beyond an entirely literary ambience have been omitted (e.g. *dialogue des sourds* smacks of affectation as an alternative to 'dialogue of the deaf'). Sometimes a foreign expression fulfils a valid function as a euphemism: *faux marbre* sounds considerably more up-market than *fake* (or *false*) *marble*. Words that are current but used only in the context of the country of origin have been looked at individually on the basis of likelihood of applications outside the particular national context; for example, *ragazza* as a word for 'girl' is most unlikely to be encountered anywhere except in a text specifically about or set in Italy, while *wagon-lit* on the other hand is much less country-specific. Greetings and polite forms of address have generally been excluded on similar grounds, *gnädige Frau* and such expressions belonging more properly in a foreign-language phrase book.

The tables given in the Appendix break down the headwords in the *Dictionary* by country of origin and century of introduction. They are intended as a snapshot of the foreign expressions for which there is evidence in twentieth-century texts and are in no sense a statistical exercise. Dates are given in abbreviated form, following the scheme used for the *New Shorter Oxford English Dictionary* (see below).

OE	Old English	pre-1149
ME	Middle English	1150–1349
LME	late Middle English	1350–1469
L15	late fifteenth century	1470–1499
E16	early sixteenth century	1500–1529
M16	mid sixteenth century	1530–1569
L16	late sixteenth century	1570–1599
E17	early seventeenth century	1600–1629
M17	mid seventeenth century	1630–1669
L17	late seventeenth century	1670–1699
E18	early eighteenth century	1700–1729
M18	mid eighteenth century	1730–1769
L18	late eighteenth century	1770–1799
E19	early nineteenth century	1800–1829
M19	mid nineteenth century	1830–1869
L19	late nineteenth century	1870–1899
E20	early twentieth century	1900–1929

M20	mid twentieth century	1930–1969
L20	late twentieth century	1970–1999
E21	early twenty-first century	2000–

Pronunciation Guide

Guidance on pronunciation follows the International Phonetic Alphabet system (IPA), and is based on the pronunciation associated especially with southern England (sometimes referred to as 'Received Pronunciation'). Many foreign words and phrases, however, have widely varying pronunciations, ranging from the wholly naturalized to a conscious attempt to reproduce what the speaker believes to be the 'foreign' pronunciation, and it is neither feasible nor particularly helpful to include every possibility.

Stress

ˈ   indicates primary stress on the following syllable

ˌ   indicates secondary stress on the following syllable

Consonants and Semivowels

b, d, f, h, k, l, m, n, p, r, s, t, v, w, and *z* all have their usual English values. Other sounds are represented by the following symbols:

g	get	x	loch	ð	this	j	yes
tʃ	chip	ŋ	ring	ʃ	she	ʤ	jar
θ	thin	ʒ	decision	ç	(German) echt		
ɲ	(French) seigneur			ɥ	(French) nuit		

(r) indicates an *r* that is sometimes sounded when a vowel follows, as in *cha-chaing*.

Vowels

The following symbols represent vowel sounds that appear in English and foreign languages:

short vowels		long vowels (: indicates length)		diphthongs	
a	cat	ɑː	arm	ʌɪ	my
ɛ	bed	ɛː	hair	aʊ	how
ə	ago	əː	her	eɪ	day
ɪ	sit	iː	see	əʊ	no
i	cosy	ɔː	saw	ɪə	near
ɒ	hot	uː	too	ɔɪ	boy
ʌ	run			ʊə	poor
ʊ	put			ʌɪə	fire
				aʊə	sour

(ə) signifies the indeterminate sound as in the final syllables of *garden, carnal,* and *rhythm.*

The following symbols are used for vowel sounds that do not occur in English:

short vowels		*long vowels* (: *indicates length*)	
ɑ	(French) passé		
e	(French) démodé (Italian) dolce	e:	(German) Wehrmacht (Italian) commedia
o	(French) auberge (German) Bildungsroman (Italian) amoretto	o:	(German) verboten (Italian) cassone
ɔ	(French) borné (German) Doppelgänger (Italian) donna		
œ	(French) boeuf	œ:	(French) accoucheur
ø	(French) bleu	ø:	(French) berceuse (German) Gasthöfe
u	(French) bijou (Italian) figurante		
y	(French) cru	y:	(German) gemütlich

The following symbols are used for other sounds that do not occur in English:

nasalized vowels (~ *indicates nasality*)		*diphthongs*	
ɒ̃	(French) cordon bleu	aɪ	(German) Gleichschaltung
ã	(French) en		
ɛ̃	(French) distingué	ɔy	(German) Hakenkreuz
ɔ̃	(French) congé		

aa /'ɑːɑː/ *noun* M19 Hawaiian ('a-'a). *Geology* Basaltic lava forming very rough, jagged masses with a light, frothy texture. Cf. PAHOEHOE.

abatis /'abətɪs/ *noun* (also **abattis** /ə'batɪs/) *plural* **abat(t)is**, **abatises** M18 French (literally 'felled (trees)', from Old French *abatre*, ultimately from Latin *batt(u)ere* to beat). *History* A defence formed by placing felled trees lengthwise one over the other with their branches pointing towards the enemy line. Also, a barricade of barbed wire.

abattoir /'abətwɑː/ *noun* E19 French (from *abattre* to fell). A slaughterhouse.

abaya /ə'beɪjə/ *noun* M19 Arabic ('abāya). A full-length sleeveless outer garment, worn by Arabs.

Abba /'abə/ *noun* LME ecclesiastical Latin (from New Testament Greek, from Aramaic 'abbā father; sense 3 is from Hindi *abbā*, from Arabic *ab*). **1** (In the New Testament) God as father. **2** A title given to bishops and patriarchs in the Syrian Orthodox and Coptic Churches. **3** (**abba**) Father (often as a familiar form of address in Muslim families). *Indian.*

abbé /'abeɪ/, *foreign* /abe/ (*plural same*) *noun* M16 French (from ecclesiastical Latin *abbat-* abbot). (In France) an abbot or other cleric.

ab initio /ab ɪ'nɪʃɪəʊ/ *adverb phrase* E17 Latin. From the beginning.
   1996 *Spectator* An unthinking agnosticism is taken for granted everywhere, so atheists are seldom called on to put their case *ab initio*.

Abitur /abi'tuːr/ *noun* (also **abitur**) M20 German (abbreviation of *Abiturientenexamen* leavers' examination). (In Germany) a set of examinations taken in the final year of secondary school (success in which formerly ensured a university place).

ablaut /'ablaʊt/ *noun* M19 German (from *ab* off + *Laut* sound). Alternation in the vowels of related word forms, especially in Germanic strong verbs (e.g., *sing, sang, sung*).

ab origine /ab ə'rɪdʒɪni/ *adverb phrase* M16 Latin (from *ab* from + *origine* ablative of *origo* beginning, source). From the beginning; from the creation of the world.

ab ovo /ab 'əʊvəʊ/ *adverb phrase* L16 Latin (= from the egg). From the very beginning.

abrazo /a'braθo/, /a'braso/, /ə'brɑːzəʊ/ *noun* plural **abrazos** /a'braθos/, /a'brasos/, /ə'brɑːzəʊz/ E20 Spanish. An embrace, a hug, especially as a salutation.

abscissa /ab'sɪsə/ *noun* plural **abscissae** /ab'sɪsiː/, **abscissas** L17 Modern Latin (*abscissa* use as noun (sc. *linea* line) of feminine past participle of *abscindere* to cut asunder). *Mathematics* (In a system of coordinates) the distance from a point to the vertical or *y*-axis, measured parallel to the horizontal or *x*-axis; the *x*-coordinate.
   ■ Originally denoted the part of a line between a point on it and the point of intersection with an ordinate.

abseil /'abzʌɪl/, /'abseɪl/ *verb & noun* M20 German (*abseilen*, from *ab* down + *Seil* rope). *Mountaineering* **A** *intransitive verb* Descend a rock face or other near-vertical surface by means of a doubled rope fixed at a higher point. **B** *noun* A descent made by abseiling.

absinth /'absɪnθ/ *noun* (also (in sense 2 usually) **absinthe**) LME French (*absinthe* from Latin *absinthium* from Greek *apsinthion* wormwood). **1** Wormwood, the plant *Artemisia absinthium* or its essence; *figuratively* bitterness, sorrow. **2** A potent green aniseed-flavoured liqueur, originally made from wormwood (which is now banned because of its toxicity). **b** A green colour resembling that of the liqueur.

absit omen /'absɪt ˌəʊmən/ *interjection* L16 Latin (= may this (ill) omen be absent). Used when referring to something undesirable, in the hope that the thing mentioned will not occur.

ab urbe condita /ab ˌəːbeɪ kɒn'dɪtə/ *adverb phrase* E17 Latin (= since the foundation of the city). (In the Roman annual dating system) since the founding of Rome.

■ The traditional date of the founding of Rome was 753 BC, which was the point of departure for the computation of dates. A variant form of the phrase is *anno urbis conditae* in the year of the founding of the city. Both versions are abbreviated AUC.

AC abbreviation of APPELLATION CON-TRÔLÉE.

academia /akə'diːmɪə/ *noun* M20 Latin (from Greek *akadem(e)ia*, adjective from *Akademos*). The environment or community concerned with the pursuit of research, education, and scholarship.

■ Akademos was the man or demigod who gave his name to the garden just outside ancient Athens where Plato conducted his philosophical school.

acanthus /ə'kanθəs/ *noun* M16 Latin (from Greek *akanthos*, from *akantha* thorn, perhaps from *akē* sharp point). **1** Any of several erect herbaceous plants belonging to the genus *Acanthus* (family Acanthaceae), having decorative spiny leaves; especially *Acanthus spinosus*, native to the Mediterranean region. **2** *Architecture* A conventionalized representation of the leaf of *Acanthus spinosus*, used especially to decorate Corinthian column capitals.

a cappella /a kə'pɛlə/, /aː/ *adjective & adverb phrase* L19 Italian (= in chapel style). (Of choral music or choirs) sung without instrumental accompaniment. Cf. ALLA CAPPELLA.

■ Used both as a premodifier and post-positively (see quotations).

1995 *Times* No doubt the uninviting weather had something to do with it [the smallness of the audience], although admittedly it is difficult to imagine a programme of 20th-century Ger-

man and Dutch *a cappella* music ever causing a traffic jam in Smith Square.

1996 *Times* He [sc. Bruce Springsteen] remained at the Ivy the other night until all other diners had left, then regaled staff with a short concert *a cappella*.

accelerando /əkˌsɛlə'randəʊ/, /əˌtʃɛlə-'randəʊ/ *adverb, adjective, & noun* E19 Italian. *Music* **A** *adverb & adjective* (Especially as a direction) with gradual increase of speed. **B** *noun* plural **accelerandos, accelerandi**. A gradual increase of speed; a passage (to be) played with a gradual increase of speed; also *figurative*.

B 1996 *Bookseller* There are fewer and fewer prerequisites to studying the humanities, but . . . the entrance exams in mathematics and physics for the first-year student, were what, less than 15 years ago, would have been post-doctoral research. That is your accelerando.

acciaccatura /əˌtʃakə'tʊərə/, *foreign* /atˌtʃakka'tuːra/ *noun* plural **acciaccaturas, acciaccature** /atˌtʃakka'tuːre/ E19 Italian (from *acciaccare* to crush). *Music* A grace note performed as quickly as possible before an essential note of a melody.

accidie /'aksɪdi/ *noun* ME Anglo-Norman (= Old French *accide* from medieval Latin *accidia*, alteration of late Latin ACEDIA). Spiritual or mental sloth, apathy. Now also, despair.

■ The term became obsolete after the 16th century, but was subsequently revived in the late 19th century.

accouchement /ə'kuːʃmɒ̃/, *foreign* /akuʃmã/ *noun* L18 French (from *accoucher* to give birth). Childbirth. *Archaic*.

accoucheur /aku:'ʃə:/, *foreign* /akuʃœːr/ (*plural same*) *noun* M18 French (from *accoucher* to give birth). A man (formerly also a woman) who acts as midwife.

accra /'akrə/, /ə'krɑː/ *noun* (also **akara** /ə'karə/) L19 Yoruba (*àkàrà* bean cake). A West African and West Indian fritter made with black-eyed peas or a similar pulse, or, especially in Trinidad, mashed fish.

acedia /ə'siːdɪə/ *noun* E17 Late Latin (*acedia* from Greek *akēdia*, from *a-* not + *kēdos* care, concern). ACCIDIE.

achar /ə'tʃɑ:/ *noun* L16 Hindi (ultimately from Persian *āchār*). (In Indian cookery) a type of pickle in which the food is preserved in spiced oil.

acharnement /aʃarnəmɑ̃/, /ə'ʃɑ:nmɒ̃/ *noun* M18 French (from *acharner* to give a taste of flesh (to dogs, a falcon, etc.)). Bloodthirsty fury; ferocity, gusto. *Archaic.*

acharya /ɑ:'tʃɑ:rjə/ *noun* E19 Sanskrit (*ācārya* master, teacher). (In the Indian subcontinent) a Hindu or Buddhist spiritual teacher or leader; an influential mentor.

à cheval /a ʃəval/, /ɑ: ʃə'val/ *adverb phrase* M19 French (= on horseback). With one foot on each side; with a stake risked equally on two chances.

achkan /'atʃk(ə)n/ *noun* E20 Hindi (*ackan*). A knee-length coat, buttoned in front, worn by men from the Indian subcontinent.

acme /'akmi/ *noun* L16 Greek (*akmē* highest point). The highest point; the point at which something is at its best or most highly developed.

■ Long after its introduction into English it was consciously used as a Greek word and written in Greek letters. It was formerly also used in the specific senses of 'the period of full growth; the flower or full bloom of life' (L16–M19) and 'the crisis of an illness' (M17–M19).

acropolis /ə'krɒpəlɪs/ *noun* E17 Greek (*akropolis*, from as *akros* tip, peak + *polis* city). The citadel or fortified part of an ancient Greek city, typically one built on a hill; (**the Acropolis**) the ancient citadel at Athens.

actualité /aktɥalite/ *noun* L20 French (= current events). Objective, existing facts.

■ As an alternative to 'truth' in the euphemism 'economical with the *actualité*' (i.e. lying). This euphemistic phrase was popularized in 1992 by the Conservative politician Alan Clark, who, under cross-examination at the Old Bailey during the Matrix Churchill case, referred to 'our old friend economical... with the *actualité*'.

actus reus /ˌaktəs 'reɪəs/ *noun phrase* E20 Latin (= guilty act). *Law* Action or conduct which is a constituent element of a crime, as opposed to the mental state of the accused. Cf. MENS REA.

acumen /'akjʊmən/, /ə'kju:mən/ *noun* L16 Latin (= point, acuteness, from *acuere* to sharpen, from *acus* needle). The ability to make good judgements and take quick decisions.

AD abbreviation of ANNO DOMINI.

adagio /ə'dɑ:(d)ʒɪəʊ/ *adverb, adjective, & noun* L17 Italian (from *ad agio* at ease). *Music* **A** *adverb & adjective* (Especially as a direction) in slow time, leisurely. **B** *noun* plural **adagios**. **1** A musical piece or movement in slow time. **2** A dance or ballet movement in slow time.

ADC abbreviation of AIDE-DE-CAMP.

addendum /ə'dɛndəm/ *noun* plural **addenda** /ə'dɛndə/ L17 Latin (= that which is to be added, neuter gerundive of *addere* to add). An item of additional material added to the end of a book or other publication.

à deux /a dɸ/ *adverb & adjective phrase* L19 French. For or involving two people: *dinner à deux*. Cf. FOLIE À DEUX, MÉNAGE.

ad hoc /ad 'hɒk/ *adverb & adjective phrase* M17 Latin (literally, 'to this'). Created or done for a particular purpose as necessary: *the discussions were on an ad hoc basis*; *the group was constituted ad hoc.*

ad hominem /ad 'hɒmɪnɛm/ *adverb & adjective phrase* L16 Latin (= to the person). **1** (Of an argument or reaction) directed against a person rather than the position they are maintaining. Cf. ARGUMENTUM AD HOMINEM. **2** Relating to or associated with a particular person.

adieu /ə'dju:/ *interjection & noun* LME French (Anglo-Norman *adeu*, Old French *adieu*, from *à* to + *Dieu* god: cf. ADIOS). **A** *interjection* Goodbye. **B** *noun* plural **adieus, adieux** /ə'dju:z/. A leave-taking; a parting word; a farewell.

ad infinitum /ad ˌɪnfɪ'nʌɪtəm/ *adverb & adjective phrase* E17 Latin (literally, 'to infinity'). Again and again in the same way; for ever.

ad interim /ad ˈɪntərɪm/ *adverb & adjective phrase* L18 Latin (*ad* to + *interim* adverb 'meanwhile' used as noun). For an intervening or temporary period of time.

adios /adɪˈəʊs/, /adɪˈɒs/ *interjection* M19 Spanish (*adiós*, from *a* to + *Dios* god: cf. ADIEU). Goodbye.

> **1996** *Times*... Señor Nuñez has decided that since he had neither cups nor courtesy from the coach, it is time to say *adios* to Mr Cruyff.

ad lib /ad ˈlɪb/ *adverb, adjective, verb, & noun* (also **ad-lib**, when used as attributive adjective or verb) E19 Latin (abbreviation of next). **A** *adverb & adjective* **1** Spoken or performed without previous preparation. **2** As much and as often as desired. **B** *transitive & intransitive verb* Speak or perform without previously preparing one's words; improvise. **C** *noun* Something extemporized; an ad-lib remark or speech.

ad libitum /ad ˈlɪbɪtəm/ *adverb & adjective phrase* E17 Latin (literally, 'according to pleasure'). **1** Spoken or performed without previous preparation. **2** As much and as often as desired.

> ▪ Often used in the abbreviated form AD LIB.
>
> *adjective phrase* **1995** *New Scientist* The joke—though it wasn't a funny joke—in our lab is that the most deadly thing we've tested has been a perfectly healthy diet given in ad libitum amounts. We literally kill them [sc. the rats] with kindness.

ad litem /ad ˈlʌɪtɛm/ *adverb & adjective phrase* M18 Latin (= for the lawsuit). *Law* (Of a guardian, etc.) appointed to act in a lawsuit on behalf of a child or other person who is not considered capable of representing themselves.

ad nauseam /ad ˈnɔːzɪam/, /ad ˈnɔːsɪam/ *adverb phrase* M17 Latin (literally, 'to sickness'). Used to refer to the fact that something has been done or repeated so often that it has become annoying or tiresome.

> ▪ The phrase was earlier (E17) introduced in the form *ad nauseam usque* (right up to sickness), and also occurs as *usque ad nauseam*, but these have been superseded by the shorter form.
>
> **1996** *Times* As we argued ad nauseam at the time, the Government should have consulted

the people when the Maastricht treaty was drummed through Parliament...

adobe /əˈdəʊb(ɪ)/ *noun* M18 Spanish (from *adobar* to plaster, from Arabic *aṭ-ṭūb*, from *al* the + *ṭūb* bricks). **1** A kind of clay used as a building material. **2** A brick formed from adobe. **3** A house built of such bricks. *United States*.

ad personam /ad pəˈsəʊnam/ *adverb & adjective phrase* M20 Latin (literally, 'to the person'). On an individual basis.

ad referendum /ad rɛfəˈrɛndəm/ *adverb phrase* L18 Modern Latin (literally, 'for reference'). Subject to the assent of a higher authority.

ad rem /ad ˈrɛm/ *adverb & adjective phrase* L16 Latin (literally, 'to the matter'). Relevant to what is being done or discussed at the time.

aduki variant of ADZUKI.

ad valorem /ad vəˈlɔːrɛm/ *adverb & adjective phrase* L17 Latin (= according to the value). (Of the levying of tax or customs duties) in proportion to the estimated value of the goods or transaction concerned.

adytum /ˈadɪtəm/ *noun* plural **adyta** /ˈadɪtə/) E17 Latin (from Greek *aduton* use as noun of neuter singular of *adutos* impenetrable). The innermost part of a temple; a private chamber, a sanctum.

adzuki /ədˈzuːki/ *noun* (also **aduki** /əˈduːki/) E18 Japanese (*azuki*). A small, round dark-red edible bean; the bushy Asian plant, *Vigna angularis*, which produces this bean.

> ▪ Also in the phrase *adzuki bean*.

aegis /ˈiːdʒɪs/ *noun* (also **egis** (chiefly United States)) E17 Latin (from Greek *aigis* shield of Zeus). **1** (In classical art and mythology) an attribute of Zeus and Athena (or their Roman counterparts Jupiter and Minerva) usually represented as a goatskin shield. **2** The protection, backing, or support of a particular person or organization.

> ▪ First used to denote armour or a shield. Now most frequently in the phrase *under the aegis of* 'under the protection of' (see quotation).

1996 *Country Life* Here under the aegis of Jan Brueghel, Roelandt Savery and Bosschaert we can see the format evolving.

aegrotat /ʌɪˈɡrə(ʊ)tat/, /ˈiːɡrə(ʊ)tat/, /iːˈɡrə(ʊ)tat/ *noun* L18 Latin (= he or she is ill, 3rd singular present indicative of *aegrotare* to be ill, from *aeger* sick, ill). In British universities, a certificate stating that a student is too ill to attend an examination; an examination pass or (*North America*) a credit awarded to a student having such a certificate.

aetatis /ʌɪˈtɑːtɪs/, /iːˈteɪtɪs/ *adjective* (usually abbreviated as **aet.** /ʌɪt/, /iːt/ or **aetat** /ˈʌɪtat/, /ˈiːtat/) E19 Latin. Of or at the age of.

■ The formula *aetatis*, *aetatis suae*, or one of the abbreviations, plus a figure, is found much earlier, in England and elsewhere, inscribed on portraits to give the age of the sitter. The full formula *anno aetatis suae* is also occasionally found.

affaire /aˈfɛr/ *noun* plural pronounced same E19 French. A temporary sexual relationship outside marriage; a love affair. Also a sensational event, case, or scandal.

■ Originally more usual in its full form *affaire de* (or *du*) *cœur* /də/, /dy/, /kœr/ (literally, 'affair of the heart'). In its more general sense, used with the definite article (either French or English), followed by the name of the person involved (see quotation 1995).

1958 A. Wilson *Middle Age of Mrs. Eliot* It would be so awful to have one of those office affaires that they have in the women's mags.
1995 *Times* Robbed of its most lurid aspect—money—*l'affaire* O.J. [sc. Simpson] may now serve a more contemplative purpose.

affairé /aferé/ *adjective* E20 French. Busy; involved.

affaire de (or **du**) **cœur** see AF-FAIRE.

affidavit /afɪˈdeɪvɪt/ *noun* M16 Medieval Latin (= he/she has affirmed, 3rd person singular perfect indicative of *affidare* to declare on oath). *Law* A written statement, confirmed by oath, to be used as evidence in court.

■ In legal phraseology a deponent *swears* an affidavit, the judge *takes* it; in popular use, however, the deponent *takes* or *makes* it.

1996 *Oldie* For my part, once I am sure that everyone knows who I am talking about, I shall sign an affidavit that all the characters are fictitious, and publish the book anonymously.

afflatus /əˈfleɪtəs/ *noun* M17 Latin (from *afflat-* past participial stem of *afflare*, from *ad* on + *flare* to blow). A divine creative impulse or inspiration.

aficionado /afɪsjəˈnɑːdəʊ/, *foreign* /aˌfiθjoˈnado/, *noun* plural **aficionados** /aˌfɪsjəˈnɑːdəʊz/, *foreign* /aˌfiθjoˈnados/ M19 Spanish (= amateur, use as noun of past participle of *aficionar* to become fond of, from *afición* from Latin *affectio* favourable disposition). **1** A devotee of bull-fighting. **2** A knowledgeable and enthusiastic follower of any activity or interest.

1 1996 *Spectator* For those of us who are *aficionados*, it is satisfying to report that the bullfight is flourishing today as never before.
2 1996 *Times* Dennis Potter *aficionados* may care to take notice of Keeley Hawes... who will be making something of a splash as the female star of *Karaoke*.

a fortiori /eɪ fɔːtɪˈɔːrʌɪ/, /fɔːtɪˈɔːriː/ *adverb phrase* E17 Latin (from *a fortiori argumento* from stronger argument). Used to express a conclusion for which there is stronger evidence than for a previously accepted one.

1961 *New Scientist* Anyone who...loses his sight after leaving school—or *a fortiori* in mid-career—cannot easily escape feelings of deep dismay.

afreet /ˈafriːt/ *noun* (also **afrit**) L18 Arabic ('*ifrīt*, colloquial '*afrīt*). A powerful jinn or demon in Arabian stories and Muslim mythology.

aga /ˈɑːɡə/ *noun* (also **agha**) M16 Turkish (*ağa* master, lord from Mongolian *aqa*). *Chiefly History* (In Muslim countries, especially under the Ottoman Empire) a military commander or official.

agal /aˈɡɑːl/ *noun* M19 Arabic (representing Bedouin pronunciation of Arabic '*iḵāl* bond, rope for hobbling a camel). A headband worn by Bedouin Arabs to keep the KEFFIYEH in position.

agape /ˈaɡəpi/ *noun* plural **agapae** /ˈaɡəpiː/, **agapes** E17 Greek (*agapē* brotherly love). **1** *Theology* Christian love, as distinct from erotic love or simple affection. **2** A communal meal held in Christian fellowship.

agar-agar /ˌeɪgɑːrˈeɪgɑː/ *noun* (in sense 2 usually simply **agar**) E19 Malay. **1** Any of certain South-East Asian seaweeds from which a gelatinous substance is extracted. **2** The substance itself, used especially as a thickener in soups and to form biological culture media.

agent provocateur /aʒã prɔvɔkatœr/ *noun phrase* plural **agents provocateurs** (pronounced same) L19 French (= provocative agent). A person employed to tempt a suspected criminal to commit a crime so that they can be convicted.

> **1996** *Times* Either try persuading people that cycling is a realistic mode of transport in London. Or—forgive me for sounding like an *agent provocateur*—start shooting motorists.

agio /ˈadʒɪəʊ/ *noun* plural **agios** L17 Italian (*ag(g)io* ease, convenience). The percentage charged on the exchange of one currency, or one form of money, into another that is more valuable.

agitato /adʒɪˈtɑːtəʊ/ *adverb & adjective* E19 Italian. *Music* (Especially as a direction) in an agitated manner.

agitprop /ˈadʒɪtprɒp/, /ˈagɪtprɒp/ *noun* (also **Agitprop**) E20 Russian (from *agit(atsiya)* agitation + *prop(aganda)* propaganda). Political (originally communist) propaganda, especially in art or literature.

agnolotti /ˌanjəˈlɒti/ *noun plural* L20 Italian. Pasta made into small square cases stuffed with a variety of fillings, like small ravioli.

Agnus Dei /ˌagnʊs ˈdeɪi:/, *in sense 1 also* /ˌanjʊs/; /ˌagnəs ˈdiːʌɪ/ *noun phrase* LME Latin (= Lamb of God). *Christian Church* **1** Part of the Mass beginning with the words *Agnus Dei*; a musical setting of this. **2** A figure of a lamb bearing a cross or flag, as an emblem of Christ.

> ■ In sense 2 the Agnus Dei is the emblem in art of St John the Baptist, who is very often depicted with it and holding a scroll with the words *ECCE AGNUS DEI* 'Behold the Lamb of God'.

a gogo /ə ˈgəʊgəʊ/ *adverb & postpositive adjective phrase* M20 French (*à gogo*, from Old French *gogue* fun). In abundance, galore. *Colloquial.*

agonistes /agəˈnɪstiːz/ *postpositive adjective* L17 Greek (= contestant, from *agōn* contest). Used as an epithet of a person who takes part in a struggle or contest.

> ■ First used in the title of John Milton's *Samson Agonistes* (1671) and imitated by later authors.

agora /ˈagɒrə/ *noun* plural **agorae** /ˈagɒriː/, **agorai** /ˈagɒrʌɪ/, **agoras** L16 Greek. (In ancient Greece) a public open space used for assemblies and markets.

> **1996** *Times* If there was ever an opportunity to create a new European *agora*, the Net's unsupervised electronic anarchy is surely the place.

aguardiente /ˌagwardiˈente/, /əˌgwɑːdɪˈɛnti/ *noun* E19 Spanish (from *agua* water + *ardiente* fiery). A distilled liquor resembling brandy, especially as made in South America from sugar cane.

AH see under HEGIRA.

ahimsa /əˈhɪmsɑː/ *noun* L19 Sanskrit (from *a* non- + *hiṃsā* violence). The doctrine in Hindu, Buddhist, and Jain philosophy that there should be no violence or killing of any living creature, however humble.

à huis clos /a yi klɔ/ *adverb phrase* E17 French. In secret, behind closed doors, IN CAMERA.

aide-de-camp /eɪddəˈkõ/, *foreign* /ɛddəkɑ̃/ *noun* (also **aid-de-camp**, **aide de camp**) plural **aides-de-camp**, **aids-de-camp** (*chiefly United States*), /eɪdzdəˈkõ/, *foreign* /ɛddəkɑ̃/ L17 French (= camp adjutant). A military officer acting as a confidential assistant to a senior officer, or assisting on a ceremonial occasion; anyone acting in a similar capacity to a more senior person.

> ■ Often abbreviated in military use to ADC.
> **1996** *Times* The culprits were John Redwood, MP for Wokingham, and his ebullient *aide de camp*, Hywel Williams.

aide-mémoire /ˌeɪdmɛm'wɑː/; *foreign* /ɛdmemwɑr/ (*plural same*) *noun* M19 French. **1** An aid to the memory, especially a book or note. **2** An informal diplomatic message.

> **1 1995** *Spectator* Then I had a bright idea and dug out of a trunk all my account books going back to the 1950s. They are a wonderful *aide-mémoire*.

aigrette /'eɪɡrɛt/, /eɪ'ɡrɛt/ *noun* M18 French (= egret). A headdress consisting of a white egret's plume or other decoration such as a spray of gems.

aiguille /'eɪɡwiːl/ *noun* M18 French (= needle). A sharply pointed peak of rock, especially in the Alps.

aikido /ʌɪ'kiːdəʊ/ *noun* M20 Japanese (*aikidō* literally 'way of adapting the spirit', from *ai* together, unify + *ki* spirit + *dō* way). A Japanese form of self-defence and martial art that uses locks, holds, throws, and the opponent's own movements.

aileron /'eɪlərɒn/ *noun* E20 French (diminutive of *aile* wing). A movable aerofoil used to control the balance of an aircraft in flight, usually a hinged flap in the trailing edge of a wing.

aioli /ʌɪ'jəʊli/, *foreign* /ajɔli/ *noun* E20 French (from Provençal *ai* garlic + *oli* oil). Mayonnaise seasoned with garlic.

akara variant of ACCRA.

akvavit variant of AQUAVIT.

à la /ɑ: lɑ:/, *foreign* /a la/ *preposition phrase* L16 French (abbreviation of À LA MODE). **1** (Of a dish) cooked or prepared in a specified way: *fish cooked à la meunière*. **2** In the style or manner of.

> ■ Followed by a French noun in standard phrases, but also often with an English noun or a person's name.
> **2 1995** *Spectator* And how long can the Labour leader go on talking about newness *à la* Newt before someone notices that, unlike with Mr Gingrich, there is no real radicalism behind the rhetoric?

à la bonne femme see BONNE FEMME.

à la carte /ɑ: lɑ: 'kɑːt/, *foreign* /a la kart/ *adverb & adjective phrase* E19 French (= according to the (menu) card). (In a restaurant) referring to food that can be ordered as separate items, rather than part of a set meal.

alameda /alə'meɪdə/ *noun* L18 Spanish. (In Spain and Spanish-speaking areas) a public walkway or promenade shaded with trees.

à la mode /ɑ: lɑ: 'məʊd/, *foreign* /a la mɔd/ *adverb & adjective phrase* L16 French (= in the fashion). **1** In or according to the fashion; fashionable. **2** *Cookery* **a** (Of beef) braised or made into a rich stew, usually with wine. **b** (Of food) served with ice cream. Chiefly *United States*.

> ■ Also in use in the mid to late 17th century as a noun (phrase), usually as one word, meaning 'a fashion, a temporary mood' or 'a thin glossy usually black silk'.
> **1 1996** *Spectator* He ends with a chapter describing what the book might have been, if it had been longer... All very much *à la mode*, but why not save the space and cut the price to the public?

albedo /al'biːdəʊ/ *noun* plural **albedos** M19 ecclesiastical Latin (= whiteness, from Latin *albus* white). The proportion of the incident light or radiation reflected by a surface, especially of a planet or moon.

albino /al'biːnəʊ/ *noun & adjective* E18 Spanish and Portuguese (from *albo* white). **A** *noun* plural **albinos** **1** A person or animal having a congenital deficiency of pigmentation in the skin and hair, which are white, and the eyes, which are usually pink. **2** An abnormally white animal or plant. **B** *adjective* Congenitally lacking in pigmentation; abnormally white.

> ■ Originally applied by the Portuguese to albinos among African blacks.

albumen /'albjʊmɪn/ *noun* L16 Latin (from *albus* white). Egg white, or the protein contained in it.

alcalde /al'kaldi/, *foreign* /al'kalde/ *noun* M16 Spanish (from Arabic *al-ḳāḍī* the judge). A mayor, magistrate, or similar administrative officer in Spain, Portugal, and parts of South America and the south-western United States.

alcazar /alkə'zɑ:/, *foreign* /al'kaθar/, /al'kasar/ *noun* plural **alcazars** /alkə'zɑ:z/, **alcazares** /al'kaθares/, /al'kasares/ E17 Spanish (*alcázar* from Arabic *al-ḳaṣr* the castle). A Spanish palace or fortress of Moorish origin.

alcheringa /altʃə'rɪŋgə/ *noun* L19 Arrernte (= in the Dreamtime). (In the mythology of some Australian Aboriginals) the 'golden age' when the first ancestors were created.

al dente /al 'dɛnti/, *foreign* /al 'dɛnte/ *adverb & adjective phrase* M20 Italian (literally, 'to the tooth'). (Of pasta, vegetables, etc.) cooked so as to be still slightly firm when bitten.

> **1995** *Spectator* [The] pasta, although it had swollen wonderfully with the pale coral juices of the seafood, was just a bit too *al dente*.

aleph /'ɑ:lɛf/ *noun* ME Hebrew ('*ālep*, literally, 'ox' (the character in Phoenician and ancient Hebrew possibly being derived from a hieroglyph of an ox's head); cf. ALPHA). The first letter of the Hebrew, Phoenician, and other Semitic alphabets.

alfalfa /ˌal'falfə/ *noun* M19 Spanish (from Arabic *al-fasfaṣa* a green fodder). A leguminous plant, *Medicago sativa*, cultivated for green fodder; lucerne.

alfresco /al'frɛskəʊ/ *adverb & adjective* (also **al fresco**) M18 Italian (*al fresco*). **A** *adverb* In the open air: *lunch was served alfresco*. **B** *adjective* Open-air: *an alfresco supper*.

alga /'algə/ *noun* plural **algae** /'aldʒi:/, /'algi:/ M16 Latin (= seaweed). Originally, seaweed; now, any of a large group of simple, non-flowering, and typically aquatic plants, including the seaweeds and many single-celled forms. Also *collectively*, the mass formed by such organisms.

alguacil /algwə'sɪl/, *foreign* /algwa'θil/, /algwa'sil/ *noun* plural **alguacils** /algwə'sɪlz/, *foreign* **alguaciles** /algwa'θiles/, /algwa'siles/ (also **alguazil** /algwə'zɪl/ plural **alguazils** /algwə'zɪlz/, **alguaziles** /algwə'zi:ləz/) E16 Spanish ((earlier *alguazil*) from Arabic *al-wazīr*, from *al* the + *wazīr* helper, aide, vizier). Each of a pair of mounted constables acting as an official at a bullfight.

alhaji /al'hadʒi/ *noun* (also as a title **Alhaji**) M20 Hausa (from Arabic *al* the + *ḥajj* pilgrimage). (In West Africa) a Muslim who has been to Mecca as a pilgrim.

alias /'eɪlɪəs/ *adverb & noun* LME Latin (= at another time, otherwise). **A** *adverb* Used to indicate that a named person is also known or more familiar under another specified name. **B** *noun* A false or assumed identity: *a spy operating under the alias of Barsad*.

alibi /'alɪbʌɪ/ *noun & verb* L17 Latin (= elsewhere). **A** *noun* **1** A claim or piece of evidence that one was elsewhere when an act, typically a criminal one, is alleged to have taken place. **2** An excuse of any kind. *Colloquial*. **B** *transitive & intransitive verb* Provide an alibi for, offer an excuse for.

> ∎ *Alibi* was originally used in English as an adverb meaning 'elsewhere', following the Latin, but during the late 18th century this usage became obsolete and was superseded by the modern noun usage.

aliquot /'alɪkwɒt/ *adjective & noun* L16 French (*aliquote* from Latin *aliquot* some, several, from *alius* one of two + *quot* how many). Originally *Mathematics*. **A** *adjective* That is contained in the whole an integral number of times. Chiefly in *aliquot part*. **B** *noun* An aliquot part, integral factor; *loosely* any fraction of a whole, a sample.

alla breve /alə 'breɪvi/ *noun phrase* M18 Italian (= according to the breve). *Music* A time signature indicating two or four minim beats in a bar.

alla cappella /alə kə'pɛlə/ *adverb & adjective phrase* M18 Italian. (Of choral music or choirs) unaccompanied.

> ∎ Introduced earlier than A CAPPELLA.

allargando /alɑːˈgandəʊ/ *adverb, adjective, & noun* L19 Italian (= broadening). *Music* **A** *adverb & adjective* (Especially as a direction) getting slower and slower and often also fuller in tone. **B** *noun* plural **allargandi** /alɑːˈgandi/, **allargandos**. A passage marked to be performed allargando.

allée /ale/ *noun* plural pronounced same M18 French. A walk or passage in a formal garden or park, usually flanked and shaded by trees or shrubs; an alley.

1996 *Country Life: Garden Year* The grotto is approached through an ominously dark *allée* of tall yews extending south of the house.

allegretto /alɪˈɡrɛtəʊ/ *adverb, adjective, & noun* M18 Italian (diminutive of ALLE-GRO). *Music* **A** *adverb & adjective* (Especially as a direction) in fairly quick time, but not as quick as allegro. **B** *noun* plural **allegrettos, allegretti** /alɪˈɡrɛti/. A movement or passage marked to be performed allegretto.

allegro /əˈleɪɡrəʊ/, /əˈlɛɡrəʊ/ *adverb, adjective, & noun* M18 Italian (= lively, gay). *Music* **A** *adverb & adjective* (Especially as a direction) in quick time; at a brisk speed. **B** *noun* plural **allegros, allegri** /əˈleɪɡri/ A movement, passage, or composition marked to be performed allegro.

allemande /ˈalmɑːnd/, /almãd/ (*plural same*) *noun* L17 French (= German (dance)). **1** A piece of music for a German dance or in its rhythm, especially one which forms a movement of a suite. **2** Any of various German dances, in particular an elaborate court dance popular in the 16th century. **b** A figure in square dancing in which adjacent dancers link arms or join hands and make a full or partial turn. Also used as a call to dancers to execute this figure turning in the specified direction.

alluvium /əˈl(j)uːvɪəm/ *noun* plural (now *rare*) **alluvia** /əˈl(j)uːvɪə/, **alluviums** M17 Latin (neuter of *alluvius* washed against, from *ad* to + *luere* to wash). A deposit of clay, silt, sand, etc., left by flowing flood water in a river valley or delta, typically producing fertile soil.

Alma Mater /ˌalmə ˈmɑːtə/, /ˈmeɪtə/ *noun phrase* (also **alma mater**) plural **Alma Maters**, (*rare*) **Almae Matres** /ˌalmʌɪ ˈmɑːtrɛz/, /ˌalmi ˈmeɪtriːz/ M17 Latin (= bounteous mother, a title given to various Roman goddesses, especially Ceres and Cybele). **1** Someone or something providing nourishment and care. **2** The university, school, or college that one formerly attended.

2 1996 *Spectator* After representing the Emperor and Empress...at King George VI's coronation, and visiting his *alma mater* at Oxford, he [sc. the Crown Prince] returned to Japan...

aloe vera /ˌaləʊ ˈvɛːrə/ *noun phrase* L20 Latin (= true aloe). A plant resembling a cactus from which an extract used in skin care and other health products is obtained.

aloha /əˈləʊhə/ *interjection & noun* E19 Hawaiian. Used in Hawaii especially at greeting or parting: love, affection.

alpaca /alˈpakə/ *noun* L18 Spanish (from Aymara *allpaca*). A domesticated South American mammal, *Lama pacos*, resembling the llama, with long fine woolly hair and usually brown and white colouring; the wool of the alpaca; fabric or a garment made from this.

alpargata /alpɑːˈɡɑːtə/ *noun* E19 Spanish. A light canvas shoe with a plaited fibre sole; an ESPADRILLE.

alpenhorn /ˈalpənhɔːn/ *noun* L19 German (= Alp horn). A long wooden horn used for signalling in the Alps.

alpenstock /ˈalpənstɒk/ *noun* E19 German (= Alp stick). A long iron-tipped staff used by hillwalkers and formerly by mountaineers.

alpha /ˈalfə/ *noun* ME Latin (from Greek). **1** The first letter (A, a) of the Greek alphabet, transliterated as 'a'; the beginning of anything. **2** Denoting the first of a series of items or categories. **3** *attributive Science* First, most important; as in *Astronomy* (preceding the genitive of the Latin name of the constellation) designating the chief star in a constellation; thus *Alpha Centauri* is the brightest star in the constellation Centaurus. **4** A first-class mark given for an examination paper or piece of school or college work.

■ In sense 1 *alpha* often appears in the phrase *the alpha and (the) omega*, which originally referred to God (see Revelation 1:8), but now is also used in the transferred sense of 'the beginning and the end' (see quotation 1996). In scientific terminology *alpha* has specialist applications in Chemistry, Medicine, and Computing, as well as Astronomy.

1 1996 *Times* The 100 metres is the alpha and omega of sport.

3 1995 *New Scientist* If the female deigns to mate, the honour goes to the senior partner, or alpha male. The junior, or beta male reaps his reward years later: when the alpha dies, the beta inherits his mentor's alpha status, and recruits his own apprentice.

alter ego /ˌaltər 'ɛgəʊ/, /ˌɒltər/, /'iːgəʊ/ *noun phrase* plural **alter egos** M16 Latin (= other self). **1** A person's secondary or alternative personality. **2** An intimate and trusted friend.

1996 *Times* If... Anne is ever-faithful Auden to Kallman's rake, then the poet could not have asked for a more sympathetic alter ego.

1996 *Oldie* 'Simply put, one of the greatest writers ever.' This is Scott Turow's considered judgment on Ruth Rendall and her alter ego Barbara Vine.

althorn /'althɔːn/ *noun* M19 German (*alt* alto + *horn* horn). A musical instrument of the saxhorn family.

altiplano /altɪ'plɑːnəʊ/, *foreign* /alti-'plano/ *noun* E20 Spanish. The high table-land of central South America.

alto /'altəʊ/ *noun & adjective* L16 Italian (from *alto (canto)* = high (song), from Latin *altus* high). *Music* **A** *noun* plural **altos** **1** (Especially in church music) the highest adult male singing voice (sometimes distinguished from the counter-tenor voice as using falsetto); a part written for such a voice. **b** A female voice of similar range, a contralto voice; a part written for such a voice. **2** A person with an alto voice. **3** An alto wind instrument (see **B**). **B** *adjective* Denoting the member of a family of similar instruments with a range or relative pitch comparable to an alto voice (among wind instruments usually the second or third highest member of the family).

alto-relievo /ˌaltəʊrɪ'liːvəʊ/ *noun* (also **alto-rilievo** /ˌaltəʊrɪ'ljeɪvəʊ/) plural **alto-relievos** M17 Italian (*alto-rilievo*). High relief; a sculpture, moulding, carving, etc., in high relief.

alumna /ə'lʌmnə/ *noun* plural **alumnae** /ə'lʌmniː/ L19 Latin (feminine of next). A female former student of a school, college, university, or other educational institution.

alumnus /ə'lʌmnəs/ *noun* plural **alumni** /ə'lʌmnʌɪ/, /ə'lʌmniː/ M17 Latin (= nursling, pupil, from *alere* to nourish). Formerly, a pupil. Now, a male former student of a school, college, university, or other educational institution.

■ In the singular, *alumnus* nearly always means a male, but the plural *alumni* can be used to refer to former students of either sex.

a.m. abbreviation of ANTE MERIDIEM.

amah /'ɑːmə/ *noun* M19 Portuguese (*ama* nurse). (In parts of the Indian subcontinent and the Far East) a nursemaid or maid.

amanuensis /əˌmanjʊ'ɛnsɪs/ *noun* plural **amanuenses** /əˌmanjʊ'ɛnsiːz/ E17 Latin (from *a manu* in *servus a manu* slave at hand + *-ensis* belonging to). A literary or artistic assistant, in particular one who takes dictation or copies manuscripts.

■ The Latin phrase *servus a manu* was used by Suetonius (Life of Julius Caesar: 74) and by the Latin legal writers to denote a slave who acted as a secretary.

amateur /'amətə/, /'amətjʊə/ *noun & adjective* L18 French (from Italian *amatore* from Latin *amator* lover). **A** *noun* **1** A person who engages in a pursuit, especially a sport, on an unpaid basis; a person who is contemptuously inept at a particular activity. **B** *adjective* Engaging or engaged in without payment, non-professional; done in an inept or unskilful way.

ambo /'ambəʊ/ *noun* plural **ambos** also written in Latin form **ambones** /am'bəʊniːz/ M17 Medieval Latin (from Greek *ambōn* rim, edge of a cup). The pulpit or reading desk in early Christian churches; an oblong enclosure with steps at both ends.

ambrosia /am'brəʊzjə/ *noun* M16 Latin (from Greek = immortality, elixir of life, from *ambrotos* immortal; in Dioscurides and Pliny applied to one or more herbs). **1** *Classical Mythology* The food of the gods. **2** Something very pleasing to taste or smell. **3** Honey or pollen used as food by bees, bee-bread. **4** A fungal product which forms the food of the pinhole borer.

ameba variant of AMOEBA.

amende honorable /amɑ̃d ɔnɔrabl/ *noun phrase* plural **amendes honorables** (pronounced same) E17 French (= honourable reparation). A public or open apology, typically with some form of reparation.

amicus curiae /aˌmʌɪkəs ˈkjʊərɪiː/ *noun phrase* plural **amici curiae** /aˌmiː siː ˈkjʊərɪiː/ E17 Modern Latin (= friend of the court). *Law* An impartial adviser to a court of law in a particular case.

1996 *Times* At the High Court's Chancery Division, the Government will argue that the traitor [sc. George Blake] has no right to royalties...Lord Lester of Herne Hill has been appointed *amicus curiae* to ensure Blake gets a fair hearing.

amigo /əˈmiːɡəʊ/ *noun* plural **amigos** M19 Spanish. A friend, a comrade.

■ Frequently used as a colloquial form of address, mainly in the United States.

1996 *Times* Herro thought the 'amigos' who had been with the brothers since time began...would never walk away from their fat-cat accoutrements, pensions, chauffeured cars, and so on. But they did.

amir /əˈmiːə/ *noun* (also **ameer**) L16 Persian and Urdu (from Arabic *'amīr* commander, governor, prince, from *amara* to command; cf. EMIR). A title of various Muslim rulers.

amnesia /amˈniːzjə/ *noun* L18 Greek (*amnēsia* forgetfulness). A partial or total loss of memory.

amoeba /əˈmiːbə/ *noun* (also **ameba**) plural **amoebas**, **amoebae** /əˈmiːbiː/ M19 Modern Latin (from Greek *amoibē* change, alternation). A single-celled aquatic protozoan, characterized by a constantly changing shape.

amok /əˈmɒk/ *adverb* (also **amuck** /əˈmʌk/, (earliest) **am(o)uco**) M17 Portuguese (*am(o)uco* from Malay *amok* rushing in a frenzy). **run amok**, behave uncontrollably and disruptively.

■ Early use was as a noun denoting a Malay in a homicidal frenzy.

amontillado /əˌmɒntɪˈlɑːdəʊ/, /əˌmɒntɪlˈjɑːdəʊ/ *noun* (also **Amontillado**) plural **amontillados** E19 Spanish (from *Montilla* a town in southern Spain where the original wine was produced). A medium dry sherry of a matured type.

amoretto /aməˈrɛtəʊ/, *foreign* /amoˈretto/ *noun* plural **amoretti** /amoˈretti/, **amoretto(e)s** /aməˈrɛtəʊz/ L16 Italian (diminutive of *amore* love). A representation of Cupid in a work of art.

amoroso /aməˈrəʊsəʊ/ *noun, adverb, & adjective* E17 Spanish and Italian (from medieval Latin *amorosus* amorous). **A** *noun* plural **amorosi** /aməˈrəʊsi/, **amorosos** A type of sweetened oloroso sherry. **B** *adverb & adjective Music* (Especially as a direction) in a loving or tender manner.

amour /əˈmʊə/, *foreign* /amur/ *noun* ME Old and Modern French (from Latin *amor*). A love affair or lover, especially one that is secret.

■ Originally used in the sense 'love, affection'. The current sense dates from the late 16th century.

1996 *Times* The final swapping of amours [in *Twelfth Night*] does not seem a tricky matter.

amour courtois /amur kurtwa/ *noun phrase* L19 French (= courtly love). A highly conventionalized medieval code of love and etiquette first developed by the troubadours among the chivalric aristocracy of southern France; courtly love.

amour fou /ˌamʊə ˈfuː/, *foreign* /amur fu/ *noun phrase* L20 French (= insane love). Uncontrollable or obsessive passion.

amour propre /ˌamʊə ˈprɒpr(ə)/, *foreign* /amur prɔpr/ *noun phrase* (also **amour-propre**) L18 French. A sense of one's own worth; self-respect.

1996 *Times* [N]ot only is hurling yourself about the court and going for every shot healthier both for body and for *amour-propre*, it is the best excuse there is for losing to those younger than you.

1996 *Spectator* Although it would be a blow to the *amour propre* of Mr Preston and friends to sell the Sunday paper after only three years, they may have to do so.

amphisbaena /ˌamfɪsˈbiːnə/ *noun* LME Latin (from Greek *amphisbaina*, from

amphis both ways + *bainein* to go, walk).
1 A fabled serpent with a head at each
end and able to move in either direction. **2** A wormlike burrowing lizard
of the genus *Amphisbaena*.

■ Pliny describes the mythical serpent in
the eighth book of his *Natural History*, and
Lucan (*Pharsalia* ix.719) lists it amongst
the poisonous monsters of Libya that
sprang from the dripping blood of the
gorgon Medusa's severed head.

amphora /'amf(ə)rə/ *noun* plural **am-
phorae** /'amf(ə)ri:/, **amphoras** ME Latin
(from Greek *amphoreus*, or French *am-
phore*). A tall ancient Greek or Roman
jar or jug with two handles and a
narrow neck.

ampoule /'ampu:l/ *noun* E20 French. A
small sealed glass capsule containing
a liquid, especially a measured quantity ready for injecting.

ampulla /am'pʊlə/ *noun* plural **ampul-
lae** /am'pʊli:/ LME Latin (diminutive of
ampora variant of AMPHORA). **1** *Roman
Antiquities* A small two-handled globu-
lar flask or bottle. **2** A flask for sacred
uses such as holding the oil for
anointing the sovereign at a coronation. **3** *Anatomy* A vessel or cavity
shaped like the ancient ampulla.

amuck variant of AMOK.

amuse-gueule /amyzɡœl/ *noun* L20
French (literally, 'amusement for the
mouth'). A small savoury item of food
served as an appetizer before a meal.
1996 *Spectator* Before our starters came an
amuse-gueule.

anabasis /a'nabəsɪs/ *noun literary* plural **anabases** /a'nabəsi:z/ E18 Greek (=
going up, from *ana-* up + *basis* going). A
military advance into the interior of a
country.

■ The original *anabasis* was that of ten
thousand Greek auxiliaries under the
Persian Cyrus the Younger into Asia in
401 BC. The Athenian writer Xenophon
narrated the story of the ill-fated expedition, which turned into a *katabasis* or
retreat in which he played a conspicuous
role, in his *Anabasis*.

anacoluthon /ˌanəkə'lu:θɒn/, /ˌanəkə-
'lu:θ(ə)n/ *noun* plural **anacolutha**
/ˌanəkə'lu:θə/ E18 Late Latin (from Greek
anakolouthon neuter singular of adjective
= lacking sequence, from *an-* not + *akolouthos*
following). A sentence or construction
in which the expected grammatical
sequence is absent, for example *while
in the garden, the door banged shut.*

anacrusis /anə'kru:sɪs/ *noun* plural
anacruses /anə'kru:si:z/ M19 Modern
Latin (from Greek *anakrousis* prelude,
from *anakrouein*, from *ana-* not + *krouein*
to strike). **1** *Prosody* One or more
unstressed syllables at the beginning
of a verse. **2** *Music* One or more
unstressed notes before the first bar
line of a piece or passage.

anaesthesia /anɪs'θi:zjə/ *noun* (also
anesthesia) E18 Modern Latin (from
Greek *anaisthēsia*, from *an-* not + *aisthēsis*
sensation). Insensitivity to pain, especially as artificially induced by the
administration of gases or the injec-
tion of drugs before surgical operations.

analgesia /an(ə)l'dʒi:zjə/ *noun* E18 Greek
(*analgēsia* painlessness, ultimately from
an- not + *algein* to feel pain). *Medicine*
The inability to feel pain; medication
that acts to relieve pain.

anamnesis /anəm'ni:sɪs/ *noun* plural
anamneses /anəm'ni:si:z/ L16 Greek
(*anamnēsis* remembrance). **1** Recollec-
tion, especially of a supposed previous
existence. **2** *Christian Church* The part
of the Eucharist in which the Passion,
Resurrection, and Ascension of Christ
are recalled. **3** A patient's account of
his or her medical history.

anamorphosis /anə'mɔ:fəsɪs/ *noun*
plural **anamorphoses** /anə'mɔ:fəsi:z/
E18 Greek (*anamorphōsis* transformation).
A distorted projection or drawing
which appears normal when viewed
from a particular point or by means of
a suitable mirror or lens; the process
by which such images are produced.

anaphora /ə'naf(ə)rə/ *noun* L16 Latin
and Greek (senses 1 and 2, Latin from
Greek = repetition, from *ana-* back, again
+ *pherein* carry; sense 3 Late Greek).
1 *Grammar* The use of a word which
refers to or stands for an earlier word

or group of words. **2** *Rhetoric* The repetition of the same word or phrase in several successive clauses. **3** *Christian Church* The part of the Eucharist which contains the consecration, anamnesis, and communion.

anastrophe /ə'nastrəfi/ *noun* M16 Greek (*anastrophē* turning back, from *ana-* back + *strephein* to turn). *Rhetoric* The inversion of the usual order of words or clauses.

anathema /ə'naθəmə/ *noun* plural **anathemas**, in sense 3 also **anathemata** /anə'θiːmətə/ E16 ecclesiastical Latin (= excommunicated person, excommunication, from Greek originally 'a thing devoted', later 'an accursed thing', originally variant of *anathēma* votive offering, from *anatithenai* to set up). **1** Something or someone that one vehemently dislikes. **2** A formal curse by a pope or council of the Church, excommunicating a person or denouncing a doctrine. **3** A strong curse.

anchoveta /antʃə'vɛtə/ *noun* M20 Spanish (diminutive of *anchova*). An anchovy found off the Pacific coasts of South America, of great commercial importance to Peru.

ancien régime /ãsjɛ̃ reʒim/ *noun phrase* L18 French (= former regime). The political and social system in France before the Revolution of 1789. More generally, a political or social system that has been displaced by another; the old system or style of things.

1995 *Spectator* Sponsored by the Home Office under the auspices of the Centre of Criminological Research at the University of Oxford, it [sc. the researchers' visitation] set the fear of God into Grendon's *ancien régime*.

andante /an'danti/ *adverb, adjective, & noun* E18 Italian (= going, present participle of *andare* to go). *Music* **A** *adverb & adjective* (Especially as a direction) in a moderately slow tempo. **B** *noun* A movement, passage, or composition marked to be performed andante.

andantino /ˌandan'tiːnəʊ/ *adverb, adjective, & noun* E19 Italian (diminutive of preceding). *Music* **A** *adverb & adjective* (Especially as a direction) lighter than andante, and usually quicker. **B** *noun* plural **andantinos**. A movement or

passage marked to be performed andantino.

■ The term was originally used to indicate a tempo slower than andante.

andouille /ãduj/ *noun* plural pronounced same E17 Old and Modern French (of unknown origin). A kind of pork sausage, usually served as a hors d'oeuvre.

angelus /'andʒ(ə)ləs/ *noun* M17 Latin (from the opening words *Angelus domini* the angel of the Lord). **1** A devotional exercise commemorating the Incarnation of Jesus, said by Roman Catholics at morning, noon, and sunset. **2** A ringing of church bells announcing the angelus.

angina pectoris /anˌdʒʌɪnə 'pɛktərɪs/ *noun* M18 Latin (*angina* quinsy (from Greek *agkhonē* strangling, assimilated to Latin *angere* to squeeze) + *pectoris* of the chest). *Medicine* A condition marked by severe pain in the chest, and often also the arms and neck, due to inadequate blood supply to the heart muscles.

■ *Angina* alone was earlier (M16) used of any condition marked by a suffocating, oppressive pain or discomfort, especially quinsy. It is now rare in this sense and is current only as a shortened form of *angina pectoris*.

anglice /'anɡlɪsi/ *adverb* (also **Anglice**) E17 Medieval Latin (from Latin *Anglus* English). In (plain) English.

angst /aŋst/ *noun* E20 German (= fear). A feeling of deep anxiety or dread, typically an unfocused one about the human condition or the state of the world in general.

1995 *Times* 'Oh, I'm seriously rich,' hoots Rhys Jones, not altogether seriously. 'I am covered in angst because I am so rich.'

anima /'anɪmə/ *noun* E20 Latin (= mind, soul). *Psychoanalysis* **1** (In Jungian psychology) the feminine part of a man's personality. Cf. ANIMUS. **2** The part of the psyche which is directed inwards, in touch with the subconscious (opposed to PERSONA).

anime /'anɪmeɪ/, /'anɪmə/ *noun* L20 Japanese. Japanese film and television animation, typically having a science-fiction theme and sometimes including violent or explicitly sexual material. Cf. MANGA.

animus /'anɪməs/ *noun* E19 Latin (= spirit, mind). **1** Hostility or ill feeling. **2** Motivation to do something. **3** *Psychoanalysis* (In Jungian psychology) the masculine part of a woman's personality. Cf. ANIMA.

1 1995 *Spectator* The greatest animus felt by British, Australian and New Zealand troops alike was against the politicians.

ankh /aŋk/ *noun* L19 Egyptian (= life, soul). An object or design resembling a cross, but with a loop in place of the upper limb, used in ancient Egyptian art as a symbol of life.

■ Also called *crux ansata*.

ankus /'aŋkəs/ *noun* L19 Hindi (*ākus, aṅkas* from Sanskrit *aṅkuśa*). (In the Indian subcontinent) a goad for elephants.

anno aetatis suae see under AETATIS.

Anno Domini /ˌanəʊ 'dɒmɪnʌɪ/, /'dɒmɪni/ *adverb & noun phrase* M16 Latin (= in the year of the Lord). **A** *adverb phrase* Of the Christian era (used to indicate that a date comes the specified number of years after the traditional date of Christ's birth). Usually written AD. **B** *noun phrase* **1** A particular year. **2** Advanced or advancing age. *Colloquial*.

B.2 1906 E. V. Lucas *Fireside and Sunshine* When the time came for A. to take the bat he was unable to do so. *Anno Domini* asserted itself.

annulus /'anjʊləs/ *noun* plural **annuli** /'anjʊlʌɪ/, /'anjʊli:/ M16 Latin (late form of *anulus* diminutive of *anus* ring). **1** *Technical* A ring-shaped object, structure, or region. **2** *Mathematics* A plane figure consisting of the area between a pair of concentric circles.

annus horribilis /ˌanəs hʊ'rɪbɪlɪs/ *noun phrase* L20 Modern Latin (= horrible year; formed after ANNUS MIRABILIS). A year of disaster or misfortune.

■ The phrase leapt into circulation after H.M. the Queen used it with reference to 1992, a year of much-publicized matrimonial troubles within the British royal family and a serious fire at Windsor Castle.

1995 *Times* Against this background, the EU has let itself in for an *annus horribilis* in 1998.

annus mirabilis /ˌanəs mɪ'rɑːbɪlɪs/ *noun phrase* M17 Modern Latin (= wonderful year). A remarkable or auspicious year.

■ The origin of the phrase is the title of Dryden's poem *Annus Mirabilis: The Year of Wonders* (1667), which chronicled events in 1666, including British naval battles against the Dutch and the Great Fire of London. Dryden's use of *mirabilis* as 'remarkable in both good and bad senses' has tended to be superseded by the more positive sense of 'marvellous' (see quotation), a tendency reinforced by the currency of ANNUS HORRIBILIS in the 1990s.

1995 *Spectator* All peoples have their *annus mirabilis*, the crucial period of their history which defines them...: great political or constitutional acts, like 1776 to the Americans or 1789 to the French, or great military events like 1812 in Russia...or 1813 in Prussia.

anomie /'anəmi/ *noun* (also **anomy**) M20 French (from Greek *anomia*, from *anomos* lawless). Lack of the usual social or ethical standards in a group or person.

■ The term was resurrected in its current sense by the French sociologist Émile Durkheim in *Suicide* (1897). It occurs in English in technical sociological contexts, but also more generally (see quotation).

1995 *Spectator* Today,...travelling to work by car is guaranteed to whip up anger, alienation and *anomie*.

anonym /'anənɪm/ *noun* (also **anonyme**) E19 French (*anonyme* from Greek *anōnumos* anonymous). **1** An anonymous person or publication. **2** A pseudonym.

anorak /'anərak/ *noun* E20 Eskimo (Greenlandic *annoraaq*). **1** A waterproof jacket, typically with a hood, of a kind originally used in polar regions. **2** A studious or obsessive person with unfashionable and largely solitary interests. *British colloquial, derogatory*.

■ The British English informal sense dates from the 1980s and derives from the anoraks worn by trainspotters, regarded as typifying this kind of person.

anorexia /anəˈrɛksɪə/ *noun* L16 Late Latin (from Greek *an-* no + *orexis* appetite). *Medicine* Lack or loss of appetite for food (as a medical condition).

■ First introduced in 1598 in the French form *anorexie*, which, like the anglicized form *anorexy*, is now obsolete. *Anorexia* now very often refers to the specific complaint of ANOREXIA NERVOSA.

anorexia nervosa /anəˌrɛksɪənəˈvəʊsə/ *noun phrase* L19 Late Latin (= nervous anorexia). An emotional disorder characterized by an obsessive desire to lose weight by refusing to eat.

Anschluss /ˈanʃlʊs/ *noun* E20 German (from *anschliessen* to join, annex). Union, annexation; *specifically* the annexation of Austria by Germany in 1938.

1958 *Economist* Ability to opt to join the Commonwealth might give certain states a valuable policy counter, when other forms of Anschluss seem to be in the offing.

ante /ˈanti/ *noun* E19 Latin (= before). **1** (In poker and similar games) a stake put up by a player before drawing cards. **2** *transferred* An advance payment; a sum of money for a payment.

■ Chiefly North American. Often in the phrase *upping* (or *to up*) *the ante*, that is, 'raising the stakes'.

2 1996 *Times* That would have balanced the market and raised the negotiating ante.

ante-bellum /antɪˈbɛləm/ *adjective* (also **antebellum**) M19 Latin (*ante bellum* before the war). Occurring or existing before a particular war, especially the American Civil War. Opposed to POST-BELLUM.

1996 *Times* Kenneth Greenberg's aim is to enlarge our understanding of a dead world... The world? The antebellum slave South.

ante meridiem /ˌantɪ məˈrɪdɪəm/ *adjective & adverb phrase* M16 Latin. Before midday; between midnight and the following noon.

■ Abbreviated to *a.m.*

ante-mortem /antɪˈmɔːtəm/ *adjective* L19 Latin (*ante mortem* before death). Made before death. Cf. POST-MORTEM.

anthemion /anˈθiːmɪən/ *noun plural* **anthemia** /anˈθiːmɪə/ M19 Greek (= flower).

An ornamental design resembling a stylized honeysuckle.

anthrax /ˈanθraks/ *noun* L19 Latin (= carbuncle, from Greek *anthrax*, *anthrak-* coal, carbuncle (with reference to the skin ulceration in humans)). A serious bacterial disease of sheep and cattle, typically affecting the skin and lungs. It can be transmitted to humans, causing severe skin ulceration or a form of pneumonia.

■ Originally (LME) with its Latin sense, but this is now rare or obsolete.

anthropophagi /anθrəˈpɒfəgʌɪ/, /ˌanθrəˈpɒfədʒʌɪ/ *noun plural* M16 Latin (*anthropophagus* from Greek *anthrōpophagos* man-eating). Cannibals, especially in legends or fables.

■ The singular *anthropophagus* is rare.

anti /ˈanti/ *noun, adjective, & preposition* L18 Greek (*anti-* = opposite, against). **A** *noun* Someone who is opposed to a particular policy, activity, or idea. **B** *adjective* Against or antagonistic to someone or something; opposed. **C** *preposition* Opposed to; against.

■ The use of *anti-* as a prefix in words adopted (ultimately) from Greek, and in English words modelled on these, long predates the use of *anti* as an independent word, and as a prefix *anti-* has been freely used with nouns and adjectives in the 20th century with the sense 'opposite, against, preventing'.

A 1996 *Spectator* In those days, the antis were marginal figures, more numerous than the League of Empire loyalists but with hardly greater purchase on the future.

antipasto /antɪˈpastəʊ/ *noun plural* **antipasti** /antɪˈpasti/, **antipastos** E17 Italian (from *anti-* before + *pasto* (from Latin *pastus* food)). (In Italian cookery) an appetizer, an hors d'oeuvre.

■ Rare before the mid 20th century. Also used figuratively (see quotation).

1996 *Times* An artistic *antipasto* can stimulate the appetite for more substantial fare.

antipodes /anˈtɪpədiːz/ *noun plural* (sense 2 also treated as *singular*) (also **Antipodes**) LME French (or late Latin from Greek plural of *antipous* having the feet opposite, from as *anti-* opposite + *pous*, *pod-* foot). **1** Australia and New Zealand (used by inhabitants of the northern hemisphere). **2** Exact opposites. Also as *singular*. (Followed by *of*, *to*.)

■ The term originally denoted the inhabitants of opposite sides of the earth. Formerly pronounced as a trisyllable /ˈantɪpəʊdz/; present pronunciation follows Greek and Latin.

antistrophe /anˈtɪstrəfi/ *noun* M16 Late Latin (from Greek *antistrophē*, from *antistrephein* to turn against). The second section of an ancient Greek choral ode or of one division of it.

■ Originally used as term in rhetoric denoting the repetition of words in reverse order.

antithesis /anˈtɪθəsɪs/ *noun* plural **antitheses** /anˈtɪθəsiːz/ LME Late Latin (from Greek, from *antitithenai*, from as *anti-* against + *tithenai* to set, place: cf. THESIS). **1** A person or thing that is the direct opposite of someone or something else. **2** A contrast or opposition between two things. **3** A rhetorical or literary device in which an opposition or contrast of ideas is expressed. **4** (In Hegelian philosophy) the negation of the THESIS as the second stage in the process of dialectical reasoning.

■ Originally denoted the substitution of one grammatical case for another.

antonomasia /ˌantənəˈmeɪzɪə/ *noun* M16 Latin (from Greek, from *antonomazein* to name instead, from as *anti-* instead + *onoma* name). **1** The substitution of an epithet or title for a proper name (e.g. *the Iron Lady* for Margaret Thatcher). **2** The use of a proper name to express a general idea (e.g. *Scrooge* for 'a miser').

AOC see under APPELLATION CONTRÔLÉE.

à outrance /a utrãs/ *adverb phrase* Also **à loutrance** /a lutrãs/, **à toute outrance** /a tut utrãs/ E17 French (= to the utmost). To the death; to the bitter end.

1996 *Spectator*...he [sc. President Clinton] may find it difficult to shift the blame onto the opposition as he did so brilliantly when Newt Gingrich unwisely engaged him in war *à outrance* over the budget.

Apache *in senses A.1, B* /əˈpatʃi/; *in sense A.2* /əˈpaʃ/, *foreign* /apaʃ/ (*plural of noun same*) *noun & adjective* M18 Mexican Spanish (probably from Zuñi *Ápachu*, literally, 'enemy'; sense A.2 through French, by association with the reputed ferocity of the American Indian people). **A** *noun* plural **Apaches**, same. **1** A member of an American Indian people living chiefly in New Mexico and Arizona; the language of this people. **2** (**apache**) A violent street ruffian, originally in Paris. **B** *adjective* Relating to the Apache or their language.

apartheid /əˈpɑːtheɪt/ *noun* M20 Afrikaans (literally, 'separateness', from Dutch *apart* apart + *-heid* -hood). The former South African policy or system of segregation or discrimination on grounds of race. Also *transferred* and *figurative*, any other form of segregation.

1996 *Times* Men became more involved in parenting and women entered the workplace. But the end of sexual apartheid brought its own problems.

aperçu /apɛrsy/ (*plural same*), /apɛːˈsjuː/ *noun* E19 French (past participle of *apercevoir* to perceive). A comment or brief reference which makes an illuminating or entertaining point; an insight, a revealing glimpse.

1995 *Spectator* Nowhere, though, have I seen mentioned one of Amis's best *aperçus*...that the surest harbinger of boredom and *longueurs* is the question, perfunctory and ominous—'Red or white, sir?'

aperitif /əˈpɛrɪtiːf/, /əpɛrɪˈtiːf/ *noun* (also **apéritif** /aperitif/ (*plural same*)) L19 French (*apéritif* (noun and adjective) from medieval Latin *aperitivus* (adjective) variant of late Latin *apertivus*, from *apertus* open). An alcoholic drink taken before a meal to stimulate the appetite.

apex /ˈeɪpɛks/ *noun* plural **apexes**, **apices** /ˈeɪpɪsiːz/ E17 Latin (= peak, tip). **1** The top or highest part of something, especially one forming a point; the vertex of a triangle, cone, etc.; *Botany* the growing point of a shoot etc. **2** The highest point of achievement; a climax.

aphasia /əˈfeɪzɪə/ *noun* M19 Greek (from *aphatos* speechless, from *a-* without + *phanai* to speak). *Medicine* Loss or impairment of the faculty of speech or of understanding of language (or both), as a result of brain damage.

aplomb /əˈplɒm/ *noun* L18 French (from *à plomb* according to a plumb line). Self-confidence or assurance, especially when in a demanding situation.

■ Originally used in English in the sense 'perpendicularity, steadiness'.

1996 *Spectator* Some ministers stamp their personality on their department with such aplomb that, ever after, they become archetypes.

Apocrypha /əˈpɒkrɪfə/ *noun* (usually treated as *singular*; rarely as *plural*, with singular **Apocryphon** /əˈpɒkrɪfɒn/) LME ecclesiastical Latin (neuter plural (sc. *scripta* writings) of *apocryphus* from Greek *apokruphos* hidden, from *apokruptein* to hide). **1** Biblical or related writings not forming part of the accepted canon of Scripture. **2** (**apocrypha**) Writings or reports not considered genuine.

à point /a pwɛ̃/ *adverb phrase* E20 French (= to the point). Especially *Cookery*. At or to exactly the right point; just enough, without overcooking or undercooking.

apologia /apəˈləʊdʒɪə/ *noun* L18 Latin. A written defence of one's own opinions or conduct.

■ The currency of *apologia* is largely due to the impact of John Henry Newman's *Apologia pro Vita Sua* (1864), charting his intellectual and spiritual progress from Anglicanism to Roman Catholicism. The complete phrase is sometimes used of an autobiography, especially one by a controversial figure.

1996 *Times* . . . we are told that there is respect for human rights in China. To prove it (and this gets very macabre), the Chinese Government has published a weird kind of apologia.

aporia /əˈpɔːrɪə/, /əˈpɒrɪə/ *noun* M16 Late Latin (from Greek, from *aporos* impassable). **1** An irresolvable internal contradiction or logical disjunction in a text, argument, or theory. **2** *Rhetoric* The expression of doubt.

a posteriori /eɪ/, /ɑː/, /pɒˌstɛrɪˈɔːrʌɪ/, /pɒˌstɪərɪɔːrʌɪ/ *adverb & adjective phrase* E17 Latin (= from what comes after). (With reference to reasoning or

knowledge) proceeding from observations or experiences to the deduction of probable causes. Opposed (to) A PRIORI.

1991 W. Charlton *The Analytic Ambition* This general belief is dispositional. It could be applied in action or prediction but here it is applied in a posteriori inference.

apotheosis /əˌpɒθɪˈəʊsɪs/ *noun* plural **apotheoses** /əˌpɒθɪˈəʊsiːz/ L16 ecclesiastical Latin (from Greek *apotheōsis*, from *apotheoun* to deify, from *apo-* + *theos* god). **1** The highest point in the development of something; a culmination or climax. **2** The elevation of someone to divine status.

apparat /apəˈrɑːt/ *noun* M20 Russian (through German from Latin *apparatus* from *apparare* to make ready). The administrative system of the Communist Party in the former USSR and other countries.

apparatchik /apəˈratʃɪk/ *noun* plural **apparatchiki** /apəˈratʃɪki/, **apparatchiks** M20 Russian (from preceding). **1** A member of a Communist Party AP-PARAT. **2** An official in a large political organization; an implementer of party or official policy.

2 1996 *Spectator* What usually happens now is that the prime minister assembles a committee of favoured ministers, placemen and apparatchiks to decide the date.

apparatus criticus /apəˌreɪtəs ˈkrɪtɪkəs/ *noun phrase* plural **apparatus critici** /apəˌreɪtəs ˈkrɪtɪsʌɪ/ M19 Modern Latin. A collection of notes, variant readings, and other matter accompanying a printed text.

1996 *Spectator* On what grounds is this a *Selected* and not a *Collected*? How much surviving comic verse [of A. E. Housman's] do we in fact have? We are not going to find out from the present apparatus criticus, so to dignify it.

appellation contrôlée /apɛlasjɔ̃kɔ̃t role/ *noun phrase* M20 French (= controlled appellation). A description awarded to a French wine guaranteeing that it was produced in the region specified, using vines and production methods which satisfy the regulating body.

■ Abbreviated to AC. Also *appellation d'origine contrôlée* /apɛlasjɔ̃ dɔriʒin kɔ̃trole/, abbreviated to AOC.

1996 *Times* Without any form of *appellation contrôlée*, the quality of what we are served in the name quickly deteriorates.

appliqué /əˈpliːkeɪ/ *noun & verb* M18 French (use as noun of past participle of *appliquer* from Latin *applicare* to apply (to)). **A** *noun* Ornamental needlework in which pieces of fabric are sewn or stuck on to a larger piece to form a picture or pattern. **B** *transitive verb* Sew or stick pieces of fabric on to (a garment or larger piece of fabric) to form a picture or patterns. Chiefly as *appliquéd* participial adjective.

appoggiatura /əˌpɒdʒəˈtʊərə/ *noun* plural **appoggiature** /əˌpɒdʒəˈtʊəreɪ/ M18 Italian (from *appoggiare* to lean upon, rest). *Music* A grace note which delays the next note of the melody, taking half or more of its written time value.

après /ˈapreɪ/, *foreign* /aprɛ/ *preposition* M20 French. Coming after in time, typically specifying a period following an activity.

■ Combined with English words in (humorous) imitation of APRÈS-SKI, as *après-bath*, *après-sex*, etc.

après nous le déluge /apre nu lə delyʒ/ *adverb phrase* M19 French (literally, 'after us the flood'). Used to express the feeling that the present state of affairs or order of things will not long survive us.

■ Attributed in the *Mémoires* of Mme de Hausset (1824) to Mme de Pompadour (1721–64), mistress of King Louis XV of France, who had premonitions of catastrophe after the French defeat by the Prussians at Rossbach in 1757. It is very often quoted by English speakers in the version *après moi le déluge*.

1995 *Times* Evidently, the only way we can truly face our own demise is by hoping that, so to speak, *après moi, le déluge*. If we have to go, then we want everyone to go with us.

après-ski /ˌapreɪˈskiː/ *noun & adjective* M20 French (= after skiing). The social activities and entertainment following a day's skiing at a resort.

a priori /eɪ prʌɪˈɔːrʌɪ/, /ɑː prɪˈɔːriː/ *adverb & adjective phrase* L16 Latin (*a priori* from

what is before). **1** Relating to or denoting reasoning or knowledge which proceeds from theoretical deduction rather than from observation or experience. Opposed to A POSTERIORI. **2** Without previous investigation; to the best of one's knowledge; as far as one knows.

2 1995 *Spectator* What would be limited is the phenomenon by which European law could be said to apply *a priori*, regardless of national legislatures.

apropos /aprəˈpəʊ/, /ˈaprəpəʊ/ *adverb, adjective, & preposition* (also **à propos** /a prɔpo/) M17 French (*à propos*, from à to + *propos* purpose). **A** *adverb* **1** To the point; at the opportune moment. **2** Incidentally, by the way. **B** *adjective* Relevant or appropriate to a particular situation; opportune, timely: *the song feels apropos to a midnight jaunt.* **C** *preposition* Concerning, with regard to.

C 1996 *Times* A propos the medicinal habits of Florence Nightingale . . . , there is convincing evidence in biographical literature that she took laudanum . . .

apsara /ˈʌpsərɑː/ *noun* M19 Hindi (*apsarā* from Sanskrit *apsarās*). *Hindu Mythology* Any of a class of celestial nymphs, frequently regarded as the wives of the gandharvas or heavenly musicians.

aqua fortis /ˌakwə ˈfɔːtɪs/ *noun phrase* (also **aquafortis**) L15 Latin (= strong water). Nitric acid; originally, any powerful solvent. Now *archaic*.

aqua regia /ˌakwə ˈriːdʒə/ *noun phrase* (also formerly **aqua regis**) E17 Latin (= royal water). *Chemistry* A concentrated mixture of nitric and hydrochloric acids, able to dissolve gold, platinum, etc.

aquarelle /akwəˈrɛl/ *noun* M19 French (from Italian *acquarella* watercolour, from *acqua* from Latin *aqua* water). A style of painting in thin, usually transparent, watercolours; a painting in this style.

aquavit /akwəˈviːt/ *noun* (also **akvavit** /akvəˈviːt/) L19 Norwegian, Swedish, Danish (*akvavit* AQUA VITAE). An alcoholic spirit distilled from potatoes or other starch-containing plants.

aqua vitae /ˌakwə ˈvʌɪtiː/, /ˈviːtʌɪ/, /ˈviːtiː/ *noun phrase* (also **aqua-vitae**) LME Latin (= water of life: cf. French *eau de vie*). Strong alcoholic spirit, especially brandy.

arabesque /arəˈbɛsk/ *noun & adjective* M17 French (from Italian *arabesco*, from *arabo* Arabic). **A** *noun* **1** Decorative work of a kind which originated in ancient Islamic art, consisting of flowing lines of branches, leaves, scrollwork, etc., fancifully intertwined; an ornamental design of this kind. **2** *Ballet* A posture in which the body is bent forwards and supported on one leg with the other leg extended horizontally backwards, with the arms extended one forwards and one backwards. **3** *Music* A passage or composition with fanciful ornamentation of the melody. **B** *adjective* (Of ornamental design) decorated with arabesques (sense 1).

arak /ˈarək/ *noun* (also **arrack**) E17 Arabic (ˈaraḳ sweat, especially in ˈaraḳ *at-tamr* fermented and distilled juice of dates). An alcoholic spirit made in Eastern countries from the sap of the coco palm or from rice.

arbiter elegantiae /ˌɑːbɪtə ɛlɪˈgantɪʌɪ/ E19 Latin (= judge of elegance). An authority on matters of artistic taste or etiquette.

■ First introduced in the form *arbiter elegantiarum* 'judge in matters of taste', which was current in English in the 19th century, but the singular form of the genitive, *elegantiae*, is now usual. It has classical sanction in being applied by Tacitus (*Annales* xvi.18) to Titus Petronius, *elegantiae arbiter* at the court of Nero.

arboretum /ɑːbəˈriːtəm/ *noun* plural **arboreta** /ɑːbəˈriːtə/, (chiefly *North American*) **arboretums** E19 Latin (= place with trees, from *arbor* tree). A botanical garden devoted to the cultivation and exhibition of trees.

arbor vitae /ˌɑːbə ˈvʌɪtiː/, /ˈviːtʌɪ/ *noun phrase* E17 Latin (= tree of life). Any of a number of North American or Far Eastern evergreen conifers, belonging chiefly to the genus *Thuja*.

arcanum /ɑːˈkeməm/ *noun* plural **arcana** /ɑːˈkeɪnə/ L16 Latin (use as noun of neuter singular of *arcanus* concealed). Usually in *plural*. **1** A hidden thing; a mystery, a profound secret. **2** Any of the supposed secrets of nature sought by alchemists; a marvellous remedy, an elixir.

> **1** **1996** *Spectator* One has always heard it bruited that such [obscene] compositions survive, shrouded away on the duskier, dustier shelves of the British and Cambridge Libraries... surely the age has now come when the arcana may finally be opened?

archi plural of ARCO.

archon /ˈɑːkən/ *noun* plural **archons**, **archontes** /ɑːˈkɒntiːz/ L16 Greek (*arkhōn*, *arkhont-* ruler, use as noun of present participle of *arkhein* to rule). The chief magistrate, or, after the time of Solon, each of the nine chief magistrates, of ancient Athens.

arco /ˈarko/, /ˈɑːkəʊ/ *noun, adverb, & adjective* M18 Italian. *Music* **A** *noun* plural **archi** /ˈarki/, **arcos** /ˈɑːkəʊz/. A bow for a stringed instrument. **B** *adverb & adjective* (Especially as a direction) played on a violin or other stringed instrument using the bow. Often contrasted with PIZZICATO.

areg plural of ERG.

arête /əˈrɛt/, /əˈreɪt/ *noun* E19 French (from Latin *arista* ear of corn, fish bone or spine). A sharp mountain ridge with steep sides.

argot /ˈɑːgəʊ/ *noun* M19 French (of unknown origin). The jargon, slang, or peculiar phraseology of a particular group or class; originally, the jargon or slang of criminals.

> **1996** *Times* European football has always had its own argot too...

argumentum ad hominem /ɑːgjʊˌmɛntəm ad ˈhɒmɪnɛm/ *noun phrase* M17 Latin. An argument, usually vilificatory, attacking the personal circumstances or character of an opponent rather than employing sound reasoning to make the point. Cf. AD HOMINEM.

■ In attributive use often shortened to *ad hominem*; see quotation.

1995 *Times* Ad hominem attacks smack of an insolence intolerable to most leaders...

arhat /ˈɑːhat/ *noun* L19 Sanskrit (*arhat*, Pali *arahat* meritorious). *Buddhism* and *Jainism* A saint of one of the highest ranks.

aria /ˈɑːrɪə/ *noun* E18 Italian (from Latin *aera* accusative of *aer* from Greek *aēr* air). *Music* A long accompanied song for a solo voice, typically one in an opera or oratorio.

arioso /arɪˈəʊsəʊ/ *adjective, adverb, & noun* E18 Italian (from ARIA). *Music* **A** *adjective* Melodious, songlike, cantabile; having something of the quality of an aria, though less formal. Also as *adverb* as a direction. **B** *noun* plural **ariosos**. A piece of vocal or instrumental music of this kind.

armada /ɑːˈmɑːdə/ *noun* (also **armado** and in sense 1b **Armada**) M16 Spanish (from Proto-Romance *armata* army). **1 a** fleet of warships. **b** *specifically* The Spanish Armada, the fleet sent by Philip II of Spain to attack England in 1588. **2** A large fleet of vessels of any kind.
■ Formerly pronounced /ɑːˈmeɪdə/.

armamentarium /ˌɑːməmɛnˈtɛːrɪəm/ *noun* plural **armamentaria** /ˌɑːməmɛnˈtɛːrɪə/ L19 Latin (= arsenal, armoury). The medicines, equipment, and techniques available to a medical practitioner.

armiger /ˈɑːmɪdʒə/ *noun* M16 Latin (= bearing arms, from *arma* arms). Originally, a person who attended a knight to bear his shield; now, a person entitled to heraldic arms.

armoire /ɑːˈmwɑː/ *noun* L16 French. A cupboard or wardrobe, typically one that is ornate or antique.

arpeggio /ɑːˈpɛdʒɪəʊ/ *noun* plural **arpeggios** E18 Italian (from *arpeggiare* to play on the harp, from *arpa* harp). *Music* The notes of a chord played in rapid succession, either ascending or descending.
1996 *Country Life*...the playfulness of Opus 110 dissolved into a moment of perfect stillness before the joyous arpeggios came bubbling back.

arrack variant of ARAK.

arrière-pensée /arjɛrpɑ̃se/ *noun* plural pronounced same E19 French (literally, 'behind-thought'). A concealed thought or intention; an ulterior motive.

arrivisme /ariːˈviːzm(ə)/ *noun* (also in Anglicized form **arrivism**) M20 French (from Old French *ariver* to arrive, ultimately from Latin *ad* to + *ripa* shore). The behaviour or character of an ARRIVISTE.

arriviste /ariːˈviːst/ *noun* plural pronounced same (also in Anglicized form **arrivist**) E20 French (from as preceding). An ambitious or ruthlessly self-seeking person.
1995 *Spectator* The shameless effrontery with which these two power-greedy *arrivistes* bought and sold office for votes quite takes one's breath away.

arrondissement /arɔ̃dismɑ̃/ *noun* plural pronounced same E19 French (from *arrondiss-* lengthened stem of *arrondir* make round). A subdivision of a French department, for local government administration; an administrative district of certain large French cities, in particular Paris.

arroyo /əˈrɔɪəʊ/ *noun* plural **arroyos** M19 Spanish. A steep-sided gully formed by the action of fast-flowing water in an arid or semi-arid region, found chiefly in the south-western US.

arsis /ˈɑːsɪs/ *noun* plural **arses** /ˈɑːsiːz/ LME Late Latin (from Greek = lifting, raising, from *airein* to raise). *Prosody* A stressed syllable or part of a metrical foot in Greek or Latin verse. Opposed to THESIS.

artel /ɑːˈtɛl/ *noun* L19 Russian (*artel'*). (In pre-revolutionary Russia) a cooperative association of craftsmen living or working together.

artiste /ɑːˈtiːst/ *noun* E19 French. A professional entertainer, especially a singer or dancer.

art nouveau /ɑː nuːˈvəʊ/, *foreign* /ar nuvo/ *noun phrase* E20 French (literally, 'new art'). A style of decorative art, architecture, and design prominent in western Europe and the United States from about 1890 until the First World War and characterized by ornamented and flowing lines. Cf. JUGENDSTIL.

1996 *Spectator* Bakst's original setting for the 1906 exhibition in Paris...gives a lift to some overripe Russian art nouveau sculpture.

ascesis /əˈsiːsɪs/ *noun* L19 Greek (*askēsis* exercise, training, from *askein* to exercise). The practice of severe self-discipline, typically for religious reasons.

ashram /ˈaʃrəm/ *noun* E20 Sanskrit (*āśrama* hermitage). **1** (In the Indian subcontinent) a hermitage, monastic community, or other place of religious retreat. **2** Any group with shared spiritual or social aims living together.

askari /əˈskɑːri/ *noun* plural **askaris**, same L19 Arabic (ˈaskarī soldier). (In East Africa) a soldier or police officer.

asphyxia /əsˈfɪksɪə/ *noun* M19 Modern Latin (from Greek *asphuxia*, from *a-* without + *sphuxis* pulsation). *Medicine* A condition arising when the body is deprived of oxygen, causing unconsciousness or death; suffocation.

assai /aˈsʌɪ/ *adverb* E18 Italian (= very much). *Music* (In directions) very: *allegro assai*.

assegai /ˈasəɡʌɪ/ *noun* (also **assagai**) E17 French (*azagaie* (now *zagaie, sagaie*)) or Portuguese (*azagaia*, Spanish *azagaya* from colloquial Arabic *az-zaġāya* from *al* the + Berber *zaġāya* spear). A slender, iron-bladed spear with a hardwood shaft used chiefly by southern African peoples.

assemblé /asɑ̃ble/ *noun* plural pronounced same L18 French (past participle of *assembler* to bring together). *Ballet* A leap in which the feet are brought together before landing.

ataman /ˈatəman/ *noun* M19 Russian. A Cossack leader. Cf. HETMAN.

ataraxia /atəˈraksɪə/ *noun* M19 Greek (= impassiveness, from *a-* not + *tarassein* to disturb). A state of serene calmness; imperturbability.

atelier /əˈtɛlɪeɪ/ *noun* L17 French (from Old French *astelle* splinter of wood, from Latin *astula*). A workshop or studio, especially one used by an artist or fashion designer.

1995 *Times* Gone are the days when...the *ateliers* of craftspeople were busy, not just with clothes and hats for a wedding, but with custom-made jewels.

a tempo /ɑː ˈtɛmpəʊ/ *adverb phrase* M18 Italian (= in time). *Music* (Especially as a direction) in the tempo indicated previously, before the direction to deviate from it.

atlantes /atˈlantiːz/ *noun plural* E17 Greek (*Atlas, Atlant-*, the Titan supposed to hold up the pillars of the universe, and a mountain range in western North Africa also regarded mythically as supporting the heavens). *Architecture* Stone carvings of male figures used as pillars to support the entablature of a Greek or Greek-style building.

■ The singular form of the word, meaning 'a person who supports a great burden', was introduced via Latin (L16) and soon afterwards (M17) became the name for 'a collection of maps or charts bound in a volume'. In this sense, and in other senses derived from it, *atlas* has long been entirely naturalized. The connection between the world-supporting Titan and the book of maps was first made in the mid 16th century, when Antonio Lafreri, a French publisher working in Rome, put together collections of maps to his customers' specifications and bound them with a standard titlepage depicting Atlas carrying the world on his shoulders. The use of 'Atlas' as a title for a book of maps originated with the Flemish geographers Gerhard and Rumold Mercator, whose complete 107-map *Atlas* was published in 1595. The Mercator *Atlas* in various versions and editions so dominated European cartography in the first half of the 17th century (it appeared in English in 1636) that the name became used generically for all such books.

atman /ˈɑːtmən/ *noun* L18 Sanskrit (*ātman* essence, breath). *Hinduism* The spiritual life principle of the universe, especially when regarded as immanent in the individual's real self; a person's soul.

atrium /ˈeɪtrɪəm/ *noun* plural **atria** /ˈeɪtrɪə/, **atriums** L16 Latin. **1** *Architecture*

An open-roofed entrance hall or central court in an ancient Roman house; a central hall in a modern building, typically rising through several stories and having a glazed roof; the forecourt of a large church built on the basilican plan. **2** *Anatomy* Each of the two upper cavities of the heart from which blood is passed to the ventricles.

> **1** 1995 *Times* Office accommodation for tenants has a separate entrance with escalators leading up to a glass and cream-coloured marble atrium.

à trois /a trwa/ *adjective & adverb phrase* L19 French. Shared by, or in a group of, three people. Cf. MÉNAGE À TROIS.

> 1996 *Spectator* In 1956 Gottfried, Budge and I went to dine *à trois* wearing black tie.

attaché /əˈtaʃeɪ/ *noun* E19 French (= attached, past participle of *attacher* to attach). A person on the staff of an ambassador having a specialized area of responsibility.

> ■ Frequently in the combination *attaché case* a small rectangular case, usually with a handle, for carrying documents.

attar /ˈatə/ *noun* (also (earlier) **otto** /ˈɒtəʊ/) M17 Persian (ʿitr, Arabic ʿitr, colloquial Arabic ʿaṭar perfume, essence). A fragrant essential oil, *especially* (more fully *attar of roses*) that obtained from rose petals.

aubade /əʊˈbɑːd/, *foreign* /obad/ (*plural same*) *noun* L17 French (from Spanish *albada*, from *alba* (= French *aube*) dawn). A piece of music or a poem written to be heard at or appropriate to dawn.

auberge /əʊˈbɛːʒ/; *foreign* /obɛrʒ/ (*plural same*) *noun* L16 French (from Provençal *alberga* lodging). An inn in a French-speaking country.

aubergine /ˈəʊbəʒiːn/ *noun & adjective* L18 French (from Catalan *alberginia*, from Arabic *al-bāḏinjān*, from *al-* the + Persian *bādingān, bādinjān* from Sanskrit *vātiṃgaṇa*). **A** *noun* **1** The fruit of the eggplant, *Solanum melongena*, eaten as a vegetable; the plant itself. Cf. BRINJAL. **2** A dark purple colour typical of the skin of the fruit. **B** *adjective* Of the colour aubergine, dark purple.

Aubusson /obysɔ̃/ *noun* plural pronounced same E20 French (Aubusson = a town in central France). A fine tapestry or carpet woven at Aubusson, especially one from the late 18th century.

AUC abbreviation of AB URBE CONDITA.

au contraire /o kɔ̃trɛr/, /əʊ kɒnˈtrɛː/ *adverb phrase* M18 French. On the contrary.

> 1995 D. Lodge *Therapy* Don't get the idea that I'm an enthusiast for British Rail's Inter-City service to London. *Au contraire*, as Amy would say.

au courant /o kurɑ̃/ *adverb & adjective phrase* M18 French (literally, 'in the (regular) course'). **1** Aware of what is going on; well informed: *they were au courant with the literary scene.* **2** Fashionable.

> ■ Usually followed by *with, of,* but can also be used on its own.
>
> 1996 *Times* . . . to find out what the in-your-face young are wearing, or were ten minutes ago when in-your-face was still an *au courant* fashion statement . . .

au fait /əʊ feɪ/, *foreign* /o fɛ/ *adverb & predicative adjective phrase* M18 French (literally, 'to the fact', 'to the point'). Having a good or detailed knowledge of something.

> 1996 *Times: Weekend* The Tuscans are not entirely au fait with the idea of walking for pleasure.

au fond /o fɔ̃/ *adverb phrase* L18 French (literally, 'at the bottom'). Basically; in essence.

> 1996 *Spectator* . . . Mrs Lancaster was *au fond* nostalgic, a sentiment she vehemently denies possessing . . .

au gratin /o gratɛ̃/ *adverb & predicative adjective phrase* E19 French (from *au* with the + GRATIN). *Cookery* Sprinkled with breadcrumbs or grated cheese and browned.

au naturel /o natyrɛl/ *adverb phrase* E19 French (literally, 'in the natural (state)'). **1** With no elaborate treatment, dressing, or preparation; in the most simple or natural way. **2** Naked.

> **1** 1996 *New Scientist* Now the company is paying people to look for weedy pastures around the state [sc. Nebraska] and pick the [milkweed] pods *au naturel*.

au pair /əʊ pɛː/ *noun phrase* L19 French (= on equal terms). A young foreign person, typically a woman, who helps with housework or childcare in exchange for food, a room, and some pocket money.

■ The phrase was originally adjectival, describing an arrangement between two parties paid for by the exchange of mutual services. The noun use dates from the 1960s.

aureola /ɔːˈriːələ/ *noun* plural **aureolae**, /ɔːˈriːəli/, **aureolas** L15 Latin (from *aureola (corona)* golden (crown), feminine of *aureolus* adjective, diminutive of *aureus* golden, from *aurum* gold). A circle of light or brightness surrounding something, especially as depicted in art around the head or body of a person represented as holy; a corona around the sun or moon.

au revoir /o rəvwɑr/, /əʊ rəˈvwɑː/ *interjection & noun phrase* L17 French (literally, 'to the seeing again'). Goodbye until we meet again; a farewell for the present.

aurora /ɔːˈrɔːrə/ *noun* (also **Aurora**) plural **aurorae** /ɔːˈrɔːriː/, **auroras** LME Latin (*Aurora* the Roman goddess of the dawn). **1** A luminous phenomenon, often taking the form of streamers of reddish or greenish light in the sky, seen in the upper atmosphere of high northern (*borealis*) and southern (*australis*) latitudes. **2** The rising light of the morning; the dawn.

aurora australis /ɔːˌrɔːrə ɔːˈstreɪlɪs/ M18 Latin (= southern dawn). The aurora of the southern polar regions, the southern lights.

■ Coined after AURORA BOREALIS.

aurora borealis /ɔːˌrɔːrə bɔːrɪˈeɪlɪs/ E18 Latin (= northern dawn). The aurora of the northern polar regions, the northern lights.

■ The phrase was coined to describe the phenomenon in 1621 by the French physicist and philosopher Pierre Gassendi (1592–1655).

Auslese /ˈaʊsleːzə/ *noun* (also **auslese**) plural **Auslesen** /ˈaʊsleːzən/, **Ausleses** M19 German (from *aus* out + *lese* picking, vintage). A white wine of German origin or style made from selected

bunches of grapes picked later than the general harvest.

auteur /otœr/ *noun* plural pronounced same M20 French (= author). A film director who so greatly influences their films as to be able to rank as their author.

1995 *Spectator* But then why would anyone go hire a writer when everyone keeps telling him that he's an *auteur*?

autobahn /ˈɔːtəbɑːn/, *foreign* /ˈaʊtobɑːn/ *noun* plural **autobahns**, **autobahnen** /ˈaʊtobɑːnən/ M20 German (from *Auto* automobile + *Bahn* path, road). A German, Swiss, or Austrian motorway.

1996 *Independent* Germany gave us prototypical motorways in Hitler's *Autobahn*.

auto-da-fé /ˌautodaˈfe/, /ˌɔːtəʊdɑːˈfeɪ/, /ˌaʊtəʊdɑːˈfeɪ/ *noun* plural **autos-da-fé** /ˌautosdaˈfe/, /ˌɔːtəʊzdɑːˈfeɪ/, /ˌaʊtəʊzdɑːˈfeɪ/, **auto-da-fés** E18 Portuguese (= act of the faith (Spanish *auto de fe*)). **1** A judicial sentence of the Spanish Inquisition, especially the public burning of a heretic. **2** Any public burning.

2 1997 G. Kepel *Allah in West* . . . television viewers saw the scenes [of the burning of Rushdie's *Satanic Verses*] differently: they recalled engravings of Inquisition bonfires or black-and-white images of Nazis burning books . . . whilst commentators in the Western press used these images to wax indignant about the *auto-da-fé* . . .

autogiro /ɔːtəʊˈdʒaɪrəʊ/ *noun* (also **autogyro**) plural **autogiros** E20 Spanish (from as *auto-* self + *giro* gyration). A type of aircraft having a propeller and freely rotating horizontal blades.

automat /ˈɔːtəmat/ *noun* L17 German (from French *automate* from Latin *automaton*, from Greek *automatos* acting of itself). A cafeteria in which food and drink is obtained from slot machines.

■ Chiefly a United States usage, dating from the early 20th century. First used in English in the late 17th century to denote an automaton.

autopista /ɔːtəˈpiːstə/, *foreign* /autoˈpista/ *noun* M20 Spanish (from *auto* automobile + *pista* track, PISTE). A motorway in a Spanish-speaking country.

autoroute /ˈɔːtəruːt/, *foreign* /otorut/ (*plural same*) *noun* M20 French (from *auto* automobile + *route* road). A French motorway.

autostrada /ɔːtəˈstrɑːdə/, *foreign* /auto ˈstrɑːda/ *noun* plural **autostradas, autostrade** /autoˈstrɑːde/ E20 Italian (from *auto* automobile + *strada* road). An Italian motorway.

avalanche /ˈavəlɑːnʃ/ *noun & verb* L18 French (from Romansh, alteration of Alpine French dialect *lavanche* (of unknown origin), by blending with *avaler* descend: cf. Provençal *lavanca*, Italian *valanga*). **A** *noun* **1** A large mass of snow, rocks, and ice, falling rapidly down a mountainside. **2** A large mass of mud or other material moving rapidly downhill. **3** A sudden arrival or occurrence of something in overwhelming quantities. **4** *Physics* A process of cumulative ionization in which each electron and ion generates further charged particles. Also more fully *Townsend avalanche*. **B** *intransitive verb* Descend in or like an avalanche.

avant-garde /ˌavɒ̃ˈgɑːd/ *noun & adjective* LME French (from *avant* forward, before + *garde* guard). **A** *noun* New and experimental ideas in art, music, or literature; a group of artists, musicians, or writers working with new and experimental ideas and methods. **B** *adjective* Favouring or introducing new and experimental ideas and methods; progressive, ultra-modern.

■ In early use, the term denoted the vanguard of an army. Current senses date from the early 20th century.

A 1996 *Times* The punk singer, who wowed the avant-garde of Madrid in the frenzied years after Franco's death, has mellowed into a chubby 45-year-old in jeans and a stripey jumper.

B 1996 *Country Life* [Stockhausen's] *Gruppen* has always been considered an avant-garde landmark.

avant la lettre /avɒ̃ la lɛtr/ *adverb phrase* M20 French (literally, 'before the letter'). Before the word or term was invented.

1995 *Spectator* He was a Eurosceptic *avant la lettre*.

avatar /ˈavətɑː/ *noun* L18 Sanskrit (*avatāra* descent, from *ava* off, away, down + *tar-* to pass over). **1** Chiefly *Hinduism* A

manifestation of a deity or released soul in bodily form on earth; an incarnate divine teacher. **2** An incarnation, embodiment, or manifestation of a person or idea. **3** *Computing* A movable icon representing a person in cyberspace or virtual reality graphics.

2 1995 *Times* Most are interpreted as avatars of anti-imperialism, which requires some dedicated pummelling into shape.

ave /ˈɑːvi/, /ˈɑːveɪ/ *noun & interjection* (also **Ave** in sense A.1) ME Latin (= fare well, imperative singular of *avere* to be or fare well, used as an expression of greeting or farewell). **A** *noun* **1** An AVE MARIA. **b** A bead on a rosary (as used for counting the number of aves recited). **2** A shout of welcome or farewell. **B** *interjection* Used to express good wishes on meeting or parting.

■ The earliest use of the noun was short for AVE MARIA.

ave atque vale /ˌɑːveɪ atkwi ˈvɑːleɪ/ *interjection* M19 Latin (= hail and farewell). Hello and goodbye, hail and farewell.

■ The concluding words of Catullus' graveside address to his dead brother (*Carmina* ci.10), the exclamation is now sometimes used humorously as a greeting to someone whom one has seen or will see for only a short time.

Ave Maria /ˌɑːvi məˈriːə/, /ˌɑːveɪ məˈriːə/ *noun phrase* (also **Ave Mary** /ˈmɛːri/) ME Latin (= hail, Mary!). A prayer to the Virgin Mary used in Catholic worship, the first line of which is adapted from Luke 1:28.

avoirdupois /avədəˈpɔɪz/, /ˌavwɑːdjuˈpwɑː/ *noun* ME Old French (*aveir de peis* goods of weight, from *ave(i)r* (modern *avoir*) use as noun of *avoir* to have (from Latin *habere*) + *de* of + *peis*, *pois* (modern *poids*) weight). **1** A system of weights based on a pound (the *avoirdupois pound*) of 16 ounces or 7,000 grains. More fully *avoirdupois weight*. **2** Weight, heaviness; *colloquially* excess bodily weight.

■ Originally denoted merchandise sold by weight. The substitution of *du* for the earlier *de* was established in the 17th century.

2 1995 *Times* It may be wish-fulfilment or simply *avoirdupois*, but Paula Yates's famously tiny waist seems to have expanded.

ayah /'ʌɪə/ *noun* L18 Portuguese (*aia* feminine of *aio* tutor). A nursemaid or nanny employed by Europeans in India or another former British territory.
> **1996** *Times: Weekend* Olive, like many children born in colonies and brought up by an *ayah*, has divided loyalties.

ayahuasca /ˌaja'waska/ *noun* L20 **South American Spanish** (from Quechua *ayawáskha* from *aya* corpse + *waskha* rope). A hallucinogenic drug made from the bark of a tropical vine found in the Amazon basin; the vine itself. Also called *yagé*.

ayatollah /ʌɪə'tɒlə/ *noun* (also (as a title) **Ayatollah**) M20 Persian (from Arabic *'āyatu-llāh* miraculous sign of God). **1** A high-ranking religious leader among Shiite Muslims, especially in Iran. **2** A dogmatic leader, an influential or powerful person.

ayurveda /ɑːjə'veɪdə/ *noun* (also **Ayurveda**) E20 Sanskrit (*āyur-veda* science of life, medicine). The traditional Hindu system of medicine (incorporated in Atharda Veda, the last of the four Vedas), which is based on the idea of balance in bodily systems and uses diet, herbal treatment, and yogic breathing.

azan /ə'zɑːn/ *noun* M19 Arabic (*'aḏān* announcement). The Muslim call to ritual prayer, often made by a muezzin or broadcast through loudspeakers from the minaret of a mosque.

azulejo /aθu'lexo/, /asu'lexo/, /azjʊ'leɪhəʊ/ *noun* plural **azulejos** /aθu'lexos/, /asu'lexos/, /azjʊ'leɪhəʊz/ M19 Spanish (from *azul* blue). A kind of coloured glazed tile traditionally used in Spanish and Portuguese buildings.

Bb

baas /bɑːs/ *noun* L18 Dutch. (In South Africa) a supervisor or employer, especially a white man in charge of coloured or black people. Often *offensive*.

■ The word was first used in English in 1625 (*Purchas his Pilgrimes* I. ii. 117) for a sea captain: 'Our Baase (for so a Dutch capitaine is called)'. It travelled to South Africa with the Dutch settlers of that country and became, in both Afrikaans and South African English, the normal form of address used by black or coloured South Africans for those in authority.

baba /ˈbɑːbɑː/ *noun* E19 French (from Polish, literally, 'married peasant woman'). A small, rich sponge cake, typically soaked in rum-flavoured spirit. More fully *rum baba* or *baba au rhum*.

babiche /bəˈbiːʃ/ *noun* E19 Canadian French (from Micmac *a:papi:č*). Raw hide, typically formed into strips, as used by North American Indians for making fastenings and animal snares.

babu /ˈbɑːbuː/ *noun* (also (as title) **Babu**) L18 Hindi (*bābū* father). **1** A respectful title or form of address for a man, especially an educated one. **2** An office worker.

babushka /bəˈbʊʃkə/ *noun* M20 Russian (= grandmother). **1** (In Russia) a grandmother, an old woman. **2** A headscarf tied under the chin, typical of those traditionally worn by Russian women. Chiefly *North American*.

bacalao /bakaˈlaʊ/ *noun* (also **bacalhau** /bakaˈjaʊ/) M16 Spanish (*bacal(l)ao*, Portuguese *bacalhau*). Codfish, especially dried or salted, as used in Spanish and Latin American cookery.

baccalaureate /bakəˈlɔːrɪət/ *noun* M17 French (*baccalauréat* or medieval Latin *baccalaureatus*, from *baccalaureus* bachelor, originally with reference to *bacca lauri* laurel berry (because of the laurels awarded to scholars)). **1** The university degree of bachelor. **2** An examination intended to qualify successful candidates for higher education in any of several countries; hence also known as the *International Baccalaureate*.

baccarat /ˈbakərɑː/ *noun* (also **baccara**) M19 French (*baccara*, of unknown origin). A gambling card game in which players hold two- or three-card hands, the winning hand being that yielding the highest remainder when its total face value is divided by 10.

bach /bɑːx/ *noun* L19 Welsh ((dialect) literally, 'little'). Used as a term of endearment, often after a personal name.

backsheesh variant of BAKSHEESH.

badinage /ˌbadɪˈnɑːʒ/ *noun* M17 French (from *badiner* to joke, from *badin* fool from Provençal, from *badar* to gape, from Proto-Romance). Humorous or witty conversation; banter.

> **1996** *Spectator* The jokes and the badinage now were for real; and so were the author's anxieties.

badmash /ˈbʌdmɑːʃ/ *noun* M19 Urdu (from Persian, from *bad* evil + Arabic *maˈāš* means of livelihood). (In the Indian subcontinent) a dishonest or unprincipled man.

bagasse /bəˈgas/ *noun* E19 French (from Spanish *bagazo* pulp). The dry pulpy residue left after the extraction of juice from sugar cane or sugar beet.

bagatelle /bagəˈtɛl/ *noun* M17 French (from Italian *bagatella* perhaps diminutive of Latin *baca* berry, or from Italian *baga* baggage). **1** A trifle, a thing regarded as too unimportant or easy to be worth much consideration. **2** A short piece of verse or music in a light style. **3** A game in which small balls are struck (usually by a mechanical striker operated by the player) towards numbered holes on a board with a semicircular end.

1 1996 *Spectator* What if I had confused a treaty? Phooey, a mere bagatelle.

bagel /ˈbeɪɡ(ə)l/ *noun* (also **beigel** /ˈbʌɪɡ(ə)l/) E20 Yiddish (*beygel*). A dense bread roll in the shape of a ring, characteristic of Jewish baking.

bagnio /ˈbɑːnjəʊ/ *noun* plural **bagnios** L16 Italian (*bagno* from Latin *balneum* bath). **1** (In the Far East) a prison. Now only *historical*. **2** A brothel. *Archaic*.

ba gua /bɑːˈɡwɑː/ *noun* (also **pa gua** /pɑːˈkwɑː/) L19 Chinese (*bāguà* (Wade–Giles *pà-kua*), from *bā* eight + *guà* divinatory symbols). **1** A Chinese decorative and religious motif incorporating the eight trigrams of *I Ching*; *specifically* an arrangement of these trigrams in a circle round the yin-yang symbol. **2** A Chinese martial art in which fighters are arranged around a circle according to the trigram sequence in positions which they must defend.

baguette /baˈɡɛt/ *noun* E18 French (from Italian *bacchetto* diminutive of *bacchio* from Latin *baculum* staff). **1** A long narrow French loaf. **2** A gem, especially a diamond, cut in a long rectangular shape. **3** *Architecture* A small moulding of semicircular section.

bahada variant of BAJADA.

bain-marie /ˌbanməˈriː/, *foreign* /bɛ̃mari/ *noun* plural **bains-marie** (pronounced same) E18 French (translation of medieval Latin *balneum Mariae* (= bath of Maria) translation of medieval Greek *kaminos Marias* (= furnace of Maria), Maria being the name of a supposed Jewish alchemist). A pan of hot water in which a cooking container is placed for slow cooking.

bajada /bəˈhɑːdə/ *noun* (also **bahada**) M19 Spanish (= descent, slope). A broad slope of alluvial material at the foot of an escarpment.

■ Originally south-western United States but subsequently more general.

baklava /ˈbɑːkləvə/ *noun* M17 Turkish. A dessert originating in the Middle East made of filo pastry filled with chopped nuts and soaked in honey.

baksheesh /bakˈʃiːʃ/ *noun* (also **backsheesh**) M18 Persian (ultimately from *bakšīš* from *bakšīdan* to give). (In parts of the Middle East, Far East, and the Indian subcontinent) a small sum of money given as alms, a tip, or a bribe.

balafon /ˈbalafɒn/ *noun* L20 Manding (*bala* xylophone + *fo* to play). A West African musical instrument similar to a xylophone.

balalaika /baləˈlʌɪkə/ *noun* L18 Russian (of Tartar origin). A Russian musical instrument like a guitar with a triangular body and from two to four strings.

baldachin /ˈbaldəkɪn/, /ˈbɔːldəkɪn/ *noun* (also **baldaquin**) M17 Italian (*baldacchino*, ultimately from *Baldacco* Italian form of *Baghdad*). A ceremonial canopy supported on columns or fixed to a roof or wall, and placed over an altar, throne, or doorway.

■ When first introduced into English (L16), *baldacchino* denoted rich brocade of a type that had originally been made in Baghdad. It was later (M17) transferred to describe a canopy made out of this material, and in current usage the canopy can be of any material.

ballade /baˈlɑːd/ *noun* LME French (from Provençal *balada* dance, song, or poem to dance to, from *balar* to dance). **1** A poem (originally for singing with accompaniment) consisting of one or more triplets of stanzas having 7, 8, or 10 lines, each usually ending with the same refrain line, and an envoy; more *generally*, a poem divided into stanzas of equal length, usually of 7 or 8 lines. **2** *Music* A piece of music in romantic style with dramatic elements, typically for the piano.

ballerina /baləˈriːnə/ *noun* plural **ballerinas** L18 Italian (feminine of *ballerino* dancing master, from *ballare* to dance). A female ballet dancer.

ballet /ˈbaleɪ/, /ˈbali/ *noun* M17 French (from Italian *balletto* diminutive of *ballo* ball). An artistic dance form performed to music, using precise and highly formalized set steps and gestures; a creative work of this form or the music written for it; a group of dancers who regularly perform ballet.

ballista /bə'lɪstə/ *noun* plural **ballistae** /bə'lɪstiː/, **ballistas** E16 Latin (ultimately from Greek *ballein* to throw). A catapult used in ancient warfare for hurling large stones and other missiles.

ballon /balɔ̃/ *noun* plural pronounced same M19 French. **1** (In dancing) the ability to appear effortlessly suspended while performing movements during a jump. **2** A spherical glass for brandy, a brandy balloon.

> **1** 1995 *Times* Tetsuya Kumakawa as the Blue Boy turns and jumps with the flashy *ballon* and clarity that has made him such a hit . . .

bal masqué /bal maske/ *noun phrase* plural **bals masqués** (pronounced same) M18 French. A masked ball.

bal musette /bal myzɛt/ *noun phrase* plural **bals musettes** (pronounced same) E20 French (originally denoting dancing outdoors to bagpipe accompaniment). (In France) a dance hall with an accordion band.

balsa /'bɒlsə/ *noun* E17 Spanish (= raft). A tropical American tree, *Ochroma pyramidale* (more fully *balsa tree*); its strong, very light wood, used for making models, rafts, floats, etc. (more fully *balsa wood*).

> ■ Originally denoting a kind of South American raft or fishing boat.

balti /'bɔːlti/, /'balti/ *noun* L20 Urdu (of uncertain origin). A type of spicy Pakistani cuisine in which the food is cooked in a small two-handled pan known as a karahi; a meal prepared in this way.

> 1994 *Guardian* Among the 8,000 restaurants now doing business, previous vogues have been superseded by balti (bucket) cuisine. 'Balti is the current fashion and it hasn't peaked yet,' he said.

bambino /bam'biːno/, /bam'biːnəʊ/ *noun* plural **bambini** /bam'biːni/, **bambinos** E18 Italian (diminutive of *bambo* silly). A young child or baby; *specifically* an image of the infant Jesus in swaddling clothes.

banco /'baŋkəʊ/ *interjection* L18 French (from Italian). (In baccarat, chemin de fer, etc.) an indication of a player's willingness to meet single-handed the banker's whole stake.

bandeau /'bandəʊ/, *foreign* /bɑ̃do/ *noun* plural **bandeaux** /'bandəʊz/, *foreign* /bɑ̃do/ E18 French (from Old French *bandel* diminutive of *bande*). A narrow band worn round the head to hold the hair in position.

banderilla /bande'rija/, /bandə'rɪljə/ *noun* plural **banderillas** /bande'rijas/, /bandə'rɪljəz/ L18 Spanish (diminutive of *bandera* banner). A decorated dart thrust into a bull's neck or shoulders during a bullfight.

banderillero /banderi'jero/, /bandərɪ'ljɛːrəʊ/ *noun* plural **banderilleros** /banderi'jeros/, /bandərɪ'ljɛːrəʊz/ L18 Spanish (from BANDERILLA). *Bullfighting* A bullfighter who uses banderillas. Also called PEON.

banderole /'bandərəʊl/ *noun* (also **banderol** /'bandərəʊl/, /'bandər(ə)l/) M16 French (*ban(n)erole*, later *banderole*, from Italian *banderuola* diminutive of *bandiera* banner). **1** A long narrow flag with a cleft end, flown from the masthead of a ship. **2** A rectangular banner borne at the funerals of public figures and placed over the tomb. **3** An ornamental streamer of the kind attached to a knight's lance. **4** A ribbon-like stone scroll bearing an inscription.

bandobast variant of BUNDOBUST.

bania /'bʌnɪə/ *noun* L18 Hindi (*baniyā* from Sanskrit *vāṇija*). (In India) a trader or merchant.

banian variant of BANYAN.

banquette /baŋ'kɛt/ *noun* E17 French (from Italian *banchetta* diminutive of *banca* bench, shelf). **1** A raised step or way running along the inside of a rampart, at the bottom of a trench, etc., on which soldiers stand to fire at the enemy. **2** A long upholstered seat along a wall, especially in a restaurant or bar.

banyan /'banɪən/, /'banjən/ *noun* (also **banian**) L16 Portuguese (from Gujarati *vāṇiyo* man of the trading caste, from Sanskrit *vāṇija* merchant). **1** In full ***banyan tree.*** An Indian fig tree, *Ficus benghalensis*, the branches of which root themselves over a wide area. **2** A loose flannel undergarment worn in India.

■ Originally denoting a Hindu merchant, the term was applied by Europeans in the mid 17th century to a particular tree of the species growing in a port on the Persian Gulf, under which such traders had built a pagoda. In 1634 Sir Thomas Herbert wrote of 'A tree... named by us the Bannyan Tree, from their adorning and adoring it with ribbons and streamers of varicoloured Taffata' (*Travels* II (1638)). The tree is not known by this name in any Indian language.

banzai /ban'zʌɪ/ *interjection & adjective* L19 Japanese (= ten thousand years (of life to you)). **A** *interjection* **1** A Japanese battle cry. **2** A form of greeting used to the Japanese emperor. **B** *adjective* **1** (Especially of troops) attacking fiercely and recklessly: *a banzai charge.* **2** Behaving wildly; berserk. *Slang.*

bara brith /ˌbarə 'brɪθ/ *noun* M20 Welsh (= speckled bread). A traditional Welsh tea bread, typically made with raisins, currants, and candied peel.

baraza /bə'rɑːzə/ *noun* L19 Kiswahili. (In East Africa) a public meeting place.

barbette /bɑː'bɛt/ *noun* L18 French (from *barbe* beard + diminutive *-ette*). **1** A fixed armoured housing at the base of a gun turret on a warship or armoured vehicle. **2** *History* A platform on which a gun was placed to fire over a parapet.

barbotine /'bɑːbətɪn/, /'bɑːbəti:n/ *noun* M19 French. Slip (liquid clay) used to decorate pottery.

barcarole /'bɑːkərəʊl/, /bɑːkə'rəʊl/ *noun* (also **barcarolle** /'bɑːkərɒl/) L18 French (*barcarolle* from Venetian Italian *barcarola* boatman's song, related to *barcarolo* gondolier, from *barca* boat). A song traditionally sung by Venetian gondoliers; a piece of music in imitation of such songs or suggestive of the rocking motion of a boat.

barchan /'bɑːk(ə)n/ *noun* (also **barchane, barkhan, barkan**) L19 Turkic (*barkhan*). A shifting crescent-shaped sand dune, concave on the leeward side.

barège /barɛʒ/ *noun* plural pronounced same E19 French (from *Barèges*, a village in south-west France, where it was originally made). A light, silky dress fabric resembling gauze, typically made from wool.

barkan, barkhan variants of BARCHAN.

bar mitzvah /bɑː 'mɪtsvə/ *noun & verb phrase* (also **Bar mitzvah**) M19 Hebrew (*bar miswāh* son of the commandment). **A** *noun phrase* The initiation ceremony of a Jewish boy who has reached the age of thirteen, regarded as ready to observe the religious precepts and eligible to take part in public worship; the boy undergoing this ceremony. Cf. BAT MITZVAH. **B** *transitive verb phrase* Administer the bar mitzvah ceremony to (a boy).

barouche /bə'ruːʃ/ *noun* E19 German (dialect *Barutsche* from Italian *baroccio* (Spanish *barrocho*) two-wheeled, ultimately from Latin *birotus*, from *bi-* two + *rota* wheel). A four-wheeled horse-drawn carriage with a collapsible hood over the rear half, a seat in front for the driver, and seats facing each other for the passengers. Chiefly *historical.*

barre /bɑː/ *noun & adjective* E20 French. **A** *noun* A waist-level horizontal bar on which ballet dancers rest a hand for support during certain exercises. **B** *adjective* *Music* Denoting a chord played using the BARRÉ method.

barré /bare/ *noun* plural pronounced same L19 French (past participle of *barrer* to bar). *Music* A method of playing a chord on the guitar or a similar instrument in which one finger is laid across all the strings at a particular fret.

barrette /ba'rɛt/ *noun* E20 French (diminutive of *barre* bar). A bar-shaped clip or ornament for a woman's or girl's hair.

1996 *Times* Jil Sander and Prada favoured twisted buns sometimes held in place with a slim barrette.

barrio /ˈbarɪəʊ/ *noun* plural **barrios** M19 Spanish (perhaps from Arabic). A district of a town in Spain and Spanish-speaking countries; (in the US) the Spanish-speaking quarter of a town or city.

bascule /ˈbaskjuːl/ *noun* L19 French ((earlier *bacule*) = see-saw, from stem of *battre* to beat + *cul* buttocks). (also **bascule bridge**) A type of bridge with a section which can be raised and lowered using counterweights; a movable section of road forming part of a bascule bridge.

■ First used in English (in the late 17th century) to denote a lever apparatus of which one end is raised when the other is lowered.

basho /ˈbaʃəʊ/ *noun* plural same, **ba-shos** L20 Japanese. A sumo wrestling tournament.

basilica /bəˈsɪlɪkə/, /bəˈzɪlɪkə/ *noun* plural **basilicas**, (*rare*) **basilicae** /bəˈsɪlɪkiː/ M16 Latin (literally, 'royal palace' from Greek *basilikē* use as noun of feminine of *basilikos* royal, from *basileus* king). **1** A large oblong hall or building, with double colonnades and a semicircular apse, used in ancient Rome for courts of law and public assemblies. **2** A building of this form used as a Christian church. Also, used as the title of certain churches granted special privileges by the Pope.

basmati /basˈmɑːti/, /baːˈzˈmɑːti/ *noun* M19 Hindi (*bāsmatī* literally, 'fragrant'). A kind of long-grain Indian rice with a delicate fragrance. More fully *basmati rice*.

bassinet /basɪˈnɛt/ *noun* (also **bassinette**) M19 French (diminutive of *bassin* basin). A wicker cradle or pram with a curved hood.

■ A buttercup is called a bassinet in Normandy, and *bacinetz* occurs in a 1509 French list of vernacular flower names. In English too, *bassinet* was for a long time (L16–E18) used solely in a botanical context, with Lyte's 1578 herbal referring to the marsh marigold as the 'Brave Bassinet'; later herbalists recorded it as a dialect name for a geranium or various species of ranunculus.

basso /ˈbasəʊ/ *noun* plural **bassos**, **bassi** /ˈbasi/ E18 Italian (= low, from Latin *bassus*). *Music* A bass voice or vocal part.

basso continuo /ˌbasəʊ kənˈtɪnjʊəʊ/ *noun phrase* plural **basso continuos** E18 Italian (BASSO + CONTINUO). *Music* (In baroque music) an accompanying part which includes a bass line and harmonies, typically played on a keyboard instrument and with other instruments such as cello or lute; a figured bass, a thorough bass.

basso profundo /ˌbasəʊ prəˈfʌndəʊ/ *noun phrase* (occasionally **profondo** /prəˈfɒndəʊ/) plural **bassi profundi** /ˌbasi prəˈfʌndi/, **bassos profundos** M19 Italian (BASSO + *profundo*, literally, 'deep'). *Music* A bass singer with an exceptionally low range.

basso-relievo /ˌbasəʊrɪˈliːvəʊ/ *noun* (also **basso-rilievo** /ˌbasəʊrɪˈljeɪvəʊ/) plural **basso-relievos** M17 Italian (*basso-rilievo*). Low relief; a sculpture, moulding, carving, etc., in low relief; bas-relief.

basta /ˈbasta/ *interjection* L16 Italian. Enough! No matter!

bastide /baˈstiːd/ *noun* E16 Old French (Provençal *bastida* (medieval Latin *bastida*) use as noun of feminine past participle of *bastir* to build). **1** *History* A fortified village or town in France. **2** A country house in southern France.

> **2 1996** *Times Magazine* . . . centuries-old village houses, abandoned *mas* or farmhouses, grand *bastides*, dressed up for today's tastes but retaining their nobility.

basuco /bəˈzuːkəʊ/, /bəˈsuːkəʊ/ *noun* (also **basuko, bazuco, bazuko**) L20 Colombian Spanish (perhaps connected with Spanish *basura* waste; or with Spanish *bazucar* to shake violently). A cheap form of impure cocaine made from adulterated coca paste and highly addictive when smoked as a drug.

■ The explosive effect of *basuco* has led to an alternative suggestion for the etymology, linking it with the English word *bazooka*, adopted in Spanish and applied figuratively to the drug and then borrowed back into English in a slightly altered form. Other names for the drug,

which first appeared in the English-speaking world in the mid 1980s, are *little devil* and *Suzuki*.
1985 C. Nicholl *The Fruit Palace* There's a big internal market; a lot of coke and basuko used by the street boys.

batata /bəˈtɑːtə/ *noun* M16 Spanish (from Taino). (In the southern Caribbean) sweet potato.

bateau /ˈbatəʊ/, *foreign* /bato/ *noun* plural **bateaux** /ˈbatəʊz/, *foreign* /bato/ E18 French (= boat). A light riverboat, especially of a flat-bottomed kind used in Canada. Cf. BATEAU MOUCHE.
■ *Bateau* is also used attributively as an alternative to 'boat' in *bateau neck, bateau-necked*, etc., used of a garment with shallow curved neckline running from shoulder to shoulder.

bateau mouche /ˌbatəʊ ˈmuːʃ/, foreign /bato muʃ/ *noun* plural **bateaux mouches** (pronounced same) E20 French (literally 'fly boat', because of the boat's mobility). A pleasure boat which takes sightseers on the Seine in Paris.

bathos /ˈbeɪθɒs/ *noun* E18 Greek (= depth). (Especially in a literary work) an effect of anticlimax created by an unintentional lapse in mood from the sublime to the trivial or ridiculous.
■ First introduced in the mid 17th century with its original Greek meaning of 'depth, lowest phase, bottom', *bathos* is now rare or obsolete in this sense, which has been superseded by the sense above. Alexander Pope was primarily responsible for this sense in *Peri Bathous: or the Art of Sinking in Poetry* (1727), a parody of the work by the ancient Greek rhetorician Longinus *On the Sublime*.

batik /ˈbatɪk/, /bəˈtiːk/ *noun & adjective* L19 Javanese (literally, 'painted'). **A** *noun* A method (originally used in Java) of making coloured designs on textiles by dyeing them, having first applied wax to the parts to be left undyed; cloth treated in this way. **B** *adjective* Executed or ornamented by this method.

batiste /bəˈtiːst/ *noun & adjective* E19 French ((earlier *batiche*) perhaps from base of *battre* to beat). A fine light cotton or linen fabric resembling cambric.

bat mitzvah /bɑːt ˈmɪtsvə/ *noun phrase* (also **Bat mitzvah**) M20 Hebrew (*bat miṣwāh* daughter of commandment, after BAR MITZVAH). The initiation ceremony of a Jewish girl who has reached the age of twelve years and one day, regarded as the age of religious maturity; the girl undergoing this ceremony. Cf. BAR MITZVAH.

baton /ˈbat(ə)n/, *in senses* 4 *and* 6 *also foreign* /batɔ̃/ *noun* E16 French (*bâton* (earlier *baston*) = Provençal, Spanish *baston* Italian *bastone* from Proto-Romance, from late Latin *bastum* stick). **1** A stick or staff used as a weapon. **b** A police officer's truncheon. **2** A thin stick used by a conductor to direct an orchestra or choir; a drum major's stick. **3** A short stick or tube carried in a relay race and passed from one participant to the next. **4** A staff carried as symbol of office, especially one carried by a field marshal. **5** *Heraldry* A narrow bend truncated at each end. **6** A long loaf or stick of bread.
■ Although *baton* or *batton* was used by Scots writers in the 16th century, the commoner spelling in England until the 19th century was *batoon*. *Baton* in the general sense 1 is now much less common than in its various specialized senses.

battement /batmɑ̃/ *plural same*, /ˈbatmɔ̃/ *noun* M19 French (= beating). *Ballet* A movement in which one leg is moved outward from the body and in again. Cf. GRAND BATTEMENT, PETIT BATTEMENT.

batterie /batri/ *noun* plural pronounced same E18 French (= beating). **1** *Ballet* The action of beating the feet or calves together during a leap. **2** Abbreviation of BATTERIE DE CUISINE.

batterie de cuisine /batri də kɥizin/ *noun phrase* L18 French (= articles for cookery). The apparatus or set of utensils for preparing or serving a meal.

battue /bəˈt(j)uː/; *foreign* /baty/ (*plural same*) *noun* E19 French (use as noun of feminine past participle of *battre* to beat). The driving of game towards the guns by beaters; a shooting party arranged so that beaters can drive the game towards the hunters.

Bauhaus /'baʊhaʊs/ *noun* E20 German (= house of architecture, from *Bau* building + *Haus* house). A German school of architecture and design founded in 1919 by Walter Gropius and closed in 1933.

bayadère /beɪjə'dɛ:/, /beɪjə'dɪə/ *noun* L16 French (from Portuguese *bailadeira*, from *bailar* to dance, related to medieval Latin *ballare* to dance). A Hindu dancing girl, especially one at a southern Indian temple.

bayou /'bʌɪu:/ *noun* M18 American French (from Choctaw *bayuk*). (In the southern United States) a marshy offshoot of a river or lake.

bazaar /bə'zɑ:/ *noun* L16 Italian (*bazarro* from Turkish from Persian *bāzār* market). **1** A market in a Middle Eastern country. **2** A fund-raising sale of miscellaneous new or second-hand goods. **3** A large shop, or arcade of shops, selling miscellaneous goods.

bazuco, bazuko variants of BASUCO.

béarnaise /beɪə'neɪz/, *foreign* /bearnɛz/ *adjective* (also **Béarnaise**) L19 French (feminine of *béarnais* of Béarn, a region of south-west France). A rich white sauce thickened with egg yolks and flavoured with tarragon. In full, *béarnaise sauce* (also *sauce béarnaise*).

beau /bəʊ/ *noun* plural **beaux** /bəʊz/, **beaus** L17 French (use as noun of adjective, ultimately from Latin *bellus* fine, beautiful). **1** A rich, fashionable young man; a fop, a dandy. **2** A boyfriend or male admirer.

beau geste /bəʊ ʒɛst/ *noun phrase* plural **beaux gestes** (pronounced same) E20 French (= splendid gesture). A noble and generous act.

beau idéal /bəʊ ʌɪ'dɪəl/ *noun phrase* E19 French (= ideal beauty). A person or thing representing the highest possible standard of excellence in a particular respect.
  ■ Now often misunderstood to mean 'beautiful ideal'.

Beaujolais nouveau /ˌbəʊʒəleɪ nu: 'vəʊ/, *foreign* /boʒɔlɛ nuvo/ L20 French (= new Beaujolais). A light, usually red, burgundy wine of the latest vintage from the Beaujolais district of France.

beau monde /bəʊ 'mɒnd/, *foreign* /bo mɔ̃d/ *noun phrase* L17 French (= fine world). Fashionable society.
  1995 *Times* Teresa Lady Rothschild was never deeply interested in the glittering *beau monde* which circled around the international banking dynasty into which she married.

beau sabreur /bo sabrœr/ *noun phrase* plural **beaux sabreurs** (pronounced same) M19 French (= fine (or handsome) swordsman). A handsome or dashing adventurer.
  ■ Originally a sobriquet of Joachim Murat (1767–1815), French cavalry officer and brother-in-law of Napoleon.

beaux arts /boz ɑr/ *noun & adjective phrase* (also **beaux-arts**) E19 French (*beaux-arts*). **A** *noun phrase plural* Fine arts. **B** *adjective phrase* Relating to the classical decorative style maintained by the *École des Beaux-Arts* in Paris in the 19th century.

beaux esprits plural of BEL ESPRIT.

beaux gestes plural of BEAU GESTE.

beaux yeux /boz jø/ *noun phrase* E19 French. Beautiful eyes; admiring glances; favourable regard.

béchamel /'beɪʃəmɛl/, *foreign* /beʃamɛl/ *noun* M18 French. A rich white sauce made with milk infused with herbs and other flavourings. More fully *béchamel sauce*.
  ■ Called after the Marquis Louis de *Béchamel*, steward to Louis XIV of France, who is said to have invented a similar sauce.

bêche-de-mer /bɛʃdə'mɛ:/ *noun* plural same, **bêches-de-mer** /bɛʃdə'mɛ:/ L18 pseudo-French (from Portuguese *bicho do mar*, literally, 'worm of the sea'). **1** A large sea cucumber eaten as a delicacy in China and Japan. **2** An English-based pidgin language used formerly as a trade language and contact vernacular in the south-west Pacific. Also *bêche-de-mer English* or *beach-la-mar*.

Bedouin /'bɛdʊɪn/ *noun & adjective* (also **Beduin, beduin**) LME Old French (*beduin* (modern *bédouin*) ultimately (through medieval Latin *beduini* plural) from Arabic *badawī*, plural *badawīn* (from *badw* desert) nomadic desert tribes). **A** *noun* **1** A nomadic Arab of the desert. **2** A person living a nomadic life. **B** *adjective* Relating to the Bedouin; nomadic, wandering.

Bedu /'bɛduː/ *noun & adjective* plural of noun same E20 Arabic (*badw*). BEDOUIN.

Beerenauslese /'beːrən‚aʊsleːzə/ *noun* (also **beerenauslese**) plural **Beeren-auslesen**, /'beːrən‚aʊsleːzən/, **Beeren-ausleses** E20 German (from *Beeren* berries, grapes + AUSLESE). A white wine of German origin or style made from selected individual grapes picked later than the general harvest.

beguine /bɪˈgiːn/ *noun* E20 West Indian French (from French *béguin* infatuation). A popular dance of West Indian origin, similar to the foxtrot.

begum /'beɪgəm/ *noun* (also (as title) **Begum**) M17 Urdu (*begam* from Early Turkic *begim*, from *beg* bey + 1st person singular possessive suffix *-im*). (In the Indian subcontinent) a Muslim woman of high rank. Also (**Begum**), a title given to a married Muslim woman (= Mrs).

beignet /'bɛnjeɪ/, /bɛnˈjɛ/, *foreign* /bɛɲɛ/ (*plural same*) *noun* M19 French. A fritter; *specifically* (*United States*) a square of fried dough sprinkled with icing sugar and eaten hot. Usually in *plural*.

> **1995** *Observer* The French beignets, golden balls of molten cheese, must rank high in the world of the fritter fancier...

bel canto /bɛl ˈkantəʊ/ *noun phrase* L19 Italian (= fine song). A lyrical style of operatic singing characterized by a full rich broad tone, smooth phrasing, and accomplished technique.

> **1996** *Spectator* Not only is his voice beautiful, but he always sings beautifully—'bel canto', in other words...

bel esprit /bɛl ɛspri/ *noun phrase* plural **beaux esprits** /boz ɛspri/ M17 French (= fine mind). A brilliant or witty person. *Archaic*.

belle /bɛl/ *noun* E17 French (feminine of *bel*, BEAU, from Latin *bella* feminine of *bellus* beautiful). A beautiful girl or woman, especially the outstanding beauty at a particular event: *the belle of the ball*.

belle époque /bɛl eɪˈpɒk/ *noun phrase* (also **belle epoque, Belle Epoque**) plural **belles epoques** /bɛlz eɪˈpɒk/ M20 French (= fine period). A period of settled comfort and prosperity.

> ■ Originally and specifically used of the period in France immediately preceding the First World War.

belles-lettres /bɛlˈlɛtr/ *noun plural* (occasionally treated as *singular*) M17 French (literally, 'fine letters'). Literary works written and read primarily for their aesthetic effect, especially essays on literary and artistic criticism.

bema /'biːmə/ *noun* plural **bemas, bemata** /'biːmətə/ L17 Greek (*bēma* a step, a raised place to speak from). **1** *Christian Church* The altar part or sanctuary in ancient and Orthodox churches; the chancel. **2** (usually **bimah**) The podium or platform in a synagogue from which the Torah and Prophets are read. **3** The platform from which orators spoke in ancient Athens.

benedicite /bɛnɪˈdʌɪsɪti/ *noun* ME Latin (2nd person plural imperative of *bene-dicere* to wish well to, bless, from *bene* well + *dicere* to say). **1** A blessing, especially a grace said at table in religious communities. **2** (**the Benedicite**) The canticle used in the Anglican service of matins, beginning *Benedicite, omnia opera* 'O all ye works [of the Lord], bless ye [the Lord]', known also as 'The Song of the Three Children'.

benthos /'bɛnθɒs/ *noun* L19 Greek (= depth of the sea). The flora and fauna of the bottom of the sea or of a lake.

ben trovato /ben troˈvaːto/ *adjective phrase* L19 Italian (literally, 'well found'). (Of a story or anecdote) invented but plausible; appropriate though untrue.

> ■ *Se non è vero, è molto ben trovato* 'if it is not true, it is a happy invention' was apparently a well-known saying in 16th-century Italy, being found for example in the writings of Giordano Bruno. Smollett

used the phrase in 1771 in the form *ben trovata*.

1952 R. M. Hare *Language of Morals* We might say that to tell a story about someone, which every one knows is *ben trovato*, is not lying.

1996 *Spectator* Beaverbrook, who was a fund of good stories (*ben trovato* anyhow), was the source for the famous story of an old friend visiting Bottomley in prison finding him mending mailbags, as was usual then.

berceuse /bɛrsøz/, /bɛːˈsəːz/ *noun* plural pronounced same L19 French (from *bercer* to rock + feminine agent-suffix *-euse*). *Music* A lullaby; an instrumental piece with a gently rocking rhythm.

beret /ˈbɛreɪ/, /ˈbɛri/ *noun* E19 French (*béret* Basque cap, from south-west French dialect and Old Provençal *berret*). A round felt or cloth cap that lies flat on the head, covering it closely (as traditionally worn by Basque peasantry); such a cap forming part of military uniform.

berg /bəːg/, *foreign* /bɛrx/ *noun* E19 Afrikaans (from Dutch (= Old English *beorg* barrow, hill)). A mountain or hill; a mountain range.

bergère /bɛrʒɛr/ *noun* plural pronounced same M18 French (= shepherdess). A long-seated upholstered armchair fashionable in the 18th century. Also, a chair with canework seat, back, and sides.

1995 *Country Life* There are at least two types of *bergère*. One is a rectangular seat with high arms sweeping up to the back, which may be caned or covered in leather....The second type is the 'curricle', which is a rounded, and usually slightly smaller, version of the same thing.

bergschrund /ˈbəːgʃrʊnd/ *noun* M19 German (from *Berg* mountain + *schrund* cleft). A crevasse or gap at the junction of a glacier or snowfield with a steep upper slope.

beta /ˈbiːtə/ *noun* ME Latin (from Greek). **1** The second letter (B, β) of the Greek alphabet, transliterated as 'b'. **2** Denoting the second of a series of items or categories. **3** *attributive Science* Second in importance; as in *Astronomy* (preceding the genitive of the Latin name of the constellation) designating the second brightest star in a constellation. **4** A

second-class mark given for a piece of work or an examination paper.

■ Like *alpha*, *beta* has a number of specialist applications in scientific terminology and often appears in the same context to designate the entity secondary to the *alpha* one.

betel /ˈbiːt(ə)l/ *noun* M16 Portuguese (from Malayalam *verrila*). The leaf of an Asian climbing evergreen shrub, which in the East is chewed as a mild stimulant. Also (more fully *betel pepper*), the plant itself, *Piper betle*.

bête noire /beɪt ˈnwɑː/, *foreign* /bɛt nwar/ *noun phrase* plural **bêtes noires** (pronounced same) M19 French (literally, 'black beast'). A person or thing that one particularly dislikes.

1995 *Spectator* [F. R. Leavis's] *bête noire*, David Cecil at Oxford, taught literature as something to be enjoyed without benefit of Leavisite scrutiny.

bêtise /bɛtiz/, /beɪˈtiːz/ *noun* (also **betise**) plural pronounced same E19 French (= stupidity, from *bête* foolish, from Old French *beste* beast). A foolish or ill-timed remark or action; a piece of folly.

1996 *Spectator* They...at once went to Zimbabwe where their *betises* included, in an attempt to portray the sundowner life, a room full of ancient people served by a black man in a fancy uniform, in the kind of grand house that scarcely existed then. Wrong on every count.

beurre blanc /bœr blɑ̃/, /bə: ˈblɒ̃/ *noun phrase* M20 French (= white butter). A creamy sauce made with butter, onions, and vinegar or lemon juice, usually served with seafood dishes.

beurre manié /bœr manje/, /bə: manˈjeɪ/ *noun phrase* M20 French (= worked butter). A mixture of flour and butter used for thickening sauces or soups.

bey /beɪ/ *noun* (also (as title) **Bey**) L16 Turkish (modern form of *beg* prince, governor). *History* The governor of a district or province in the Ottoman Empire. Also (**Bey** following name) formerly used in Turkey and Egypt as a courtesy title.

bhajan /ˈbʌdʒ(ə)n/ *noun* E20 Sanskrit (*bhajana*, from *bhaj* to worship). *Hinduism* A devotional song.

bhaji /'bɑːʤi/ *noun* L20 Hindi (*bháji* fried vegetables, from Sanskrit *bhrajj* to fry). (In Indian cuisine) a small flat cake or ball of vegetables, fried in butter.

bhakti /'bʌkti/ *noun* M19 Sanskrit. *Hinduism* Religious devotion or piety as a means of salvation.

bhang /bɑːŋ/ *noun* (also **bang**) L16 Persian and Urdu (*bang* (through Portuguese *bangue*), later assimilated to Hindi *bhān* from Sanskrit *bhaṅg*). The leaves and flower tops of the cannabis or Indian hemp plant (*Cannabis sativa*), used as an intoxicating or hallucinogenic drug or for medicinal purposes.

bhangra /'bɑːŋgrə/ *noun* M20 Punjabi (*bhāngrā*). **1** A type of Punjabi folk dance for men associated with the harvest. **2** A style of popular music combining Punjabi folk music with Western pop music.

■ In Britain *bhangra* (also known as *bhangra beat*) originated in the Asian communities in the 1980s, but by the end of the decade had won a wider following.

2 1987 *Independent* An up and coming group...set the seemingly incompatible rhythmic stridency of funk and Bhangra dance to a compulsive harmony.

bhikkhu /'bɪkuː/ *noun* (also **bhikku**) M19 Pali (*bhikkhu*, from Sanskrit *bhikṣu* beggar). A Buddhist monk or religious devotee.

bibelot /'bɪbəlaʊ/, *foreign* /biblo/ (*plural same*) *noun* L19 French (from reduplication of *bel* beautiful). A small, decorative ornament or trinket.

1996 *Times* Nor can he tell us who is the famous actress and beauty who slid bibelots into her handbag at Sir Harold Acton's villa outside Florence...

bibi /'biːbiː/ *noun* E19 Urdu (*bībī* from Persian). (In the Indian subcontinent) a mistress of a household, a man's wife; *dated* a non-European female consort.

bibliotheca /ˌbɪblɪə'θiːkə/ *noun* E18 Latin (from Greek *bibliothēkē* library, from *biblion* book + *thēkē* repository). A collection of books or treatises; a library; a bibliographer's catalogue.

■ Following St Jerome, *bibliotheca* was used in both medieval Latin and Old English to mean 'the Bible'. In Anglo-Latin it occurs interchangeably with *biblia* in an 11th-century catalogue of the library of Lindisfarne, but by the time of the compilation of the 13th-century Durham catalogue only *biblia* appears. By the end of that century the Middle English *bibul* and its many variants, from which Modern English *bible* derives, had replaced *bibliotheca* in the vernacular. The modern reintroduction into English of *bibliotheca* in a bibliographical sense is thus entirely separate from the earlier biblical sense and relies on learned Latin usage. *Bibliotheca annua* (1700–4), an annual catalogue of English and Latin books published in England, was an early example. Since the 19th century *bibliotheca* has been used in titles of series (e.g. *Bryophytorum bibliotheca*; *Bibliotheca Americana Vetustissima*) or individual bibliographies (e.g. *Bibliotheca arcana* (1885), a catalogue of banned erotica; *Bibliotheca chemica* (1906), a catalogue of alchemical works).

bibliothèque /biblijɔtɛk/ *noun* plural pronounced same M16 French (from Greek *bibliothēkē* library, from *biblion* book + *thēkē* repository). A library.

■ Formerly naturalized, but now treated as French.

bidet /'biːdeɪ/ *noun* M17 French (from earlier sense 'pony', from *bider* to trot, of unknown origin). **1** A small horse. *Archaic*. **2** A low oval basin used for washing one's genital and anal area.

■ The evolution of sense 2 from sense 1 is explained in Grose's definition of *bidet* in his *Dictionary of the Vulgar Tongue* (1785): 'commonly pronounced biddy, a kind of tub, contrived for ladies to wash themselves, for which purpose they bestride it like a little French poney,... called in France bidets.'

bidonville /'biːd(ə)nvɪl/; *foreign* /bidɔ̃vil/ (*plural same*) *noun* M20 French (from *bidon* container for liquids + *ville* town). A shanty town built of oil drums or other metal containers, especially a slum on the outskirts of a French or North African city.

biennale /biːɛ'nɑːli/ *noun* M20 Italian (from Latin *biennis* of two years). A large art exhibition or music festival, especially one held every two years.

■ Originally used as the name of a specific international art exhibition, the Biennale, held biennially in Venice, Italy.

biennium /baɪˈɛnɪəm/ noun plural **bienniums**, **biennia** /baɪˈɛnɪə/ E20 Latin (from as bi- two + annus year). A specified period of two years.

bien pensant /bjɛ̃ pɑ̃sɑ̃/ adjective & noun phrase Also **bien-pensant** (plural pronounced same) E20 French (bien well, pensant present participle of penser to think). **A** adjective phrase Conventional or orthodox in attitude; right-thinking. **B** noun phrase A conventional or orthodox person.

■ Often with a derogatory implication of timorous or mindless compliance with current intellectual or moral fashion.
A 1996 Spectator I ask him if Ms Roddick's liberal embrace of every bien-pensant cause does not lead to jumping on every passing bandwagon.
B 1996 Times In this form of journo-speak, a Tory 'right winger' is someone who believes in: hanging, low taxes, large armies, standards in schools,...and a rag-bag of other items which offend the bien pensants.

bierhaus /ˈbiːrhaʊs/ noun plural **bierhäuser** /ˈbiːrhɔyzər/ M20 German (from Bier beer + Haus house). (In a German-speaking country) a public house or alehouse.

bijou /ˈbiːʒuː/, foreign /biʒu/ noun & adjective M17 French (from Breton bizoù finger ring, from biz finger). **A** noun plural **bijoux** /ˈbiːʒuː(z)/, foreign /biʒu/. A jewel or trinket. **B** adjective (Especially of a house or flat) small and elegant.

■ In its adjectival use, bijou has become well-known as a euphemistic piece of estate agents' jargon to describe a house or flat that is uncomfortably small and cramped.
B 1996 Bookseller Shops dealing exclusively in English language books in the south of France tend to be bijou in size.

bijouterie /biʒutri/ noun E19 French. Jewellery or trinkets.

Bildungsroman /ˈbɪldʊŋzroˌmɑːn/ noun plural **Bildungsromane** /ˈbɪldʊŋzroˌmɑːnə/ E20 German (from Bildung education

+ Roman novel). A novel dealing with one person's formative years or spiritual education.
1995 Times His long, indulgent autobiography, What's It All About?, is a kind of bildungsroman about how Maurice Joseph Micklewhite, Jr. became Michael Caine.

billabong /ˈbɪləbɒŋ/ noun M19 Aboriginal (Billibang Bell River, from billa water + bang channel dry except after rain). (In Australia) a branch of a river forming a backwater or stagnant pool, made by water flowing from the main stream during a flood.

billet-doux /bɪlɪˈduː/ noun plural **billets-doux** /bɪlɪˈduːz/ L17 French (literally, 'sweet note'). A love letter.

■ Now dated or humorous.

biltong /ˈbɪltɒŋ/ noun E19 Afrikaans (from Dutch bil buttock + tong tongue). (In South Africa) lean meat cut into strips and dried.

bimbo /ˈbɪmbəʊ/ noun plural **bimbos**, **bimboes** E20 Italian (= small child, baby). **1** A chap, especially a young and foolish one. **2** An attractive but unintelligent or frivolous young woman.

■ Now used in a slang and almost always derogatory sense, bimbo was originally a direct borrowing from Italian. P. G. Wodehouse used it in sense 1 (see quotation 1947), but it was already current in the 1920s with the sense of a pretty but brainless tart. Bimbo was revived in the 1980s media to designate a young woman who has an affair with a rich or famous man and then sells the 'revelations' to the popular press. The word has also spawned a number of derivatives: bimbette (a teenage bimbo), bimboy (a male bimbo), bimboland, etc.
1 1947 P. G. Wodehouse Full Moon...bimbos who went about the place making passes at innocent girls after discarding their wives.
2 1988 Independent In the strict sense the bimbo exists on the fringes of pornography, and some cynics might say she has the mental capacity of a minor kitchen appliance.

bint /bɪnt/ noun M19 Arabic (= daughter, girl). A girl, a woman; (formerly) a girl friend.

■ Originally British servicemen's slang, used by personnel stationed in Egypt and elsewhere in the Middle East during the two world wars; usually derogatory.

1958 K. Amis *I Like It Here* As the R.A.F. friend would have put it, you could never tell with these foreign bints.

biretta /bɪˈrɛtə/ *noun* L16 Italian (*berretta* or Spanish *birreta*, feminine diminutives corresponding to Old Provençal *berret* beret, based on late Latin *birrus*, *birettum* hooded cape or cloak, perhaps of Celtic origin). A square cap with three flat projections on top, worn by Roman Catholic clergymen (black by priests, purple by bishops, red by cardinals).

biriani variant of BIRYANI.

biryani /bɪˈrjɑːni/, /bɪrrˈɑːni/ *noun* (also **biriani** and other variants) M20 Urdu (from Persian *biryānī*, from *biriyān* fried, grilled). A dish of the Indian subcontinent consisting of highly seasoned rice and meat, fish, or vegetables.

bis /bis/ *adverb* E17 French and Italian (from Latin *bis* twice). *Music* (As a direction) again, i.e. indicating that a passage is to be repeated.

bismillah /bɪsˈmɪlə/ *interjection* L18 Arabic (*bi-smi-llāh(i)*, the first word of the Koran). In the name of God (an invocation used by Muslims at the beginning of any undertaking).

bisque /bɪsk/ *noun* 1 M17 French (of unknown origin). An extra turn or stroke allowed to a weaker player in croquet.

■ Originally a term in real tennis.

bisque /bɪsk/ *noun* 2 M17 French (from Old French *bescuit*, *besquit*, ultimately from Latin *bis* twice + *coctus* past participle of *coquere* to cook). A variety of unglazed white porcelain used for statuettes etc. Also porcelain that has undergone firing but no other treatment; biscuit.

bisque /bɪsk/, /biːsk/ *noun* 3 (also **bisk** /bɪsk/) M17 French (= crayfish soup). A rich shellfish soup, typically made from lobster.

bistre /ˈbɪstə/ *noun* (also **bister**) E18 French (of unknown origin). A brownish-yellow pigment made from the soot of burnt wood; the colour of this pigment.

bistro /ˈbiːstrəʊ/, /ˈbɪstrəʊ/ *noun* plural **bistros** E20 French. A small, inexpensive restaurant.

bivouac /ˈbɪvʊak/, /ˈbɪvwak/ *noun & verb* E18 French (probably from Swiss German *Bîwacht*, literally, 'extra watch'). **A** *noun* Originally, a night watch by a whole army. Later, a temporary camp, usually for the night, without tents or cover, used especially by soldiers or mountaineers. **B** *intransitive verb* Inflected **bivouack**. Stay in a bivouac.

■ The Swiss word is said to have been used in Aargau and Zürich to denote a patrol of citizens to assist the ordinary town watch.

bizarre /bɪˈzɑː/ *adjective* M17 French (from Italian *bizzarro* angry, of unknown origin. Cf. Spanish and Portuguese *bizarro* handsome, brave). Very strange or unusual.

blague /blag/ *noun* M19 French. A joke or piece of nonsense.

blagueur /blagœr/ *noun* plural pronounced same L19 French (from BLAGUE). A person who talks nonsense; a joker, a teller of tall stories.

blanc /blɑ̃/ *adjective* M18 French (= white). (Of wine) white.

blancmange /bləˈmɒnʒ/, /bləˈmɑːnʒ/ *noun* (also (earlier) **blancmanger**) LME Old French (*blanc mangier* (modern *blancmanger*), from *blanc* white + *mang(i)er* food, use as noun of *mang(i)er* to eat). A sweet opaque jelly-like dessert made with flavoured cornflour and milk.

■ Originally used to denote a dish of white meat or fish in a cream sauce. The terminal 'r' was dropped in the 18th century.

blanquette /blɑ̃kɛt/ *noun* plural pronounced same M18 French (from Old French *blanchet* from *blanc*, *blanche* white). A dish of light meat, especially veal, cooked in a white sauce.

blasé /ˈblɑːzeɪ/ *adjective* E19 French (= cloyed). Unimpressed with or indifferent to something because one has experienced or seen it so often before.

1996 *Oldie* We have also survived scares about yoghurt..., microwave cookers, television sets, computers, salami (contains nitrate), etc, and have now got blasé about it all.

blin /blɪn/ *noun* plural **blini, bliny** /'blɪni/, **blinis** /'blɪnɪz/ L19 Russian. A kind of pancake made from buckwheat flour and served with sour cream. Cf. BLINTZE.

blintze /blɪn(t)s/ *noun* E20 Yiddish (*blintse* from Russian *blinets* diminutive of *blin*). A thin rolled pancake filled with cheese or fruit and then fried or baked. Cf. BLIN.

blitzkrieg /'blɪtskriːg/ *noun* (also **Blitz-krieg**) M20 German (from *Blitz* lightning + *Krieg* war). An intense, violent military campaign intended to bring about a swift victory.
  ■ Used specifically of the German military campaigns in World War Two, *Blitzkrieg* is usually found in the abbreviated form *Blitz* with reference to the Luftwaffe's bombardment of British cities. Both *blitzkrieg* and *blitz* are in general metaphorical use (see quotation).
  1996 *New Scientist* The Japanese blitzkrieg on Western markets was in full swing in the early 1980s.

bloc /blɒk/ *noun* E20 French (= block, from Middle Dutch *blok*, Middle and Modern Low German *block*, of unknown origin). A group of countries or political parties with common interests who have formed an alliance.

blonde /blɒnd/ *adjective & noun* (also **blond**) L15 Old and Modern French (from medieval Latin *blundus, blondus* yellow, perhaps of Germanic origin). **A** *adjective* (Especially of the hair) fair or pale yellow; (of the complexion) light-coloured with fair hair. **B** *noun* A person (especially a woman) with blonde hair.
  ■ The form *blond* dates from the late 15th century. The feminine form *blonde* was introduced from French in the 17th century, but the masculine/feminine distinction is often not observed in English usage, with *blonde* being used of both men and women.

blouson /'bluːzɒn/, *foreign* /bluzɔ̃/ (*plural same*) *noun* E20 French. A short jacket fitting loosely on the body like a blouse and finishing at the waist.

bocage /bə'kɑːʒ/, *foreign* /bɔkaʒ/ (*plural same*) *noun* L16 French. **1** (In France) pastureland divided into small hedged fields interspersed with groves of trees. **2** The modelling of leaves, flowers, and plants in clay, especially for porcelain figurines.

bodega /bə'diːgə/, *foreign* /bo'dega/ *noun* M19 Spanish (from Latin *apotheca* from Greek *apothēkē* storehouse; *cf.* BOUTIQUE). A cellar or shop selling wine and food, especially in a Spanish-speaking country or area.

Boer /bɔː/, /'bəʊə/, /bʊə/ *noun & adjective* (also **boer**) M19 Dutch (*boer* farmer). **A** *noun* **1** A member of the Dutch and Huguenot population which settled in southern Africa in the late 17th century; an Afrikaner. **2** (**boer**) An Afrikaner farmer; (under apartheid) a member of the police, prison service, or security forces. *South African.* **B** *adjective* Relating to the Boers.

boerewors /'bɔːrəvɔːs/ *noun* M20 Afrikaans (from *boer* farmer + *wors* sausage). A type of coarse sausage made with beef and pork seasoned with spices.
  1950 L. G. Green *Land of Afternoon* Boerewors is another farm product which some still make in the old way; a sausage in which the meat has been pounded with a wooden stamper rather than minced.

bœuf /bœf/ *noun* E20 French (= beef). *Cookery* Used in the names of various beef dishes.

bœuf bourguignon /bœf burgiɲɔ̃/ *noun phrase* E20 French (= beef of Burgundy). A casserole of beef cooked slowly in red wine.

boîte /bwat/ *noun* plural (pronounced same) E20 French (= box). A small (French) restaurant or nightclub.

bolas /'bəʊləs/ *noun singular* (with plural **bolases**) or *plural* (also *singular* **bola** /'bəʊlə/) E19 Spanish and Portuguese (plural of *bola* ball). (Especially in South America) a missile consisting of a number of balls connected by a strong cord, which is thrown to entangle the legs of a quarry.

bolero /bə'lɛːrəʊ/, *in sense 2 also* /'bɒlərəʊ/ *noun* plural **boleros** L18 Spanish. **1** A lively Spanish dance; a piece of music for this dance. **2** A short jacket just reaching the waist, worn by men in Spain; a woman's short open jacket, with or without sleeves.

boletus /bə'li:təs/ *noun* (also anglicized as **bolet** /bə'lɛt/, **bolete** /bə'li:t/) E16 Latin (*boletus* from Greek *bōlitēs*, perhaps from *bōlos* lump). A mushroom or toadstool of the large genus *Boletus*, having the underside of the cap full of pores.

Bolshevik /'bɒlʃɪvɪk/ *noun & adjective* (also **bolshevik**) E20 Russian (*bol'shevik* = member of the majority, from *bol'she* greater, from *bol'shoĭ* big). **A** *noun* **1** *History* A member of the majority faction of the Russian Social Democratic Party, which seized power in the October Revolution of 1917. **2** *general* A person with politically subversive or radical views; a revolutionary. **B** *adjective* Relating to or characteristic of Bolsheviks or Bolshevism.

bolus /'bəʊləs/ *noun* M16 Late Latin (from Greek *bōlos* clod, lump of earth). **1** A small rounded mass of a substance, especially of chewed food at the moment of swallowing. **2** A type of large pill used in veterinary medicine. **3** *Medicine* A single dose of a drug or other medicinal given all at once.
  ■ Originally denoted a large pill.

boma /'bəʊmə/ *noun* L19 Kiswahili. (In eastern and southern Africa) a defensible enclosure, especially for animals; hence, a police or military post; a magistrate's office.

bombe /bɒmb/, *foreign* /bɔ̃b/ (*plural* same) *noun* L19 French (= bomb). A frozen dome-shaped dessert; a dome-shaped mould in which a bombe is made.

bombé /bɔ̃be/ *adjective* E20 French (past participle of *bomber* to swell out). (Especially of furniture) rounded, convex.

bombora /bɒm'bɔːrə/ *noun* M20 Aboriginal. (In Australia and New Zealand) a dangerous stretch of water where waves break over a submerged offshore reef or rock.

bon /bɔ̃/ *adjective* L16 French (= good (masculine; cf. BONNE)). Good.

■ In various phrases used in English (see entries below).

bona fide /ˌbəʊnə 'fʌɪdi/ *adjective & adverb phrase* M16 Latin (= with good faith). **A** *adjective phrase* Genuine; real: *a bona fide money-back guarantee.* **B** *adverb phrase* Chiefly *Law*. Without intention to deceive: *the court will assume that they have acted bona fide.*
  A *1996 Times* We hear echoes of it in Top 40 songs, but we seldom, if ever, see a bona fide gospel singer in the chart shows.

bona fides /ˌbəʊnə 'fʌɪdi:z/ *noun phrase* L18 Latin (= good faith). **1** A person's honesty and sincerity of intention: *he went to great lengths to establish his liberal bona fides.* **2** (erroneously treated as plural) Documentary evidence showing that a person is what they claim to be; credentials.

bonanza /bə'nanzə/ *noun & adjective* E19 Spanish (= fair weather, prosperity, from Latin *bonus* good). **A** *noun* A situation which creates a sudden increase in wealth, good fortune, or profits; a large amount of something desirable. **B** *adjective* Greatly prospering or productive.
  ■ Originally used among miners in the United States for 'a rich find' or 'lucky strike'.
  A *1996 Country Life* Daffodil growers..., who missed their usual £10 million bonanza on Mothering Sunday because cold weather delayed flowering, are setting their sights on Easter.

bon appétit /bɒn apeti/, /bɒn apə'ti:/ *interjection* M19 French. Good appetite!
  ■ Used as a salutation to people about to eat.

bonbon /'bɒnbɒn/ *noun* L18 French (literally, 'good-good'). A piece of confectionery, a sweet.

bonbonnière /bɔ̃bɔnjɛr/ *noun* plural pronounced same E19 French. A fancy box or lidded jar for holding sweets.
  1996 Country Life As an amusement, I would far rather have had a bonbonnière by an unidentified 18th-century German factory. It was of a crouching and concentrating cat...

bondieuserie /bɔ̃djøzri/ *noun* plural pronounced same M20 French (from *bon* good + *Dieu* God). A church ornament or devotional object, especially one of little artistic merit; such objects collectively.

■ The French journalist and novelist Jules Vallès (1832–85) is credited with the invention of the term.

bongo /ˈbɒŋgəʊ/ *noun* plural **bongo(e)s** E20 American Spanish (*bongó*). Either of a pair of small deep-bodied drums, usually held between the knees and played with the fingers. Also *bongo drum(s)*.

bonhomie /ˈbɒnəmiː/ *noun* (also formerly written **bonhommie**) L18 French (from *bonhomme* good man, from medieval Latin *bonus homo* + suffix *-ie*). Good-natured friendliness, geniality.

1992 A. Lambert *A Rather English Marriage* Reginald was bluff and cheery, spreading enough *bonhomie* to fuel a party.

bonito /bəˈniːtəʊ/ *noun* plural **bonitos** (also **boneta** /bəˈniːtə/) L16 Spanish. Any of various striped tuna, especially *Sarda sarda* of the Atlantic and Mediterranean.

bonjour /ˈbɔːʒur/ *interjection* L16 French. Good day! Hello!

■ Used as a general greeting.

bon mot /bɔ̃ məʊ/ *noun phrase* plural **bons mots**, **bon mots** (pronounced same or /bɔ̃ məʊz/) M18 French (literally, 'good word'). A clever or witty remark.

1995 *Spectator* When King Louis-Philippe was told that Talleyrand had died he was heard to mutter: 'Died, has he? I wonder what he meant by that.' It seems a shame to deprive Louis-Philippe of some of his few recorded *bons mots* and ascribe it to Talleyrand, who has plenty to his credit.

bonne /bɔn/ *adjective & noun* E16 French (feminine of BON). **A** *adjective* Good. **B** *noun* A nursemaid or housemaid, typically a French one.

■ Use as an adjective has long been restricted to certain phrases adopted from French (see below) and the nominal use too is now rare.

bonne bouche /bɔn buʃ/ *noun phrase* (also **bonne-bouche**) plural **bonnes bouches** (pronounced same) M18 French (literally, 'good mouth'). An appetizing item of food, especially some-thing sweet eaten at the end of a meal; a dainty morsel, a titbit; also *figurative*.

■ In French the sense is 'a pleasing taste in the mouth', which has been understood in English as the delicacy that gives this.

1996 *Times* Let us begin with a *bonne-bouche* before we tuck in.

bonne femme /bɔn fam/ *adjective phrase* E19 French (literally, 'in the manner of a good housewife'). *Cookery* (Of fish dishes, stews, and soups) cooked in a simple way.

■ Also in the fuller form *à la bonne femme*, both used postpositively, as in 'sole *bonne femme*'.

bonsai /ˈbɒnsʌɪ/ *noun* plural same E20 Japanese (from *bon* tray + *sai* planting). The art of growing ornamental, artificially dwarfed varieties of trees and shrubs in pots; an ornamental tree or shrub grown in such a way.

bon vivant /bɔ̃ vivɑ̃/ *noun phrase* plural **bons vivants**, **bon vivants** (pronounced same) L17 French (literally, '(a person) who lives well'). A person with a sociable and luxurious lifestyle; a gourmand, an epicure.

■ In contemporary usage *bon vivant* and BON VIVEUR appear interchangeably in a general sense of someone with a self-indulgent lifestyle (see quotation).

1996 *Times* Nor does it mean that the *bon vivant* has renounced his ways. 'Don't worry, . . . [the] fun and sex are not over yet.'

bon viveur /bɔ̃ vivœr/ *noun phrase* plural **bons viveurs**, **bon viveurs** (pronounced same) M19 pseudo-French (formed after BON VIVANT). A person who indulges a taste for the good things of life.

1995 *Spectator* Roy Hattersley, politician, man of letters, *bon viveur*, is one of public life's polymaths.

bon voyage /bɒn vwaˈjɑːʒ/ *interjection* L17 French (literally, 'good journey'). Pleasant journey!

■ Used to express good wishes to someone about to set off on a journey.

bonze /bɒnz/ *noun* L16 French (*bonze* or Portuguese *bonzo* probably from Japanese *bonzō*, *bonsō* priest). A Japanese or Chinese Buddhist religious teacher.

boomerang /ˈbuːməraŋ/ *noun & verb* E19 Dharuk. **A** *noun* A curved flat piece of wood that can be thrown so that it will return to the thrower, traditionally used by Australian Aboriginals as a hunting weapon. **B** *intransitive verb* (Of a plan or action) recoil on the originator: *misleading consumers about quality will eventually boomerang on a carmaker.*

boondocks /ˈbuːndɒks/ *noun plural* M20 Tagalog (*bundok* mountain). Rough or isolated country; remote parts.

■ North American slang, originally used by service personnel. It appears infrequently in the singular, more usually in the plural, and often in the phrase (*out) in the boondocks.*

bordello /bɔːˈdɛloʊ/ *noun* plural **bordellos** L16 Italian (from medieval Latin *bordellum*). A brothel.

1996 *Times* The management skills involved in running a chain of hotels, discotheques, pubs or theme restaurants are no different from those needed for bordellos.

borscht /bɔːʃt/ *noun* (also **borsch** /bɔːʃ/) E19 Russian (*borshch*). A Russian or Polish soup made with beetroot and usually served with sour cream.

bossa nova /ˌbɒsə ˈnəʊvə/ *noun phrase* M20 Portuguese (*bossa* tendency, *nova* feminine singular of *novo* new). A style of Brazilian music related to the samba; a dance to this music.

bouchée /ˈbuːʃeɪ/ *noun* plural pronounced same M19 French (= mouthful, from *bouche* mouth). A small pastry with a sweet or savoury filling.

■ Usually in plural.

bouclé /ˈbuːkleɪ/ *noun* L19 French (= buckled, curled). Yarn with a looped or curled ply, or fabric woven from this yarn.

boudin /ˈbuːdɪn/, *foreign* /budɛ̃/ (*plural same*) *noun* M19 French. **1** A French type of black pudding. **2** *Geology* Any of a number of roughly parallel elongated sections resulting from the fracturing of a sedimentary rock stratum during folding.

boudoir /ˈbuːdwɑː/ *noun* L18 French (literally 'place to sulk in', from *bouder* to pout, sulk). A woman's bedroom or small private room.

bouffant /ˈbuːfɑ̃/ *adjective & noun* E19 French (= swelling, present participle of *bouffer* to swell). **A** *adjective* (Of a person's hair) styled so as to stand out from the head in a rounded shape. **B** *noun* A bouffant hairstyle.

B 1996 *Times* Hoddle has come a long way since the days when he sported first a Keeganesque bouffant and then hair straggling sweatily down his neck.

bougie /ˈbuːʒi/ *noun* M18 French (literally 'wax candle', from *Bougie* (Arabic *Bijāya*) a town in Algeria which carried on a trade in wax). *Medicine* A thin, flexible surgical instrument for exploring or dilating a passage of the body.

bouillabaisse /buːjəˈbeɪs/, *foreign* /bujabɛs/ *noun* M19 French (from Modern Provençal *bouiabaisso*). A rich, spicy stew or soup made with various kinds of fish, originally from Provence. Also *figurative.*

1996 *Times* Emerging from this *bouillabaisse* of complaints, however, is one certainty.

bouilli /ˈbuːji/, *foreign* /buji/ *noun* E17 French (use as noun of past participle of *bouillir* to boil). Boiled or stewed meat, especially beef.

■ Since the mid 18th century often anglicized as *bully*, especially when referring to beef in the form used for army rations.

bouillon /ˈbuːjɒ̃/, *foreign* /bujɔ̃/ *noun* M17 French (= liquid in which something has boiled, from *bouillir* to boil). Thin soup or stock made by stewing meat, fish, or vegetables in water. See also COURT BOUILLON.

boule /ˈbuːli/ *noun* 1 M19 Greek (*boulē* senate). A legislative body of ancient or modern Greece.

boule /buːl/, *foreign* /bul/ *noun* 2 plural **boules** (pronounced same) E20 French (= bowl). (*singular* and in *plural*) A French form of bowls played on rough ground, usually with metal bowls.

■ Originally denoted a form of roulette.

boulevard /ˈbuːləvɑːd/, *foreign* /bulvar/ (*plural same*) *noun* M18 French ((originally) = rampart, (later) a promenade on the site of this). A broad street in a town or city, typically one lined with trees.

boulevardier /bulvardje/ *noun* plural pronounced same L19 French (from *boulevard* + *-ier*). A person who frequents (French) boulevards; a wealthy, fashionable socialite.

bouleversement /bulvɛrsəmã/ *noun* plural pronounced same L18 French (from *bouleverser* to turn as a ball). An inversion, especially a violent one; an upset, a reversal of fortune.

boulle variant of BUHL.

bouquet /buˈkeɪ/, /bəʊˈkeɪ/, /ˈbʊkeɪ/ *noun* E18 French ((earlier = clump of trees), from dialectal variant of Old French *bos, bois* wood). **1** An attractively arranged bunch of flowers, especially one presented as a gift or carried at a ceremony. **b** An expression of approval; a compliment. **2** The characteristic scent of a wine or perfume.

bouquet garni /bʊkeɪ ˈgɑːni/ *noun phrase* M19 French (literally, 'garnished bouquet'). A bunch of assorted herbs, typically encased in a muslin bag, used for flavouring a stew or soup.

bourdon /ˈbʊəd(ə)n/ *noun* (also **burdoun**) ME Old and Modern French (= drone, from Proto-Romance, of imitative origin). A low-pitched stop in an organ or harmonium; the drone pipe of a bagpipe; the lowest-pitched in a peal of bells.

■ *Bourdon* was first used in the sense 'the drone of a bagpipe' or 'the bass or undersong of a melody'. This sense soon merged with the same sense of *burden* and the word is now rare or obsolete with its original meaning. The modern use is a reintroduction.

bourgeois /ˈbʊəʒwɑː/, *foreign* /burʒwa/ *adjective & noun* M16 French. **A** *adjective* **1** Belonging to or characteristic of the middle class; conventionally respectable and unimaginative; selfishly materialistic. **2** (In Marxist contexts) upholding the interests of capitalism; not communist. **B** *noun* plural same. **1** Originally, a (French) citizen or freeman of a city or burgh, as distinct from a peasant or a gentleman. Now,

any member of the middle class. **2** (In Marxist contexts) a capitalist, an exploiter of the proletariat. **3** A socially or aesthetically conventional person, a philistine.

bourgeoise /ˈbʊəʒwɑːz/, *foreign* /burʒwaz/ *noun & adjective* plural of noun pronounced same L18 French (feminine of preceding). **A** *noun* A female member of the bourgeoisie. **B** *adjective* Belonging to or characteristic of female members of the bourgeoisie.

bourgeoisie /ˌbʊəʒwɑːˈziː/, *foreign* /burʒwazi/ *noun* E18 French (from BOURGEOIS). The bourgeois collectively; the middle class.

bourrée /ˈbʊəreɪ/, *foreign* /bure/ (*plural same*) *noun* L17 French (= faggot of twigs (the dance being performed around a fire made with such twigs)). **1** A lively dance of French origin, resembling the gavotte; a piece of music for this dance or in its rhythm, especially one which forms a movement of a suite. **2** *Ballet* A series of very fast little steps, with the feet close together, usually performed on the tips of the toes and giving the impression that the dancer is gliding over the floor.

bourse /bʊəs/ *noun* L16 French (= purse). A stock market in a non-English-speaking country, especially France; (**the Bourse**) the Paris stock exchange.

1996 *Times* For diplomats used to trading sovereignty for 'influence in the Brussels *bourse*, the thought that sovereignty might be retrieved, and independence asserted, is deeply uncongenial.

boustrophedon /baʊstrəˈfiːd(ə)n/, /buːstrəˈffiːd(ə)n/ *adverb & adjective* E17 Greek (= as the ox turns in ploughing, from *bous* ox + *strophos* twist + adverbial suffix *-don*). (Of written words) from right to left and from left to right in alternate lines.

boutade /buːˈtɑːd/ *noun* E17 French (from *bouter* to thrust). A sudden outburst or outbreak.

boutique /buːˈtiːk/ *noun* M18 French (= small shop, from Old Provençal *botica* (Italian *bottega*) from Latin *apotheca* from Greek *apothēkē* storehouse: cf. BODEGA). **1** A small shop, or a department in a large store, selling fashionable clothes or accessories. **2** A business serving a sophisticated or specialized clientele.

bouton /'buːtɒn/ *noun* M20 French (= button). *Anatomy* An enlarged part of a nerve fibre or cell, especially an axon, where it forms a synapse with another nerve.

boutonnière /ˌbuːtɒnˈjɛː/, *foreign* /butɔnjɛr/ (*plural same*) *noun* L19 French (= button-hole). A spray of flowers worn in a lapel buttonhole.

> **1996** *Times: Weekend* Reno is noted for being a wedding factory town, where one enterprising local chapel offers an all-inclusive nuptial special for $129 . . . in addition to a free *boutonnière* for the groom . . .

bouzouki /buˈzuːki/ *noun* M20 Modern Greek (*mpouzouki*: cf. Turkish *bozuk* spoilt, i.e. roughly made (instruments)). A long-necked Greek form of mandolin much used in traditional Greek folk music.

boyar /bəʊˈjɑː/ *noun* L16 Russian (*boyarin* grandee). *History* A member of an order of Russian aristocracy (abolished by Peter the Great), next in rank to a prince.

braai /'brɑːɪ/ *noun & verb* M20 Afrikaans (abbreviation of next). **A** *noun* (In South Africa) a barbecue, a BRAAIVLEIS; a structure on which a fire can be made for the outdoor grilling of meat. **B** *transitive & intransitive verb* Grill (meat) over an open fire.

braaivleis /'brɑːɪflfleɪs/ *noun* M20 Afrikaans (= grilled meat, from *braai* to grill + *vleis* meat). (In South Africa) a picnic or barbecue where meat is grilled over an open fire; meat cooked in this way.

braggadocio /braɡəˈdəʊtʃɪəʊ/ *noun* plural **braggadocios** L16 pseudo-Italian (fictional name formed from *brag* or *braggart* + Italian augmentative suffix *-occio*). Empty boasting, bluster.

> ■ This word was originally used in the sense 'a loud-mouthed braggart, an idle boaster'. It comes from *Braggadocchio*, the name of a cowardly braggart in Spenser's *Faerie Queene*, the first part of which was published in 1590: 'Proud *Braggadocchio*, that in vaunting vaine / His glory did repose, and credit did maintaine' (III. viii.11).

> **1996** *Spectator* He drank unwisely and not too well, went in for a deal of Celtic fist-flaying and had a bully's *braggadocio* . . .

brahman /'brɑːmən/ *noun* (also **brahma** /'brɑːmə/, **brahm**, **Brahman**) L18 Sanskrit (*bráhman* sacred utterance). (In Hindu philosophy) the ultimate reality underlying all phenomena.

brandade /brɑ̃dad/ *noun* E19 French (from Modern Provençal *brandado*, literally, 'thing which has been moved or shaken'). A Provençal dish made from salt cod mixed into a purée with olive oil and milk.

brasserie /'brasəri/ *noun* M19 French ((originally = brewery), from *brasser* to brew). A restaurant in France or in a French style; an informal or inexpensive restaurant.

brassière /'brasɪə/, /'brazɪə/ *noun* (also **brassiere**) E20 French (= child's reins, camisole, etc.). A woman's shaped undergarment worn to support the breasts.

> ■ The abbreviation *bra* is almost universal in informal contexts.

bratwurst /'bratwəːst/, /'brɑːtvəːst/ E20 German (from *Brat* a spit (*braten* roast etc.) + *Wurst* sausage). A type of mild-flavoured German pork sausage that is generally fried or grilled.

bravo /'brɑːvəʊ/ *noun* 1 plural **bravo(e)s** L16 Italian (= bold). A thug or hired assassin.

bravo /brɑːˈvəʊ/, /'brɑːvəʊ/ *interjection & noun* 2 M18 French (from as preceding). **A** *interjection* Used to express approval when a performer or other person has done something well. **B** *noun* plural **bravos**. A cry of 'bravo!', a cheer.

> **B 1996** *Country Life* There was silence at the close, broken finally by bravos.

bravura /brəˈv(j)ʊərə/ *noun & adjective* M18 Italian (from *bravo* brave). **A** *noun* **1** Great technical skill and brilliance shown in a performance or activity: *the recital ended with a blazing display of bravura.* **2** The display of great daring. **B** *adjective* Showing great technical skill and brilliance: *a bravura performance.*

> **A 2 1996** *Spectator* But behind all the bravura lies a new novelist of prodigious talent; one whose voice, only audible when his own

comedy has subsided, is a moving, melancholic one.

breccia /'brɛtʃə/, /'brɛtʃɪə/ *noun* L18 Italian (= gravel, rubble, cognate with French *brèche*, German *brechen* from Germanic base of break). *Geology* Rock consisting of angular fragments of stones cemented together e.g. by lime.

bric-à-brac /'brɪkəbrak/ *noun* (also **bric-a-brac**) M19 French (from obsolete *à bric et à brac* at random). Miscellaneous objects and ornaments of little value.

> **1996** *Spectator* For many years the great auction houses of London sold only fine art in all its forms. If you wanted to dispose of the bric-à-brac of life you had to look for others to sell it for you.

bricolage /brɪkə'lɑːʒ/, *foreign* /brɪkɔlaʒ/ (*plural same*) *noun* M20 French (from *bricoler* to do odd jobs, repair). (In art or literature) construction or creation from whatever is immediately available for use; something constructed or created in this way, an assemblage of haphazard or incongruous elements.

bricoleur /brɪkə'lə:/; *foreign* /brikɔlœr/ (*plural same*) *noun* M20 French (= handyman, from *bricoler* to do odd jobs). A person who engages in BRICOLAGE; a constructor or creator of bricolages.

brinjal /'brɪndʒaːl/ *noun* E17 Anglo-Indian (ultimately from Portuguese *berinjela*, from as AUBERGINE). (Especially in the Indian subcontinent) an aubergine.

brio /'briːəʊ/ *noun* M18 Italian. Vigour or vivacity of style or performance.

> **1996** *Country Life* At a time when the RSC has been looking a bit wobbly, it restores some much-needed brio and confidence to Stratford Shakespeare.

brioche /bri:'ɒʃ/, /'bri:ɒʃ/ *noun* E19 French. A light sweet yeast bread typically in the form of a small round roll.

briquette /brɪ'kɛt/ *noun* (also **briquet**) L19 French (diminutive of *brique* brick). A small block or slab, especially of compressed coal dust, peat, or other flammable material for use as fuel.

brisé /brize/ *noun* plural pronounced same L18 French (= brɔken, past participle of *briser* to break). *Ballet* A jump in which the dancer sweeps one leg into the air to the side while jumping off the other, brings both legs together in the air, and beats them before landing.

brochette /brɒ'ʃɛt/ *noun* L15 French (diminutive of *broche* spit). **1** A skewer or spit on which chunks of meat or fish are barbecued, grilled, or roasted: *beef and lamb en brochette*; a dish of meat or fish chunks cooked in this way. **2** A pin or bar used to fasten medals, orders, etc., to clothing; a set of decorations worn in this way.

brochure /'brəʊʃə/, /brɒ'ʃʊə/ *noun* M18 French (literally, 'stitching, stitched work', from *brocher* to stitch + -*ure*). A booklet or pamphlet containing pictures and information about a product or service.

> ■ The literal French meaning refers to the fact that, before the days of staplers, such a pamphlet would have been made by stitching a few sheets of paper together.

broderie anglaise /ˌbrəʊd(ə)rɪ ɒŋ'gleɪz/ *noun phrase* M19 French (= English embroidery). Open embroidery, typically in floral patterns, on fine white cotton or linen; fabric so embroidered.

brogan /'brəʊg(ə)n/ *noun* M19 Irish (*brógán*, Gaelic *brógán* diminutive of *bróg* brogue). A coarse stout leather shoe reaching to the ankle.

bronco /'brɒŋkəʊ/ *noun & adjective* (also **broncho**) M19 Spanish (= rough, rude). **A** *noun* plural **broncos**. A wild or half-tamed horse, especially of the western United States. **B** *adjective* Wild, uncontrollable, rough. *United States, colloquial.*

brouhaha /'bruːhɑːhɑː/ *noun* L19 French (probably imitative). A noisy and over-excited reaction or display of interest; a commotion or uproar.

bruit /bruːt/, *in sense 2 of noun foreign* /brɥi/ (*plural same*) *noun & verb* LME Old and Modern French (use as noun of past participle of *bruire* to roar, from Proto-Romance alteration of Latin *rugire* to roar, by association with Proto-Romance source of 'bray'). **A** *noun* **1** Rumour, report. *Archaic.* **2** *Medicine* A sound (especially an abnormal one) heard through a stethoscope; a murmur. **B** *transitive verb* Spread (a report or rumour) widely.

brunette /bruːˈnɛt/, /brʊˈnɛt/ *noun* (United States also **brunet**) M16 French (*brunet* masculine, *brunette* feminine, diminutive of *brun* brown). A woman or girl with dark brown hair.

bruschetta /brʊˈskɛtə/ *noun* M20 Italian (from *bruscare* to toast). Toasted Italian bread drenched in olive oil and served typically with garlic or tomatoes.

brusque /brʊsk/, /bruːsk/ *adjective* (also **brusk**) M17 French (= lively, fierce, harsh, from Italian *brusco* sour, tart, use as adjective of noun = Spanish, Portuguese *brusco* butcher's broom (a spiny bush) from Proto-Romance). Abrupt or offhand in manner or speech.
■ Earliest (only in E17) in the sense of 'tart'.

brut /bruːt/, *foreign* /bryt/ *adjective* L19 French (= raw, rough). (Of sparkling wine) unsweetened, very dry.

bubo /ˈbjuːbəʊ/ *noun* plural **buboes** LME Latin (from Greek *boubōn* groin, swelling in the groin). A swollen inflamed lymph node especially in the groin or armpit.

buckaroo see VAQUERO.

buckling /ˈbʌklɪŋ/ *noun* E20 German (*Bückling* bloater). A smoked herring.

buckra /ˈbʌkrə/ *noun* M18 Ibibio and Efik ((*m*)*bakara* European, master). A white person, especially a man.
■ Used in the West Indies and southern United States and frequently derogatory.

buffet /ˈbʊfeɪ/ *noun* E18 French (from Old French *bufet* stool, of unknown origin). **1** A meal consisting of several dishes from which guests serve themselves. **2** A room or counter in a station, hotel, or other public building selling light meals or snacks; (also **buffet car**) a railway carriage selling light meals or snacks.
■ Originally denoted a sideboard or recessed cupboard for china, plate, etc.

buffo /ˈbʊfəʊ/ *noun & adjective* M18 Italian (= puff of wind, buffoon, from *buffare* to puff, from Proto-Romance verb of imitative origin). **A** *noun* plural **buffos**. A comic actor in Italian opera, a singer in OPERA BUFFA. **B** *adjective* Of or typical of Italian comic opera; comic, burlesque.

buhl /buːl/ *noun* (also **boulle, Buhl**) E19 German (*buhl*, French *boule*, from André Charles *Boulle* (1642–1732), French cabinetmaker). Brass, tortoiseshell, or other material cut into ornamental patterns for inlaying furniture; furniture or other work inlaid in this way.

bulgar /ˈbʌlɡə/ *noun* (also **bulgur, bulgar wheat**) M20 Turkish (= Persian *bulġur* bruised grain). A cereal food made from whole wheat partially boiled then dried, eaten especially in Turkey.

bundobust /ˈbʌndəbʌst/ *noun* (also **bandobast**) L18 Urdu (from Persian *band-o-bast* tying and binding). (In the Indian subcontinent) arrangements or organization.

bunyip /ˈbʌnjɪp/ *noun* M19 Aboriginal. (In Australia) a mythical amphibious monster said to inhabit swamps and lagoons; an imposter or pretender.

bureau /ˈbjʊərəʊ/ *noun* plural **bureaux** /ˈbjʊərəʊz/, **bureaus** L17 French (Old French *burel*, originally = woollen stuff, baize (used for covering writing desks), probably from *bure*, variant of *buire* dark brown, from Proto-Romance alteration of Latin *burrus* fiery red, from Greek *purros* red). **1** A writing desk with drawers and typically an angled top opening downwards to form a writing surface. **b** A chest of drawers. *North America*. **2** An office or department for transacting particular business; a government department.

burette /bjʊˈrɛt/ *noun* (also **buret**) M19 French. A graduated glass tube with a tap at one end, used for measuring small quantities of liquid in chemical analysis.

burghul /bəˈɡuːl/ *noun* E20 Arabic (*burġul* from Persian *burġūl* variant of *bulġūr*). BULGAR.

burin /ˈbjʊərɪn/ *noun* M17 French (related to Italian *burino* (*bulino*), perhaps connected

with Old High German *bora* boring tool).
A hand-held tool for engraving on
copper or wood.

burka /ˈbʊəkə/ *noun* (also **burkha,
burqa**) M19 Urdu (Persian *burk̲a̲ʻ* from
Arabic *burk̲u̲ʻ*). A long, loose garment
covering the whole body from head to
feet, worn in public by women in
many Muslim countries.

burlesque /bəːˈlɛsk/ *noun & verb* M17
French (from Italian *burlesco*, from *burla*
ridicule, joke, fun, of unknown origin).
A *noun* **1** An absurd or comically
exaggerated imitation of something,
especially in a literary or dramatic
work; a parody or caricature. **2** A
variety show, frequently featuring
striptease. Originally and chiefly *United States*. **B** *transitive verb* Parody or
imitate in an absurd or comically
exaggerated way; caricature.

burnous /bəːˈnuːs/ *noun* (also **bur-
noose** and other variants) L16 French
(from Arabic *burnus, burnūs*). A long,
loose hooded cloak worn by Arabs.

burra /ˈbʌrə/ *adjective* E19 Hindi (*baṛā,
bārā* great, greatest). (In the Indian
subcontinent) high-ranking, important, great.

■ Occurs only in phrases such as *burra
sahib* and *burra memsahib*, used to refer to
important people.

burrito /bʊˈriːtəʊ/ *noun* plural **burritos**
M20 American Spanish (diminutive of *burro*

donkey). A Mexican dish consisting of
a tortilla rolled round a filling of
spiced beef or beans.

burro /ˈbʊrəʊ/ *noun* plural **burros** E19
Spanish. A small donkey used as a pack
animal. Chiefly *North American*.

bushido /ˈbuːʃɪdəʊ/, /bʊˈʃiːdəʊ/ *noun* L19
Japanese (= military knight's way). The
code of honour and morals developed
by the Japanese samurai.

bustier /ˈbʌstɪeɪ/, /ˈbʊstɪeɪ/, *foreign*
/bystje/ (*plural same*) *noun* L20 French
(from *buste* bust). A close-fitting usually
strapless bodice or top worn by women.

■ The revival of the *bustier* as a fashion
item in the 1980s was closely associated
with the rock star Madonna, who frequently wore one for her public appear-
ances.
1987 *London Evening News*...bustiers in
scarlet and black sat atop wafts of brightly
coloured chiffon skirts for evening.

butte /bjuːt/ *noun* M19 French. *Geography*
(In North America) an isolated hill
with steep sides and a flat top, similar
to but narrower than a MESA.

bwana /ˈbwɑːnə/ *noun* L19 Kiswahili. (In
East Africa) master, boss, sir.

■ Frequently used, particularly in colonial times, as a term of respectful address
by a black person to a white man.

c., ca. abbreviations of CIRCA.

cabala variant of CABBALA.

caballero /kabə'ljɛːrəʊ/ *noun* plural **caballeros** M19 Spanish (= gentleman, horseman, based on Latin *caballus* horse). A Spanish gentleman.

cabana /kə'bɑːnə/ *noun* (also **cabaña** /kə'bɑːnjə/) L19 Spanish (*cabaña* from late Latin *capanna*, *cavana* cabin). A hut, cabin, or shelter at a beach or swimming pool. Chiefly *United States*.

> **1957** F. Richards *Practise to Deceive* He asked why Lane had gone into the bath-house cabaña.

cabaret /'kabəreɪ/, /kabə'reɪ/ (*plural same*) *noun* M17 Old and Modern French (originally Walloon and Picard, from Middle Dutch variant of *camaret*, *cambret* from Old Picard *camberet* little room). Entertainment held in a nightclub or restaurant while the audience eat or drink at tables; a nightclub or restaurant where cabaret is performed.

> ■ Originally denoted a French inn. Current senses date from the early 20th century.

Cabbala /kə'bɑːlə/, /'kabələ/ *noun* (also **Cabala, Kabbala**) E16 Medieval Latin (*cab-(b)ala* from rabbinical Hebrew *qabbālāh* tradition, from *qibbēl* to receive, accept). The ancient Jewish tradition of mystical interpretation of the Bible, first transmitted orally and using esoteric methods (including ciphers).

cabildo /ka'bildo/, /kə'bɪldəʊ/ *noun* plural **cabildos** /ka'bildos/, /kə'bɪldəʊz/ E19 Spanish (from late Latin *capitulum* chapter house). (In Spain and Spanish-speaking countries) a town council or local government council; a town hall.

cabochon /'kabəʃɒn/ *adjective & noun* M16 Old and Modern French (diminutive of *caboche*, Picard variant of Old French *caboce* head, of unknown origin). A gem that has been polished but not faceted.

> ■ Also in the phrase EN CABOCHON.

cabotage /'kabətaːʒ/, /'kabətɪdʒ/ *noun* M19 French (from *caboter* to sail along a coast, perhaps ultimately from Spanish *cabo* cape, promontory). The right to operate sea, air, or other transport services within a particular territory; restriction of the operation of sea, air, or other transport services within or into a particular country to that country's own transport services.

> ■ Originally used in the sense 'coastal trade'.

cabriole /'kabrɪəʊl/, *foreign* /kabrijɔl/ (*plural same*) *noun* L18 French (= light leap, from *cabrioler*, earlier *caprioler*, from Italian *capriolare* to leap; cf. CAPRIOLE). **1** *Ballet* A jump in which one leg is extended and the other brought up to meet it, and the dancer lands on the second foot. **2** A kind of curved leg characteristic of Chippendale and Queen Anne furniture.

> ■ Sense 2 is so named from the resemblance to the front leg of a leaping animal.

cabriolet /'kabrɪəleɪ/ *noun* M18 French (from *cabriole* goat's leap, from *cabrioler* to leap (so named because of the carriage's motion)). **1** A light two-wheeled carriage with a hood, drawn by one horse. Chiefly *historical*. **2** A car with a roof that folds down.

cache /kaʃ/ *noun & verb* L18 French (from *cacher* to hide). **A** *noun* **1** A collection of valuables, provisions, or ammunition stored in a hidden or inaccessible place. **2** A hidden or inaccessible storage place for valuables, provisions, or ammunition. **3** *Computing* An auxiliary memory from which high-speed retrieval is possible. Also *cache memory*. **B** *transitive verb* Place or store in a cache.

> **B 1986** *Personal Computer World* Window images are normally cached in a form to allow fast screen redraw.

cachepot /kaʃpo/ (*plural same*), /ˈkaʃp-ɒt/ *noun* L19 French (*cache-pot*, from *cacher* to hide + *pot* pot). An ornamental holder for a flowerpot.

cache-sexe /kaʃsɛks/ (*plural same*), /ˈkaʃsɛks/ *noun* E20 French (from *cacher* to hide + *sexe* sex). A covering for the genitals, typically worn by erotic dancers or tribal peoples.

cachet /ˈkaʃeɪ/ *noun* E17 French (from *cacher* (in sense 'press', represented now in *écacher* to crush) from Proto-Romance alteration of Latin *coactare* to constrain). **1** The state of being respected or admired; prestige, high status. **2** A distinguishing mark or seal. **3** A small digestible capsule enclosing a dose of medicine.

1 1995 *Times* Suddenly perfume is losing its luxury cachet and becoming an everyday purchase—and buyers are no longer showing brand loyalty.

cachou /ˈkaʃuː/, /kəˈʃuː/ *noun* L16 French (from Portuguese *cachu* from Malay *kacu*). A pleasant-smelling lozenge sucked to mask bad breath. *Dated*.

■ Originally in the sense 'catechu' (a tannin-rich vegetable extract used in tanning). The current sense dates from the early 18th century.

cacique /kəˈsiːk/ *noun* M16 Spanish or French (from Taino). **1** (In Latin America or the Spanish-speaking Caribbean) a native chief. **2** (In Spain or Latin America) a local political boss.

cacodemon /kakəˈdiːmən/ *noun* (also **cacodaemon**) L16 Greek (*kakodaimōn* from as *kako-* evil + *daimōn* spirit). A malevolent spirit or person.

cacoethes /kakəʊˈiːθiːz/ *noun* M16 Latin (from Greek *kakoēthes* use as noun of adjective *kakoēthēs* ill-disposed, from as *kako-* evil + *ēthos* disposition). An urge to do something inadvisable.

■ Although also formerly used of a malignant tendency in a medical sense, *cacoethes* mainly occurs in English with reference to the Latin poet Juvenal (*Satire* vii): *tenet insanabile multos* / *scribendi cacoethes* 'the incurable itch to write grips many'.

cadeau /kado/ *noun* plural **cadeaux** plural pronounced same L18 French. A gift.

cadenza /kəˈdɛnzə/ *noun* M18 Italian. *Music* A virtuoso solo passage inserted into a movement in a concerto or other musical work, typically near the end.

cadet /kəˈdɛt/ *noun* E17 French (earlier *capdet* from Gascon dialect (= Provençal *capdel*) from Proto-Romance diminutive of Latin *caput* head). **1** A young trainee in the armed services or police force. **2** A boy or girl of 13–18 who undergoes voluntary army, navy, or air force training together with adventure training. **3** A younger son or daughter; a junior branch of a family.

■ First used in English in sense 3. The notion 'little head' or 'inferior head' gave rise to that of 'younger, junior'.

cadi /ˈkɑːdi/, /ˈkeɪdi/ *noun* (also **kadi**, **qadi**) L16 Arabic ((*al-*)*ḳāḍī*). A civil judge in an Islamic country.

cadre /ˈkɑːdə/, /ˈkɑːdr(ə)/, /ˈkadri/ *noun* M19 French (from Italian *quadro* from Latin *quadrus* square). **1** A small group of people specially trained for a particular purpose or profession. **2** A group of activists in a communist or other revolutionary organization. **3** A member of an activist group.

caduceus /kəˈdjuːsɪəs/ *noun* plural **caducei** /kəˈdjuːsɪʌɪ/ L16 Latin (*caduceus*, *caduceum* from Doric Greek *karuk(e)ion* = Attic *kērukeion* neuter adjective used as noun, from *kērux* herald). An ancient Greek or Roman herald's wand; *specifically* the wand carried by the messenger god Hermes or Mercury, usually represented with two serpents twined round it.

caesura /sɪˈzjʊərə/ *noun* M16 Latin (*caesura*, from *caes-* past participial stem of *caedere* to cut). **1** *Prosody* (In Greek and Latin verse) a break between words within a metrical foot; (in modern verse) a pause near the middle of a line. **2** *generally* A break, a stop, an interruption.

cafard /kaˈfɑː/, *foreign* /kafar/ *noun* M16 French (= cockroach, hypocrite, probably from late Latin *caphardum*). Melancholia.
■ Originally used in the sense 'hypocrite'.

café /ˈkafeɪ/, /ˈkafi/; *also colloquial* /kaf/, /keɪf/ *noun* (*also* **cafe** and (reflecting colloquial pronunciation) **caf(f)**) E19 French (= coffee (house)). A small restaurant selling light meals and drinks; a bar or nightclub (*United States*).
■ The 'coffee' sense of the French occurs in English in such phrases as *café au lait* and *café noir*.

café au lait /kafe o lɛ/ *noun & adjective phrase* M18 French (= coffee with milk). **A** *noun phrase* Coffee with milk, white coffee. **B** *adjective phrase* Of the light brown colour of this.

café noir /kafe nwar/ *noun phrase* M19 French (= black coffee). Coffee without milk, black coffee.

cafeteria /kafɪˈtɪərɪə/ *noun* M19 American Spanish (*cafetería*, from *café* coffee). A restaurant in which customers serve themselves from a counter and pay before eating, often as part of the facilities in a workplace, institution, or public building.
■ Originally United States, but apparently spread to Europe in the 1920s, when the *Glasgow Herald* (30 July 1925) observed that 'Cafeterias, although a commonplace in America, are just beginning to have a hold in Paris.'

cafetière /kaftjɛr/ *noun plural* pronounced same M19 French (from *café* coffee). A coffee pot containing a plunger made of fine mesh with which the grounds are pushed to the bottom when the coffee is ready to be poured.
1996 *Times Magazine* Every household member believes that he or she is the only person who ever…deals with coffee-grounds in the cafetière….

caffè latte see LATTE.

caffè macchiato see MACCHIATO.

caftan variant of KAFTAN.

cagoule /kəˈguːl/ *noun* (*also* **kagoule**) M20 French (literally, 'cowl'). A light-weight, hooded, thigh-length waterproof jacket.

caique /kʌɪˈiːk/, /keɪˈiːk/ *noun* E17 French (*caïque* from Italian *caicco* from Turkish *kayík*). **1** A light rowing boat or skiff used on the Bosporus. **2** A small eastern Mediterranean sailing ship.

caisson /ˈkeɪs(ə)n/, /kəˈsuːn/ *noun* L17 French (= large chest, from Italian *cassone* with assimilation to *caisse* case). **1** A large watertight chamber open at the bottom, from which the water is kept out by air pressure, used in laying foundations under water. **b** A floating vessel or watertight structure used as a dock gate. **2** *History* An ammunition chest; an ammunition wagon.

calabrese /ˈkaləbriːs/ *noun* M20 Italian (= Calabrian). A variety of usually green sprouting broccoli.

calamari /kaləˈmɑːri/ *noun plural* L20 Italian (plural of *calamaro* squid). Squid served as food.

calando /kəˈlandəʊ/, *foreign* /kaˈlando/ *adverb* E19 Italian (= slackening). *Music* (Especially as a direction) gradually decreasing in speed and volume.

caldarium /kalˈdɛːrɪəm/ *noun plural* **caldaria** /kalˈdɛːrɪə/ M18 Latin. A hot room in an ancient Roman bath.

caldera /kalˈdɛːrə/, /kalˈdɪərə/ *noun* L17 Spanish (from late Latin *caldaria* pot for boiling). A volcanic crater of great size, especially one formed by a major eruption leading to the collapse of the mouth of the volcano.

calliope /kəˈlʌɪəpi/ *noun* M19 Greek (*Kalliopē* literally, 'beautiful-voiced') the Muse of epic poetry). An American keyboard instrument resembling an organ but with the notes produced by steam whistles, formerly used on showboats and in travelling fairs.

callus /ˈkaləs/ *noun* M16 Latin (more commonly *callum*). **1** A thickened and hardened part of the skin or soft tissue, especially in an area that has been subject to friction. **2** *Medicine* The bony healing tissue which forms around the ends of broken bone. **3** *Botany* A hard formation of tissue, especially new tissue formed over a wound.

calque /kalk/ *noun & verb* M20 French (= copy, tracing, from *calquer* to trace, from Italian *calcare* from Latin *calcare* to tread). **A** *noun* An expression adopted by one language from another in a more or less literally translated form; a loan translation (*of, on*). **B** *transitive verb* Form as a calque. Usually in *passive* (followed by *on*).

■ A modern example of a calque is 'that goes without saying', which is calqued on French *cela va sans dire*.

1957 G. V. Smithers *Kyng Alisaunder Fecche mood*... is evidently a calque on OF. *porter ire*, as in *Chanson de Roland*.

calumet /'kaljʊmɛt/ *noun* L17 French (dialectal variant of *chalumeau* from late Latin *calamellus* diminutive of *calamus* reed). A North American Indian tobacco pipe with a clay bowl and reed stem, smoked especially as a sign of peace; a symbol of peace.

calvados /'kalvədɒs/ *noun* E20 French (*Calvados*, a department in Normandy, France). Apple brandy, traditionally made in the Calvados region; a drink of this.

calyx /'kalɪks/, /'kelɪks/ *noun* plural **calyces** /'kalɪsiːz/, **calyxes** L17 Latin (*calyx, -yc-* from Greek *kalux* shell, husk, pod, from base of *kaluptein* to hide). *Botany* The sepals of a flower, typically forming a whorl that encloses the petals and forms a protective layer around a flower in bud.

calzone /kal'tsəʊni/ *noun* L20 Italian (literally, 'trouser leg', with reference to the shape of the pizza). A type of pizza that is folded in half before cooking to contain the filling.

camaraderie /kaməˈrɑːd(ə)ri/, /kaməˈrɑːd(ə)riː/ *noun* M19 French (from *camarade* comrade). The mutual trust and friendship among people who spend a lot of time together.

1995 *Spectator* Banter goes on across tables. The camaraderie is palpable and so is the air. Everybody smokes.

camarilla /kaməˈrɪlə/, /kaməˈrɪljə/ *noun* M19 Spanish (diminutive of *camara* chamber). A small group of people, especially a group of advisers to a ruler or politician, with a shared purpose; a cabal, a clique.

camera lucida /ˌkam(ə)rə ˈluːsɪdə/ *noun phrase* plural **camera lucidas** M18 Latin (= bright chamber). An instrument by which the rays of light from an object are reflected by a prism and produce an image on a sheet of paper placed beneath the instrument, from which a drawing can be made.

camera obscura /ˌkam(ə)rə ɒbsˈkjʊ ərə/ *noun phrase* plural **camera obscuras** E18 Latin (= dark chamber). A darkened box or enclosure with an aperture for projecting an image of external objects on a screen placed at the focus of the lens; a building containing such a box or enclosure.

camisole /'kamɪsəʊl/ *noun* E19 French (from Italian *camiciola* or Spanish *camisola*, diminutive of (respectively) *camicia*, *camisa* from late Latin *camisia* shirt, nightgown). A woman's loose-fitting undergarment for the upper body, typically held up by shoulder straps and embroidered or otherwise ornamentally trimmed.

Camorra /kəˈmɔːrə/, /kəˈmɒrə/ *noun* (also **camorra**) M19 Italian (perhaps from Spanish *camorra* dispute, quarrel). A secret criminal society akin to the Mafia operating in the Neapolitan district; *generally* any organized body engaged in extortion or other dishonest activities.

camouflage /'kaməflɑːʒ/ *noun & verb* E20 French (from *camoufler* (thieves' slang) to cover up, from Italian *camuffare* disguise, deceive, perhaps associated with French *camouflet* whiff of smoke in the face). **A** *noun* **1** The disguising or concealment of military personnel, equipment, and installations by painting or covering them to make them blend in with their surroundings; clothing or materials used as a camouflage. **2** The natural colouring or form of an animal which enables it to blend in with its surroundings. **3** Actions or devices intended to disguise or mislead: *much of my apparent indifference was merely protective camouflage.*

B *transitive verb* Hide or disguise by camouflage.

campanile /kampə'ni:li/ *noun* M17 Italian (from *campana* bell + *-ile*). An Italian bell tower, especially a free-standing one.

campesino /kampe'sino/, /kampə'si: nəʊ/ *noun* plural **campesinos** /kam pe'sinos/, /kampə'si:nəʊz/ M20 Spanish. (In Spain and Spanish-speaking countries) a peasant farmer.

campo /'kampəʊ/ *noun* plural **campos** M19 American Spanish or Portuguese (= field, open country, from Latin *campus*). **1** (In South America, especially Brazil) a grass plain with occasional stunted trees; a savannah. **2** A square in an Italian or Spanish town.

campus /'kampəs/ *noun* L18 Latin (= field). The grounds and buildings of a university or college, especially where forming a distinct area; university or college life.

■ Originally used of the grounds of Princeton University, New Jersey, then of similar open spaces in other United States universities, and now worldwide.

canaille /kanaj/ *noun* L16 French (from Italian *canaglia*, literally, 'pack of dogs', from *cane* dog). The common people, the rabble, the masses.

canapé /'kanəpeɪ/, /'kanəpi/ *noun* L19 French. **1** A small piece of bread or pastry with a savoury topping, served with drinks at receptions or formal parties. **2** A decorative French antique sofa.

■ In sense 2 the history of the Romance word *canapé* is closely linked to that of English *canopy*, both of them deriving from medieval Latin *canopeum* baldachin, a variant of classical Latin *conopeum* bed with net curtains, from Greek *kōnōpeion* Egyptian bed with mosquito curtains, from *kōnōps* mosquito. In English the sense of *canopy* has adhered to the 'curtain' sense of the Latin, while *canapé* in the Romance languages (Spanish and Portuguese as well as French) has retained the primary sense of 'couch, sofa'. By the late 18th century sense 1, now by far the more familiar in English, had evolved in French. It is a figurative

extension of the earlier sense, a 'couch' on which to place toppings.

canard /kə'nɑ:d/, /kanɑd/ *noun* M19 French (literally, 'duck', also 'hoax'). **1** An unfounded rumour or story. **2** A small wing-like projection attached to an aircraft forward of the main wing to provide extra stability or control, sometimes replacing the tail.

1 1995 *New Scientist* This is a common misunderstanding and is a canard on a par with the belief that long ago insurance companies which provided fire engines would not put out fires unless the building displayed their company's mark.

canasta /kə'nastə/ *noun* M20 Spanish (= basket, ultimately from Latin *canistrum* bread (or flower) basket). A two-pack card game of the rummy family and of Uruguayan origin, usually played by four in two partnerships; a meld of seven or more cards in this game.

cancan /'kankan/ *noun* M19 French (child's word for *canard* duck). A lively, high-kicking stage dance originating in 19th-century Parisian music halls and performed by women in long skirts and petticoats.

candelabrum /kandɪ'lɑ:brəm/, /kandɪ 'leɪbrəm/ *noun* plural **candelabra** /kan dɪ'lɑ:brə/, **candelabrums** (also **candelabra**, plural same, **candelabras**) E19 Latin (from *candela* candle). A large usually branched ornamental candlestick or lamp holder carrying several lights.

candida /'kandɪdə/ *noun* M20 Modern Latin (feminine of Latin *candidus* white). A yeast-like parasitic fungus of the genus *Candida* that can sometimes cause thrush.

cannelloni /kanə'ləʊni/ *noun plural* M20 Italian (augmentative plural of *cannello* stalk, tube). Rolls of pasta stuffed with a meat or vegetable mixture; an Italian dish consisting largely of this and usually a sauce.

cannelure /'kan(ə)ljʊə/ *noun* M18 French (from *canneler* to groove, flute, from *canne* reed). A groove round the cylindrical part of a bullet.

cantabile /kan'tɑ:bɪli/ *adverb, adjective, & noun* E18 Italian (= that can be sung).

Music **A** *adverb & adjective* In a smooth flowing style, as if singing. **B** *noun* Cantabile style; a piece or movement in this style.

cantaloupe /'kantəlu:p/ *noun* (also **cantaloup**) L18 French (*cantaloup*). A small round ribbed variety of melon, with orange flesh. Also called *rock melon*.

■ The French name is taken from *Cantaluppi*, the name of the place near Rome, where, on its introduction from Armenia, the melon was first grown in Europe.

cantata /kan'tɑːtə/ *noun* E18 Italian (from *cantata (aria)* sung (air), from *cantare* to sing). *Music* A medium-length narrative or descriptive piece of music with vocal solos and usually a chorus and orchestra.

cantilena /kantɪ'leɪnə/,   /kantɪ'liːnə/ *noun* M18 Italian (or Latin *cantilena* song). *Music* The part carrying the melody in a composition.

cantina /kan'tiːnə/ *noun* L19 Spanish and Italian. (In Spain, Spanish-speaking countries, and the south-western United States) a bar, a saloon; (in Italy) a wine shop.

canto /'kantəʊ/ *noun* plural **cantos** L16 Italian (literally, 'song', from Latin CANTUS). One of the sections into which certain long poems are divided.

canton /'kantɒn/, /kan'tɒn/ *noun* E16 Old and Modern French (= corner, from Provençal from oblique case of Proto-Romance variant of Latin *cant(h)us*). A subdivision of a country established for political or administrative purposes; a small district; *specifically* one of the several states which form the Swiss Confederation.

cantor /'kantɔː/, /'kantə/ *noun* M16 Latin (= singer, from *canere* to chant). **1** An official who sings liturgical music and leads prayer in a synagogue, a HAZZAN. **2** (In formal Christian worship) a person who sings solo verses or passages to which the choir or congregation respond.

cantoris /kan'tɔːrɪs/ *noun* M17 Latin (genitive of CANTOR). The section of a church or cathedral choir convention-

ally placed on the north side and taking the second or lower part in antiphonal singing (cf. DECANI).

cantus /'kantəs/ *noun* plural **cantus** /'kantuːs/, /'kantəs/ L16 Latin (= song). The highest voice in polyphonic choral music.

cantus firmus /ˌkantəs 'fəːməs/ *noun phrase* plural **cantus firmi** /'fəːmʌɪ/ M19 Medieval Latin (= firm song). *Music* A melody used as the basis for a polyphonic composition.

canyon /'kanjən/ *noun* M19 Spanish (*cañón* tube, pipe, gun barrel, etc., based on Latin *canna* reed). A deep gorge (especially in the United States or Mexico), frequently with a river flowing through it.

canzona /kan'tsəʊnə/ *noun* L19 Italian (from next). An instrumental arrangement of a French or Flemish song, typical of 16th-century Italy.

canzone /kan'tsəʊni/ *noun* plural **canzoni** /kan'tsəʊni/ L16 Italian (= song (corresponding to Old and Modern French *chanson*) from Latin *cantio(n-)* singing, from *cant-* past participle of *canere* to sing). An Italian or Provençal song or ballad; a style of lyric resembling a madrigal.

caoutchouc /'kaʊtʃʊk/ *noun* L18 French (from obsolete Spanish *cauchuc* from Quechua *kauchuk*). Natural rubber that has not been vulcanized.

cap-à-pie /kapə'piː/ *adverb* E16 Old French (*cap a pie* (Modern French *de pied en cap*)). From head to foot, fully (armed, ready, etc.). Now *archaic*.

capo /'kapəʊ/ *noun* plural **capos** M20 Italian (from Latin *caput* head). The head of a crime syndicate, especially the Mafia, or one of its branches. Chiefly *United States*.

capo abbreviated form of CAPO TASTO.

capot /kə'pɒt/ *noun & verb* M17 French (perhaps from *capoter* dialectal variant of *chapoter* to castrate). *Piquet* **A** *noun* The winning of all the tricks by one player; a score awarded for this. **B** *transitive verb* Win all the tricks from.

■ Formerly stressed on the first syllable. *Capot* is the source of the German *kaputt*, from which the dated English slang KAPUT is taken.

capo tasto /kapəʊ ˈtastəʊ/ *noun* plural **capo tastos** (also **capotasto**) L19 Italian (literally, 'head stop'). *Music* A clamp fastened across all the strings of a fretted musical instrument to raise their tuning by a chosen amount.

■ Generally known as a *capo*.

capote /kəˈpəʊt/ *noun* E19 French (diminutive of *cape* cape, cloak). A long cloak or coat with a hood, worn especially as part of an army or company uniform.

cappuccino /kapʊˈtʃiːnəʊ/ *noun* plural **cappuccinos** M20 Italian (literally 'Capuchin', a Franciscan friar (because the drink's colour resembles that of a Capuchin's habit)). A type of coffee made with milk that has been frothed up with pressurized steam.

capriccio /kəˈprɪtʃɪəʊ/ *noun* plural **capriccios** E17 Italian (literally, 'head with the hair standing on end', (hence) horror; later (by association with *capra* goat) sudden start, from *capo* head + *riccio* hedgehog, ultimately from Latin *(h)ericius* urchin). **1** A lively piece of music, typically one that is short and free in form. **2** A painting or other work of art representing a fantasy or a mixture of real and imaginary features.

■ Originally denoted a sudden change of mind.

capriccioso /kəprɪtʃɪˈəʊsəʊ/ *adverb* M18 Italian (literally, 'capricious'). *Music* (Especially as a direction) in a free and impulsive style.

caprice /kəˈpriːs/ *noun* M17 French (from CAPRICCIO). **1** A sudden and unaccountable change of mind or behaviour; a whim. **b** Inclination or disposition to such changes etc.; capriciousness. **2** *Music* A CAPRICCIO.

capriole /ˈkaprɪəʊl/ *noun* & *verb* L16 French ((now *cabriole*), from Italian *capriola*, from *capriolare* to leap, from *capriolo* roebuck, from Latin *capreolus* diminutive of *caper* goat). **A** *noun* **1** A movement performed in classical riding, in which the horse leaps from the ground and

kicks out with its hind legs. **2** A leap or caper in dancing, especially a CABRIOLE. **B** *intransitive verb* Perform a capriole; skip, leap, caper.

caput mortuum /ˌkapət ˈmɔːtuːəm/ *noun phrase* M17 Latin (= dead head). *Alchemy* The residue remaining after distillation or sublimation.

carabinero /ˌkarabiˈnero/, /ˌkarəbɪˈnɛːrəʊ/ *noun* plural **carabineros** /ˌkarabiˈneros/, /ˌkarabɪˈnɛːrəʊz/ M19 Spanish (literally, 'carabineer'). A Spanish or South American frontier guard or customs officer.

carabiniere /ˌkarabiˈnjere/, /ˌkarəbɪˈnjɛːri/ *noun* plural **carabinieri** /ˌkarabɪˈnjeri/ M19 Italian (literally, 'carabineer'). An Italian soldier in a corps serving as a police force.

> **1995** *Times* Away from skiing, Tomba is facing possible expulsion from the Italian *carabinieri* after a photographer, who had sold nude photographs of him to a magazine, alleged that the Italian had thrown a heavy glass trophy at him after a World Cup race on Sunday.

caracole /ˈkarəkəʊl/ *noun* (also **caracol** /ˈkarəkɒl/) E17 French (*caracol(e)* snail's shell, spiral). *Equestrianism* A half-turn or wheel to the right or left by a horse or rider. Formerly also, a series of such turns alternately to right and left.

■ The word was also formerly used in English for short periods in senses deriving directly from its basic French meanings: 'a spiral shell' (only E17) and in architectural contexts 'a helical staircase' (E18).

caracul variant of KARAKUL.

carafe /kəˈraf/, /kəˈrɑːf/ *noun* L18 French (from Italian *caraffa*, probably based on Arabic *garafa* draw water). An open-topped glass flask used for serving wine or water in a restaurant.

caramba /kəˈrambə/, *foreign* /kaˈramba/ *interjection* M19 Spanish. An expression of surprise or dismay. *Colloquial*, often *humorous*.

caravanserai /karəˈvansərʌɪ/, /karə-ˈvansəri/ *noun* (also **caravansary**, **caravansery**, and other variants) L16 Persian (*kārwānsarāy*, from *kārvān* (desert) caravan + SERAI). **1** An inn with a central courtyard for travellers in the desert regions of Asia or north Africa. **2** A group of people travelling together; a caravan.

carcinoma /kɑːsɪˈnəʊmə/ *noun* plural **carcinomas**, **carcinomata** /kɑːsɪˈnəʊmətə/ E18 Latin (from Greek *karkinōma* from *karkinos crab* + *suffix -oma*). *Medicine* A cancer; now *specifically* a malignant tumour of epithelial origin.

caret /ˈkarət/ *noun* L17 Latin (= is lacking, 3rd person singular present indicative of *carere* to be without, lack). A mark (strictly ^) placed below a line of text to indicate a proposed insertion.

cariad /ˈkarɪad/ *noun* L19 Welsh (= love). Darling, sweetheart.

caries /ˈkɛːriːz/ *noun* plural same L16 Latin. Decay and crumbling of a tooth or bone.

carillon /ˈkarɪljən/, /ˈkarɪlɒn/, /kəˈrɪljən/ *noun* L18 French (alteration of Old French *car(e)ignon*, *quarregnon*, from Proto-Romance = peal of four bells). **1** A set of bells sounded either from a keyboard or by an automatic mechanism similar to a piano roll. **2** A tune played on such bells.

carioca /karɪˈəʊkə/ *noun* M19 Portuguese. **1** A native of Rio de Janeiro, Brazil. **2** A Brazilian dance resembling a samba; a piece of music for this dance.

cariole variant of CARRIOLE.

carnet /ˈkɑːneɪ/, *foreign* /karnɛ/ (*plural same*) *noun* E20 French (= notebook). **1** A book of tickets for use on public transport in some countries. **2** A customs permit allowing a motorist to drive across a frontier for a limited period.

carousel /karəˈsɛl/, /karəˈzɛl/ *noun* M17 French (*carrousel* from Italian *carosello*, *garosello*). **1** A merry-go-round; a roundabout. Chiefly *North American*. **2** A conveyor system at an airport from which arriving passengers collect their luggage. **3** *History* A kind of tournament in which variously dressed companies of knights took part in demonstrations of equestrian skills.

carpaccio /kɑːˈpatʃɪəʊ/, *foreign* /karˈpattʃo/ *noun* L20 Italian (named after Vittore *Carpaccio*, from his use of red pigments, resembling raw meat). An Italian hors d'oeuvre consisting of thin slices of raw beef or fish served with a sauce.

carpe diem /kɑːpeɪ ˈdiːɛm/, /kɑːpeɪ ˈdʌɪɛm/ *interjection* E19 Latin (literally 'seize the day!', a quotation from Horace (*Odes* I.xi)). Used to urge someone to make the most of the present time and give little thought to the future.

carriole /ˈkarɪəʊl/ *noun* (also **cariole**) M18 French (from Italian *carriuola*, diminutive of *carro* car). **1** A small open carriage for one; a covered light cart. Chiefly *historical*. **2** (In Canada) a kind of sledge pulled by a horse or dogs.

carte blanche /kɑːt ˈblɑːnʃ/, *foreign* /kart blɑ̃ʃ/ *noun phrase* plural **cartes blanches** /kɑːts ˈblɑːnʃ/, *foreign* /kart blɑ̃ʃ/ L17 French (= blank paper). **1** Complete freedom to act as one wishes. **2** *Cards* In piquet and bezique, a hand containing no court cards as dealt, and attracting a compensatory score.

■ The term originally referred to a blank sheet of paper to be filled in as one wishes, particularly one's own terms for an agreement.

1 1996 *Times* That is greatly to the credit of the company, which gave *carte blanche* to…an experienced American business academic who spent 60 days coming up with a more down-to-earth 'audit' than sceptics might have expected.

carte-de-visite /ˌkɑːtdəvɪˈziːt/ *noun* plural **cartes-de-visite** (pronounced same) M19 French (= visiting-card). A small photographic portrait of a person, mounted on a piece of card. Now *archaic* or *historical*.

cartel /kɑːˈtɛl/ *noun* M16 German (*Kartell*, from French *cartel*, from Italian *cartello* placard, challenge, diminutive of *carta* from Latin *carta*). A manufacturers' agreement or association formed to maintain prices at a high level and restrict competition.

■ Originally used to refer to the coalition of the Conservatives and National

Liberal parties in Germany (1887), and hence any political combination. In later use the word came to denote a trade agreement.

cartes blanches, cartes-de-visite plural of CARTE BLANCHE, CARTE-DE-VISITE.

cartonnage /'kɑ:t(ə)nɪʤ/ *noun* M19 French (from *carton* cardboard (from Italian *cartone* augmentative of *carta*, from Latin *c(h)arta* paper) + *-age*). An ancient Egyptian mummy case made of tightly fitting layers of linen or papyrus glued together.

cartouche /kɑ:'tu:ʃ/ *noun* E17 French (from Italian *cartoccio* from *carta* paper). **1** A carved tablet or drawing representing a scroll with rolled-up ends or edges, used ornamentally or bearing an inscription. **b** A decorative architectural feature, such as a modillion or corbel, resembling a scroll. **2** An ornate frame around a design or inscription in the shape of such a scroll. **3** *Archaeology* An oval or oblong enclosing a group of Egyptian hieroglyphs, typically representing the name and title of a monarch.

casbah variant of KASBAH.

cascara sagrada /ka'skɑ:rə sə‚grɑ:də/ *noun phrase* L19 Spanish (*cáscara sagrada*, literally, 'sacred bark'). The bark of a Californian buckthorn, *Rhamnus purshiana*; an extract of this, used as a purgative.
■ Often shortened to *cascara*.

casino /kə'si:nəʊ/ *noun* plural **casinos** M18 Italian (diminutive of *casa* house, from Latin *casa* cottage). **1** Originally, a public room used for social meetings; *especially* a public music or dancing saloon. Now, a public room or building where gambling games are played. **2** A summer house (*specifically* in Italy).
2 1996 *Spectator* [Sir William Hamilton] took a *casino* on the beach at Posillipo for sea-bathing...

casque /kɑ:sk/ *noun* L17 French (from Spanish *casco*). **1** A piece of armour to cover the head; a helmet. Now *historical* or *poetical*. **2** *Zoology* A helmet-like

structure, such as the bill of a hornbill or the head of a cassowary.

cassareep /'kasəri:p/ *noun* M19 Caribbean. A thick brown syrup prepared by boiling down the juice of grated cassava with sugar, spices, etc.

cassata /kə'sɑ:tə/ *noun* E20 Italian. A Neapolitan ice cream containing candied or dried fruit and nuts.

casserole /'kasərəʊl/ *noun* & *verb* E18 French (extension of *cassole* diminutive of *casse* spoon-like container, from Provençal *casa*, from late Latin *cattia* ladle, pan, from Greek *kuathion*, *kuatheion* diminutive of *kuathos* cup). **A** *noun* A kind of stew that is cooked slowly in an oven; a large covered heatproof dish used for cooking casseroles. **B** *transitive verb* Cook (food) slowly in a casserole.

cassis /ka'si:s/, /'kasɪs/ *noun* L19 French (= blackcurrant, apparently from Latin *cassia*). A syrupy blackcurrant liqueur produced mainly in Burgundy.

cassone /ka'səʊni/, *foreign* /kas'so:ne/ *noun* plural **cassones** /ka'səʊniz/, **cassoni** /kas'so:ni/ L19 Italian (= large chest, from *cassa* chest). (In Italy) a large chest, especially one used to hold a bride's trousseau.

cassoulet /'kasʊleɪ/ *noun* M20 French (diminutive of dialect *cassolo* stew pan, tureen). A stew made with meat and beans.

castrato /ka'strɑ:təʊ/ *noun* plural **castrati** /ka'strɑ:ti/ M18 Italian (use as noun of past participle of *castrare* to castrate). *History* An adult male singer castrated in boyhood so as to retain a soprano or alto voice.

casus belli /‚kɑ:sʊs 'bɛli:/, /‚keɪsəs 'bɛlaɪ/ *noun phrase* M19 Latin (from *casus* case + *belli* genitive of *bellum* war). An act or situation that justifies or provokes a war.
1996 *Spectator* There must be clear provocation, a satisfactory *casus belli*.

catafalque /'katəfalk/ *noun* (also (now *rare*) **catafalco** /katə'falkəʊ/, plural **catafalco(e)s** M17 French (from Italian *catafalco*, of unknown origin). **1** A decorated wooden framework supporting the coffin of a distinguished person during a funeral service or for a lying in state. **2** A structure on which a coffin is drawn in procession.

catalogue raisonné /katalɔg rezɔne/ *noun phrase* plural **catalogues raisonnés** (pronounced same) L18 French (= explained catalogue). A descriptive catalogue of works of art with explanations and scholarly comments; *figurative* an exhaustive account.

> **1996** *Country Life* Paul McCarron has produced a *catalogue raisonné* of the prints of Martin Lewis...
> *figurative* **1995** *Spectator* That is the import of *The Sleaze File* by Judith Cook, a new *catalogue raisonné* of British scandal and microscandal over the last two or three years.

catalysis /kəˈtalɪsɪs/ *noun* plural **catalyses** /kəˈtalɪsiːz/ M19 Modern Latin (from Greek *katalusis*, from *kataluein* to dissolve). *Chemistry* The action or effect of a substance in increasing the rate of a chemical reaction without itself undergoing any permanent chemical change; an instance of this.

catamaran /ˌkatəməˈran/, /ˈkatəmaran/ *noun* E17 Tamil (*kaṭṭumaram*, literally, 'tied wood'). A yacht or other boat with twin hulls side by side.

catechesis /katɪˈkiːsɪs/ *noun* plural **catecheses** /katɪˈkiːsiːz/ M18 ecclesiastical Latin (from Greek *katēkhēsis* oral instruction, from *katēkhein*). Religious instruction given with a catechism in preparation for Christian baptism or confirmation; (in Roman Catholic use) religious instruction in general.

catechumen /katɪˈkjuːmɛn/ *noun* LME Old and Modern French (*catéchumène* or ecclesiastical Latin *catechumenus* from Greek *katēkhoumenos* being instructed, present participle passive of *katēkhein*). A person who is receiving instruction in preparation for Christian baptism or confirmation.

catenaccio /katəˈnatʃɪəʊ/ *noun* L20 Italian (= bolt, from *catena* chain + the pejorative suffix *-accio*). *Soccer* A very defensive system of play, especially one employing a sweeper.

catharsis /kəˈθɑːsɪs/ *noun* plural **catharses** /kəˈθɑːsiːz/ E19 Modern Latin (from Greek *katharsis*, from *kathairein* to cleanse, from *katharos* pure). **1** The process of releasing, and thereby providing relief from, strong or repressed emotions. **2** *Medicine* Purgation. Now *rare*.

> ■ The notion of 'release' through drama (sense 1) derives from Aristotle's *Poetics*.

catheter /ˈkaθɪtə/ *noun* E17 Late Latin (*catheter* from Greek *kathetēr*, from *kathienai* to send or let down). *Medicine* A flexible tube which can be passed into the bladder or other body cavity or canal to allow the draining of fluid.

cathexis /kəˈθɛksɪs/ *noun* E20 Greek (*kathexis* holding, retention). *Psychoanalysis* The concentration of mental energy on one particular person, idea, or object (especially to an unhealthy degree).

> ■ A rendering of Freud's German term *Libidobesetzung*.

caudillo /kaʊˈdiːljəʊ/ *noun* plural **caudillos** M19 Spanish (from late Latin *capitellum* diminutive of *caput* head). (In Spain and Spanish-speaking countries) a military or political leader.

> ■ The title *El Caudillo*, 'the leader', was assumed by General Franco of Spain in 1938.

cause célèbre /koz selɛbr/ *noun phrase* plural **causes célèbres** (pronounced same) M18 French (literally, 'famous case'). A controversial issue that attracts a great deal of public attention.

> **1996** *Times* The rape of Artemisia Gentileschi is a cause célèbre in art history.

causerie /kozri/ *noun* plural pronounced same E19 French (from *causer* to talk). An informal article or talk, typically in a literary subject.

causes célèbres plural of CAUSE CÉLÈBRE.

cavatina /kavəˈtiːnə/ *noun* E19 Italian. *Music* A short operatic aria in simple style without repeated sections; a similar piece of lyrical instrumental music.

cave /ˈkeɪvi/ *interjection* M19 Latin (imperative singular of *cavere* to beware). Look out! British school slang, *dated*.

■ Also used in the phrase *keep cave*, act as a lookout.

caveat /'kavɪat/, /'keɪvɪat/ *noun* M16 Latin (= let a person beware, 3rd person singular present subjunctive of *cavere* to beware). **1** A warning or proviso of specific stipulations, conditions, or limitations. **2** *Law* A notice, especially a probate, that certain actions may not be taken without informing the person who gave notice.

■ Also formerly as a transitive verb (M17) in legal terminology or an intransitive verb (M17) in fencers' jargon meaning 'disengage'. Current verbal use is confined to the phrase CAVEAT EMPTOR.
1 1996 *Times* I started to offer Wiesenthal Lord Shawcross's objections, but he stopped me with a caveat about using the euphemism 'war criminals'.

caveat emptor /ˌkavɪat 'ɛmptɔː/ *noun phrase* E16 Latin (= let the buyer beware!). The principle that the buyer alone is responsible for checking the quality and suitability of goods before a purchase is made.

■ Frequently invoked in the context of horse-dealing—the earliest recorded use in English is in J. Fitzherbert's *A newe tracte...for all husbande men* (1523)—this ancient principle fails to find much favour under modern consumer protection legislation.
1950 T. H. Marshall *Citizenship and Social Class* The principle of caveat emptor is at least plausible when you are buying a horse.

cedilla /sɪ'dɪlə/ *noun* (formerly (L16–M19) also **cerilla**) L16 Spanish ((now *zedilla*), diminutive of *zeda* letter Z). The diacritic mark , written under the letter *c*, especially in French, to show that it is pronounced like an *s* rather than a *k* (e.g. *façade*); a similar mark under *s* in Turkish and other oriental languages.

ceilidh /'keɪlɪ/ *noun* L19 Irish (*céilidhe* (now *céili*), Gaelic *cèilidh*, from Old Irish *céilide* visit, act of visiting, from *céile* companion). A social event with Scottish or Irish folk music and singing, traditional dancing, and storytelling.

celadon /'sɛlədɒn/ *noun* M18 French (*céladon*). **1** A willow-green colour; pale greyish green. **2** A glaze of this colour used on (especially Chinese) pottery or porcelain; ceramic ware made with celadon glaze.

■ From the name of the shepherd-hero of D'Urfé's immensely popular pastoral romance *L'Astrée* (1607–27).

celesta /sɪ'lɛstə/ *noun* L19 pseudo-Latin (based on French *céleste* heavenly). A small keyboard instrument in which felted hammers strike on steel plates, producing an ethereal bell-like sound.

celeste /sɪ'lɛst/ *noun* L19 French (*céleste* heavenly, from Latin *caelestis* from *caelum* heaven). **1** A stop on an organ or harmonium with a soft tremulous tone (French *voix céleste*). Also, a form of soft pedal on a piano. **2** A CELESTA.

cella /'kɛlə/ *noun* plural **cellae** /'kɛliː/ L17 Latin. *Architecture* The inner area of a Greek or Roman temple housing the hidden cult image; a similar part of other ancient temples.

cembalo /'tʃɛmbələʊ/ *noun* plural **cembalos** M19 Italian (abbreviation of *clavicembalo*). A harpsichord.

cenacle /'sɛnək(ə)l/ *noun* LME Old and Modern French (*cénacle* from Latin *cenaculum*, from *cena* dinner). **1** A place where a discussion group, literary clique, etc., meets; the group itself. **2** The room in which the Last Supper was held.

cenote /se'note/ *noun* M19 Yucatan Spanish (from Maya *tzonot*). A natural underground reservoir of water, such as occurs in the limestone of Yucatan, Mexico.

census /'sɛnsəs/ *noun* E17 Latin (from *censere* to assess). An official count or survey, especially of a population.

■ In Latin the word was applied to the registration of citizens and their property in ancient Rome, usually for taxation purposes. It was first used in English to denote a poll tax. The current English sense dates from the mid 18th century.

cento /'sɛntəʊ/ *noun* plural **centos** E17 Latin (literally, 'patchwork garment'). **1** A piece of patchwork; a patchwork garment. Now *obsolete*. **2** A hotchpotch, a medley; *specifically* a literary work made up of quotations from other authors.

centrifuge /'sɛntrɪfju:dʒ/ *noun & verb*
E18 French (from Modern Latin *centrifugus*
centrifugal). **A** *noun* A machine with a
rapidly rotating container that applied
centrifugal force to its contents, typically to separate fluids of different
densities or liquids from solids. **B** *transitive verb* Subject to centrifugal motion;
separate by means of a centrifuge.

cep /sɛp/ *noun* (also **cèpe** /sɛp/ (*plural
same*)) M19 French (*cèpe* from Gascon *cep*
tree-trunk, mushroom, from Latin *cippus*
stake). An edible European mushroom
with a smooth brown cap and pores
rather than gills.

cerebellum /sɛrɪ'bɛləm/ *noun* M16 Latin
(diminutive of CEREBRUM). *Anatomy* The
part of the brain at the back of the
skull, which coordinates and regulates
muscular activity.
> **1996** *Oldie* We are all so dull, without
> discernment... But flabby cerebellums, arise!
> Address yourselves to a new noise.

cerebrum /'sɛrɪbrəm/ *noun* E17 Latin (=
brain). *Anatomy* The principal part of
the brain, located in the front area of
the skull, responsible for voluntary
activity and mental processes.

cerise /sɛ'ri:z/, /sɛ'ri:s/ *noun & adjective*
M19 French (= cherry). **A** *noun* A light
clear red colour. **B** *adjective* Of a light
clear red colour.

cervelat /'sə:vəla:/ *noun* E17 French
((now *cervelas*) from Italian *cervellata* Mila-
nese sausage). A kind of smoked pork
sausage.

cervix /'sə:vɪks/ *noun* plural **cervices**
/'sə:vɪsi:z/ M18 Latin. *Anatomy* **1** The
narrow neck-like passage forming
the lower end of the womb adjacent
to the vagina. **2** The neck. *Archaic.*

c'est la guerre /,seɪ la 'gɛ:/ *interjection*
E20 French (= that's war). Used to express
resigned acceptance; 'that's the kind
of thing that happens!'.

c'est la vie /,seɪ la 'vi:/ *interjection* E20
French (= that's life). Used to express
acceptance or resignation in the face
of a difficult or unpleasant situation.
> **1995** *Country Life* Thanks to my inattention,
> and a low-flying helicopter..., I was bucked off
> this morning. *C'est la vie.*

cestui /'sɛti/ *noun* M16 Anglo-Norman and
Old French (from Proto-Romance, from
Latin *ecce* lo! + *iste* that (one), with
element *-ui* as in *cui* dative of *quis* who).
Law The person (who), he (who).
> ■ Only in the following legal phrases:
> *cestui que trust*, *cestui que use* the person for
> whose benefit something is given in
> trust to another; *cestui que vie* a person
> for whose lifetime an estate or interest in
> property is held by another.

ceteris paribus /,keɪtərɪs 'parɪbəs/,
/,sɛtərɪs 'parɪbəs/, /,si:tərɪs 'parɪbəs/ *adverb phrase* E17 Modern Latin. With other
conditions remaining the same; other
things being equal.
> **1995** *Spectator* The new Rowntree Trust
> report merely gives the latest gloss on the
> problem. Thousands of years from now,
> Rowntree-type people will be producing,
> *ceteris paribus*, similar gloomy reports.

ceviche /sɛ'vi:tʃeɪ/ *noun* (also **seviche**)
M20 South American Spanish (*seviche, ce-
biche*). A South American dish of marinaded raw fish or seafood, usually
garnished and served as a starter.

cha-cha /'tʃɑ:tʃɑ:/ *noun & verb* (also **cha-
cha-cha** /tʃɑ:tʃɑ:'tʃɑ:/ M20 American Spanish. **A** *noun* A type of ballroom dance
with small steps and swaying hip
movements, performed to a Latin
American rhythm; a piece of music
for this dance. **B** *transitive verb* Perform
this dance.
> **A 1996** *Times* Ballroom dancing is divided into
> Latin (cha-cha, jive, rumba, samba, paso
> doblé) and Modern...

chacham variant of HAHAM.

chaconne /ʃə'kɒn/ *noun* L17 French
(from Spanish *chacona*). *Music* A moderately slow musical composition on a
ground bass, usually in triple time; a
dance to this music. Cf. PASSACAGLIA.
> **1996** *Country Life*..a theme by Bach is
> worked into a *chaconne* which is one of the
> wonders of 19th-century music.

chacun à son goût /ʃakœ̃ a sɔ̃ gu/
interjection L19 French. Each to their own
taste.
> ■ Also occasionally in the form usual in
> French: *à chacun son goût*.
> **1996** *Country Life* People must think I'm totally
> halfwitted. There are some who would give

their eye-teeth to fish this beautiful stretch of river. But *chacun à son goût.*

chador /'tʃɑːdə/ *noun* (also **chaddar, chuddar** /'tʃʌdə/, and other variants) E17 Urdu (*chādar, chaddar* from Persian *čādar* sheet, veil). A large piece of cloth that is wrapped around the head and upper body leaving only the face exposed, worn especially by Muslim women.

chaebol /keɪ'bɒl/ *noun* L20 Korean (= money clan). (In the Republic of Korea) a large family-owned business conglomerate.

chagrin /'ʃagrɪn/ *noun & verb* M17 French (literally, 'rough skin', of unknown origin). **A** *noun* Annoyance or distress at having failed or been disappointed. **B** also /ʃə'griːn/ *transitive verb* Affect with chagrin. Usually in *passive.*

■ This word was originally used in English in the sense 'melancholy'. The spelling *shagreen* of the noun is an obsolete variant that is now used solely in senses that retain the literal French meaning, being applied to a kind of untanned leather with a rough granular surface (often dyed green) or to the rough scaly skin of sharks or rays especially as used for polishing.

chaîné /ʃene/ *noun* M20 French (= linked). *Ballet* A quick step or turn from one foot to the other, or a series of these, performed in a line.

chaise /ʃeɪz/ *noun* plural pronounced same M17 French (variant of *chaire* chair). **1** A horse-drawn carriage for one or two people, typically one with an open top and two wheels. Chiefly *historical.* **2** A CHAISE LONGUE.

chaise longue /ʃeɪz 'lɒŋɡ/, *foreign* /ʃɛz lɔ̃ɡ/ *noun phrase* plural **chaise longues** /ʃeɪz 'lɒŋɡz/, **chaises longues** /ʃeɪz 'lɒŋɡ(z)/, *foreign* /ʃɛz lɔ̃ɡ/ E19 French (= long chair). A kind of sofa with a backrest at only one end.

chakra /'tʃʌkrə/ *noun* L18 Sanskrit (*cakra* wheel, circle; cf. Greek *kuklos* cycle). (In Indian thought) each of seven centres of spiritual power in the human body.

chal /tʃal/ *noun* M19 Romany (= person, fellow). A male Gypsy.

chalet /'ʃaleɪ/ *noun* L18 Swiss French (diminutive of Old French *chasel* farmstead, from Proto-Romance derivative of Latin *casa* hut, cottage). **1** A wooden house with overhanging eaves, typically found in the Swiss Alps. **2** A small cabin or house used by holiday-makers, forming a unit within a holiday complex.

challah /'hɑːlə/, *foreign* /'xɑːlɑː/ *noun* L20 Hebrew. A plaited loaf of white leavened bread, traditionally baked to celebrate the Jewish Sabbath.

chalumeau /ʃalymo/ *noun* plural **chalumeaux** /ʃalymo/ E18 French (from late Latin *calamellus* diminutive of *calamus* reed). A reed instrument of the early 18th century, the forerunner of the clarinet. Also (in full *chalumeau register*), the lowest register of the clarinet.

cham /kam/ *noun* LME French (*cham, chan* from Turkic *kān* KHAN). A khan. Now only *transferred* and *figurative*, an autocrat, a dominant critic, etc.

■ The transferred use alludes to an expression of the Scottish author Tobias Smollett, who, in a letter to John Wilkes in 1759, referred to Samuel Johnson as the 'great Cham of literature'.

chambré /ʃɒmbreɪ/, *foreign* /ʃɑ̃bre/ *adjective* M20 French (past participle of *chambrer* to bring to room temperature, from Old French *chambre* from Latin *camera* room). (Of red wine) at room temperature. Usually *predicative.*
1952 B. Pym *Excellent Women* My only fear is that it will scarcely be chambré by the time I shall want to drink it.

chametz /hɑːˈmɛts/, /ˈxɑːmɛts/ *noun* (also **chometz**) M19 Hebrew (*hāmēṣ*). Leaven or food mixed with leaven, prohibited during the Passover.

chamois /'ʃamwɑː/; *in sense 2, usually* /ʃami/ *noun* (sense 2 also **shammy** /'ʃami/) plural same /'ʃamwɑːz/, /'ʃamɪz/ M16 Old and Modern French (probably ultimately from Swiss Proto-Romance; cf. Gallo-Latin *camox*). **1** An agile goat-like antelope, *Rupicapra rupicapra*, found in the mountains of Europe from Spain to the Caucasus. **2** Soft pliable leather from the chamois or (now more usually) from sheep, goats, or deer; a piece of this, used for washing windows or cars. More fully *chamois leather*.

champignon /tʃam'pɪnjən/, /'ʃampɪnjɔ̃/; *foreign* /ʃãpiɲɔ̃/ (*plural same*) *noun* L16 French ((earlier *champaignon*), diminutive of Old French *champagne* open country). A small edible mushroom with a light brown cap, growing in short grass in both Eurasia and North America and often forming fairy rings.

champlevé /'ʃampləveɪ/, *foreign* /ʃãləve/ *noun* M19 French (from *champ* field + *levé* raised). Enamel work in which the colours in the pattern are set into hollows made in the surface of the metal base. Cf. CLOISONNÉ.

1996 *Country Life* An example... is a Limoges engraved copper, gilt and *champlevé* enamel statue of the Virgin and Child.

chancre /'tʃaŋkə/ *noun* L16 French (from Latin *cancer* crab, creeping ulcer). *Medicine* A painless ulcer, particularly one that develops on the genitals in venereal disease.

chandelier /ʃandə'lɪə/ *noun* M17 French (from *chandelle* candle, from Latin *candela*). A large, decorative hanging light with branches for several light bulbs or candles.

changement /ʃãʒmã/ *noun* plural pronounced same M19 French (from *changer* to change). *Ballet* A leap during which the dancer changes the position of the feet. In full *changement de pieds* /ʃãʒ mãdə pje/ (literally, 'changing of feet').

chanson /ʃãsɔ̃/ *noun* plural pronounced same L15 Old and Modern French (from Latin *cantio* song). A French song.

chanson de geste /ʃãsɔ̃ də ʒɛst/ *noun* *phrase* plural **chansons de geste** (pronounced same) M19 French (= song of heroic deeds). A medieval French historical verse romance, dealing with chivalric and heroic subjects.

■ The earliest was the *Chanson de Roland*, written about 1100.

chanterelle /tʃa:ntə'rɛl/ *noun* (also **chantarelle**) L18 French (from Modern Latin *cantharellus* diminutive of *cantharus* from Greek *kantharos* drinking vessel). An edible woodland mushroom with a

yellow funnel-shaped cap, *Cantharellus cibarius*.

chanteuse /ʃɑ̃tøz/ *noun* plural pronounced same M19 French. A female singer of popular songs, originally in France.

1996 *Times Magazine* Stylistically, the work is a throwback to the golden age of confessional chanteuse à la Joni Mitchell...

chaparejos /ʃapə'reɪhəʊs/, /'tʃapə'reɪhəʊs/ *noun* plural (also **chaparreras** /ʃapə-'rɛːrəs/, /tʃapə'rɛːrəs/) M19 Mexican Spanish (*chaparreras*, from *chaparra, chaparro* dwarf evergreen oak). Tough leather over-trousers worn by cowboys to protect the legs, especially against thorny vegetation.

■ *Chaparejos* is a later form than *chaparreras* and is probably influenced by Spanish *aparejo* 'equipment'. In the United States the abbreviation *chaps* has been commonly used from the late 19th century onwards.

chaparral /ʃapə'ral/, /tʃapə'ral/ *noun* M19 Spanish (from *chaparra* dwarf evergreen oak). (In United States) vegetation consisting chiefly of tangled shrubs and thorny bushes.

chaparreras variant of CHAPAREJOS.

chapatti /tʃə'pɑːti/, /tʃə'pati/ *noun* (also **chapati, chupatti**, and other variants) E19 Hindi (*capātī*, from *capānā* to flatten, roll out, ultimately from Dravidian). (In Indian cookery) a thin pancake of unleavened wholemeal bread cooked on a griddle.

chapeau-bras /ʃapobra/ *noun* plural **chapeaux-bras** (pronounced same) M18 French (from *chapeau* (Old French *c(h)apel*, from Latin *cappellum* diminutive of *cappa* cap) hat + *bras* arm). *History* A man's three-cornered flat silk hat able to be carried under the arm.

chaperone /'ʃapərəʊn/ *noun & verb* (also **chaperon**) LME Old and Modern French (from *chape* cape, hood, ultimately from Latin *caput* head). **A** *noun* **1** A person who accompanies and looks after another person or group of people. **2** An older woman responsible for decorous behaviour of a young unmarried girl at social occasions. *Dated.* **B** *transitive verb* Accompany and look after or supervise; act as a chaperone to.

■ Originally denoted a hood or cap, regarded as giving protection.

chappal /ˈtʃap(ə)l/ *noun* (also **chappli** /ˈtʃapli/) L19 Hindi (*cappal, capli*). (In the Indian subcontinent) a slipper or sandal.

chaprasi /tʃəˈprasi/ *noun* plural **chaprasi(e)s** E19 Hindi (from *caprās* official badge, from Persian *čaprāst*). (In the Indian subcontinent) a junior office worker who carries messages.

charabanc /ˈʃarəbaŋ/ *noun* (also **char-à-banc**) E19 French (*char-à-bancs* literally, 'carriage with seats'). An early form of bus, used typically for pleasure trips. Now *archaic* or *humorous*.

charade /ʃəˈrɑːd/ *noun* L18 French (from Modern Provençal *charrado* conversation, from *churra* chatter, perhaps of imitative origin). **1** An absurd pretence intended to create a pleasant or respectable appearance. **2** (in *plural* usually treated as *singular*) A game in which players guess a word or phrase from a written or acted clue given for each syllable and for the whole item.

charcuterie /ʃarkytri/ (*plural same*), /ʃaːˈkuːt(ə)riː/ *noun* M19 French (from *char* (modern *chair*) *cuite* cooked flesh). Cold cooked meats; a shop selling these.

1996 *Times* He is capable of appreciating the elaborate display of a *charcuterie*...

chargé /ˈʃaːʒeɪ; *foreign* /ʃarʒe/ (*plural same*) *noun* M19 French. Abbreviation of CHARGE D'AFFAIRES.

chargé d'affaires /ˌʃaːʒeɪ daˈfɛː/, *foreign* /ʃarʒe dafɛr/ *noun phrase* plural **chargés d'affaires** (pronounced same) (also **chargé des affaires**) M18 French (= (a person) in charge of affairs). **1** An ambassador's deputy; a state's diplomatic representative in a minor country. **2** A person temporarily in charge.

charisma /kəˈrɪzmə/ *noun* plural (sense 2) **charismata** /kəˈrɪzmətə/ M17 ecclesiastical Latin (from Greek *kharisma, -mat-*, from *kharis* favour, grace). **1** Compelling attractiveness or charm that can inspire devotion in others. **2** *Christian*

Theology A divinely conferred power or talent.

1 1996 *Times* In the entertainment world, the Sagittarian's charisma is matched by a determination to be different, to stamp originality on the most mundane or unlikely material.

charivari /ʃaːrɪˈvaːriː/ *noun* M17 French (of unknown origin). **1** A cacophonous mock serenade, typically performed by a group of people in derision of an unpopular person or in celebration of a marriage. **2** A discordant medley of sounds, a hubbub.

■ The variant *shivaree* is mainly found in the United States.

charlotte /ˈʃaːlət/ *noun* L18 French (from the female given name). A pudding made of stewed fruit with a casing or covering of bread, biscuits, sponge cake, or breadcrumbs.

■ Usually with defining word, as in *apple charlotte, rhubarb charlotte,* etc. Cf. CHARLOTTE RUSSE.

charlotte russe /ˈʃaːlət ˌruːs/ *noun phrase* plural **charlottes russes, charlotte russes** M19 French (= Russian CHARLOTTE). A pudding with flavoured custard or cream inside a moulded sponge cake or sponge finger casing.

charmeuse /ʃaːˈməːz/, *foreign* /ʃarmøz/ *noun* E20 French (feminine of *charmeur* charmer, from Old French *charme* charm, from Latin *carmen* song, incantation). A soft smooth silky dress fabric.

charpoy /ˈtʃaːpɔɪ/ *noun* M17 Urdu (*chārpāī* from Persian). (In the Indian subcontinent) a light bedstead.

charro /ˈtʃaːrəʊ/ *noun* plural **charros** E20 Mexican Spanish (from Spanish = rustic). A traditionally dressed Mexican cowboy.

chartreuse /ʃaːˈtrəːz/, *foreign* /ʃartrøz/ (*plural same*) *noun* E19 French (feminine of *Chartreux*). **1** A green or yellow liqueur of brandy and aromatic herbs, originally made by the monks of La Grande Chartreuse, near Grenoble, France. **2** A pale yellow or green colour. **3** A dish made in a mould using pieces of meat, game, vegetables, or (now most often) fruit enclosed in jelly.

chasse /ʃas/, /ˈʃɑːs/ *noun* plural **chasses** /ʃas/, /ˈʃɑːsɪz/ M18 French (abbreviation of *chasse-café*, literally, 'chase-coffee'). A liqueur drunk after coffee; a chaser.

■ The full form *chasse-café* (E19) is now rare.

chassé /ˈʃase/ (*plural same*), /ˈʃaseɪ/ *noun* E19 French (= chased). A sliding step in dancing in which one foot displaces the other.

■ A mainly North American alteration is *sashay* (noun and verb), '(to perform) a *chassé* in square dancing'; as a verb *sashay* also has a general colloquial sense of 'to walk with an ostentatiously gliding or swinging step').

1995 *Times* A group of couples appear, confident in their skaters' *chassé* steps, with only one of the men later falling over.

chasseur /ʃaˈsəː/; *foreign* /ʃasœr/ (*plural same*) *noun* M18 French (= huntsman, from *chasser* to hunt). **1** *History* A soldier equipped and trained for rapid movement, especially in the French army. **2** A dish of poultry or game served with a rich dark sauce with wine and mushrooms: *chicken chasseur*.

chassid variant of HASID.

chassis /ˈʃasi/, /ˈʃasiː/ *noun* plural same /ˈʃasɪz/, /ˈʃasiːz/ M17 French (*châssis* frame, from Proto-Romance, from Latin *capsa* case, box). **1** The base frame of a car, carriage, or other wheeled vehicle. **2** The outer structural framework of a piece of audio, radio, or computer equipment. **3** The human or animal frame, the body. *Slang*.

château /ˈʃatəʊ/, *foreign* /ʃato/ *noun* plural **châteaux** /ˈʃatəʊz/, *foreign* /ʃato/ M18 French. A large French country house or castle; *especially* one giving its name to wine made in its neighbourhood.

■ Sometimes also used humorously with the owner's name of an ostentatious or pretentious house anywhere, e.g. Château Jones.

1996 *Times Magazine* Buying en primeur... is often the only chance that claret lovers will get to buy their favourite châteaux.

Chateaubriand /ʃatobrijɑ̃/ *noun* plural pronounced same L19 French. A thick fillet of beef steak, grilled and garnished with herbs etc.

■ Called after François René, Vicomte de *Chateaubriand* (1768–1848), French writer and statesman, whose chef is said to have created the dish. Also *Chateaubriand steak* or *steak à la Chateaubriand*.

chatelaine /ˈʃatəleɪn/ *noun* M19 French (*châtelaine* feminine of *châtelain*). **1** A woman in charge of a large house or castle. **2** *History* A set of short chains attached to a woman's belt for carrying keys, a watch, a pencil, etc.

1 1995 *Times* If the chatelaine had spent all day lying down zonked out with Valium, these were suppers that required a minimum of preparation.

chatoyant /ʃəˈtɔɪənt/, *foreign* /ʃatwajɑ̃/ *adjective* L18 French (present participle of *chatoyer* to shimmer). (Of a gem, especially when cut *en cabochon*) showing a band of bright lustre caused by reflection from inclusions in the stone.

■ Now *rare*.

chauffeur /ˈʃəʊfə/ *noun & verb* L19 French (= stoker (by association with steam engines), from *chauffer* to heat). **A** *noun* A person employed to drive a private or hired car. **B** *transitive verb* Drive (a car or a passenger in a car) as a chauffeur.

■ First used in English in the general sense 'motorist'.

chaukidar variant of CHOKIDAR.

chayote /tʃeɪˈəʊti/, *noun* L19 Spanish (from Nahuatl *chayotli*). A tropical American vine, *Sechium edule*, cultivated elsewhere for its fruit; the succulent green pear-shaped fruit of this vine. Also called *chocho*.

cheder /ˈhɛdə/, /ˈxɛdə/ *noun* (also **heder**) plural **chedarim** /hɛˈdɑːrɪm/, **cheders** L19 Hebrew (*ḥēder* room). A school for Jewish children in which Hebrew and religious knowledge are taught.

cheechako /tʃiːˈtʃɑːkəʊ/ *noun* L19 Chinook Jargon (= newcomer). A recently arrived immigrant to the mining districts of Alaska or north-west Canada; a greenhorn.

■ North American colloquial.

chee-chee variant of CHHI-CHHI.

chef /ʃɛf/ *noun* E19 French (= head). A professional cook, typically the chief cook in a restaurant or hotel.

■ Also in combinations such as *sous-chef* 'under-chef', COMMIS *chef*, etc.

chef d'école /ʃɛf dekɔl/ *noun phrase* plural **chefs d'école** (pronounced same) M19 French (= head of school). The initiator or leader of a school or style of music, painting, or literature.

1995 *Spectator* He found himself an unwilling and unsuitable *chef d'école*—unsuitable because his search for a modern language in painting became increasingly idiosyncratic.

chef d'équipe /ʃɛf dekip/ *noun phrase* plural **chefs d'équipe** (pronounced same) L20 French (= head of team; cf. ÉQUIPE). The manager of a sports team responsible for practical arrangements especially when travelling.

1996 *Times* Long after she [sc. Pat Smythe] had been forced to give up showjumping she remained involved in the sport as an international selector, and sometimes, chef d'equipe of British teams abroad.

chef-d'œuvre /ʃɛdœvr/ *noun* plural **chefs-d'œuvre** (pronounced same) E17 French (= chief (piece) of work). The greatest work of an artist etc.; a masterpiece.

chef d'orchestre /ʃɛf dɔrkɛstr/ *noun phrase* plural **chefs d'orchestre** (pronounced same) M19 French (= head of orchestra). The leader or conductor of an orchestra.

chela /ˈtʃeɪlə/ *noun* M19 Hindi (*celā*). A follower and pupil of a guru.

chemin de fer /ʃ(ə)mɛ̃ də fɛr/, /ʃə'mɑ̃ də fɛː/ *noun* L19 French (= railway, literally, 'road of iron'). A card game which is a variety of baccarat.

chemise /ʃə'miːz/ *noun* ME Old and Modern French (from late Latin *camisia* shirt, nightgown). **1** A woman's loose-fitting undergarment or dress hanging straight from the shoulders. **2** A priest's alb or surplice. **3** *History* A smock.

chemisette /ˌʃɛmɪ'zɛt/ *noun* E19 French (diminutive of CHEMISE). A woman's undergarment similar to a camisole.

chenille /ʃə'niːl/ *noun* M18 French (literally, 'hairy caterpillar', from Latin *canicula* diminutive of *canis* dog). A tufty velvety cord or yarn, used for trimming furniture and made into carpets or clothing.

cheongsam /tʃɪɒŋ'sam/, /tʃɒŋ'sam/ *noun* M20 Chinese (Cantonese (= Mandarin *chángshān*)). A straight, close-fitting silk dress with a high neck and slit skirt, worn by Chinese and Indonesian women.

cherchez la femme /ʃɛrʃe la fam/ *interjection* L19 French (= look for the woman). The principle that there is certain to be a woman at the bottom of a problem or mystery.

■ A catchphrase of Alexandre Dumas *père* in *Les Mohicans de Paris* (1864).

1996 *Times* [Lady Hollis] was credited with influencing Alan Howarth's decision to cross the floor—a canard put out by credulous Tories playing *cherchez la femme*.

cherimoya /tʃɛrɪ'mɔɪə/ *noun* (also **chirimoya** /tʃɪrɪ'mɔɪə/) M18 Spanish (from Quechua, from *chiri* cold, refreshing + *muya* circle). **1** A kind of custard apple with scaly green skin and a flavour resembling that of pineapple. **2** The small tree, *Annona cherimola*, which bears this fruit, native to the Andes of Peru and Ecuador.

chernozem /ˈtʃəːnəzɛm/ *noun* (also **chernosem**) M19 Russian (from *chërnyĭ* black + Slavonic base *zem-* (cf. Russian *zemlya*) earth). A dark, humus-rich, fertile soil characteristic of temperate or cool grassland.

■ Originally used of the soil of the Russian steppes, now generally for soils of this type.

Chetnik /ˈtʃɛtnɪk/ *noun* E20 Serbo-Croat (*četnik*, from *četa* band, troop). A member of a Slavic nationalist guerrilla force in the Balkans, especially during the Second World War.

cheval /ʃəval/, /ʃə'val/ *noun* plural **chevaux** /ʃəvo/, /ʃə'vəʊ/ L15 French (= horse, frame). Horse; frame.

■ Never independently naturalized in English, *cheval* occurs in the combination *cheval glass* (a tall glass set on a pivot in an upright frame) and in phrases such as À CHEVAL and CHEVAL DE BATAILLE.

cheval de bataille /ʃəval də bataj/ *noun phrase* plural **chevaux de bataille** /ʃəvo də bataj/ E19 French (literally, 'battle horse'). An obsession, a pet subject; something made boring by repetition or overuse.

　■ Native English equivalents are 'hobby horse' or 'warhorse', depending on context; see quotation for 'warhorse' sense.
　1942 E. Blom *Music in England* The chief *chevaux de bataille* for new sopranos [are] the heroines in 'La Sonnambula' and 'Lucia di Lammermoor'.

chevalier /ʃɛvə'lɪə/, *foreign* /ʃəvalje/ (*plural same*) *noun* LME Anglo-Norman (*chevaler*, Old and Modern French *chevalier*, from medieval Latin *caballarius*, from Latin *caballus* horse). **1** *History* A horseman, *especially* a mounted knight. **2** A member of certain orders of knighthood, or of the French Legion of Honour, etc.

　■ Sometimes in the phrase *chevalier sans peur et sans reproche* literally, 'a knight without fear or stain', a perfect gentleman; see also SANS PEUR.

chevaux de frise /ʃəvo də friz/ *noun phrase* L17 French (literally, 'horses of Friesland'). Iron spikes closely set in timber, originally to repel cavalry; a similar device, often with the spikes rotating around a rod, now set along the tops of walls, fences, etc. to deter intruders.

　■ The name is an ironical reference to the fact that the Frieslanders possessed no cavalry and relied upon such devices to beat off the cavalry of others. Although the phrase is plural in form it is often treated as singular.

chevet /ʃə've1/, *foreign* /ʃəvɛ/ (*plural same*) *noun* E19 French (= pillow). (In large churches) an apse with an ambulatory giving access behind the high altar to a series of chapels set in bays.

chèvre /ʃɛvr/ *noun* M20 French (= goat, she-goat). French cheese made with goat's milk.

chevron /'ʃɛvrən/ *noun* LME Old and Modern French (from Proto-Romance, from Latin *caper* goat; cf. Latin *capreoli*

pair of rafters). **1** A V-shaped line or stripe, especially one on the sleeve of a uniform indicating rank or length of service. **2** *Heraldry* A charge consisting of a bent bar of an inverted V shape.

chez /ʃe/, *before a vowel* /ʃez/ *preposition* M18 French (from Old French *chiese* from Latin *casa* cottage). At the house or home of.

　1996 *Spectator* The predominant political leaning *chez* Hart suggested that a special musical selection was called for—perhaps a K-Tel collection of Top Tunes for Troubled Tories.

chhi-chhi /'tʃiː'tʃiː/ *interjection* (also **chee-chee**) L18 Indian (perhaps from Hindi *chī-chī* shame on you!). Used to express disgust. *Indian*.

chiaroscuro /kɪˌɑːrə'skʊərəʊ/ *noun* plural **chiaroscuros** M17 Italian (from *chiaro* clear, bright + *oscuro* dark, obscure). **1** A style of painting in which only light and shade are represented; black and white. **2** The treatment or disposition of the light and shade, or brighter and darker masses, in a picture; an effect or contrast of light and shade in a picture or in nature. **3** *figurative* The use of contrast in literature etc.

chiasmus /kʌɪ'azməs/, /kɪ'azməs/ *noun* plural **chiasmi** /kʌɪ'azmʌɪ/ M17 Modern Latin (from Greek *khiasmos* from *khiazein* mark with a chi, from *khi* chi). *Rhetoric* The inversion in a second phrase or clause of the order of words in the first.

　■ First used in English in the sense 'crosswise arrangement'.

chibouk /tʃɪ'buːk/ *noun* (also **chibouque**) E19 French ((*chibouque* from) Turkish *çubuk*, (earlier) *çıbık* tube, pipe). A long Turkish tobacco pipe.

chic /ʃiːk/ *noun & adjective* M19 French (probably from German *Schick* skill). **A** *noun* Stylishness and elegance, typically of a specified kind. **B** *adjective* Stylishly and elegantly fashionable.

chicane /ʃɪ'keɪn/ *noun & verb* L17 French (from *chicaner* to pursue at law, quibble, of unknown origin). **A** *noun* **1** A sharp double bend created to form an obstacle on a motor-racing track. **2** *Cards* A hand without cards of one

particular suit as dealt; a void. *Dated.*
3 The use of deception or subterfuge;
chicanery. *Archaic.* **B** *verb* **1** *intransitive
verb* Employ chicanery; quibble, cavil.
Archaic. **2** *transitive verb* Deceive by
chicanery, cheat.

chicano /tʃɪˈkɑːnəʊ/, /ʃɪˈkɑːnəʊ/, /tʃɪ
ˈkeɪnəʊ/, /ʃɪˈkeɪnəʊ/ *noun & adjective*
(also **Chicano**) M20 Spanish (alteration
of *mejicano* Mexican, from *Méjico* Mexico).
A *noun* plural **chicanos** (feminine
chicana /tʃɪˈkɑːnə/) A North American
of Mexican origin or descent. **B** *adjective* Relating to chicanos; Mexican
American.

chicha /ˈtʃɪtʃə/ *noun* E17 American Spanish
(from Kuna). (In South and Central
America) a kind of beer made typically
from maize.

chicharron /tʃiːtʃəˈrəʊn/, *foreign* /tʃɪtʃa
ˈrron/ *noun* plural **chicharrones** /tʃiːtʃə
ˈrəʊnɪz/, *foreign* /tʃɪtʃaˈrrones/ M19 American
Spanish (*chicharrón*). (In Mexican cooking)
a piece of fried pork crackling.

chichi /ˈʃiːʃiː/ *adjective & noun* E20 French
(of imitative origin). **A** *adjective* Attempting stylish elegance but achieving
only an over-elaborate preten-
tiousness; showy, frilly, fussy. **B** *noun*
Pretentious and over-elaborate refine-
ment.

chicle /ˈtʃɪk(ə)l/, /ˈtʃɪkli/ *noun* L19 American Spanish (from Nahuatl *tzictli*). The
milky latex of the sapodilla, *Manilkara
zapota*, and several related trees,
which forms the basis of chewing
gum.

chiffon /ˈʃɪfɒn/ *noun & adjective* M18
French (from *chiffe* rag). **A** *noun* A light,
transparent fabric of silk, nylon, etc.
B *adjective* **1** Made of chiffon; light in
weight. **2** (Of a cake or dessert) made
with beaten eggs to give a light
consistency.

■ Originally used in the plural, denoting
trimmings on a woman's dress.

chiffonade /ʃɪfəˈnɑːd/, *foreign* /ʃifɔnad/
(*plural same*) *noun* (also **chiffonnade**)
L19 French (from *chiffonner* to crumple). A
selection of shredded or finely cut
vegetables, used especially as a garnish for soup.

chiffonier /ʃɪfəˈnɪə/ *noun* M18 French
(*chiffonnier*, *chiffonière*, collecter of scraps,
ragpicker, also denoting a chest of
drawers for odds and ends). **1** A low
cupboard either used as a sideboard or
with a raised bookshelf on top. **2** A
tall chest of drawers. *North American.*

chignon /ˈʃiːnjɒ̃/ *noun* L18 French (originally = nape of the neck, from Proto-Romance variant of Latin *catena* chain). A
knot or coil of hair arranged on the
back of a woman's head.

chikan /ˈtʃɪk(ə)n/ *noun* L19 Urdu (*chikan*
from Persian *čikin*). (In the Indian subcontinent) a type of hand embroidery
using cutwork and shadow work.

chile relleno /ˌtʃɪli rɛˈljeɪnəʊ/ *noun
phrase* E20 Spanish (= stuffed chilli). (In
Mexican cuisine) a stuffed chilli pepper, typically battered and deep-fried.

■ Sometimes abbreviated to *relleno* plural *rellenos*.

chilli /ˈtʃɪli/ *noun* (also **chile**, **chili**)
plural **chil(l)ies**, **chiles** E17 Spanish (*chile*
from Nahuatl *chilli*). A small hot-tasting
pod of a variety of capsicum, *Capsicum
annuum* var. *longum*, used in sauces,
relishes, and spice powders. Also *chilli
pepper*. **b** Chilli powder. **c** CHILLI CON
CARNE.

chilli con carne /ˌtʃɪli kɒn ˈkɑːni/ *noun
phrase* (also **chile con carne**, **chili con
carne**) M19 Spanish (= chilli with meat).
A stew of minced beef and beans
flavoured with chilli powder.

chimera /kʌɪˈmɪərə/, /kɪˈmɪərə/ *noun*
(also **chimaera**) LME Latin (*chimaera*
from Greek *khimaira* she-goat, monster,
from *khimaros* he-goat). **1** *Greek Mythology* A fire-breathing monster, with a
lion's head, a goat's body, and a
serpent's tail. **2** Any mythical animal
formed from parts of various animals.
3 A thing which is hoped for but is
illusory or impossible to achieve.
4 (Usually **chimaera**.) Any cartilagi-
nous marine fish of the family Chi-
maeridae. **5** *Biology* An organism
whose cells are not all derived from
the same zygote.

chinchilla /tʃɪnˈtʃɪlə/ *noun* E17 Spanish
(probably from Aymara or Quechua).

1 A small South American rodent of the genus *Chinchilla*, with very soft grey fur. **2** A cat of a silver-grey breed. **3** A rabbit of a variety bred for its grey fur. **4** The fur of the South American chinchilla or of the chinchilla rabbit.

chino /'tʃiːnəʊ/ *noun* plural **chinos** M20 American Spanish (= toasted). A cotton twill cloth, usually khaki-coloured; in *plural*, casual trousers made of this.

■ Originally United States.

chinoiserie /ʃɪn'wɑːzəri/, *foreign* /ʃin wazri/ (*plural same*) *noun* L19 French (from *chinois* Chinese + *-erie*). A decorative style in Western art, furniture, and architecture, especially in the 18th century, characterized by the use of Chinese motifs and techniques; objects or decorations in this style.

chipolata /tʃɪpə'lɑːtə/ *noun* L19 French (from Italian *cipollata* dish of onions, from *cipolla* onion). In full *chipolata sausage*. A small thin sausage.

chipotle /tʃɪr'pɒtleɪ/ *noun* L20 Mexican Spanish. A smoked hot chilli pepper used in Mexican cooking.

chi-rho /kʌɪ'rəʊ/ *noun* M19 Greek (twenty-second letter of the alphabet *chi* + seventeenth letter *rho*). A monogram of chi (X) and rho (P), representing the first two letters of Greek *Khristos* Christ.

■ The *chi-rho* was adopted in AD 312 by the Byzantine emperor Constantine the Great as a device for his military banners, following on a vision in which he was told 'By this sign you shall conquer'. During the following centuries the *chi-rho* became ubiquitous in Christian art.

chirimoya variant of CHERIMOYA.

chitarrone /kɪtə'rəʊni/ *noun* plural **chitarroni** /kɪtə'rəʊni/ M18 Italian (= large guitar, from *chitarra* guitar). A double-necked lute of great length, similar to a theorbo.

chiton /'kʌɪtɒn/, /'kʌɪt(ə)n/ *noun* E19 Greek (*khitōn* tunic; in sense 1 through Modern Latin *Chiton* genus name). **1** A marine mollusc of the class Polyplacophora, characterized by a broad oval foot and a shell composed of a series of eight overlapping plates. **2** A long woollen tunic worn in ancient Greece.

chocolatier /tʃɒkə'latɪə/, *foreign* /ʃɔk ɔlatje/ (*plural same*) *noun* L19 French (from *chocolat* (or Spanish *chocolate* from Nahuatl *chocolatl* item of food made from caocao seeds)). A maker or seller of chocolate.

chokidar /'tʃəʊkɪdɑː/ *noun* (also **chaukidar** /'tʃəʊkɪdɑː/) E17 Urdu (*chaukīdār*, from Hindi *cauki* toll, police station + Urdu and Persian *-dār* keeper). (In the Indian subcontinent) a watchman or gatekeeper.

chola see CHOLO.

cholent /'tʃʊl(ə)nt/, /'ʃʊl(ə)nt/ *noun* M20 Yiddish (*tscholnt*). A Jewish Sabbath dish of slowly baked meat and vegetables, prepared on a Friday and cooked overnight.

choli /'tʃəʊli/ *noun* E20 Hindi (*coli*). An Indian woman's short-sleeved bodice of a type worn under a SARI.

cholo /'tʃəʊləʊ/ *noun* (also **Cholo**; feminine **chola** /'tʃəʊlə/) plural **cholos** M19 American Spanish (from *Cholollán*, now *Cholula*, a district of Mexico). A Latin American man with American Indian blood; a mestizo; *United States* (frequently *derogatory*) a lower-class Mexican, especially in an urban area; *United States* a member of a Mexican street gang.

chometz variant of CHAMETZ.

chop suey /tʃɒp'suːɪ/ *noun* L19 Chinese ((Cantonese) *tsaâp sui* mixed bits). A Chinese-style dish of meat stewed and fried with bean sprouts, bamboo shoots, and onions, and served with rice.

chorea /kɒ'rɪə/ *noun* L17 Latin (from Greek *khoreia* dancing in unison). *Medicine* A neurological disorder characterized by jerky involuntary movements.

chorizo /tʃə'riːzəʊ/ *noun* plural **chorizos** M19 Spanish. A spicy Spanish pork sausage.

chota /'tʃəʊtə/ *adjective* E19 Anglo-Indian (Hindi *choṭā*). Small, little; younger, junior; lower in rank or importance.

■ Occurs often in such phrases as *chota hazri* (a light early breakfast) and *chota peg* (a small drink of whisky).

chou see CHOUX.

choucroute /ʃukrut/ *noun* M19 French (from German dialect *Surkrut* SAUER-KRAUT, influenced by French *chou* cabbage). Pickled cabbage; sauerkraut.

choux /ʃuː/, *foreign* /ʃu/ *noun* (also **chou** (pronounced same)) plural **choux** E18 French (= cabbage, from Latin *caulis*). A round cream-filled pastry.

■ *Choux pastry* is very light pastry made with egg, typically used for éclairs and profiteroles.

chow mein /tʃaʊ 'meɪn/ *noun phrase* L19 Chinese (*chǎo miàn* fried noodles). A Chinese-style dish of fried noodles usually in a sauce with shredded meat and vegetables.

chroma /'krəʊmə/ *noun* L19 Greek (*khrōma* colour). Purity or intensity as a colour quality, especially in colour television etc.

chuddar variant of CHADOR.

chupatti variant of CHAPATTI.

chuppah /'xʊpə/ *noun* L19 Hebrew (*ḥuppāh* cover, canopy). A canopy beneath which Jewish marriage ceremonies are performed.

churinga /tʃə'rɪŋɡə/ *noun* (also **tjurunga** /tʃə'rʊŋɡə/) plural **churingas**, same L19 Arrernte (*tywerrenge*). (Among Australian Aboriginals) a sacred object, *specifically* an amulet.

churrasco /tʃʊ'rasko/, /tʃʊ'raskəʊ/ *noun* L20 South American Spanish (probably from dialect *churrascar* to burn; cf. Spanish *soccarar* to scorch). A South American dish of steak barbecued over a wood or charcoal fire.

chutzpah /'xʊtspə/, /'hʊtspə/ *noun* L19 Yiddish (from Aramaic *ḥuṣpā*). Extreme self-confidence or audacity (usually used approvingly).

1995 *Times* Celtic oratory—brooding, bombastic, and with a touch of Hergé's Captain Haddock . . .—meets a metropolitan Londoner's smoothness, zest and chutzpah.

chypre /ʃipr/ *noun* L19 French (= Cyprus, where perhaps originally made). A heavy perfume made from sandalwood.

ciabatta /tʃə'bɑːtə/, *foreign* /tʃa'batta/ *noun* plural **ciabattas**, **ciabatte** /tʃa'ba:tte/ L20 Italian ((dialect) literally, 'slipper' (from the shape of the loaf)). A type of moist aerated Italian bread made with olive oil; a loaf of this.

ciao /tʃaʊ/ *interjection* E20 Italian (dialectal alteration of *schiavo* (I am your) slave, from medieval Latin *sclavus* slave). Used as a greeting at meeting or parting.

■ A colloquial expression widespread in continental Europe, now also used as a casual greeting between Anglophones.

ciborium /sɪ'bɔ:rɪəm/ *noun* plural **ciboria** /sɪ'bɔ:rɪə/ M16 Medieval Latin (from Greek *kibōrion* cup-shaped seed-vessel of the Egyptian water lily, a drinking-cup made from this; sense 1 probably influenced by Latin *cibus* food). 1 *Christian Church* A receptacle for holding the Eucharist, shaped like a shrine, or a cup with an arched cover. 2 *Architecture* A canopy over an altar in a church, standing on four pillars; a canopied shrine.

cicada /sɪ'kɑ:də/ *noun* LME Latin (*cicada, cicala*). A large bug with long transparent wings, the males of which make a loud, shrill droning noise after dark.

■ The Old Provençal name *cigala* (cf. French *cigale*) was the usual form in English during the 17th and 18th centuries.

cicatrice /'sɪkətrɪs/ *noun* (also (especially *Medicine and Botany*) **cicatrix** /'sɪkətrɪks/) plural **cicatrices** /'sɪkətrɪsiz/, *especially Medicine and Botany* /sɪkə'trʌɪsiːz/ LME Old and Modern French (or Latin *cicatrix, cicatric-*). 1 The scar of a healed wound, burn, etc.; a scar on the bark of a tree. 2 *Botany* A mark on a stem left after a leaf or other part has become detached.

cicerone /tʃɪtʃə'rəʊni/, /sɪsə'rəʊni/ *noun & verb* plural **ciceroni** /tʃɪtʃə'rəʊni/, /sɪsə'rəʊni/, **cicerones** E18 Italian (from Latin name *Cicero, -onis*). A *noun* A guide who gives information about places of interest to sightseers. B *transitive verb* Act as a cicerone to.

■ Marcus Tullius Cicero (106–43 BC) was renowned for his eloquence and learning, and it is surmised that English Grand Tourists dubbed the local Italian antiquaries who showed them round the sites *cicerones*, that is 'Ciceros'. The actual historical origin of the word is uncertain, as the earliest English use of *cicerone* (Addison was apparently the first, in 1726) antedates its appearance in Italian dictionaries.

1996 *Country Life* He made a good profit on the... 'Portland' vase bought from the Roman cicerone James Byres for £1,000...

cicisbeo /ʧɪʧɪzˈbeɪəʊ/ *noun* plural **cicisbei** /ʧɪʧɪzˈbeɪiː/, **cicisbeos** E18 Italian (of unknown origin). A married woman's male companion or lover.

ci-devant /sidvɑ̃/ *adjective* E18 French (= heretofore). From or in an earlier time; former: *her ci-devant pupil, now her lover.*

■ Used with the person's earlier name or status.

cigala see under CICADA.

cilantro /θiˈlantro/, /siˈlantro/ *noun* L20 Spanish. Coriander used as a seasoning or garnish. *North American.*

cilium /ˈsɪlɪəm/ *noun* plural **cilia** /ˈsɪlɪə/ E18 Latin. **1** An eyelash. **2** *Biology* A short microscopic hair-like vibrating structure which is found in large numbers on the surfaces of some cells, and in many organisms is used in locomotion.

cimbalom /ˈsɪmb(ə)l(ə)m/ *noun* L19 Hungarian (from Italian *cymbalo* dulcimer). A large Hungarian dulcimer.

cinéaste /ˈsɪneɪast/, *foreign* /sineast/ (*plural same*) *noun* (also **cineast(e)** /ˈsɪnɪast/) E20 French (from *ciné* cine + *-aste* as in *enthousiaste* enthusiast). A person who is fond of or knowledgeable about the cinema.

1995 *Spectator* It is outwardly the unfilmable script, far more imaginary than real, of a would-be English cinéaste, one Richard Arthur Thornby (RAT), currently lecturing in Texas on the cinema.

cinematheque /sɪnɪməˈtɛk/ *noun* (also **cinémathèque** /sinematɛk/ (*plural same*)) M20 French (*cinémathèque*, from *cinéma* cinema, after *bibliothèque* library).

A film library or archive. Also, a small cinema showing artistic films.

cinéma-vérité /sinemɑverite/, /ˌsɪnɪmˈə'vɛrɪteɪ/ *noun* M20 French (= cinema truth). A style of film-making characterized by realistic, typically documentary films which avoid artificiality and artistic effect and are generally made with simple equipment.

ciné-vérité /sineverite/, /sɪnɪ'vɛrɪteɪ/ *noun* M20 French. CINÉMA-VÉRITÉ.

cinq-à-sept /sɛ̃k a sɛt/ *noun* (also **cinq à sept**) L20 French (literally, 'five to seven'). A visit to a mistress or a brothel, traditionally made between five and seven p.m.

1996 *Spectator* The English like to stand around a pool table and guffaw rather loudly. Continental men prefer *le cinq à sept.*

cinquecento /ˌʧɪŋkwɪ'ʧɛntəʊ/ *noun* M18 Italian (= five hundred). The 16th century as a period of Italian art, architecture, or literature, with a reversion to classical forms.

■ Shortened from *milcinquecento* '1500', used with reference to the years 1500–99.

cipolin /ˈsɪpəlɪn/ *noun* (also **cipollino** /ˌʧɪpə'liːnəʊ/, plural **cipollinos**) L18 French ((*cipolin* from) Italian *cipollino*, from *cipolla* onion (Latin *cepa*); so called because its structure, having thin veins of other materials, resembles onion skin). An Italian marble with veins of talc, mica, quartz, etc., showing alternating white and green streaks.

circa /ˈsəːkə/ *preposition* M19 Latin. About, approximately in or at (with dates etc.).

■ Frequently in abbreviated form before a date: *c.* or *ca.*

ciré /ˈsiːreɪ/ *noun* E20 French (= waxed). A fabric with a smooth polished surface, obtained especially by heating and waxing.

cire perdue /sir pɛrdy/ *noun phrase* L19 French (= lost wax). A method of casting bronze by pouring molten metal over a wax-surfaced core within a mould, to form a model in the space created by the melting and running out of wax.

cirque /sə:k/ *noun* E17 French (from Latin *circus* circle, circus, corresponding to Greek *kirkos* ring, circle). **1** *Geology* A large bowl-shaped hollow of glacial origin at the head of a valley or on a mountainside. **2** A circle, a ring, a circlet. *Literary*.

cirrus /'sɪrəs/ *noun* (also **cirrhus**) plural **cirri** /'sɪrʌɪ/ E18 Latin (= curl, fringe). **1** *Meteorology* A cloud-type occurring at high altitude and having the appearance of wispy filamentous tufts. **2** *Zoology* A slender tendril or hair-like filament, e.g. the limb of a cirripede, a barbel of certain fishes. **3** *Botany* A tendril.

clachan /'klax(ə)n/ *noun* LME Gaelic and Irish (*clachán*). (In Scotland and Northern Ireland) a small village, a hamlet.

clair-de-lune /klɛrdəlyn/, /klɛ:də'lu:n/ *noun* L19 French (literally, 'moonlight'). A soft white or pale blue-grey colour; a Chinese porcelain glaze of this colour.

clairvoyance /klɛ:'vɔɪəns/ *noun* M19 French (from *clair* clear + *voir* to see). The supposed faculty of perceiving things or events in the future or beyond normal sensory contact.

clairvoyant /klɛ:'vɔɪənt/ *adjective & noun* (occasionally feminine **clairvoyante**) L17 French (from *clair* clear + *voyant* present participial adjective of *voir* to see). **A** *adjective* Having or exhibiting the faculty of clairvoyance. **B** *noun* A person who claims to have a supernatural ability to perceive events in the future or beyond normal sensory contact.

■ Originally used in the sense 'clear-sighted, perceptive'. The current sense dates from the mid 19th century.

claque /klak/, /klɑːk/; *foreign* /klak/ (*plural same*) *noun* M19 French (from *claquer* to clap). **1** A group of sycophantic followers. **2** A group of people hired to applaud (or heckle) a performer or public speaker.

■ The practice of paying members of an audience for their support originated at the Paris opera.

1995 *Times* [The organizers] of events decreed that before every open race there would be competitions for juveniles and juniors. This encourages the young to participate, feeds talent into the sport and provides an enthusiastic claque to cheer on the stars.

claqueur /kla'kə:/, *foreign* /klakœr/ (*plural same*) *noun* M19 French (from *claquer* to clap). A member of a claque.

clarschach /'klɑ:ʃax/ *noun* L15 Scottish Gaelic (*clàrsach*). The traditional Celtic harp strung with wire.

classico /'klasɪkəʊ/ *adjective* L20 Italian. (Of an Italian wine) produced in the region from which the type takes its name, and thus of a higher standard than a regional wine without the designation.

■ Used after the name of a wine, as in *Bardolino classico*.

clave /kleɪv/, /klɑ:v/ *noun* E20 American Spanish (from Spanish *clave* keystone, from Latin *clavis* key). Either of a pair of hardwood sticks used to make a hollow sound when struck together.

■ Usually in plural.

clementine /'klɛm(ə)ntʌɪn/, /'klɛm(ə)nti:n/ *noun* E20 French (*clémentine*). A tangerine of a deep orange-red North African variety which is grown around the Mediterranean and in South Africa.

clepsydra /'klɛpsɪdrə/ *noun* plural **clepsydras**, **clepsydrae** /'klɛpsɪdri:/ LME Latin (from Greek *klepsudra*, from *kleps-* combining form of *kleptein* to steal + *hudōr* water). An instrument used in antiquity to measure time by the flow of water; a water clock.

cliché /'kli:ʃeɪ/ *noun* M19 French (use as noun of past participle of *clicher* to stereotype, perhaps of imitative origin). **1** A phrase or opinion that is overused and betrays a lack of original thought. **2** A very predictable or unoriginal thing or person.

■ This was originally a term used in printing for a metal stereotype or electrotype block.

1 1996 *Spectator* [The] novel . . . simultaneously underlines and overturns whole layers of class clichés.

clientele /ˌkli:ɒn'tɛl/, *foreign* /kliᾱtɛl/ *noun* (also **clientèle**) M16 Latin and French (either, directly from Latin *clientela*, from *cliens, -ntis* (earlier *cluens*) client, use as noun of present participle of *cluere* to hear, obey; or, later, from French *clientèle* from Latin). Clients collectively; the customers of a shop, bar, or place of entertainment.

clique /kliːk/ *noun* E18 Old and Modern French (from *cliquer* to make a noise, from Middle Dutch *klikken* to click). A small close-knit group of people who do not readily allow others to join them; a coterie.

■ Possibly related to CLAQUE.

cloaca /kləʊˈeɪkə/ *noun* plural **cloacae** /kləʊˈeɪkiː/, **cloacas** L16 Latin (*cloaca, cluaca* related to *cluere* to cleanse). **1** An underground conduit for drainage, a sewer. *Archaic.* **2** *Zoology* A common cavity at the end of the digestive tract for the release of both excretory and genital products in birds, reptiles, amphibians, most fish, and monotremes.

clochard /klɔʃar/ *noun* plural pronounced same M20 French (from *clocher* to limp). (In France) a beggar, a vagrant.

1996 *Times* When, after the war, he went back to France, he lived for years—legend has it—more or less as a *clochard*, looked after, for a time, by the French Communist Party.

cloche /klɒʃ/, /kləʊʃ/ *noun* L19 French (= bell). **1** A small translucent (especially glass) cover for forcing or protecting outdoor plants; a bell glass. **2** A woman's close-fitting bell-shaped hat. In full *cloche hat*.

cloisonné /klwazɔne/ *adjective & noun* M19 French (past participle of *cloisonner* to partition, from *cloison* division). More fully *cloisonné enamel*. Enamel work in which the different colours in the pattern are separated by strips of flattened wire placed edgeways on a metal backing. Cf. CHAMPLEVÉ.

cloqué /ˈkləʊkeɪ/ *noun* (also anglicized as **cloky** /ˈkləʊki/) E20 French (literally, 'blistered'). A fabric with an irregularly raised or embossed surface.

clou /klu/ *noun* L19 French (literally, 'nail, stud'). The chief attraction, the point of greatest interest, the central idea.

1959 *Observer* The *clou* of the ballet is to be found in these four female solos.

coccyx /ˈkɒksɪks/ *noun* plural **coccyxes, coccyges** /ˈkɒksɪʤiːz/ L16 Latin (from Greek *kokkux* (originally) cuckoo (from its resemblance (in humans) to a cuckoo's beak)). *Anatomy* The small triangular bone forming the lower end of the spinal column in humans and some apes.

coco de mer /ˌkəʊkəʊdəˈmɛː/ *noun* E19 French (*coco-de-mer* coco from the sea (because the tree was first known from the nuts found floating in the sea)). A tall palm tree, *Lodoicea maldivica*, native to the Seychelles; its immense woody nut.

cocotte /kɒˈkɒt/ *noun* M19 French (sense 1 from a child's name for a hen; sense 2 from French *cocasse* from Latin *cucuma* cooking vessel). **1** A fashionable prostitute. *Archaic.* **2** A small heatproof dish for cooking and serving an individual portion of food. Usually in phrase *en cocotte* /ɑ̃ kɒˈkɒt/.

coda /ˈkəʊdə/ *noun* M18 Italian (from Latin *cauda* tail). **1** *Music* The concluding passage of a piece or movement, typically forming an addition to the basic structure. **2** *Ballet* The final section of a classical *pas de deux*; the finale of a ballet in which the dancers parade before the audience. **3** A concluding event, remark, or section.

codex /ˈkəʊdɛks/ *noun* plural **codices** /ˈkəʊdɪsiː/, /ˈkɒdɪsiː/ L16 Latin (*codex, codic-* block of wood, block split into leaves or tablets, book). **1** An ancient manuscript text in book form. **2** An official list of drugs, chemicals, etc.

■ Originally denoted a collection of statutes or set of rules, a legal code.

cogida /koˈxiða/, /kəˈhiːdə/ *noun* E20 Spanish (literally, 'a gathering of the harvest', use as noun of feminine past participle of *coger* to seize, from Latin *colligare* to bind together). (In bullfighting) a tossing of a bullfighter by a bull.

cogito /ˈkɒʤɪtəʊ/ *noun* M19 Latin (= I think, 1st person present of *cogitare* to cogitate). *Philosophy* The principle establishing the existence of the thinker

71

from the fact of his or her thinking or awareness.

■ The principle derives from the formula *cogito, ergo sum* 'I think (*or* I am thinking), therefore I am' of the French philosopher René Descartes (1596–1650).

cognomen /kɒɡˈnəʊmən/ *noun* plural **cognomens,** (earlier) **cognomina** E17 Latin (*cognomen* from as *co-* with + (*g*)*nomen* name). **1** A nickname or surname; a name. **2** An extra personal name given to an ancient Roman citizen, functioning rather like a nickname and typically passed down from father to son.

cognoscenti /kɒɲɒˈʃɛntɪ/ L18 Italian ((now *conoscenti*), literally, 'people who know', from Latin *cognoscent-* present participial stem of *cognoscere* to know). People who are especially well informed about a particular subject.

1995 *Country Life* This steep, deep and funky resort [sc. Taos] is an extraordinary amalgam of Swiss, Pueblo Indian and Spanish cultures and attracts skiing *cognoscenti* from round the globe.

cohabitation /kəʊˌhabɪˈteɪʃ(ə)n/, *in sense 3 foreign* /kɔabitasjɔ̃/ *noun* LME French. **1** Living together; community of life. *Archaic.* **2** Living together and having a sexual relationship without being married. **3** *Politics* An alliance dictated by expediency between office-holders of differing political views (originally in France).

■ Fully naturalized in senses 1 and 2, the word in its general literal meaning, as used in Middle English, is now almost entirely superseded by the particular sense 2. As a recent introduction from the French political scene, sense 3 is often written in italics to differentiate it from sense 2 and is therefore accorded a version of the French pronunciation.

3 1995 *Times* That experience will be all the more important in dealings with the new Duma, where the election result will force *cohabitation à la russe.*

coiffeur /kwaˈfəː/, /kwɒˈfəː/, *foreign* /kwafœr/ (*plural same*) *noun* M19 French (from *coiffer* to arrange the hair). A hairdresser.

coiffure /kwaːˈfjʊə/, /kwɒˈfjʊə/, *noun also foreign* /kwafyr/ (*plural same*) *noun*

& *verb* M17 French (*coiffe* from Old French *coife* headdress, from late Latin *cofia* helmet). **A** *noun* The way the hair is arranged or (formerly) the head decorated or covered; a person's hairstyle. **B** *transitive verb* Style or arrange hair. Chiefly as *coiffured* participial adjective.

coitus /ˈkəʊɪtəs/ *noun* M19 Latin. Sexual intercourse.

coitus interruptus /kəʊɪtəs ɪntəˈrʌptəs/ *noun* M19 Latin (from COITUS + *interruptus* interrupted). Sexual intercourse in which the penis is withdrawn before ejaculation.

cojones /koˈxones/, /kəˈhəʊneɪz/ *noun* plural M20 Spanish (plural of *cojón* testicle). **1** Testicles. **2** Courage, guts.

■ Colloquial, and in figurative use often euphemistic for 'balls' (see quotation 1996). The word, in both the literal and figurative uses, is more common in American English than British English.

1932 E. Hemingway *Death in the Afternoon* It takes more cojones to be a sportsman where death is a closer party to the game.

1996 *Times Magazine* Corrigan is working his *cojones* off to give us kidneys, liver, sweetbreads, anything that has not been banned which might be banned.

col /kɒl/ *noun* M19 French (from Latin *collum* neck). **1** A depression in the summit-line of a mountain chain; a saddle between two peaks. **2** *Meteorology* A region of slightly elevated pressure between two anticyclones.

collage /kɒˈlɑːʒ/ *noun* E20 French (– *gluing*). **1** A form of art in which various materials such as photographs and pieces of paper or fabric are arranged and stuck to a backing; a work in this form. **2** A jumbled collection or combination of impressions, events, styles, etc.

collectanea /kɒlɛkˈtɑːnɪə/, /kɒlɛkˈteɪnɪə/ *noun* M17 Latin (*collectanea* neuter plural (from *collect-*, past participial stem of *colligere* to assemble) as used as adjective in *Dicta collectanea* of Caesar, and as noun in *Collectanea* of Solinus). As *plural*, passages, remarks, and other pieces of text collected from various sources. As *singular*, a miscellany.

collegium /kəˈliːdʒɪəm/ *noun* plural **collegia** /kəˈliːdʒɪə/ L19 Latin (= association). **1** A society of amateur musicians, especially one attached to a German or American university. In full *collegium musicum* /ˈmjuːzɪkəm/, plural *collegia musica* /ˈmjuːzɪkə/. **2** *History* (representing Russian *kollegiya*) An advisory or administrative board in Russia.

col legno /kɒl ˈlɛnjəʊ/ *adverb* E17 Italian (= with the wood (of the bow)). *Music* (With reference to a bowed instrument) played by hitting the strings with the back of the bow.

colloquium /kəˈləʊkwɪəm/ *noun* plural **colloquia** /kəˈləʊkwɪə/, **colloquiums** L16 Latin (from *colloqui* to converse, from *col-* together + *loqui* to speak). An academic conference or seminar.

■ Originally used in English to denote a conversation or dialogue.

colluvium /kəˈl(j)uːvɪəm/ *noun* M20 Latin (from *colluvies* confluence of matter. *Geology* Material which accumulates at the foot of a steep slope.

colophon /ˈkɒləf(ə)n/ *noun* E17 Late Latin (from Greek *kolophōn* summit, finishing touch). **1** A publisher's emblem or imprint on the title page of a book. **2** A statement at the end of a manuscript or printed book, sometimes with a printer's emblem, giving information about its authorship, production, etc.

■ Originally denoted a crowning or finishing touch.

coloratura /kɒlərəˈtjʊərə/, /kɒlərə ˈtʊərə/ *noun* M18 Italian (= colouring, from late Latin *coloratura*, from *colorat-* past participial stem of *colorare* to colour). **1** Florid passages in vocal music (especially in operatic singing), with runs, trills, etc.; the singing of these. **2** A singer skilled in singing of this kind, especially a soprano.

1 1996 *Spectator* Thus Zerbinetta's display piece in *Ariadne auf Naxos* is every bit as riveting as the frustrated composer's outcry earlier on...its coloratura expresses the feelings of a free spirit...

colossus /kəˈlɒsəs/ *noun* plural **colossi** /kəˈlɒsʌɪ/ **colossuses** LME Latin (from Greek *kolossos* applied by Herodotus to the statues of Egyptian temples). **1** A statue of considerably more than life size. **2** A person or thing of enormous size, importance, or ability.

■ The Colossus of Rhodes, a gigantic statue of the Hellenistic period that is said to have straddled the harbour entrance on the island of Rhodes, was one of the Seven Wonders of the World.

2 1996 *New Scientist* Freud was a colossus, a massive intellect, the keenest clinical observer of mental disorders in the past 200 years.

colostrum /kəˈlɒstrəm/ *noun* (also (earlier) **colostra**) L16 Latin. The first milk of a mammal after giving birth.

colportage /ˈkɒlpɔːtɪdʒ/ *noun* M19 French (from *colporter* to hawk, peddle (see next)). The work of a colporteur; the peddling of books, newspapers, bibles, etc.

colporteur /ˈkɒlpɔːtə/, /kɒlpɔːˈtə/ *noun* L18 French (from *colporter*, probably alteration of *comporter* from Latin *comportare* transport, from as *com-* with + *portare* to carry). A person who sells books, newspapers, and similar literature; a person employed by a religious society to distribute bibles and other religious tracts.

columbarium /kɒl(ə)mˈbɛːrɪəm/ *noun* plural **columbaria** /kɒl(ə)mˈbɛːrɪə/, **columbariums** M18 Latin (*columbarium* pigeon-house, from *columba* dove, pigeon + *-arium*). A vault or building with niches for funeral urns to be stored.

coma /ˈkəʊmə/ *noun* 1 M17 Modern Latin (from Greek *kōma*, *kōmat-*, related to *koitē* bed, *keisthai* to lie down). A state of prolonged deep unconsciousness, caused especially by severe injury or illness; a state of extreme lethargy or sleepiness.

coma /ˈkəʊmə/ *noun* 2 plural **comae** /ˈkəʊmiː/ E17 Latin (from Greek *komē* hair of the head). **1** *Astronomy* A diffuse cloud of gas and dust surrounding the nucleus of a comet. **2** An optical aberration causing the image of an off-axis point to be flared, like a comet with a diverging tail; the flared image itself.

■ First used in English in the botanical sense 'tuft of hairs on a seed'.

comedienne /kə,miːdɪˈɛn/, /kə,mɛdɪ ˈɛn/ *noun* (also **comédienne** /kə,meɪdɪ ˈɛn/) M19 French (feminine of *comédien* comedian). A female comedian.

commando /kəˈmɑːndəʊ/ *noun* plural **commandos** L18 Portuguese ((now *comando*), from *commandar* to command). A soldier specially trained for carrying out raids; a unit of commandos.

■ The term is recorded from the late 18th century, denoting a militia, originally consisting of Boers in South Africa.

comme ci, comme ça /kɒm si kɒm sa/ *adverb phrase* M20 French (literally, 'like this, like that'). Used, especially in answer to a question, to convey that something is neither very good nor very bad.

commedia dell'arte /kɒm,meːdia dɛll ˈarte/, /kɒ,mɛdɪə dɛlˈɑːteɪ/ *noun phrase* L19 Italian (= comedy of art). An improvised kind of popular comedy in Italian theatres between the 16th and 18th centuries, based on stock characters.

comme il faut /kɒm il fo/, /kɒm iːl fəʊ/ *adjective phrase* M18 French (literally, 'as it is necessary'). Correct in behaviour or etiquette.

1984 A. Brookner *Hotel du Lac* It was implied that prolonged drinking, whether for purposes of business or as a personal indulgence, was not *comme il faut*...

commendatore /,kɒmɛndəˈtɔːri/ *noun* L19 Italian. A knight of an Italian order of chivalry.

commère /kɒmɛr/, /ˈkɒmɛː/ *noun* plural pronounced /kɒmɛr/, /ˈkɒmɛːz/ E20 French (literally 'godmother'). A female COMPÈRE.

commis /ˈkɒmi/ *noun* plural same (pronounced same, /ˈkɒmiːz/) L16 French (= deputy, clerk, past participle of *commettre* to entrust). A junior chef. Also **commis chef**.

commissar /kɒmɪˈsɑː/ *noun* E20 Russian (*komissar*, from French *commissaire*, from medieval Latin *commissarius* commissary). *History* An official of the Communist Party, especially in the former Soviet Union or present-day China, respon-

sible for political education and organization; a head of a government department in the former Soviet Union before 1946; *figurative* a strict or prescriptive figure of authority.

1996 *Spectator* She assumed that because she was a commissar, she could exercise rights which she wished to deny to her constituents.

commissionaire /kə,mɪʃəˈnɛː/ *noun* (also **commissionnaire** M17 French (*commissionnaire*, from medieval Latin *commissarius* person in charge, from Latin *committere* to entrust). A uniformed door attendant at a hotel, theatre, office, etc.

■ The Corps of Commissionaires was founded in London in 1859 as an organization through which pensioned (originally wounded) soldiers could find light employment as messengers, porters, etc.

1996 *Times* The commissionaire, mistaking him for a bum, refused him access.

communard /ˈkɒmjʊnɑːd/ *noun* L19 French. A member of a commune; *especially* (**Communard**) a supporter of the Paris Commune (the socialist government March–May 1871).

communautaire /,kɒmjʊnəʊˈtɛː/ *adjective* L20 French. Attentive to or serving the best interests of the wider community (usually with reference to the European Union).

1995 *Spectator* [A united Ireland] simply isn't going to come about in any foreseeable future unless the Protestants are physically expelled from Ulster, and that would be a little tricky for the Irish to carry out in their new enlightened and *communautaire* pose.

communiqué /kəˈmjuːnɪkeɪ/ *noun* M19 French (use as noun of past participle of *communiquer* to communicate). An official announcement or statement reporting on a meeting, conference, etc.

compadre /kɒmˈpɑːdri/ *noun* M19 Spanish (= godfather, (hence) benefactor, friend). Companion, friend.

■ Chiefly United States, often used as a form of address. The extension of meaning from 'godfather' to 'friend' is paralleled in the evolution of the native English word *gossip* from late Old English *godsibb* (from *god* God + *sib* kin) meaning a 'godparent' to mid-14th-century *gossip* 'a familiar acquaintance'. (The usual modern sense of *gossip* follows from the restriction of the word to specifically *female friends*, and thence to mean the sort of talk enjoyed by women amongst themselves.)

compendium /kəm'pɛndɪəm/ *noun* plural **compendiums**, **compendia** /kəm'pɛndɪə/ L16 Latin (originally, 'profit, saving', from *compendere* to weigh together). **1** A collection of concise but detailed information about a particular subject, especially in a book or other publication. **2** A collection or set of similar items. **3** A box containing assorted table games. **b** A package of stationery for letter-writing.

compère /'kɒmpɛː/ *noun & verb* (also **compere**) E20 French (originally, 'godfather in relation to the actual parents', from medieval Latin *compater* from *com-* with + *pater* father). **A** *noun* A person who introduces the performers or contestants in a variety show. **B** *transitive & intransitive verb* Act as compère (to a show).

compos mentis /ˌkɒmpɒs 'mɛntɪs/ *adjective phrase* E17 Latin. Having full control of one's mind; sane: *are you sure he was totally compos mentis?*. Cf. NON COMPOS MENTIS.

■ Usually used predicatively and sometimes shortened to *compos*.

compote /'kɒmpəʊt/, /'kɒmpɒt/ *noun* (also **compôte**) L17 French (Old French *composte* mixture, from Latin *compos(i)ta*, *compos(i)tum* use as noun of feminine and neuter past participle of *componere* to place together, compound). **1** Fruit preserved or cooked in a syrup. **2** A bowl-shaped dessert-dish with a stem.

compte rendu /kɔ̃t rɑ̃dy/ *noun phrase* plural **comptes rendus** (pronounced same) E19 French (= account rendered). A formal report or review.

con abbreviation of CONTRA.

con amore /kɒn ə'mɔːreɪ/, *foreign* /kɔn a'moːrɛ/ *adverb phrase* M18 Italian (= with love). *Music* (Especially as a direction) with tenderness.

con brio /kɒn 'briːəʊ/, *foreign* /kɔn 'brio/ *adverb phrase* E19 Italian. *Music* (Especially as a direction) with vigour. Also *figurative*.

1996 *Times* He also signed autographs by the dozen—it is, incidentally, a signature that is bold, sweeping and exuberant, written *con brio*.

conceptus /kən'sɛptəs/ *noun* M18 Latin (= conception, embryo, from *concept-* past participial stem of *concipere* to conceive). The embryo in the womb, especially in the early stages of pregnancy.

concertante /kɒntʃə'tanti/ *adjective* E18 Italian (= harmonizing, from *concertare* to harmonize). *Music* **1** Denoting a piece of music containing one or more solo parts, typically of less prominence than in a concerto. **2** Denoting prominent instrumental parts present throughout a piece of music, especially in baroque and early classical compositions.

concerti plural of CONCERTO.

concerti grossi plural of CONCERTO GROSSO.

concertino /kɒntʃə'tiːnəʊ/ *noun* plural **concertinos** L18 Italian (diminutive of CONCERTO). *Music* **1** A simple or short concerto. **2** A solo instrument or solo instruments playing with an orchestra.

concerto /kən'tʃəːtəʊ/, /kən'tʃɛːtəʊ/ *noun* plural **concertos**, **concerti** /kən'tʃəːti/ E18 Italian (from *concertare* to harmonize). *Music* Originally, a composition for various combinations of instruments. Now a composition for a solo instrument or instruments accompanied by an orchestra, especially one conceived on a relatively large scale.

concerto grosso /kən‚tʃəːtəʊ 'grɒsəʊ/ *noun phrase* plural **concerti grossi** /kən‚tʃəːti 'grɒsiː/ E18 Italian (= big concerto). *Music* A baroque concerto characterized by the use of a small group of solo instruments alternately with the full orchestra; a modern imitation of this.

concessionaire /kən‚sɛʃə'nɛː/ *noun* (also **concessionnaire**) M19 French (*concessionnaire*, from Latin *concessio(n)-* (from *concess-* past participial stem of *concedere* to concede) + *-aire*). The holder of a concession or grant, especially of the use of land or commercial premises or for trading rights.

concierge /ˈkɒnsɪɛːʒ/; *foreign* /kɔ̃sjɛrʒ/ (*plural same*) *noun* M16 French (from Old French *cumcerges* etc. = medieval Latin *consergius*, probably ultimately from Latin *conservus* fellow slave). **1** (Especially in France) a resident caretaker of a block of flats or a small hotel. **2** A hotel employee whose job is to assist guests by booking tours, making theatre and restaurant reservations, etc.

■ In early use denoted the warden of a house, castle, prison, or palace.

concordat /kənˈkɔːdat/ *noun* E17 French or Latin (*concordatum* something agreed upon, neuter past participle of *concordare* to be of one mind). An agreement or treaty; *especially* one between the Vatican and a secular government relating to matters of mutual interest.

1996 *New Scientist* The lot of contract researchers was improved last week when universities and major research sponsors signed a concordat to give them some of the benefits enjoyed by permanent staff...

concours d'élégance /kɔ̃kur deleɡɑ̃s/ *noun phrase* plural same M20 French (= contest of elegance). An exhibition or parade of vintage or classic motor vehicles in which prizes are awarded for those in the best or most original condition.

■ Sometimes shortened to *concours*, especially when used attributively (see quotation).

1996 *Times* ...Rolls-Royce would complete the work to *concours* condition and deliver the car 'in perfect working order, free of charge' in return for the right to use it for publicity.

condominium /kɒndəˈmɪnɪəm/ *noun* E18 Modern Latin (from *con-* together with + *dominium* right of ownership, rule). **1** Joint control of a state's affairs by two or more other states. **2** A building or complex of buildings containing a number of individually owned apartments or houses; each of the individual apartments or houses in a condominium. *North American*.

condottiere /kɔndotˈtjere/ *noun* plural **condottieri** /kɔndotˈtjeri/ (also **condottiero**) L18 Italian (from *condotta* a con- tract, from feminine past participle of *condurre* to conduct). *History* A leader or member of a troop of mercenaries, especially in Italy.

confetti /kənˈfɛti/ *noun* E19 Italian (= sweets, plural of *confetto* sweet, bonbon, from Latin *confectum* something prepared). Small pieces of coloured paper traditionally showered on the bride and bridegroom by the guests after a marriage ceremony.

■ Originally plural but now usually treated as singular. The term was first used in English to denote the real or imitation sweets thrown during Italian carnivals.

confiture /ˈkɒnfɪtjʊə/; *(foreign)* /kɔ̃fityr/ (*plural same*) *noun* M16 French (Old French *confit*). A preparation of fruit preserved in sugar; a confection.

■ The word was a rare import from Old French in the Middle English period with the meaning of 'a preparation of drugs'. In its present sense the forms *confiture* and *comfiture* were both used until the form in *-n-* was readopted (E19) from Modern French.

confrère /ˈkɒnfrɛː/ *noun* LME French (Old French from medieval Latin *confrater*, from *con* together + *frater* brother). **1** A fellow member of a brotherhood or fraternity. **2** A fellow member of a profession, scientific body, etc.

2 1996 *Bookseller* His is a surprisingly Thatcherite credo, given how many of his confrères are running for cover in the face of the impending Tory bloodbath.

conga /ˈkɒŋɡə/ *noun & verb* M20 American Spanish (from Spanish feminine of *congo* Congolese). **A** *noun* **1** A Latin American dance usually performed by people in single file who take three steps forward and then kick. **2** In full *conga drum*. A tall, narrow, low-toned drum that is beaten with the hands. **B** *intransitive verb* (past tense and participle **conga'd**, **congaed**). Perform the conga.

congé /kɔ̃ʒe/ (*plural same*), /ˈkɔ̃ʒeɪ/, /ˈkɒnʒeɪ/ *noun* LME Old French (*congié* (modern *congé*) from Latin *commeatus* passage, leave of absence, from *commeare* to go and come). An unceremonious dismissal or rejection of someone. Chiefly *humorous*.

■ Originally used in the general sense 'permission to do something'.

con moto /kɒn ˈməʊtəʊ/, *foreign* /kɔn ˈmoto/ *adverb phrase* E19 Italian (= with movement). *Music* (Especially as a direction) with spirited movement.

connoisseur /kɒnəˈsəː/ *noun* E18 French ((now *connaisseur*), from Old French *conoiss-* present participial stem of *conoistre* (modern *connaître*) to know). A person with a thorough knowledge and critical judgement of a subject, especially one of the fine arts; an expert in any matter of taste, e.g. wines, foods.

■ Often followed by *of*, *in*.

1996 *Country Life* Happily, this exhibition now re-unites more than 200 objects associated with Hamilton, attesting to the excellence of the connoisseur's taste...

conquistador /kɒnˈkwɪstədɔː/ *noun* plural **conquistadors**, **conquistadores** /kɒnˌkwɪstəˈdɔːrɪz/ M19 Spanish. A conqueror; *specifically* any of the Spanish conquerors of Mexico and Peru in the 16th century.

1995 *New Scientist* Pauling's style was that of a conquistador in the realm of science, much as Freud had claimed him to be.

consensus /kənˈsɛnsəs/ *noun* M17 Latin (= agreement, from *consens-* past participial stem of *consentire* to assent). A general agreement, a collective opinion.

1996 *Country Life* Life is moving faster than the consensus of how to behave.

conservatoire /kənˈsəːvətwɑː/, *foreign* /kõsɛrvatwar/ (*plural same*) *noun* L18 French (from Italian CONSERVATORIO). A college for the study of classical music or other performing arts, typically in the continental European tradition.

■ Such an academy may also be called a CONSERVATORIO and CONSERVATORIUM in other parts of Europe (see below), while *conservatory* in this sense is chiefly North American.

conservatoria plural of CONSERVATORIUM.

conservatorio /kənˌsəːvəˈtɔːrɪəʊ/ *noun* plural **conservatorios** L18 Italian (from late Latin *conservatorium* use as noun of

neuter of adjective *conservatorius* from *conservat-* past participial stem of *conservare* to conserve). An Italian or Spanish college for the study of classical music or other performing arts. Cf. CONSERVATOIRE, CONSERVATORIUM.

conservatorium /kənˌsəːvəˈtɔːrɪəm/ *noun* plural **conservatoriums**, **conservatoria** /kənˌsəːvəˈtɔːrɪə/ M19 German and Modern Latin (from as CONSERVATORIO *noun*). A college for the study of classical music or other performing arts, especially in Germany, Austria, or Australia. Cf. CONSERVATOIRE, CONSERVATORIO.

consigliere /kɒnsɪˈljɛːreɪ/ *noun* plural **consiglieri** pronunciation same M20 Italian (= a member of a council). A member of a Mafia family who serves as an adviser to the leader and resolves disputes within the family.

consommé /kənˈsɒmeɪ/ *noun* E19 French (use as noun of past participle of *consommer* from Latin *consummare* to finish up). A clear soup made with concentrated stock.

con sordino /kɒn sɔːˈdiːnəʊ/ *adverb & adjective phrase* E19 Italian. *Music* (Especially as a direction) played with the use of a mute.

consortium /kənˈsɔːtɪəm/ *noun* plural **consortia** /kənˈsɔːtɪə/, **consortiums** E19 Latin (from *consors, consort-* having an equal share with). **1** An association, typically of several companies. **2** *Law* The companionship, affection, and assistance which each spouse in a marriage is entitled to receive from the other.

■ Originally used in the sense 'partnership, association'.

conspectus /kənˈspɛktəs/ *noun* M19 Latin (from *conspectus* past participial stem of *conspicere* to view, look at attentively). A summary or overview of a subject.

contadina /kontaˈdiːna/, /kɒntəˈdiːnə/ *noun* plural **contadine** /kontaˈdiːne/, /kɒntəˈdiːni/, **contadinas** E19 Italian (feminine of next). An Italian peasant girl or peasant woman.

contadino /konta'di:no/, /kʊntə'di:nəʊ/ noun plural **contadini** /konta'di:ni/, **contadinos** M17 Italian (from contado county, (peasant population of) agricultural area round a city). An Italian peasant or countryman.

conte /kɔ̃t/ noun plural pronounced same L19 French. A short story as a form of literary composition, specifically a medieval narrative tale.

> **1996** Bookseller [Authors' agents] were always ready with scurrilous gossip or a mucky conte.

contessa /kɒn'tɛsə/ noun (also (especially in titles) **Contessa**) E19 Italian (from medieval Latin comitissa). An Italian countess.

continua plural of CONTINUUM.

continuo /kən'tɪnjʊəʊ/ noun plural **continuos** E18 Italian (= continuous). (In baroque music) an accompanied part which includes a bass line and harmonies, typically played on a keyboard instrument and with other instruments such as a cello or lute; a figured bass, a thorough bass (= BASSO CONTINUO).

continuum /kən'tɪnjʊəm/ noun plural **continua** /kən'tɪnjʊə/ M17 Latin (use as noun of neuter singular of Latin continuus continuous, unbroken). A continuous sequence in which adjacent elements are not perceptibly different from each other, but the extremes are quite distinct.

contra /'kɒntrə/ adverb, preposition, & noun LME Latin (= against (adverb and preposition), ablative feminine of a comparative from com, cum with). **A** adverb On or to the contrary; contrariwise. Chiefly in pro and con(tra) 'for and against'. **B** preposition Against. **C** noun **1** The opposing or opposite (side); an opposing factor or argument. **2** (Also Contra.) A member of a counter-revolutionary guerrilla force in Nicaragua, especially one opposing the left-wing Sandinista government (1979–90).

> ■ Often in abbreviated form in the noun phrase pros and cons (the points for and against (something)).

contralto /kən'traltəʊ/ noun (plural **contraltos**) M18 Italian (from as contra- + ALTO). Music The lowest female singing voice; a singer with such a voice; a part written for such a voice.

contra mundum /ˌkɒntrə 'mʌndəm/ adverb phrase M18 Latin (= against the world). Defying or opposing everyone else.

> **1995** Country Life Perhaps journalists and country people should gang up together. Us contra mundum.

contrapposto /kontrap'posto/ noun plural **contrapposti** /kontrap'posti/ E20 Italian (past participle of contrapporre from Latin contraponere tó place against). In the visual arts, an arrangement of a human figure in which the line of the arms and shoulders contrasts as strongly as possible with that of the hips and legs; a twisting of a figure on its own axis.

contra proferentem /ˌkɒntrə prɒfə'rɛntɛm/ adverb phrase E20 Latin (= against (the person) mentioning). Law (Of the interpretation of an ambiguous contract) against the party which proposed or drafted the contract or clause.

contredanse /'kɒntrədɑːns/, foreign /kɔ̃trədɑ̃s/ (plural same) noun E19 French (alteration of country dance by association with contre against, opposite). A French form of country dance, originating in the 18th century and related to the quadrille; a piece of music for such a dance.

contre-jour /'kɔ̃trəʒʊə/ adjective & adverb E20 French (from contre against + jour daylight). Photography Having or involving the sun or other light source behind the subject: a glorious contre-jour effect.

contretemps /'kɔ̃trətɒ̃:/, /'kɒntrətɔ̃:/ noun plural pronounced same L17 French (originally 'motion out of time', from contre against + temps time). **1** A minor dispute or disagreement. **2** An unexpected or untoward occurrence, especially of an embarrassing kind; a hitch, a mishap.

> ■ Originally a fencing term, denoting a thrust made at an inopportune moment

or at the same time as one's opponent makes one. The term is still used in fencing to denote a feint made with the intention of inducing a counter-thrust.

convenance /kɔ̃vnãs/ *noun* plural pronounced same L15 French (from *convenir* from Latin *convenire* to agree with). Conventional propriety or usage; in *plural*, the proprieties. *Archaic*.

conversazione /ˌkɒnvəsatsɪ'əʊni/ *noun* plural **conversaziones, conversazioni** /ˌkɒnvəsatsɪ'əʊni/ M18 Italian (= conversation). A scholarly social gathering held for discussion of the arts, literature, etc.; an educational soirée.

> **1995** *New Scientist* It [sc. the Royal Albert Hall] was to host science *conversaziones* and agricultural, industrial and scientific exhibitions.

cooee /'ku:ɪ/, /'ku:i:/ *interjection & verb* L18 Aboriginal. **A** *interjection* Used to attract attention, especially at a distance. **B** *intransitive verb* Make a call to attract attention.

> ■ Chiefly Australia and New Zealand, imitative of a signal used by Aboriginals and copied by settlers.

cooncan /'ku:nkan/ *noun* L19 Spanish (perhaps from *con quién?* with whom?). A card game for two players, originally from Mexico, similar to rummy.

copaiba /kəʊ'pʌɪbə/ *noun* (also **copaiva** /kəʊ'pʌɪvə/) E17 Portuguese (*copaíba* (whence Spanish *copaíba*) from Tupi *copaiba*, Guarani *cupaíba*). A balsam of aromatic odour and acrid taste obtained from South American leguminous trees of the genus *Copaifera* and used in medicine and the arts. Formerly also, a tree yielding this.

copal /'kəʊp(ə)l/ *noun* L16 Spanish (from Nahuatl *copalli* incense). A hard translucent resin obtained from various tropical trees and used to make a fine transparent varnish. Also *gum copal*.

copita /kəʊ'pi:tə/ *noun* M19 Spanish (diminutive of *copa* from popular Latin *cuppa* cup). A tulip-shaped sherry glass of a type traditionally used in Spain; a glass of sherry.

copra /'kɒprə/ *noun* L16 Portuguese and Spanish (from Malayalam *koppara*). Dried coconut kernels, from which oil is obtained.

copula /'kɒpjʊlə/ *noun* E17 Latin (= connection, linking of words, from as *co-* together + *apere* to fasten). *Logic* and *Grammar* A connecting word, in particular a form of the verb *be* connecting a subject and complement.

coq au vin /kɒk əʊ vɛ̃/ *noun phrase* M20 French (literally, 'cock in wine'). A casserole of chicken pieces cooked in red wine.

coquette /kɒ'kɛt/ *noun* M17 French (feminine of *coquet* wanton). **1** A flirtatious woman. **2** A crested Central and South American hummingbird of the genus *Lophornis*.

> **1 1996** *Spectator* . . . she can mock, tease, play the coquette . . .

coquina /kəʊ'ki:nə/ *noun* M19 Spanish (= shellfish, cockle, from Old Spanish *coca* from medieval Latin by-form of Latin *concha* shell). A soft white limestone composed of broken marine shells cemented together and used in roadmaking in the Caribbean and Florida. Also *coquina rock*, *coquina stone*.

coquito /kəʊ'ki:təʊ/ *noun* plural **coquitos** M19 Spanish (diminutive of *coco* coconut). The Chilean wine palm, *Jubaea chilensis*, which yields large amounts of sweet sap (palm honey) and fibre. Also *coquito palm*.

coram /'kɔ:rəm/ *preposition* M16 Latin. Before, in the presence of.

> ■ Occurs in various archaic legal phrases used in English, such as CORAM JUDICE, *coram nobis* 'in our presence', *coram populo* 'in the presence of the people' (i.e. in public).

coram judice /ˌkɔ:rəm 'ju:dɪsi/ *adverb phrase* E17 Latin (= in the presence of a judge). In a properly constituted or an appropriate court of law.

cor anglais /kɔ:r 'ɑ:ŋgleɪ/, /kɔ:r 'ɒŋgleɪ/ *noun phrase* L19 French (literally, 'English horn'). An alto woodwind musical instrument like an oboe but lower in pitch; a player of this. Also, an organ stop of similar quality.

corbeille /kɔː'beɪ/ *noun* E19 French (= basket). An elegant basket of flowers or fruit.

cordillera /kɔːdɪ'ljɛːrə/ *noun* E18 Spanish (from *cordilla* diminutive of *cuerda* from Latin *chorda* cord). Each of a series of parallel mountain ridges or chains, especially in the Andes or the Rockies; an extensive belt of mountains, valleys, etc., especially as a major continental feature.

cordon bleu /ˌkɔːdō 'blə:/ *adjective & noun phrase* M18 French (*cordon* ribbon + *bleu* blue). **A** *adjective phrase* **1** (Of cooking) of the highest class: *a cordon bleu chef.* **2** Denoting a dish consisting of an escalope of veal or chicken rolled, filled with cheese and ham, and then fried in breadcrumbs. **B** *noun phrase* plural **cordons bleus** (pronounced same). A cook of the highest class.

■ In French history, a blue ribbon signified the highest order of chivalry under the Bourbon kings.

cordon sanitaire /ˌkɔːdō sanɪ'tɛ:/ *noun phrase* plural **cordons sanitaires** (pronounced same) M19 French (*cordon* ribbon, band + *sanitaire* sanitary). **1** A guarded line placed around an area affected by disease in order to prevent anyone from leaving the area and thus spreading the disease. **2** A measure designed to prevent communication or the spread of undesirable influences.

■ Earlier (E19) simply *cordon*.
2 1996 *Spectator* Working in oils is a moosy, smelly business which demands a *cordon sanitaire* from the rest of the household.

cordovan /'kɔːdəv(ə)n/ *noun* L16 Spanish (*cordován* (now *cordobán*) noun, *cordovano* adjective, from *Córdova* (now *Cordoba*) from Latin *Corduba* Córdoba). A kind of pliable fine-grained leather used especially for shoes, made originally at Córdoba from goatskin and now from horse hide.

corniche /'kɔːnɪʃ/, /kɔː'niːʃ/ *noun* M19 French. A road along the edge of a cliff, especially one running along a coast. Also *corniche road.*

cornucopia /kɔːnjʊ'kəʊpɪə/ *noun* E16 Late Latin (*cornucopia* from Latin *cornu copiae* horn of plenty (a mythical horn able to provide whatever is desired)). **1** A symbol of plenty consisting of a goat's horn overflowing with flowers, fruit, and corn; an ornamental container or other representation of this. **2** An abundant supply of good things of a specified kind: *the festival offers a cornucopia of pleasures.*

corps /kɔː/, *foreign* /kɔr/ *noun* plural same /kɔz/, *foreign* /kɔr/ L16 French (from Latin *corpus* body). **1** A main subdivision of an army in the field, consisting of two or more divisions; a branch of an army assigned to a particular kind of work (medical, ordnance, intelligence, etc.). See also ESPRIT DE CORPS. **2** A body of people engaged in a particular activity: *the press corps.* **3** CORPS DE BALLET.

■ The first appearance of *corps* in English was in the phrase *corps de garde*, a small body of soldiers set as a guard. It was apparently first used as an independent word by Addison in 1711 in the *Spectator* in a letter peppered with up-to-the-minute military jargon, which was largely the product of the Duke of Marlborough's campaigns in Europe. It was probably at first pronounced as the English word *corpse*, and Johnson's *Dictionary* (1755) gives *corps* and *corpse* as alternative spellings. The desirability of distinguishing between the two sorts of 'body' has ensured that the French pronunciation and spelling have been retained for the 'group of people' sense.

corps de ballet /kɔr də balɛ/, /ˌkɔː də 'baleɪ/ *noun phrase* plural same E19 French. The members of a ballet company who dance together as a group; the members of the lowest rank of dancers in a ballet company.

corps d'élite /kɔr delit/, /ˌkɔː deɪ'liːt/ *noun phrase* plural same L19 French. A select group of people.

corps diplomatique /kɔr diplɔmatik/, /ˌkɔː dɪpləmɑ'tiːk/ *noun phrase* plural **corps diplomatiques** (*pronounced same*) L18 French. The body of diplomats representing other countries in a particular state; the diplomatic corps.

corpus /'kɔ:pəs/ *noun* plural **corpora** /'kɔ:p(ə)rə/, **corpuses** LME Latin (= body).
1 A collection of written texts, especially the entire works of a particular author or a body of writing on a particular subject. **b** A collection of written or spoken material in machine-readable form, assembled for the purpose of linguistic research. **2** *Anatomy* The main body or mass of a structure; the central part of the stomach, between the fundus and the antrum.

■ Originally used in English to denote the body of a person or animal. Sense 1 dates from the early 18th century.

1 **1996** *Oldie* Some exercise of this sort… needs to be applied to the corpus of architectural criticism.

corpus delicti /kɔ:pəs dɪ'lɪktʌɪ/ *noun* M19 Latin (= body of offence). *Law* The facts and circumstances constituting a crime.

corral /kə'rɑːl/ *noun & verb* L16 Spanish and Old Portuguese (*corral*, Portuguese *curral*: cf. KRAAL). **A** *noun* **1** An enclosure for livestock, especially cattle or horses, on a farm or ranch. Chiefly *North American*. **2** *History* A defensive enclosure formed of wagons in an encampment. **B** *transitive verb* inflected *-ll-*. **1** Put or keep (livestock) in a corral. **2** Gather (a group of people or things) together. **3** *History* Form (wagons) into a corral.

corrida /kɔ:'ri:də/, *foreign* /ko'rrida/ *noun* L19 Spanish (literally, 'running (of bulls)'). A bullfight; bullfighting. In full *corrida de toros* /də 'tɔ:rəʊz/, *foreign* /ðe 'toros/.

corrigendum /kɒrɪ'dʒɛndəm/ *noun* plural **corrigenda** /kɒrɪ'dʒɛndə/ E19 Latin (neuter gerundive of *corrigere* to correct). Something requiring correction, typically an error in a printed book. In *plural especially* errors listed with the corrections alongside.

corroboree /kə'rɒbəri/ *noun* L18 Dharuk (*garaabara*, denoting a style of dancing). **1** An Australian Aboriginal dance ceremony which may take the form of a sacred ritual or an informal gathering. **2** A party or other lively social gathering. Chiefly *Australian*.

corsetière /'kɔ:sɪtjɛ:/ *noun* M19 French (feminine of *corsetier*, from as Old French *cors* (modern *corps*) body + *-ière*). A woman who makes or fits corsets.

Corso /'kɔ:səʊ/ *noun* (also **corso**) plural **Corsos** L17 Italian (= course, main street from Latin *cursus* course). (In Italy and some other Mediterranean countries) a social promenade; a street given over to this, or where races and parades were formerly held.

cortège /kɔ:'teɪʒ/ *noun* M17 French (from Italian *corteggio*, from *corteggiare* to attend court, from *corte* court). A solemn procession, especially for a funeral; a person's entourage or retinue.

cortex /'kɔ:tɛks/ *noun* plural **cortices** /'kɔ:tɪsiːz/ LME Latin (= bark). An outer layer of a part in an animal or plant; *specifically*: *Anatomy* the outer layer of the cerebrum, composed of folded grey matter and playing an important role in consciousness; *Botany* an outer layer of plant tissue immediately below the epidermis of a stem or root.

cortile /kor'ti:le/, /kɔ:'ti:li/ *noun* E18 Italian (derivative of *corte* court). (In Italy) an enclosed usually roofless and arcaded area within or attached to a building.

1984 A. G. Lehmann *European Heritage* …for all the classical exhibition in the *cortile*, when it comes to furnishing their private apartments, the Medici lean rather towards the tastes of a European market, not a classical revival at all.

corvée /'kɔ:veɪ/ *noun* ME Old and Modern French (= Provençal *corroada*, based on Latin *corrogare* to ask for, collect). A day's unpaid labour owed by a vassal to his feudal lord; forced labour exacted as a tax, *specifically* that on public roads in France before 1776; *figurative* an unpleasant duty, an onerous task.

corvette /kɔ:'vɛt/ *noun* M17 French (ultimately diminutive of Middle and Modern Dutch *korf* basket, kind of ship). **1** A small warship used especially for protecting convoys against submarines in the war of 1939–45. **2** A type of sailing warship with a flush deck and one tier of guns. Now *historical*.

coryphée /ˈkɒrɪfeɪ/ *noun* E19 French (from Greek *koruphaios* leader of a chorus, from *koruphē* head, top). A leading dancer in a CORPS DE BALLET.

coryza /kəˈrʌɪzə/ *noun* E16 Latin (from Greek *koruza* nasal mucus, catarrh). *Medicine* Acute catarrhal inflammation of the mucous membrane in the nose, caused especially by a cold or by hay fever.

Cosa Nostra /ˌkəʊzə ˈnɒstrə/ *noun phrase* M20 Italian (= our thing). A US criminal organization resembling and related to the Mafia.

cosmos /ˈkɒzmɒs/ *noun* ME Greek (*kosmos* order, ornament, world). **1** The universe seen as a well-ordered whole. **2** An ordered system of thought or ideas.

costa /ˈkɒstə/ *noun* (also **Costa**) M20 Spanish (= coast). A coast, *especially* one developed as a holiday resort.

   ■ On the pattern of genuine place names such as *Costa Brava* or *Costa del Sol*, humorous usage creates pseudo-Spanish names such as *Costa Geriatrica* (a seaside resort or area mainly populated by elderly people) or *Costa del Crime* (an area favoured by criminals for enjoying their ill-gotten gains in luxury while remaining beyond the reach of extradition laws).

   1995 *Times: Weekend* Goa is a long way yet from becoming another Spanish costa but the beach will become crowded and there will no longer be any sense of solitude.

costumier /kɒˈstjuːmɪə/ *noun* M19 French (from *costumer* to costume). A person or company that makes or supplies theatrical or fancy-dress costumes.

coterie /ˈkəʊt(ə)ri/ *noun* E18 French ((in Old French = tenants holding land together), ultimately from Middle Low German *kote* cote, cottage). A small group of people with shared interests or tastes, especially one that is exclusive of other people.

cotillion /kəˈtɪljən/ *noun* (in sense 1 also **cotillon** /kəˈtɪljən/, *foreign* /kɔtijõ/ (*plural same*)) E18 French (*cotillon* petticoat dance, diminutive of *cotte* coat). **1** Any of several dances with elaborate steps and figures. **2** A formal ball, especially one at which débutantes are presented. *United States.*

cotta /ˈkɒtə/ *noun* M19 Italian (from Proto-Romance, from Frankish, of unknown origin). A short garment resembling a surplice, worn typically by Catholic priests and servers.

   1996 *Oldie* I . . . feel deeply uncomfortable with its atmosphere of unguents, incense, bells, mortifications and prayers directed at a world infected with cassocks and cottas . . .

couchant /ˈkaʊtʃ(ə)nt/ *adjective* LME Old and Modern French (present participle of *coucher* to couch, lie down). *Heraldry* (Of an animal) lying on its belly with its head up. Usually *postpositive*, as in *lion couchant*.

couchette /kuːˈʃɛt/, *foreign* /kuʃɛt/ (*plural same*) *noun* E20 French (literally, 'little bed', diminutive of *couche*). A railway carriage in which the seats convert into sleeping berths; a berth in such a carriage.

coudé /kuːˈdeɪ/ *adjective* L19 French (past participle of *couder* to bend at right angles, from *coude* elbow from Latin *cubitum* cubit). Relating to or denoting a telescope in which the rays are bent to focus at a fixed point off the axis.

coulée /kuːˈleɪ/, /ˈkuːli/ *noun* (also **coulee**, **coulie** /ˈkuːli/) E19 French (= (lava) flow, from Latin *colare* to filter, strain, (in Proto-Romance) flow, from *cōlum* strainer). A deep ravine. *North American.*

coulis /ˈkuːli/ *noun* L20 French (from *couler* to flow). A thin, flowing fruit or vegetable sauce.

   1996 *Spectator* . . . a cassata . . . was very good, though I was less keen on the strawberry coulis draped around it.

coulisse /kuːˈliːs/ *noun* E19 French (use as noun of feminine of *coulis* sliding (from *coulisser* to slide); cf. *portcullis* literally, 'sliding door'). **1** A flat piece of scenery at the side of the stage in a theatre. **2** (In *plural*) the spaces between these pieces of scenery, the wings.

couloir /ˈkuːlwɑː/, *foreign* /kulwar/ (*plural same*) *noun* E19 French (= channel, from *couler* to pour, from Latin *colare* to filter).

A steep, narrow gully on a mountain-side.

coup /ku:/, *foreign* /ku/ (*plural same*) *noun* L18 French (from medieval Latin *colpus* blow, from Latin *colaphus* from Greek *kolaphos* blow with the fist). **1** A COUP D'ÉTAT. **2** An instance of successfully achieving something difficult; an unusual or unexpected but successful tactic in card play. **3** *Billiards* The direct pocketing of the cue ball, which is a foul stroke. **4** *History* (Among North American Indians) an act of touching an enemy, as a deed of bravery; an act of first touching an item of the enemy's in order to claim it.

coup de foudre /ku də fudr/ *noun phrase* plural **coups de foudre** (*pronounced same*) L18 French (literally, 'stroke of lightning'). A sudden unforeseen event, in particular an instance of love at first sight.

coup de grâce /ˌku: də ˈɡrɑ:s/ *noun phrase* plural **coups de grâce** (*pronounced same*) L17 French (literally, 'stroke of grace'). A blow by which a mortally wounded person or animal is mercifully killed; *figurative* a decisive finishing stroke.

1996 *Times* It was de Villiers who administered the *coup de grâce*, dismissing Cork, Martin and Gough in successive overs...

coup de main /ku də mɛ̃/ *noun phrase* plural **coups de main** (*pronounced same*) M18 French (literally, 'stroke of hand'). A sudden surprise attack, especially one made by an army during war.

coup de maître /ˌku: də ˈmɛ:tr(ə)/ *noun phrase* plural **coups de maître** (*pronounced same*) M17 French (literally, 'master stroke'). A master stroke.

coup d'état /ku: deɪˈtɑ:/, *foreign* /ku detɑ/ *noun phrase* plural **coups d'état** /ku:z deɪˈtɑ:/, *foreign* /ku detɑ/, **coup d'états** /ku: deɪˈtɑ:z/ M17 French (literally, 'blow of state'). A sudden, violent, and illegal seizure of power from a government.

■ Now often abbreviated to *coup* in all but the most formal contexts.

1996 *Spectator* Andreotti was once asked whether there could be a coup d'état in Italy. 'No,' he replied. 'There is no état.'

coup de théâtre /ku də teatr/ *noun phrase* plural **coups de théâtre** (*pronounced same*) M18 French (literally, 'blow of theatre'). **1** A sudden dramatic turn of events or action, especially in a play. Also *figurative* (see quotations). **2** A theatrical hit.

1 1995 *Spectator*...the finale of the scene—where the Prince's girlfriend is shot dead—looks rather forced, instead of being a *coup de théâtre*.

1 *figurative* 1995 *Times* Tony Blair's most unexpected *coup de théâtre* this week was his announcement of a deal with British Telecom...

coup d'œil /ku dœj/ *noun phrase* M18 French (literally, 'stroke of eye'). A glance that takes in a comprehensive view; a general view.

1996 *Country Life* Also, they [sc. the rooms] are seen at the correct angles in the first views, with the chimneypieces being part of the first *coup d'œils* in all of them.

coupe /ku:p/ *noun* L19 French (= goblet, from medieval Latin *cuppa*). **1** A shallow glass or glass dish, typically with a stem, in which desserts or champagne are served. **2** A dessert served in such a dish.

coupé /ˈku:peɪ/ *noun* (in sense 1 also **coupe** /ku:p/) M19 French (past participle of *couper* to cut; sense 2 abbreviation of *carrosse coupé*, literally, 'cut carriage'). **1** A car with a fixed roof, two doors, and a sloping rear. **2** A four-wheeled carriage with a seat for two inside and an outside seat for the driver. Chiefly *historical*. **3** (In South Africa) an end compartment in a railway carriage with seats on only one side.

courante /kʊˈrɒ̃t/, /kʊˈrɑ:nt/ *noun* (also **courant** /kʊˈrant/) L16 French (use as noun of feminine present participle of *courir* to run). **1** A 16th-century court dance consisting of short advances and retreats, later developed into a rapid gliding dance in quick triple time. **2** *Music* A piece of music written for or in the style of this dance, typically one forming a movement of a suite.

courbette /kʊəˈbɛt/ *noun* M17 French (from Italian *corvetta* little curve). (In classical riding) a movement in which the horse performs a series of jumps on the hind legs without the forelegs touching the ground.

coureur /kurœr/ *noun* plural pronounced same E18 French (= (wood-)runner). *History* A woodsman or trader of French origin in Canada and the northern United States. In full *coureur de bois* /də bwa/.

courgette /kʊəˈʒɛt/ *noun* M20 French (diminutive of *courge* gourd). A small variety of vegetable marrow, harvested and eaten at an early stage of growth. Also called ZUCCHINI.

court bouillon /kur bujɔ̃/ *noun phrase* M17 French (from *court* short + BOUILLON). A stock made from wine, vegetables, etc., typically used in fish dishes.

couscous /ˈkuːskuːs/ *noun* (also **kouskous, couscoussou** /ˈkuːskuːsuː/) E17 French (from Arabic *kuskus, kuskusū* millet grain, probably of Berber origin). A type of North African semolina in granules made from crushed durum wheat; a spicy dish made by steaming or soaking couscous and adding meat, vegetables, or fruit.

couture /kuːˈtjʊə/ *noun* E20 French (= sewing, dressmaking, from Old French *cousture* sewing from late Latin *consutura*, from Latin *consutus* past participle of *consuere* to sew together). The design and manufacture of fashionable clothes to a client's specific requirements and measurements; fashionable made-to-measure clothes.

couvade /kuːˈvɑːd/ *noun* M19 French (from *couver* to hatch from Latin *cubare* to lie). A custom in some cultures by which a man takes to his bed and goes through certain rituals when his wife bears a child, as though he were physically affected by the birth.

■ Adopted in French in this sense (M19) owing to a misunderstanding of the expression *faire le couvade* 'to sit doing nothing' in earlier writers.

couverture /ˈkuːvətjʊə/ *noun* M20 French (= covering). Chocolate made with extra cocoa butter to give a high gloss, used for coating sweets and cakes.

coyote /ˈkɔɪəʊt/, /kɔrˈəʊti/ *noun* plural same, **coyotes** M18 Mexican Spanish (from Nahuatl *coyotl*). **1** A small nocturnal wolf-like animal, *Canis latrans*, of western North America, noted for its mournful howling. Also called *prairie wolf*. **2** A person who smuggles people from Latin America across the United States border, typically for a very high fee. *North American colloquial*.

craic /krak/ *noun* (also **crack**) L20 Irish (*craic* entertaining conversation). Enjoyable social activity; a good time.

crannog /ˈkranəg/ *noun* E17 Irish (*crannóg*, Gaelic *crannog* timber structure, from *crann* tree, beam). (In Scotland and Ireland) an ancient fortified dwelling constructed in a lake or marsh on an artificial island made from timber.

craquelure /ˈkrakljʊə/, *foreign* /kraklyr/ *noun* E20 French (from *craqueler* to crackle). A network of fine cracks in the pigment or varnish on the surface of a painting.

crèche /krɛʃ/, /kreɪʃ/ *noun* L18 French (from Old French *creche* wooden feeding rack for animals, from Proto-Romance from Germanic base related to *crib*). **1** A nursery where babies and young children are cared for during the working day. **2** A representation of the Nativity scene.

■ *Crib* is now the more usual word for sense 2.

credenza /krɪˈdɛnzə/ *noun* L19 Italian (from medieval Latin *credentia* from Latin *credent-* present participial stem of *credere* to believe; see quotation 1996). A sideboard or cupboard.

> **1996** *Country Life* ... although I knew what a credenza was—a sideboard or display cabinet with a blind door flanked by shelves or glazed cupboards—I was unsure of the derivation. A 'credence' in English furniture terminology began as a church table ... but now means something more like a card-table. Although the Italian *credenza* shares the same origin, it developed into a sideboard, and the name was anglicized when such cabinets became popular in the 19th century.

credo /ˈkriːdəʊ/, /ˈkreɪdəʊ/ *noun* plural **credos** ME Latin (*credo* I believe). **1** A statement of the beliefs or aims which guide someone's actions. **2** (**Credo**) A creed of the Christian Church in

Latin (from the first word); a musical setting of the Nicene Creed, typically as part of a mass.

1 1996 *Bookseller* To any critic they can always call on their shabby mass-market credo, 'If that's what people want, who am I to patronise them by offering what someone else might think is better?'

crème /krɛm/ (*plural same*), /kreɪm/ *noun* (also **crême**) E19 French (= cream). **1** Cream; a cream, a custard. Used especially in names of desserts and liqueurs (see following entries). **2** The CRÈME DE LA CRÈME.

crème anglaise /krɛm ɑ̃'gleɪz/ *noun phrase* E19 French (= English cream). A rich egg custard.

crème brûlée /krɛm bryle/, /kreɪm 'bruːleɪ/ *noun phrase* L19 French (literally, 'burnt cream'). A cream or custard dessert topped with caramelized sugar.

crème caramel /krɛm karamɛl/, /kreɪm 'karəmɛl/ *noun phrase* E20 French. A custard dessert made with whipped cream and eggs and topped with caramel.

■ Earlier (M19) as *crème au caramel*.

crème de cacao /krɛm də kakao/, /ˌkreɪm də kə'kaʊ/ *noun phrase* M20 French. A chocolate-flavoured liqueur.

crème de la crème /krɛm də la krɛm/, /kreɪm də lɑː kreɪm/ *noun phrase* M19 French (literally, 'cream of the cream'). The best person or thing of a particular kind.

1996 *Spectator* In 1988, they played Liverpool, then seen as the *crème de la crème* of Europe, in the FA Cup Final.

crème de menthe /krɛm də mɑ̃t/, /kreɪm də 'mɑːnt/, /kreɪm də 'mɒnθ/ *noun phrase* E20 French (= cream of mint). A peppermint-flavoured liqueur.

crème fraîche) /krɛm frɛʃ/ *noun phrase* (also **creme fraiche**) L20 French (= fresh cream). A type of thick cream made from double cream with the addition of buttermilk, sour cream, or yogurt.

creole /'kriːəʊl/ *noun & adjective* (also (especially in strict use of senses 1 and 2 of the noun and corresponding uses of the adjective) **Creole**) E17 French (*créole*, earlier *criole* from Spanish *criollo* probably from Portuguese *crioulo* black person born in Brazil, home-born slave, from *criar* to nurse, breed, from Latin *creare* to create). **A** *noun* **1** A person of mixed European and black descent, especially in the Caribbean. **2** A descendant of Spanish or other European settlers in the Caribbean or Central or South America; a white descendant of French settlers in the southern United States, especially Louisiana. **3** A mother tongue formed from the contact of a European language (especially English, French, Spanish, or Portuguese) with local languages (especially African languages spoken by slaves in the West Indies). **B** *adjective* Relating to a creole or creoles.

crêpe /kreɪp/, (sense A.3) /krɛp/ *noun & adjective* (also **crepe**) L18 French (earlier *crespe*, use as noun of Old French *crespe* curled, frizzed, from Latin *crispus* curled). **A** *noun* **1** A light, thin fabric with a wrinkled surface. **2** A type of raw rubber rolled into thin sheets with a wrinkled surface, used for the soles of shoes. More fully *crêpe rubber*. **3** A very thin pancake. **B** *attributive* or as *adjective* Made of crêpe; resembling crêpe.

■ The anglicized spelling *crape* was current in the 17th century in sense A.1, but later came to be restricted to a specific kind of black silk cloth used especially for mourning dresses and funereal drapes.

crêpe de Chine /kreɪp də ʃiːn/ *noun phrase* L19 French. A fine crêpe of silk or similar fabric. Also called *China crêpe*.

crêpe Suzette /kreɪp suːˈzɛt/ *noun phrase* plural **crêpes Suzette** (*pronounced same*) E20 French. A thin dessert pancake flamed and served in alcohol.

crépinette /kreɪpɪˈnɛt/ *noun* L19 French (diminutive of *crêpine* caul). A kind of flat sausage consisting of minced meat and savoury stuffing wrapped in pieces of pork caul.

crépon /'kreɪpən/ *noun* L19 French (from as CRÊPE). A fabric resembling crêpe, but heavier and with a more pronounced crinkled effect.

crescendo /krɪˈʃɛndəʊ/ *noun, adverb, adjective, & verb* L18 Italian (present participle of *crescere* to increase from Latin *crescere* to grow). **A** *noun* plural **crescendos, crescendi. 1** *Music* A gradual increase in loudness in a piece of music; a passage of music marked or performed with a crescendo. **2** The loudest point reached in a gradually increasing sound. **3** A progressive increase in intensity. **4** The most intense point reached; a climax. **B** *adverb & adjective Music* (Especially as a direction) with a gradual increase in loudness. **C** *intransitive verb* Increase gradually in loudness or intensity.

> **B 1995** *Spectator*... the composer Percy Grainger used the word 'louden', where less Australian musicians are content with 'crescendo'...

cretonne /krɛˈtɒn/, /ˈkrɛtɒn/ *noun* L19 French (of unknown origin). A heavy cotton fabric printed on one or both sides with a (usually large floral) pattern, used for chair covers, curtains, etc.

crevasse /krɪˈvas/ *noun* E19 French (Old French *crevace*). **1** A deep open crack, especially one in a glacier. **2** A breach in the bank or levee of a river, canal, etc. *United States.*

cri de cœur /kri də kœr/ *noun phrase* plural **cris de cœur** (pronounced same) E20 French (= cry from the heart). A passionate appeal, complaint, or protest.

> **1996** *Times* Newcastle's social sides are not going down without a final *cri de cœur* for the essential amateurism which they... believe can co-exist with professional rugby.

crime passionnel /krim pasjɔnɛl/ *noun phrase* plural **crimes passionnels** (pronounced same) E20 French (= crime of passion). A crime, especially murder, committed in a fit of sexual jealousy.

criollo /krɪˈɒləʊ/ *noun* (also **Criollo**) plural **criollos** L19 Spanish (= native to the locality). **1** A person from Spanish South or Central America, especially one of pure Spanish descent. **2** A horse or other domestic animal of a South or Central American breed. **3** A

cacao tree of a variety producing thin-shelled beans of high quality.

crise /kriz/ *noun* plural pronounced same LME French. Crisis.
> ■ Formerly fully naturalized, it now occurs only in the following phrases or as an abbreviation of them.

crise de conscience /kriz də kɔ̃sjɑ̃s/ *noun phrase* M20 French. A crisis of conscience.

crise de nerfs /kriz də nɛr/ *noun phrase* (also **crise des nerfs**) E20 French (= crisis of nerves). An attack of anxiety.
> **1970** *New Yorker* She has been a splendid advertisement for the benefits of a happy marriage—conspicuously more relaxed, far less subject to those old *crises des nerfs*.

critique /krɪˈtiːk/ *noun & verb* Originally **critic** M17 French (ultimately from Greek *kritikē* (sc. *tekhnē*) the critical art, criticism). **A** *noun* A detailed analysis and assessment of something, especially a literary, philosophical, or political theory. **B** *verb* Evaluate a theory or practice in a detailed and analytical way.

crochet /ˈkrəʊʃeɪ/, /ˈkrəʊʃɪ/ *noun & verb* M19 French (diminutive of *croc* with *-ch-* from *crochié, crochu* hooked). **A** *noun* A handicraft in which yarn is made up into a textured fabric by means of a hooked needle; crocheted fabric or items. **B** *verb* **1** *transitive verb* Make (a garment or piece of fabric) using crochet. **2** *intransitive verb* Do crochet work.

croissant /ˈkrwasɒ̃/ *noun* L16 French. A flaky pastry roll in the shape of a crescent, eaten for breakfast.
> ■ Earlier (L16–L17) found as an occasional variant of *crescent*, especially with reference to the crescent moon, *croissant* is now solely used for the pastry roll.

cromlech /ˈkrɒmlɛk/ *noun* L17 Welsh (from *crom* feminine of *crwm* bowed, arched + *llech* (flat) stone). (In Wales) a megalithic tomb consisting of a large flat stone laid on upright ones; a dolmen.

croque-monsieur /ˈkrɔk məˌsjəː/ *noun* M20 French (literally 'bite (a) man').

A fried or grilled ham-and-cheese sandwich.

croquette /krɒˈkɛt/ *noun* E18 French (from *croquer* to crunch). A small ball or roll of vegetable, minced meat, or fish, fried in breadcrumbs.

crostini /krɒsˈtiːnɪ/ *noun plural* L20 Italian (plural of *crostino* little crust). Small pieces of toasted or fried bread served with a topping as a starter or canapé.

crotale /ˈkrəʊt(ə)l/ *noun* M20 French (from Latin *crotalum* denoting an ancient type of castanet). A small tuned cymbal.

croupade /kruˈpeɪd/ *noun* M17 French (from Italian *groppata* (with assimilation to French *croupe* croup)). A movement performed in classical riding, in which the horse leaps from the ground with its legs tucked under its body.

croupier /ˈkruːpɪə/, /ˈkruːpɪeɪ/ *noun* E18 French ((originally a person who rides behind on a horse's croup), from *croupe* from Proto-Romance from Germanic base related to *crop*). 1 The person in charge of a gaming table, responsible for raking in and paying out the money or tokens. 2 The assistant chairman at a public dinner, seated at the lower end of the table. Now *historical*.

■ Originally used to denote a person standing behind a gambler to give support and advice.

croustade /kruˈstɑːd/ *noun* M19 French (from Old French *crouste* (modern CROÛTE) or Italian *crostata* tart (from *crosta* crust)). A crisp piece of bread or pastry hollowed to receive a savoury filling.

croûte /kruːt/ *noun plural* pronounced same E20 French. A crisp piece of toasted or fried bread on which savoury snacks can be served. See also EN CROÛTE.

croûton /ˈkruːtɒn/, /kruːtɔ̃/ *(plural same) noun* (also **crouton**) E19 French (from CROÛTE). A small piece of toasted or fried bread served with soup or as a garnish.

cru /kry/ *(plural same)*, /kruː/ *noun* (also **crû**) E19 French (from *crû* past participle of *croître* grow). (In France) a vineyard

or wine-producing region, especially one of recognized superior quality; the grade or quality of wine produced in such a vineyard or region.

■ Often in phrases (see quotation); see also GRAND CRU, PREMIER CRU.

1966 P. V. Price *France, Food & Wine Guide* Just below the classed growths come the *crus bourgeois*...then the *crus artisans*.

crudités /krydite/, /ˈkruːdɪteɪ/ *noun plural* M20 French. Assorted raw vegetables served as an hors d'oeuvre, typically with a sauce into which they may be dipped.

crumhorn variant of KRUMMHORN.

crux /krʌks/ *noun plural* **cruxes** /ˈkrʌksɪz/, **cruces** /ˈkruːsiːz/ M17 Latin (= cross). 1 The decisive or most important point at issue; a particular point of difficulty. 2 (Usually **Crux**) The constellation of the Southern Cross, the most familiar one to observers in the southern hemisphere.

■ In early use *crux* referred to a representation of a cross, chiefly in *crux ansata* 'ankh' (literally 'cross with a handle'). See ANKH.

csardas /ˈtʃɑːdɑːʃ/, /ˈzɑːdəs/ *noun* (also **czardas**) plural same M19 Hungarian (*csárdás*, from *csárda* inn). A Hungarian dance usually having a slow start and a rapid wild finish, with many turns and leaps; a piece of music for this dance.

cuadrilla /kwadˈrija/, /kwɒdˈriːljə/ *noun* plural **cuadrillas** /kwadˈrijas/, /kwɒdˈriːljəz/ M19 Spanish. A matador's team.

cueca /ˈkwɛkə/ *noun* E20 American Spanish (from *zamacueca*, also denoting a dance performed especially in Chile). A lively South American dance.

cuesta /ˈkwɛstə/ *noun* E19 Spanish (= slope, from Latin *costa* rib, flank). Originally (*United States dialect*), a steep slope that terminates a gently sloping plain; a plain in this configuration. Now (*Geography*), a ridge with a gentle slope (dip) on one side and a steep one (scarp) on the other.

cui bono /kwiː ˈbɒnəʊ/, /kuːɪ ˈbɒnəʊ/, /kuːɪ ˈbəʊnəʊ/ *interjection* E17 Latin (= to whom (is it) a benefit?). Who stands to gain (from a crime, and so might have been responsible for it)?

> **1996** *Spectator* Then, from the 1960s to the 1980s, yet more scholars... put the attribution back to Raphael and authenticated the Dürer inscription, to the general satisfaction. *Cui bono*? Well, it gave large numbers of dons and students... something to do.

cuisine /kwɪˈziːn/ *noun* L18 French (= kitchen, from Latin *coquina, cocina*, from *coquere* to cook). A style or method of cooking, especially as characteristic of a particular country, region, or establishment; food cooked in a certain way. Cf. HAUTE CUISINE, NOUVELLE CUISINE.

cul-de-sac /ˈkʌldəsak/, /kʊldəˈsak/ *noun* plural **culs-de-sac** (pronounced same), **cul-de-sacs** M18 French (= bottom of a sack). **1** A street or passage closed at one end. **2** A route or course leading nowhere.

> ■ This was originally a term in anatomy, referring to a vessel, tube, or sac that was open only at one end, or to the closed end of such a vessel.
> **2 1995** *New Scientist* Lock up the DNA libraries and information will simply not be available to other researchers. Life-saving research could then become stuck in a cul-de-sac.

culmen /ˈkʌlmɛn/ *noun* M17 Latin (contraction of *columen* top, summit, etc). The upper ridge of a bird's bill.

culottes /kjuːˈlɒt(s)/, *foreign* /kylɔt/ *noun plural* M19 French (= knee breeches; cf. SANSCULOTTE). Woman's knee-length trousers, cut with full legs to resemble a skirt; a divided skirt.

culpa /ˈkʌlpə/ *noun* M19 Latin. *Law* Neglect resulting in damage, negligence.

> ■ See also FELIX CULPA.

cultus /ˈkʌltəs/ *noun* M19 Latin (from past participial stem of *colere* to honour with worship). A system of religious worship or ritual; a cult.

cum /kʌm/ *preposition* L19 Latin (= with). **1** Combined with. Used in names of combined parishes (e.g. *Horton-cum-Studley*). **2** With. Chiefly in Latin phrases and English ones imitating them (e.g. *cum dividend*). **3** And also.

Denoting a combined role, nature, or function.

> **3 1996** *New Scientist* ... she [sc. Sylvia Earle] co-founded Deep Ocean Technology and Deep Ocean Engineering,... apparently running them as director-cum-secretary from her kitchen table.

cum grano salis /kʌm ˈɡrɑːnəʊ ˈsɑːlɪs/ *adverb & adjective phrase* M17 Latin (= with a grain of salt). (In the phrase *take something cum grano salis*) another way of saying *take something with a pinch of salt*.

cum laude /kʌm ˈlɔːdi/, /kʌm ˈlaʊdeɪ/ *adverb & adjective phrase* L19 Latin (= with praise). With distinction, with honours (with reference to university degrees and diplomas).

> ■ Chiefly North American; cf. MAGNA CUM LAUDE, SUMMA CUM LAUDE.

cumulus /ˈkjuːmjʊləs/ *noun* plural **cumuli** /ˈkjuːmjʊlʌɪ/, /ˈkjuːmjʊliː/ M17 Latin (= heap). *Meteorology* Cloud forming rounded masses heaped on each other and having a horizontal base at usually a low altitude. Also *cumulus cloud*.

> ■ Originally denoting a heap or pile, or an accumulation.

cunnilingus /kʌnɪˈlɪŋɡəs/ *noun* L19 Latin (from *cunnus* vulva + *lingere* to lick). Stimulation of a woman's genitals with the tongue or lips.

cupola /ˈkjuːpələ/ *noun* M16 Italian (from late Latin *cupula* little cask, small burying vault, diminutive of *cupa* cask). **1** A rounded dome forming or adorning a roof or ceiling. **b** Something likened to such a dome. **2** A cylindrical, originally domed, furnace for refining metals. Also *cupola furnace*. **3** A gun turret.

curandero /kuranˈdero/ *noun* plural **curanderos** /kuranˈderos/ (feminine **curandera** /kuranˈdera/) M20 Spanish (from *curar* to cure, from Latin *curare*). (In Spain and Latin America) a healer who uses folk remedies.

curare /kjʊˈrɑːri/ *noun* L18 Spanish and Portuguese (from Carib word represented also by *wourali*). A resinous bitter substance obtained from the bark and stems of various tropical and subtropical South American plants, which paralyses the motor nerves and is traditionally used by some Indian peoples to poison their arrows and blowpipe darts.

curé /kyre/ *noun* plural pronounced same M17 French (from medieval Latin *curatus* a person who has a cure or charge (of a parish)). (In France and French-speaking countries) a parish priest.

curettage /kjʊəˈrɛtɪdʒ/, /kjʊərɪˈtɑːʒ/ *noun* L19 French (from as next). *Surgery* The scraping or cleaning of an internal surface of an organ or body cavity with a curette.

▪ Often in the phrase *dilatation and curettage* (colloquially abbreviated *d&c*), a common operation on the lining of the uterus which consists of this.

curette /kjʊəˈrɛt/ *noun & verb* M18 French (from *curer* to take care of, clean, from Latin *curare* to heal). *Surgery* **A** *noun* A small instrument resembling a scoop used to remove material by a scraping action, especially from the uterus. **B** *transitive & intransitive verb* Scrape or clean with a curette.

Curia /ˈkjʊərɪə/ *noun* M19 Latin (*curia*). The papal court at the Vatican, by which the Roman Catholic Church is governed, comprising tribunals, congregations, and other institutions and departments.

▪ Originally *curia* denoted one of the divisions into which each of the three tribes of ancient Rome was divided; also (by extension) the senate of any ancient Italian city other than Rome. Later the term came to denote a feudal or Roman Catholic court of justice.

curiosa /kjʊərɪˈəʊsə/ *noun* plural L19 Latin (*curiosa* neuter plural of *curiosus*). Curiosities, oddities; *specifically* erotic or pornographic books or articles.

1996 *Independent on Sunday* It has beautiful women:...an absent-minded, gloriously disorganised, plump and pretty *assistante* sprung to life from the pages of some piece of Victorian *curiosa*.

currach /ˈkʌrə(x)/ *noun* (also **curragh, corrack**) LME Irish (Gaelic *curach* small boat, coracle). (In Ireland and Scotland) a small boat made of slats or laths covered with watertight material (for-

merly hide, now usually tarred canvas); a coracle.

curragh /ˈkʌrə(x)/ *noun* M17 Irish (*currach* marsh, Manx *curragh* moor, bog, fen). (In Ireland and the Isle of Man) a stretch of marshy waste ground.

curriculum /kʌˈrɪkjʊləm/ *noun* plural **curricula** /kʌˈrɪkjʊlə/ E19 Latin (= running, course, racing chariot, from *currere* to run). The subjects making up a course of study in a school or college.

curriculum vitae /kʌˌrɪkjʊləm ˈviːtʌɪ/, /ˈvʌɪtiː/ *noun phrase* plural **curricula vitae** /kʌˈrɪkjʊlə/ E20 Latin (= course of life). A brief account of one's education, qualifications, and previous occupations, typically sent with a job application.

▪ In job advertisements and colloquial contexts usually abbreviated to *CV*.

1996 *Times* None of the usual 'seeking other business opportunities', no attempt to deny a rift or gild the *curriculum vitae* for the benefit of future employers.

cursillo /kurˈsijo/; /kʊəˈsiːjəʊ/, /kurˈsiːljəʊ/ *noun* plural **cursillos** /kurˈsijos/, /kurˈsijəʊz/, /kurˈsiːljəʊz/ M20 Spanish (literally, 'little course'). A short informal spiritual retreat by a group of Roman Catholics, especially in Spain or Latin America.

cuspidor /ˈkʌspɪdɔː/ *noun* M18 Portuguese (= spitter, from *cuspir* to spit, from Latin *conspuere*). A spittoon. Chiefly *North American*.

custos /ˈkʌstɒs/ *noun* plural **custodes** /kʌˈstəʊdiːz/, (originally) **custoses** /kʌˈstəʊsiːz/ LME Latin. A keeper, a guardian, a custodian.

▪ Now chiefly in titles from Modern Latin, as in *custos rotulorum* (literally, 'keeper of the rolls'), a title given to the chief Justice of the Peace in an English county, who has nominal responsibility for the records of the commission of the peace in that county.

cuvée /kjuːˈveɪ/, *foreign* /kyve/ (*plural* same) *noun* M19 French (= vatful, from *cuve* from Latin *cupa* cask, vat). A type, blend, or batch of wine, especially champagne.

cuvette /kju:'vɛt/ *noun* E18 French (diminutive of *cuve* cask, vat). *Biochemistry* A straight-sided clear container for holding liquid samples in a spectrophotometer or other instrument.

cwm /kʊm/ *noun* M19 Welsh (= coomb). A bowl-shaped valley or hollow in Welsh mountains; a CIRQUE.

cyanosis /sʌɪə'nəʊsɪs/ *noun* plural **cyanoses** /sʌɪə'nəʊsiːz/ M19 Modern Latin (from Greek *kuanōsis* blueness). *Medicine* A blue discoloration of the skin due to poor circulation or deficient oxygenation of the blood.

cyme /sʌɪm/ *noun* E18 French (*cyme, cime* summit, top, from popular variant of Latin *cyma*). *Botany* A flower cluster with a central stem bearing a single terminal flower which develops first, the other flowers in the cluster developing as terminal buds of lateral stems.

czar variant of TSAR.

czardas variant of CSARDAS.

czarevich, czarina, etc. variants of TSAREVICH, TSARINA, etc.

Dd

da capo /dɑː ˈkɑːpəʊ/ *adverb phrase* E18 Italian (= from the head). *Music* (Especially as a direction) repeat from the beginning. Compare with DAL SEGNO.

dacha /ˈdatʃə/ *noun* (also **datcha**) M19 Russian (= grant of land). A small country house or villa in Russia, typically used as a second or holiday home.

> **1996** *Oldie* The Russians, who did not enjoy their time in Yemen, built *dachas* and Black Sea style hotels.

dacoit /dəˈkɔɪt/ *noun* L18 Hindi (ḍakait, from ḍākā gang-robbery). (In India or Burma (Myanmar)) a member of a band of armed robbers.

dado /ˈdeɪdəʊ/ *noun* plural **dados** M17 Italian (= die, cube, from Latin *datum* something given, starting point). **1** The lower part of an interior wall when faced or coloured differently from the upper part. **2** *Architecture* The plain portion of a pedestal between the base and the cornice.

daemon /ˈdiːmən/, /ˈdʌɪməʊn/ *noun* (also formerly **demon**) M16 Latin (medieval Latin *demon*, Latin *daemon* from Greek *daimōn* divinity, genius). **1** *Greek Mythology* A being of a nature between that of gods and humans, a spirit; the soul of a deceased person regarded as a minor divinity. **2** An inner or attendant spirit or inspiring force; a DAIMON.

> ■ *Demon*, meaning specifically 'an evil spirit' or 'devil', was naturalized in Middle English, and this spelling was also occasionally used in Early Modern English in the senses above. However, the usefulness of being able to differentiate between an evil spirit and other morally neutral entities taken over from pagan classical religion ensured that the spelling *daemon* has survived in the latter senses. A similar consideration lay behind the later (M19) introduction of DAIMON. The form *daemon* has been popularized by Philip Pullman's use of the term in his *His Dark Materials* trilogy (1995–2000), where it refers to a companion in animal form that attends each human, a physical embodiment of their spirit or soul.

dagga /ˈdagə/ *noun* L17 Afrikaans (from Khoikhoi *dachab*). (In South Africa) cannabis.

daimon /ˈdʌɪməʊn/ *noun* M19 Greek (*daimōn*). An inner or attendant spirit or inspiring force.

> ■ The direct transliteration of the Greek is intended to evoke the pagan classical concept of the personal spirit, unencumbered by the nuances of the earlier usages of d(a)emon; see also DAEMON.

daimyo /ˈdʌɪmɪəʊ/, /ˈdʌɪmjəʊ/ *noun* (also **daimio**) plural **daimyos** E18 Japanese (from *dai* great + *myō* name). (In feudal Japan) one of the chief landowning nobles who were vassals of the shogun.

dak /dɑːk/, /dɔːk/ *noun* (also **dawk**) E18 Hindi (ḍāk). The postal service in the Indian subcontinent, originally delivered by a system of relay runners.

dal variant of DHAL.

dal segno /dal ˈseɪnjəʊ/ *adverb phrase* L19 Italian (= from the sign). *Music* (Especially as a direction) repeat from the point marked by a sign (not the beginning). Compare with DA CAPO.

damna plural of DAMNUM.

damnosa hereditas /damˌnəʊsə hɪˈrɛdɪtas/ *noun phrase* M19 Latin (= inheritance that causes loss). An inheritance or tradition bringing more burden than profit.

> **1955** *Times* The rule that an executor was not compelled to accept a *damnosa hereditas* did not provide a reliable guide.

damnum /ˈdamnəm/ *noun* plural **damna** /ˈdamnə/ E19 Latin (= hurt, harm, damage). *Law* A loss, a wrong.

dan /dan/ *noun* M20 Japanese. Each of the ten grades of advanced proficiency in judo or karate; a person who has reached a specified dan grade. Cf. KYU.

danse macabre /dɑ̃s makabr/ *noun phrase* plural **danses macabres** (pronounced same) L19 French. The dance of death; a musical piece or passage representing or suggestive of this.

■ Earlier (LME) anglicized as *dance (of) macabre* (cf. MACABRE). As an allegory, the Dance of Death (called TOTENTANZ in German-speaking areas) was very popular in the late Middle Ages. Medieval and Renaissance representations of it show Death in the form of a skeleton approaching young and old, rich and poor, powerful and obscure, and leading them all away in a dance to the grave. The most famous of these images is the series of 50 woodcuts by Hans Holbein the Younger designed in the early 1520s and published at Lyons in 1538.
figurative **1996** *Spectator* ... less like all-out war, more like a stately minuet between the command structure of the British state and that of the IRA, a *danse macabre* whose ritual bows to certain unwritten understandings about the rules of engagement.

danseur /dɑ̃sœr/ *noun* plural pronounced same E19 French (from *danser* to dance). *Ballet* A male dancer.

danseur noble /dɑ̃sœr nɔbl/ *noun phrase* plural **danseurs nobles** (pronounced same) M20 French (from as *danseur* + *noble* noble). *Ballet* A principal male dancer, especially one who is particularly suited by bearing or physique to princely roles.
1996 *Spectator* Wildor is now a complete ballerina.... Similarly, Trevitt is a true *danseur noble* who coped brilliantly with the complexities of the part...

danseuse /dɑ̃søz/ *noun* plural pronounced same E19 French. A female dancer; a ballerina.

dariole /'darɪəʊl/ *noun* LME Old and Modern French. **1** An individual sweet or savoury dish of various kinds; now *specifically* one made in a dariole mould. **2** A small metal mould shaped like a flowerpot and used for making such a dish. In full *dariole mould*.

darshan /'dɑːʃən/ *noun* E20 Hindi (pronunciation of Sanskrit *darśana* sight, seeing, from *dṛś-* to see). *Hinduism* An opportunity to see or an occasion of seeing a holy person or the image of a deity.

Dasein /'dɑːzem/ *noun* M19 German (from *dasein* to exist, from *da* there + *sein* to be). *Philosophy* In Hegelian terms, existence, determinate being; in existentialism, human existence, the being of a person in the world.

dashiki /'dɑːʃɪki/ *noun* M20 West African (probably Yoruba from Hausa: cf. Krio *da(n)shiki*). A loose brightly coloured shirt or tunic, originally from West Africa.

data /'deɪtə/ *noun* M17 Latin (plural of DATUM). *plural and collective singular* **1** Facts, especially numerical facts, collected together for reference or information. **2** The quantities, characters, or symbols on which operations are performed by computers and other automatic equipment, and which may be stored and transmitted in the form of electrical signals, records on magnetic, optical, or mechanical recording media, etc. **3** Things given or granted; things known or assumed as facts, and made the basis of reasoning or calculation.
1 **1996** *New Scientist* Much of the modern craze for collecting data is to avoid having to admit that we are just using our judgment.

datcha variant of DACHA.

datum /'deɪtəm/ *noun singular* plural **data** /'deɪtə/ M18 Latin (neuter past participle of *dare* to give). A thing given or granted; a thing known or assumed as a fact, and made the basis of reasoning or calculation; a fixed starting point for a series of measurements etc.
■ Now much more frequent in the plural DATA.

daube /dəʊb/, *foreign* /dob/ (*plural same*) *noun* E18 French. A stew of meat, typically beef, braised slowly in wine.

dauphin /'dɔːfɪn/, /'dəʊfɑ̃/ *noun* (also **Dauphin**) LME French ((Old French *daulphin*), family name of the lords of Dauphiné, an area of south-east France). *History* (The title of) the eldest son of the King of France, from 1349 to 1830.
■ Dauphiné ultimately derives from a nickname meaning 'dolphin'.

dauphinois /dəʊfɪ'nwʌ/ *adjective* (also **dauphinoise** /dəʊfɪ'nwʌz/) E20 French

(= from the province of Dauphiné). (Of potatoes or other vegetables) sliced and cooked in milk, typically with topping of cheese.

dazibao /ˈdɑːdzəbaʊ/ *noun* plural same M20 Chinese (*dàzìbào*, from *dà* big + *zi* character + *bào* newspaper, poster). (In the People's Republic of China) a wall poster written in large characters, expressing a political opinion.

débâcle /deɪˈbɑːk(ə)l/, /dɪˈbɑːk(ə)l/ *noun* (also **debacle**) E19 French (from *débâcler* to unbar, from *dé-* + *bâcler* to bar). **1** A sudden and ignominious collapse or defeat; a humiliating and embarrassing situation. **2** A breaking-up of ice in a river; a sudden flood or rush of water carrying along debris.
▸ **1** 1996 *Times Magazine* Fred Vermorel emerges from this débâcle as a sad individual trading on the reflected glory of his association with people from a bygone time.

debitage /dɛbɪˈtɑːʒ/ *noun* M20 French (*débitage* cutting of stone). *Archaeology* Waste material produced in the making of prehistoric stone implements.

debris /ˈdɛbriː/, /ˈdeɪbriː/ *noun* (also **débris**) E18 French (*débris*, from *débriser* to break down, break up, from *dé-* + *briser* to break). **1** Scattered pieces of rubbish or remains. **2** Loose natural material consisting especially of broken pieces of rock.

début /ˈdeɪb(j)uː/, /ˈdɛb(j)uː/; /ˈdeɪˈbjuː/, /dɛˈbjuː/ *noun, adjective, & verb* (also **debut**) M18 French (from *débuter* to lead off). **A** *noun* **1** A person's first appearance or performance in a particular capacity or role. **2** The first appearance of a débutante in society. **B** *adjective* Denoting the first recording or publication of a group, singer, or writer: *a debut album.* **C** *intransitive verb* Perform in public for the first time.

débutant /ˈdɛbjʊtɒ̃/, /ˈdeɪbjʊtɒ̃/ *noun* (also **debutant**) E19 French (present participle of *débuter* to lead off). A man making his first public appearance, especially in sport.

débutante /ˈdɛbjʊtɑːnt/, /ˈdeɪbjʊtɑːnt/ *noun* (also **debutante**) E19 French (feminine of *débutant*: see preceding). **1** An upper-class young woman making her first appearance in fashionable society. **2** A woman making her first public appearance, especially in sport.

decani /dɪˈkeɪnʌɪ/ *noun* M18 Latin (genitive of *decanus* dean). The section of a church or cathedral choir conventionally placed on the south side and taking the first or higher part in antiphonal singing (cf. CANTORIS).

decennium /dɪˈsɛnɪəm/ *noun* plural **decennia** /dɪˈsɛnɪə/, **decenniums** L17 Latin (from *decennis*, from *decem* ten + *annus* year). A period of ten years, a decade.

déclassé /deklase/ (*plural same*), /deɪˈklaseɪ/ *adjective* (feminine **déclassée**) L19 French (past participle of *déclasser* to (re)move from a class). Having fallen in social class or status.
▸ 1995 *Spectator* Forte (having for so long been accused of being too *déclassé* to own the Savoy) could point out the incongruity of a company whose most famous hostelry is the Rover's Return in *Coronation Street* becoming the landlord of the Grosvenor House in Park Lane.

décolletage /dekɔltaʒ/, /deɪkɒlˈtɑːʒ/ *noun* L19 French (from *décolleter* to expose the neck). **1** A low-cut neckline on a woman's dress or top. **2** Exposure of the neck and shoulders by such a neckline.
▸ **2** 1995 *Times Pride and Prejudice* convinced a nation of bra burners that a heaving décolletage was the only way to attract a Mr Darcy in time for Christmas.

décolleté /dekɔlte/, /deɪˈkɒl(ə)teɪ/ *adjective* (also **décolletée**) M19 French ((feminine *décolletée*), from *décolleter* to expose the neck, from *dé-* + *collet* collar of a dress etc). (Of a woman's dress or top) having a low-cut neckline; (of a woman) wearing a low-necked dress or top.

décor /ˈdeɪkɔː/ *noun* (also **decor**) L19 French (from *décorer* to decorate). **1** The decoration and furnishings of a room, building, etc. **2** The scenery and furnishings of a theatre stage; the set.

découpage /dekupaʒ/ *noun* plural pronounced same M20 French (from *découper* to cut up, cut out). The decoration of a surface of an object with cut-out paper patterns or illustrations; an object so decorated.

1977 A. Jeffs *Creative Crafts* As découpage traveled through Europe in the 18th century, it was enthusiastically adopted by the women of the courts who amused themselves by imitating the then fashionable Chinese lacquerwork.

decrescendo /di:krɪˈʃɛndəʊ/ *adverb, adjective, noun, & intransitive verb* plural of noun **decrescendos** E19 Italian (present participle of *decrescere* to decrease). DIMINUENDO.

de facto /deɪ ˈfaktəʊ/, /di:/ *adverb & adjective phrase* E17 Latin (= of fact). **A** *adverb phrase* In fact, whether by right or not. Often contrasted with DE JURE. **B** *adjective phrase* Existing or holding a specified position in fact but not necessarily by legal right: *the de facto president of the republic.*
B 1996 *Times* Old Compton Street on a Saturday night has become a *de facto* pedestrian precinct. It is thronged with people and almost impossible to drive down.

dégagé /degaʒe/, /deɪˈgɑːʒeɪ/ *adjective* (feminine **dégagée**) L17 French (past participial adjective of *dégager* to set free). Unconstrained, relaxed; detached, unconcerned.

dégringolade /degrɛ̃gɔlad/ *noun* plural pronounced same L19 French (from *dégringoler* to descend rapidly). A rapid descent or deterioration; decadence.
1996 *Spectator* After the happy Venetian years before the last war and the hardly less happy postwar ones..., there followed the ghastly and grotesque *dégringolade* of the final years.

de gustibus non est disputandum
/deɪ ɡʌstɪbəs nɒn ɛst dɪspjuːˈtandəm/ *interjection* L18 Latin (= there is no disputing about tastes). There is no accounting for tastes.

de haut en bas /də o ã bɑ/ *adverb and adjective phrase* L17 French (= from above to below). In a condescending or superior manner.
1995 *Spectator* Maynard Keynes... had a very *de haut en bas* view that he knew best what forms of culture should be supported (opera and ballet)...

dehors /dəɔr/, /dəˈhɔ:/ *preposition* E18 French (in Old French used as a preposition (Modern French as adverb and noun)). *Law* Other than, not including, or outside the scope of.

Dei gratia /deɪɪ ˈɡrɑːtɪə/, /di:ʌɪ ˈɡreɪʃə/ *adverb phrase* E17 Latin. By the grace of God.

déjà vu /deʒa vy/, /ˌdeɪʒɑː ˈvuː/ *noun phrase* E20 French (= already seen). A feeling of having already experienced the present situation.
1995 *Spectator* Huddled in the international departure lounge at Waterloo underneath a Eurostar board proudly exhibiting its cancelled trains, I felt a sudden nostalgic twinge of *déjà-vu* [sic].

déjeuner /deʒœne/ (*plural same*), /ˈdeɪʒəneɪ/ *noun* L18 French (use as noun of infinitive = to break one's fast). **1** A morning meal (early or late) in France or elsewhere; breakfast or (usually) lunch. **2** A set of cups, saucers, plates, etc., for serving breakfast, breakfast service.
∎ *Petit déjeuner* is commonly used for 'breakfast'.

de jure /di: ˈdʒʊəri/, /deɪ ˈjʊəreɪ/ *adverb & adjective phrase* M16 Latin (= of law). **A** *adverb phrase* According to rightful entitlement or claim; by right. Often contrasted with DE FACTO. **B** *adjective phrase* Existing or holding a specified position by legal right: *a de jure claim to the territory.*

dekko /ˈdɛkəʊ/ *noun* plural **dekkos** L19 Hindi (*dekho* polite imperative of *dekhnā* to look). A quick look or glance.
∎ Originally British army slang in India. Although the word also existed (L19) as a transitive and intransitive verb, the verbal sense is usually expressed by *have* (or *take*) *a dekko.*

delicatessen /ˌdɛlɪkəˈtɛs(ə)n/ *noun* L19 German (*Delikatessen* plural or Dutch *delicatessen* plural, from French *délicatesse* delicacy). A shop, or shop counter or department, selling cooked meats, cheeses, and unusual or foreign prepared foods.
∎ Originally used in the United States, denoting the prepared foods themselves. Now often abbreviated colloquially to *deli.*

delirium tremens /dɪˌlɪrɪəm ˈtri:mənz/, /dɪˌlɪrɪəm ˈtrɛmənz/ *noun phrase* E19 Modern Latin (= trembling delirium). A psychotic condition typical of withdrawal in chronic alcoholics, involving tremors, hallucinations, anxiety, and disorientation.

■ A term invented by a Dr T. Sutton in 1813 for a type of delirium that was worsened by bleeding but alleviated by opium; later medical writers established its modern sense. In informal use often abbreviated to *DTs*.

delta /'dɛltə/ *noun* ME Latin (from Greek). **1** The fourth letter of the Greek alphabet (Δ, δ), transliterated as 'd'. **2** A triangular tract of sediment deposited at the mouth of a river, typically where it diverges into several outlets; originally (*the Delta*) *specifically* that of the River Nile. **3** A triangle; a triangular area or formation. Usually *attributive*, as in *delta connection* (*Electricity*) and *delta wing* (*Aeronautics*). **4** Denoting the fourth of a series of items or categories. **5** *attributive Science* Fourth; as in *Astronomy* (preceding the genitive of the Latin name of the constellation) designating the fourth brightest star in a constellation; (**b**) *delta rays*, rays of low penetrative power consisting of slow electrons released from atoms by other particles; (**c**) *delta rhythm*, *delta waves*, slow electrical activity of the unconscious brain. **6** A fourth-class mark given for an examination paper or piece of school or college work.

de luxe /dɪ 'lʌks/, /'lʊks/, /də/ *adjective phrase* E19 French (= of luxury). Luxurious or sumptuous; of a superior kind.

■ Used either postpositively (see quotation 1996) or as a premodifier (see quotation 1970). Cf. POULE DE LUXE.

1970 K. Chesney *Victorian Underworld* These places were often little businesses engaged in a de luxe trade, glovers, bonnet makers, perfumers and so on.
1996 *Spectator* Margaret Cooper, at the age of about 500 and as pretty as springtime, is a catalyst de luxe.

démarche /demarʃ/ (*plural same*), /deɪ'mɑːʃ/ *noun* M17 French (from *démarcher* to take steps, from *dé-* + *marcher* to march). A political or diplomatic action or initiative.

1996 *Spectator* John Lloyd... and Barry Cox... urged Mr Blair to stand against John Smith.... Mr Blair was right to disregard their

advice... But the Cox/Lloyd *démarche* is interesting...

démenti /demãti/ *noun* plural pronounced same L16 French (from *démentir* to contradict, from *dé-* from + *mentir* to lie). A contradiction, a denial; now *especially* an official denial of a published statement.

demi-caractère /ˌdɛmikarək'tɛː/, *foreign* /dəmikaraktɛr/ (*plural same*) *noun* L18 French (literally, 'half character'). *Ballet* A style of ballet having elements of character dance, but executed with steps based on the classical technique.

demi-glace /'dɛmɪglas/ *noun* E20 French (literally, 'half-glaze'). *Cookery* A rich, glossy brown sauce from which the liquid has been partially evaporated, typically flavoured with wine and served with meat. In full *demi-glace sauce*.

demilune /'dɛmɪluːn/ *noun & adjective* E18 French (literally, 'half-moon'). **A** *noun* A crescent or half-circle, or a thing of this shape. **B** *adjective* Crescent-shaped, semicircular.

demi-mondaine /dəmimõden/ (*plural same*), /ˌdɛmɪmɒn'deɪn/ *noun* L19 French (from as next). A woman considered to belong to the DEMI-MONDE.

1996 *Spectator* Most of my romantic entanglements have been less *demi-mondaine* than mundane.

demi-monde /dəmimõd/, /ˌdɛmɪ'mɒnd/, /'dɛmɪmɒnd/ *noun* M19 French (literally, 'half world'). **1** (In 19th-century France) a class of women considered to be of doubtful social standing and morality. **2** A group of people on the fringes of respectable society.

■ *Le Demi-monde* was the title of a novel (1855) by the younger Alexandre Dumas.
1988 K. Adler *Unknown Impressionists* La Grenouillère was well known as a favourite place for Parisian bourgeois men to meet women of the demi-monde....

demi-pension /dəmipãsjõ/ *noun* M20 French. (Originally in France and French-speaking countries) hotel accommodation with bed, breakfast, and one main meal per day; half-board.

attributive **1995** D. Lodge *Therapy* We were on *demi-pension* terms at the hotel.

demi-sec /dɛmɪ'sɛk/, *foreign* /dəmisɛk/ *adjective* M20 French (literally, 'half-dry'). (Of wine) medium dry.

demitasse /'dɛmɪtas/, *foreign* /dəmitas/ (*plural same*) *noun* M19 French (literally, 'half-cup'). (The contents of) a small coffee cup.

démodé /demɔde/, /deɪ'məʊdeɪ/ *adjective* L19 French (past participle of *démoder* to send, go out of fashion, from *dé-* from + *mode* fashion). Out of fashion, unfashionable.

demoiselle /dɛmwɑː'zɛl/ *noun* E16 French (= damsel). **1** A small Old World crane, *Anthropoides virgo*, with a black head and breast and white ear tufts, breeding in south-east Europe and central Asia. Now usually more fully *demoiselle crane*. **2** A damselfly, especially an agrion. **3** A damselfish.

■ Originally used in the archaic or literary sense 'a young woman'.

Demos /'diːmɒs/ *noun* plural **Demoi** /'diːmɔɪ/ L18 Greek (*dēmos*). The common people of an ancient Greek State; the populace of a democracy as a political unit.

dengue /'dɛŋgi/ *noun* (also **denga** /'dɛŋgə/) E19 West Indian Spanish (from Kiswahili *denga*, *dinga* (in full *kidinga-popo*), identified with Spanish *dengue* fastidiousness, prudery, with reference to the dislike of movement by affected patients). A debilitating tropical viral disease, transmitted by mosquitoes, and causing sudden fever and acute pains in the joints. Also *dengue fever*.

de nos jours /də no ʒur/ *postpositive adjective phrase* E20 French (= of our days). Of the present time; contemporary.

1995 *Times* Much was made in the late Eighties about comics being the rock stars *de nos jours* and so forth.

denouement /deɪ'nuːmɒ̃/, /deɪ'nuːmɒn/ *noun* (also **dénouement**) M18 French (*dénouemont*, from *dénouer* to unknot). The final part of a play, novel, or other narrative in which the strands of the plot are drawn together and matters are explained or resolved; the outcome of a situation, when something is decided or made clear.

1996 *Times* The denouement [of *An Ideal Husband*] depends on the accidental discovery of a brooch the villainess has stolen, by the very man who years before bought it.

de novo /deɪ 'nəʊvəʊ/, /diː/ *adverb & adjective phrase* E17 Latin (= from new). Starting again from the beginning.

1995 *Country Life* A splendid example of a private Jacobean chapel built *de novo* for Anglican worship is that at Hatfield House, Hertfordshire, created for Robert Cecil, 1st Earl of Salisbury, in 1607–12.

deoch an doris /dɒx (ə)n 'dɒrɪs/, /dɒk/ *noun phrase* (also **doch an doris**) M17 Gaelic (*deoch an doruis* (Irish *deoch an dorais*) a drink at the door). (In Scotland and Ireland) a final drink taken before parting, a stirrup cup.

Deo gratias /deɪəʊ 'grɑːtɪəs/, /'grɑːʃɪəs/ *interjection* L16 Latin (= (we give) thanks to God). Thanks be to God.

Deo volente /ˌdeɪəʊ vɒ'lɛnteɪ/ *adverb phrase* M18 Latin. God willing; if nothing prevents it.

■ Abbreviated to *d.v.*

dépaysé /depeize/ *adjective* (feminine **dépaysée**) E20 French (= (removed) from one's own country). Removed from one's habitual surroundings.

de profundis /deɪ prə'fundiːs/ *noun & adverb phrase* LME Latin (= from the depths). **A** *noun phrase* **1** A psalm of penitence; specifically Psalm 130. **2** A cry of appeal from the depths of sorrow or anguish. **B** *adverb phrase* Out of the depths. Used to convey that one's most heartfelt feelings of sorrow or anguish are being expressed.

■ The initial words of Psalm 130: 'Out of the deep have I called unto thee O Lord' (Book of Common Prayer). *De Profundis* was the title of Oscar Wilde's posthumously published apologia written after being sentenced to a term of imprisonment in Reading Gaol, and modern use of the phrase often contains an unspoken allusion to Wilde's work (see quotation).

A 1996 *Times* Johnson has given us an excellent Profession of Faith: his *De Profundis* has yet to come.

déraciné /derasine/ (*plural same*), /deɪ'rasɪneɪ/ *adjective & noun* (feminine **déracinée**) E20 French (= uprooted, past participial adjective of *déraciner*). **A** *adjective* Uprooted from one's environment; displaced geographically or socially. **B** *noun* A *déraciné* person.

derailleur /dɪˈreɪlə/, /dɪˈreɪljə/ *noun* M20 French (*dérailleur*, from *dérailler* to cause (a train) to run off the rails). A bicycle gear which works by lifting the chain from one sprocket wheel to another of a different size.

de rigueur /də rigœr/, /də rɪˈgəː/ *predicative adjective phrase* M19 French (literally, 'in strictness'). Required by etiquette or current fashion.
> **1995** *Spectator* It was *de rigueur* to dream on the eve of a battle, before giving birth to a hero, or before one's own assassination.

dernier cri /dɛrnjeˈkri/, /ˌdəːnjeɪ ˈkriː/ *noun phrase* (also **le dernier cri**) L19 French (literally, '(the) last cry'). The very latest fashion.
> **1996** *Times* I loathed every minute of the staging, while recognising that it is probably the *dernier cri* (this week) of the producer's art.

derrière /dɛrjɛr/, /dɛrɪˈɛː/ (*plural same*) *noun* L18 French (= behind). The buttocks.
> ■ Usually only in humorous or colloquial use.
> **1995** *Times* At the autumn fashion collections, hourglass girls sashayed down the catwalk all décolletage and derrière with only a wasp waist to separate them.

dervish /ˈdəːvɪʃ/ *noun* L16 Turkish (*derviş* from Persian *darvīš* poor, a religious mendicant). A Muslim (specifically Sufi) religious man or woman who has taken vows of poverty and austerity. Dervishes first appeared in the 12th century; they were noted for their wild or ecstatic rituals and were known as *dancing*, *whirling*, or *howling dervishes* according to the practice of their order.

desaparecido /ˌdesapareˈsido/ *noun* plural **desaparecidos** /ˌdesapareˈsidos/ L20 Spanish (= (one who has) disappeared). (In Argentina) a person who disappeared during the period of military rule between 1976 and 1983, presumed killed by members of the armed services or the police; a child removed from his or her arrested parents and placed with another family without consent.
> ■ By extension, the word is now also applied to any persons who have vanished or been separated from their real families under totalitarian regimes in South America.
> **1987** *New Yorker* People whose children or husbands or wives were *desaparecidos*—disappeared ones—would go to Cardinal Arns, and the Cardinal would stop whatever he was doing and drive to the prisons, the police, the Second Army headquarters.

descamisado /ˌdeskamiˈsado/, /dɛsˌkamiˈsaːdəʊ/ *noun* plural **descamisados** /ˌdeskamiˈsados/, /dɛsˌkamiˈsaːdəʊz/ M19 Spanish (= shirtless). *History* An extreme liberal in the Spanish Revolutionary War of 1820–3; *transferred* an impoverished revolutionary, a very poor person.
> ■ A similar sartorial deficiency gave rise to the earlier French Revolutionary equivalent, SANSCULOTTE.
> **1979** J. M. Taylor *Evita Perón* His speech declared Eva the martyr of the descamisados, an example given by God to the Argentinian people of self-sacrifice and faith.

déshabillé /dezabije/ (*plural same*) *noun* (also **deshabille**, **déshabille** /deɪzə ˈbiːl/, /deɪzaˈbiːjeɪ/, **dishabille** /dɪsəˈbiːl/) L17 French (= undressed). The state of being only partly or scantily clothed. Chiefly in *in dishabille*, *en déshabillé*.

desideratum /dɪˌzɪdəˈraːtəm/, /dɪˌzɪdə ˈreɪtəm/, /dɪˌsɪdəˈraːtəm/ *noun* plural **desiderata** /dɪˌzɪdəˈraːtə/, /dɪˌzɪdəˈreɪtə/, /dɪˌsɪdəˈraːtə/ M17 Latin (= something desired, neuter singular of past participle of *desiderare* to feel the lack of, desire). A thing for which desire is felt; a thing lacked and wanted, a requirement.
> **1995** *Spectator* Stalin's demands changed remarkably little between 1939 and 1945; all that altered was his ability to obtain his desiderata.

détente /deɪˈtãː(n)t/, /deɪˈtã(n)t/, /deɪ ˈtɑːnt/, /deɪˈtɒnt/ *noun* E20 French (= loosening, relaxation). The easing of hostility or strained relations, especially between countries.

détenu /deɪtəˈnuː/; *foreign* /detəny/ (*plural same*) *noun* (also **detenu**) E19 French (use as noun of past participle of *détenir* to detain). A person held in custody, a detainee, now especially in the Indian subcontinent.

detour /'di:tʊə/ *noun & verb* (also **détour** /'deɪtʊə/) M18 French (*détour* change of direction, from *détourner* to turn away). **A** *noun* **1** A long or roundabout route that is taken to avoid something or to visit somewhere along the way. **2** An alternative route for use by traffic when the usual road is temporarily closed. **B** *verb* **1** *intransitive* Make a detour. **2** *transitive* Bypass, make a detour round.

de trop /də tro/, /də 'trəʊ/ *adjective phrase* M18 French (literally, 'excessive'). Not wanted, unwelcome.

> **1996** *Oldie* But now blackboards and chalk are rapidly becoming *de trop*, replaced by whiteboards and markers.

deus absconditus /ˌdeɪəs ab'skʊnd ɪtəs/, /ˌdi:əs/ *noun phrase* M20 Latin (= hidden god). *Theology* A divine being that is inaccessible to human perception.

> ∎ Cf. Isaiah 45:15 'Verily thou art a God that hidest thyself, O God of Israel...'

deus ex machina /ˌdeɪəs ɛks 'makɪnə/, /ˌdi:əs ɛks 'makɪnə/ *noun phrase* L17 Modern Latin (translation of Greek *theos ek mēkhanēs*, literally, 'god from the machinery'). An unexpected power or event arriving in the nick of time to save a seemingly hopeless situation, especially as a contrived plot device in a play or novel.

> ∎ The 'machine' was originally the device by which actors representing gods were suspended above the stage in the theatre in classical antiquity. The denouement of the play was brought about by their intervention.
>
> *attributive* **1996** *Spectator* The *deus ex machina* resolution of the drama may provide one of the most feeble dénouements in all opera...

deva /'deɪvə/ *noun* E19 Sanskrit (= a god, (originally) a shining one). Any of a class of deities in Vedic mythology; any of the lower-level gods in Hinduism and Buddhism.

devadasi /deɪvə'dɑ:si/ *noun* E19 Sanskrit (*devadāsī*, literally, 'female servant of a god' (cf. preceding)). A hereditary female dancer in a Hindu temple.

développé /devlɔpe/ *noun plural* pronounced same E20 French (use as noun of past participle of *développer* to develop). *Ballet* A movement in which one leg is raised and then kept in a fully extended position.

dhal /dɑ:l/ *noun* (also **dal**) L17 Hindi (*dāl*). (In Indian cookery) split pulses (especially the seed of the pigeon-pea, *Cajanus cajan*).

dhamma /'dɑ:mə/, /'dʌmə/ *noun* E20 Pali (from as *dharma*). Especially among Theravada Buddhists, DHARMA.

dharma /'dɑ:mə/, /'də:mə/ *noun* L18 Sanskrit (= something established, decree, custom; cf. DHAMMA). (In *Hinduism*) social or caste custom, right behaviour, law; justice, virtue; natural or essential state or function, nature. (In *Buddhism*) universal truth or law, especially as proclaimed by Buddha.

dharmsala /'dɑ:msɑ:lə/, /'də:mʃɑ:lɑ:/ *noun* (also **dharmasala** /'dɑ:məsɑ:lə/, /'də:məʃɑ:lɑ:/) E19 Sanskrit (representing Hindi pronunciation of Sanskrit *dharma-śālā*, from *dharma* + *śālā* house). (In the Indian subcontinent) a building devoted to religious or charitable purposes, especially a rest house for travellers.

dhobi /'dəʊbi/ *noun* (also **dhoby, dhobie**) M19 Hindi (*dhobī*, from *dhob* washing). (In the Indian subcontinent) a washerman or washerwoman.

dhoti /'dəʊti/ *noun* (also formerly **dhootie** /'du:ti/ and other variants) E17 Hindi (*dhotī*). A cloth worn by male Hindus, the ends being passed through the legs and tucked in at the waist.

dhow /daʊ/ *noun* L18 Arabic (*dāwa*, probably related to Marathi *dāw*). A lateen-rigged sailing vessel with one or two masts, used chiefly in the Arabian region.

diablerie /dɪ'ɑ:bləri/ *noun* (also **diablery**) M18 French (from ecclesiastical Latin *diabolus* devil). **1** The quality of being reckless or wild in a charismatic way. **2** Sorcery supposedly assisted by the devil.

diabolo /dɪ'abələʊ/, /dʌɪ'abələʊ/ *noun* plural **diabolos** E20 Italian (from ecclesiastical Latin *diabolus* devil). A game in which a two-headed top is thrown up and caught on a string stretched between two sticks; the top used in this game.

■ The game was formerly called *devil on two sticks*.

diabolus in musica /dɪˈɑːbələs in ˌmjuːˈziːkə/ *noun phrase* M20 Latin (literally, 'the devil in music'). *Music* The interval of the diminished fifth.

■ So called because of its displeasing or unsettling effect.

attributive **1995** J. D. Barrow *Artful Universe* An acoustic form of this perceptual ambiguity exists with musical chord sequences displaying the *diabolus in musica* phenomenon.

diaeresis /daɪˈɪərɪsɪs/, /daɪˈɛrɪsɪs/ *noun* (also **dieresis**) plural **diaereses** /daɪˈɪərɪsiːz/ L16 Latin (from Greek *diairesis* noun of action from *diairein* to take apart, divide). **1** The sign placed over a vowel to indicate that it is pronounced separately, as in *Brontë*, *naive*. **2** The division of one syllable into two, especially by sounding a diphthong as two vowels. **3** *Prosody* A natural rhythmic break in a line of verse where the end of a metrical foot coincides with the end of a word or phrase.

diamanté /dɪəˈmɒnteɪ/, *foreign* /djamɑ̃tɛ/ (*plural of noun same*) *adjective & noun* E20 French (past participle of *diamanter* to set with diamonds, from *diamant* diamond). **A** *adjective* Decorated with glass cut to resemble diamonds. **B** *noun* Costume jewellery or fabric made or decorated with glass that is cut to resemble diamonds.

diaspora /daɪˈasp(ə)rə/ *noun* (also **Diaspora**) L19 Greek (from *diaspeirein* to disperse, scatter). **1** The dispersion of the Jews beyond Israel; Jews living outside Israel. **2** The dispersion or spread of any people from their original homeland; people who have spread or been dispersed from their homeland.

■ The main diaspora began in the 8th–9th centuries BC, and even before the sack of Jerusalem in AD 70 the number of Jews dispersed by the diaspora was greater than that living in Israel. Thereafter, Jews were dispersed even more widely throughout the Roman world and beyond.

dictum /ˈdɪktəm/ *noun* plural **dicta**, /ˈdɪktə/, **dictums** L16 Latin (= something

said). **1** A formal pronouncement from an authoritative source. **2** *Law* An expression of opinion by a judge which is not essential to the decision and so has no binding authority as precedent. See also OBITER DICTUM. **3** A short statement that expresses a general truth or principle.

1 1996 *Spectator* Conan Doyle's dictum— 'When you have eliminated the impossible, whatever remains, *however improbable*, must be the truth'—simply doesn't apply.

didgeridoo /ˌdɪdʒ(ə)rɪˈduː/ *noun* (also **didjeridoo, didgeridu**) E20 Aboriginal (of imitative origin). An Australian Aboriginal wind instrument in the form of a long wooden tube, traditionally made from a hollow branch, which is blown to produce a deep, resonant sound.

dieresis variant of DIAERESIS.

Dies Irae /ˌdiːeɪz ˈɪərʌɪ/, /ˌdiːeɪz ˈɪərəɪ/ *noun phrase* E19 Latin (= day of wrath). A Latin hymn sung in a Mass for the dead.

■ The text of which *Dies irae* is the opening phrase is attributed to Thomas of Celano (*c.*1250).

dies non /ˈdʌɪiːz ˈnɒn/ *noun phrase* plural same E19 Latin (literally, 'a non day'). A day on which no legal business can be done, or which does not count for legal purposes.

■ Used in its original legal sense, it is an abbreviated form of the following, but it is also applied in other contexts.

dies non juridicus /ˌdʌɪiːz nɒn dʒʊəˈrɪdɪkəs/ *noun phrase* plural **dies non juridici** /ˌdʌɪiːz nɒn dʒʊəˈrɪdɪsʌɪ/ E17 Latin (literally, 'non-judicial day'). *Law* A day on which no legal business is enacted.

differentia /dɪfəˈrɛnʃɪə/ *noun* plural **differentiae** /dɪfəˈrɛnʃɪiː/ L17 Latin (= difference). **1** A distinguishing mark or characteristic. **2** *Logic* An attribute that distinguishes a species from other species of the same genus.

digamma /dʌɪˈgamə/ *noun* L17 Latin (from Greek, from *di-* twice + *gamma* (from the shape of the letter, a GAMMA with a doubled cross-stroke)). The sixth letter of the original Greek alphabet, probably equivalent to W, later dis-used.

digestif /diʒɛstif/ (plural same), /dʌɪ-'dʒɛstɪf/ noun E20 French (= digestive). A drink, especially an alcoholic one, drunk before or after a meal in order to aid the digestion.

diktat /'dɪktat/ noun M20 German (from Latin dictatum use as noun of neuter past participle of dictare to dictate). **1** An order or decree imposed by someone in power without popular consent; a severe settlement, especially one imposed by a victorious nation on a defeated one. **2** A categorical assertion.

dilettante /dɪlɪ'tanti/ noun & adjective plural **dilettanti** /dɪlɪ'tanti/, **dilettantes** M18 Italian (use as noun of verbal adjective from dilettare from Latin delectare to delight). **A** noun **1** A person who takes an interest in a subject merely as a pastime and without serious study, a dabbler. **2** A lover of the fine arts; a person who cultivates the arts as an amateur. Archaic. **B** adjective Relating to or characteristic of a dilettante; amateur.

■ The English use of the word is linked to the 18th-century British fashion for wealthy young aristocrats to travel to Italy on the so-called Grand Tour to study the remains of classical antiquity there and to purchase sculptures, coins, and other objects for their personal collections. In 1733–4 'some gentlemen who had travelled in Italy, desirous of encouraging, at home, a taste for those objects which had contributed so much to their entertainment abroad' founded the Society of Dilettanti. Despite Horace Walpole's unkind observation that the nominal qualification for membership of the Dilettanti was 'having been in Italy, and the real one, being drunk', the society subsequently financed some major expeditions and publications and generally played a key role in developing British knowledge of the ancient world.
A.2 1996 Spectator . . . the show is an oasis of antique elegance and calm—where would-be dilettanti can take wistful refuge from the mêlée of not-so-grand tourists in the Museum's entrance hall, and wish themselves transported to 18th-century Naples.

diminuendo /dɪˌmɪnjʊ'ɛndəʊ/ noun, adverb, adjective, & verb L18 Italian (= diminishing, present participle of diminuire from Latin deminuere to lessen). Music **A** noun plural **diminuendos, diminuendi** /dɪˌmɪnjʊ'ɛndi/ A gradual decrease in loudness in a piece of music; a passage to be performed with a gradual decrease in loudness. **B** adverb & adjective (Especially as a direction) with a gradual decrease in loudness. **C** intransitive verb Decrease in loudness or intensity.

dim sum /dɪm 'sʌm/ noun phrase (also **dim sim** /dɪm 'sɪm/ and other variants) plural **dim sum(s)** etc. M20 Chinese (Cantonese) (tǐm sam, from tǐm dot + sam heart). A Chinese dish of small steamed or fried savoury dumplings containing various fillings.

dinero /dɪ'nɛːrəʊ/ noun plural **dineros** L17 Spanish (= coin, money from Latin denarius a silver coin). **1** History Formerly, a monetary unit in Spain and Peru, now disused. **2** Money. United States slang.

Ding an sich /dɪŋ an 'zɪç/ noun phrase M19 German (= thing in itself). Philosophy A thing as it is in itself, not mediated through perception by the senses or conceptualization, and therefore unknowable. Cf. NOUMENON.

Directoire /dɪ'rɛktwɑː/, foreign /dirɛk'war/ (plural of noun same) noun & adjective L18 French (from Late Latin directorium use as noun of neuter singular of directorius from director person who directs) **A** noun History The French Directory (1795–9). **B** adjective Also **directoire**. Relating to a neoclassical decorative style intermediate between the more ornate Louis XVI style and the Empire style, prevalent at the time of the Directory.

■ The adjective is often found in the phrase directoire knickers or drawers (women's knee-length knickers elasticated at the knee and waist).

dirigisme /diriʒism/ noun (also **dirigism** /'dɪrɪdʒɪz(ə)m/) M20 French (from diriger from Latin dirigere to direct). State control of economic and social matters.

1996 Times French dirigisme preserved their oyster. English laissez faire turned the oyster from poor man's food into an impossible luxury.

dirigiste /diriʒist/ *adjective & noun* M20 French (as preceding). **A** *adjective* Relating to DIRIGISME. **B** *noun* A proponent of DIRIGISME.

A 1995 *New Scientist* But it is surely off-beam to suggest an outright ban is somehow less dirigiste than piecemeal regulation.
B 1995 *Times* The European Community, which had been designed to make Europe more competitive, was already moving towards a bureaucratic model based on those old European *dirigistes* Bismarck and Colbert.

dirndl /'də:nd(ə)l/ *noun* M20 German (dialect, diminutive of *Dirne* girl). **1** A dress in the style of Alpine peasant costume with a bodice and full skirt. **2** A full wide skirt with a tight waistband. More fully *dirndl skirt*.

discobolus /dɪ'skɒbələs/ *noun* plural **discoboli** /dɪ'skɒbəlʌɪ/, /dɪ'skɒbɑ:li:/ E18 Latin (from Greek *diskobolos*, from *diskos* discus + *-bolos* throwing, from *ballein* to throw). A discus-thrower in ancient Greece; a statue representing one in action.

discothèque /'dɪskətɛk/ *noun* (also **discotheque**) M20 French (originally = record library (after *bibliothèque*)). A place or event at which recorded pop music is played for dancing.

■ Now almost universally abbreviated to *disco*.

diseuse /di:'zə:z/, *foreign* /dizøz/ *noun* plural pronounced same L19 French (= talker, feminine of *diseur*, from *dire* to say). A female artiste who specializes in monologue.

dishabille variant of DÉSHABILLÉ.

disinvoltura /ˌdisinvɔl'tu:ra/ *noun* M19 Italian (from *disinvolto* unembarrassed, from *disinvolgere* to unwind). Self-assurance; lack of constraint.

disjecta membra /dɪsˌjɛktə 'mɛmbrə/ *noun phrase plural* (also **disiecta membra**) E18 Latin. Scattered fragments, especially of written work.

■ Alteration of Latin *disjecti membra poetae* 'limbs of a dismembered poet' (Horace *Satires* I.iv.62). The word order *membra disjecta* is apparently a later (M20) variant.

dissensus /dɪ'sɛnsəs/ *noun* M20 Latin (= disagreement; or from *dis-* + *(con)sensus*). Widespread dissent; the reverse of consensus.

distingué /dɪ'staŋɡeɪ/, *foreign* /distẽge/ *adjective* (feminine **distinguée**) E19 French (= distinguished). Having an air of distinction; having a distinguished appearance or manner.

distrait /dɪ'streɪ/, /'dɪstreɪ/, *foreign* /distrɛ/ *adjective* (feminine **distraite** /dɪ'streɪt/, /'dɪstreɪt/, *foreign* /distrɛt/) LME French (from Old French *destrait* past participle of *destraire* from Latin *distrahere* to distract). **1** Distracted in mind. **2** Divided, separated. **3** Absent-minded, distracted; not paying attention.

■ Sense 3 represents an 18th-century reborrowing from French after *distrait* had become obsolete in English in its two earlier senses.

3 1996 *Spectator* On my visit, ... the place was crowded, though emptying, and the young, slightly inept staff *distrait*.

dithyramb /'dɪθɪram(b)/ *noun* (also in Latin form **dithyrambus** /ˌdɪθɪ'rambəs/, plural **dithyrambi** /ˌdɪθɪ'rambʌɪ/) E17 Latin (*dithyrambus* from Greek *dithurambos*). **1** A wild choral hymn of ancient Greece, especially one dedicated to Dionysus. **2** A passionate or inflated poem, speech, or other writing.

ditto /'dɪtəʊ/ *noun* plural **dittos** E17 Italian (dialect (Tuscan) variant of *detto* said, from Latin *dictus* past participle of *dicere* to say). **1** The same thing again (used in lists and accounts and often indicated by two apostrophes or commas under the word or figure to be repeated). **2** Used to indicate that something already said is applicable a second time. *Colloquial*.

■ The word is recorded from the early 17th century in the sense 'in the aforesaid month'.

2 1996 *Times* Anyway, neither Carman, QC, nor Gray, ditto, is going to beg his bread in the gutter...

diva /'di:və/ *noun* L19 Italian (from Latin *diva* goddess). A celebrated female opera singer; a famous female singer of popular music; a woman regarded as temperamental or haughty.

1995 *Times* In person, she [sc. Dawn Upshaw] has few diva tendencies. The morning after her Berlin recital, she came to her interview minutes after stepping from the shower—hair still wet, face scrubbed.

divertimento /dɪˌvəːtɪˈmɛntəʊ/, /dɪˌvɛːtɪˈmɛntəʊ/ *noun* plural **divertimenti** /dɪˌvəːtɪˈmɛnti/, **divertimentos** M18 Italian (= diversion). *Music* A light and entertaining composition, typically one in the form of a suite for chamber orchestra.

■ The word was first used in English (in the early 18th century) to refer to a diversion or amusement.

divertissement /ˌdiːvɛːˈtiːsmɒ̃/, *foreign* /divertismɑ̃/ (*plural pronounced same*) *noun* E18 French (from *divertiss-* stem of *divertir* to divert). **1** A minor entertainment or diversion. **2** A short dance within a ballet that displays a dancer's technical skill without advancing the plot or character development.

1996 *Spectator*...the ballroom scene is constructed as a conventional 19th-century *divertissement*, where the well-regulated choral dancing frames virtuoso duets...

divisi /diˈviːsi/ *adjective & noun* M18 Italian (= divided, plural past participial adjective of *dividere* to divide). *Music* **A** *adjective* With a section of players divided into two or more groups each playing a different part: *violas divisi.* **B** *noun* A passage written or played in this manner.

divorcee /dɪvɔːˈsiː/ *noun* (also (earlier) **divorcé**, feminine **divorcée**, /dɪvɔːˈseɪ/ (*plural same*)) E19 French (partly from *divorcé(e)* use as noun of past participial adjective of *divorcer* to divorce, partly from *divorce* + *-ee* after the French). A divorced person.

djellaba /ˈdʒɛləbə/ *noun* (also **djellabah**, **jellaba**, **jellabah**) E19 Arabic ((Moroccan) *jellāb(a)*, *jellābiyya*). A loose hooded long-sleeved usually woollen cloak of a kind worn originally by Arab men in North Africa.

djibba(h) variant of JIBBA.

djinn see JINN.

docent /ˈdəʊs(ə)nt/ *foreign* /doˈtsɛnt/ *noun* L19 German (*Docent*, *Dozent*, from Latin *docent-* present participial stem of *docere* to teach). **1** (In certain United States and European universities and colleges) a member of the teaching staff immediately below professorial rank. **2** A person who acts as a guide, typically on a voluntary basis, in a museum, art gallery, or zoo.

doch an doris variant of DEOCH AN DORIS.

doctrinaire /ˌdɒktrɪˈnɛː/ *adjective & noun* E19 French (from *doctrine* + *-aire*). **A** *adjective* Seeking to impose a doctrine in all circumstances without regard to practical considerations. **B** *noun* A doctrinaire person.

A 1996 *Country Life* [It] would be easy to imagine this tear-jerking technique being used for propaganda purposes. A clever, doctrinaire film-maker could have a wonderful time with fox cubs.

doek /dʊk/ *noun* L18 South African Dutch, from Dutch (= cloth). (In South Africa) a headscarf.

doge /dəʊ(d)ʒ/ *noun* M16 French ((monosyllabic) from Italian (disyllabic) from Venetian Italian *doze* ultimately from Latin *dux*, *duc-* leader). *History* The chief magistrate in the former republics of Venice and Genoa.

dojo /ˈdəʊdʒəʊ/ *noun* plural **dojos** M20 Japanese (from *dō* way, pursuit + *-jō* a place). A room or hall in which judo or other martial arts are practised; an area of padded mats for the same purpose.

dolce far niente /ˌdɒltʃe far niˈɛnte/ *noun phrase* E19 Italian (= sweet doing nothing). Pleasant idleness.

■ Also in the shortened form *far niente.*

dolce vita /ˌdɒltʃe ˈviːta/, /ˌdəʊltʃeɪ ˈviːtə/ *noun phrase* M20 Italian (= sweet life). A life of luxury, pleasure, and self-indulgence.

■ Frequently preceded by *the* or *la* /la/. The phrase may have been popularized in English by Federico Fellini's film *La Dolce Vita* (1960), which starred Marcello Mastroianni and Anita Ekburg.

1996 *Country Life*...his talent and prospects were regularly undermined by his taste for *la dolce vita.*

doli capax /ˌdɒlɪ ˈkapaks/ *adjective phrase* L17 Latin (from *doli* genitive singular of *dolus* guile, fraud + *capax* capable). *Law* Deemed capable of forming the intent to commit a crime or tort, especially by reason of age (ten years old or older).

doli incapax /ˌdɒlɪ ɪnˈkapaks/ *adjective phrase* L17 Latin (from as DOLI CAPAX). *Law* Deemed incapable of forming the intent to commit a crime or tort, especially by reason of age (under ten years old).

> *attributive* **1996** *Times* . . . the House of Lords shied away from changing the *doli incapax* rule concerning the criminal liability of children.

dolma /ˈdɒlmə/ *noun* plural **dolmas**, **dolmades** /dɒlˈmɑːdɛz/ L17 Modern Greek (*ntolmas* from Turkish *dolma*, from *dolmak* to fill, be filled). A Greek and Turkish delicacy in which ingredients such as spiced rice, meat, and bread are wrapped in vine or cabbage leaves.

dolman /ˈdɒlmən/ *noun* (in sense 1 also written (earlier) **doliman**) L16 French (in sense 1 from French *doliman*; in sense 2 from French *dolman* from German from Hungarian *dolmány*; both ultimately from Turkish *dolama(n)*). **1** A long Turkish robe open in front and with narrow sleeves. **2** A hussar's jacket worn with the sleeves hanging loose. **3** A woman's loose cloak with cape-like sleeves. **4** A loose sleeve cut in one piece with the body of a garment. In full *dolman sleeve*.

dolmus /ˈdɒlmʊʃ/ *noun* M20 Turkish (*dolmuş* filled, (as noun) dolmus). (In Turkey) a shared taxi.

dolus /ˈdɒləs/ *noun* Latin. *Law* Deceit; intentional damage. Cf. DOLI CAPAX.

domaine /dəˈmeɪn/ *noun* M20 French. A vineyard.

> ■ Often in the phrase *domaine-bottled*, indicating that the wine has been bottled at the estate where the grapes of which it is made were grown.

dominee /ˈduːmɪni/, /ˈdʊəmɪni/ *noun* (also (especially as a title) **Dominee**) M20 Afrikaans and Dutch (from Latin *domine*, vocative of *dominus* lord, master). (In South Africa) a pastor of the Dutch Reformed Church.

dominie in *sense 1* /ˈdɒmɪni/; in *sense 2* /ˈdəʊmɪni/, /ˈdɒmɪni/ *noun* L17 Latin (alteration of Latin *domine!* master!, sir!, from *dominus* lord, master, formerly used

as a polite form of address to a clergyman or member of one of the professions). **1** A schoolmaster. Now chiefly *Scottish*. **2** A pastor or clergyman. *United States*.

dominium /dəˈmɪnɪəm/ *noun* M18 Latin. *Law* chiefly *United States*. Ownership and control of property.

> ■ Chiefly in the phrases *dominium directum* 'direct ownership' and *dominium utile* 'ownership of use', differentiating the rights of the owner and those of the tenant who has the use only of something.

don /dɒn/ *noun* E16 Spanish ((in sense 2c Italian) from Latin *dominus* lord, master). **1** (At British universities, especially Oxford and Cambridge) a university teacher, especially a senior member of a college. **2** (**Don**) Used as a title of respect preceding the forename of a Spanish man (originally one of high rank) or (formerly, *humorous*) preceding the name or designation of any man. **b** A Spanish lord or gentleman. **c** A high-ranking or powerful member of the Mafia. *North American slang*.

donatio mortis causa /dəˌneɪʃɪəʊ ˌmɔːtɪs ˈkɔːzə/ *noun phrase* plural **donationes mortis causa** /dəˌneɪʃɪˈəʊniːz/ M17 Latin (= gift by reason of death). *Law* A gift of personal property made by someone who expects to die in the immediate future, taking full effect only after the donor dies.

doner kebab /ˌdɒnə kɪˈbab/, /ˌdəʊnə/, /kəˈbab/, /kəˈbɑːb/ *noun phrase* M20 Turkish (*döner kebab*, from *döner* rotating + *kebap* KEBAB). A Turkish dish consisting of spiced lamb cooked on a vertical rotating spit and served in slices, typically with pitta bread.

donga /ˈdɒŋɡə/ *noun* L19 Nguni. **1** A dry gully, formed by the eroding action of running water. *South Africa* and *Australia*. **2** A makeshift shelter; a temporary dwelling. *Australia*. **3** The bush, the remote countryside. *Australia*.

donnée /dɔne/, /ˈdɒneɪ/ *noun* (also **donné**) L19 French (feminine past participial adjective of *donner* to give). **1** A subject, theme, or motif of a literary work. **2** A basic fact or assumption.

1 **1995** *Spectator* In a preface, Vansittart reveals that he received the *donné* for his novel some 50 years before actually embarking on it.

doosra /ˈduːzrə/ *noun* L20 Hindi and Punjabi (= second, other). *Cricket* A ball which breaks from the leg (to a right-handed batsman), though bowled with an apparent off-break action in order to deceive the batsman.

dop /dɒp/ *noun* L19 South African Dutch (= shell, husk). **1** (In South Africa) brandy, especially of a cheap or inferior kind. In full *dop brandy*. **2** A tot of liquor, especially of wine as given to farm labourers in the Cape Province of South Africa.

doppelgänger /ˈdɔpəlˌgɛŋər/, /ˈdɒp(ə)l ˌgɛŋə/, /ˈdɒp(ə)lˌgaŋə/ *noun* (also **dop-pelganger**) M19 German (literally, 'dou ble-goer'). An apparition or double of a living person.

> **1962** O. Sitwell *Tales My Father Taught Me* I was never able myself to discern the mysterious stranger, and my own feeling was that he must be . . . my father's Narcissus-like *doppelgänger*, a projection from and of his own personality . . .

dos-à-dos /dozadoʊ/, /dəʊzəˈdəʊ/ *adjective, noun, & adverb* (also **do-se-do** /dəʊzɪˈdəʊ/, /dəʊsɪˈdəʊ/, **do-si-do**) M19 French (= back to back). **A** *adjective* (Of two books) bound together with a shared central board and facing in opposite directions. **B** *noun* plural same. A seat or carriage in which the occupants sit back to back. **C** *adverb* Back to back.

dot /dɒt/ *noun* M19 Old and Modern French (from Latin *dos, dot-* dowry). A dowry from which only the interest or annual income was available to the husband. *Archaic.*

double entendre /ˌduːb(ə)l ɒˈtɒːdr(ə)/, *foreign* /dubl ɑ̃tɑ̃dr/ *noun phrase* plural **double entendres** (pronounced same) L17 French (now obsolete (modern *double entente*) = double understanding). A word or phrase open to two interpretations, one of which is usually risqué or indecent. Also, humour using such words or phrases.

> **1996** *Spectator* It seemed as if only I was vulgar enough to be aware of the *double entendre*; one or two other ladies confessed that they were plonkers too.

doublure /dəˈbluə/, /duˈbluə/, *foreign* /dublyr/ (*plural same*) *noun* L19 French (= lining, from *doubler* to line). An ornamental lining, usually of leather, on the inside of a book cover.

douce /duːs/ *adjective* ME Old French (*dous* (modern *doux*), feminine *douce* from Latin *dulcis* sweet). Quiet, sober, sedate. *Scottish* and *northern* (dialect).

> ■ Originally used in Middle English in the sense 'pleasant, sweet'.

douceur /dusœr/, /duːˈsə/ *noun* LME French (from Proto-Romance variant of Latin *dulcor* sweetness). **1** A conciliatory present; a financial inducement, a bribe. **2** A tax benefit available to a person who sells a work of art by private treaty to a public collection rather than on the open market.

> **1** **1996** *Times: Magazine* Journalists . . . take a stern, principled, even po-faced stance against bribery, corruption, inducements and *douceurs*.

douceur de vivre /dusœr də vivr/ *noun phrase* (also **douceur de (la) vie** /dusœr də (la) vi/) M20 French (literally, 'sweetness of living'). A way of living that is pleasant and free from worries.

> **1995** *Spectator L'Heure de Gloire* is also a panorama of the Belle Epoque and the years of *douceur de vivre* that were brought to an end by the first world war.

douche /duːʃ/ *noun & verb* M18 French (from Italian *doccia* conduit pipe, from *docciare* to pour by drops, from Proto-Romance from Latin *ductus* duct). **A** *noun* **1** A shower of water. **2** A jet of liquid applied to part of the body, as a form of bathing or for medicinal purposes; a device for washing out the vagina, as a contraceptive measure. **B** *verb* **1** *transitive verb* Spray or shower with water; administer a douche to. **2** *intransitive verb* Use a douche as a contraceptive measure.

doyen /ˈdɔɪən/, /ˈdwaːjɑ̃/ *noun* L17 French (Old French *d(e)ien* from Late Latin *decanus* chief of a group of ten, from Latin *decem* ten, after *primanus* member of the first legion). The most respected or prominent person in a particular field.

> ■ Found as a rare borrowing from Old French in the Late Middle English period, with the sense of 'a leader or commander

of ten', the word became obsolete after this period and was then reintroduced from Modern French in its modern sense. The English word *dean* (from Anglo-Norman *de(e)n*) is closely related.

1996 *Oldie* Any art critic who goes on the telly to talk about art runs the risk of being compared with the doyen of telly-savants, the late Lord Clark.

doyenne /'dɔɪɛn/, /dɔɪ'ɛn/, /dwɑː'jɛn/ *noun* M19 French (feminine of DOYEN). The most respected or prominent woman in a particular field, a female doyen.

1996 *Times* Elma Browne, the wartime doyenne of London nightclubs, was impressed and offered her a two-week engagement at the Pigalle Club...

dragée /'drɑːʒeɪ/, *foreign* /draʒe/ (*plural same*) *noun* L17 French (Old French *dragie*, from medieval Latin *drageia*, *dragetum*, perhaps from Latin *tragemata* sweetmeats, from Greek). A sweet consisting of a centre covered with some coating, such as a sugared almond; a small silver-coated sugar ball for decorating a cake.

dramatis personae /ˌdramətɪs pəː'səʊnʌɪ/, /ˌdramətɪs pəː'səʊniː/ *noun plural* (frequently treated as *singular*) M18 Latin (= persons of the drama). The characters in a play, novel, or narrative; *figurative* the participants in an event etc.

1996 *Spectator* Rebecca...is the only one of these films in which the terror seems to rise organically from character and psychology and situation—rather than just being imposed on the *dramatis personae* by the dictates of the formula.
figurative **1996** *Times* The *dramatis personae* are the usual cast of Catalan and Basque nationalists.

dramaturge /'dramatəːʤ/ *noun* (also **dramaturg** /drama'təːg/) M19 French (*dramaturge*, German *Dramaturg*, from Greek *dramatourgos*, from *dramat-* drama + *-ergos* worker). A dramatist; *specifically* a literary editor on the staff of a theatre who liaises with authors and edits texts.

Drang nach Osten /ˌdraŋ nax 'ɔstən/ *noun phrase* E20 German (literally, 'drive towards the east'). *History* The German imperialist policy of eastward expansion, especially that espoused under Nazi rule; *transferred* any political or economic drive eastwards.

dreck /drɛk/ *noun* (also **drek**) E20 Yiddish (from *drek* filth, dregs, from a Germanic base shared by Old English *threax*; probably related to Greek *skatos* dung). Rubbish; trash. *Colloquial*.

dreidel /'dreɪd(ə)l/ *noun* (also **dreidl**) M20 Yiddish (*dreydl*, from Middle High German *dræ(je)n* (German *drehen*) to turn). A small four-sided spinning-top with a Hebrew letter on each side, used in Jewish gambling games, especially at Hanukkah. Chiefly *North American*.

dressage /'drɛsɑːʒ/, /'drɛsɑːʤ/ *noun* M20 French (literally, 'training', from *dresser* to train, drill). The art of riding and training a horse in a manner that develops obedience, flexibility, and balance; the execution by a horse of precise movements in response to its rider.

droit /drɔɪt/, *foreign* /drwa/ *noun* LME Old and Modern French (from Proto-Romance use as noun of variant of Latin *directum* neuter of *directus* past participle of *dirigere* to direct, guide). A right; a legal claim; something to which one has a legal claim; a due.

droit de seigneur /ˌdrwa də sɛn'jəː/, *foreign* /drwa də sɛɲœr/ *noun phrase* (also **droit du seigneur**) E19 French (literally, 'lord's right'). The alleged right of a medieval feudal lord to have sexual intercourse with a vassal's bride on her wedding night.

1996 *Times* Droit de seigneur may be harder to trace in fact than in The Marriage of Figaro, but it represents the popular myth of lordly immorality.

dromos /'drɒmɒs/ *noun plural* **dromoi** /'drɒmɔɪ/ M19 Greek (= course, running, avenue). An avenue or passage leading into an ancient Greek temple or tomb, often between rows of columns or statues.

droshky /'drɒʃki/ *noun* (also **drosky** /'drɒʃki/) E19 Russian (*drozhki* plural, diminutive of *drogi* wagon, hearse, plural of *droga* centre pole of a carriage). A low four-wheeled open carriage of a kind formerly used in Russia; any horse-drawn passenger vehicle.

duce /ˈduːtʃeɪ/ *noun* (also **Duce**) E20 Italian. A leader.

■ *Il* (Italian = the) *Duce* was the title assumed by Benito Mussolini (1883–1945), creator and leader of the Fascist State in Italy; hence *duce* in English usage generally has derogatory overtones.

duchesse /duːˈʃɛs/, /ˈdʌtʃɪs/, /ˈdʌtʃɛs/, *foreign* /dyʃɛs/ (*plural same*) *noun* (also **Duchesse**) L18 French (from medieval Latin *ducissa* feminine from Latin *dux* leader). **1** A chaise longue consisting of two facing armchairs connected by a detachable footstool. **2** A dressing table with a pivoting mirror. More fully *duchesse dressing table*. **3** More fully *duchesse satin*, *satin duchesse*. A soft, heavy, glossy kind of satin, usually of silk.

■ Also in several English phrases: e.g. *duchesse lace* (a kind of fine Brussels pillow lace characterized by bold floral patterns worked with a fine thread); *duchesse potatoes* (mashed potatoes mixed with egg, moulded into small cakes and baked or fried); *duchesse set* (lace mats for a dressing table); *duchesse sleeve* (a two-thirds-length sleeve with an elaborate trim).

duende /duːˈɛndeɪ/, *foreign* /ˈdwende/ *noun* E20 Spanish (contraction of *duen de casa*, from *dueño de casa* owner of the house). **1** A quality of passion and inspiration. **2** A spirit, a ghost.

duenna /djuːˈɛnə/ *noun* M17 Spanish (*dueña*, *duenna* from Latin *domina* lady, mistress). An older woman acting as a governess and companion to one or more girls, especially within a Spanish family; a chaperone.

du jour /dy ʒur/ *postpositive adjective phrase* L20 French (= of the day). Used to describe something that is enjoying great but probably short-lived popularity or publicity.

dulciana /dʌlsɪˈɑːnə/ *noun* L18 Medieval Latin (from Latin *dulcis* sweet). *Music* An organ stop, typically with small conical open metal pipes.

dulia /djuˈlʌɪə/ *noun* LME Medieval Latin (from Greek *douleia* servitude, from *doulos* slave). *Roman Catholic Church* The reverence accorded to saints and angels.

■ Cf. LATRIA. Similar distinctions in degrees of veneration obtain in the Orthodox Churches, *dulia* being the honour paid to icons as representative of the saints.

duma /ˈduːmə/, /ˈdjuːmə/ *noun* L19 Russian. *History* A Russian elective municipal council; *specifically* the elective legislative council of state of 1906–17; the Russian parliament.

dummkopf /ˈdʊmkʊpf/ *noun* (also **domcop**) E19 German (from *dumm* stupid + *Kopf* head; obsolete variant *domcop* from Dutch). A stupid person, a blockhead.

■ Slang, originating in the United States.

duo /ˈdjuːəʊ/ *noun* plural **duos** L16 Italian ((whence also French) from Latin = two). **1** *Music* A duet. **2** A pair of people or things, especially in music or entertainment.

duodecimo /ˌdjuːəʊˈdɛsɪməʊ/ *noun* plural **duodecimos** M17 Latin ((*in*) *duodecimo* in a twelfth (sc. of a sheet), from Latin *duodecimus* twelfth). A size of book or paper in which each leaf is one twelfth of the size of a standard printing sheet; a book of this size. (Abbreviation *12mo*.)

duomo /ˈdwəʊməʊ/, *foreign* /ˈdwomo/ *noun* (also (earlier) **domo**) plural **duomos** /ˈdwəʊməʊz/, **duomi** /ˈdwomi/ M16 Italian (= dome). An Italian cathedral.

durbar /ˈdəːbɑː/ *noun* E17 Urdu (from Persian *darbār* court). A public reception held by an Indian prince or by a British governor or viceroy in India. Also, the court of an Indian ruler.

durchkomponiert /ˌdʊrçkɔmpoˈniːrt/ *adjective* L19 German (from *durch* through + *komponiert* composed). *Music* (Of a composition, especially a song) not based on repeated sections or verses, especially having different music for each verse. Also called through-composed.

duumvir /djuːˈʌmvə/ *noun* plural **duumvirs**, in Latin form **duumviri** /djuːˈʌmvɪrʌɪ/ E17 Latin (singular from *duum virum* of the two men). (In ancient Rome) either of a pair of magistrates or officials holding a joint office; *generally* either of two people with joint authority, a coalition of two people.

duvet /ˈdjuːveɪ/, /ˈduːveɪ/ *noun* M18 French (= down). A thick soft quilt filled with down, feathers, or synthetic fibre, used instead of other bedclothes.

dux /dʌks/ *noun* plural **duces** /ˈdjuːsiːz/, **duxes** M18 Latin (= leader). The top pupil in a class or school. Chiefly in *Scotland, New Zealand*, and *South Africa*.
■ Originally used, in the mid 18th century, to denote the leading voice or instrument in a fugue or canon.

duxelles /ˈdʌks(ə)lz/, *foreign* /dyksɛl/ *noun* L19 French (Marquis *d'Uxelles*, 17th-century French nobleman). *Cookery* A preparation of mushrooms sautéed with onions, shallots, garlic, and parsley and used to make stuffing or sauce.

d.v. abbreviation of DEO VOLENTE.

dybbuk /ˈdɪbʊk/ *noun* (also **dibbuk**) plural **dybbukim** /ˈdɪbʊkɪm/, **dybbuks** E20 Yiddish (*dibek* from Hebrew *dibbûq*, from *dāḇaq* to cling, cleave). (In Jewish folklore) a malevolent wandering spirit that enters and possesses the body of a living person until exorcized.

dysphoria /dɪsˈfɔːrɪə/ *noun* M19 Greek (*dusphoria* malaise, discomfort, from *dusphoros* hard to bear, from *dus-* + *pherein* to bear). *Psychiatry* a state of unease or generalized dissatisfaction with life. Opposed to euphoria.

dyspnoea /dɪspˈniːə/ *noun* (also **dyspnea**) M17 Latin (from Greek *duspnoia*, from *dus-* + *pnoē* breathing). *Medicine* Difficulty in breathing or shortness of breath, as a symptom of disease.

dystopia see UTOPIA.

eau /əʊ/, *foreign* /o/ *noun* plural **eaux** pronounced same E19 French. Water.

■ Occurs in English only in various phrases, mainly the names of liquids used in medicine or perfumery.

eau de Cologne /ˌəʊdəkə'ləʊn/ *noun* E19 French (= water of Cologne). A toilet water with a strong scent, originally produced at Cologne, Germany.

eau de Nil /ˌəʊdə'niːl/, *foreign* /odnil/ *noun phrase* L19 French (*eau-de-Nil*, literally, 'water of the Nile'). A pale greenish colour (purportedly resembling the waters of the River Nile).

eau de toilette /ˌəʊ də twaː'lɛt/, *foreign* /o də twalɛt/ *noun phrase* E20 French (= toilet water). A dilute form of perfume; toilet water.

eau de vie /ˌəʊdə'viː/, *foreign* /odvi/ *noun phrase* M18 French (*eau-de-vie*, literally, 'water of life'). Brandy.

écarté /eɪ'kɑːteɪ/, *foreign* /ekarte/ *noun* E19 French (past participle of *écarter* to discard, from *é-* + *carte* card). **1** A card game for two people, originating in 19th-century France, in which thirty-two cards are used and cards may be discarded in exchange for others. **2** *Ballet* A position in which the dancer, facing diagonally towards the audience, extends one leg in the air to the side with the arm of the same side raised above the head and the other arm extended to the side.

Ecce Homo /ˌɛki 'həʊməʊ/ *interjection & noun phrase* E17 Latin. **A** *interjection* Behold the Man! **B** *noun phrase Art* A portrayal of Jesus wearing the crown of thorns.

■ The source is the Latin text of the account of the presentation of Jesus to the crowd after his trial by Pontius Pilate: 'Then came Jesus forth, wearing the crown of thorns, and the purple robe. And Pilate saith unto them, Behold the man!' (John 19:5).

echelon /'ɛʃəlɒn/, /'eɪʃəlɒn/ *noun* (also **echellon**) L18 French (*échelon*, from *échelle* ladder, from Latin *scala*). **1** A level or rank in an organization, a profession, or society. **2** *Military* A formation of troops, ships, aircraft, or vehicles in parallel lines such that the end of each line is stepped somewhat sideways from that in front; *generally* a formation of people or things arranged, individually or in groups, in a similar stepwise fashion. **3** A part of a military force differentiated by position in battle or by function: *the rear echelon*.

■ Originally used, in the late 18th century, in sense 2.

echinus /ɪ'kʌɪnəs/ *noun* plural **echini** /ɪ'kʌɪnʌɪ/ LME Latin (sense 1 from Greek *ekhinos* hedgehog, sea urchin; the origin of sense 2 (also in Latin and Greek) is unknown). **1** A sea urchin. **2** *Architecture* A rounded moulding next below the abacus on a Doric or Ionic capital.

echt /ɛxt/, *foreign* /ɛçt/ *adjective & adverb* E20 German. **A** *adjective* Authentic, genuine, typical. **B** *adverb* Authentically, genuinely, typically.

> **B** 1995 *Spectator* 'He [sc. Newt Gingrich] doesn't say he's a conservative, he says he's allied to the conservatives' is how Paul Weyrich, head of the *echt*-conservative Free Congress Foundation, explains the relationship.

éclair /eɪ'klɛː/, /ɪ'klɛː/ *noun* M19 French (literally, 'lightning'). A small finger-shaped cake of choux pastry, filled with cream and topped with chocolate icing.

éclaircissement /eklɛrsismã/ *noun* plural pronounced same M17 French (from *éclaircir* to clear up, from *é* (expressing a change of state) + *clair* clear). An enlightening explanation of something that has hitherto been obscure or inexplicable.

éclat /ɛ'klɑ:/, /'eɪklɑ:/, *foreign* /ekla/ *noun*
L17 French (from *éclater* to burst out).
1 Radiance, dazzling effect (now only
figurative); brilliant display. **2** Social
distinction; celebrity, renown. **3** Conspicuous success; universal acclama-
tion. Chiefly as *with* (*great* etc.) *éclat*.

1 1996 *Times* Puccini's La Rondine, staged with
old-fashioned theatrical *éclat* by John Copley…,
was almost as enjoyable.

écorché /'ɛkɔ:ʃeɪ/, *foreign* /ekɔrʃe/ (*plural same*) *noun* M19 French (past participle
of *écorcher* to flay). *Art* A painting or
sculpture of a human figure with the
skin removed to display the muscula-
ture.

écossaise /ɛkɒ'seɪz/, *foreign* /ekɔsɛz/
noun plural pronounced same M19
French (feminine of *écossais* Scottish). An
energetic country dance in duple time
in which couples form lines facing
each other.

ecru /'eɪkru:/, /ɛ'kru:/ *noun* M19 French
(*écru* raw, unbleached). The light fawn
colour of unbleached linen.

editio princeps /ɪˌdɪʃɪəʊ 'prɪnsɛps/
noun phrase plural **editiones principes**
/ɪˌdɪʃɪˌəʊniːz 'prɪnsɪpiːz/ E19 Modern Latin
(from Latin *editio* publication + *princeps*
first). The first printed edition of a
book.

effendi /ɛ'fɛndi/ *noun* E17 Turkish (*efendi*
from Modern Greek *aphentē* vocative of
aphentēs from Greek *authentēs* lord, master). A man of high education or social
standing in an eastern Mediterranean
or Arab country. Frequently (usually
historical) as a title of respect or
courtesy in Turkey or (former) Turkish
territory.

e.g. abbreviation of EXEMPLI GRATIA.

égalité /egalite/ *noun* L18 French (= equality, from *égal* from Latin *aequalis* equal).
The condition of having equal rank,
power, etc. with others.

■ Historically, as part of the rallying cry
of the French Revolution: *Liberté, égalité,
fraternité* 'Liberty, equality, brotherhood'.

ego /'i:ɡəʊ/, /'ɛɡəʊ/ *noun* plural **egos** E19
Latin (= I (pronoun)). **1** A person's sense
of self-esteem or self-importance.

2 *Psychoanalysis* That part of the mind
which has a sense of individuality and
is most conscious of self. **3** *Metaphysics*
Oneself, the conscious thinking subject.

1 1997 *Daily Telegraph* Mum can nurture her
ego by fulfilling the career role set for her…

eheu fugaces /ˌeɪhju: fu:'ɡɑ:si:z/ *interjection* M19 Latin (= alas, the fleeting (years
are hurrying by)). An expression of
regret for the rapidity with which life
passes.

■ The words are from the opening line of
one of Horace's *Odes* (II.xiv).

Eid /i:d/ *noun* (also **Id**) L17 Arabic ('*īd* feast,
festival, from Aramaic). A Muslim festi-
val; *specifically* that marking the end of
the fast of Ramadan (in full *Eid ul-Fitr*
/'i:dʊlfɪtrə/).

eidolon /ʌɪ'dəʊlɒn/ *noun* plural **eidola**
/ʌɪ'dəʊlə/, **eidolons** E19 Greek (*eidōlon*,
from *eidos* form). **1** An idealized person
or thing. **2** A spectre, a phantom.

Einfühlung /'ʌɪnfy:lʊŋ/, /'ʌɪnfu:ləŋ/
noun E20 German (from *ein-* into + *Fühlung*
feeling, from *fühlen* to feel). Empathy.

eisteddfod /ʌɪ'stɛðvɒd/, /ʌɪ'stɛdvəd/
noun plural **eisteddfods, eisteddfodau**
/ʌɪ'stɛðvɒdʌɪ/ E19 Welsh (= session). A
competitive festival of music and
poetry in Wales.

Eiswein /'ʌɪsvʌɪn/ *noun* M20 German
(from *Eis* ice + *Wein* wine). Wine made
from ripe grapes picked while covered
with frost.

ejecta /ɪ'dʒɛktə/ *noun* plural (treated as
plural or *singular*) L19 Latin (= things
thrown out, neuter plural of past participle of *e(j)icere* to eject). **1** *Geology* and
Astronomy Material that is forced or
thrown out, especially as a result of
volcanic eruption, meteoritic impact,
or stellar explosion. **2** Material discharged from the body, *especially* vomit.

■ An earlier (M19) synonym for sense
1 was *ejectamenta*.

ejido /e'xido/, /eɪ'hi:dəʊ/ *noun* plural
ejidos /e'xidos/, /eɪ'hi:dəʊz/ L19 Mexican
Spanish (from Spanish = common land
(on the road leading out of a village),
from Latin *exitus* going out). (In Mexico)

a piece of land farmed communally under a system supported by the state.

ekdam /eɪkˈdʌm/ *adverb* L19 Hindi (from *ek* one + Urdu *dam* breath). Completely, totally: *his bravado was ekdam finished*. *Indian colloquial*.

élan /eɪˈlɒ̃/, /eɪˈlan/, *foreign* /elɒ̃/ *noun* M19 French (from *élancer* to dart). Energy, style, and enthusiasm.

> **1996** *Country Life* Boucher's two canvases with their dramatic *élan* and beautifully painted landscape backgrounds are the best of the series.

élan vital /elɒ̃ vital/, /eɪˈlɒ̃ viːˈtɑːl/ *noun phrase* E20 French. An intuitively perceived life-force; any mysterious life-force, especially one supposed to have caused the variations from which new species have emerged.

> ■ The French philosopher Henri Bergson (1859–1941) posited the *élan vital*, as opposed to inert matter, in *L'Évolution créatrice* (1907); as philosophical concept it has frequently been attacked for its lack of content (see quotation), but the phrase remains current in English in more general use.
>
> **1996** *Times L'évolution créatrice* has had much less impact than it deserves. Perhaps, nearly 100 years later, people will now realise that the *élan vital* exists on Mars.

elenchus /ɪˈlɛŋkəs/ *noun* plural **elenchi** /ɪˈlɛŋkʌɪ/ M17 Latin (from Greek *elegkhos* argument of refutation). *Logic* A logical refutation; the Socratic method of eliciting truth by question and answer, especially as used to refute an argument.

élite /eɪˈliːt/, /ɪˈliːt/ *noun & adjective* (also **elite**) L18 French (= selection, choice, from *élire*, *eslire* from Proto-Romance variant of Latin *eligere* to elect). **A** *noun* **1** A group of people considered to be superior in a particular society or organization. **2** (Usually *elite*.) A size of letter in typewriting, having twelve characters to the inch (about 4.7 to the centimetre). **B** *attributive adjective* Of or belonging to an élite; exclusive.

> **A.1 1996** *Spectator* Gone are the good old days: now only Soho . . . is the resting place of the élite.

El Niño /ɛl ˈniːnjəʊ/ *noun phrase* (also **el Niño**, **El Nino**) L19 Spanish (*El Niño* (de *Navidad*) the (Christmas) child, with reference to beginning in late December). Formerly, an annual warm southward current off northern Peru. Now, an irregularly occurring southward current in the equatorial Pacific Ocean, associated with weather changes and ecological damage; these associated phenomena.

> **1992** *Economist* The effects of El Nino are not limited to the countries of the Pacific rim.

embargo /ɛmˈbɑːɡəʊ/, /ɪmˈbɑːɡəʊ/ *noun & verb* (also formerly **imbargo**) E17 Spanish (from *embargar* to arrest, impede, from Proto-Romance, from Latin *in-* + *barra* bar). **A** *noun* plural **embargoes**. **1** An official ban on trade or other commercial activity with a particular country. **2** An official ban on any activity. **3** *History* An order prohibiting foreign ships from entering or leaving a country's ports, usually issued in anticipation of war. **B** *transitive verb* **1** Impose an official ban on (trade or a country or commodity); officially ban the publication of. **2** Seize, requisition, or impound (ships or goods) for the service of the state.

embarras de choix /ābara də ʃwa/ *noun phrase* L19 French (literally, 'embarrassment of choice'). More choices than one knows what to do with.

embarras de richesse /ābara də riʃɛs/ *noun phrase* (also **embarrass de richesses**) M18 French (literally, 'embarrassment of riches'). More options or resources than one knows what to do with.

> ■ *L'embarras des richesses* (1726) was the title of a work by the Abbé d'Allainval, and the earliest recorded use in English (1751) is in one of Lord Chesterfield's letters. *Richesse* as an independent noun is found earlier (ME–L17) with the meanings 'wealth' or 'richness' and also (L15) 'a group of martens', but it has long been archaic as an independent noun.
>
> **1995** *Spectator* There is an *embarras de richesse* of rose gardens to visit in June.

embolus /ˈɛmbələs/ *noun* plural **emboli** /ˈɛmbəlʌɪ/, /ˈɛmbəliː/ M17 Latin (= piston of a pump, from Greek *embolos* peg, stopper). *Medicine* A blood clot, air bubble, or other object or substance which has been carried in the bloodstream to lodge in a vessel and cause an embolism.

■ Originally used in the mid 17th century to denote something inserted or moving within another, specifically the plunger of a syringe. The current sense dates from the mid 19th century.

embonpoint /ãbɔ̃pwɛ̃/ *noun* L17 French (phrase *en bon point* in good condition). The plump or fleshy part of a person's body, in particular a woman's bosom.

> **1995** *Times* It was Kissinger's bad luck, but our good fortune, that a photographer caught the moment as the learned doctor peered, astonished, at the Princess's embonpoint.

embouchure /ãbuʃyr/, /ˈɒmbʊʃʊə/ *noun* M18 French (from *s'emboucher* to discharge itself by a mouth, from *emboucher* put in or to the mouth, from as *em* into + *bouche* mouth). **1** *Music* The manner in which a player applies their mouth to the mouthpiece of a brass or wind instrument, especially as it affects the production of the sound. **b** The mouthpiece of a musical instrument, especially of a flute. **2** The mouth of a river or valley. *Archaic*

> **1.a 1996** *Times* But my composer friend was right about my trombone-playing.... The problem is my embouchure, you see: it's just not the same with a false tooth.

embourgeoisement /ãburʒwazmã/ *noun* M20 French (from *embourgeoiser* to make or become BOURGEOIS). The proliferation in a society of values perceived as characteristic of the middle class, especially of materialism; bourgeoisification.

> **1996** *Spectator* He [sc. Liam Gallagher] is undergoing the same *embourgeoisement* which affected the late John Lennon when he embraced domesticity and started baking his own bread.

embrasure /ɪmˈbreɪʒə/, /ɛmˈbreɪʒə/ *noun* E18 French (from obsolete *embraser* (modern *ébraser*) to widen (a door or window opening), of unknown origin). **1** *Military* An opening in a parapet that widens towards the exterior, made to fire a gun through. **2** A slanting or bevelling of the wall on either side of a door or window opening so as to form a recess; the area contained between such walls.

emeritus /ɪˈmɛrɪtəs/ *adjective* M18 Latin (past participle of *emereri* to earn (one's discharge) by service, from *e-* + *mereri* to deserve). (Of a former office-holder, especially a university professor) retired but allowed to retain his or her title as an honour.

■ Often postpositive (see quotation).

> **1995** *Spectator* Sir Michael Richardson, Savoy director emeritus and pastmaster dealmaker, is just the man to go round with the hat.

emigré /ˈɛmɪgreɪ/ *noun & adjective* (also **émigré**) L18 French (*émigré*, past participle of *émigrer* from Latin *emigrare* to emigrate). **A** *noun* Originally, a French emigrant, especially one escaping the Revolution of 1789–99. Now, any person who has left their own country in order to settle in another, typically for political reasons. **B** *adjective* That is an emigré; composed of emigrés.

éminence grise /eminãs griz/ *noun phrase* plural **eminences grises** (pronounced same) M20 French (literally, 'grey eminence'. A person who exercises power or influence though holding no official position. Also, a confidential adviser.

■ The term was originally applied to Cardinal Richelieu's grey-cloaked private secretary, Père Joseph (1577–1638).

> **1995** *New Scientist* A young researcher talking about her work today would be an invaluable resource for some future investigator about to interview the same person when an elderly *éminence grise* of science.

emir /ɛˈmɪə/ *noun* L16 French (*émir* from Arabic *'amīr*). A title of certain Muslim rulers; a Muslim (usually Arab) military commander or local chief.

■ Originally denoting a male descendant of Muhammad.

empanada /ɛmpəˈnɑːdə/, *foreign* /em paˈnada/ *noun* M20 Spanish (use as noun of feminine past participle of *empanar* to bake or roll in pastry, from as *em-* + *pan* bread, from Latin *panis*). *Cookery* A Spanish or Latin American pastry turnover with a filling of meat, cheese, or vegetables.

en bloc /ã blɔk/, /ɒn blɒk/ *adverb phrase* M19 French (literally, 'as a block'). All together or all at the same time.

1984 A. G. Lehmann *European Heritage* ... the civil service moves, *en bloc*, and with no changes, from serving the Kaiser to serving the republic—equally without enthusiasm.

en brosse /ā brɔs/ *adverb & adjective phrase* E20 French (literally, 'as a brush'). (Of hair) cut short and bristly.

1996 *Times: Weekend* Middle-aged men wore Newcastle United shirts, ear-rings, hair *en brosse* or back-to-front baseball caps.

en cabochon /ā kabɔʃɔ̃/ *adverb phrase* E19 French. (Of a gem) cut as a CABO-CHON, with curved surfaces rather than facets.

enceinte /āsɛ̃t/, /ŏ'sãt/ *noun* plural pronounced same E18 French (from Latin *incincta* feminine past participle of *incingere* to gird in). The main enclosure or enclosing wall of a fortified place.

enceinte /āsɛ̃t/, /ŏ'sãt/ *adjective* (also in legal use) **ensient** E17 French (from medieval Latin *incincta* ungirded, from Latin *in-* + *cincta* feminine past participle of *cingere* to gird). (Of a woman) pregnant.

■ Now archaic or euphemistic.

enchaînement /āʃɛnmā/ *noun* plural pronounced same M19 French (literally = a chaining up, a concatenation). *Ballet* A linked sequence of steps or movements constituting a phrase.

enchilada /ɛntʃɪ'lɑːdə/ *noun* M19 American Spanish (feminine of *enchilado* past participle of *enchilar* to season with chilli). A tortilla served with chilli sauce and a filling of meat or cheese.

■ In informal North American English, *the big enchilada* is 'a person or thing of great importance', while *the whole enchilada* is 'the whole situation, everything'.

enchiridion /ˌɛnkʌɪ'rɪdɪən/ *noun* LME Late Latin (from Greek *egkheiridion*, from as *en-* + *kheir* hand + diminutive suffix *-idion*). A book containing essential information on a subject; a handbook, a manual.

en clair /ā klɛr/ *adverb & adjective phrase* L19 French. (Especially of a telegram or official message) in ordinary language, not in code or cipher; also *figurative*.

figurative **1995** *Spectator* Franks worked *en clair*, Goodman in code.

enclave /'ɛnkleɪv/, *formerly also* /āklav/ *noun* M19 French (from Old and Modern French *enclaver* to enclose, from popular Latin *in-* + *clavis* key). **1** A portion of territory surrounded by a larger territory whose inhabitants are culturally or ethnically distinct. **2** A place or group that is different in character from those surrounding it.

encomium /ɛn'kəʊmɪəm/ *noun* plural **encomiums, encomia** L16 Latin (from Greek *egkōmion* eulogy, from as *en-* + *komos* revel). A formal or high-flown expression of praise.

■ Earlier (M16) anglicized as *encomy*.

1996 *Bookseller* I was miffed, incidentally, not to be among the luminaries asked to provide a 10th birthday encomium for Serpent's Tail.

encore /'ɒŋkɔː/ *noun, interjection, & verb* E18 French (= still, again). **A** *noun* An audience's demand for an item to be performed again or for a further item at the end of a concert or other performance. Also an item performed thus. **B** *interjection* Again! (as called by an audience at the end of a concert or other performance). **C** *transitive verb* Call for a repeated or additional performance of (an item) at the end of a concert or other performance.

■ The origin is uncertain. The Italian equivalent *ancora* 'still' was also formerly used (E18) but neither it nor *encore* occurs in this context in the original languages.

encourager les autres see POUR ENCOURAGER LES AUTRES.

en croûte /ā krut/ *adverb & adjective phrase* L20 French. In a pastry crust: *salmon en croûte*.

en daube /ā dob/ *adverb & adjective phrase* L20 French (cf. DAUBE). (Of meat) braised slowly in wine.

en échelon /ān eʃlɔ̃/ *adjective & adverb phrase* (also **en echelon**) E19 French. *Chiefly Geology* In approximately parallel formation at an oblique angle to a particular direction; in an ECHELON.

en face /ā fas/ *adverb phrase* M18 French. **1** With the face to the front, facing forwards. **2** *Bibliography* On the facing page.

en famille /ã famij/, /ɒn faˈmiː/ *adverb phrase* E18 French (= in family). With one's family, or as a family.

1996 *Times: Weekend* Though mostly in their fifties or sixties, there was a sprinkling of teenagers *en famille*.

enfant gâté /ãfã gate/ *noun phrase* plural **enfants gâtés** (pronounced same) E19 French (= spoilt child). A person who is excessively flattered or indulged.

enfant terrible /ãfã tɛribl/ *noun phrase* plural **enfants terribles** (pronounced same) M19 French (= terrible child). A person who behaves in an unconventional or controversial way.

1996 *Country Life* Seven years on, Mr Barr has lost none of his impishness; he remains one of the *enfants terribles*, the young Turks of the wine-writing world, still tweaking the nose of the Establishment...

en fête /ã fɛt/ *predicative adjective phrase* M19 French (= in festival). Prepared for or holding a party or celebration.

enfilade /ɛnfrˈleɪd/, /ˈɒnfɪlɑːd/ *noun & verb* E18 French (from *enfiler* to thread on a string, pierce or traverse from end to end, from as *en-* + *fil* thread). **A** *noun* **1** A volley of gunfire directed along a line from end to end. **2** A suite of rooms with doorways in line with each other; a vista between rows of trees etc. **B** *transitive verb* Direct a volley of gunfire along the whole length of (a target).

■ The term was originally used to denote the position of a military post commanding the length of a line.

A.2 1995 *Country Life* Hopetoun's Great Apartment is arranged in a standard enfilade running north from the entrance hall, and incorporating a spectacular five-bay drawing room...

engagé /ãgaʒɛ/, /ˌɒŋgaˈʒeɪ/ *adjective* M20 French (past participle of *engager* to engage). (Of a writer or artist) morally committed to a particular cause.

1996 *Spectator* They know where they are with other directors: Truffaut? Wry. Godard? *Engagé*.

en masse /ã mas/, /ɒn mas/ *adverb phrase* L18 French (= in a mass). In a group; all together: *the cabinet immediately resigned en masse*.

1996 *Spectator* Rereading the stories *en masse* brings out Rose Tremain's strengths as a short story writer...

ennui /ɒnˈwiː/, *foreign* /ãnɥi/ *noun* M18 French (from Latin *in odio* in *mihi in odio est* it is hateful to me). Mental weariness and dissatisfaction arising from a lack of occupation or excitement; boredom.

1996 *Country Life* [February] epitomises that rural ennui which is distinguished by its lack of distinguishedness.

enosis /ɪˈnəʊsɪs/, /ˈɛnəsɪs/ *noun* M20 Modern Greek (*henōsis*, from *hena* one). The political union of Greece and Cyprus, as an aim or ideal of certain Greeks and Cypriots.

en pantoufles /ã pãtufl/ *adverb phrase* E20 French (literally, 'in slippers'). Relaxed, off guard; in a free and easy manner or atmosphere.

en papillote /ɒ ˈpapɪjɒt/ *adjective & adverb* E19 French. (Of food) cooked and served in a paper wrapper: *fish en papillote.*

en passant /ã pasã/, /ɒ̃ paˈsɒnt/ *adverb phrase* E17 French (= in passing). By the way, incidentally.

1996 *Bookseller* Michael Schwanhauser of Walthari in Freiburg commented almost *en passant* that his twice-weekly orders for British books arrived within four days.

en pension /ã pãsjõ/ *adverb and adjective phrase* E19 French. Living as a boarder or lodger in a small hotel or private house.

■ Formerly (L16 onwards) anglicized as *in* or *on pension*; cf. PENSION.

en plein air /ã plɛn ɛr/ *adverb phrase* L19 French. In the open air.

■ Especially with reference to the working methods of the French Impressionist painters, as compared with their academic *confrères* who worked in studios and from posed models; cf. PLEIN-AIR.

1988 K. Adler *Unknown Impressionists* Many of them wished to learn from Pissarro's example, ... and they watched him at work, often *en plein air*, and discussed ideas about art.

en pointe /ã pwɛ̃t/ *adjective & adverb phrase* M19 French. *Ballet* On the tips of the toes. Cf. POINTE.

en poste /ã pɔst/ *adverb phrase* M20 French. In an official diplomatic position at a particular place.

1996 *Spectator* Nathaniel Hawthorne, who actually did get a cushy job as consul, turned out nothing while he was *en poste*.

en primeur /ā primœr/ *adverb & adjective phrase* L20 French (= as being new). (Of vegetables) fresh, new; (of wine) newly produced and made available. Cf. PRIMEUR.

1996 *Country Life* If you have not bought *en primeur* before, get as many merchants' lists as you can and compare the tasting notes.

en prise /ā priz/ *adverb phrase* E19 French. *Chess* In a position to be taken.

en rapport /ā rapɔr/ *adjective phrase* E19 French. Having a close and harmonious relationship. Cf. RAPPORT.

en route /ā rut/, /ɒn ruːt/ *adverb phrase* L18 French. On the way; during the course of a journey.

1996 *Spectator* On one occasion, . . . the Prince marched through the meeting in a towel *en route* to the bathroom.

ensemble /ɒn'sɒmb(ə)l/, *foreign* /āsābl/ (*plural same*) *noun* M18 Old and Modern French (from Proto-Romance from Latin *insimul*, from *in-* into, in + *simul* at the same time). **1** A group of musicians, actors, or dancers who perform together. **b** A piece of music or passage written for performance by a whole cast, choir, or group of instruments. **c** The coordination between performers executing an ensemble passage. **2** A group of items viewed as a whole rather than individually. **3** A set of (usually women's) clothes chosen to harmonize when worn together. **4** *Science* A notional collection of systems of identical constitution but not necessarily in the same state.

■ Originally (LME) introduced in the adverbial sense of 'together, at the same time', which it retains in French, but this has long been rare in English.

1 **1996** *Country Life* Once a small ensemble of distinct individuals, this company now resembles a large precision instrument...

ensient variant of ENCEINTE.

ensilage /'ɛnsɪlɪdʒ/, /ɛn'sʌɪlɪdʒ/ *noun & verb* L19 French (from *ensiler* from Spanish *ensilar*, from *en-* + *silo* silo). **A** *noun* **1** The process of making silage. **2** Silage. **B** *transitive verb* Treat (fodder) by ensilage; turn into silage.

en suite /ɒn 'swiːt/, *foreign* /ā sɥit/ *adverb, adjective, & noun phrase* (also (especially as adjective & noun phrase) **ensuite** /õswiːt/) L18 French (= in sequence). **A** *adverb & adjective phrase* (Of a bathroom) immediately adjoining a bedroom and forming part of the same set of rooms. **B** *noun phrase* An en suite bathroom.

■ Introduced in the late 18th century in the sense 'in agreement or harmony', now rare or obsolete.

entasis /'ɛntəsɪs/ *noun* plural **entases** /'ɛntəsiːz/ M17 Modern Latin (from Greek, from *enteinein* to strain). *Architecture* A slight convex curve in the shaft of a column (introduced to correct the visual illusion of concavity produced by a straight shaft).

entente /ɒn'tɒnt/, *foreign* /ātāt/ *noun* M19 French (= understanding). A friendly understanding or informal alliance between states or factions; a group of states in an informal alliance.

1995 *Times* France has its own, largely German, reasons for wanting a new entente with Britain; both countries know that a close bilateral relationship is essential.

entente cordiale /ātāt kɔrdjal/, /ˌɒntɒnt kɔːdɪˈɑːl/ *noun phrase* plural **ententes cordiales** (pronounced same) M19 French (= friendly understanding). An entente, specifically the understanding between Britain and France reached in 1904, forming the basis of Anglo-French cooperation in the First World War.

1995 *Times* But the selection of a chap with such a friendly disposition towards Europe can only serve to strengthen the new *entente cordiale* between John Major and Jacques Chirac.

entourage /'ɒntʊrɑːʒ/, /ˌɒntʊ(ə)'rɑːʒ/ *noun* M19 French (from *entourer* to surround, from *entour* surroundings, use as noun of adverb = 'round about'). A group of people attending or accompanying someone important.

entr'acte /'ɒntrakt/, *foreign* /ātrakt/ (*plural same*) *noun* M19 French (now obsolete (modern *entracte*), from *entre* between + *acte* act). The interval between two acts of a play or opera; a piece of music or dance performed during an interval.

en travesti /ā travɛsti/ *adverb phrase* M20 French (= (dressed) in disguise). *Theatre* Dressed as a member of the opposite sex.

1996 *Spectator* Carabosse, traditionally performed by a man *en travesti*, becomes an unbearable over-gesticulating drag queen.

entrechat /ātrəʃa/ (*plural same*), /ˈɒnt rəʃa:/ *noun* L18 French (from Italian (*capriola*) *intrecciata* complicated (caper)). *Ballet* A vertical jump during which the dancer repeatedly crosses the feet and beats them together while in the air.

entrecôte /ˈɒntrəkəʊt/, *foreign* /ātrəkot/ (*plural same*) *noun* M19 French (literally = between rib). A boned steak cut off the sirloin. More fully *entrecôte steak*.

entrée /ˈɒntreɪ/, *foreign* /ātre/ (*plural same*) *noun* E18 French. **1** The main course of a meal; *British* a dish served between the first and main courses at a formal dinner. **2** The right to enter or join a particular sphere or group.

■ First used in English (in the early 18th century) to denote a piece of instrumental music forming the first part of a suite or divertissement, or introducing a character etc. on stage.

2 1996 *Times* His upper-class accent and eminently recognisable surname...had not only given him an entrée to the profession, it had allowed him to land a good royal story...

entremets /ātrəmɛ/ *noun plural* L15 French (from *entre* between + *mets* dish). A light dish served between two courses of a formal meal.

entre nous /ātrə nu/ *adverb phrase* L17 French. Between ourselves; in private.

entrepôt /ˈɒntrəpəʊ/, *foreign* /ātrəpo/ (*plural same*) *noun* E18 French ((earlier *entrepost*, *entrepos*), from *entreposer* to store, from *entre* among + *poser* to place). A port, city, or other centre to which goods are brought for import and export, and for collection and distribution.

entrepreneur /ˌɒntrəprəˈnəː/ *noun* E19 French (from *entreprendre* to undertake). **1** A person who sets up a business or businesses, taking on financial risks in the hope of profit. **2** A promoter in the entertainment industry.

■ Originally used to denote the director of a musical institution.

entresol /ˈɒntrəsɒl/, *foreign* /ātrəsɔl/ (*plural same*) *noun* (also **entersole**, **intersole**) E18 French (from Spanish *entresuelo*, from *entre* between + *suelo* storey). A low storey between the ground floor and the first floor of a building; a mezzanine floor.

en ventre sa mère /ā vātr sa mɛr/ *adverb phrase* (also **en ventre sa mere**) L18 French (= in its mother's womb). *Law* In the mother's womb.

environs /ɪnˈvʌɪrənz/, /ɛnˈvʌɪrənz/, /ˈɛnvɪrənz/ *noun plural* M17 French (plural of *environ* surrounding(s)). The surrounding area or district: *the picturesque environs of the loch.*

envoi /ˈɛnvɔɪ/ *noun* (also (earlier) **envoy**) LME Old and Modern French (from *envoyer* to send, from phrase *en voie* on the way). The concluding part of a literary work, *especially* a short stanza concluding a ballade; *archaic* an author's concluding words, dedication, etc.; *generally* a conclusion.

1996 *Country Life* She ended with a brief piece by Elgar...an apt *envoi* to an evening where landscape, architecture and music met in peculiarly English harmony.

eo ipso /ˌeɪəʊ ˈɪpsəʊ/ *adverb phrase* L17 Latin (ablative of *id ipsum* the thing itself). By that very act or quality; through that alone; thereby. Cf. IPSO FACTO.

épater /epate/ *transitive verb* E20 French (= flabbergast). Startle, shock.

■ Only used in the infinitive, especially in phrase below or English phrases based upon it.

épater les bourgeois /epate lɛ burʒwa/ *adverb phrase* (also **épater le bourgeois**) E20 French (= to amaze the bourgeois). To shock people who have attitudes or views perceived as conventional, narrow-minded, or complacent.

■ 'Je les ai épatés, les bourgeois' is attributed to Alexandre Private d'Anglemont (d. 1859).

1995 *Times* Because it takes more than a urinal to *épater les bourgeois* now, the real things that are being hauled into galleries grow ever more provocative: turds, frozen foetuses and used sanitary towels...

epaulette /ˈɛpəlɛt/, /ˈɛpɔːlɛt/, /ɛpəˈlɛt/ *noun* (also **epaulet**) L18 French (*épaulette* diminutive of *épaule* shoulder, from Latin *spatula*, (in Late Latin) shoulder-blade). An ornamental shoulder piece on an item of clothing, especially on the coat or jacket of a military uniform, usually as a sign of rank.

épée /ˈeɪpeɪ/, *foreign* /epe/ (*plural same*) *noun* L19 French (= sword, from Old French *espee*). A sharp-pointed duelling sword used (with the end blunted) in fencing; the art of fencing with this.

ephemera /ɪˈfɛm(ə)rə/, /ɪˈfiːm(ə)rə/ *noun plural* L16 Greek (plural of *ephemeron*, neuter of *ephēmeros* lasting only one day). **1** Things that exist or are used or enjoyed for only a short time. **2** Collectable items that were originally expected to have only short-lived usefulness or popularity.

■ Recorded in English from the late 16th century as the plural of *ephemeron*, from Greek As a singular noun, the word originally denoted a plant said by ancient writers to last only one day, or an insect with a short lifespan, and hence was applied (late 18th century) to a person or thing of short-lived usefulness or interest. Current use has been influenced by plurals such as *trivia* and *memorabilia*.

ephemeris /ɪˈfɛm(ə)rɪs/, /ɪˈfiːm(ə)rɪs/ *noun plural* **ephemerides** /ɛfɪˈmɛrɪdiːz/ E16 Latin (from Greek, from *ephēmeros* lasting only a day). A table or book of tables giving the calculated positions of celestial bodies on a daily or regular basis over a particular period; an astronomical almanac.

epithalamium /ɛpɪθəˈleɪmɪəm/ *noun* (also (earlier) **epithalamion** /ɛpɪθəˈleɪmɪən/) plural **epithalamiums, epithalamions, epithalamia** /ɛpɪθəˈleɪmɪə/ L16 Latin (from Greek *epithalamion* use as noun of neuter of *epithalamios* nuptial, from *epi-* upon + *thalamos* bridal chamber). A song or poem in celebration of a wedding.

epitome /ɪˈpɪtəmi/, /ɛˈpɪtəmi/ *noun* E16 Latin (from Greek *epitomē*, from *epitemnein* to cut into, cut short, from *epi-* in addition + *temnein* to cut). **1** A person or thing that is a perfect example of a particular quality or type. **2** A summary or abstract of a written work; a condensed account. **3** A thing representing something else in miniature. *Archaic.*

e pluribus unum /eɪ ˌplʊərɪbʊs ˈjuː nʊm/ *interjection* L18 Latin. One out of many (the motto of the United States).

epode /ˈɛpəʊd/ *noun* E17 French (*épode* or Latin *epodos* from Greek *epōidos*, from *epi-* upon + *ōidē* ode). **1** A Greek lyric poem composed of couplets in which a long line is followed by a shorter one; a serious poem. **2** The third section of an ancient Greek choral ode, or of one division of such an ode.

epsilon /ˈɛpsɪlɒn/, /ɛpˈsʌɪlɒn/ *noun* E18 Greek (*e psilon*, literally, 'bare e', short e written ε). **1** The fifth letter (E, ε) of the Greek alphabet, transliterated as 'e'. **2** *Astronomy* (preceding the genitive of the Latin name of the constellation) the fifth brightest star in a constellation. **3** An examiner's fifth-class mark; a person of low intelligence.

epyllion /ɪˈpɪlɪən/, /ɛˈpɪlɪən/ *noun* plural **epyllia** /ɪˈpɪlɪə/, /ɛˈpɪlɪə/ L19 Greek (*epullion* diminutive of *epos* word, song, from *eipein* to say). A narrative poem resembling an epic poem in style or matter but of shorter extent.

équipe /ekip/ *noun* (also **equipe**) plural pronounced same M20 French (= group, team, from as *équiper* to equip (cf. Anglo-Norman *eskipeson*, medieval Latin *eschipare* to man (a vessel)), probably from Old Norse *skipa* to man (a vessel), fit up, from *skip* ship). A motor-racing stable; a team, especially of sports players.

equivoque /ˈiːkwɪvəʊk/, /ˈɛkwɪvəʊk/ *noun* (also **equivoke**) LME Old and Modern French (*équivoque* or late Latin *aequivocus*). **1** An expression capable of more than one meaning; a pun; wordplay, punning. **2** The fact of having more than one meaning or interpretation; ambiguity.

■ Earlier (LME–M17) as an adjective meaning 'equivocal'.

erg /əːɡ/ *noun* plural **ergs** or **areg** /'arɛɡ/ L19 French (from Arabic *'irk̟*, *'erg*). An area of shifting desert sand dunes, especially in the Sahara.

ergo /'əːɡəʊ/ *adverb* LME Latin. Therefore.

■ Later (L16) there was also a nominal sense of *ergo*, meaning 'a use or occurrence of *ergo*, as in a logical conclusion', but this sense has long been rare. In modern use, *ergo* is often used to introduce a conclusion that seems to follow logically from a preceding statement, though the writer or speaker is aware that such a conclusion may be an oversimplification or absurdity.

    1995 *Spectator* Thus, if the US Federal Government committed a crime (the Waco massacre), everyone who works for the Federal Government shares in its guilt; ergo it is permissible to bomb a Federal Government building because the people in it are by definition guilty.

ergot /'əːɡɒt/ *noun* L17 French (= cock's spur, from Old French *ar(i)got*, *argoz* of unknown origin). **1** A fungal disease of rye and other cereals in which black elongated fruiting bodies grow in the ears of the cereal, giving the appearance of cock's spur; a fungus causing such a disease. **2** The fruiting bodies of the ergot fungus, used as a source of certain medicinal alkaloids, especially for inducing contraction of the uterus or controlling post-partum bleeding. **3** A small horny protrusion on the back of the fetlock of most horses.

erh hu /əː 'huː/ *noun phrase* (also **erhu**) E20 Chinese (*èrhú*, from *èr* two + *hú* bowed instrument). A Chinese two-stringed musical instrument held in the lap and played with a bow.

Eros /'ɪərɒs/, /'ɛrəʊz/ *noun* plural **Erotes** /ɪ'rəʊtɛz/, **Eroses** /'ɪərɒsɪz/, /'ɛrəʊzɪz/ (also **eros**) L17 Latin (from Greek). **1** Love; the god of love, Cupid; sexual love or desire. **2** (In Freudian psychology) the urge for self-preservation and sexual pleasure; the life instinct.

errata /ɛ'rɑːtə/, /ɛ'reɪtə/ *noun* L16 Latin (plural of ERRATUM). **1** *plural* of ERRATUM. **2** A list of corrected errors appended to a book or published in a subsequent issue of a journal.

erratum /ɛ'rɑːtəm/, /ɛ'reɪtəm/ *noun* plural **errata** /ɛ'rɑːtə/ M16 Latin (= error, use as noun of neuter past participle of *errare* to err). An error in a printed or written text; *especially* one of a list of corrected errors appended to a book or published in a subsequent issue of a journal.

ersatz /'əːsats/, /'ɛːsats/, *foreign* /ɛr'zats/ *adjective* L19 German (= compensation, replacement). **1** Made or used as a substitute (typically an inferior one) for something else: *ersatz coffee*. **2** Not real or genuine: *ersatz emotion*.

    2 1996 *Spectator* . . . to judge from recent Australian movies, the old pro-British cringe, which was at least rooted in historical and cultural reality, has been replaced by an *ersatz* Americanisation, rooted in nothing but commercial calculation.

eruv /ə'rʌv/ *noun* plural **eruvim** /ər ʌ'vim/ or **eruvs** L20 Hebrew. An urban area enclosed by a wire boundary which symbolically extends the private domain of Jewish households into public areas, permitting activities within it that are normally forbidden in public on the Sabbath.

    1993 *Guardian* Most major American cities now have eruvim—the White House is even in Washington's.

escargot /ɛ'skɑːɡəʊ/, /ɪ'skɑːɡəʊ/ *noun* plural pronounced same L19 French (from Old French *escargol* from Provençal *escaragol*). The edible snail, especially as an item on a menu.

escarole /'ɛskərəʊl/ *noun* E20 French (from Italian *scar(i)ola* from late Latin *(e)scariola*, from Latin *escarius* used as food, from *esca* food). A variety of endive with broad undivided leaves and a slightly bitter flavour, used in salads.

■ Mainly North American.

escritoire /ˌɛskriː'twɑː/ *noun* L16 Old French (= study, writing box (modern *écritoire* writing desk) from medieval Latin *scriptorium* writing room). A small writing desk with drawers and compartments, a bureau.

esophagus variant of OESOPHAGUS.

esoterica /ɛsə'tɛrɪkə/, /iːsə'tɛrɪkə/ *noun plural* E20 Greek (*esōterika* neuter plural of *esōterikos* esoteric). Items or publications intended only for the initiated or appropriate only to an inner circle; esoteric details.

espada /ɛ'spɑːdə/ *noun plural same* Spanish (via Portuguese) (from Latin *spatha* sword). A scabbardfish, especially as caught for food in Madeira and elsewhere.

espadrille /ɛspə'drɪl/, /'ɛspədrɪl/ *noun* L19 French (from Provençal *espardi(l)hos*, from *espart* esparto). A light canvas shoe with plaited fibre sole, originally worn in the Pyrenees; an ALPARGATA.

espalier /ɪ'spaljə/, /ɛ'spaljə/ *noun* M17 French (from Italian *spalliera*, from *spalla* shoulder, from Latin *spatula*, (in late Latin) shoulder blade). **1** A fruit tree or ornamental shrub whose branches are trained to grow flat against a wall, supported on a lattice. **2** A lattice on which a tree or shrub is trained in this way.

esparto /ɛ'spɑːtəʊ/, /ɪ'spɑːtəʊ/ *noun plural* **espartos** M19 Spanish (from Latin *spartum* from Greek *sparton* rope). A tough grass, *Stipa tenacissima*, growing in Spain and North Africa and used in paper-making. Also *esparto grass*.

esplanade /ɛsplə'neɪd/, /ɛsplə'nɑːd/ *noun* L16 French (from Italian *spianata* from feminine of Latin *explanatus* flattened, levelled, past participle of *explanare*). **1** A long, open, level area, typically beside the sea, along which people may walk for pleasure. **2** An open, level space separating a fortress from a town.
 ■ Originally denoted an area of flat ground on the top of a rampart.

espressivo /ˌɛsprɛ'siːvəʊ/ *adverb & adjective* L19 Italian (from Latin *expressus* distinctly presented, past participle of *exprimere* to express). *Music* (Especially as a direction) with expression of feeling.

espresso /ɛ'sprɛsəʊ/ *noun* (also **expresso** /ɛk'sprɛsəʊ/) plural **espressos** M20 Italian ((*caffè*) *espresso*, from *espresso* squeezed, pressed out, from Latin *expres-* sus (see preceding)). A type of strong black coffee made by forcing steam through ground coffee beans.

esprit /ɛspri/, /ɛ'spriː/, /'ɛspriː/ *noun* L16 French (from Latin *spiritus* spirit). The quality of being lively, vivacious, or witty.
 1995 *Times* So you walk back to the Rigaud portrait [of Lord Nelson], the slight figure with colourless hair and arched brows and a face full of nervous *esprit* and determination.

esprit de corps /ɛˌspriː də 'kɔː/, /ˌɛspriː/ *noun phrase* L18 French (= spirit of the body). A feeling of pride and mutual loyalty shared by the members of a group; team spirit.
 1995 *Spectator* An *esprit de corps* was emerging fast. As we sped into the Channel Tunnel, the businessman on the next table cracked open a bottle of champagne and handed round paper cups.

esprit de l'escalier /ɛspri də lɛskalje/ *noun phrase* (also **esprit descalier**) E20 French (literally, 'wit of the staircase'). The fact of a witty remark or rejoinder coming to mind only after the opportunity to make it has passed.
 ■ The phrase was coined by the French philosopher Denis Diderot (1713–84) in *Paradoxe sur le Comédien*. The staircase was the one descending from the salon, and *esprit d'escalier* was the witty saying that came to mind only as one was departing down it.
 1995 *Times Magazine* With my usual dunderheaded *esprit d'escalier* I will realise later that the correct response is simply to walk on past...

esse /'ɛsi/ *noun* M16 Latin (use as noun of *esse* to be). *Philosophy* Essential nature, essence.

estaminet /ɛstaminɛ/ *noun plural* **estaminets** pronounced same E19 French (from Walloon *staminé* byre, from *stamo* pole to which a cow is tethered in a stall, probably from German *Stamm* stem, trunk). Originally, a café where smoking was allowed. Now, a small unpretentious café selling wine, beer, etc.

estancia /ɛ'stansɪə/, *foreign* /e'stanθia/, /e'stansia/ *noun* M17 Spanish (literally, 'station' = Old French *estance* dwelling, from medieval Latin *stantia*, from Latin *stant-* present participial stem of *stare* to stand). A cattle ranch in Latin America or the southern United States.

1996 *Oldie* In the pampas cattle and sheep farmers made their fortunes on huge estancias.

estrus variant of OESTRUS.

estufa /e'stufa/ *noun* M19 Spanish (probably based on Greek *tuphos* steam, smoke). **1** A heated chamber in which Madeira wine is stored and matured. **2** An underground chamber in which a fire is kept permanently alight, used as a place of assembly by Pueblo Indians.

et /ɛt/ *conjunction* ME Latin. And.

■ In Modern English only in medieval and Modern Latin phrases; see ET AL., ET CETERA, etc.

eta /'iːtə/ *noun* LME Greek (*ēta*). **1** The seventh letter (H, η) of the Greek alphabet, transliterated as 'e' or 'ē'. **2** *attributive Astronomy* (Preceding the genitive of the Latin name of the constellation) denoting the seventh brightest star in a constellation.

etagere /ɛtə'ʒɛː/ *noun* (also **étagère**) plural pronounced same M19 French (*étagère*, from *étage* shelf, stage). A piece of furniture with a number of open shelves for displaying ornaments.

et al. /ɛt al/ *adverb phrase* L19 Latin (*et* and + abbreviation of *alii, aliae, alia* masculine, feminine, and neuter plural of *alius* other). And others.

■ Often used in bibliographies in cases of works by several authors; the formula 'Smith et al.' avoids having to list all the authors' names in full.

1996 *Spectator* [There] is a long succession of recreated theatrical 'flats' ... with original costumes and astonishingly flamboyant designs by Bakst, Benois, Goncharova *et al.*

et cetera /ɛt'sɛt(ə)rə/, /ɪt'sɛt(ə)rə/ *adverb & noun* (also **etcetera**, **et caetera**) ME Latin (from *et* and + *cetera* the rest, neuter plural of *ceterus* remaining over). **A** *adverb* **1** And the rest; and so on (used at the end of a list to indicate that further, similar items are included). **2** Indicating that a list is too tedious or clichéd to give in full: *we've all got to do our duty, pull our weight, et cetera, et cetera.* **B** *noun* (In *plural*.) Unspecified or typical extra items.

■ Often abbreviated to *etc.* or *&c.*

etiquette /'ɛtɪkɛt/, /ɛtɪ'kɛt/ *noun* M18 French (*étiquette* list of ceremonial observances of a court; etiquette; label, ticket). The customary code of polite behaviour in society or among members of a particular profession or group.

■ Also formerly (M19) in the primary French sense of 'a label, ticket', but this is rare in English. The sense of 'a rule of etiquette', 'an observance prescribed by etiquette' was also briefly (L18–E19) current in English, generally in the plural. From the word's history in French it is not entirely clear how the transition between the primary and secondary senses was effected, although the English colloquial expressions 'just the ticket' and 'not quite the ticket' (*ticket* here meaning 'the accepted (or needed) thing') suggest how it could have come about.

etrier /'eɪtrɪə/, *foreign* /etrije/ (*plural same*) *noun* (also **étrier**) M20 French (*étrier* stirrup, etrier). *Singular* and in *plural*. A short rope ladder with a few rungs of wood or metal, used by climbers.

et seq. /ɛt sɛk/ *noun phrase* plural **et seqq.** (pronounced same) L19 Latin (*et* and + present participle of *sequi* to follow; abbreviation of *et sequentes* (Latin masculine and feminine plural of *sequens*) and *et sequentia* (neuter plural of *sequens*)). And what follows (used in page references): *see volume 35, p. 329 et seq.*

Et tu, Brute /ɛt 'tuː ˌbruːteɪ/ *interjection* L16 Latin (= and you, Brutus). An expression of reproach to a friend who has betrayed one's trust and gone over to the enemy.

■ The words spoken by Caesar in Shakespeare's *Julius Caesar* (III.i) when he sees his friend Brutus amongst his assassins. Another name is sometimes humorously substituted for that of Brutus (see quotation 1995(2)).

1995 *Times* The cry *Et tu, Brute?* has been the death rattle of many a fallen king.

1995 *Times* The penalty shoot-out, the Boland decision, and all such pack-'em-in modifications to a sport ... betray competition for fun. Each one is a betrayal: a knife in the heart of sport. *Et tu,* Illingworth?

étude /'eɪtjuːd/, /eɪ'tjuːd/, *foreign* /etyd/ (*plural same*) *noun* M19 French (= study). A short musical composition, typically for one instrument, designed as an exercise to improve the technique or demonstrate the skill of the player.

etui /ɛ'twi:/ *noun* (also **etwee**) E17 French (*étui*, Old French *estui* prison, from Old French *estuier* to shut up, keep, save). A small usually ornamental case for needles, cosmetics, and other articles. Formerly also, a case for surgical instruments.

euchre /'ju:kə/ *noun & verb* E19 German (dialect *Jucker(spiel)*). **A** *noun* **1** A North American card game for two to four players in which the highest cards are the joker (if used), the jack of trumps, and the other jack of the same colour in a pack with the lower cards removed, the aim being to win at least three of the five tricks played. **2** An instance of euchring or being euchred. **B** *transitive verb* **1** Prevent (a bidder) from winning three or more tricks at euchre, thereby scoring points oneself. **2** Cheat, trick (*into*, *out of*); deceive, outwit. **3** Exhaust; ruin, finish, do for (a person). Usually in *passive*. *Australian*.

eureka /jʊ(ə)'ri:kə/ *interjection & noun* (also **Eureka**) E17 Greek (*heurēka* (= I have found it), from *heuriskein* to find). **A** *interjection* A cry of joy or satisfaction when one finds or discovers something. **B** *noun* **1** A cry of *eureka!*; a fortunate discovery. **2** (**Eureka**) (Proprietary name for) an alloy of copper and nickel used for electrical filament and resistance wire.

■ The exclamation supposedly uttered by the Sicilian Greek philosopher Archimedes (*c*.287–*c*.212 BC) when he hit upon a method of determining the purity of gold, an inspiration which, according to tradition, occurred to him as he was taking a bath.

événement /evenmã/ *noun* plural pronounced same M20 French (= event, happening). Politically motivated civil disorder involving mass demonstrations.

■ Usually plural. The word became current in English with reference to the French strikes and student riots of 1968 and received a further boost from the wave of strikes and demonstrations in France in 1995, though it is no longer necessarily confined to the French political scene (see quotation 1995(2)).

1995 *Times* The French media are full of comparisons with the *événements* of 1968, when students and workers suddenly took to the streets for no very obvious reason.
1995 *Spectator* The next few months will show whether the Ilidza *événements* join the heady days of Belgrade 1941 in the annals of Serb defiance.

Ewigkeit /'e:vɪçkaɪt/, /'eɪvɪgkʌɪt/ *noun* (also **ewigkeit**) L19 German. Eternity; infinity.

ex /ɛks/ *noun & adjective* plural **exes**, **ex's** /'ɛksɪz/ E19 Latin (from prefix *ex*-former(ly)). **A** *noun* A former husband, wife, or other partner in a relationship. **B** *adjective* Former; outdated.

ex /ɛks/ *preposition* M19 Latin (= out of) **1** (Of goods) sold direct from (a ship, warehouse, etc.). **2** Without; excluding.

exacta /ɪg'zaktə/, /ɛg'zaktə/ *noun* M20 American Spanish (*quiniela exacta* exact quinella). *Betting* (In North America) a PERFECTA.

exalté /ɛgzalte/ *noun & adjective* (feminine **exaltée**) plural of noun pronounced same M19 French (past participial adjective of *exalter* to exalt, from as *ex*- up(wards) + *altus* high). **A** *noun* A person who is elated or impassioned. **B** *adjective* Inspiring or stimulating.

ex ante /ɛks 'antɪ/ *adjective & adverb phrase* M20 Modern Latin (from *ex* from + *ante* before). Chiefly *Economics* **A** *adjective phrase* Based on prior assumptions or expectations; predicted, prospective. **B** *adverb phrase* Before the event, in advance, beforehand.

■ The opposite of EX POST.
B 1992 *New York Review of Books* Ex ante, the thing looks dubious. *Ex post* it is, disconcertingly, a surprising success…

ex cathedra /ɛks kə'θi:drə/, /ɛks 'kaθɪdrə/ *adverb & adjective phrase* E17 Latin (= from the (teacher's) chair, from *ex* (preposition) + *cathedra* chair). With the full authority of office (especially that of the Pope, implying infallibility as defined in Roman Catholic doctrine).

1996 *New Scientist* Something of a pattern emerges about deception that will reassure the ex cathedra theoreticians.

excelsior /ɛk'sɛlsɪɔ:/ *interjection & noun* (also **Excelsior**) L18 Latin (comparative of *excelsus* from *ex-* + *celsus* lofty). **A** *interjection* Go higher! **B** *noun* **1** A person who or thing which reaches or aspires to reach higher. Used in the names of hotels and products to indicate superior quality. **2** Curled shavings of soft wood for stuffing furniture or packing fragile goods. Originally *United States*.

excreta /ɪk'skri:tə/, /ɛk'skri:tə/ *noun plural* M19 Latin (use as noun of neuter plural of *excretus* past participle of *excernere* to excrete). Waste matter discharged from the body, especially faeces and urine.

excursus /ɪk'skə:səs/, /ɛk'skə:səs/ *noun* plural **excursuses, excursus** /ɪk'skə:su:s/ E19 Latin (= excursion, from *excurs-* past participial stem of *excurrere* to run out). **1** A fuller treatment in an appendix of some point in the main text of a book, especially an edition of the classics. **2** A digression within a narrative in which some point is discussed at length.

exeat /'ɛksɪat/ *noun* E18 Latin (= let him or her go out, 3rd person singular present subjunctive of *exire* to go out). **1** A permission for temporary absence from a college, boarding school, or other institution. **2** A permission granted by a bishop to a priest to move to another diocese.

1 1984 A. Brookner *Hotel du Lac* The tall thin beauty with the dog was never visible in the daytime and it was impossible to imagine her doing anything except eating ice cream and smoking, like a child on an exeat from school.

exedra /'ɛksɪdrə/, /ɪk'si:drə/, /ɛk'sɪdrə/ *noun* (also **exhedra** /'ɛkshɪdrə/, /ɪks'hi:drə/, /ɛks'hɪdrə/) plural **exedrae** /'ɛksɪdri:/ E18 Latin (from Greek, from as *ex-* + *hedra* seat). *Architecture* A room, portico, or arcade with a bench or seats where people may converse, especially in ancient Roman and Greek buildings.

exegesis /ɛksɪ'dʒi:sɪs/ *noun* plural **exegeses** /ɛksɪ'dʒi:si:z/ E17 Greek (*exēgēsis*, from *exēgeisthai* to interpret). Critical explanation or interpretation of a text, especially scripture.

1996 *Spectator* And his films resist the easy exegesis of critics . . .

exempla plural of EXEMPLUM.

exempli gratia /ɪgˌzɛmpli 'greɪʃə/, /ɛgˌzɛmpli/ *adverb phrase* M17 Latin (from genitive of *exemplum* example + ablative of *gratia* grace). For example; for instance.

■ Abbreviated to *e.g. Exempli gratia* and its ubiquitous abbreviation have entirely superseded *exempli causa* (literally, 'by reason of example'), although the latter was the earlier (M16) in English.

exemplum /ɪg'zɛmpləm/, /ɛg'zɛmpləm/ *noun* plural **exempla** /ɪg'zɛmplə/ L19 Latin. An example or model, especially a story told to illustrate a moral point.

exequatur /ɛksɪ'kweɪtə/ *noun* E17 Latin (= let him or her perform, 3rd person singular present subjunctive of *exequi* to carry out, execute). An official recognition of a consul by a foreign government, authorizing him or her to exercise office.

exergue /ɪk'sə:g/, /ɛk'sə:g/, /'ɛksə:g/ *noun* L17 French (from medieval Latin *exergum*, from Greek *ex-* + *ergon* work). *Numismatics* A small space on a coin or medal, usually on the reverse below the principal emblem, for the date, the engraver's initials, etc.; the inscription placed there.

exeunt /'ɛksɪʌnt/ *verb & noun* L15 Latin (= they go out, 3rd person plural present indicative of *exire* to go out). **A** *intransitive verb* Used as a stage direction in a play to indicate that a group of actors leaves the stage: *exeunt Hamlet and Polonius.* Cf. EXIT (verb 1). **B** *noun* A collective EXIT; a departure by more than one person.

■ Also in the phrase *exeunt omnes* 'all leave the stage' at the end of a scene or play.
B 1996 *Times* Usually when the critics slink off to the pub during the last act, their excuse to the paying customers they are forcing to stand up for their exeunt is that they have to catch the early editions.

ex gratia /ˌɛks ˈgreɪʃə/ *adverb & adjective phrase* M18 Latin (= from favour, from *ex* from + *gratia* grace). (Referring to a payment) done from a sense of moral obligation rather than because of any legal requirement.

> **1996** *New Scientist* We can only ask that the government provide ex gratia payments to all affected.

exhedra variant of EXEDRA.

ex hypothesi /ˌɛks hʌɪˈpɒθəsʌɪ/ *adverb phrase* E17 Modern Latin (from Latin *ex* from + ablative of late Latin HYPOTH-ESIS). According to the hypothesis proposed; supposedly.

exit /ˈɛksɪt/, /ˈɛgzɪt/ *noun* L16 Latin (*exitus*; cf. EXIT. (verb 1)) **1** A departure of an actor etc. from the stage during a scene; *figurative* a person's death. **2** *generally* An act of leaving a place; a departure from a particular situation. **3** A way out of a building, room, or passenger vehicle; an outlet, a way out. **b** A place where traffic can leave a major road or roundabout. **4** *Cards* (especially *Bridge*) The action of deliberately losing the lead; a card enabling one to do this.

exit /ˈɛksɪt/, /ˈɛgzɪt/ *verb* 1 *(intransitive)* M16 Latin (3rd person singular present indicative of *exire* to go out, from as *ex-* out + *ire* to go). Used as a stage direction in a play to indicate that an actor leaves the stage: *exit Pamela*. Cf. EXEUNT.

exit /ˈɛksɪt/, /ˈɛgzɪt/ *verb* 2 E17 Latin (from EXIT (noun)). **1** *intransitive verb* Make one's exit or departure, especially from a stage; leave any place; *figurative* die. **2** *intransitive verb Cards* (especially *Bridge*). Lose the lead deliberately. **3** *transitive verb* Leave, get out of. **4** *intransitive verb Computing* Terminate a process or program. **5** *transitive verb Computing* Terminate (a process or program).

ex libris /ɛksˈlɪbrɪs/, /ɛksˈliːbrɪs/, /ɛksˈlʌɪbrɪs/, /ɛksˈliːbriːs/ *adverb & noun phrase* L19 Latin (literally, 'out of the books *or* library (of —)'. **A** *adverb phrase* Used as an inscription on a bookplate to show the name of the book's owner: *ex libris Edith Wharton*. **B** *noun phrase*

plural same. A bookplate inscribed in such a way.

ex machina see DEUS EX MACHINA.

ex nihilo /ɛks ˈniːhɪləʊ/, /ˈnʌɪhɪləʊ/ *adverb phrase* L16 Latin. Out of nothing.

> **1996** *New Scientist* Atheists are equally alarmed, because the notion of the Universe coming into being from nothing looks suspiciously like the creation, *ex nihilo*, of Christianity.

exodus /ˈɛksədəs/ *noun* OE ecclesiastical Latin (*Exodus* from Greek *exodos*, from as *ex-* out + *hodos* way). **1** (*Exodus*) (The name of) the second book of the Bible, relating the departure of the Israelites from slavery in Egypt and their journey to Canaan. **2** A mass departure of people; *specifically* the departure of the Israelites from Egypt.

ex officio /ˌɛks əˈfɪʃɪəʊ/ *adverb & adjective phrase* M16 Latin (from *ex* out of, from + *officium* duty, office). By virtue of one's position or status.

exordium /ɪgˈzɔːdɪəm/, /ɛgˈzɔːdɪəm/ *noun* plural **exordiums**, **exordia** /ɪgˈzɔːdɪə/ L16 Latin (from *exordiri* to begin). The beginning or introductory part, especially of a discourse or treatise.

exotica /ɪgˈzɒtɪkə/, /ɛgˈzɒtɪkə/ *noun plural* L19 Latin (neuter plural of *exoticus* exotic, foreign). Objects considered interesting because they are out of the ordinary, especially because they originated in a distant foreign country; exotic things.

> **1995** *Country Life* This year's hot summer is not principally responsible for the increase in insect life... The exotica survived because of the mildness of the winter.

ex parte /ɛks ˈpɑːti/ *adverb & adjective phrase* (as adjective frequently **ex-parte**) E17 Latin (= from a side). *Law* With respect to or in the interests of one side only or of an interested outside party.

ex pede Herculem /ɛks ˌpɛdi ˈhəːkjʊlɛm/ *adverb phrase* M17 Latin (= Hercules from his foot). Inferring the whole of something from an insignificant part.

■ The ancient Greek mathematician Pythagoras is supposed to have calculated the height of the hero Hercules from the size of his foot.

explicit /'ɛksplɪsɪt/ *noun* M17 Late Latin (either = here ends, 3rd person singular indicative of *explicare* to unfold (plural *explicunt*); or abbreviation of *explicitus est liber* = the book is finished). The end; the conclusion.

■ Originally used by medieval scribes to denote the end of a Latin manuscript or work, *explicit* was sometimes also placed (ME–M19) at the end of a printed book, chapter, etc.

exposé /ɪk'spəʊzeɪ/, /ɛk'spəʊzeɪ/, *foreign* /ɛkspoze/ (*plural same*) *noun* (also **expose**) E19 French (past participle of *exposer* to set out, display). A report in the media that reveals something discreditable.

1996 *Spectator*...his relentless research has produced something much more than an exposé of a single rogue...

ex post /ɛks 'pəʊst/ *adjective & adverb phrase* M20 Modern Latin (from *ex* from + Latin *post* after). Chiefly *Economics*. **A** *adjective phrase* Based on past events or actual results; occurring afterwards; actual rather than predicted; retrospective. **B** *adverb phrase* After the event; retrospectively.

■ The opposite of EX ANTE.

ex post facto /ˌɛks pəʊst 'faktəʊ/ *adverb & adjective phrase* M17 Latin (erroneous division of Latin *ex postfacto* in the light of subsequent events, from *ex* from, out of + ablative of *postfactum* that which is done subsequently). **A** *adverb phrase* After the event, after the fact; retro-

spectively. **B** *adjective phrase* Done after another thing; *especially* (of a law) applied retrospectively.

expresso variant of ESPRESSO.

ex silentio /ɛks sɪ'lɛntɪəʊ/, /ɛks sɪ'lɛnʃɪəʊ/ *adverb phrase* E20 Latin (= from silence). (With reference to an argument or theory) based on lack of evidence to the contrary.

extrados /ɪks'treɪdɒs/, /ɛks'treɪdɒs/ *noun* L18 French (from Latin *extra* outside + French *dos* back). *Architecture* The upper or outer curve of an arch; *especially* the upper curve of the voussoirs which form the arch. Cf. INTRADOS.

extraordinaire /ɪkˌstrɔːdɪ'nɛː/, /ɛkˌstrɔːdɪ'nɛː/, *foreign* /ɛkstraɔrdinɛr/ *postpositive adjective* M20 French (= extraordinary). Remarkable, outstanding; (of a person) unusually active or successful in a specified respect.

1996 *Times* This brings up the unfortunate truth that Roger Daltry, trout-farmer extraordinaire, is cooler than Cobain...

exuviae /ɪg'zjuːvɪiː/, /ɛg'zjuːvɪiː/ *noun plural* M17 Latin (= clothing stripped off, skins of animals, spoils, from *exuere* to divest oneself of). *Zoology* The cast or sloughed skin of an animal, especially of an insect larva; *figurative* remnants, remains.

ex-voto /ɛks'vəʊtəʊ/ *noun* plural **ex-votos** L18 Latin (*ex voto* from *ex* out of, from + *voto* ablative singular of *votum* vow). Something offered in fulfilment of a vow previously taken.

f abbreviation of FORTE *(musical direction).*

fabliau /ˈfablɪəʊ/, /fablijo/ *noun* plural **fabliaux** /ˈfablɪəʊz/, /fablijo/ E19 French. *Literature* A verse tale, typically a bawdily humorous one, from the early period of French poetry.

■ The word is also used to denote a similar verse tale of sex and trickery in medieval English, particularly the tales of the Miller, Reeve, Summoner, Merchant, and Shipman in Chaucer's *Canterbury Tales.*

facade /fəˈsɑːd/ *noun* (also **façade**) M17 French (*façade*, from *face* face). **1** The principal front of a building, that faces on to a street or open space. **2** A deceptive outward appearance.

facetiae /fəˈsiːʃɪiː/ *noun plural* E16 Latin (plural of *facetia* jest). **1** Witticisms; humorous sayings. *Archaic.* **2** *Bookselling* Pornographic literature.

facia variant of FASCIA.

facies /ˈfeɪʃɪiːz/ *noun* plural same E17 Latin (= face). **1** *Medicine* The facial expression of an individual that is characteristic of a particular illness. **2** *Science* A general aspect, appearance, or character. **b** *Geology* The character of a rock expressed by its formation, composition, and fossil content.

factotum /fakˈtəʊtəm/ *noun* M16 Medieval Latin (from *fac* imperative of *facere* to do, make + *totum* the whole). A person who does all kinds of work; a servant or other employee who manages all the employer's affairs.

■ Originally in the now obsolete phrases *dominus factotum* or *magister factotum* (translating roughly as 'master of everything') or *Johannes factotum* ('John do-it-all' or 'Jack of all trades'), now most often in the phrase *general factotum.*

fado /ˈfadu:/, /ˈfɑːdəʊ/ *noun* plural **fados** /ˈfadu:ʃ/, /ˈfɑːdəʊz/ E20 Portuguese (literally, 'fate'). A type of popular Portuguese song, usually with a melancholy theme and accompanied by mandolins or guitars; the music for a fado.

faïence /fʌɪˈʊ̃s/, /feɪˈʊ̃s/, /fʌɪˈɑːns/ *noun & adjective* (also **faience**, **fayence**) L17 French (from Faïence, the French name for Faenza, a town in the northern Italian province of Emilia-Romagna). Glazed ceramic ware, in particular decorated tin-glazed earthenware of the type made in Faenza, especially between *c.*1450 and 1520.

faille /feɪl/ *noun* M19 French. A soft, light-woven fabric having a ribbed texture, originally of silk.

■ When originally introduced (M16) it denoted a kind of hood or veil worn by women.

fainéant /ˈfeɪneɪ̃/, foreign /fɛneɑ̃/ (*plural same*) *noun* (also **faineant**) E17 French (from *fait* 3rd person singular of *faire* to do + *néant* nothing). An idle or ineffective person. *Archaic.*

faisandé /fəzɑ̃de/ *adjective* E20 French (literally = (of game) hung until high). Affected, artificial.

1958 *Observer* He plays the part in a *faisandé* Cockney accent straight out of Bruce Bairnsfather's Old Bill cartoons.

fait accompli /fɛt akɔ̃pli/, /feɪt əˈkɔpli/, /feɪt əˈkɒmpli/ *noun phrase* plural **faits accomplis** (pronounced same) M19 French (= accomplished fact). A thing that has already happened or been decided before those affected hear about it, leaving them with no option but to accept it.

1996 *Spectator* He [sc. Konrad Adenauer] governed . . . by a mixture of persuasion, accusation, *faits accomplis* and pressure.

fajitas /fəˈhiːtəz/, foreign /faˈxitas/ *noun plural* L20 Mexican Spanish (literally, 'little strips'). A dish of Mexican origin consisting of strips of spiced beef or chicken, chopped vegetables, and grated cheese, wrapped in a soft tortilla and often served with sour cream.

fakir /ˈfeɪkɪə/, /ˈfakɪə/ *noun* (also formerly **faquir**) E17 Arabic (= poor (man); partly through French *faquir*). A Muslim (or *loosely* Hindu) religious ascetic who lives solely on alms.

falafel /fəˈlɑːf(ə)l/ *noun* (also **felafel**) plural same M20 Arabic (colloquial Egyptian). A Middle Eastern dish of spiced mashed chickpeas or other pulses formed into balls or fritters and deep-fried, usually eaten with or in pitta bread.

falsetto /fɔːlˈsɛtəʊ/, /fɒlˈsɛtəʊ/ *noun & adjective* L18 Italian (diminutive of *falso* false, from Latin *falsus*). *Music* **A** *noun* A method of voice production used by male singers, especially tenors, to sing notes higher than their normal range; a singer using this method; a voice or sound that is unusually high. **B** *attributive* or as *adjective* Above the natural register; high-pitched.

famille jaune /famij ʒɔn/ *noun phrase* L19 French (literally, 'yellow family'). A type of Chinese enamelled porcelain of which the predominant colour is yellow, dating from the 18th century.

famille noire /famij nwar/ *noun phrase* L19 French (literally, 'black family'). A type of Chinese enamelled porcelain of which the predominant colour is black, dating from the 18th century.

famille rose /famij roz/ *noun phrase* L19 French (literally, 'pink family'). A type of Chinese enamelled porcelain of which the predominant colour is pink, dating from the reign of Yongzheng (1723–35).

famille verte /famij vɛrt/ *noun phrase* L19 French (literally, 'green family'). A type of Chinese enamelled porcelain of which the predominant colour is green, dating from the reign of Kangxi (1662–1722).

famulus /ˈfamjʊləs/ *noun* plural **famuli** /ˈfamjʊlʌɪ/, /ˈfamjʊliː/ L19 Latin (= servant). An assistant or servant, especially one working for a scholar or magician.

fandango /fanˈdaŋɡəʊ/ *noun* plural **fandangos** or **fandangoes** M18 Spanish. **1** A lively Spanish dance for two in 3/4 or 6/8 time, usually accompanied by guitars and castanets; a piece of music for this dance. **2** An elaborate or complicated process or activity.

fanfaronade /ˌfanfarəˈneɪd/, /ˌfanfarə-ˈnɑːd/ *noun* (also **fanfaronnade**) M17 French (*fanfaronnade* from *fanfaron* a braggart). **1** Arrogant, swaggering talk; bluster. **2** A fanfare.

fantasia /fanˈteɪzɪə/, /fantəˈziːə/ *noun* E18 Italian (= fantasy). A musical or other composition with a free form and often an improvisatory style; a piece of music based on a familiar tune or tunes; a thing composed of a mixture of different forms or styles.

faquir variant of FAKIR.

farandole /ˌfar(ə)nˈdəʊl/, /ˈfar(ə)ndəʊl/ *noun* M19 French (from modern Provençal *farandoulo*). A lively Provençal communal dance in which the dancers join hands and wind in and out in a chain; a piece of music for this dance.

farce /fɑːs/ *noun* E18 French (= stuffing). *Cookery* Forcemeat, stuffing.

■ In medieval cookbooks the word appears in the form *fars*. It was reintroduced into English in its modern form in Richard Bradley's *Family Dictionary* (1725), which was a translation of Chomel's *Dictionaire oeconomique*. The use of *farce* to denote a type of comic dramatic work derives from this 'forcemeat' sense. The word came to be used metaphorically for comic interludes 'stuffed' into the texts of religious plays, leading to the current usage.

farceur /farsœr/ (*plural same*), /fɑːˈsəː/ *noun* (feminine **farceuse**) plural pronounced same L17 French. **1** A joker or buffoon; a comedian. **2** A writer of or actor in farces.

2 1996 *Country Life* . . . it is more than a little odd for British culture to be represented by a detective writer, an actor-producer, a TV mogul, a violinist and a Whitehall *farceur*.

farfalle /fɑːˈfaleɪ/, /fɑːˈfali/ *noun* plural L20 Italian (plural of *farfalla* butterfly). Small pieces of pasta shaped like bows or butterflies' wings.

farouche /fəˈruːʃ/ *adjective* M18 French (ultimately from Latin *foras* out-of-doors). Sullen or shy in company, ill at ease.

> **1996** *Country Life* The farouche and unintentionally dangerous colt... has become a biddable, lovable and, when handled firmly, quite gentle creature.

farrago /fəˈrɑːgəʊ/, /fəˈreɪgəʊ/ *noun* plural **farragos**, (chiefly United States) **farragoes** M17 Latin (= mixed fodder for cattle, hence *figurative*, a medley). A jumble; a hotchpotch; a confused situation.

> **1995** *Spectator* Only one man, in this entire farrago, appears to have been corrupt in the word's fullest sense, in that he broke the law for the sake of personal financial gain.

farruca /fəˈruːkə/ *noun* E20 Spanish (feminine of *farruco* Galician or Asturian, from *Farruco* pet form of male forename *Francisco*). A type of flamenco dance.

fartlek /ˈfɑːtlɛk/ *noun* M20 Swedish (from *fart* speed + *lek* play). A method of training used by middle- and long-distance runners in which the terrain and pace are continually varied.

fasces /ˈfasiːz/ *noun* plural L16 Latin (plural of *fascis* bundle). **1** In ancient Rome, rods tied in a bundle with an axe, carried before the leading magistrates as a symbol of power, and later used as an emblem of authority in Fascist Italy. **2** (Emblems of) power or authority.

> **2 1996** *Times* And our VIPs are at heart no more eager than the Italians to give up their fasces of authority.

fascia /ˈfaʃɪə/, /ˈfeɪʃɪə/, /ˈfaʃə/ *noun* (also (except sense 4) **facia**) plural **fasciae** /ˈfeɪʃiː/ (sense 4), **fascias** M16 Latin (= band, door frame). **1** A board covering the ends of rafters or other fittings. **2** A signboard on a shopfront. **3** (In classical architecture) a long flat surface between mouldings on an architrave. **4** *Anatomy* A thin sheath of fibrous tissue enclosing a muscle or other organ. **5** The dashboard of a motor vehicle; a board or panel of controls on any piece of equipment. **6** A covering, typically a detachable one, for the front part of a mobile phone.

fata morgana /ˌfɑːtə mɔːˈgɑːnə/ *noun phrase* E19 Italian (= fairy Morgan (Morgan le Fay)). A kind of mirage often seen in the Strait of Messina between Italy and Sicily, formerly attributed to supernatural agency; an illusion.

■ According to the northern European Arthurian legends, Morgan le Fay was the sister of Britain's King Arthur and possessed magical powers. Her legend was taken to Sicily by the Normans when they conquered the island in the eleventh century.

fatwa /ˈfatwɑː/ *noun* (also **Fatwa, fatwah**) E17 Arabic. A ruling on a point of Islamic law given by a recognized authority.

■ Although it was first used in English in the 17th century (in the form *fetfa*), the word came into general currency in the English-language media after February 1989, when Ayatollah Khomeini of Iran issued a *fatwa* condemning the Indian-born British writer Salman Rushdie and his publishers to death on account of Rushdie's novel *The Satanic Verses* (1988), which many Muslims held to be blasphemous and deeply objectionable in its treatment of the Koran. Because of the circumstances of the *fatwa* on Rushdie, the word is sometimes wrongly thought to mean 'a death sentence'. Since its revitalization in English, *fatwa* has moved far beyond its original Islamic context and is often used figuratively to indicate any strong denunciation (see quotation 1995).

> **1989** *Bookseller* The... International Committee... have capitalized on the outrage felt at the notorious *fatwa* to drive forward... the long-nurtured campaign for total abolition of blasphemy laws in this country.
>
> **1989** *Independent* This Fatwa... was written and signed by the Grand Ayatollah of Shia in Iraq, explaining his position regarding the executions of 16 Kuwaiti Pilgrims...
>
> **1995** *Times* That the bishops should choose to intone on a subject as morally trivial as the lottery is itself indicative of that order of priorities which so often flummoxes the Christian on the Clapham omnibus. *Fatwas* against the lottery reveal once more the confusion.

faubourg /fobur/ (*plural same*), /ˈfəʊbʊəg/ *noun* L15 French (cf. medieval Latin *falsus burgus* not the city proper). A suburb, especially a suburb of Paris; formerly that part of a town or city lying just outside the walls.

fauna /'fɔ:nə/ *noun* plural **faunae** /'fɔ:ni:/, **faunas** L18 Modern Latin (application of *Fauna*, an ancient Italian rural goddess, sister of the god *Faunus*, who was equated with the Greek god Pan). **1** *collective singular and in plural* The animals and animal life of a particular region, habitat, or geological period; cf. FLORA. **2** A book or other work detailing the animal life of a region.

faute de mieux /fot də mjə/ *adjective & adverb phrase* M18 French. For want of a better alternative.
1995 *Times* The dinner party is dead. Enter, *faute de mieux*, the age of the supper party.

fauteuil /fotœj/ *noun* plural pronounced same M18 French. A wooden seat in the form of an armchair with open sides and upholstered arms.

fauve /fəʊv/ *noun & adjective* (also **Fauve**) plural pronounced same E20 French (literally, 'wild beast'). **A** *noun* An adherent of fauvism, a style of painting notable for its vivid expressionistic and non-naturalistic use of colour, originating in the early 20th century with the work of Henri Matisse (1869–1954) and his followers; a fauvist. **B** *adjective* Relating to fauvism or fauvists.
■ The term was coined by the French art critic Louis Vauxcelles at the Autumn Salon in Paris in 1905, who, seeing a traditional Renaissance-type statue exhibited amidst the works of Matisse and his adherents, exclaimed, '*Donatello au milieu des fauves!*' ('*Donatello among the wild beasts!*')
1984 A. G. Lehmann *The European Heritage* Matisse, even if called a '*fauve*', can convey a wonderful serenity...

faux /fəʊ/ *adjective* L20 French (= false). Made in imitation; artificial.
■ Also *faux-* as first element in combinations, as in *faux-soul*, *faux-painted*, etc.
1993 W. Self *My Idea of Fun* I ran the length of the new hallway, with its Wilton carpeting, faux hunting prints and brocaded wallpaper.
transferred 1996 *Spectator* The *faux* egalitarianism of Gap matches the *faux* illusion of the age of Clinton.

faux amis /ˌfəʊz 'əmi:/ *noun phrase* plural M20 French (literally, 'false friends'). Pairs of words in two different languages (especially French and English) that have a similar form but which have entirely different meanings.
■ The term derives from *Les Faux Amis ou les Trahisons du vocabulaire anglais*, the title of a book with a collection of such terms made in 1928 by M. Koessler and J. Derocquigny. An example is English *defiance* and French *défiance* 'distrust'.

faux-naïf /fonaif/, /ˌfəʊnʌɪˈi:f/ *noun & adjective* (also **faux-naif**) plural pronounced same M20 French (from *faux* false + *naïf* ingenuous, naive). **A** *noun* A person who pretends to be ingenuous. **B** *adjective* Artificially or affectedly simple or naive.
1996 *Times* When she attempts the old, cheerful faux-naïf trick, it doesn't work.

faux pas /fo pa/, /fəʊ 'pɑ:/ *noun phrase* plural same L17 French (from *faux* false + *pas* step). An embarrassing or tactless act or remark in a social situation; a social blunder.
1995 *Times* I never gave formal dinner parties and never liked them with their implications that they were to do with somehow showing off at the same time as being a minefield of *faux pas*.

favela /fa'vela/ *noun* M20 Portuguese. A Brazilian shack or shanty town.
■ Usually in plural *favelas* 'a slum'.
1961 G. Mikes *Tango* In the midst of all this beauty and elegance, you discover the *favelas*...A *favela* is a wretched, ramshackle, filthy hut run up out of sticks, rotting planks, dirty rags and cardboard, as a rule in less than twenty-four hours.

fazenda /fə'zɛndə/ *noun* E19 Portuguese. (In Portugal, Brazil, and Portuguese-speaking countries) a large farm or estate; the homestead belonging to such an estate.
■ The equivalent in Spanish-speaking countries is a HACIENDA.

fazendeiro /ˌfazɛn'dɛ:rəʊ/ *noun* E19 Portuguese. A person who owns or lives on a FAZENDA.

fedayeen /ˌfɛdʌɪˈji:n/ *noun* plural L19 Arabic ((or Persian) = those who sacrifice their lives for others or for a cause, from *fada* ransom). Arab guerrillas operating especially against Israel.
■ The singular *fedai* had previously been used (late 19th century) to denote an Ismaili Muslim assassin.

feijoa /feɪ'(d)ʒəʊə/ *noun* L19 Modern Latin (named after the Brazilian naturalist J. da Silva Feijó). An evergreen shrub or small tree that bears edible green fruit resembling guavas; the fruit of the feijoa.

feijoada /feɪ'(d)ʒwadə/, /feɪ'(d)ʒwadə/ *noun* M20 Portuguese (from *feijão*, from Latin *phaseolus* bean). A Brazilian or Portuguese stew made with black beans, pork, and sausage and served with rice.

feis /fɛʃ/, /feɪʃ/ *noun* (in sense 1 also **fes(s)**) plural **feiseanna** /fɛʃənə/ L18 Irish (= wedding feast, festival). **1** An assembly of kings and chieftains, formerly believed to be a kind of early Celtic parliament. **2** An Irish or Scottish festival of music and dancing, similar to the Welsh EISTEDDFOD.

felafel variant of FALAFEL.

feldsher /'fɛldʃə/ *noun* (also **feldscher**) L19 Russian (*fel'dsher* from German *Feldscher* a field surgeon). In Russia and the former USSR: a person with practical training in medicine and surgery, but lacking professional medical qualifications; an assistant to a physician or surgeon; a medical auxiliary.

felix culpa /ˌfiːlɪks 'kʌlpə/, /ˌfeɪlɪks 'kʊlpɑː/ *noun phrase* M20 Latin (literally, 'happy fault'). **1** *Theology* The sin of Adam viewed as fortunate, because it brought about the blessed outcome of the redemption of mankind by Jesus Christ. **2** An apparent error or disaster with ultimately happy consequences.

■ The phrase is taken from the Exultet, which forms part of the Roman Catholic liturgy for Holy Saturday (Easter Eve).
1987 D. Hall *Seasons at Eagle Pond* And, *felix culpa*, Fall is the most beautiful season—at least in New Hampshire.

fellah /'fɛlə/ *noun* plural **fellaheen, fellahin** /'fɛləhiːn/, **fellahs** M18 Arabic (*fallah* colloquial plural *fallahin* tiller of the soil). A peasant in Egypt and other Arabic-speaking countries.

felo de se /ˌfiːləʊ dɪ 'siː/, /ˌfɛləʊ də 'seɪ/ *noun phrase* plural **felones de se** /fɪˌləʊniːz dɪ 'siː/, **felos de se** /ˌfɛləʊz də 'seɪ/ E17 (Anglo-)Latin (literally, 'felon of himself'). **1** A person who commits

suicide (formerly in the UK a criminal act) or intentionally brings about his or her own death. **2** Suicide.

felucca /fɛ'lʌkə/ *noun* E17 Italian (*feluc(c)a* perhaps from an Arabic word via Spanish). A small sailing vessel with lateen sails and oars, formerly widely used in the Mediterranean area and still used on the River Nile.

feme covert /fiːm 'kʌvət/ *noun phrase* (also **femme couverte**) plural **femes coverts** (pronounced same) M16 Old French (literally 'a covered woman' (i.e. protected by marriage)). *Law* A married woman.

■ The technical spelling is *feme*, but the Modern French *femme* is also found.

feme sole /fiːm 'səʊl/ *noun phrase* plural **femes soles** (pronounced same) M16 Old French (literally 'a woman alone'). *Law* An unmarried woman, especially a divorcée; *historical* a married woman who carries on a business in her own right, independently of her husband.

femme /fɛm/ *noun* (also **fem**) M20 French (= woman). A lesbian who takes a traditionally feminine sexual role. *Colloquial*.

femme couverte see FEME COVERT.

femme fatale /fam fatal/, /ˌfɛm fa'tɑːl/ *noun phrase* plural **femmes fatales** (pronounced same) E20 French (literally, 'disastrous woman'). An attractive and seductive woman, especially one who will ultimately cause distress to a man who becomes involved with her.
1995 *Big Issue* Furthermore, the entrance of the femme fatale—embodied by such cat-like sirens as Lauren Bacall and Barbara Stanwyck—exposed male fears of the newly empowered woman . . .

fenestella /ˌfɛnɪ'stɛlə/ *noun* LME Latin (diminutive of *fenestra* window). A niche in an interior wall of a church, usually on the south side of the altar and containing the PISCINA.

feng-shui /ˌfɛŋ 'ʃuːi/, /ˌfʌŋ 'ʃuːi/ *noun* L18 Chinese (from *feng* wind + *shui* water). (In Chinese thought) a system of laws considered to govern spatial arrangement and orientation in relation to the flow of energy (chi), and whose favourable or unfavourable effects are taken into account when siting or designing buildings.

ferae naturae /ˌfɪəri: nəˈtʃʊəriː/, /ˌfɛrʌɪ nəˈtʃʊərʌɪ/ *noun phrase* M17 Latin (= of wild nature). Chiefly *Law* Undomesticated or wild animals.

fer de lance /ˌfɛː də ˈlaːns/ *noun* plural **fers de lance** (pronounced same), **fer de lances** L19 French (= iron (head) of a lance). A highly venomous tropical pit viper, *Bothrops atrox*, native to Central and South America.

feria /ˈfɪərɪə/, /ˈfɛrɪə/ *noun* LME Latin (= holiday; in sense 2 through Spanish). **1** *Ecclesiastical* A weekday, especially one on which no festival falls. **2** (In Spain and Spanish-speaking countries) a fair.
> **2 1996** *Spectator* . . . live television coverage of the [bull]fights at the major *ferias* has become commonplace.

fermata /fəˈmɑːtə/ *noun* plural **fermatas**, **fermate** /fəˈmɑːteɪ/ L19 Italian (from *fermare* to stop). *Music* A pause of unspecified length on a note or rest; a sign indicating a prolonged note or rest.

ferronnière /fɛrɒnjɛr/ (*plural same*), /fɛˌrɒnɪˈɛː/ *noun* (also **feronière**) M19 French (literally, 'blacksmith's wife'; a frontlet). A piece of jewellery comprising a decorative chain worn around the head with a pendant on the centre of the forehead; a frontlet.
> ■ The name derives from Leonardo da Vinci's portrait known as *La Belle Ferronnière*, which shows a woman wearing this sort of ornament.

fest /fɛst/ *noun* (also **Fest**) M19 German (= festival). A special occasion; a celebration, a celebratory gathering.
> ■ Originally United States, it is chiefly used as the second element in a combination, as in *filmfest*, *gabfest* (a gathering for talk; a conference), *glamfest* (= glamourfest), *songfest*, *talkfest*, etc.
> **1995** *Times* The elegance of the *ancien régime* is taken further in M Saint Laurent's own office, a glamfest of mirrors, gilt and velvet.
> **1995** *Times* By dawn the *mediafest* which had been gathering outside Westminster on College Green was already setting up its cameras.

festina lente /fɛsˈtiːnə ˌlɛnteɪ/ *interjection* L17 Latin (= make haste slowly (imperative singular of *festinare* to hasten + *lente* slowly)). Urging caution; more haste, less speed!
> ■ According to Suetonius (*Life of Augustus Caesar* xxv), the Greek form of this tag was a favourite with Augustus with reference to military operations and the qualities he looked for in a commander.
> **1996** *Times* Why so long? Must *festina lente* always be the exchange's watchword?

Festschrift /ˈfɛs(t)ʃrɪft/ *noun* (also **festschrift**) plural **Festschriften** /ˈfɛs(t)ʃrɪftən/, **Festschrifts** L19 German (literally, 'celebration-writing'). A collection of writings published in honour of a scholar, usually presented to mark an occasion in his or her life.
> **1994** W. D. Hackmann and A. J. Turner *Learning, Language and Invention* The mere existence of a *festschrift* is evidence of esteem for its recipient as it is for his stature in his profession.
> *figurative* **1995** *Spectator* Charm is an underrated quality in public life, as is humour. Goodman had both, as this week's *festschrift* of Goodman stories has indicated.

feta /ˈfɛtə/ *noun* (also **fetta**) M20 Modern Greek. A white salty Greek cheese made from the milk of ewes or goats.

fête /feɪt/, /fɛt/ *noun & verb* (also **fete**) LME French (from Old French *feste*). **A** *noun* **1** A public function, typically held outdoors and organized to raise funds for a charity, including entertainment and the sale of goods and refreshments. *British.* **2** A celebration or festival. *Chiefly North American.* **B** *transitive verb* Honour or entertain (a person) lavishly: *she was an instant celebrity, fêted by the media.*
> ■ Originally used in the sense 'festival, fair'.

fête champêtre /fɛt ʃɑ̃pɛtr/ *noun phrase* plural **fêtes champêtres** (pronounced same) L18 French (= a rural festival). An outdoor or pastoral entertainment; a garden party.
> **1996** *Spectator* . . . no one before had painted prostitutes instead of goddesses, drunks and urban café scenes in the place of *fêtes champêtres*.

fête galante /fɛt galɑ̃t/ *noun phrase* plural **fêtes galantes** (pronounced same) E20 French (= an elegant festival). An outdoor entertainment or rural festival, especially as depicted in an 18th-century French genre of painting; a painting in this genre.

■ The subject matter of young ladies and gentlemen in elaborate or theatrical dress making music, flirting, and dancing in Arcadian surroundings is particularly associated with Jean Antoine Watteau (1684–1721).

1996 *Country Life* It is surprising that rather than call on the talents of the two great animal painters Oudry and Desportes, the artists chosen were history painters or painters of *fêtes galantes*.

fêtes champêtres, fêtes galantes plural of FÊTE CHAMPÊTRE, FÊTE GALANTE.

fetta variant of FETA.

fettuccine /fɛtʊˈtʃiːni/ *noun plural* (also **fettucini**) E20 Italian (plural of *fettuccina*, diminutive of *fetta* slice, ribbon). Pasta in the form of ribbons; an Italian dish consisting mainly of this, usually with a sauce.

feu de joie /fø də ʒwa/ *noun phrase* plural **feux de joie** (pronounced same) E17 French (literally, 'fire of joy'). **1** A rifle salute fired by soldiers on a ceremonial occasion, each soldier firing in succession along the ranks to make a continuous sound. **2** *figurative* A joyful occasion; a celebration.

feu follet /fø fɔlɛ/ *noun phrase* plural **feux follets** (pronounced same) M19 French (literally, 'frolicsome fire'). A will-o'-the-wisp, an IGNIS FATUUS. Usually *figurative*.

feuilleton /ˈfəːɪtɒ̃/, *foreign* /fœjtɔ̃/ *noun* M19 French (from *feuillet*, diminutive of *feuille* leaf). A section of a newspaper or magazine devoted to fiction, criticism, light reading, etc.; an article or story suitable for or printed in that section.

fez /fɛz/ *noun* plural **fezzes** E19 Turkish (*fes*, perhaps through French *fez*). A flat-topped conical brimless red hat with a tassel, worn by men in some Muslim countries.

■ Named after *Fez* (now *Fès*) in Morocco, once the principal place of manufacture, the fez was the national headgear of the Turks until the reforms of Kemal Atatürk in the 1920s.

ff abbreviation of FORTISSIMO *(musical direction)*.

fiancé /fɪˈɒnseɪ/, /fɪˈɑːnseɪ/, /fɪˈɒ̃seɪ/ *noun* M19 French (from (Old) French *fiancer* to betroth). A man to whom a woman is engaged to be married.

fiancée /fɪˈɒnseɪ/, /fɪˈɑːnseɪ/, /fɪˈɒ̃seɪ/ *noun* M19 French (see preceding). A woman to whom a man is engaged to be married.

fianchetto /fɪənˈtʃɛtəʊ/, /fɪənˈkɛtəʊ/ *noun & verb* M19 Italian (diminutive of *fianco* flank). *Chess* **A** *noun* plural **fianchettoes** The development of a bishop by moving it one square to a long diagonal of the board. **B** *transitive verb* Develop (a bishop) in this way.

fiasco /fɪˈaskəʊ/ *noun* plural **fiascos** M19 Italian (from phrase *far fiasco*, literally, 'make a bottle'). A complete failure, especially a ludicrous or humiliating one.

■ The word was originally used of a theatrical or musical performance. The allusion in the Italian phrase is unexplained.

fiat /ˈfʌɪat/ *noun* LME Latin (3rd person singular present subjunctive of *fieri* = let it be done, let there be made). **1** A formal authorization for a proposed arrangement, etc.; generally, any authoritative pronouncement, decree. **2** A command by which something is brought into being.

■ In sense 2 *fiat* is short for or an allusion to *fiat lux* = let there be light (Vulgate Genesis 1:3).

fichu /ˈfiːʃuː/ *noun* M18 French (from *ficher* to fix, pin). A triangular piece of lace or fine fabric worn by women round the neck or shoulders, and formerly also over the head.

fidus Achates /ˌfʌɪdəs əˈkeɪtiːz/ *noun phrase* L16 Latin (= faithful Achates). A trusted friend or devoted follower.

■ Quotation from Virgil *Aeneid* vi.158. Achates was the loyal and trusted companion of the poem's hero, Aeneas.

fiesta /fɪˈɛstə/ *noun* M19 Spanish (= feast). **1** (In Spanish-speaking countries) a religious festival. **2** An event marked by festivities or celebration.

figura /fɪˈgjʊərə/ *noun* plural **figurae** /fɪˈgjʊariː/ M20 Latin (= figure). (In literary theory) a person or thing representing or symbolizing a fact or ideal.

figurant /figyrɑ̃/ (*plural same*), /ˈfɪgjʊr(ə)nt/ *noun* (feminine **figurante**) L18 French (present participial adjective of *figurer* to figure). A supernumerary actor with a walk-on role in a theatrical performance.

■ A *figurant* was originally a ballet dancer; in the context of ballet now the term usually denotes a non-dancing performer with a supporting role.

filé /ˈfiːleɪ/ *noun* M19 French (past participle of *filer* twist). (In the United States) powdered or pounded sassafras leaves used to flavour and thicken soup, especially gumbo.

■ Earliest use in *gumbo filé*.

1996 *Times Magazine* If you can get powdered *file*, so much the better. This dried and powdered sassafras is what gives the gumbo its thick and shiny texture.

filet /ˈfiːleɪ/, /fɪlɪt/, *foreign* /filɛ/ (*plural same*) *noun* L19 French (= net). A kind of net or lace with a square mesh.

filet de boeuf /ˌfiːleɪ də ˈbəːf/, *foreign* /filɛ də bœf/ *noun phrase* M19 French. A fillet of beef; *United States* a tenderloin.

filet mignon /ˌfiːleɪ ˈmiːnjɒ̃/, *foreign* /filɛ miɲɔ̃/ *noun phrase* plural **filet mignons** (pronounced same) E20 French (= dainty fillet). A small tender piece of beef from the end of the undercut.

1995 *Times* Succulent as *filet mignon* but low in fat and cholesterol...

filioque /fɪlɪˈəʊkweɪ/ *noun* (also **Filioque**) M19 Latin (= and from the Son). *Christian Church* The statement in the Nicene Creed that the Holy Spirit proceeds not only from God the Father but also from the Son.

■ *Filioque* appeared as an addition to the Creed in the Western Church in the sixth century, possibly originating in Spain. It gradually became a source of contention between the theologians of Rome and Constantinople, since it was accepted in the West but rejected by the Eastern Orthodox Churches. It was one of the central issues in the Great Schism of 1054.

fille de joie /fij də ʒwa/ *noun phrase* plural **filles de joie** (pronounced same) E18 French (literally, 'girl of pleasure'). A prostitute.

film noir /film nwar/, /fɪlm ˈnwɑː/ *noun phrase* plural **films noirs** (pronounced same) M20 French (literally, 'black film'). A style or genre of cinematographic film of a pessimistic, cynical, and sombre character; a film of this type.

■ The typical *film noir* was a black-and-white Hollywood movie of the late 1940s or early 1950s with gloomy lighting, a menacing urban setting, and a fatalistic loner as the anti-hero. The phrase is sometimes abbreviated to simply *noir*, with examples of the revival of the genre since the 1990s being dubbed *neo noir*.

1995 *Big Issue* Film noir was a particular, time-specific genre, a shock antidote to the Techni-color musicals and 'aw-shucks' family dramas that dominated Forties Hollywood.

filo /ˈfiːləʊ/ *noun* (also **phyllo**) M20 Modern Greek (*phullo* leaf). Dough that can be stretched into very thin sheets, used in layers to make both sweet and savoury pastries, especially in eastern Mediterranean cookery.

fils /fis/ *noun* L19 French (= the son). The son, the younger, junior.

■ *Fils* is appended to a name to distinguish between father and son of the same name; cf. PÈRE.

1996 *Bookseller* Amis *fils* was believed to have been unhappy about the ... serialisation of a diary Mr Jacobs had kept of his last meetings with Amis *père*.

finale /fɪˈnɑːli/ *noun* M18 Italian (use as noun of adjective from Latin *finalis* from *finis* end). The last part of a piece of music, an entertainment, or a public event, especially when particularly dramatic or exciting.

1996 *Country Life* By now, the orchestra in the pit had reached its finale, rending the air with thundering timpani.

finca /ˈfiŋka/, /ˈfiŋkə/ *noun* E20 Spanish (from *fincar* to cultivate). (In Spain and Spanish-speaking countries) a country estate; a ranch.

fin de siècle /fɛ̃ də sjɛkl/ *adjective phrase & noun phrase* (also **fin-de-siè-cle**) L19 French (= end of century). **A** *adjective phrase* Relating to or characteristic of the final years of a century, especially the 19th century; decadent. **B** *noun phrase* plural **fins de siècle** (pronounced same). The end of a century, especially the 19th century.

    A 1995 *Spectator* [Isaiah] Berlin is acutely aware of the pathology of nationalism, of the distortions of *fin-de-siècle* Romantic voluntarism that lie at the root of Nazi paganism.
    B 1995 *Spectator* Fins de siècle don't have too good a reputation.

fine /fin/ *noun* plural pronounced same E20 French (abbreviation of FINE CHAMPAGNE). French brandy of high quality made from distilled wine rather than from pomace; specifically, FINE CHAMPAGNE.

fine champagne /fin ʃɑ̃paɲ/ *noun phrase* M19 French (= fine (brandy from) Champagne). Brandy from the Champagne district of the Cognac region of which half or more of the content comes from the central Grande Champagne.

    ■ The abbreviation FINE is also found in English.

fines herbes /finz ɛrb/, /fiːnz ˈɛːb/ *noun phrase plural* M19 French (= fine herbs). Fresh mixed herbs (usually parsley, tarragon, chervil, and chives) chopped and used in cooking.

    ■ Frequently used in adjective phrase with *aux*, as in *omelette aux fines herbes*.

finesse /fiˈnɛs/ *noun & verb* LME French. **A** *noun* **1** Impressive delicacy and skill. **2** Great subtlety and tact in handling or manipulating people or difficult situations. **3** (In bridge and whist) an attempt to take a trick with a card that is not a certain winner. **B** *transitive verb* **1** Bring about or deal with (something) by using great delicacy and skill. **2** Slyly attempt to avoid blame or censure when dealing with (a situation or problem). *Chiefly North American*. **3** (In bridge and whist) play (a card) as a finesse.

finis /ˈfiːnɪs/, /ˈfɪnɪs/, /ˈfʌɪnɪs/ *noun* LME Latin (= end). **1** The end (printed at the end of a book or shown at the end of a film). **2** The finish, the conclusion; the end of life, death.

    ■ In the Latin tag *finis coronat opus* 'the end crowns the work', *finis* is used in sense 2.

fino /ˈfiːnəʊ/ *noun* plural **finos** M19 Spanish (= fine *adjective*). A type of pale-coloured dry sherry.

finocchio /fɪˈnɒkɪəʊ/ *noun* (also **finochio**) E18 Italian (from a popular Latin variant of *faeniculum* fennel). A form of fennel with swollen leaf bases eaten as a vegetable.

fiord variant of FJORD.

fioritura /fɪˌɔːrɪˈtʊərə/ *noun* plural **fioriture** /fɪˌɔːrɪˈtʊəri/, /fɪˌɔːrɪˈtʊəreɪ/ M19 Italian (= flowering, from *fiorire* to flower). *Music* An embellishment of a melody, especially as improvised by an operatic singer.

firn /fɪən/ *noun* M19 German ('(snow) of the previous year', from Old High German *firni* old, related to Old Saxon *fern* past, *forn* formerly, Old Norse *forn* ancient). The granular snow on the upper part of a glacier which is in the process of being compressed into ice. Also called NÉVÉ.

fjord /fjɔːd/, /ˈfjɔːd/ *noun* (also **fiord**) L17 Norwegian. A long, narrow, deep inlet of the sea between steep cliffs, as on the Norwegian coast.

fl. abbreviation of FLORUIT.

flacon /flakɔ̃/ *noun* plural pronounced same. E19 French. A small stoppered bottle, especially one for perfume.

flagellum /fləˈdʒɛləm/ *noun* plural **flagella** /fləˈdʒɛlə/ E19 Latin (diminutive of *flagrum* scourge). *Biology* A slender thread-like structure, especially a microscopic whip-like appendage which enables many protozoa, bacteria, spermatozoa, etc. to swim.

    ■ Originally used in the sense 'a whip or scourge'.

flageolet /flaʤə'lɛt/, /'flaʤəlɪt/ *noun* 1 M17 French. A very small flute-like instrument resembling a recorder but with four finger holes on top and two thumb holes below; a tin whistle.

flageolet /flaʤə'lɛt/, /flaʒɔlɛ/ (*plural same*) *noun* 2 L19 French (ultimately from Latin *phaseolus* bean). A small kind of French kidney bean used in cooking. Also *flageolet bean*.

flambé /flãbe/, /'flɒmbeɪ/ *adjective & verb* L19 French (past participle of *flamber* singe, pass through flame). **A** *adjective* 1 *Cookery* (Of food) set alight after being drenched in brandy or other spirit and served while still flaming. 2 Denoting or characterized by a lustrous red copper-based porcelain glaze with purple streaks. **B** *transitive verb* Drench (food) in spirit and set alight.

flambeau /'flambəʊ/ *noun* plural **flambeaus**, **flambeaux** /'flambəʊz/ M17 French (diminutive of *flambe*, from Latin *flammula*, diminutive of *flamma* flame). 1 A flaming torch, especially one made of several thick wicks dipped in wax. 2 A large candlestick with several branches.

flamenco /flə'mɛŋkəʊ/ *noun* plural **flamencos** L19 Spanish (= like a Gypsy, literally = Fleming). A style of Spanish music, played especially on the guitar and accompanied by singing and dancing; a style of spirited, rhythmical dance performed to flamenco music, often with castanets.

flâneur /flɑnœr/ *noun* (also **flaneur**) plural pronounced same. M19 French (from *flâner* to lounge, saunter idly). An man about town who saunters around observing society.

> **1995** *Times* The more Vidal tries to tell us that he is only a *flaneur*, the more real and thorough is his work and life.

fleadh /'flɑː/ *noun* M20 Irish (from *fleadh ceoil* music festival). A festival of Irish or Celtic music, dancing, and culture.

flèche /flɛʃ/, /fleɪʃ/ *noun* (also **fleche**) M19 French (= arrow). 1 A slender spire, typically over the intersection of the nave and the transept of a church. 2 Any of the twenty-four points on a

backgammon board. 3 *Fencing* A running attack. In full *flèche attack*.

fléchette /fleɪ'ʃɛt/ *noun* (also **flechette**) E20 French (diminutive of *flèche* arrow). A type of ammunition resembling a small dart, shot from a gun.

fleur-de-lis /ˌflə:də'li/ *noun phrase* (also **fleur-de-lys**) plural **fleurs-de-lis** (pronounced same) ME French (Old French *flour de lys*, literally, 'flower of the lily'). 1 *Art* and *Heraldry* A stylized lily composed of three petals bound together near their bases, especially known from the former royal arms of France, in which it appears in gold on a blue field. 2 A European iris.

fleuron /'flʊərɒn/, /'flə:rɒn/, *foreign* /flœrɔ̃/ (*plural same*) *noun* LME French (from Old French *floron*, from *flour* flower). 1 A decorative motif in the form of a stylized flower, used especially in printing, architecture, or coinage. 2 A small piece of puff pastry used for garnishing.

flic /flɪk/, *foreign* /flik/ (*plural same*) *noun* L19 French. A French police officer. *Slang*.

flicflac /'flɪkflak/ *noun* M19 French (imitative of a succession of sharp sounds). *Ballet* A lashing movement of the leg related to the FOUETTÉ.

flor. abbreviation of FLORUIT.

flora /'flɔːrə/ *noun* plural **floras**, **florae** /'flɔːriː/ E16 Latin (*flos* flower, plural *flora*; *Flora*, an ancient Italian goddess of fertility and flowers). 1 The personification of nature's power to produce flowers. 2 The plants of a particular region, habitat, or geological period; cf. FAUNA. 3 A treatise on or a list of such plant life.

floreat /'flɒreɪat/, /'flɔːreɪat/ *interjection* Latin (= let he/she/it flourish (3rd person singular present subjunctive of *florere* to flourish)). Used before a name to express one's desire that the specified institution or person will thrive and prosper.

> ■ Originally used in *Floreat Etona!* ('May Eton flourish!'), the motto of Eton College.

florentine /ˈflɒr(ə)ntiːn/ *adjective* E20 French (*Florentine*, of Florence). (Of eggs, fish, etc.) served on a bed of spinach or with a spinach sauce: *eggs florentine*.

flore pleno /ˌflɔːrɪ ˈpleɪnəʊ/, /ˌflɔːrɪ ˈpliːnəʊ/ *adjective phrase* L19 Latin (literally, 'with a full flower'). (Of a plant variety) double-flowered.

■ Used after the names of certain garden flowers that exist in both single- and double-flowered versions.

florilegium /flɒrɪˈliːdʒɪəm/, /flɔːrɪˈliːdʒɪəm/ *noun* plural **florilegia** /flɒrɪˈliːdʒɪə/, **florilegiums** E17 Modern Latin (literally, 'bouquet', from Latin *flori-* combining form of *flos* flower + *legere* to gather, translating Greek *anthologion* anthology). A collection of choice extracts from literature; an anthology.

floruit /ˈflɒrʊɪt/, /ˈflɔːrʊɪt/ *verb & noun* M19 Latin (= he/she/it flourished (3rd person singular perfect indicative of *florere* to flourish)). **A** *verb* Used in conjunction with a specified period or set of dates to indicate when a particular historical figure lived, worked, or was most active. **B** *noun* The period during which a historical figure lived and worked; heyday, period of greatest activity or prosperity.

■ Often abbreviated to *fl.* or *flor.* and used in cases where a person's birth and death dates are unknown or uncertain.

flotilla /fləˈtɪlə/ *noun* E18 Spanish (diminutive of *flota* fleet). A small fleet of ships or boats.

flügelhorn /ˈfluːɡ(ə)lhɔːn/ *noun* (also **flugelhorn**, **flugel horn**) M19 German (*Flügelhorn*, from *Flügel* wing + *horn* horn). A valved brass musical instrument with a cup-shaped mouthpiece and a wide conical bore.

■ Also abbreviated to *flugel*.

focaccia /fɒˈkatʃa/ *noun* plural **focacce** /fɒˈkatʃe/ L20 Italian. A type of flat Italian bread made with olive oil and flavoured with herbs.

1996 *Times* Rivals include olive and tomato breads, focaccia and the more established baguette.

föhn /fəːn/ *noun* (also **foehn**) M19 German (in Old High German *phonno*, Middle High German *foenne*, ultimately from Latin

(*ventus*) *Favonius* mild west wind (Favonius being the Roman personification of the west or west wind)). **1** A hot southerly wind which blows down valleys on the northern slopes of the Alps. **2** *Meteorology* A warm dry wind of this type developing on the lee side of a mountain range as a result of air moving across the range. Also *föhn wind*.

foie gras /fwɑ ˈɡrɑ/ *noun phrase* (also **foie-gras**) E19 French. Abbreviation of PÂTÉ DE FOIE GRAS.

folie à deux /ˌfɒli ɑ ˈdəː/, *foreign* /fɔli a dø/ *noun phrase* E20 French (= shared madness). Delusion or mental illness shared by two people in close association; a shared act of folly between two people.

folie de grandeur /ˌfɒli də ɡrɒˈdəː/, *foreign* /fɔli də ɡrɑ̃dœr/ *noun phrase* (also **folie des grandeurs**) L19 French. Delusions of grandeur or importance.

■ Often applied to something built or created as a result of someone's sense of their own importance, such as a grandiose building or monument.

1995 *Times* ...either this comet is vast and about to obliterate us; or it is a small comet that has suddenly brightened ...All experts admit that a diminutive comet with *folie de grandeur* is the likeliest explanation.

fondant /ˈfɒnd(ə)nt/ *noun* L19 French (use as noun of present participle of *fondre* to melt). A thick paste made of sugar and water, often flavoured or coloured, used in the making of sweets and the icing and decoration of cakes; a sweet made of fondant.

fondue /ˈfɒnd(j)uː/ *noun* M19 French (feminine past participle of *fondre*; cf. FONDANT). A dish in which small pieces of food are cooked, usually at table, by being dipped into a hot sauce or a hot cooking medium such as oil or broth.

fons et origo /ˌfɒnz ɛt ˈɒrɪɡəʊ/, /ˌfɒnz ɛt ɒˈrʌɪɡəʊ/ *noun phrase* E19 Latin. The source and origin of something.

■ Earliest use is in the phrase *fons et origo mali* the source and origin of evil.

1996 *Times Magazine* Half a mile northwest we come to Bedford Park ...the *fons et origo* of every planned suburb between its inception in 1875 and the First World War.

foo yong /fuː ˈjɒŋ/ *noun phrase* M20 Chinese (Cantonese *foo yung*, literally, 'hibiscus'). A Chinese dish made with eggs mixed and cooked with vegetables and other ingredients.

force majeure /fɔrs maʒœr/ *noun phrase* L19 French (= superior strength). **1** *Law* Unforeseeable circumstances that prevent someone from fulfilling a contract. **2** Irresistible compulsion or superior strength.

> **1 1995** *Times* The oil companies... realised that their position was untenable. Therefore, they invoked *force majeure* and agreed new contracts with their customers...

forte /ˈfɔːteɪ/, /ˈfɔːtɪ/, /fɔːt/ *noun* **1** M17 French (use as noun of feminine of *fort* strong). **1** *Fencing* The stronger part of a sword blade, from the hilt to the middle. **2** The strong point of a person; the thing in which one excels.

> ■ The word entered English in its masculine form *fort*, but the feminine form *forte* was later substituted. The modern pronunciation has been influenced by Italian *forte* (see next).

forte /ˈfɔːtɪ/ *adverb, adjective, & noun* **2** E18 Italian (= strong, loud, from Latin *fortis* strong). *Music* **A** *adverb & adjective* (Especially as a direction) loud or loudly. **B** *noun* A passage performed or marked to be performed loudly.

> ■ As a direction, usually abbreviated to *f*.

forte piano /ˌfɔːtɪ pɪˈanəʊ/ *noun, adverb, & adjective* M18 Italian. *Music* **A** *noun* (**fortepiano**) An early form of the pianoforte. **B** *adverb & adjective* (Especially as a direction) loud and then immediately soft.

> ■ As a musical instrument often shortened to PIANO (*noun* 2); as a musical direction, usually abbreviated to *fp*.

fortissimo /fɔːˈtɪsɪməʊ/ *adverb, adjective, & noun* E18 Italian (superlative of FORTE loud(ly)). *Music* **A** *adverb & adjective* (Especially as a direction) very loud or loudly. **B** *noun* plural **fortissimos, fortissimi** /fɔːˈtɪsɪmi/ A passage performed or marked to be performed very loudly.

> ■ As direction, usually abbreviated to *ff*.
> **A** *transferred* **1995** *Times* Defending himself yesterday, Mr Portillo conceded that his speech had been a 'fortissimo' expression of the Government's newly-sceptical European policy.

fouetté /fwete/ (*plural same*), /ˈfwɛteɪ/ *noun* M19 French (past participle of *fouetter* to whip). *Ballet* A pirouette performed with a circular whipping movement of the raised leg to the side; a quick shift of direction of the upper body, performed with one leg extended.

foulard /ˈfuːlɑː/, /ˈfuːlɑːd/ *noun* M19 French. **1** A lightweight printed or checked material of silk or silk and cotton. **2** A tie or handkerchief made from this.

fourchette /fʊəˈʃɛt/ *noun* M18 French (diminutive of *fourche* fork). *Anatomy* A thin fold of skin at the back of the vulva.

foyer /ˈfɔɪeɪ/, *foreign* /fwaje/ (*plural same*) *noun* L18 French (= hearth, home, ultimately from Latin *focus* hearth). An entrance hall or other open area in a building used by the public, especially a hotel or theatre; *North American* an entrance hall in a house or flat.

> ■ Originally denoted the centre of attention or activity.

fp abbreviation of FORTE PIANO (musical direction).

fracas /ˈfrakɑː/ *noun* plural same /ˈfrakɑːz/ E18 French (from *fracasser* from Italian *fracassare* to make an uproar). A noisy disturbance or quarrel.

Fraktur /ˈfraktʊə/ *noun* (also **fraktur**) L19 German (from Latin *fractura* fracture, because of the type's angularity). *Typography* A German style of black-letter type, the normal type used for printing German from the 16th to the mid 20th century.

framboise /frɒmˈbwɑːz/ *noun* L16 French (= raspberry, ultimately from a conflation of Latin *fraga ambrosia* ambrosian strawberry). **1** (In cookery) a raspberry. **2** A white brandy distilled from raspberries. **3** A shade of pink; raspberry colour.

franc tireur /frɑ̃ tirœr/ *noun phrase* plural **francs tireurs** (pronounced same) E19 French (= free shooter). An irregular soldier, a guerrilla fighter; *historically* a member of an irregular

French light infantry corps, originating in the wars of the French Revolution.

franglais /frɑ̃glɛ/ *noun* (also **Franglais**) M20 French (blend of *français* French + *anglais* English). A blend of French and English, either French speech that makes excessive use of English expressions, or unidiomatic French spoken by an English person.

■ The problem, as perceived by the French, of their language being sullied by the influx of Anglo-Saxon words was aired under this name in R. Etiemble's *Parlez-vous Franglais* (1964). Despite various campaigns to exclude them, interlopers such as *le weekend* appear firmly entrenched and likely to remain.

frankfurter /ˈfraŋkfəːtə/ *noun* (also (chiefly *United States*) **frankfurt**) L19 German (*Frankfurter Wurst* Frankfurt sausage). A seasoned sausage made of smoked beef and pork, originally made at Frankfurt am Main in Germany.

frappé /frape/, /ˈfrapeɪ/ *adjective & noun* M19 French (past participle of *frapper* in the sense of 'to ice (drinks)'). **A** *adjective* (Chiefly of wine) iced, chilled; (of a drink) served with crushed ice. **B** *noun* A drink (especially coffee) served with crushed ice or partially frozen to a slushy consistency.

Frau /frau/ *noun* (also **frau**) plural **Frauen** /frauən/, **Fraus** E19 German. A title or form of address for a married or widowed German-speaking woman.

Fräulein /ˈfrɔɪlʌɪn/, *foreign* /ˈfrɔɪlaɪn/ *noun* (also **fraulein**) L17 German (diminutive of FRAU). A title or form of address for an unmarried German-speaking woman, especially a young woman.

frazil /ˈfreɪz(ə)l/, /frəˈzil/ *noun* L19 Canadian French (*frasil* = snow floating on water, from French *fraisil* cinders). Slush consisting of small ice crystals formed in water too turbulent to freeze solid. Also *frazil ice.*

fresco /ˈfrɛskəʊ/ *noun & verb* L16 Italian (= cool, fresh). **A** *noun* plural **frescos**, **frescoes** **1** A method of painting by which watercolour is applied to damp,

freshly laid plaster on a wall or ceiling, so that the colours penetrate and become fixed as the plaster dries. **2** A painting produced by this method. **B** *transitive verb* Paint in fresco.

■ Earliest English use in the phrase *in fresco*, representing Italian *affresco* or *al fresco* 'on the fresh (plaster)'.

fresco secco /ˌfresko ˈsekko/ *noun phrase* M19 Italian (= dry fresco). The process or technique of painting on dry plaster with pigments mixed with water.

■ Sometimes abbreviated to *secco* (M19).

fricandeau /ˈfrɪkandəʊ/ *noun & verb* E18 French. **A** *noun* plural **fricandeaux** /ˈfrɪkandəʊz/ E18 *Cookery* A slice of veal or other meat cut from the leg; a dish consisting of a veal fillet stewed or fried and served with sauce. **B** *transitive verb* Make into fricandeaux.

fricassée /ˈfrɪkəsiː/, /frɪkəˈsiː/ *noun & verb* M16 French (feminine past participle of *fricasser* to cut up and stew in sauce). **A** *noun* *Cookery* A dish of stewed or fried pieces of meat served in a thick white sauce. **B** *transitive verb* Make a fricassée of (meat).

frigidarium /frɪdʒɪˈdɛrɪəm/ *noun* plural **frigidariums, frigidaria** /frɪdʒɪˈdɛrɪə/ E18 Latin (from *frigidus*, from *frigere* to be cold, from *frigus* cold). The room in ancient Roman baths containing the final, cold bath.

frijoles /friˈxoles/, /frɪˈhəʊlɛs/ *noun plural* L16 Spanish (plural of *frijol* bean, ultimately from Latin *phaseolus*). (In Mexican cookery) a dish of beans.

frisée /ˈfriːzeɪ/ *noun* L20 French ((feminine) past participle of *friser* to curl). Curly endive.

■ Abbreviation of French *chicorée frisée*.

frisson /frisɔ̃/, /ˈfrɪsɒn/ *noun* plural pronounced same L18 French (= shiver, thrill). A sudden strong feeling of excitement or fear; an emotional thrill.

1995 *Country Life* In the 18th century, some followers of the Picturesque movement used to enjoy the frisson of terror experienced when they beheld an unusually 'horrid' landscape; their fear became pleasurable from the

French

English abounds in words of French origin, many dating back to the years following the Norman Conquest, when French first became established as the language of government, law, the church, and public proceedings. Most words introduced at this time have subsequently become fully anglicized (such as *beef, crown, judge, river*), but there are hundreds of words and phrases, mainly those arriving within the last three hundred years or so, that have not been assimilated in this way and that still feel recognizably 'French'.

French is pre-eminently the language of cooking, food, and wine. There are numerous such terms used in kitchens and restaurants on a daily basis. They include *appellation contrôlée, au gratin, bain-marie, béchamel, bistro, bouillabaisse, bouillon, casserole, chanterelle, chef-d'œuvre, compote, cordon bleu, coulis, crème brûlée, croquette, crudités, entrecôte, flambé, gateau, goujon, haute cuisine, hollandaise, julienne, jus, maître d'hôtel, mangetout, mousse, nouvelle cuisine, petits pois, ragout, ratatouille, roulade, roux, sauté, sommelier, soufflé, tournedos, vinaigrette,* and *vin de table.* As this list demonstrates, French provides English not only with the names of dishes and styles of cooking but also with the language of food and meals generally. Other examples include *à la carte, aperitif, bon appétit, chef, cuisine, entrée, gourmet, hors d'oeuvre, plat du jour,* and *restaurateur.*

The vocabulary of art and literature is also rich in French terms: *art nouveau, avant-garde, beaux arts, belles-lettres, collage, conservatoire, coup de théâtre, dramaturge, entr'acte, genre, gouache, mise en scène, objet trouvé, œuvre, roman-à-clef, roman-fleuve,* and *trompe l'oeil.* Ballet terminology owes even more to French: *arabesque, barre, battement, brisé, chaîné, corps de ballet, entrechat, fouetté, pas de deux, pirouette, plié, port de bras, relevé, tour en l'air,* and many more. And French contributions to the language of film-making include *auteur, cinéaste, film noir, montage,* and *nouvelle vague.*

French terms also crop up in the field of conversation and verbal sparring (*bon mot, esprit de l'escalier, mot juste, riposte, touché*) and are indispensable in describing a certain kind of casual confidence or style (*aplomb, insouciance, nonchalant, panache, sangfroid, savoir faire*). One fascinating group of French borrowings is made up of terms relating to romance, sexual behaviour, and indecency. These include *affaire, amour, billet-doux, cinq-à-sept, crime passionel, décolletage, double entendre, femme fatale, grande horizontale, liaison, ménage à trois, risqué, roué,* and *soixante-neuf.*

Finally, French has traditionally been the language of diplomacy, hence the prevalence of terms such as *chargé d'affaires, communiqué, corps diplomatique, détente,* and *entente cordiale.*

knowledge that they were only going to look at the bleak scene before them, not live in it.

frittata /frɪˈtɑːtə/ *noun* L20 Italian. An Italian dish made from fried beaten eggs, resembling a Spanish omelette.

fritto misto /ˌfritto ˈmisto/ *noun phrase* E20 Italian (= mixed fry). A dish of various foods, typically seafood, deep-fried in batter.

froideur /frwadœr/ *noun* L20 French (from *froid* cold). Coolness or reserve between people.

1995 *Times* When one interviewer… suggested that she [sc. Catherine Deneuve] seemed a little over-controlled herself, her response was a flash of ironic *froideur* that might have been scripted by Buñuel himself.

fromage blanc /ˌfrɒmɑːʒ ˈblɒ̃/, *foreign* /frɔmaʒ blɑ̃/ *noun phrase* L20 French

137

fromage frais | führer

(= white cheese). A type of soft French cheese made from cow's milk and having a creamy sour taste.

fromage frais /ˌfrɒma:ʒ 'freɪ/, *foreign* /frɔmaʒ frɛ/ *noun phrase* L20 French (= fresh cheese). A type of smooth soft fresh cheese, with the consistency of thick yogurt.

▪ In France this type of cheese is generally known as PETIT SUISSE.

fronde /frɔd/ *noun* (usually **Fronde** in sense 1) plural pronounced same L18 French (literally, 'sling', of the type used in a children's game played in the streets of Paris at the time). **1** *French History* A political party in France during the mid 17th century, which initiated violent uprisings against the administration of Cardinal Mazarin during the minority of Louis XIV. **2** *transferred* A malcontent or disaffected party; violent political opposition.

frondeur /frɔdœr/ *noun* (usually **Frondeur** in sense 1) plural pronounced same L18 French (from FRONDE). **1** *French History* A participant in the Fronde. **2** *transferred* A political rebel.

fronton /'frʌnt(ə)n/ *noun* L17 French (from Italian *frontone*, from *fronte* forehead; in sense 2 Spanish *frontón*). **1** *Architecture* A pediment. **2** A building in which pelota or jai alai is played.

frottage /'frɒta:ʒ/, *foreign* /frɔtaʒ/ *noun* M20 French (= rubbing, friction). **1** The practice of rubbing against or touching the clothed body of another person (usually in a crowd) as a means of obtaining sexual gratification. **2** *Art* The technique or process of taking a rubbing from an uneven surface, such as grained wood, to form the basis of a work of art; a work of art produced by taking a rubbing from an uneven surface.

frotteur /frɒ'tə:/, *foreign* /frɔtœr/ *noun* plural pronounced same L19 French. A person who indulges in FROTTAGE (sense 1).

frottola /'frɒtələ/, *foreign* /'frɔttola/ *noun* plural **frottole** /'frɒtəleɪ/, *foreign* /'frɔttole/ M19 Italian (literally, 'fib, tall story'). *Music* A form of Italian comic or

amorous song, especially from the 15th and 16th centuries.

frou-frou /'fru:fru:/ *noun* L19 French (imitative of the soft rustling sound of a woman walking in a dress). Frills or other ornamentation, particularly of women's clothes. Also *attributive*.

attributive **1946** B. Spencer *Aegean Islands* 'Yachts on the Nile' [Yachts] . . . fresh as a girl at her rendezvous, and wearing frou-frou names, Suzy, Yvette or Gaby.

fruits de mer /ˌfrwi:də'mɛ:/ *noun phrase* M20 French (= fruits of the sea). *Cookery* Seafood, especially a dish made up of mixed shellfish.

frustum /'frʌstəm/ *noun* (also **frustrum**) plural **frustums, frusta** /'frʌstə/ M17 Latin (= piece cut off). *Mathematics* The portion of a solid figure, such as a cone or pyramid, which remains after the upper part has been cut off by a plane parallel to the base.

fuehrer variant of FÜHRER.

fugato /fjuː'gɑ:təʊ/ *adverb, adjective, & noun* M19 Italian (= fugued, from *fuga* FUGUE). *Music* **A** *adverb & adjective* In the style of a fugue, but not in strict or complete fugue form. **B** *noun* plural **fugatos** A passage in this style.

fugu /'fu:gu:/ *noun* M20 Japanese. A type of pufferfish that is eaten as a Japanese delicacy, after some highly poisonous parts have been removed.

fugue /fju:g/ *noun* L16 French (or, its source, Italian *fuga*, from Latin *fuga* flight). **1** *Music* A contrapuntal composition in which a short melody or phrase (the subject) is introduced by one part and successfully taken up by others and developed by interweaving the parts. **2** *Psychiatry* A loss of awareness of one's identity, often coupled with flight from one's usual environment, associated with certain forms of hysteria and epilepsy.

führer /'fjʊərə/ *noun* (also **fuehrer**) M20 German (= leader). A tyrannical leader; a dictator.

▪ Hitler, in his role as leader of the Third Reich, is often alluded to under his assumed title of *the* (or) *der Führer*, and the transferred use of the word in

English usually has strongly negative implications.

furioso /ˌfjʊərɪˈəʊzəʊ/, foreign /furiˈoːso/ adjective, adverb, & noun M17 Italian (from Latin furiosus enraged, furious). **A** adjective & adverb Music (Especially as a direction) furiously and wildly. **B** noun plural **furiosos** A furious person.

furore /fjʊəˈrɔːri/, /fjʊəˈrɔː/ noun L18 Italian (from Latin furor, from furere to rage). An outbreak of public anger or excitement; an uproar or fuss.
  ■ Originally used to denote a wave of enthusiastic admiration or a craze.

furor scribendi /ˌfjʊərɔː skrɪˈbɛndi/ noun phrase M19 Latin (= frenzy of writing). An irresistible urge to write.
  1975 S. Perelman Vinegar Puss The all-consuming urge to create, the furor scribendi, is upon him and will not be stilled.

fusain /ˈfjuːzeɪn/, also foreign /fyzɛ̃/ (plural same) noun L19 French (= spindle tree, charcoal). Art Artists' charcoal (made from the wood of the spindle tree); a charcoal drawing.

fusee /fjuːˈziː/ noun L16 French (fusée spindleful, ultimately from Latin fusus spindle). **1** A conical pulley or wheel onto which a chain is wound so as to equalize the power of the mainspring in a mechanical watch or clock. **2** A large-headed match for lighting a cigar or pipe. **3** North American A railway signal flare.

fuselage /ˈfjuːzəlɑːʒ/, /ˈfjuːzəlɪdʒ/ noun E20 French (from fuseler to shape into a spindle, from fuseau spindle). The elong-

ated body section of an aircraft in which the crew and passengers or cargo are carried.

fusillade /fjuːzɪˈleɪd/, /fjuːzɪˈlɑːd/ noun & verb E19 French (from fusiller to shoot). **A** noun A series of shots fired or missiles thrown all at the same time or in quick succession; figurative a sustained barrage of criticism, etc. **B** transitive verb Fire a fusillade at (a place or person). Archaic.

fusilli /ˈfuːsɪli/ noun plural L20 Italian (plural of diminutive of fuso spindle). Pasta in the form of small twists or spirals.

fustanella /fʌstəˈnɛlə/ noun M19 Italian (from Modern Greek phoustani, phoustánela, Albanian fustan, probably from Italian fustagno fustian). A stiff white kilt formerly worn by men in Albania and Greece and still part of Greek ceremonial military dress.

futon /ˈfuːtɒn/ noun (also **futong**) L19 Japanese. A padded unsprung mattress originating in Japan, that can be rolled up or folded in two.
  ■ The word has occurred in accounts of Japanese culture since the 19th century, but its introduction as a fashionable item of Western furniture dates from the 1980s. In modern Western furnishing the futon often includes a slatted wooden base capable of conversion into a seat by day.
  1996 Times Minimalists believe they will be redeemed by the futon, that they can meditate in the kitchen and create the metaphysical from the hygienic.

gabion /ˈɡeɪbɪən/ *noun* M16 French (from Italian *gabbione*, from *gabbia* cage). A cylinder of wicker or woven metal bands filled with earth or stones for use in civil engineering works or (formerly) fortifications.

gaffe /ɡaf/ *noun* (also **gaff**) E20 French (literally 'boat-hook', used colloquially to mean 'blunder'). A blunder, a clumsy or indiscreet act or remark.

> **1996** *Times* It's not that Bottomley is alone in making such photographic gaffes—remember John Gummer stuffing a hamburger down his daughter in 1990 to allay fears of mad cow disease affecting humans?

gaga /ˈɡɑːɡɑː/, /ˈɡaɡə/ *adjective* (also **ga-ga**) E20 French (= senile, a senile person). Slightly mad, typically as a result of old age, infatuation, or excessive enthusiasm. *Slang.*

gaijin /ɡʌɪˈdʒɪn/ *noun & adjective* M20 Japanese (contraction of *gaikoku-jin*, from *gaikaku* foreign country + *jin* person). **A** *noun* plural same. (In Japan) a foreigner. **B** *attributive* or as *adjective* Foreign, alien (to the Japanese).

> **A 1995** *Times* The dollars-for-bonds deal is designed to insure both against a collapse, but it is hard to say who is most put out—the Americans, forced to shore up their biggest economic competitor, or the Japanese, coming cap-in-hand to the *gaijin* for financial help.

gala /ˈɡɑːlə/, /ˈɡeɪlə/ *noun* E17 French (or its source in Italian from Spanish from Old French *gale* merrymaking). **1** A social occasion with special entertainments or performances. **2** (In Britain) a special sports meeting, especially a swimming competition.

> ■ Originally used in English in the sense 'fine or showy dress'.

galactico /ɡəˈlaktɪkəʊ/ *noun* **galacticos** E21 Spanish (= galactic, person from another galaxy). (In sport, especially football) one of a team's star players, especially an expensive signing.

> ■ Chiefly associated with the Spanish club Real Madrid, whose high-profile signings Luis Figo, Zinedine Zidane, Ronaldo, and David Beckham were collectively dubbed *Los Galácticos*.

galant /ɡaˈlã/, /ɡəˈlɑːnt/ *adjective* L19 French and German. **1** *Music* Relating to or denoting a light and elegant style of 18th-century music. **2** Courteous, attentive to women.

> **2 1995** D. Lodge *Therapy* Laurence remains wonderfully *galant*.

galère /ɡalɛr/ *noun* plural pronounced same M18 French (= galley). A coterie; an undesirable group of people; an unpleasant situation.

> ■ The primary literal sense of *galère* as 'a ship powered by oars' in which criminals were condemned to be rowers explains its use as a metaphor for a disagreeable situation or bad company. The figurative use is a reference to Molière's *Scapin* (II xi): '*Que diable allait-il faire dans cette galère?*'
> **1995** *Bookseller* I grow a-weary of...the whole *galère* of head honchos, smart-alec agents, insanely overpaid writers, etc.

galette /ɡəˈlɛt/ *noun* L18 French. A savoury pancake made from grated potatoes or a buckwheat flour.

galipot /ˈɡalɪpɒt/ *noun* L18 French (*galipot*, *garipot*: cf. Provençal *garapot* pine-tree resin). A kind of hardened turpentine formed on the stem of the maritime pine.

galleria /ɡaləˈriːə/ *noun* L19 Italian. A shopping arcade in an Italian city or designed in imitation of one of these; a collection of small shops under a single roof.

> ■ The idea of the shopping arcade on the Italian *galleria* principle became fashionable among urban architects in the English-speaking world during the 1960s, but the word *galleria* only became a fashionable synonym for 'arcade' in the 1980s. The term is also applied to shops-within-a-shop.

1990 *Times* The winning scheme... incorporated the inevitable 'galleria'.

galop /'galəp/, /gə'lɒp/ *noun* M19 French (= gallop). A lively ballroom dance in 2/4 time, popular in the late 18th century; a piece of music for this dance.

gamba /'gambə/ *noun* L16 Italian (= leg; short for VIOLA DA GAMBA). A VIOLA DA GAMBA.

gamelan /'gaməlan/ *noun* E19 Javanese. A traditional instrumental ensemble in Java and Bali, including many bronze percussion instruments.

gamin /'gamɪn/, /'gamã/, *foreign* /gamɛ̃/ (*plural same*) *noun & adjective* M19 French. **A** *noun* A street urchin, a waif; a streetwise or impudent child. **B** *adjective* Of or resembling a gamin.

gamine /ga'miːn/, *foreign* /gamin/ (*plural same*) *noun & adjective* L19 French. **A** *noun* **1** A female street urchin. **2** A small, attractively informal, mischievous, or elfin young woman. **B** *adjective* (Of a girl) attractively boyish.
1984 A. Brookner *Hotel du Lac* In her navy linen trousers and her, perhaps too tight, white jersey, Jennifer was determinedly *gamine*.

gamma /'gamə/ *noun* LME Latin (from Greek). **1** The third letter (Γ, γ) of the Greek alphabet, transliterated as 'g'. **2** Denoting the third of a series of items or categories. **3** *attributive Science* Third in importance; as in *Astronomy* (preceding the genitive of the Latin name of the constellation) designating the third brightest star in a constellation. **4** A third-class mark given for an examination paper or piece of school or college work. **5** *Physics* Relating to gamma rays, penetrating electromagnetic radiation of shorter wavelength than X-rays.

gangue /gaŋ/ *noun* E19 French (from German *Gang* way, course, vein or lode of metal). The commercially valueless material in which ore is found.

ganja /'gandʒə/, /'gɑːndʒə/ *noun* (also **ganga**) E19 Hindi (*gājā*). Cannabis.

garam masala /ˌgʌrəm mə'sɑːlə/ *noun phrase* M20 Urdu (*garam maṣāla*). A spice mixture used in Indian cookery.

garbanzo /gɑː'banzəʊ/ *noun* plural **garbanzos** M18 Spanish. A chickpea.

garçon /garsɔ̃/ *noun* plural pronounced same E17 French (= boy). A waiter, especially in a French restaurant or hotel.

garçonnière /garsɔnjɛr/ *noun* plural pronounced same E20 French. A bachelor's flat or set of rooms.

garimpeiro /garim'peiru/ *noun* M19 Portuguese. (In Brazil) an independent prospector for diamonds, gold, etc.

garuda /'garʊdə/ *noun* L19 Sanskrit (*garuḍa*). *Hinduism* A fabulous bird, half-eagle, half-man, ridden by the god Vishnu.

Gastarbeiter /'gast,ɑːrbaɪtər/ *noun* plural **Gastarbeiters**, same M20 German (from *Gast* guest + *Arbeiter* worker). A person with temporary permission to work in another country, especially in Germany.

Gasthaus /'gasthaʊs/ *noun* plural **Gasthäuser** /'gasthɔyzər/ M19 German (from *Gast* guest + *Haus* house). A small inn or hotel in a German-speaking country.

Gasthof /'gastho:f/ *noun* plural **gasthofs**, **Gasthöfe** /'gasthøːfə/ M19 German (from *Gast* guest + *Hof* hotel, large house). A hotel in a German-speaking country, usually larger than a GASTHAUS.

gateau /'gatəʊ/ *noun* (also **gâteau**) plural **gateaux** /'gatəʊ(z)/, **gateaus** M19 French (*gâteau* cake). A rich cake, typically one with layers of cream or fruit eaten as a dessert.
■ The word also applies to other recipes, such as a *gâteau de riz* /ˌgatəʊ də 'riːz/ (= of rice) (M19), a rich rice dessert in the shape of a cake, or to meat or fish baked and served in the form of a cake (L19); both usages are now rare.

gauche /gəʊʃ/ *adjective* M18 French (literally, 'left(-handed)'). Lacking in tact or ease of manner, awkward, blundering; lacking in subtlety or skill, crude, unsophisticated.
1995 *Country Life* It was an astounding performance from someone who had once been so gauche as to be an embarrassment before the television cameras.

gaucherie /ˈgəʊʃ(ə)ri/ *noun* L18 French (from *gauche*; see preceding). Gauche or awkward manner; a gauche action.

gaucho /ˈgaʊtʃəʊ/ *noun* plural **gauchos** E19 American Spanish (probably from Araucanian *kaučú* friend). A cowboy from the South American pampas, usually of mixed European and American Indian descent.

> 1996 *Oldie* The hotel bars would have been lined with gauchos with moustaches and bad teeth much as they are today.

gavotte /gəˈvɒt/ *noun* L17 French (from modern Provençal *gavoto*, from *Gavot* an inhabitant of the Alps). **1** A medium-paced dance popular in the 18th century. **2** A piece of music for this dance, composed in common time with each phrase beginning on the third beat of the bar; a piece of music in this rhythm, especially one which forms a movement of a suite.

gazpacho /gəsˈpɑːtʃəʊ/, *foreign* /gaθˈpatʃo/, *noun* plural **gazpachos**, /gəsˈpɑːtʃəʊz/, *foreign* /gaθˈpatʃos/, /gasˈpatʃos/ E19 Spanish. A Spanish soup made from tomatoes, peppers, cucumber, garlic, etc., and served cold.

gefilte fish /gəˈfɪltə fɪʃ/ *noun phrase* (also **gefüllte fish**) L19 Yiddish (= stuffed fish, from *gefilte* inflected past participle of *filn* to fill). A dish either of stewed or baked stuffed fish or of fish cakes boiled in a fish or vegetable broth.

gelato /dʒəˈlɑːtəʊ/ *noun* (also) plural **gelati** /dʒəˈlɑːti/, **gelatos** L20 Italian. An ice cream.

■ Originally in Italy and Italian-speaking countries and now also United States.

Gemeinschaft /gəˈmaɪnʃaft/ *noun* M20 German (from *gemein* common, general + *-schaft* -ship). Sociology A form of social integration based on close personal and family ties; community.

gemütlich /gəˈmyːtlɪç/, /gəˈmuːtlɪʃ/ *adjective* (also **gemutlich**) M19 German. Pleasant, cheerful; cosy, snug, homely; genial, good-natured.

> 1996 *Spectator* Austria wins hands down. The people are nicer, the villages more 'gemutlich' . . .

Gemütlichkeit /gəˈmyːtlɪçkaɪt/, /gəˈmuːtlɪʃkaɪt/ *noun* M19 German (cf. preceding). The quality of being *gemütlich*; geniality; cosiness; cheerfulness.

gendarme /ˈʒɒndɑːm/, *foreign* /ʒɑ̃darm/ (*plural same*) *noun* plural **gendarmes**, (now *historical*) **gens d'armes** /ʒɑ̃ darm/ M16 French (a singular from the plural (now *historical*) gens *d'armes* men of arms). **1** A paramilitary police officer in France and other French-speaking countries. **2** A rock pinnacle on a mountain, occupying and blocking an arête.

■ Originally denoting a mounted officer in the French army. Sense 1 dates from the late 18th century.

gendarmerie /ʒɒnˈdɑːməri/, *foreign* /ʒɑ̃ darməri/ (*plural same*) *noun* M16 French (from *gendarme*; see preceding). A force of gendarmes; the headquarters of such a force.

genera plural of GENUS.

generalissimo /ˌdʒɛn(ə)rəˈlɪsɪməʊ/ *noun* plural **generalissimos** E17 Italian (superlative of *generale* general). The commander of a combined military, naval, and air force, or of several armies.

genie /ˈdʒiːni/ *noun* plural **genii** /ˈdʒiːnɪaɪ/, **genies** M17 French (*génie* from Latin *genius* attendant spirit present from one's birth, innate ability or inclination). A spirit of Arabian folklore, as depicted traditionally imprisoned within a bottle or oil lamp, and capable of granting wishes when summoned. Cf. JINN.

■ Originally used in English to denote a guardian or protective spirit. *Génie* was adopted in the current sense by the 18th-century French translators of *The Arabian Nights' Entertainments*, because of its resemblance in form and sense to Arabic *jinnī* 'jinn'.

genitor /ˈdʒɛnɪtə/ *noun* LME Latin (*genitor* (Old French *géniteur*) from base of *gignere* to beget). **1** A male parent. *Archaic*. **2** *Anthropology* A person's biological as opposed to legal father.

■ Long archaic in the general sense 1, *genitor* in sense 2 was revived in the specific context of the distinction between biological and legal fatherhood; cf. PATER sense 2.

genius loci /ˌdʒiːnɪəs ˈləʊsʌɪ/, /ˈlɒkiː/ *noun phrase* E17 Latin (= spirit of the place). The presiding god or spirit of a place; the prevailing character or atmosphere of a place.

> **1995** *Oldie* Betjeman was a genius in the popular literary sense of the word, but he was also a *genius loci*—a sort of tutelary deity who looked after a particular bit of earth, in his case these poor old islands of ours.
> **1996** *Spectator* At best, it [sc. a picnic] is as much the product of *genius loci* as the food, drink and company. The best one I have ever had was in Russia on the sprawling meadows of Tolstoy's Yasnaya Polyana estate.

genizah /gɛˈniːzə/ *noun* (also **geniza**) L19 Hebrew (literally, 'a hiding, hiding place', from *gānaz* to set aside, hide). A room attached to a synagogue, housing damaged, discarded, or heretical texts and sacred relics.

genre /ˈʒɑːrə/, /ˈʒɒnrə/ *noun & adjective* E19 French (= a kind). **A** *noun* A style or category of art, music, or literature. **B** *adjective* Denoting a style of painting depicting scenes from ordinary life, typically domestic situations.

gens /dʒɛnz/ *noun* plural **gentes** /ˈdʒɛnti:z/, /ˈdʒɛnteɪz/ M19 Latin (from base of *gignere* to beget). **1** (In ancient Rome) a group of families with a supposed common origin, a common name, and common religious rites. Also, a similar group of families in other cultures. **2** *Anthropology* A kinship group composed of people related through their male ancestors.

genus /ˈdʒɛnəs/, /ˈdʒiːnəs/ *noun* plural **genera** /ˈdʒɛn(ə)rə/, **genuses** M16 Latin (= birth, family, nation). **1** *Biology* A grouping of organisms having common characteristics distinct from those of other such groupings. The genus is a principal taxonomic category that ranks above species and below family. **2** (In philosophical and general use) a class of things which have common characteristics and which can be divided into subordinate kinds.

georgette /dʒɔːˈdʒɛt/ *noun* E20 French (from Mme *Georgette* de la Plante (flourished *c.*1900), French dressmaker). A thin plain-woven crêpe dress material, usually of silk.

gesso /ˈdʒɛsəʊ/ *noun* plural **gessoes** L16 Italian (from Latin *gypsum* gypsum). A hard compound of plaster of Paris or whiting in glue, used in sculpture or as a base for gilding or painting on wood.

gestalt /gəˈʃtɑːlt/, /gəˈʃtalt/ *noun* (also **Gestalt**) E20 German (= form, shape). Chiefly *Psychology*. An organized whole that is perceived as functionally more than the sum of its parts.

German

Given that both the Austrian psychotherapist Sigmund Freud and his Swiss collaborator Carl Jung were German speakers, it is appropriate that the language has furnished a number of useful terms to describe human psychology and emotions. Among these are *angst*, *Weltanschauung*, *Weltschmerz*, and *Zeitgeist*. German borrowings also include words for a number of concepts for which there is no straightforward English equivalent, such as *realpolitik* (politics based on practical considerations), *Schaden-freude* (pleasure derived from someone else's misfortune), and *wanderlust* (a strong desire to travel).

Familiar items of German food (many bought from the *delicatessen*, another German word) include *bratwurst*, *frankfurter*, *pretzel*, *pumpernickel*, *sauer-kraut*, *schnitzel*, *strudel*, and *wurst*. Inevitably, a number of German words associated with warfare were adopted into English in the 20th century as a result of the Second World War. These include *blitzkrieg*, *führer*, *Gestapo*, *panzer*, and *Reich*. Among the dozens of other common words borrowed from German are *abseil*, *doppelgänger*, *ersatz*, *gesundheit*, *kaput*, *kindergarten*, *kitsch*, *leitmotiv*, *poltergeist*, *spiel*, *spritzer*, *über-*, and *umlaut*.

Gestapo /gə'stɑːpəʊ/ *noun* plural **Gestapos** M20 German (acronym, from *Geheime Staatspolizei* Secret State Police). The German secret police under Nazi rule. It ruthlessly suppressed opposition to the Nazis in Germany and occupied Europe, and sent Jews and others to concentration camps. Also *transferred*.

> **1995** *Country Life* …one expects nothing better than charred raw meat and discomfort at barbecues. Why the environmental health officers, our wonderful germ gestapo, have not stamped them out long since is a mystery.

gesundheit /gɛ'zʌndhʌɪt/, *foreign* /gɛ-'zʊnthaɪt/ *interjection* E20 German (from *Gesundheit* health). Used to wish good health to a person who has just sneezed.

gharana /gə'rɑːnə/ *noun* M20 Hindi (*gharānā* family). (In the Indian subcontinent) any of the various specialist schools or methods of classical music or dance.

ghat /gɑːt/, /gɔːt/ *noun* (also **ghaut**) E17 Hindi (*ghāṭ*). **1** (In the Indian subcontinent) a mountain pass. **2** (In the Indian subcontinent) a flight of steps leading to a river bank; a landing place. **3** A level place at the top of a river-bank ghat where Hindus cremate their dead. In full *burning ghat*.

ghazal /'gazal/ *noun* (also **ghazel**) L18 Persian (from Arabic *ġazal*). (In Middle Eastern and Indian literature and music) a lyric poem with a fixed number of verses and a repeated rhyme, typically on the theme of love, and normally set to music.

ghazi /'gɑːzi/ *noun* (also (as a title) **Ghazi**) plural **ghazis** M18 Arabic (*al-ġāzī* active participle of *ġazā* to invade, raid). A Muslim fighter against non-Muslims. Frequently as an honorific title.

ghee /giː/ *noun* M17 Hindi (*ghī*, from Sanskrit *ghṛta* past participle of *ghṛ-* to sprinkle). Clarified butter made from the milk of a buffalo or cow, used in Indian cooking.

gherao /gɛ'raʊ/ *noun & verb* M20 Hindi (from *ghernā* to surround, besiege). **A** *noun* plural **gheraos**. (In India and Pakistan) a form of protest or harassment in labour disputes whereby employers are prevented by workers from leaving the place of work until certain demands are met. **B** *transitive verb* Detain (a person) in this manner.

ghetto /'gɛtəʊ/ *noun* plural **ghetto(e)s** E17 Italian (origin uncertain: perhaps abbreviation of Italian *borghetto* diminutive of *borgo* borough, or from Italian *getto* foundry, where the first ghetto established in Venice, in 1516, was sited). **1** *History* The quarter in a city, originally in Italy, to which Jews were restricted. **2** A part of a city, especially a slum area, occupied by a minority group or groups; an isolated or segregated social group or area.

ghibli /'gɪbli/ *noun* (also **qibli**) E19 Arabic (*ḳiblī* southern). A hot dry southerly wind of North Africa.

gibber /'gɪbə/ *noun* L18 Aboriginal. (In Australia) a stone or boulder forming part of a boulder plain; any small stone.

gigolo /'ʒɪgələʊ/, /'dʒɪgələʊ/ *noun* plural **gigolos** E20 French (formed as masculine of *gigole* dancehall woman). A professional male dancing partner or escort; a young man paid or financially supported by a (usually older) woman to be her escort or lover.

gigot /'dʒɪgət/ *noun* E16 French (diminutive of dialect *gigue* leg, from *giguer* to hop, jump, of unknown origin). **1** A leg of mutton or lamb. **2** A leg-of-mutton sleeve. More fully *gigot sleeve*.

gigue /ʒiːg/ *noun* L17 French (= jig). A lively piece of music in the style of a dance, typically of the Renaissance or baroque period, and usually in compound time.

gilet /ʒiːlɛ/ *noun* plural pronounced same L19 French (= waistcoat). A light sleeveless padded jacket.

gilgai /'gɪlgʌɪ/ *noun* (also **ghilgai**) M19 Aboriginal ((Kamilaroi) *gilgaay*). (In Australia) a shallow depression between mounds or ridges, in which rainwater collects; a waterhole.

ginseng /'dʒɪnsɛŋ/ *noun* M17 Chinese (*rénshēn* (Wade–Giles *jên shên*), from *rén* man + *shēn* kind of herb (because of the supposed resemblance of the forked root to a person)). **1** A plant tuber credited, especially in the Far East, with various tonic and medicinal properties. **2** The source of this root, any of several plants of the genus *Panax* (family Araliaceae), native to east Asia and North America.

girandole /ˈdʒɪr(ə)ndəʊl/ *noun* M17 French (from Italian *girandola*, from *girare* from late Latin *gyrare* to gyrate). A branched support for candles or other lights which either stands on a surface or projects from a wall.

▪ Originally used in English to denote a revolving cluster of fireworks.

girasol /ˈdʒɪrəsɒl/, /ˈdʒɪrəsəʊl/ *noun* (also **girasole** /ˈdʒɪrəsəʊl/) L16 French (or Italian *girasole*, from *girare* to gyrate + *sole* sun). **1** A variety of opal which reflects a reddish glow, a fire opal. **2** A Jerusalem artichoke. *North America.*

▪ Originally used in the sense 'sunflower', the derivation coming from the fact that the sunflower turns to follow the path of the sun.

giro /ˈdʒʌɪrəʊ/ *noun* plural **giros** L19 German (from Italian = circulation (of money)). **1** A system of electronic credit transfer used in Europe and Japan, involving banks, post offices, and public utilities. **2** A cheque or payment by giro; *specifically* in Britain, a social security payment.

gîte /ʒiːt/ *noun* (also **gite**) plural pronounced same M20 French. A small furnished holiday house in France, typically in a rural district.

gjetost /ˈjɛtɒst/ *noun* E20 Norwegian (from *gjet, geit* goat + *ost* cheese). A very sweet, firm golden-brown Norwegian cheese, traditionally made from goat's milk.

glacé /ˈɡlaseɪ/ *adjective & noun* M19 French (past participle of *glacer* to ice, give a gloss to, from *glace* ice). **A** *adjective* **1** (Of fruit) covered with icing or sugar. (Of icing) made with icing sugar and water. **2** (Of cloth or leather) smooth, highly polished, glossy. **B** *noun* Glacé silk, glacé leather.

glacis /ˈɡlasɪs/, /ˈɡlasi/ *noun* plural same /ˈɡlasɪz/, /ˈɡlasiːz/ L17 French (from Old French *glacier* to slip, slide, from *glace* ice, from Proto-Romance alteration of Latin *glacies* ice). **1** A gently sloping bank; *specifically* in *Fortification*, a natural or artificial bank sloping down from the covered way of a fort so as to expose attackers to the defenders' missiles. **b** *figurative* A zone or area acting as a protective barrier or buffer between two (potential) enemies. **2** A sloping piece of armour plate protecting an opening etc. in a ship. In full *glacis plate.*

glasnost /ˈɡlaznɒst/, /ˈɡlɑːsnɒst/ *noun* L20 Russian (*glasnost'* the fact of being public). (In the former Soviet Union) the policy or practice of more open consultative government and wider dissemination of information. Also *transferred.*

▪ *Glasnost* is an old Russian word, but its connotation of 'freedom of information' only evolved in the latter years of the Soviet regime. A debate on the subject started by the state newspaper *Izvestiya* in January 1985 was taken up by Mikhail Gorbachev in his speech in March the same year accepting the post of General Secretary of the Communist Party and expressing his commitment to reform. *Glasnost* was one of the key concepts in the Gorbachev reform programme (see also PERESTROIKA), and English-speaking political commentators, finding that there was no English word exactly equivalent to *glasnost*, opted to use the Russian one. It became widely current in the late 1980s and was soon applied to mean 'openness', in particular 'openness in government', in a variety of situations quite outside its original context.

1986 *New York Times* Exposés of corruption, shortages and economic problems appear virtually daily in the [Soviet] press. It is a change that became evident after Mikhail S. Gorbachev came to office last March and called for more 'glasnost', or openness, in covering domestic affairs.

transferred **1996** *Guardian* For royal correspondents, used to being fobbed off, lied to, and told off like naughty boys, Atkinson and Vulliamy represented a new *glasnost* in Palace PR.

glaucoma /ɡlɔːˈkəʊmə/ *noun* M17 Greek (*glaukōma*, from *glaukos* bluish-green, bluish-grey (because of the grey-green haze in the pupil)). *Medicine* An eye condition characterized by increased pressure within the eyeball and a gradual impairment or loss of sight.

Gleichschaltung /ˈglaɪçˌʃaltʊŋ/ *noun* (also **gleichschaltung**) M20 German. The standardization of political, economic, and cultural institutions in authoritarian states.

glissade /glɪˈsɑːd/, /glɪˈseɪd/ *noun & verb* M19 French (from *glisser* to slip, slide). **A** *noun* **1** *Mountaineering* A way of sliding down a steep slope of snow or ice, usually on the feet with the support of an ice axe. **2** *Ballet* A step consisting of a glide or slide in any direction, usually a joining step. **B** *verb Mountaineering* Slide down a steep slope of snow or ice by means of a glissade.

glissando /glɪˈsandəʊ/ *noun* plural **glissandi** /glɪˈsandi/, **glissandos** L19 Italian (from French *glissant* present participle of *glisser* to slip, slide). *Music* A continuous slide upwards or downwards between two notes.

> **1996** *Times* The hour was late; the booze was strong; the notes on my trombone part seemed very small . . . I felt my *glissandi* getting limper and limper.

glissé /glise/ *noun* plural pronounced same E20 French (past participle of *glisser* to slip, slide). *Ballet* A sliding step in which the flat of the foot is often used. More fully *pas glissé* /pɑ glise/.

glockenspiel /ˈglɒk(ə)nʃpiːl/, /ˈglɒk(ə)nspiːl/, *noun* E19 German (= bell-play). A musical percussion instrument having a set of tuned metal bars mounted on a horizontal frame and struck with small hammers.

■ The term was originally used to denote an organ stop imitating the sound of bells.

glögg /glœg/, /glɒg/ *noun* (also **glugg** /glʌg/) E20 Swedish. A Scandinavian winter drink, consisting of hot sweetened red wine with brandy, almonds, raisins, and spices.

Gloria /ˈglɔːrɪə/ *noun* ME Latin (= glory). Any of several Christian liturgical hymns or formulae, as the hymn beginning *Gloria in excelsis Deo* ('Glory be to God in the highest'), forming a set part of the Mass, and the doxology beginning *Gloria Patris* ('Glory be to the Father'), used after psalms and in formal prayer. **b** The music to which any of these is set.

glugg variant of GLÖGG.

glühwein /ˈglyːvaɪn/, /ˈgluːvʌɪn/ *noun* (also **gluhwein**) L19 German (from *glühen* to mull, glow + *wein* wine). Mulled wine.

gneiss /nʌɪs/ *noun* (also (earlier) **kneiss**) M18 German (from Old High German *gneisto* (= Old English *gnāst*, Old Norse *gneisti*) spark (because of the rock's sheen)). A metamorphic rock with a banded or foliated structure, typically coarse-grained and consisting mainly of feldspar, quartz, and mica.

gnocchi /ˈn(j)ɒki/, /ˈgnɒki/, *foreign* /ˈɲokki/ *noun* plural L19 Italian (plural of *gnocco*, from *nocchio* knot in wood). (In Italian cooking) small dumplings made with flour, semolina, or potato, usually served with a sauce.

gnomon /ˈnəʊmɒn/ *noun* M16 French (or Latin *gnomon*, from Greek *gnōmōn* inspector, indicator, carpenter's square). **1** The projecting piece on a sundial that shows the time by the position of its shadow. **2** *Astronomy* A structure, especially a column, used in observing the sun's meridian attitude. **3** *Geometry* The part of a parallelogram left after a similar parallelogram is taken away from one of its corners.

gnosis /ˈnəʊsɪs/ *noun* plural **gnoses** /ˈnəʊsiːz/ L16 Greek (*gnōsis* investigation, knowledge, from *gno-* base of *gignōskein* to know). Knowledge of spiritual mysteries.

go /gəʊ/ *noun* L19 Japanese. A Japanese board game of territorial possession and capture. Cf. WEI CH'I.

godet /gəʊˈdɛt/, /ˈgəʊdeɪ/ *noun* L19 French. A triangular piece of material inserted into a dress, glove, or other garment to make it flared or for ornamentation.

goitre /ˈgɔɪtə/ *noun* (also **goiter**) E17 French (either (i) from Old French *goitron* from Provençal from Proto-Romance, from Latin *guttur* throat, or (ii) back-formation from French *goitreux* goitred, from Latin adjective from *guttur*).

A swelling of the neck due to enlargement of the thyroid gland.

goldwasser /'gəʊldvasə/, *foreign* /'gɔltvasər/ *noun* E20 German (= gold water). A liqueur containing particles of gold leaf, originally made at Gdańsk in Poland.

golem /'gəʊləm/, /'gɔɪləm/ *noun* L19 Yiddish (*goylem* from Hebrew *gōlem* shapeless mass). (In Jewish legend) a human figure of clay supernaturally brought to life; an automaton, a robot.

golgotha /'gɒlgəθə/ *noun* E17 Late Latin ((Vulgate), from Greek by metathesis from Aramaic *gōgolṭâ*, perhaps under influence of Hebrew *gulgōleṭ* skull). A place of interment; a graveyard, a charnel house.

■ In the New Testament, Golgotha is the name of the site of the crucifixion of Jesus. According to Matthew 27:33, 'And they were come unto a place called Golgotha, that is to say, a place of a skull'.

gondola /'gɒndələ/ *noun* M16 Italian ((Venetian) from Rhaeto-Romance *gondolà* to rock). **1** A light asymmetric flat-bottomed boat used on the Venetian canals, having a high pointed prow and stern and usually propelled by a single oar at the stern. **2** A large light flat-bottomed riverboat; a lighter, used also as a gunboat. *United States.* **3** An enclosed compartment suspended from a dirigible or airship; something resembling this. **4** An open railway goods wagon with low sides. More fully *gondola car*, *gondola wagon. United States.* **5** The seating compartment in a ski lift. **6** A free-standing block of shelves used to display goods in a supermarket.

gondolier /ˌgɒndə'lɪə/ *noun* E17 French (from Italian *gondoliere*, from GONDOLA). A person who propels and steers a Venetian gondola.

gonfalonier /ˌgɒnf(ə)lə'nɪə/ *noun* L16 French (Old French *gonfanonier*). A standard bearer; *specifically* (a) the Pope's standard bearer; (b) *History* any of various officials or magistrates in the Italian city states.

gonzo /'gɒnzəʊ/ *adjective & noun* L20 Italian (= foolish, or perhaps Spanish *ganso*

goose, fool). **A** *adjective* **1** Relating to or denoting journalism of an exaggerated, subjective, and fictionalized style. **2** Bizarre, crazy. **B** *noun* plural **gonzos** Gonzo journalism; a journalist writing in this style; *generally* a crazy or foolish person.

■ Originally and chiefly United States slang.

goombay /'gu:mbeɪ/ *noun* L18 West Indian creole (cf. Kikongo *ngoma* a kind of drum, Twi *gumbe* drum music). (In the West Indies) a goatskin drum with a round or squared top, played with the fingers (rather than with sticks); the calypso-style music associated with the playing of goombay drums.

goonda /'gu:ndə/ *noun* (also **goondah**) E20 Hindi (*guṇḍā* rascal). (In the Indian subcontinent) a hired thug or bully.

gopura /'gəʊpʊrə/ *noun* (also **gopuram** /'gəʊpʊrəm/) M19 Sanskrit (*gopura* city gate, from *go* cow, cattle + *pura* city, quarter). (In southern India) the great pyramidal tower over the entrance gate to a temple precinct.

Gorsedd /'gɔːsɛð/ *noun* L18 Welsh (= mound, throne, assembly). A council of Welsh or other Celtic bards and druids, especially the assembly that meets before the eisteddfod.

Götterdämmerung /'gœtərˌdɛmərʊŋ/, /gʊtə'damərʊŋ/ *noun* E20 German (literally, 'twilight of the gods'). *Germanic mythology* The downfall of the gods; *generally* a cataclysmic collapse of a regime, institution, etc. Cf. RAGNAROK.

■ *Götterdämmerung* is the title of the final opera in Wagner's Ring cycle.

gouache /gu:'ɑ:ʃ/, *foreign* /gwaʃ/ *noun* L19 French (from Italian *guazzo*). A method of opaque watercolour painting, in which the pigments are bound by a glue-like substance to form a sort of paste; a painting executed in this way; paint of this kind, opaque watercolour.

goujon /'guːʤ(ə)n/, *foreign* /guʒõ/ (*plural same*) *noun* M20 French (from Latin *gobio(n)*-, from *gobius* goby). *Cookery* In *plural.* Narrow strips of fish, especially sole, or of chicken, usually for deep-frying.

goulash /ˈguːlaʃ/ *noun* M19 Hungarian (*gulyás(hús)*, from *gulyás* herdsman + *hús* meat). **1** A highly seasoned Hungarian soup or stew of meat and vegetables, flavoured with paprika. **2** *Bridge* A fresh deal of unshuffled cards, usually three or more at a time, after the hands have been thrown in without bidding.

gourmand /ˈgʊəmənd/, /ˈgɔːmənd/, *foreign* /gurmɑ̃/ (*plural same*) *noun & adjective* (occasionally feminine **gourmande** /ˈgʊəmɒnd/, /ˈgɔːmɑːnd/, *foreign* /gurmɑ̃ːd/ (*plural same*)) LME Old and Modern French (of unknown origin). **A** *noun* **1** A person who is overfond of eating; a glutton. **2** A person who is fond of, or a judge of, good food; a GOURMET. **B** *adjective* Gluttonous, greedy; fond of eating.

gourmet /ˈgʊəmeɪ/, /ˈɡɔːmeɪ/, *foreign* /gurmɛ/ (*plural same*) *noun & adjective* E19 French (formerly = wine-merchant's assistant, wine-taster, influenced in sense by GOURMAND). **A** *noun* A connoisseur in eating and drinking; a judge of good food. **B** *attributive* or as *adjective* Of a kind or standard suitable for a gourmet.

goy /ɡɔɪ/ *noun* plural **goyim** /ˈɡɔɪɪm/, **goys** M19 Hebrew (*gōy* people, nation). (Among Jews) a non-Jew, a Gentile.
■ Usually derogatory.

gradus /ˈɡreɪdəs/ *noun* M18 Latin (*gradus* step(s)). *History* A manual of classical prosody formerly used in schools to help in writing Greek and Latin verse.
■ This category of schoolbook took its name from the title of a manual of Latin prosody, the *Gradus ad Parnassum* 'Step(s) to Parnassus', which appeared in England in many editions from the late 17th century onwards and inspired a *Greek Gradus* and other imitations.

Graf /ɡrɑːf/ *noun* M17 German. A German nobleman corresponding in rank to a European count or British earl.
■ Chiefly in titles. The feminine equivalent is *Gräfin*.

graffiti /ɡrəˈfiːti/ *transitive verb* L20 Italian (from plural of next). Apply graffiti to; write as graffiti.

graffito /ɡrəˈfiːtəʊ/ *noun* plural (frequently used as *singular*) **graffiti** /ɡrəˈfiːti/ M19 Italian (from *graffio* scratching). **1** A drawing, writing, or scribbling on a wall etc., originally *specific* on an ancient wall, as at Rome and Pompeii. Usually in *plural.* **2** A method of decoration or design produced by scratching through a plaster layer to reveal a different colour below.

grand battement /ɡrɑ̃ batmɑ̃/, /ˈɡrɒ̃ ˈbatmɒ̃/ *noun phrase* plural **grands battements** (pronounced same) M19 French. *Ballet* A movement in which both legs are kept straight and one leg is kicked outwards from the body and in again.

grand cru /ɡrɑ̃ kry/, /ɡrɒ̃ ˈkruː/ *noun & adjective phrase* plural **grands crus** /ɡrɑ̃ kry/, **grand crus** /ɡrɒ̃ ˈkruːz/ E20 French (= great growth). (Chiefly in French official classifications) a wine of the most superior quality, or the vineyard which produces it.
1996 *Times Magazine* At the top of the pyramid are those glorious grands crus wines that dreams are made of.

grande dame /ɡrɑ̃d dam/ plural **grandes dames** (pronounced same) M18 French (= grand lady). A woman holding an influential position within a particular sphere.
1995 *Times* The latest lifestyle tip from the grandes dames of chic: take your dog to work. The offices of *Tatler* are overrun . . .

grande horizontale /ɡrɑ̃d ɔrizɔ̃tal/ *noun phrase* plural **grandes horizontales** (pronounced same) L19 French (= great horizontal). A courtesan or prostitute.
1970 *New Yorker* He is overshadowed throughout by Aunt Augusta, the still unretired grande horizontale of seventy-three.

Grand Guignol /ˌɡrɒ̃ ɡiːˈnjɒl/, *foreign* /ɡrɑ̃ ɡiɲɔl/ *noun phrase* E20 French (= Great Punch). A dramatic entertainment in which short horrific or sensational pieces are played successively; a literary work with similar characteristics.
■ In France *Guignol* is a marionette drama equivalent to the English Punch and Judy show. *Grand Guignol* takes its name from a theatre in Paris.
1996 *Spectator* Many novelists who specialise in *grand guignol* . . . might just as well be writing

love stories, or crime stories, or something else without the gratuitous details of blood and gore.

grand jeté /grã ʒɛte/, /grɒ ˈʒəteɪ/ *noun phrase* plural **grands jetés** (pronounced same) M20 French. *Ballet* A jump in which a dancer springs from one foot to land on the other with one leg forward of their body and the other stretched backwards while in the air.

grand mal /grɒ ˈmal/, *foreign* /grã mal/ *noun phrase* L19 French (literally, 'great sickness'). A serious form of epilepsy with muscle spasms and prolonged loss of consciousness. Cf. PETIT MAL.

Grand Prix /grɒ ˈpriː/ *noun phrase* plural **Grands Prix** (pronounced same) M19 French (= great or chief prize). **1** An international horse race for three-year-olds, founded in 1863 and run annually in June at Longchamps, Paris. In full *Grand Prix de Paris* /də paˈriː/. **2** Any of a series of motor-racing or motorcycling contests forming part of a world championship series, held in various countries under international rules. Also, an important competitive event in various other sports.

grand seigneur /grã sɛɲœr/, /ˌgrɒ semˈjə/ plural **grands seigneurs** (pronounced same) E17 French (= great lord). A man whose rank or position allows him to command others.

grand siècle /grã sjɛkl/, /ˌgrɒ sɪˈɛk(ə)l/ M19 French (literally, 'great century or age'). A classical or golden age; *especially* the reign of Louis XIV (1643–1715), seen as France's period of political and cultural pre-eminence.

granita /graˈniːtə/, *foreign* /graˈnita/ *noun* plural **granite** /graˈniːti/, *foreign* /graˈnite/ M19 Italian. An Italian-style water ice with a granular texture; a drink made with crushed ice.

gran turismo /gran tuˈrizmo/, /ˌgran tʊəˈrizməʊ/ *noun* M20 Italian (literally, 'great touring'). A comfortable high-performance model of car.

■ Abbreviated to *GT*.

grappa /ˈgrapə/ *noun* L19 Italian (= grape stalks). A brandy distilled from the fermented residue of grapes after wine-making.

graticule /ˈgratɪkjuːl/ *noun* L19 French (from medieval Latin *graticula* for (also classical Latin) *craticula* small gridiron, diminutive of Latin *cratis* hurdle). **1** A network of lines representing meridians and parallels, on which a map or plan can be represented. **2** A series of fine lines or fibres in the eyepiece of an optical device, such as a microscope, or on the screen of an oscilloscope, used as a measuring scale or an aid in locating objects.

gratin /ˈgratɛ̃/, /ˈgratã/ *noun* M17 French (from *gratter*, earlier *grater* to grate). **1** A method of cooking, or a dish cooked, with a lightly browned crust of breadcrumbs or melted cheese. Cf. AU GRATIN. **2** The highest class of society.

■ For sense 2, cf. the English metaphorical phrase 'the upper crust'.

2 1959 *Sunday Times* She belonged to the Edwardo-Georgian *gratin*.

gratiné /gratine/ (*plural same*), /gratɪˈneɪ/ *adjective* (also **gratinée**) E20 French (past participial adjective of *gratiner* to cook *au gratin*). AU GRATIN.

gratis /ˈgratɪs/, /ˈgrɑːtɪs/, /ˈgreɪtɪs/ *adverb & adjective* LME Latin (*gratis* contraction of *gratiis* out of favour or kindness, ablative plural of *gratia* grace, favour). **A** *adverb* Without charge; free. **B** *adjective* Given or done for nothing; free; gratuitous.

graupel /ˈgraʊp(ə)l/ *noun* L19 German. *Meteorology* Soft hail, small snow pellets with a fragile ice crust.

gravadlax variant of GRAVLAX.

gravamen /grəˈveɪmɛn/ *noun* plural **gravamens**, **gravamina** /grəˈveɪmɪnə/ E17 Late Latin (*gravamen* physical inconvenience, (in medieval Latin) grievance, from Latin *gravare* to weigh on, oppress, from *gravis* heavy, grave). **1** *Chiefly Law* The essence or most serious part of a complaint or accusation. **2** A grievance.

■ Originally an ecclesiastical term denoting the formal presentation of a grievance.

gravida /ˈgravɪdə/ *noun* M20 Latin (use as noun of feminine of *gravidus* gravid). *Medicine* A woman who is pregnant; (with preceding or following numeral) a woman who has had the specified number of pregnancies, including a present one.

gravitas /ˈgravɪtɑːs/, /ˈgravɪtas/ *noun* E20 Latin (from *gravis* serious). Dignity, seriousness, or solemnity of manner.

> **1996** *Times* It [sc. the appointment of a lord to a directorship] may well give added gravitas to the board, but gravitas does not equal competence.

gravlax /gravˈlaks/ *noun* (also **gravlaks**, **gravadlax** /ˌgravadˈlaks/) M20 Swedish (from *grav* grave, trench + *lax* salmon (from the former practice of burying the salmon in salt in a hole in the ground)). A Scandinavian dish of dry-cured salmon marinated in herbs.

grenadine /ˈɡrɛnədiːn/ *noun* L19 French ((*sirop de*) *grenadine* from *grenade* pomegranate). A sweet cordial made in France from pomegranates.

grillade /ɡrɪˈleɪd/, /ɡrɪˈjɑːd/, /ˈɡriːɑːd/ *noun* M17 French. A kind of meat stew usually made with beef steak, typical of French regional and Cajun cookery.

grimoire /ɡrɪmˈwɑː/ *noun* M19 French (alteration of *grammaire* grammar). A book of magic spells and incantations.

gringo /ˈɡrɪŋɡəʊ/ *noun* plural **gringos** M19 Spanish (= foreign, foreigner, gibberish). A white person from an English-speaking country (used in Spanish-speaking countries, chiefly Central and South America).

> ■ Usually derogatory.

griot /ˈɡriːəʊ/ *noun* E19 French. A member of a class of travelling poets, musicians, and storytellers who maintain a tradition of oral history in parts of West Africa.

grippe /ɡrɪp/, *foreign* /grip/ *noun* L18 French. Influenza.

grisaille /ɡrɪˈzeɪl/, /ɡrɪˈzeɪli/, *foreign* /ɡrizɑj/ (*plural same*) *noun* M19 French (from *gris* grey). A method of painting in grey monochrome, used to represent objects in relief or to decorate stained glass; a stained-glass window or painting of this kind.

grisette /ɡrɪˈzɛt/ *noun* E18 French (from *gris* grey). **1** A common edible woodland mushroom with a brown or grey cap, a slender stem, and white gills. **2** A young working-class Frenchwoman. *Archaic*.

> ■ Sense 2 derives from the grey dress material typically worn by such women.

grissino /grisˈsiːno/, /ɡrɪˈsiːnəʊ/ *noun* plural **grissini** /grisˈsiːni/ M19 Italian. A thin, crisp Italian breadstick.

> ■ Usually in plural.

grosgrain /ˈɡrəʊɡreɪn/, *foreign* /ɡroɡrɛ̃/ (*plural same*) *noun* M19 French (= coarse grain). A heavy ribbed fabric, typically of silk or rayon.

gros point /ɡro pwɛ̃/ *noun phrase* M19 French (= large stitch). A type of needle-point embroidery consisting of stitches crossing two or more threads of the canvas in each direction.

> ■ From *gros point de Venise*, a type of lace originally from Venice, worked in bold relief. The current sense dates from the 1930s.

gruppetto /grupˈpetto/, /ɡrʊˈpɛtəʊ/ *noun* plural **gruppetti** /grupˈpetti/, **gruppettos** M19 Italian (diminutive of *gruppo* group). *Music* A melodic ornament consisting of a group of three, four, or five notes, comprising the principal note and the notes one degree above and below it; a turn.

GT abbreviation of GRAN TURISMO.

guacamole /ɡwɑːkəˈməʊli/ *noun* (also **guacomole**) E20 American Spanish (from Nahuatl *ahuacamolli*, from *ahuacatl* avocado + *molli* sauce). A dish of mashed avocado mixed with onions, tomatoes, chillies, and seasoning.

guaiacum /ˈɡwʌɪəkəm/ *noun* M16 Modern Latin (from Spanish *guayaco, guayacan*, from Taino *guayacan*). **1** Any of various trees and shrubs of the genus *Guaiacum* native to the West Indies and tropical America. **2** The hard very heavy wood of such a tree; lignum vitae. **3** A resin obtained from such a tree, formerly used to treat gout and rheumatism, now as a flavouring and in varnishes.

guano /ˈɡwɑːnəʊ/ *noun* plural **guanos** E17 Spanish (or South American Spanish *huano*, from Quechua *huanu* dung). **1** The excrement of sea birds as found especially in thick deposits on the islands off Peru and Chile and used as fertilizer. **2** An artificial fertilizer resembling natural guano, especially one made from fish.

guarache variant of HUARACHE.

guarana /gwəˈrɑːnə/, /ˈgwɑːrənə/ *noun* M19 Portuguese (from Tupi *guaraná*). A Brazilian liana, *Paullinia cupana*, of the soapberry family; a paste prepared from the seeds of this shrub, used as a food or medicine and especially to make a drink resembling coffee.

guerrilla /gəˈrɪlə/ *noun & adjective* (also **guerilla**) E19 Spanish (diminutive of *guerra* war). **A** *noun* A member of a small independent group taking part in irregular fighting, typically against larger regular forces. **B** *adjective* **1** (Of fighting) carried on by small irregular bands; (of a person) taking part in such fighting. **2** Referring to actions or activities performed in an impromptu way, often without authorization: *guerrilla gigs*.

■ Introduced into France and England during the Peninsular War (1808–14), when the Spaniards fought such campaigns against the vastly superior invading forces of Napoleon.

guidon /ˈgʌɪd(ə)n/ *noun* M16 French (from Italian *guidone*, from *guida* guide). A pennant narrowing to a point or fork at the free end, especially one used as the standard of a light cavalry regiment.

guilloche /gɪˈləʊʃ/, /gɪˈlɒʃ/ *noun* M19 French (*guillochis* guilloche, or *guilloche* the tool used in making it). An architectural or metalwork ornament imitating braided or interlaced ribbons.

> **1996** *Country Life* … the guilloche has a clarity that recalls the appearance of that ornament in borders to the plates in D'Hancarville's *Collection of Etruscan, Greek and Roman Antiquities* …

guillotine /ˈgɪlətiːn/, /gɪləˈtiːn/ *noun & verb* L18 French (from Joseph-Ignace *Guillotin* (1738–1814)). **A** *noun* **1** An instrument for beheading consisting of a heavy blade with a diagonal cutting edge that is allowed to drop between two tall grooved uprights, used in France during the Revolution. **b** *the guillotine* Execution by means of a guillotine. **2** A surgical instrument with a blade that slides in a long groove. **3** A device for cutting that incorporates a descending or sliding blade, used typically for cutting paper, card, or sheet metal. **4** A method used in a legislative assembly for preventing obstruction of a bill by fixing times at which its different parts must be voted on. **B** *transitive verb* **1** Behead by means of a guillotine. **2** Cut with a guillotine; *figuratively* cut short.

■ Guillotin suggested the use of this instrument as a means of capital punishment in 1789 on the grounds that executions should be as swift and painless as possible. Such devices had been in operation earlier in England, Scotland (where it was called a 'maiden'), Germany (called a *Diele* or *Hobel*), and Italy (called a *mannaia*), but by the 18th century they seem to have fallen out of use until Guillotin's recommendation aroused new interest. There was a period of experimentation using dead bodies, during which the machine was referred to as *La Petite Louison* or the *Louisette*, but after its first public use in April 1792 it speedily and universally became known as *la guillotine*.

guimpe /gɪmp/, *foreign* /gɛp/ *noun* (also **guimp**) M19 French. A high-necked blouse or undergarment worn showing beneath a low-necked dress.

guipure /gɪˈpjʊə/ *noun* M19 French (from *guiper* to cover with silk, wool, etc., from Germanic base meaning 'wind round'). A heavy lace consisting of embroidered motifs held together by large connecting stitches.

guiro /ˈgwʌɪrəʊ/ *noun* L19 Spanish (= gourd). A musical instrument with a serrated surface which gives a rasping sound when scraped with a stick, originally made from a gourd and used in Latin American music.

Gulag /ˈguːlag/, *foreign* /guˈlak/ *noun* (also **gulag**) M20 Russian (acronym, from Glavnoe upravlenie ispravitel'no-trudo-vykh *lagereĭ* Chief Administration for Corrective Labour Camps). A system of labour camps maintained in the Soviet Union from 1930 to 1955 in which many people died; a camp in the Gulag system, or any political labour camp; *figurative* an oppressive environment.

■ The word became widely known in the West in the 1960s and 1970s with the translation of Alexander Solzhenitsyn's works, notably *The Gulag Archipelago.*
1996 *New Scientist* He [sc. Lysenko] was a shrewd political manipulator, gradually rising in communist circles as his opponents were exiled to the gulags.

gung-ho /gʌŋˈhəʊ/ *adjective* M20 Chinese (*gōnghé,* taken as 'work together'). Unthinkingly enthusiastic and eager, especially about taking part in fighting or warfare.

■ Adopted as a slogan in the war of 1939–45 by the United States Marines fighting in the Pacific. General Evans Carlson (1896–1947) organized 'kunghoi' meetings to discuss general problems and explain orders in order to promote cooperation.
1996 *Country Life* . . . the banished Duke is neatly played by Robert Demeger as a gung-ho figure cheering up his fellow-exiles during an Arctic winter . . .

gunyah /ˈgʌnjə/ *noun* E19 Aboriginal. (In Australia) an Aboriginal bush hut, typically made of sheets of bark and branches.

gurdwara /gʊəˈdwɑːrə/, /gəːˈdwɑːrə/ *noun* E20 Punjabi (*gurduārā,* from Sanskrit GURU + *dvāra* door). A Sikh place of worship.

guru /ˈgʊruː/, /ˈguːruː/ *noun* E17 Sanskrit (*guru* elder, teacher). **1** A Hindu spiritual teacher. **2** Anyone looked up to as a source of wisdom or knowledge; an influential teacher or popular expert.

2 1995 *Country Life* Some guru—in Yorkshire, maybe—has warned that we are to have a hard winter.

gusto /ˈgʌstəʊ/ *noun* plural **gusto(e)s** E17 Italian (from Latin *gustus* taste). Keen enjoyment displayed in doing something; relish, zest.

■ Often in the phrase *with (great) gusto* (see quotation). The other early (E17) sense of *gusto* as 'an individual fondness or preference' and the art critical sense (M17) of 'the style in which a work of art is executed' (especially in *great* or *grand gusto* (= Italian *gran gusto*)) are both now archaic.
1996 *Spectator* He is not a wild, untempered spirit; he cooks with gusto, but not without formality.

gutta-percha /gʌtəˈpəːtʃə/ *noun* M19 Malay (*getah perca,* from *getah* gum + *perca* strips of cloth (which it resembles); altered by association with obsolete *gutta* gum, from Latin *gutta* a drop). **1** The coagulated latex of certain Malaysian trees, a hard tough thermoplastic substance consisting chiefly of a hydrocarbon isomeric with rubber and now used especially in dentistry and for electrical insulation. **2** Any of the trees, of the sapote family, which yield gutta-percha.

gyro /ˈdʒaɪrəʊ/, /ˈdʒɪərəʊ/ *noun* plural **gyros** L20 Modern Greek (*guros* turning). A sandwich of pitta bread filled with slices of spiced meat cooked on a spit, tomatoes, onions, etc.

■ Mainly United States.

Hh

dados /asɛn'dɑːdəʊz/, *foreign* /aθen 'daðos/ M19 Spanish. The owner of a HACIENDA.

hachure /ha'ʃjʊə/ *noun & verb* M19 French (from *hacher* to hatch). *Cartography* **A** *noun* Any of a number of short lines of shading on a map running in the direction of a slope and indicating steepness by their closeness and thickness. Also *hachure line*. Usually in *plural*. **B** *transitive verb* Shade (a map) with hachures.

hacienda /hasɪ'ɛndə/, *foreign* /aθi 'endə/, /asi'endə/ *noun* M18 Spanish (from Latin *facienda* things to be done, from *facere* to do). (In Spain and Spanish-speaking countries) a large estate or plantation with a dwelling house.

haciendado variant of HACENDADO.

Hadith /ha'diːθ/ *noun* E18 Arabic (ḥadīṯ statement, tradition). A collection of traditions containing sayings of the prophet Muhammad which, with accounts of his daily practice (the Sunna), constitute the major source of guidance for Muslims apart from the Koran; any of the sayings from the Hadith.

hafiz /'hɑːfɪz/ *noun* M17 Persian (from Arabic ḥāfiz present participle of ḥafiẓa to guard, know by heart). A Muslim who knows the Koran by heart.

ha-ha /'hɑːhɑː/ *noun* E18 French (said to be from the cry of surprise on suddenly discovering the obstacle). A ditch with a wall on its inner side below ground level, forming a boundary to a garden or park without interrupting the view from within.

haham /'hɑːhəm/ *noun* (also **chacham** /'xɑːxəm/ and other variants) L17 Hebrew (ḥākām wise). A spiritual leader among Sephardic Jews, or, more generally, a person learned in Jewish law.

haiku /'hʌɪkuː/ *noun* plural same, **haikus** L19 Japanese (abbreviation of *haikai no ku* unserious or comic verse). A Japanese poem of seventeen syllables, in three lines of five, seven, and five, traditionally evoking images of the natural world; a poem in English written in the form of a haiku. Cf. HOKKU.

habanera /habə'nɛːrə/, /ɑːbə'nɛːrə/ *noun* L19 Spanish (short for *danza habanera* Havanan dance, feminine of *habanero* of Havana the capital of Cuba). A slow Cuban dance and song in duple time.

habeas corpus /ˌheɪbɪəs 'kɔːpəs/ *noun phrase* LME Latin (= you shall have the body (in court)). *Law* A writ requiring a person under arrest to be brought before a judge or into court, especially to secure the person's release unless lawful grounds are shown for their detention; the legal right to apply for such a writ.

> **1996** *Times* It is ironic that the American President who was most influenced by…the values of legalism was compelled by civil war to suspend the writ of habeas corpus and defy Chief Justice Taney.

habitat /'habɪtat/ *noun* L18 Latin (literally, 'it dwells', 3rd person singular present of *habitare* to dwell in). The natural home or environment of an animal, plant, or other organism.

habitué /abitɥe/ (*plural same*); /hə 'bɪtjʊeɪ/ *noun* E19 French (past participle of *habituer* from Latin *habituare* to frequent). A resident of or frequent visitor to a particular place.

> **1996** *Spectator* John became a habitué and, quite literally, sang its praises.

háček /'hɑːtʃɛk/, /'hatʃɛk/ *noun* M20 Czech (diminutive of *hák* hook). A diacritic mark (ˇ) placed over a letter to indicate modification of the sound in Slavic and other languages.

hacendado /asɛn'dɑːdəʊ/, *foreign* /aθen'dado/, /asen'dado/ *noun* (also **haciendado** /ˌasɪɛn'dɑːdəʊ/, *foreign* /aθien'dado/, /asjen'daðo/ plural **hacen-**

hajj /hadʒ/ *noun* (also **haj**) E18 Arabic ((*al-*) *ḥajj* (the Great) Pilgrimage). The pilgrimage to the Sacred Mosque at Mecca, which takes place in the twelfth month of the Muslim year and which all Muslims are expected to make at least once during their lifetime if they can afford to do so.

figurative **1995** *Times* The international conference has become a modern form of world pilgrimage, the haj of the leisure classes.

hajji /ˈhadʒiː/ *noun* (also (feminine) **hajja** /ˈhadʒə/; **haji**) E17 Persian (Turkish *ḥājjī*, *ḥājī* pilgrim, from as preceding). (The title given to) a person who has undertaken the hajj. Cf. ALHAJI.

haka /ˈhɑːkə/ *noun* M19 Maori. A Maori ceremonial war dance involving chanting.

▪ Best known through its adoption by New Zealand international rugby teams as a pre-match ritual.

hakama /ˈhakəmə/, /ˈhɑːkəmə/ *noun* M19 Japanese. Loose trousers with many pleats in the front, forming part of Japanese formal dress.

Hakenkreuz /ˈhɑːkənkrɔyts/ *noun* (also **hakenkreuz**) plural **Hakenkreuze** /ˈhɑːkənkrɔytsə/ M20 German (from *Haken* hook + *Kreuz* cross). A swastika, especially in its clockwise form as a Nazi symbol.

hakim /ˈhɑːkɪm/ *noun* 1 E17 Arabic (*ḥākim* ruler, governor, judge from *ḥakama* to pass judgement). (In Muslim countries and formerly in India) a judge, ruler, or governor.

hakim /haˈkiːm/ *noun* 2 (also **hakeem**) M17 Arabic (*ḥakīm* wise man, philosopher, physician, from as preceding). A physician using traditional remedies in India and Muslim countries.

halal /həˈlɑːl/ *adjective & noun* M19 Arabic (*ḥalāl* according to religious law). **A** *adjective* **1** Killed or prepared in the manner prescribed by Muslim law. **2** Religiously acceptable according to Muslim law. **B** *noun* Halal meat.

haldi /ˈhʌldi/ *noun* M19 Hindi (from Sanskrit *haridrā*). The plant *Curcuma longa*, of the ginger family, whose powdered tubers yield turmeric. Also, turmeric itself.

halma /ˈhalmə/ *noun* L19 Greek (= leap). A game played by two or four people on a chequerboard of 256 squares, with pieces advancing from one corner to the opposite corner by being moved over other pieces into vacant squares.

haltere /halˈtɪə/ *noun* plural **halteres** /halˈtɪəriːz/ M16 Greek (*haltēres* (plural), from *hallesthai* to jump). *Entomology* Either of the two knobbed filaments which in two-winged insects take the place of posterior wings. Also called *balancer*, *poiser*. Usually in *plural*.

▪ Originally used in the plural to denote a pair of weights like dumb-bells held in the hands to give impetus when jumping.

halva /ˈhalvɑː/, /ˈhalvə/ *noun* (also **halvah** M17 Yiddish (*hal(a)va*, modern Hebrew *ḥalbāh*, modern Greek *khalbas*, Turkish *helva*, etc., from) Arabic (and Persian) *ḥalwā* sweetmeat). A Middle Eastern sweet confection made of sesame flour and honey.

hamartia /haˈmɑːtɪə/ *noun* L18 Greek (= fault, failure, guilt). The fault or error leading to the downfall of the tragic hero or heroine of a play, novel, etc.

▪ The term was used in Aristotle's *Poetics* with reference to ancient Greek tragedy.

hamel /ˈhɑːm(ə)l/ *noun* M19 Afrikaans (= Dutch *hamel*, German *Hammel*, from Old High German *hamal* mutilated). (In South Africa) a castrated ram, a wether.

hammam /ˈhamam/, /həˈmɑːm/, /ˈhʌmʌm/ *noun* (also **hummum** /ˈhʌmʌm/) E17 Turkish (or its source Arabic *hammām* bath, from *ḥamma* to heat). An establishment where one may take a Turkish bath.

hamza /ˈhamzə/ *noun* E19 Arabic (literally, 'compression'). (In Arabic script) a symbol representing a glottal stop; a glottal stop.

hanepoot /ˈhɑːnəpʊət/ *noun* L18 Afrikaans (from Dutch *haan* cock + *poot* foot). **1** A variety of sweet muscat grape, grown in South Africa and used for making wine or raisins. **2** The sweet white wine made from these grapes.

hangi /'haŋi/, /'hɑːŋi/ *noun* M19 Maori. An earth-oven in which food is cooked on heated stones; the food cooked in such an oven; a meal or gathering at which such food is cooked and served.

■ Chiefly New Zealand.

Hanse /hans/ *noun* (also **hanse**) ME Middle Low German (*hanshūs* and medieval Latin *hansa* from Old High German *hansa*, Middle and Modern High German *hanse* (whence Middle Low German *hanse*) Gothic *hansa* company, crowd, from Germanic, whence also Finnish *kansa* people, company). *History* **1** A medieval guild of merchants. **b** *Specifically* the Hanseatic League, a medieval association of north German cities, formed in 1241 and surviving until the 19th century. **2** A membership fee payable to a merchant guild; a trading fee imposed on non-members of the guild.

hapax legomenon /ˌhapaks lɛ'gʊmənɒn/ *noun phrase* plural **hapax legomena** /ˌhapaks lɛ'gʊmənə/ M17 Greek (= (a thing) said only once). A word, form, etc., of which only one recorded instance is known.

■ Used in Greek characters until the late 19th century and sometimes abbreviated *hapax*.

hara-kiri /harə'kɪri/ *noun* (also (corruptly) **hari-kiri** /harɪ'kɪri/) M19 Japanese (from *hara* belly + *kiri* cutting). A ritual form of suicide by disembowelment with a sword, formerly practised in Japan by samurai as an honourable alternative to disgrace or execution. Also, suicide practised voluntarily from a sense of shame, as a protest, etc.

haram /hɑː'rɑːm/ *noun & adjective* E17 Arabic (*ḥarām* forbidden; cf. HAREM). **A** *noun* A Muslim sacred place, forbidden to non-Muslims. **B** *adjective* (Of food) forbidden under Islamic law. Opposed to HALAL.

harem /'hɑːriːm/, /hɑː'riːm/, /'hɛːrəm/ *noun* M17 Turkish and Arabic (originally from Turkish *harem* from Arabic *ḥaram* (that which is) prohibited, (hence) sacred or inviolable place, sanctuary, women's apartments, wives, women; later also

from Arabic *ḥarīm* with same meaning, both from *ḥaruma* to be prohibited or unlawful). **1** The separate part of a Muslim household reserved for wives, concubines, and female servants. **2** The wives (or concubines) of a polygamous man. **b** A group of female animals sharing a single mate.

haricot /'harɪkəʊ/ *noun* M17 French (in sense 1 in *febves de haricot*, perhaps from Aztec *ayacotli*; in sense 2 Old French *hericoq*, *hericot (de mouton)*, probably related to *harigoter* to cut up). **1** A leguminous plant, *Phaseolus vulgaris*, native to tropical America but having numerous widely cultivated varieties; the edible pod or seed of this plant; *especially* white varieties of the dried seed. More fully *haricot bean*. **2** A ragout, especially of mutton or lamb.

harmattan /hɑː'mat(ə)n/ *noun* L17 Akan (*haramata*). A very dry, dusty easterly or north-easterly wind on the West African coast from December to February. Also *harmattan wind*.

hartal /'hɑːtɑːl/, /'hɜːtɑːl/ *noun* E20 Hindi (*hartāl*, *hartāl*, for *haṭṭal*, literally, 'locking of shops' (Sanskrit *haṭṭa* shop, *tāla* lock, bolt)). (In the Indian subcontinent) the organized closing of shops and offices as a mark of protest or as an act of mourning.

1920 *Blackwoods Magazine* What I had seen there of the crowds at the Hartal...had made me nervous.

hashish /'haʃiːʃ/, /'haʃɪʃ/, /ha'ʃiːʃ/ *noun* L16 Arabic (*ḥašīš* dry herb, hay, powdered hemp leaves, intoxicant made from this). Cannabis.

hasid /'hasɪd/ *noun* (also **chassid** /'xasɪd/, **hassid**, and with initial capital) plural **hasidim** /'hasɪdɪm/ E19 Hebrew (*ḥāsîd* pious, pietist). A member of a strictly orthodox Jewish sect in Palestine in the third and second centuries BC which opposed Hellenizing influences on their faith and supported the Maccabean revolt.

hasta la vista /ˌasta la 'vista/ *interjection* M20 Spanish. Goodbye, until we meet again.

■ This Spanish farewell was popularized in English by its use (in the form 'hasta la vista, baby') by the Austrian-born US film actor Arnold Schwarzenegger in the 1991 science-fiction film *Terminator 2: Judgment Day*.

hatha yoga /ˌhʌtə ˈjəʊɡə/, /ˌhatə/ *noun phrase* E20 Sanskrit (from *haṭha* force + *yoga*). A system of physical exercises and breathing control used in YOGA.

hatha yogi /ˌhʌtə ˈjəʊɡi/, /ˈhatə/ *noun phrase* M20 Sanskrit (from *haṭha* force + *yogi*). A person who practises HATHA YOGA.

hausfrau /ˈhaʊsfraʊ/ *noun* plural **hausfraus, hausfrauen** /ˈhaʊsfraʊən/ L18 German (from *Haus* house + *Frau* wife, woman). A German housewife; a woman regarded as overly domesticated.
   1995 *Times* If you saw her on the street she could be a *hausfrau*. It's very hard to relate her to the terrible things you are hearing about.

haute bourgeoisie /ot burʒwazi/, /ˌəʊt bʊəʒwɑːˈziː/ *noun phrase* L19 French (literally, 'high bourgeoisie'). The upper middle class.
   1996 *Spectator* There is a thesis to be written on why all crime stories devised for the haute bourgeoisie have to present their viewers' class in a generally unfavourable light.

haute couture /ot kutyr/, /ˌəʊt kuˈtjʊə/ *noun phrase* E20 French (literally, 'high dressmaking'). The designing and making of high-quality fashionable clothes by leading fashion houses; clothes of this kind.
   1995 *Times* Here, at the office of Yves Saint Laurent, is the genuine article, the haute couture attainable by almost no one, where the likes of Catherine Deneuve and Elizabeth Taylor are fitted for dresses which will cost £25,000.

haute cuisine /ot kɥizin/, /ˌəʊt kwɪˈziːn/ *noun phrase* E20 French (literally, 'high cookery'). The preparation and cooking of high-quality food following the style of traditional French cuisine; food produced in such a way.
   1996 *Times* Haute cuisine was followed by nouvelle cuisine...

haute école /ot ekɔl/, /ˌəʊt erˈkɒl/ *noun phrase* M19 French (literally, 'high school'). The art or practice of advanced classical dressage.

hauteur /əʊˈtə:/, *foreign* /otœr/ *noun* E17 French (from *haut* high). Proud haughtiness of manner.
   1996 *Times* To the dismay of her mother— who held out with an old-fashioned hauteur against her daughter's taking to the stage— Helene Cordot decided to embark upon a career as a cabaret artiste...

haut monde /o mɔ̃d/, /əʊ ˈmɒnd/ *noun phrase* M19 French (literally, 'high world'). Fashionable society. Cf. BEAU MONDE.

haut-relief /orəljɛf/, /əʊrɪˈliːf/ *noun* M19 French (literally, 'high relief'). ALTO-RELIEVO.

havildar /ˈhavɪldɑː/ *noun* L17 Urdu (*hawildār* from Persian *hawāl(a)dār* charge holder, from *hawāl*, from Arabic *hawāl(a)* charge, assignment + Persian *hawāl(a)-dār* holding, holder). (In the Indian subcontinent) a soldier or police officer corresponding to a sergeant.

hazzan /xəˈzɑːn/, /ˈhɑːz(ə)n/ *noun* (also **chaz(z)an, hazan**) plural **hazzanim** /xəˈzɑːnim/ M17 Hebrew (*hazzān* beadle, cantor, probably from Assyrian *hazannu* overseer or governor). A CANTOR in a synagogue.

Hebe /ˈhiːbi/ *noun* E17 Greek (*hēbē* youthful beauty, *Hēbē* the Greek goddess of youth and spring, daughter of Zeus and Hera, and cupbearer of Olympus). **1** A young woman resembling Hebe; a waitress. **2** (**hebe**) Any of numerous New Zealand evergreen shrubs constituting the genus *Hebe* (formerly included in *Veronica*), with spikes of mauve, pink, or white flowers.

heder variant of CHEDER.

hegemon /ˈhɛɡɪmɒn/, /ˈhiːɡɪmɒn/, /ˈhɛʤɪmɒn/ *noun* E20 Greek (*hēgemōn* leader, from *hēgeisthai* to lead). A supreme leader.

hegira /ˈhɛʤɪrə/ *noun* (also **Hegira, hejira, hijra** /ˈhɪʤrə/) L16 Medieval Latin (from Arabic *hijra* departure from one's home and friends, from *hajara* to separate, emigrate). **1** Muhammad's departure from Mecca to Medina in AD 622, marking the consolidation of the first Muslim community; the Muslim era reckoned from Muhammad's departure from Mecca. **2** Any exodus or departure.

■ The abbreviation AH (for *anno Hegirae*) is used in Islamic dates.

hejira variant of HEGIRA.

hélas /eˈlɑːs/ *interjection* LME French (later form of *ha las*, *a las* alas). Expressing grief, sadness, regret, etc.

Heldentenor /ˌhɛldənteˈnoːr/ *noun* plural **Heldentenöre** /ˌhɛldənteˈnørə/ E20 German (= hero tenor). A powerful tenor voice suited to heroic roles, especially in Wagnerian opera; a singer with a Heldentenor voice.

helix /ˈhiːlɪks/ *noun* plural **helices** /ˈhɛlɪsiːz/, /ˈhiːlɪsiːz/, **helixes** M16 Latin (*helix, helicis* from Greek *helix*). **1** An object having a three-dimensional shape like that of a wire wound uniformly in a single layer around a cylinder or cone, as in a corkscrew or spiral staircase. **2** *Geometry* A three-dimensional curve on a conical or cylindrical surface which would become a straight line if the surface was unrolled into a plane. **3** *Biochemistry* An extended spiral chain of atoms in a protein, nucleic acid, or other polymeric molecule. **4** *Chiefly Architecture*. A spiral ornament, a volute. **5** *Anatomy* The curved fold which forms the rim of the external ear.

helot /ˈhɛlət/ *noun* L16 Latin (*Helotes* plural from Greek *Heílōtes* (plural of *Heílōs*), also *Hilotae* from Greek *Heílōtai* (plural of *Heílōtēs*): usually derived from *Helos*, a town in Laconia whose inhabitants were enslaved). *Greek History* **1** (*Helot*) A member of a class of serfs in ancient Sparta, intermediate in status between slaves and citizens. **2** *transferred* and *figurative* A serf, a slave.

hendiadys /hɛnˈdʌɪədɪs/ *noun* L16 Medieval Latin (from Greek *hen dia duoin* 'one through two'). A figure of speech in which a single complex idea is expressed by two words usually connected by *and*.

■ An example of *hendiadys* is *nice and warm* for *nicely warm*.

herpes /ˈhəːpiːz/ *noun* LME Latin (= shingles, from Greek, literally, 'creeping', from *herpein* to creep). Originally, any skin disease characterized by the formation of groups of vesicles. Now, any of a group of virus diseases affecting the skin (often with blisters) or the nervous system.

Herrenvolk /ˈhɛːrənfɒlk/, /ˈhɛr(ə)nfɒlk/, /ˈhɛːrənfəʊk/ *noun* M20 German (= master race, from *Herren*, plural of *Herr*, from Old High German *hērro*, comparative of *hēr* exalted + *volk* race). The German nation as considered by the Nazis to be innately superior to others.

hetaera /hɪˈtɪərə/ *noun* (also **hetaira** /hɪˈtʌɪrə/, plural **hetairas**, **hetairai** /hɪˈtʌɪrʌɪ/) plural **hetaeras**, **hetaerae** /hɪˈtɪəriː/ E19 Greek (*hetaira* feminine of *hetairos* companion). A courtesan or mistress, especially an educated one in ancient Greece.

hetman /ˈhɛtmən/ *noun* M18 Polish (probably from German *Hauptmann* (earlier *Heubtman*) headman, captain). A Polish or Cossack military commander. Cf. ATAMAN.

Heuriger /ˈhɔyrɪɡər/ *noun* (also **Heurige** /ˈhɔyrɪɡə/) plural **Heurigen** /ˈhɔyrɪɡən/ M20 German ((southern and Austrian) = new (wine); vintner's establishment). **1** (In Austria) wine from the latest harvest. **2** An Austrian establishment where wine from the latest harvest is served.

hexapla /ˈhɛksəplə/ *noun* (also **hexaple** /ˈhɛksəp(ə)l/) E17 Greek ((*ta*) *hexapla* (title of Origen's edition of the Old Testament) neuter plural of *hexaplous* sixfold). A sixfold text in parallel columns, especially of the Old Testament.

hiatus /hʌɪˈeɪtəs/ *noun* plural same, **hiatuses** M16 Latin (= gaping, opening, from *hiare* to gape). **1** A pause or break in continuity in a sequence or activity. **2** *Grammar* and *Prosody* A break between two vowels which come together without an intervening consonant in successive words or syllables, as in *the ear* and *cooperative*.

■ Originally used in English to denote a physical gap or opening.

hibachi /hɪˈbatʃi/, /ˈhɪbətʃi/ *noun* M19 Japanese (from *hi* fire + *hachi* bowl, pot). **1** (In Japan) a large earthenware pan or brazier in which charcoal is burnt to provide indoor heating. **2** A portable

157

hibakusha | **hoi polloi**

cooking apparatus similar to a small barbecue.

hibakusha /ˈhɪbəkuːʃə/ *noun* plural same M20 Japanese (from *hi* suffer + *baku* explosion + *sha* person). (In Japan) a survivor of either of the atomic explosions at Hiroshima or Nagasaki in 1945.

hic jacet /hɪk ˈdʒeɪsɛt/, /ˈjakɛt/ *noun phrase* E17 Latin (literally, 'here lies', the first two words of a Latin epitaph). An epitaph.

hidalgo /hɪˈdalgəʊ/ *noun* plural **hidalgos** L16 Spanish (formerly also *hijo dalgo* contraction of *hijo de algo*, literally, 'son of something' (i.e. of an important person)). A gentleman in a Spanish-speaking country.

hijab /ˈhɪdʒab/ *noun* L20 Arabic. A head covering worn in public by some Muslim women; the religious code which governs the wearing of such clothing.
1995 *Times* Western women observing this rush for the *hijab* (headscarf) tend to stare in disbelief, broadcasting the worst excesses of 'Muslim chauvinism'.

hijra variant of HEGIRA.

hippocampus /ˌhɪpə(ʊ)ˈkampəs/ *noun* plural **hippocampi** /ˌhɪpə(ʊ)ˈkampʌɪ/ L16 Latin (from Greek *hippokampos*, from *hippos* horse + *kampos* sea monster). **1** A mythical sea monster, half horse and

half fish or dolphin, represented as drawing the chariot of Neptune. **2** *Anatomy* The elongated ridges on the floor of each lateral ventricle of the brain, thought to be the centre of emotion, memory, and the autonomic nervous system.

hippodrome /ˈhɪpədrəʊm/ *noun* L16 Old and Modern French (Latin *hippodromus* from Greek *hippodromos*, from *hippos* horse + *dromos* race, course). **1** (In ancient Greece or Rome) a stadium for chariot or horse races. **2** (*Hippodrome*) (The name of) a theatre or concert hall.
■ The early sense led to the term's use as a grandiose name for a modern circus, later applied to other places of popular entertainment.

hiragana /hɪrəˈɡɑːnə/ *noun* (also **hirakana** /hɪrəˈkɑːnə/) E19 Japanese (from *hira* plain + KANA). The more cursive form of kana (syllabic writing) used in Japanese, primarily used for function words and inflections. Cf. KATAKANA.

hogan /ˈhəʊɡ(ə)n/ *noun* L19 Navajo. A traditional Navajo Indian hut of logs and earth.

hoi polloi /hɔɪ ˈpɒlɔɪ/, /hɔɪ pɒˈlɔɪ/ *noun phrase* M17 Greek (= the many). The majority, the masses; the common people.

Hindi and Urdu

That a large number of words have been borrowed from Hindi and Urdu into English is in large measure a legacy of British colonial rule in India from 1858 to 1947, known as the *Raj* (itself a Hindi word meaning 'reign'). Anglo-Indian words that gained currency during this period include *sahib* (an Urdu word), which became familiar as a polite title or form of address for a man, and *wallah* (Hindi), used to describe a person involved with a specified task, as in 'rickshaw-wallah'. *Dekko*, meaning 'a quick look or glance', is a Hindi word originally used by British soldiers in India. Although *pukka*, also from Hindi, first appeared in English in the 17th century, its revival in the 1990s was due to its being a favourite word of the popular television chef Jamie Oliver. Other familiar words from the Indian subcontinent include *purdah*, *sari*, and *sitar*.

Since Indian and Pakistani independence in 1947, the contribution of these two languages to English has continued. These items on the menu of an Indian restaurant are all Hindi words: *basmati*, *bhaji*, *chapatti*, *dhal*, *ghee*, *pakora*, *raita*, and *roti*. The following, on the other hand, all come from Urdu: *balti*, *biryani*, *korma*, *nan*, *rogan josh*, *samosa*, and *tandoori*.

■ Frequently with *the* in English. Since *hoi* is the Greek word for the definite article, some traditionalists insist that *hoi polloi* should not be used with *the*, strictly speaking an unnecessary duplication of the word.

1996 *Spectator* Why do people who can afford to run their businesses from anywhere . . . rush . . . to join city hoi polloi once the Ides of March approach.

hokku /ˈhɒkuː/ *noun* plural same, **hokkus** L19 Japanese (= 'opening verse (of a linked sequence of comic verses)'). A HAIKU.

hollandaise /hɒlənˈdeɪz/, *attributively* also /ˈhɒləndeɪz/ *adjective* M19 French (feminine of *hollandais* Dutch, from *Hollande* Holland). Designating a creamy sauce made with butter, egg yolks, vinegar or white wine, and lemon juice, usually served with fish.

hom /həʊm/ *noun* (also **homa** /ˈhəʊmə/) M19 Persian (obsolete *hōm* (modern *hūm*), Avestan *haoma* = Sanskrit *soma* SOMA). The soma plant; the juice of the soma plant as a sacred drink of the Parsees.

hombre /ˈɒmbreɪ/ *noun* M19 Spanish (= man, from Latin *homo*, *homin-* human being). A man, especially one of a particular type.

■ Chiefly in United States slang. The word originally denoted a man of Spanish descent.

1996 *Spectator* All newspapers periodically put tough hombres into the accounts department.

homme moyen sensuel /ɔm mwajɛ̃ sɑ̃sɥɛl/ *noun phrase* (also **homme sensuel moyen**) E20 French (= man of average appetites). The average man; the man in the street.

Homo /ˈhəʊməʊ/, /ˈhɒməʊ/ *noun* plural **homos** L16 Latin (= man). The genus of primates to which human beings (HOMO SAPIENS) and certain of their fossil ancestors belong. Also with Latin specific epithets in names of (proposed) species, and with Latin or pseudo-Latin adjectives (in imitation of zoology nomenclature) in names intended to personify, often humorously, some aspects of human life or behaviour.

1961 *Times* Symbolizing . . . this concept of *homo turisticus*, the new Hilton hotel . . . will

have 500 rooms—all with a view of the Parthenon.

1996 *Times* But as for homo *loquens* [speaking] we seem to be little closer to knowing when, where, why, or how this stage was reached.

Homo sapiens /ˌhəʊməʊ ˈsapɪɛnz/, /ˌhɒməʊ ˈsapɪɛnz/ *noun phrase* (also **homo sapiens**) E19 Modern Latin (= wise man). The primate species to which modern humans belong; humans regarded as a species.

■ Term introduced in Linnaeus' *Systema Naturae* (10th edn. 1758), and thence into English via the translation of Linnaeus' book.

1996 *Times* She valuably reviews the anthropological, archaeological, and palaeontological evidence for the emergence of homo sapiens in the Rift Valley.

homunculus /hɒˈmʌŋkjʊləs/ *noun* plural **homunculi** /hɒˈmʌŋkjʊlʌɪ/, /hɒˈmʌŋkjʊliː/ M17 Latin (diminutive of *homo* man). A very small human or humanoid creature.

■ Formerly also applied to a foetus considered as a fully formed human being.

honcho /ˈhɒntʃəʊ/ *noun & verb* M20 Japanese (*hanchō* group leader). **A** *noun* plural **honchos**. The leader of a small group or squad; a leader or manager; the person who is in charge: *the company's head honcho in the US.* **B** *transitive verb* Oversee; be in charge of (a project or situation).

■ Chiefly North American slang. The term was brought back to the US by servicemen stationed in Japan during the occupation following the Second World War.

honi soit qui mal y pense /ɒnɪ ˌswɑː ki: mal i: ˈpɑ̃s/ *interjection* LME French. Shame on him who thinks evil of it.

■ The motto of the Order of the Garter, the highest order of English knighthood, founded by Edward III *c*.1344. According to tradition, the garter was that of the Countess of Salisbury, which the king placed on his own leg after it fell off while she was dancing with him. *Honi soit qui mal y pense* was the king's comment to those present, subsequently adopted as the motto of the order.

honnête homme /ɔnɛt ɔmɛ/ *noun phrase* plural **honnêtes hommes** (pronounced same) M17 French (= honest man). A decent, cultivated man of the world; a gentleman.

> **1960** J. Bayley *Characters of Love* Iago... is in many ways a terrible parody of the Augustan *honnête homme.*

honorarium /ɒnəˈrɛːrɪəm/ *noun* plural **honorariums, honoraria** /ɒnəˈrɛːrɪə/ M17 Latin (*honorarium* gift made on being admitted to public office, use as noun of neuter of *honorarius* honorary). A payment given for professional services that are rendered nominally without charge.

> **1996** *Country Life* Mrs Young radiates enjoyment of her job, for which she is paid a reasonable honorarium...

honoris causa /ɒˌnɔːrɪs ˈkaʊzə/ *adverb phrase* E17 Latin (= for the sake of honour). As a mark of esteem, especially in reference to an honorary degree at a university.

hookah /ˈhʊkə/ *noun* M18 Urdu (from Arabic *ḥuḳḳa* small box, container, pot, jar). An oriental tobacco pipe with a long, flexible tube which draws the smoke through water contained in a bowl.

horchata /orˈtʃata/, /ɔːˈtʃɑːtə/ *noun* M19 Spanish. (In Spain and Latin American countries) a milky drink made from tiger nuts.

horresco referens /hɒˌrɛskəʊ rɛˈfəːrɛnz/ L17 Latin (= I shudder to relate, from *horrescere* to stand on end (of hair) + *referens*, present participle of *referre* to relate). Expressing horror at a memory.

■ The expression comes from Virgil's *Aeneid* (ii. 204), at the point when the hero Aeneas is relating how giant sea serpents killed the priest Laocoon for attempting to warn the Trojans against taking the Greeks' wooden horse into their city.

> **1995** *Spectator* I ended up bolting down a bowl of spaghetti bolognese the nastiness of which *horresco referens.*

horribile dictu /hɒˌrɪbɪleɪ ˈdɪktuː/, /hɒˌriːbɪliː/ *adverb phrase* M19 Modern Latin (by analogy with MIRABILE DICTU). Horrible to relate.

horror vacui /ˌhɒrə ˈvakjuːʌɪ/ *noun phrase* M19 Modern Latin (= the horror of a vacuum). A fear or dislike of leaving empty spaces, especially in an artistic composition.

> **1972** E. Lucie-Smith *Eroticism in Western Art* Nudes... fill the whole picture-space as if the artist suffered from *horror vacui.*

hors concours /ɔr kɔ̃kur/ *adverb &* predicate *adjective phrase* L19 French (= out of the competition). **1** Engaged in a contest but not competing for a prize. **2** Without a rival, in a class of its own.

■ Both senses are also present in modern French.

> **2 1941** V. Nabokov *Real Life of Sebastian Knight* Most husbands are fools, but that one was *hors concours.*

hors de combat /ɔr də kɔ̃ba/ *adjective phrase* M18 French (= out of the fight). Out of action due to injury or damage.

hors d'oeuvre /ɔr dœvr/, /ɔː ˈdəːvr(ə)/ *noun phrase* plural same, **hors d'oeuvres** M18 French (literally, 'outside the work'). A small savoury dish, typically one served as an appetizer or starter; in *plural* also, (usually mixed) items of food served as such a dish. Also *figurative* a preliminary.

horst /hɔːst/ *noun* L19 German (= heap, mass). *Geology* An elongated block of the earth's surface bounded by faults on some or all sides and raised relative to the surrounding land.

horti sicci plural of HORTUS SICCUS.

hortus siccus /ˌhɔːtəs ˈsɪkəs/ *noun phrase* plural **horti sicci** /ˌhɔːtʌɪ ˈsɪkʌɪ/, /ˌhɔːtiː ˈsɪkiː/ L17 Latin (= dry garden). An arranged collection of dried plants, a herbarium; *figurative* a collection of uninteresting facts etc.

hotelier /həʊˈtɛlɪeɪ/, /həʊˈtɛlɪə/ *noun* E20 French (*hôtelier*). A person who owns or runs a hotel or group of hotels.

houmous variant of HUMMUS.

houp-la /ˈhuːplɑː/ *interjection &* noun (also **hoop-la**) L19 French (*houp-là!*, from *houp* interjection + *là* there). **A** *interjection* Accompanying or drawing attention to a quick or sudden movement. **B** *noun* An exclamation of 'houp-la!'; *slang* a commotion, ballyhoo, pretentious nonsense.

houri /ˈhʊəri/ *noun* M18 French (from Persian *ḥūrī* from Arabic *ḥūr* plural of *'aḥwar*, feminine *ḥawrā'* having eyes with a marked contrast of white and black). Any of the virgins of the Muslim paradise, promised as wives to believers; *transferred* a voluptuously beautiful woman.

howdah /ˈhaʊdə/ *noun* L18 Urdu (*haudah* from Arabic *hawdaj* a litter carried by a camel). (In the Indian subcontinent) a seat for riding on the back of an elephant or camel, typically with a canopy and accommodating two or more people.

huarache /waˈrɑːtʃi/ *noun* (also **guarache** /gwaˈrɑːtʃi/) L19 Mexican Spanish. A leather-thonged sandal, originally worn by Mexican Indians.

hubris /ˈhjuːbrɪs/ *noun* L19 Greek. Presumption, insolence; pride, excessive self-confidence.

■ The earliest instance of *hubris* in a nonspecialist English text, a newspaper of 1884, refers to it as 'Academic slang' and defines it as 'a kind of high-flown insolence'. In its original context in ancient Greek literary texts it indicated insolence towards the gods, manifested either in spiritual pride or by behaviour that flouted divine or social law; thus the arrogant and riotous conduct of Penelope's suitors in Homer's *Odyssey* is an instance of hubris that met its due when they were almost all slaughtered by the returned Odysseus.

huevos rancheros /ˌwɛvɒs ranˈtʃɛːrɒs/ *noun phrase* L20 (Mexican) Spanish (= rancheros' eggs). A dish of fried or poached eggs served on a tortilla with a spicy tomato sauce, originating in Mexico.

hui /ˈhuːi/ *noun* M19 Maori and Hawaiian. (In New Zealand) a large social or ceremonial gathering; (in Hawaii) a formal club or association.

hula /ˈhuːlə/ *noun* (also **hula-hula**) E19 Hawaiian. A dance performed by Hawaiian women, characterized by six basic steps, undulating hips, and gestures symbolizing or imitating natural phenomena or historical or mythological subjects.

hummus /ˈhʊməs/ *noun* (also **houmous**) M20 Arabic (*ḥummuṣ*). A thick paste or spread made from ground chickpeas and sesame seeds, olive oil, lemon, and garlic, made originally in the Middle East.

humus /ˈhjuːməs/ *noun* L18 Latin (= soil). The organic constituent of soil, formed by the decomposition of leaves and other plant material.

hwyl /ˈhuːɪl/ *noun* L19 Welsh. (In Welsh use) a stirring feeling of emotional motivation and energy.

hydria /ˈhʌɪdrɪə/, /ˈhɪdrɪə/ *noun* plural **hydriae** /ˈhʌɪdriːiː/ ME Old French (*idr(i)e*, from Latin *hydria*, from Greek *hudria*). Formerly, a water pot. Now (*Archaeology*), a three-handled pitcher of ancient Greece.

hyperbaton /hʌɪˈpɑːbətɒn/ *noun* M16 Latin (from Greek *huperbaton* overstepping, from *huperbainein*, from as *hyper-* beyond, over + *bainein* to walk). *Grammar* and *Rhetoric* A figure of speech in which the normal order of words or phrases is inverted, especially for the sake of emphasis, as in the sentence '*this I must see*'.

hyperbole /hʌɪˈpɜːbəli/ *noun* LME Latin (from Greek *huperbolē* excess, exaggeration, from as *hyper-* beyond, over + *ballein* to throw). A figure of speech consisting in exaggerated or extravagant statement, used to express strong feeling or produce a strong impression and not meant to be taken literally; an instance of this; *generally* overstatement.

1996 *New Scientist* Hyperbole seems to be the order of the day: this phenomenon is called colossal magnetoresistance.

hypogeum /ˌhʌɪpə(ʊ)ˈdʒiːəm/ *noun* (also **hypogaeum**) plural **hypog(a)ea** /ˌhʌɪpə(ʊ)ˈdʒiːə/ M17 Latin (*hypogeum, hypogaeum* from Greek *hupogeion, hupogaion* use as noun of neuter singular of *hupogeios* underground). An underground chamber or vault.

hypothesis /hʌɪˈpɒθɪsɪs/ *noun* plural **hypotheses** /hʌɪˈpɒθɪsiːz/ L16 Late Latin (from Greek *hupothesis* foundation, base, from as *hypo-* + *thesis* placing). **1** A supposition or proposed explanation made on the basis of limited evidence as a starting point for further investigation. **2** *Philosophy* A proposition made as a basis for reasoning, without any assumption of its truth.

hysteron proteron /ˌhɪstərɒn ˈprɒtərɒn/ *noun phrase* M16 Late Latin (from Greek *husteron proteron* the latter (put in place of) the former). **1** *Rhetoric* A figure of speech in which what would naturally come last is put first, for example *'I die! I faint! I fail!'*. **2** *generally* Position or arrangement of things in the reverse of their natural or rational order.

Ii

id /ɪd/ *noun* E20 Latin (= that, translating German *es*). *Psychoanalysis* The part of the mind in which innate instinctive impulses and primary processes are manifest. In Freudian theory, it interacts with the ego and the superego.

■ The term was first used in this sense by Freud, following the use in a similar sense by his contemporary Georg Groddeck.

1996 *Spectator* . . . talk of leaving Europe is the politics of the id: a regression to infantile fantasy.

iambus /ʌɪ'ambəs/ *noun* plural **iambuses**, **iambi** /ʌɪ'ambʌɪ/ L16 Latin (from Greek *iambos* iambus, lampoon, from *iaptein* to assail in words). *Prosody* A metrical foot consisting of one short (or unstressed) syllable followed by one long (or stressed) syllable.

■ The metre known as the iambic trimeter was first used by the ancient Greek satirists, hence the connection with lampoons.

ibid /'ɪbɪd/ *adverb* M17 Latin (abbreviation of next). IBIDEM.

ibidem /'ɪbɪdɛm/, /ɪ'bʌɪdɛm/ *adverb* M18 Latin (= in the same place, from *ibi* there + demonstrative suffix *-dem*, as in *idem*, *tandem*, etc). In the same book, chapter, passage, etc. (used to save space in textual references to a quoted work which has been mentioned in a previous reference).

■ The abbreviated form *ibid* is in more general use in bibliographies etc.

ichor /'ʌɪkɔ:/ *noun* M17 Greek (*ikhōr*). **1** *Greek Mythology* A fluid supposed to flow like blood in the veins of the gods. **2** A watery discharge from a wound or sore. *Archaic.*

iconostasis /ʌɪkə'nɒstəsɪs/ *noun* plural **iconostases** /ʌɪkə'nɒstəsiːz/ M19 Modern Greek (*eikonostasis*, from as *icono-* (combining form of) icon + *stasis*, literally, 'standing'). A screen separating the sanctuary or altar from the nave in most Orthodox churches and used to display icons.

Id see EID.

idée fixe /ide fiks/, /ˌiːdeɪ 'fiːks/ *noun phrase* plural **idées fixes** (pronounced same) M19 French (= fixed idea). An idea or desire that dominates the mind, an obsession.

1995 *Spectator* I had not realised that Cézanne's numerous bathers were such an *idée fixe.*

idée reçue /ide rəsy/, /ˌiːdeɪ rə'sjuː/ *noun phrase* plural **idées reçues** (pronounced same) M20 French (= received idea). A generally accepted concept or idea.

idem /'ɪdɛm/, /'ʌɪdɛm/ *adverb* LME Latin (= the same). Used in citations to indicate an author or work that has just been mentioned.

id est /ɪd 'ɛst/ *adverb phrase* L16 Latin (= that is). That is to say (used to add explanatory information or to state something in different words).

■ Usually abbreviated to *i.e.*

idiot savant /idjo savɑ̃/ *noun phrase* plural **idiots savants** (*pronounced same*) L20 French (= learned idiot). A person who has a mental disability or learning difficulties but is extremely gifted in a particular way, such as the performing of feats of memory or calculation; a person who is extremely unworldly but displays natural wisdom and insight.

1995 *New Scientist* She is no idiot savant like the Dustin Hoffman character in *Rain Man* who could memorise a casino-full of cards but could do nothing with the information . . .

Id ul-fitr see EID.

i.e. abbreviation of ID EST.

igloo /'ɪglu:/ *noun* M19 Inuit (*iglu* house). A dome-shaped Eskimo house, typically built from blocks of solid snow.

ignis fatuus /ˌɪgnɪs 'fatjʊəs/ *noun phrase* plural **ignes fatui** /ˌɪgni:z 'fatjʊʌɪ/, /ˌɪgneɪz 'fatjʊi:/ M16 Modern Latin (= foolish fire, so called from its erratic flitting from place to place). **1** A phosphorescent light seen hovering or floating over marshy ground, perhaps due to the combustion of methane; a will-o'-the-wisp. **2** A delusive guiding principle, hope, or aim.

ignoramus /ɪgnə'reɪməs/ *noun* L16 Latin (= we do not know, (in legal use) we take no notice of it). An ignorant or stupid person.

■ The word is recorded from the late 16th century, as the endorsement made by a grand jury on an indictment considered backed by insufficient evidence to bring before a petty jury. The modern sense may derive from the name of a character in George Ruggle's *Ignoramus* (1615), a satirical comedy exposing lawyers' ignorance.

ignoratio elenchi /ɪgnə,reɪʃɪəʊ ɪ'lɛŋkʌɪ/ *noun phrase* plural **ignorationes elenchi** /ˌɪgnəreɪʃɪ'əʊni:z/ L16 Medieval Latin (translation of Greek *hē tou elegkou agnoia* ignorance of the conditions of valid proof). *Philosophy* A logical fallacy which consists in apparently refuting an opponent while actually disproving something not asserted; *generally* any argument which is irrelevant to its professed purpose.

ignotum per ignotius /ɪg,nəʊtəm pər ɪg'nəʊtɪəs/ *noun phrase* LME Late Latin (literally, 'the unknown by means of the more unknown'). An explanation which is harder to understand than what it is meant to explain.

ikat /'i:kɑ:t/ *noun* M20 Malay (literally, 'tie, fasten'). Fabric made using an Indonesian technique of textile decoration in which warp or weft threads, or both, are tie-dyed before weaving.

ikebana /ɪkɪ'bɑːnə/ *noun* E20 Japanese (literally, 'living flowers'). The art of Japanese flower arrangement, with formal display according to strict rules.

ilang-ilang variant of YLANG-YLANG.

illuminati /ɪˌlu:mɪ'nɑːti/ *noun plural* (also **Illuminati**) L16 Italian (= the enlightened ones; plural of Italian *illuminato* or Latin *illuminatus* enlightened, but in German context translating German *Illuminaten*). **1** (*Illuminati*) A sect of 16th-century heretics who claimed special religious enlightenment. **2** (*Illuminati*) A Bavarian secret society founded in 1776, organized like the Freemasons. **3** People claiming to possess special enlightenment or knowledge of something.

imago /ɪ'meɪgəʊ/ *noun* plural **imagines** /ɪ'meɪdʒɪni:z/, **imagos** L18 Latin (= image). **1** *Entomology* The final and fully developed adult stage of an insect after passing through all stages of metamorphosis. **2** *Psychoanalysis* An unconscious idealized mental image of someone, especially a parent, which influences a person's behaviour.

imam /ɪ'mɑːm/ *noun* E17 Arabic ('*imām* leader, from '*amma* to lead the way). **1** The person who leads prayers in a mosque. **2** (**Imam**) A title of any of various Muslim leaders, especially one succeeding Muhammad as the leader of Shiite Islam.

imam bayildi /ɪˌmɑːm 'bɑːjɪldi/ *noun phrase* (also **Imam Bayildi**) M20 Turkish (*imam bayıldı*, literally, 'the imam fainted'). A dish, originating in Turkey, consisting of aubergines stuffed with a garlic-flavoured onion-and-tomato mixture and baked.

■ Whether the *imam* fainted from pleasure and repletion or because he was overcome by horror at the cost of the dish seems to be a moot point.

imbroglio /ɪm'brəʊlɪəʊ/ *noun* (also **embroglio**) plural **imbroglios** M18 Italian (from *imbrogliare* to confuse, corresponding to French *embrouiller* to embroil). **1** An extremely confused, complicated, or embarrassing situation. **2** A confused heap. *Archaic*.

1 1996 *Spectator* If the royal imbroglio does end in a tragedy, Major will have blood on his hands.

immortelle /ɪmɔː'tɛl/ *noun* M19 French (from *fleur immortelle* everlasting flower).

An everlasting flower, especially *Xeranthemum annuum*.

impasse /amˈpɑːs/, /ˈampɑːs/, *foreign* /ɛ̃pɑs/ *noun* M19 French (from negative *im-* not + stem of *passer* to pass). A situation in which no progress is possible, especially because of disagreement; a deadlock.

> **1996** *New Scientist*... the only thing that can help developing countries escape this impasse is a second revolution.

impasto /ɪmˈpastəʊ/ *noun* L18 Italian (from *impastare*, from *im-* in + *pasta* paste). The process or technique of laying on paint or pigment thickly so that it stands out from a surface; paint applied thickly.

> *transferred* **1996** *Spectator* As the swirling impasto of adjectives, similes and metaphors becomes increasingly thick and clotted, so the picture becomes less and less distinct.

impedimenta /ɪmˌpɛdɪˈmɛntə/ *noun plural* E17 Latin (plural of *impedimentum* impediment, from *impedire* shackle the feet of). Equipment for an activity or expedition, especially when considered as bulky or an encumbrance.

> **1996** *Times* On the walls and hanging from the ceiling were the impedimenta of many sports: stuffed baseball players in New York Mets shirts, hang gliders, surf boards, caps, bats and gloves.

imperium /ɪmˈpɪərɪəm/ *noun* M17 Latin (= command, authority, empire). Absolute power; supreme or imperial power; empire.

> ■ Used especially of the rule of the Roman emperors.

impi /ˈɪmpi/ *noun* M19 Zulu (= regiment, armed band). A body of Zulu warriors; an armed band of Zulus involved in urban or rural conflict.

impluvium /ɪmˈpluːvɪəm/ *noun plural* **impluvia** /ɪmˈpluːvɪə/ E19 Latin (from *impluere* to rain into). The square basin in the centre of the atrium of an ancient Roman house, which received rainwater from an opening in the roof.

impresario /ˌɪmprɪˈsɑːrɪəʊ/ *noun plural* **impresarios** M18 Italian (from *impresa* undertaking). A person who organizes and often finances concerts, plays, or operas; the manager of a musical, theatrical, or operatic company.

> **1996** *Spectator* [Diaghilev] became an impresario, inspirer and explainer—of Russia to the West and the West to Russia.

imprimatur /ˌɪmprɪˈmeɪtə/, /ˌɪmprɪˈmɑːtə/, /ˌɪmprɪˈmɑːtʊə/ *noun* M17 Latin (= let it be printed, 3rd person singular present subjunctive passive of *imprimere* to imprint). An official licence issued by the Roman Catholic Church for the printing of an ecclesiastical or religious work etc.; *generally* official approval, an official sanction.

> *figurative* **1995** *Times* Without America's imprimatur, inward investment to Northern Ireland would wither away.

impromptu /ɪmˈprɒm(p)tjuː/ *adverb, adjective & noun* M17 French (from Latin *in promptu* at hand, in readiness, from *promptus* readiness). **A** *adverb* Without preparation; on the spur of the moment; extempore. **B** *adjective* Composed, uttered, or done without being planned or rehearsed; improvised. **C** *noun* A short piece of instrumental music, especially a solo, having the character of an improvisation.

imshi /ˈɪmʃi/ *transitive verb* (*imperative*) (also **imshee**) E20 Arabic ((from colloquial) *'mši* imperative of *miši* to go). Go away!

> ■ Military slang, recorded (1916) during World War I as being used to street hawkers in Cairo by the Australasian Corps.

in absentia /ɪn abˈsɛntɪə/, /ɪn abˈsɛnʃɪə/ *adverb phrase* L19 Latin (= in absence). While not present at the event being referred to.

> ■ Almost always in a legal context modifying the verbs 'try' or 'convict' (see quotation).
> **1996** *Times* The court is trying 71 members of the Dergue, of whom 25... are being tried in absentia.

inamorata /ɪˌnaməˈrɑːtə/ *noun* (also **enamorata**) M17 Italian ((now *innamorata*), feminine of INAMORATO). A person's female lover.

> **1996** *Spectator* Paula Yates... estranged wife of Bob Geldof, inamorata of rock star has-been Michael Hutchence...

inamorato /ɪˌnaməˈrɑːtəʊ/ *noun* (also **enamorato**) *plural* **inamoratos** L16 Italian (now *innamorato*, past participle of *innamorare* to fall in love with). A person's male lover.

in camera /ɪn ˈkam(ə)rə/ *adverb phrase* E19 Late Latin (= in the chamber). In private, in particular taking place in the private chambers of a judge, with the press and public excluded.

incipit /ˈɪnsɪpɪt/ *noun* L19 Latin (= (there) begins, 3rd person singular present indicative of *incipere* to begin). The opening words of a manuscript, early printed book, or chanted liturgical text.

▪ The word used by medieval scribes to indicate the beginning of a new treatise, poem, division, etc. Cf. EXPLICIT.

incognito /ˌɪnkɒgˈniːtəʊ/, /ɪnˈkɒgnɪtəʊ/ *adjective, adverb, & noun* M17 Italian (from Latin *incognitus* unknown, from as *in-* un- + *cognitus*, past participle of *cognoscere* to know). **A** *adjective* (Of a person) concealed under a disguised or assumed identity; unknown. **B** *adverb* Under a disguised or assumed identity. **C** *noun* plural **incognitos 1** A person who conceals his or her identity; an anonymous or unknown person. **2** The condition of being unknown, anonymity; assumed or pretended identity.

B 1996 *Spectator* Surely anyone could see it is my duty [as a restaurant critic] to travel incognito.

incommunicado /ˌɪnkəmjuːnɪˈkɑːdəʊ/ *adjective & adverb* (also in Spanish form **incomunicado** *also foreign* /ˌinkomuniˈkado/) M19 Spanish (*incomunicado* past participle of *incomunicar* to deprive of communication). **A** *adjective* Not able, wanting, or allowed to communicate with other people; *especially* (of a prisoner) held in solitary confinement. **B** *adverb* Without means of communication with other people.

inconnu /ˈɪŋkənuː/, *foreign* /ɛ̃kɔny/ (*plural same*) *noun* (in sense 1 feminine **inconnue**, plural (in sense 1) **inconnu(e)s**, (in sense 2) same) E19 French (= unknown). **1** An unknown person or thing; a stranger. **2** An edible predatory freshwater white fish related to the salmon, *Stenodus leucichthys*, native to Eurasian and North American lakes close to the Arctic Circle.

incubus /ˈɪŋkjʊbəs/ *noun* plural **incubuses**, **incubi** /ˈɪŋkjʊbʌɪ/ ME Late Latin (= Latin *incubo* nightmare, from *incubare* to lie on). **1** A male demon believed to have sexual intercourse with sleeping women. **2** An oppressive nightmare; something which oppresses or troubles like a nightmare; a cause of difficulty or anxiety.

2 1996 *Times* She has no incubus of accumulated policies and attitudes.

incunabulum /ˌɪnkjʊˈnabjʊləm/ *noun* plural **incunabula** /ˌɪnkjʊˈnabjʊlə/ E19 Latin (*incunabula* neuter plural swaddling-clothes, cradle, from as *in-* in + *cunae* cradle). A book printed at an early date, especially one printed before 1501.

indecorum /ɪndɪˈkɔːrəm/ *noun* L16 Latin (use as noun of neuter singular of *indecorus* unseemly). Failure to conform to good taste, propriety, or etiquette; lack of decorum.

index librorum prohibitorum /ˌɪndɛks lɪˌbrɔːrəm prəʊˌhɪbɪˈtɔːrəm/ *noun phrase* (also **Index Librorum Prohibitorum**) M17 Latin (= index of forbidden books). *Roman Catholic Church* The official list of books that Roman Catholics were forbidden to read or which were to be read only in expurgated editions, as contrary to Catholic faith or morals.

▪ The first *Index Librorum Prohibitorum* was issued in 1557, and the list was revised at intervals until it was abolished in 1966. It was also referred to simply as *the Index*.

indicia /ɪnˈdɪsɪə/ *noun* plural E17 Latin (plural of *indicium*, from *index* informer, sign). Signs, indications, or distinguishing marks.

indumentum /ˌɪndjʊˈmɛntəm/ *noun* plural **indumenta** /ˌɪndjʊˈmɛntə/ M19 Latin (= garment, from *induere* to put on). *Botany* and *Zoology* A covering of hairs, scales, feathers, etc., on an animal or plant, especially when dense.

induna /ɪnˈduːnə/ *noun* M19 Xhosa and Zulu (from nominal prefix *in-* + *duna* councillor, headman, overseer, captain). **1** A tribal councillor or headman among the Nguni peoples of southern Africa. **2** An African foreman; a person in authority.

in esse /ɪn 'ɛsi/ *adjective phrase* L16 Latin. In actual existence.

in excelsis /ɪn ɛk'selsɪs/, /ˌɛks'tʃɛlsɪs/ *adverb phrase* LME Latin (= in the highest (places); cf. EXCELSIOR). In the highest.
■ Often in the phrase *Gloria in excelsis Deo* 'Glory to God in the highest!'

in extenso /ɪn ɪk'stɛnsəʊ/ *adverb phrase* E19 Latin (from *in* in + *extenso* ablative of *extensus* past participle of *extendere* to stretch out). In full, at length.

in extremis /ɪn ɛk'striːmɪs/, /ɪn ɪk'striːmɪs/ *adverb phrase* M16 Latin (from *in* in + *extremis* ablative plural of *extremus* last, uttermost). In an extremely difficult situation; at the point of death.
1996 *Spectator* I can still recall the glorious sight of his headlong dive to the ground and the altogether unexpected knowledge of English he revealed *in extremis*.

infanta /ɪn'fantə/ *noun* L16 Spanish (Portuguese feminine of INFANTE). *History* A daughter of the ruling monarch of Spain or Portugal; *specifically* the eldest daughter who is not heir to the throne.

infante /ɪn'fanteɪ/ *noun* M16 Spanish and Portuguese (from Latin *infans*, *infant-* child). *History* A son of the ruling monarch of Spain or Portugal other than the heir to the throne; *specifically* the second son.

inferno /ɪn'fəːnəʊ/ *noun* plural **infernos** M19 Italian (from Christian Latin *infernus* below, subterranean). **1** Hell. **2** A scene of horror or distress; *especially* a large fire that is dangerously out of control.
■ Reference to hell as *the inferno* is generally in allusion to Dante's *Divine Comedy*.

in fine /ɪn 'fʌɪni/, /'fiːni/ *adverb phrase* M16 Latin. Finally, in short, to sum up.
1996 *Spectator* Alfred, *in fine*, created a well-spring of instinctive Tory-voting monarchists.

in flagrante /ɪn flə'granti/ *adverb phrase* E17 Latin (abbreviation of next or similar Latin phrase). In the very act. *Colloquial.*
1996 *Oldie* Abby herself attempts to commit suicide on finding her agent *in flagrante* with his secretary.

in flagrante delicto /ɪn flə,granti dɪ'lɪktəʊ/ *adverb phrase* L18 Latin (= in the heat of the crime, in blazing crime).

In the very act of committing an offence, especially in an act of adultery or other sexual misconduct.
1996 *Spectator* ... his sacking as editor... was more abrupt since he was caught *in flagrante delicto* with his pretty secretary...

influenza /ˌɪnflʊ'ɛnzə/ *noun* M18 Italian (literally, 'influence', from medieval Latin *influentia* influence). A highly contagious viral infection of the respiratory passages causing fever, weakness, muscular aches, coughing, and watery catarrh, and often occurring in epidemics.
■ Generally abbreviated to *flu* in all but the most formal usage. The Italian word *influenza* also has the sense 'an outbreak of an epidemic', hence 'epidemic'. It was applied specifically to an influenza epidemic which began in Italy in 1743, later adopted in English as the name of the disease.

infra /'ɪnfrə/ *adverb* L19 Latin. (In a written document) below; further on: *see note, infra.*

infra dig /ˌɪnfrə 'dɪg/ *adjective phrase* E19 Latin (abbreviation of Latin *infra dignitatem* beneath (one's) dignity). Beneath the dignity of one's position; demeaning, undignified. *Colloquial.*
1996 *Times* Hoping that this didn't look too infra dig, I duly grasped the mane on our final attempt, all but letting go of the reins...

ingénue /ˌanʒer'njuː/; *foreign* /ɛ̃ʒeny/ (*plural same*) *noun* (also **ingenue**) M19 French (feminine of *ingénu* ingenuous). An innocent or unsophisticated young woman, especially as a stage role; an actress playing such a role.
1995 *Times* She is 60, that awkward age, too old for ingenues, too young for crones.

ingesta /ɪn'dʒɛstə/ *noun* plural E18 Latin (neuter plural of *ingestus* past participle of *ingerere* to carry in, pour in). *Medicine* and *Zoology.* Substances taken into the body as nourishment; food and drink.

in loco parentis /ɪn ˌləʊkəʊ pə'rɛntɪs/ *prepositional phrase* E19 Latin (= in place of a parent). Assuming the responsibilities of a parent.
1995 *Spectator* One of us was in agony and one of us was *in loco parentis*, so it was a very sticky wait.

in medias res /ɪn ˌmɛdɪɑːs ˈreɪz/, /ˌmiːdɪɑːs/ *adverb phrase* L18 Latin (= in the middle of things). Into the middle of a narrative, without preamble; into the middle of things.

in memoriam /ɪn mɪˈmɔːrɪam/ *prepositional & noun phrase* M19 Latin. **A** *prepositional phrase* To the memory of, in memory of. **B** *noun phrase* An article or poem written in memory of a dead person; an obituary.

■ The fashion for poems with this title was set by Tennyson's sequence of poems (1850), written in memory of his friend A. H. Hallam, who died in 1833.

innuendo /ɪnjʊˈɛndəʊ/ *noun* plural **innuendo(e)s** M16 Latin (= by nodding at, pointing to, intimating, ablative gerund of *innuere* to nod to, signify, from as *in-* + *nuere* to nod). An allusive or oblique remark or hint, typically a suggestive or disparaging one.

■ The word is recorded from the mid 16th century, as an adverb in the sense 'that is to say, to wit', used in legal documents to introduce an explanation. The noun dates from the late 17th century, originally denoting an explanation of, or construction put upon, a word or expression, especially (in an action for libel or slander) the injurious meaning alleged to be conveyed by a word or expression not in itself actionable.

in parvo /ɪn ˈpɑːvəʊ/ *adverb phrase* E20 Latin. In little, in miniature, on a small scale.

in personam /ɪn pəˈsəʊnam/ *adjective phrase* L18 Latin (= against a person). *Law* Made or availing against or affecting a specific person only; imposing a personal liability. Frequently *postpositive*. Cf. IN REM.

in potentia /ɪn pəˈtɛnʃɪə/ *adverb phrase* E17 Latin (= in potentiality). As a possibility; potentially.

in propria persona /ɪn ˌprəʊprɪə pəˈsəʊnə/ *adverb phrase* M17 Latin. In his or her own person.

in re /ɪn ˈreɪ/ *preposition phrase* E17 Latin (= in the matter of). In the legal case of; with regard to. Cf. RE.

1996 *Times Magazine* . . . there are plenty of fathers around who feel they've been handed the post-marital short straw by the judiciary *in re* who gets to keep the children and who gets to pay for same.

in rem /ɪn ˈrɛm/ *adjective phrase* M18 Latin (= against a thing). *Law* Made or availing against or affecting a thing, and therefore other people generally; imposing a general liability. Frequently *postpositive*. Cf. IN PERSONAM.

inro /ˈɪnrəʊ/ *noun* plural **inros**, same E17 Japanese (*inrō*, from *in* seal + *rō* basket). An ornamental box with compartments for items such as seals and medicines, worn suspended from a girdle as part of traditional Japanese dress.

inselberg /ˈɪnsəlbəːɡ/ *noun* plural **inselbergs**, **inselberge** /ˈɪnsəlbəːɡə/ E20 German (from *Insel* island + *Berg* mountain). *Geography* An isolated hill or mountain which rises abruptly from the surrounding landscape, especially from an arid plain.

inshallah /ɪnˈʃalɑː/ *interjection* M19 Arabic (in *šā' Allāh*). If Allah wills it.

■ The Muslim equivalent of DEO VOLENTE.

in situ /ɪn ˈsɪtjuː/ *adverb & adjective phrase* M18 Latin (= in place). In the original or appropriate position.

1996 *Country Life* Among these are sundry cranesbills . . . whose ends of root, accidentally left *in situ* when a plant is moved, will often sprout and grow anew.

insomnia /ɪnˈsɒmnɪə/ *noun* (also earlier) **insomnie**, **insomnium** /ɪnˈsɒmnɪəm/) E17 Latin (from *insomnis* sleepless (from as negative *in-* + *somnus* sleep)). Habitual sleeplessness; inability to sleep.

insouciance /ɪnˈsuːsɪəns/, *foreign* /ɛ̃suːsjɑ̃s/ *noun* L18 French (from as next). Casual lack of concern; indifference.

1995 *Times* With each tightening of the regulations to prevent the spread of BSE, it [sc. the British government] has been forced into an almost furtive admission that earlier scare stories had more substance to them than its studied insouciance admitted.

insouciant /ɪnˈsuːsɪənt/, *foreign* /ɛ̃susjɑ̃/ *adjective* E19 French (from as negative *in-* + *souciant* present participle of *soucier* to care, from Latin *sollicitare* to disturb). Casually unconcerned.

inspan /ɪnˈspan/ *transitive verb* E19 Afrikaans (from Dutch *inspannen*, from *in-* + *spannen* to span, fasten). **1** Yoke (oxen, horses, etc.) in a team to a vehicle; harness an animal or animals to (a vehicle). **2** *figurative* Persuade (a person) to give assistance or service; use as a makeshift. *South African*.

2 1971 *Rand Daily Mail* Mrs Barton often gets on the telephone and inspans private householders to help out.

instanter /ɪnˈstantə/ *adverb* L17 Latin. Immediately, at once.

■ Now archaic or humorous.

in statu pupillari /ɪn ˌstatjuː pjuːˈpɪlɑː riː/ *adjective phrase* M19 Latin. **1** Under guardianship, especially as a pupil. **2** In a junior position at a university; not having a master's degree.

intacta /ɪnˈtaktə/ *adjective* M20 Latin (feminine of *intactus*, extracted from VIRGO INTACTA). Inviolate, unaffected; not spoiled or sullied.

intaglio /ɪnˈtaliəʊ/, /ɪnˈtɑːliəʊ/ *noun & verb* (also **intaglia**) M17 Italian (from *intagliare* to engrave). **A** *noun* plural **intaglios**. **1** A design incised or engraved into a material. **2** A thing ornamented with incised work; *especially* a gem having a design cut on its surface. **3** A printing process in which the type or design is etched or engraved, such as photogravure. **B** *transitive verb* Engrave or represent by an engraving.

intarsia /ɪnˈtɑːsɪə/ *noun* (in senses 1 and 2 also **intarsio** /ɪnˈtɑːsɪəʊ/, plural **intarsios**) M19 Italian (*intarsio*). **1** An elaborate form of marquetry using inlays in wood, especially as practised in 15th-century Italy. **2** Similar inlaid work in stone, metal, or glass. **3** A method of knitting with a number of colours, in which a separate length or ball of yarn is used for each area of colour (as opposed to the different yarns being carried at the back of the work). Frequently *attributive*.

intelligentsia /ɪnˌtɛlɪˈdʒɛntsɪə/ *noun* E20 Russian (*intelligentsiya*, from Polish *inteligencja*, from Latin *intelligentia* intelli-gence). The part of a nation (originally in pre-revolutionary Russia) having aspirations to intellectual activity, a section of society regarded as possessing culture and political influence; *plural* intellectuals or highly educated people as a group.

1996 *Country Life* The view that what happens on the screen can influence what happens in life—so long resisted by the liberal intelligentsia—is gaining ground.

intendant /ɪnˈtɛnd(ə)nt/ *noun* (also **intendent**) M17 French (from Latin *intendent-* present participial stem of *intendere* to direct, promote). **1** *History* A title given to a high-ranking official or administrator, especially in France, Spain, Portugal, or one of their colonies. **2** The administrator of an opera house or theatre.

2 1996 *Spectator* He seems incapable of the smarmy two-facedness of the majority of opera house *Intendants*...

inter alia /ˌɪntə(r) ˈeɪlɪə/, /ˈalɪə/ *adverb phrase* M17 Latin (from *inter* among + *alia* accusative neuter plural of *alius* another). Among other things.

1996 *Times: Weekend* He recommends, *inter alia*, that sumps should be drained and refilled, fuel tanks should be drained...that the spark plug is removed and 'an eggspoon of oil' is dropped on the piston head.

inter alios /ˌɪntə(r) ˈeɪlɪəʊs/, /ˈalɪəʊs/ *adverb phrase* M17 Latin (from *inter* among + *alios* accusative masculine plural of *alius* another). Among other people.

interim /ˈɪnt(ə)rɪm/ *noun, adjective, & adverb* M16 Latin ((adverb), from *inter* between + adverbial ending *-im*). **A** *noun* **1** The intervening time; *the* meantime. **2** An interim dividend or profit. **B** *adjective* **1** Done, made, or provided in or for the meantime; provisional, temporary. Formerly (of time), intervening. **2** Relating to less than a full year's business activity: *an interim dividend*. **C** *adverb* In the meantime; meanwhile. *Archaic*.

■ First used in the mid 16th century to denote a provisional arrangement, originally for the adjustment of religious difference between the German Protestants and the Roman Catholic Church.

intermedium /ɪntəˈmiːdɪəm/ *noun* plural **intermedia** /ɪntəˈmiːdɪə/, **inter-**

mediums L16 Late Latin (use as noun of neuter singular of Latin *intermedius* intermediate). *Zoology* (modern Latin *os intermedium*). (In tetrapods) a carpal in the centre of the wrist joint, or a tarsal in the centre of the ankle joint.

■ Originally used to denote an intervening action or performance.

intermezzo /ɪntəˈmɛtsəʊ/ *noun* plural **intermezzi** /ɪntəˈmɛtsi/, **intermezzos** L18 Italian (from as INTERMEDIUM; cf. MEZZO). **1** A short connecting instrumental movement in an opera or other musical work; a similar piece performed independently; a short piece for a solo instrument. **2** A short light dramatic, musical, or other performance inserted between the acts of a play or (formerly) an opera.

interregnum /ɪntəˈrɛɡnəm/ *noun* plural **interregnums**, **interregna** /ɪntəˈrɛɡnə/ L16 Latin (from as *inter-* between + *regnum* reign). **1** Temporary authority or rule exercised during a vacancy of the throne or a suspension of the normal government. **2** An interval during which the normal government is suspended, especially during the period between the end of a monarch's rule and the accession of his or her successor; any period of cessation or suspension of rule, authority, etc. **3** An interval, a pause, a break.

■ In English history, the Interregnum was the period from the execution of Charles I in 1649 to the Restoration of Charles II in 1660.

inter vivos /ˌɪntə ˈviːvəʊs/ *adverb & adjective phrase* M19 Latin. (Especially of a gift as opposed to a legacy) between living people.

intifada /ɪntɪˈfɑːdə/ *noun* L20 Arabic (*intifāḍa* shaking off). An uprising by Arabs; *specifically* that begun by Palestinians in 1987 against Israeli occupation of the West Bank and Gaza Strip.

■ The word had earlier been current among Islamic groups, for instance in Lebanon, but only began to appear in English-language reports of events on the West Bank in the late 1980s.
1988 *Independent* The Palestinians have succeeded for the first time in bringing the *intifada* in the occupied territories within Israel's pre-1967 boundaries.
1995 *Spectator* Such patterns are common in wars of national liberation, as exemplified . . . by the very high proportion of Palestinian casualties inflicted by their compatriots during the *Intifada*.

intimism /ˈɪntɪmɪz(ə)m/ *noun* (also **intimisme** /ɛ̃timism/) E20 French (*intimisme*, from Latin *intimus* innermost). A style of painting showing intimate views of domestic interiors using Impressionist techniques, used by artists such as Bonnard in the early 20th century.

intimist /ˈɪntɪmɪst/ *noun & adjective* (also **intimiste** /ɛ̃timist/ (*plural same*)) E20 French (from *intimisme*, from Latin *intimus* innermost). **A** *noun* A painter following the principles of intimism. **B** *adjective* Relating to intimism.

in toto /ɪn ˈtəʊtəʊ/ *adverb phrase* L18 Latin. As a whole; in all; overall.
1995 *Spectator* This does not mean, however, that what the feminists said, *in toto*, was wrong—just as the theory of pure communism contained some benevolent and pertinent points.

intrados /ɪnˈtreɪdɒs/ *noun* L18 French (from as *intra-* inside + *dos* back). *Architecture* The lower or inner curve of an arch; *especially* the lower curve of the voussoirs which form the arch. Cf. EXTRADOS.

intriguant /ˈɪntrɪɡ(ə)nt/, *foreign* /ɛ̃triɡɑ̃/ (*plural same*) *noun* (also **intrigant**) L18 French (present participle of *intriguer* to scheme). A person who makes secret plans to do something illicit or detrimental to someone else.

introit /ˈɪntrɔɪt/ *noun* LME Old and Modern French (*introït* from Latin *introitus* entrance, from *introire* to enter, from as *intro-* + *ire* to go). *Ecclesiastical* An antiphon or psalm sung or said while the priest approaches the altar to celebrate the Eucharist. Also, the first two or three words of the office of a particular day.

■ Used originally in English to denote an entrance or the act of going in.

in utero /ɪn ˈjuːtərəʊ/ *adverb & adjective phrase* E18 Latin. In the womb; before birth.

1996 *Times* . . . the study tells us nothing about the route of maternal transmission, which could be *in utero*, at birth or soon after birth.

in vacuo /ɪn ˈvakjʊəʊ/ *adverb phrase* M17 Latin. **1** In a vacuum. **2** Away from or without the normal context or environment: *instead of dealing with individual aspects of life-style in vacuo, social factors are taken into account.*

in vino veritas /ɪn ˌviːnəʊ ˈvɛrɪtɑːs/ *interjection* L16 Latin (= truth in wine). Under the influence of alcohol, a person tells the truth.

invita Minerva /ɪnˌvʌɪtə mɪˈnəːvɑː/ *adverb phrase* L16 Latin (= Minerva (being) unwilling). When one is not in the mood; without inspiration.
  ■ Minerva was the Roman goddess of learning and patroness of arts and handicrafts, so her blessing was considered essential to enterprises in these fields.
  1954 M. Cost *Invitation from Minerva* It is always a mistake to do anything invita Minerva . . . Briefly, against the grain.

in vitro /ɪn ˈviːtrəʊ/ *adjective & adverb phrase* L19 Latin (literally, 'in glass'). *Biology* (Of processes or reactions) taking place in a test tube, culture dish, or elsewhere outside a living organism.
  attributive **1995** *New Scientist* A couple from the north of England are hoping that their embryos, conceived by in vitro fertilisation, will be the first to be screened for a gene that could cause cancer in later life.

in vivo /ɪn ˈviːvəʊ/ *adjective & adverb phrase* E20 Latin (= in a living thing). *Biology* (Of processes) taking place within a living organism.
  1996 *New Scientist* . . . it is not possible, at present, to determine directly the impact, in vivo, of Prozac on a particular individual's serotonin receptors.

inyanga /ɪnˈjɑːŋə/ *noun* M19 Zulu (= doctor, herbalist). (In South Africa) a traditional healer or diviner, especially one specializing in herbalism.

ion /ˈʌɪən/ *noun* M19 Greek (neuter present participle of *ienai* to go). *Physics* and *Chemistry* An atom or molecule having a net electric charge (either positive or negative) due to loss or gain of one or more electrons.

iota /ʌɪˈəʊtə/ *noun* LME Greek (*iôta*, of Phoenician origin; cf. Hebrew *yod*). **1** The ninth letter (I, ɪ) of the Greek alphabet, transliterated as 'i'. **2** *figurative* An extremely small amount or part.

Islam

Many words imported into English from Arabic and Persian, particularly those that have only gained currency since the end of the 20th century, relate to Islamic practices and customs. Among the most well-known of these are *Eid*, *fatwa*, *hajj*, *halal*, *imam*, *jihad*, and *Ramadan*. A *fatwa* is an authoritative ruling on a point of Islamic law, not, as is often wrongly assumed, a death sentence specifically. Ayatollah Khomeini of Iran famously issued a fatwa in 1989 calling for the death of the British novelist Salman Rushdie following the publication of *The Satanic Verses*, a novel believed by many Muslims to be blasphemous. Similarly, *jihad* is usually taken to refer to a holy war waged on behalf of Islam against unbelievers, but it can also be applied to the spiritual struggle within oneself. In recent years there has been a debate surrounding the issue of the wearing of veils and headscarves by Muslim women in non-Muslim countries such as Britain and France. As a result of this the terms for various garments have become much more widely known beyond the Islamic community. These include the *hijab* (a head covering worn by some Muslim women), the *jilbab* (a full-length outer garment, traditionally covering the head and hands), the *niqab* (which leaves only the area round the eyes clear), and the *burka* (which covers the entire face and body).

Italian

Many of the Italian words commonly used in English relate to Italian food and cooking. Examples include *al dente*, *calamari*, *cappuccino*, *ciabatta*, *espresso*, *gnocchi*, *lasagne*, *macchiato*, *mozzarella*, *pasta* (and the names of all its varieties), *pepperoni*, *pesto*, *pizza*, *ricotta*, *risotto*, *salami*, *saltimbocca*, *scampi*, and *tiramisu*.

Italian is indisputably the language of music. Historically this is because it was in Italy that sheet music was first printed during the Renaissance. Mostly dating from the 18th and 19th centuries, the following terms (and many more) form an essential part of all classical musicians' vocabulary: *a cappella*, *adagio*, *allegro*, *andante*, *aria*, *arpeggio*, *basso profundo*, *bel canto*, *cadenza*, *cantabile*, *cantata*, *coda*, *con brio*, *concerto*, *contralto*, *crescendo*, *diminuendo*, *diva*, *falsetto*, *forte*, *fortissimo*, *glissando*, *intermezzo*, *largo*, *legato*, *lento*, *libretto*, *maestro*, *mezzo*, *moderato*, *obbligato*, *oratorio*, *pianissimo*, *piano*, *pizzicato*, *portamento*, *presto*, *prima donna*, *rallentando*, *rubato*, *scherzo*, *sforzando*, *sinfonietta*, *soprano*, *sostenuto*, *stretto*, *tanto*, *tempo*, *toccata*, *tremolo*, and *vibrato*.

Italian words are also widespread in art and literature, especially those associated with Renaissance painting and poetry, for example *canto*, *chiaroscuro*, *fresco*, *gesso*, *impasto*, *intaglio*, *Pietà*, *putto*, *scenario*, *stanza*, and *tempera*. *Cupola*, *portico*, and *stucco* are part of the vocabulary of architecture.

La dolce vita (literally 'the sweet life') is a life of pleasure and luxury. Other Italian borrowings that are used in the context of festivity and celebration include *confetti*, *gala*, and *regatta*.

Finally, films such as *The Godfather* and *Goodfellas* have familiarized English speakers with such examples of the arcane language of the *Mafia* as *consigliere*, *Cosa Nostra*, *Mafioso*, and *omertà*.

■ Sense 2 arose because *iota* is the smallest letter of the Greek alphabet.
2 1996 *Spectator* In fact, I have never known him change his mind one iota.

ipecacuanha /ˌɪpɪkakjʊˈanə/ *noun* E17 Portuguese (from Tupi-Guarani *ipekaaguéne*, from *ipe* small + *kaa* leaves + *guíne* vomit). **1** The root of *Cephaelis ipecacuanha*, a Brazilian plant of the madder family; an extract or preparation of this, formerly much used as an emetic and expectorant. Also, the plant itself. **2** Any of various other plants with emetic roots; a preparation of such a root.

ippon /ˈɪpɒn/ *noun* M20 Japanese. A score of one full point in judo, karate, and other martial sports.

ipse dixit /ˌɪpsi: ˈdɪksɪt/, /ˌɪpseɪ/ *noun* plural **ipse dixits** L16 Latin (literally, 'he himself said it', translation of Greek *autos epha*). An unproved assertion resting only on the authority of a speaker; a dogmatic statement.
■ The Greek expression was used of the sayings of Pythagoras by his followers.

ipsissima verba /ɪpˌsɪsɪmə ˈvəːbə/ *noun phrase* E19 Latin (= the very words themselves). The precise words used by a writer or speaker.

ipso facto /ˌɪpsəʊ ˈfaktəʊ/ *adverb phrase* M16 Latin (= by the fact itself). By that very fact or act; thereby. Cf. EO IPSO.

isangoma variant of SANGOMA.

isblink /ˈiːsblɪŋk/ *noun* L18 Swedish (or from corresponding words in Danish, German, Dutch). A luminous appearance on the horizon caused by the reflection from a distant ice sheet.
■ Also in anglicized form as *iceblink*.

issei /'iːseɪ/ *noun* plural same M20 Japanese (= generation). A Japanese immigrant to North America. Cf. NISEI, SANSEI.

item /'ʌɪtəm/ *adverb* LME Latin (= just so, similarly, moreover, from *ita* thus, so). Likewise, also.

■ Chiefly used to introduce and draw attention to a new statement, particular, or entry, especially in a list or formal document. From this is derived the fully anglicized noun meaning 'an individual thing, article, or unit included in a set, list, computation, etc.'.

izzat /'ɪzʌt/ *noun* (also **izzut**) M19 Persian (Urdu *'izzat*, from Arabic *'izza* glory). Honour, reputation, credit, prestige.
1953 E. M. Forster *Hill of Devi* In every remark and gesture, does not the Indian prince either decrease his own 'izzat' or that of his interlocutor?

jabot /ˈʒabəʊ/ *noun* plural pronounced same E19 French (= bird's crop, shirt-frill, probably from a Proto-Romance base meaning 'crop, maw, gullet'). **1** A frill on the front of a man's shirt, edging the opening. Now chiefly *historical*. **2** An ornamental frill or ruffle on a woman's bodice.

jacal /həˈkɑːl/ *noun* M19 Mexican Spanish (from Nahuatl *xacalli* contraction of *xamitl calli* adobe house). A hut built of erect stakes filled in with wattle and mud, common in Mexico and the southwestern United States; an adobe house.

j'accuse /ʒakyz/ *noun* M20 French (= I accuse). An accusation, particularly one of injustice against an authority.

■ The opening words of Émile Zola's famous letter to the newspaper *L'Aurore* (13 Jan 1898) denouncing the French military establishment for wrongly condemning the Jewish army officer Alfred Dreyfus for treason in 1894 and then attempting to suppress the facts that proved that a miscarriage of justice had taken place.
1996 *Times* . . . this comes as something of a surprise . . . an authorial disclaimer designed to retract at the last minute what a few pages earlier looked like becoming a grandiloquent *j'accuse*.

jacquard /ˈdʒakɑːd/, /ˈdʒakəd/ *adjective & noun* (also **Jacquard**) E19 French. **A** *adjective* **1** Designating an attachment to a loom which enables the pattern in the cloth to be produced automatically by means of punched cards. **2** Designating a fabric, article, or pattern made with the aid of this; of an intricate variegated design. **B** *noun* **1** A jacquard fabric, pattern, or article. **2** A jacquard attachment or loom.

■ The loom attachment is called after its inventor, Joseph-Marie Jacquard (1787–1834).

jacquerie /ˈdʒeɪk(ə)ri/, *foreign* /ʒakri/ (*plural same*) *noun* E16 Old and Modern French (from male forename *Jacques*). A communal uprising or revolt.

■ The original *jacquerie* was the revolt of the peasants of northern France against the nobles in 1357–8. *Jacques* was the former French name for a villein or peasant.

j'adoube /ʒadub/ *interjection* E19 French (= I adjust). *Chess* Indicating that a player wishes to adjust the placing of a piece without making a move with it.

jai alai /ˌhʌɪ əˈlʌɪ/ *noun phrase* E20 Spanish (from Basque *jai* festival + *alai* merry). A game like pelota played with large curved wicker baskets.

jalap /ˈdʒaləp/, /ˈdʒɒləp/ *noun* M17 French (from Spanish *jalapa*, in full *purga de Jalapa*, from *Jalapa*, *Xalapa* a Mexican city). **1** A purgative drug obtained from the tuberous roots of a Mexican climbing plant, *Ipomoea purga*, and from certain other plants of the bindweed family. **2** The plant yielding this drug; (with specifying word) any of certain other plants yielding a similar drug.

jalapeño /haləˈpeɪnjəʊ/, /haləˈpiːnəʊ/ *noun* plural **jalapeños** M20 Mexican Spanish. A very hot green chilli pepper, used especially in Mexican-style cooking. Also *jalapeño pepper*.

jalebi /dʒəˈleɪbi/ *noun* M19 Hindi (*jalebī*). An Indian sweet made by frying a coil of batter and then soaking it in syrup.

jaleo /xaˈleo/ *noun* M19 Spanish (literally, 'halloo'). A lively Andalusian dance, or the music or handclapping which accompanies it.

jalfrezi /dʒalˈfreɪzi/ *noun* plural **jalfrezis** L20 Bengali (from *jhal* hot). A medium-hot Indian dish consisting of chicken or lamb with fresh chillies, tomatoes, and onions.

jalousie /ˌdʒaluˈziː/ *noun* M18 French (literally, 'jealousy'; also, a type of blind or shutter, associated with the screening of women from view in the Middle East). A blind or shutter made from a row of angled slats to exclude sun and rain and control the entry of air and light.

1961 I. Fleming *Thunderball* Inside the small room, the jalousies threw bands of light and shadow over the bed.

jambalaya /ˌdʒambəˈleɪə/, /ˌdʒambə ˈlaɪə/ *noun* L19 Louisiana French (from Provençal *jambalaia*). A Cajun dish composed of rice mixed with shrimps, ham, chicken, turkey, etc.; *figurative* a mixture, a jumble. Originally *United States*.

jardinière /ˌdʒɑːdɪrˈnjɛː/ *noun* M19 French (literally, 'female gardener'). **1** An ornamental pot or stand for the display of growing or cut flowers. **2** *Cookery* A garnish of mixed vegetables.

jargonelle /ˌdʒɑːgəˈnɛl/ *noun* L17 French (diminutive of *jargon* from Italian *giargone*, usually identified ultimately with zircon). An early-ripening (originally inferior) variety of pear.

jaspé /ˈdʒaspeɪ/, *foreign* /ʒaspe/ *noun* M19 French (past participle of *jasper* to marble). Randomly marbled, mottled, or variegated, like jasper.

jatha /ˈdʒəˈtɑː/ *noun* E20 Punjabi and Hindi (*jāthā*). **1** (In the Indian subcontinent) an armed parade, especially of Sikhs. **2** A long march, usually aimed at spreading a message.

jati /ˈdʒɑːti/ *noun* L19 Hindi (*jāt*, *jāti* from Sanskrit *jāti* birth). (In the Indian subcontinent) a caste or subcaste.

jaune /ʒon/ *adjective* LME French (from Latin *galbinum* greenish-yellow). Yellow.

■ Although formerly fully naturalized, *jaune* is now obsolete in English except in the names of pigments, such as *jaune brilliant* cadmium yellow.

jebel /ˈdʒɛbɛl/ *noun* M19 Arabic (*jabal*, (colloquial) *jebel*, plural *jibāl*, mountain). (In the Middle East and North Africa) a mountain or hill, a range of hills.

■ Frequently in place names.

jehad variant of JIHAD.

jellaba(h) variant of DJELLABA.

je ne sais quoi /ʒənsɛkwa/, /ˌdʒə nə seɪ ˈkwɑː/ *noun phrase* M17 French (literally, 'I do not know what'). A quality that cannot be described or named easily.

■ Often used in the phrase *a certain je ne sais quoi*.

1996 *Times* Of course, computer-generated images have been a part of movies for several years now... But it had always been thought... that human actors possessed a

---

Japanese

Most of the Japanese words that have entered the English language relate specifically to Japanese culture, food, and history. These include *basho*, *haiku*, *kamikaze*, *kimono*, *sake*, *shiitake*, *sumo*, *sushi*, *teriyaki*, *tofu*, and *yakuza*. Words particularly associated with the *samurai* period of Japanese history include *bushido*, *hara-kiri*, *katana*, *ninja*, and *seppuku*.

Sometimes a product or concept has been imported into British life from Japan, together with the Japanese word for it. Examples are *bonsai*, *futon*, *karaoke*, *manga*, *origami*, *reiki*, *shiatsu*, *sudoku*, and *tamagotchi*. And much of the language of martial arts is Japanese in origin: for example, *aikido*, *dan*, *dojo*, *ippon*, *judo*, *ju-jitsu*, *karate*, and *kendo*.

Since the 1980s a number of Japanese business terms have become familiar in English-speaking countries. *Kanban*, for example, is a just-in-time manufacturing system evolved in Japan, in which the supply of components is regulated by the use of instruction cards. *Kaizen* is a Japanese business philosophy of continuous improvement of working practices and personal efficiency. A *keiretsu* is a conglomeration of closely associated Japanese companies linked by cross-shareholdings. *Karoshi*, however, is a rather alarming word meaning 'death caused by overwork'.

certain *je ne sais quoi* that would save them from being consigned to the scrapheap by the relentless advance of the techno-bores.

jeté /ʒɛˈteɪ/, *foreign* /ʒəte/ (*plural same*) *noun* M19 French (past participle of *jeter* to throw). *Ballet* A jump in which a dancer springs from one foot to land on the other with one leg extended outwards from the body while in the air. Cf. GRAND JETÉ.

jetton /ˈdʒɛtən/ *noun* M18 French (*jeton*, from *jeter* to cast up (accounts), calculate). A counter or token used as a gambling chip or to operate a slot machine.

jeu d'esprit /ʒø dɛspri/ *noun phrase* plural **jeux d'esprit** /ʒø dɛspri/ E18 French (literally, 'game of the mind'). A light-hearted display of wit and cleverness, especially in a work of literature.

> **1995** *Spectator* When the Stone of Scone was stolen from Westminster Abbey in the 1950s, E. V. Knox in *Punch* in a *jeu d'esprit* confessed that Inspector Lestrade was baffled and injected Sherlock Holmes into the case...

jeunesse dorée /ʒœnɛs dɔre/ *noun phrase* M19 French (literally, 'gilded youth'). Young people of wealth and fashion.

> ■ The original *jeunesse dorée* was a group of fashionable counter-revolutionaries in France during the Revolution, following the fall of Robespierre.
> **1996** *Spectator* Sadly, neither *jeunesse dorée*, nor even golden oldies, still flock there.

jhil /dʒiːl/ *noun* (also **jheel**) E19 Hindi (*jhīl*). (In the Indian subcontinent) a pool or lake left after a flood.

jibba /ˈdʒɪbə/ *noun* (also **jibbah, djibba, djibbah**) M19 Egyptian Arabic (variation of Arabic *jubba*). A type of long open cloth coat with wide sleeves worn by Muslim men.

jihad /dʒɪˈhɑːd/, /dʒɪˈhad/ *noun* (also **jehad**) M19 Arabic (*jihād*, literally, 'effort', expressing, in Muslim thought, struggle on behalf of God and Islam). **1** Religious warfare or a war for the propagation or defence of Islam; (in Islam) the spiritual struggle within oneself against sin. **2** A fervent campaign in some cause.

> **2 1995** *Spectator* The religious impulse, which can no longer attach itself to traditional religions, is satisfied by the taking up of a

cause... The jihad against the export of veal calves is a case in point.

jilbab /dʒɪlˈbaːb/ *noun* L20 Persian (*jilbāb*, from Arabic (= garment, dress, veil)). A full-length outer garment, traditionally covering the head and hands, worn in public by some Muslim women.

Jina /ˈdʒɪnə/ *noun* E19 Sanskrit (*jina*). Jainism A great Jain teacher who has attained liberation from KARMA; a sculptured representation of such a teacher.

jinn /dʒɪn/ *noun* plural same or **jinns** (also **djinn**) E19 Arabic (*jinnī* masculine singular, plural *jinn*). (In Arabian stories and Muslim mythology) an intelligent spirit of an order lower than the angels, able to appear in human or animal form and to possess humans. Cf. GENIE.

jinricksha /dʒɪnˈrɪkʃə/ *noun* (also **jinrikisha** /dʒɪnˈrɪkɪʃə/) L19 Japanese (*jin-riki-sha*, from *jin* man + *riki* strength, power + *sha* vehicle). A rickshaw.

jiu-jitsu variant of JU-JITSU.

joie de vivre /ʒwadəvivr/, /ˌʒwɑː də ˈviːvrə/ *noun phrase* L19 French (= joy of living). Exuberant enjoyment of life.

> **1996** *Times Magazine* '... Is she as proud as she says she is of being a spinster?' It is hard to judge beneath the joie de vivre.

jojoba /həˈhəʊbə/, /həʊˈhəʊbə/ *noun* E20 Mexican Spanish. A desert shrub, *Simmondsia chinensis* (family Simmondsiaceae), of Mexico and the southwestern United States, whose seeds yield an oil used as a lubricant and in cosmetics.

> ■ The word was familiar in the United States long before it became current in British English, which happened only from the mid 1970s onwards, when its value as a substitute for sperm whale oil and its properties as an ingredient in cosmetics and soaps became more widely appreciated.

jolie laide /ʒɔli lɛd/ *noun & adjective phrase* plural **jolies laides** (pronounced same) L19 French (from feminine adjectives *jolie* pretty + *laide* ugly). **A** *noun phrase* An attractively or fascinatingly ugly woman. **B** *adjective phrase* (Of a woman) attractively or fascinatingly ugly.

■ The masculine form *joli laid* is also occasionally found.

1996 *Spectator* We passed through unrecommendable, dull Downham Market, whose only points are a Victorian town clock and squat 100-year-old outlying houses in yellow stone which could be called *jolie laide*.

jong /jɒŋ/ *noun* E17 Afrikaans (= young (man)). Originally (*History*), a young black male slave or servant. Now, a form of address to a young man or woman, expressing affection or exasperation.

■ South African colloquial, used especially among young people.

jongleur /ʒɔ̃glœr/ *noun* plural pronounced same L18 French (alteration of *jougleur* juggler (Old French *jogleor* accusative of *joglere*) from Latin *joculator* jester). *History* An itinerant minstrel.

jota /ˈxota/ *noun* M19 Spanish. A northern Spanish folk dance performed by one or more couples in rapid triple time; a piece of music for this dance.

jotun /ˈjəʊt(ə)n/ *noun* M19 Old Norse (*jǫtunn* = Old English *eoten*, from Germanic). (In Scandinavian mythology) a member of the race of giants, enemies of the gods.

joual /ʒwal/, /ʒuːˈɑːl/ *noun* M20 Canadian French (dialect form of French *cheval* horse (apparently from the way *cheval* is pronounced in rural areas of Quebec). Demotic Canadian French characterized by non-standard pronunciations and grammar, and influenced by English vocabulary and syntax.

jubilate /ˌdʒuːbɪˈleɪti/, /ˌjuːbɪˈlɑːteɪ/ *noun* (also **Jubilate**) ME Latin (imperative of *jubilare* to call, halloo, (in Christian writers) shout for joy). **1** Psalm 100 (90 in the Vulgate), beginning *Jubilate Deo* ('rejoice in God'), especially as used as a canticle in the Anglican service of matins; a musical setting of this. **2** A call to rejoice; an outburst of joyous triumph.

Judenrat /ˈjuːd(ə)nˌrɑːt/ *noun* plural **Judenrate** /ˈjuːd(ə)nˌrɑːtə/ M20 German (= Jewish council). A council representing a Jewish community, especially in German-occupied territory during the Second World War.

judenrein /ˈjuːd(ə)nˌraɪn/ *adjective* M20 German (= free of Jews). From which Jews are excluded (originally with reference to organizations in Nazi Germany).

1951 H. Arendt *Origins of Totalitarianism* When Hitler came to power, the German banks were already almost *judenrein*.

judo /ˈdʒuːdəʊ/ *noun* L19 Japanese (from *jū* gentle + *dō* way). A sport of unarmed combat derived from ju-jitsu and intended to train the body and mind. It involves using holds and leverage to unbalance the opponent.

judoka /ˈdʒuːdəʊkə/ *noun* M20 Japanese (from JUDO + -*ka* person, profession). A person who practises or is an expert in judo.

Jugendstil /ˈjuːɡəntˌʃtiːl/ *noun* E20 German (from *Jugend* youth + *Stil* style). German ART NOUVEAU.

■ *Die Jugend* was the name of an influential German magazine started in 1896 in Munich.

ju-jitsu /dʒuːˈdʒɪtsuː/ *noun* (also **jiu-jitsu**, **ju-jutsu** /dʒuːˈdʒʌtsuː/) L19 Japanese (*jūjutsu*, from *jū* gentle + *jutsu* skill). A Japanese system of unarmed combat using an opponent's strength and weight to his or her disadvantage, now also practised as physical training. Cf. JUDO.

juju /ˈdʒuːdʒuː/ *noun* (also **ju-ju**) E17 West African (probably from French *joujou* plaything, reduplicated form from *jouer* to play from Latin *jocare*). A charm, amulet, or cult object in some West African belief systems; the supernatural force believed to be associated with such objects. Also, the system of observances associated with such objects.

jujube /ˈdʒuːdʒuːb/ *noun* LME French (or medieval Latin *jujuba*, ultimately from Latin *zizyphum* from Greek *zizuphos*, *zizuphon* *zizyphus* (tree)). **1** An edible berrylike fruit of a Eurasian plant, formerly taken as a cough cure. **b** The shrub or small tree which produces this fruit, *Ziziphus jujuba*, native to the warmer regions of Eurasia. Also *jujube bush*. **2** A jujube-flavoured lozenge or sweet. *North America*.

jukskei /ˈjœkskeɪ/ *noun* E19 South African Dutch (from *juk* yoke + *skei* pin, peg). (In South Africa) a game in which a peg is thrown at a stake.

■ The game was originally played with sticks from an animal's yoke.

juku /ˈdʒuːkuː/ *noun* L20 Japanese. (In Japan) a private school or college attended in addition to an ordinary educational institution.

> **1992** *Economist* The best Japanese *juku* are so hard to get into that there is a booming secondary industry of cramming people to get into cramming schools.

julienne /ˌdʒuːlɪˈɛn/, *foreign* /ʒyljɛn/ (*plural same*) *noun* E18 French (from male forename *Jules* or *Julien*). A portion of food cut into short, thin strips: *a julienne of vegetables*.

■ Originally used as an adjective designating soup made of chopped vegetables, especially carrots.

jumar /ˈdʒuːmə/ *noun* M20 Origin unknown (originally Swiss). *Mountaineering* A clamp which when attached to a fixed rope automatically tightens when weight is applied and relaxes when it is removed, thus facilitating the climbing of the rope; a climb using such clips.

jumbie /ˈdʒʌmbi/ *noun* E19 Kikongo (*zumbi* fetish; cf. *zombie*). A spirit of a dead person, typically an evil one. Chiefly *West Indies*.

junker /ˈjʊŋkə/ *noun* M16 German (earlier *Junkher(r)*, from Middle High German *junc* young + *herre* (modern *Herr*) lord). A German nobleman or aristocrat, especially a member of the reactionary party of the Prussian aristocracy who aimed to maintain the exclusive privileges of their class; a narrow-minded, overbearing (younger) member of the German aristocracy.

■ Obsolete except in historical contexts.

junta /ˈdʒʌntə/, /ˈhʊntə/ *noun* E17 Spanish and Portuguese (*junta* (whence French *junte*) from Italian *giunta* from Proto-Romance use as noun of Latin *juncta* feminine past

participle of *jungere* to join). **1** *History* A Spanish or Portuguese deliberative or administrative council or committee. **2** A body of people combined for a common (especially political) purpose; a self-elected committee or council, a cabal. Now frequently *specifically*, a political or military clique or faction taking power after a revolution or *coup d'état*.

■ The alternative form *junto*, modelled on Spanish nouns in *-o*, was also once used to denote a political grouping or faction, especially in 17th- and 18th-century Britain.

jus /ʒy/ *noun* M20 French (= juice). (Especially in French cuisine) a thin gravy or sauce made from meat juices.

> **1996** *Country Life* Smooth, creamy bread sauce... and a thin *jus*-like gravy flavoured with a little red Burgundy are the classic accompaniments.

jus cogens /ˌdʒʌs ˈkəʊdʒenz/ *noun phrase* L19 Latin (= compelling law). *Law* The principles of international law which cannot be set aside by agreement or acquiescence.

> **1996** T. Alexander *Unravelling Global Apartheid* There is no definitive list of laws covered by *jus cogens*, but aggression by one state against another, piracy, war crimes, slavery and genocide are generally accepted as illegal.

jus gentium /ˌdʒʌs ˈdʒenʃɪəm/ *noun phrase* M16 Latin (= law of nations). *Law* International law.

jus primae noctis /ˌdʒʌs ˌprʌɪmiː ˈnɒktɪs/ *noun* L19 Latin (= right of the first night). DROIT DE SEIGNEUR.

juste milieu /ʒyst miljø/ *noun phrase* M19 French (literally, 'the right mean'). A happy medium, the golden mean; judicious moderation, especially in politics.

juvenilia /ˌdʒuːvəˈnɪlɪə/ *noun plural* E17 Latin (neuter plural of *juvenilis* juvenile). Literary or artistic works produced by an author or artist while still young.

Kk

Kabbala variant of CABBALA.

kabloona /kə'blu:nə/ *noun* L18 Inuit (*kabluna* big eyebrow). (Among Canadian Inuit people:) a person who is not a member of the Inuit; a white person.

kabuki /kə'bu:ki/ *noun* L19 Japanese (originally (as verb) to act dissolutely; later interpreted as from *ka* song + *bu* dance + *ki* art, skill). A form of traditional Japanese drama with highly stylized song, mime, and dance, performed by male actors only.

kachina /kə'tʃi:nə/ *noun* L19 Hopi (*kacína* supernatural, from Keresan). A deified ancestral spirit in North American Pueblo Indian mythology.

Kaddish /'kadɪʃ/ *noun* E17 Aramaic (*qaddīš* holy). An ancient Jewish prayer sequence regularly recited in the synagogue, including thanksgiving and praise and concluding with a prayer for universal peace.

kadi variant of CADI.

Kaffeeklatsch /'kafeklatʃ/ *noun* (also **kaffee-klatch** /'kafɪklatʃ/) L19 German (from *Kaffee* coffee + *Klatsch* gossip; cf. KLATCH). Gossip over coffee cups; an informal social gathering at which coffee is served.

kaffiyeh variant of KEFFIYEH.

kaftan /'kaftan/, /kaf'tɑ:n/ *noun* (also **caftan**) L16 Turkish (*kaftan* from Persian ḵaftān, partly through French *cafetan*). **1** A man's long belted tunic, worn in countries of the Near East. **2** A long loose dress; a loose-fitting shirt.

2 1996 *Times* Quant simply was not a kaftan sort of person, nor was she a glitzy shoulder-padded woman either.

kagoule variant of CAGOULE.

kahuna /kə'hu:nə/ *noun* L19 Hawaiian. **1** (In Hawaii) a wise man or shaman. **2** An important person; the person in charge. *North American colloquial.* **3** (In surfing) a very large wave. *North American colloquial.*

kai /kʌɪ/ *noun* M19 Maori. Food.

■ New Zealand colloquial. Also in reduplicated form *kaikai* or *kai-kai*, meaning the same or 'feasting'.

kaikai variant of KAI.

kairos /'kʌɪrɒs/ *noun* M20 Greek (= right or proper time). A propitious moment for decision or action.

■ The word became current in English through the writings of the German-born American theologian Paul Tillich (1886–1965).

Kaiser /'kʌɪzə/ *noun* M19 German (in modern use and in this form; ultimately from Latin *Caesar*, but cf. Old English *cāsere*, Old Frisian *keisar*, Old Saxon *kēsur*, *kēsar*, Old Norse *keisari*, Gothic *kaisar*, Dutch *keizer*). *History* (The title of) the German Emperor, the Emperor of Austria, or the Head of the Holy Roman Empire.

■ Current in various spellings from the OE period, the word in its modern form reflects a Bavarian spelling which supplanted the more usual *keiser* in the 17th century. Its use in modern English appears to be because it was the form favoured by the 19th-century historian Thomas Carlyle.

kaizen /kʌɪ'zɛn/ *noun* L20 Japanese (= improvement). A Japanese business philosophy of continuous improvement of working practices, personal efficiency, etc.

1996 *Times* Standard Chartered Bank has decided to teach its executives Japanese *kaizen* teamwork and continuous self-appraisal.

kakemono /kakɪ'məʊnəʊ/ *noun* plural **kakemonos** L19 Japanese (from *kake-* hang + *mono* thing). A Japanese unframed painting made on silk or paper and displayed as a wall hanging.

kalimba /kəˈlɪmbə/ *noun* M20 Bantu. An African musical instrument played with the thumbs, consisting of metal strips mounted on a small hollow piece of wood.

kalpa /ˈkalpə/ *noun* L18 Sanskrit. (In Hindu and Buddhist tradition) an immense period of time, reckoned as 4,320 million human years, and considered to be the length of a single cycle of the cosmos (or 'day of Brahma') from creation to dissolution.

Kama Sutra /ˌkɑːmə ˈsuːtrə/ *noun phrase* L19 Sanskrit (from *kāma* love, desire + *sūtra* SUTRA). (The title of) an ancient Sanskrit treatise on the art of love and sexual technique; a sex manual.

kameez /kəˈmiːz/ *noun* (also **kameeze**) E19 Arabic (*ḳamīṣ*, perhaps from late Latin *camisia* shirt, nightgown). A loose long-sleeved shirt or tunic worn, especially by Muslims, in the Indian subcontinent, and by some Muslims elsewhere. Cf. SALWAR.

kamerad /ˈkamərɑːd/, *foreign* /kaməˈrɑːt/ *interjection* E20 German (literally, 'comrade', from French *camerade*, *camarade*). (Expression used by a German-speaking soldier:) notifying to an enemy a wish to surrender.

■ The word was current between combatants in this situation during the 1914–18 war and became a cliché of war films.

kami /ˈkami/ *noun* plural same E17 Japanese. A divine being in the Shinto religion.

kamikaze /kamɪˈkɑːzi/ *noun & adjective* L19 Japanese (= divine wind, from as KAMI + *kaze* wind). **A** *noun* **1** (In the Second World War) a Japanese aircraft, usually loaded with explosives, making a deliberate suicidal crash on an enemy target; the pilot of a kamikaze; a suicide pilot or plane. **2** A person who behaves in a recklessly or potentially self-destructive way. **3** *Surfing* A deliberately taken wipe-out. **B** *adjective* **1** Relating to or denoting a kamikaze attack or pilot. **2** Recklessly or potentially self-destructive.

■ In Japanese tradition, the 'divine wind' was the gale that destroyed the fleet of invading Mongols in 1281.
A.2 *transferred* **1971** *Observer* The stand of the *kamikazes* means that in any critical division of the Government is assured of a working majority.
B.2 **1996** *Times Magazine* While these long odds will attract the odd kamikaze punter, . . . the horse cannot be considered a plausible contender for the big race.

kana /ˈkɑːnə/ *noun* plural same E18 Japanese. The system of syllabic writing used for Japanese, having two forms, HIRAGANA and KATAKANA.

kanat variant of QANAT.

kanban /ˈkanban/ *noun* L20 Japanese (= billboard, sign). **1** A just-in-time manufacturing system evolved in Japan in which the supply of components is regulated through the use of an instruction card sent along the production line. In full *kanban system*. **2** An instruction card used in a kanban system.

1 **1993** *New Scientist* Like most other Japanese businesses, Asahi operates on the Kanban—or just-in-time—principle of stock control, which reduces stockholding to an absolute minimum.

kanga variant of KHANGA.

kanji /ˈkandʒi/, /ˈkɑːndʒi/ *noun* plural same E20 Japanese (from *kan* Chinese + *ji* letter, character). A system of Japanese writing using Chinese characters, used primarily for content words. Cf. KANA.

kanzu /ˈkanzuː/ *noun* E20 Kiswahili. A long white cotton or linen robe worn by East African men.

kaolin /ˈkeɪəlɪn/ *noun* E18 French (from Chinese *gāolǐng*, literally 'high hill', the name of a mountain in Jiangxi province where it is found). A fine soft white clay resulting from the decomposition of other clays or feldspar, used to make porcelain and china, as a filler in paper and textiles, and in medicinal adsorbents and poultices. Also called *china clay*.

kapai /ˈkɑːpʌɪ/ *adjective & adverb* M19 Maori (*ka pai*). **A** *adjective* Very pleasant; good, fine. **B** *adverb* In a pleasant way; very well.

■ New Zealand. Also used as interjection, expressing pleasure or approval.

kapellmeister /kəˈpɛlmʌɪstə/ *noun* M19 German (from *Kapelle* court orchestra, from medieval Latin *capella* chapel + *Meister* master). **1** (In German-speaking countries) the leader or conductor of an orchestra or choir. **2** *History* A leader of a chamber ensemble or orchestra attached to a German court.

kappa /ˈkapə/ *noun* LME Greek. The tenth letter (Κ, κ) of the Greek alphabet, transliterated as 'k'.

kapu /ˈkapu/ *noun* M20 Hawaiian. (In Hawaiian traditional culture and religion) a set of rules and prohibitions for everyday life. Cf. TABOO.

kaput /kəˈpʊt/ *adjective* (also **kaputt**) L19 German (*kaputt* from French (*être*) *capot* (to be) without tricks in piquet etc.; cf. CAPOT). Finished, worn out; dead, destroyed; rendered useless or unable to function; broken.

■ Slang. The allusion by an English writer in 1914 to *kaputt* as 'the Germans' favourite word about their foe, meaning done' (Duchess of Sutherland *Six Weeks at the War*) indicates the historical background to the word's entrance into the English-speaking consciousness.

karabiner /karəˈbiːnə/ *noun* M20 German (abbreviation of German *Karabiner-haken* spring hook). A metal oval or D-shaped coupling link with a closure protected against accidental opening, used by rock climbers.

karakul /ˈkarəkʊl/ *noun* (also **caracul**) M19 Russian (*karakul'*, from the name of an oasis in Uzbekistan and of two lakes in Tadzhikistan, apparently ultimately from Turkic). **1** An Asian breed of sheep with a dark curled fleece when young. **2** Cloth or fur made from or resembling the fleece of the karakul. Also called *Persian lamb*.

karanga /ˈkarəŋə/ *noun* E20 Maori. A Maori ritual chant of welcome. *New Zealand*.

karaoke /karəˈəʊki/, /karɪˈəʊki/ *noun* L20 Japanese (from *kara* empty + *oke* abbreviation of *ōkesutora* orchestra). A form of entertainment (originating in Japan) offered typically by bars and clubs, in which people take turns to sing popular songs into a microphone over pre-recorded backing tracks.

■ Introduced in both the United States and Britain during the 1980s, *karaoke* became hugely popular. The word is often used attributively, as in *karaoke bar*, an establishment in which the management provides the *karaoke machine* or jukebox that plays the backing tracks.

karate /kəˈrɑːti/ *noun* M20 Japanese (from *kara* empty + *te* hand). A Japanese system of unarmed combat using the hands and feet to deliver and block blows, widely practised as a sport.

karezza /kəˈrɛtsə/ *noun* (also **carezza**) L19 Italian (*carezza* caress). Sexual intercourse in which ejaculation is avoided.

karma /ˈkɑːmə/, /ˈkəːmə/ *noun* E19 Sanskrit (*karman* action, effect, fate). Fate or destiny following as effect from cause; good or bad luck, viewed as resulting from one's actions.

■ *Karma* has specific meanings within the religions of the Indian subcontinent: in Buddhism and Hinduism, it is the sum of a person's actions, especially intentional actions, in this and previous states of existence, regarded as determining that person's fate in future existences; in Jainism it is subtle physical matter which binds the soul as a result of bad actions.
1996 *Times Magazine* The whole complex will, Spielberg hopes, be imbued with world-beating creative karma.

karoshi /kəˈrəʊʃi/ *noun* L20 Japanese (from *ka* excess + *rō* labour + *shi* death). (In Japan) death caused by overwork or job-related exhaustion.
1991 *New Age* Thousands of workers have become victims of *karoshi*, or death by overwork.

kaross /kəˈrɒs/ *noun* M18 South African Dutch (from Khoikhoi *karos*). A rug or blanket of sewn animal skins, formerly worn as a garment by African people, now used as a bed or floor covering.

Karren /ˈkar(ə)n/ *noun plural* L19 German. *Geology* The furrows or fissures of a KARRENFELD.

Karrenfeld /'kar(ə)nfɛlt/, /'kar(ə)nfɛld/ *noun* plural **Karrenfelder** /'kar(ə)n fɛldə/, **Karrenfelds** /'kar(ə)nfɛldz/ L19 German (from preceding + *Feld* field). *Geology* An area or landscape, usually of limestone bare of soil, which has been eroded by solution so as to have an extremely dissected surface with conspicuous furrows and fissures, often separated by knifelike ridges.

karst /kɑːst/ *noun* L19 German (*der Karst* (perhaps related to Slovene *Krâs*) a limestone plateau region in Slovenia). *Geology* Landscape underlain by limestone which has been eroded by dissolution, producing ridges, towers, fissures, sinkholes, and other characteristic landforms.

kasbah /'kazbɑː/ *noun* (also **casbah**) M18 French (*casbah* from Maghribi pronunciation of Arab *kaṣaba* fortress). The citadel of a North African city; the area surrounding a North African citadel.

kasha /'kaʃə/ *noun* (also (earlier) **casha**) E19 Russian. (In Russia and Poland) porridge made from cooked buckwheat or similar grain; uncooked buckwheat groats.

kashrut /kaʃ'ruːt/ *noun* (also **kashruth** /kaʃ'ruːθ/) E20 Hebrew (= legitimacy (in religion), from as KOSHER *adjective*). The body of Jewish religious laws relating to the suitability of food, ritual objects, etc.; the observance of these laws.

kata /'kɑːtɑː/ *noun* M20 Japanese. A system of basic exercises or postures and movements used to teach and improve the execution of techniques in karate and other martial arts; an individual training exercise in karate and other martial arts.

katakana /katə'kɑːnə/ *noun* (also **katagana**) E18 Japanese (from *kata* side + KANA). An angular form of kana (syllabic writing), used in modern Japanese mainly for writing words of foreign origin and for emphasis. Cf. HIRAGANA.

katana /kə'tɑːnə/ *noun* E17 Japanese. A long, single-edged sword used by Japanese samurai.

katharevousa /ˌkaθərə'vuːsə/, /ˌkaθə 'rɛvʊsə/ *noun* E20 Modern Greek (*kathareuousa*

feminine of *kathareuōn* present participle of Greek *kathareuein* to be pure, from *katharos* pure). The purist form of modern Greek.

▪ This is a heavily archaized form of modern Greek used in traditional literary writing, as opposed to the form which is spoken and used in everyday writing (called demotic).

katsura /kat'sʊərə/ *noun* E20 Japanese. **1** A type of Japanese wig worn mainly by women. **2** A type of romantic Noh play with a woman as the central character. In full *katsuramono* /kat,-sʊərə'məʊnəʊ/ (*mono* piece, play). **3** An ornamental East Asian tree which has leaves that resemble those of the Judas tree and light, fine-grained timber.

katzenjammer /'kats(ə)njamə/ *noun* M19 German (from *Katzen* (combining form of *Katze* cat) + *Jammer* distress, wailing). **1** A hangover; a severe headache. **2** Confusion, disorder; clamour, uproar.

▪ United States colloquial. The currency of the word has been promoted by the comic strip called *The Katzenjammer Kids*, first drawn in 1897 by Rudolph Dirks for the *New York Journal*, featuring two incorrigible children.

kava /'kɑːvə/ *noun* L18 Tongan. A narcotic sedative drink made in Polynesia from the crushed roots of a plant of the pepper family; the Polynesian shrub, *Piper methysticum*, from which kava is obtained.

kayak /'kʌɪak/ *noun & verb* M18 Inuit (*qayaq*). **A** *noun* **1** An Inuit canoe, made of a framework of light wood covered with sealskins, and having a small watertight opening in the top to sit in. **2** A small covered canoe modelled on this, used for touring or sport. **B** *intransitive verb* Travel by kayak, paddle a kayak.

kazachoc /kazə'tʃɒk/ *noun* E20 Russian (diminutive of *kazak* cossack). A Slavic, chiefly Ukrainian, dance with a fast and usually quickening tempo, and employing the step PRISIADKA.

kebab /kɪ'bab/, /kə'bab/, /kɪ'bɑːb/ *noun* (also (earlier) **cabob** /kə'bɒb/) L17 Arabic (*kabāb* (perhaps ultimately from Persian), partly through Urdu, Persian, and Turkish). A dish consisting of pieces of meat, fish, or vegetables grilled or roasted on a skewer or spit.

■ The arrangement of the meat pieces on the skewer has given rise (L20) to the use of *kebab* for components of a similar polymer structure in physical chemistry.

kef variant of KIF.

keffiyeh /kəˈfiː(j)ə/ *noun* (also **kaffiyeh, kuffiyeh** and other variants) E19 Arabic (*kūfiyya*, (colloquial) *keffiyya*). A headdress worn by Arab men, consisting of a square of fabric fastened by a band round the crown of the head.

keftedes /kɛfˈtɛdiːz/ *noun plural* (also **keftedhes**) E20 Modern Greek (*kephtes*, plural *kephtedes* from Turkish *köfte* from Persian KOFTA). (In Greek cookery) small meatballs made with herbs and onions.

keiretsu /ˈkeirɛtsu/ *noun* L20 Japanese (from *kei* systems + *retsu* tier). (In Japan) a group of closely associated business companies linked together by cross-shareholdings to form a robust corporate structure.

1993 *Seattle Times* Some companies seem to be trying to join whatever *keiretsu* is forming just out of fear that they won't back the right horse.

kelim variant of KILIM.

kenaf /kəˈnaf/ *noun* L19 Persian (variant of *kanab* hemp). The brown fibre of the *Hibiscus cannabinus* plant used to make rope and coarse cloth.

kendo /ˈkɛndəʊ/ *noun* E20 Japanese (from *ken* sword + *dō* way). A Japanese sport of fencing with two-handed bamboo staves, originally developed as a safe form of sword training for samurai.

kenosis /kɪˈnəʊsɪs/ *noun* L19 Greek (*kenōsis* an emptying). *Christian Theology* Christ's full or partial renunciation of his divine nature or powers in the Incarnation.

■ The reference is to the Greek New Testament text of Philippians 2:7 *heauton ekenōse*, literally, 'he emptied himself'.

kente /ˈkɛntə/ *noun* M20 Akan (= cloth). A brightly coloured cloth consisting of separate strips sewn together, made in Ghana; a long garment made from this

material, loosely draped on or worn around the shoulders and waist.

kepi /ˈkɛpi/, /ˈkeɪpi/ *noun* M19 French (*képi* from Swiss German *Käppi* diminutive of *Kappe* cap). A French military cap with a flat circular top which slopes towards the front and a horizontal peak.

kermes /ˈkəːmɪz/ *noun* L16 French (*kermès* from Arabic *ḳirmiz*). **1** A small evergreen oak, *Quercus coccifera*, of the Mediterranean region. More fully *kermes oak*. **2** A red dye obtained from the crushed dried bodies of adult females of a scale insect, which form hard berry-like galls on the kermes oak; the scale insect *Kermes ilicis* from which this dye is obtained.

kermis /ˈkəːmɪs/ *noun* L16 Dutch (*kermis, kermisse*, from *kerk* church + *misse* mass). A summer fair held in towns and villages in the Netherlands. Also *(United States)*, a fair or carnival, especially one held to raise money for charity.

■ Originally a *kermis* was a mass held annually on the anniversary of the dedication of a church, when a fair was also held.

khadi /ˈkadi/ *noun* (also **khaddar** /ˈkadə/) E20 Punjabi (*khaddar*, Hindi *khādar*, *khādī*). An Indian homespun cotton cloth.

khaki /ˈkɑːki/ *adjective & noun* M19 Urdu (*ḳākī* dust-coloured, from *ḳāk* dust from Persian). **A** *adjective* Dust-coloured; dull brownish yellow. Also, made of khaki. **B** *noun* **1** Dust-colour; dull brownish yellow. **2** A strong cotton or wool fabric of a dull brownish-yellow colour, used especially for army uniforms. **3** A soldier dressed in khaki; *specifically* (*South African slang*) a British soldier in the Boer War of 1899–1902. **4** In *plural* Khaki trousers; khaki clothes.

khalsa /ˈkɑːlsə/ *noun* (also **khalsah**) L18 Urdu (from Persian *ḳāl(i)ṣa* crown land, revenue department, from feminine of Arabic *ḳāliṣ* pure, free (from), belonging (to)). **1** The governmental revenue department in a state in the Indian subcontinent. **2** The body or company of fully initiated Sikhs, to which devout orthodox Sikhs are ritually admitted at puberty.

khamsin /ˈkamsɪn/ *noun* (also **hamsin** /ˈhamsɪn/) L17 Arabic (*kamāsīn*, from *kamsīn, kamsūn* fifty (from the approximate number of days on which it blows)). An oppressive hot southerly wind, which blows in Egypt at intervals for about fifty days in March, April, and May, and fills the air with sand from the desert.

khan /kɑːn/, /kan/ *noun* LME Persian (*kān*). (In the Middle East) an inn for travellers, built around a central courtyard; a caravanserai.

khanga /ˈkaŋɡə/ *noun* (also **kanga**) M20 Kiswahili. A light East African cotton fabric printed in various colours and designs with borders, used especially for women's clothing.

khat /kɑːt/ *noun* (also **kat, qat**) M19 Arabic (*kāt*). **1** The leaves of an Arabian shrub of the spindle tree family, which are chewed (or drunk as an infusion) as a stimulant. **2** The shrub, *Catha edulis*, that produces khat, growing in mountainous regions and often cultivated.
　1996 *Oldie* Our own cook was a wild-eyed northerner whose cheeks bulged night and day with qat.

Khoja /ˈkəʊʤə/ *noun* E17 Turkish ((*hoca* from) Persian *kʷāja*). A member of an Ismaili sect found mainly in western India.
　■ Originally used in the sense 'Muslim scribe or teacher'.

kia ora /ˌkiə ˈɔːrə/ *interjection* L19 Maori. A greeting wishing good health. *New Zealand.*

kibbutz /kɪˈbʊts/ *noun* plural **kibbutzim** /kɪˈbʊtsɪm/, (occasionally) **kibbutzes** M20 Modern Hebrew (*qibbūṣ* gathering). A collective (especially farming) settlement in Israel, owned communally by its members, and organized on cooperative principles.

kibbutznik /kɪˈbʊtsnɪk/ *noun* M20 Yiddish (from as KIBBUTZ + Polish and Russian noun suffix -*nik* person connected with (something)). A member of a kibbutz.

kibitz /ˈkɪbɪts/ *intransitive verb* E20 Yiddish (from German *kiebitzen*, from *Kiebitz* lapwing, pewit, interfering onlooker at cards). Look on at cards, or some other activity, especially offering unwanted advice; speak informally, chat.
　■ Slang, chiefly in North American use.

kiblah variant of QIBLA.

kiddush /ˈkɪdʊʃ/ *noun* (also **Kiddush**) M18 Hebrew (*qiddūš* sanctification). A ceremony of prayer and blessing over wine, performed by the head of a Jewish household at the meal ushering in the Sabbath (on a Friday night) or a holy day or at the lunch preceding it.

kielbasa /kiːlˈbasə/, /kjɛlˈbasə/ *noun* M20 Polish (*kiełbasa* sausage). A type of highly seasoned Polish sausage, usually containing garlic.

kierie /ˈkɪri/ *noun* (also (earlier) **kirri**) M18 Nama. A short thick stick with a knobbed head, traditionally used as a club or missile by the indigenous peoples of South Africa.
　■ The South African English word *knobkerrie*, by which this weapon is also known, is from Afrikaans *knop* knob + *kierie*.

kif /kiːf/ *noun & adjective* (also (noun) **kef** /kɛf/) E19 Arabic (representing colloquial pronunciation of *kayf*). **A** *noun* A substance, especially cannabis, smoked to produce a drowsy state; a state of drowsiness or dreamy intoxication produced by the use of cannabis etc. **B** *adjective* Very good (used as a general term of approval). *South African colloquial.*

kikoi /kɪˈkɔɪ/ *noun* M20 Kiswahili. A distinctive East African striped cloth with an end fringe; a garment made of kikoi, worn round the waist.

kilim /kɪˈliːm/ *noun* (also **kelim**) L19 Turkish (*Kilim* from Persian *gelīm*). A flat-woven carpet or rug, made in Turkey, Kurdistan, and neighbouring areas.

kimchi /ˈkɪmtʃi/ *noun* L19 Korean. A Korean dish of spicy pickled cabbage.

kimono /kɪˈməʊnəʊ/ *noun* plural **kimonos** M17 Japanese (from *ki* wearing + *mono* thing). A long, loose traditional Japanese robe with wide sleeves, tied with a sash; a similar garment worn elsewhere as a dressing gown.

kinder, kirche, küche /ˌkɪndər ˌkɪrçə ˈkyːçə/ *noun phrase plural* L19 German (literally, 'children, church, kitchen'). The domestic and religious concerns traditionally regarded as appropriate for a woman.

■ Doubly discredited by its association with the Nazi ideal of womanhood and by the agenda of modern feminism, *kinder, kirche, küche* is now most frequently used ironically.

1996 *Times Magazine* But theirs is also the quaintly strident *kinder, kirche, küche* voice of Alf Garnett...

kindergarten /ˈkɪndəgaːt(ə)n/ *noun* M19 German (literally, 'children's garden'). **1** (In Britain and Australia) an establishment where children below the age of compulsory education play and learn; a nursery school. **2** (In North America) a class or school that prepares children, usually five- or six-year-olds, for the first year of formal education.

■ The term *kindergarten* was coined in 1840 by Friedrich Fröbel (1782–1852) for a school for teaching young children according to his method of stimulating their intelligence by means of interesting objects, exercises with toys, games, singing, etc.

kinesis /kɪˈniːsɪs/, /kʌɪˈniːsɪs/ *noun* plural **kineses** /kɪˈniːsiːz/ E17 Greek (*kinēsis* movement). **1** Movement, motion. **2** *Biology* An undirected movement of a cell, organism, or part that occurs in response to an external stimulus. **3** *Zoology* Mobility of the bones of the skull, as in some birds and reptiles.

kippa /kɪˈpaː/ *noun* (also **kipa(h)**, **kippah**) M20 Modern Hebrew (*kippāh*). A skullcap, usually of crocheted thread, worn by Orthodox male Jews.

Kir /kɪə/, /kəː/ *noun trademark* M20 French (personal name). A drink made from dry white wine and cassis.

■ Called after Canon Félix *Kir* (1876–1968), mayor of Dijon in France, who is said to have invented the recipe.

kirpan /kəːˈpɑːn/ *noun* E20 Punjabi and Hindi (*kirpān* from Sanskrit *kṛpāṇa* sword). A short sword or knife with a curved blade, worn (sometimes in miniature form) as one of the five distinguishing signs of the Sikh Khalsa.

kirsch /kɪəʃ/ *noun* M19 German (abbreviation of *Kirsch(en)wasser* from *Kirsche* cherry + *Wasser* water). An alcoholic spirit distilled, chiefly in Germany and Switzerland, from the fermented juice of cherries.

■ Earlier (E19) in English in the fuller form *Kirschenwasser*.

kisan /kɪˈsɑːn/ *noun* M20 Hindi (*kisān* from Sanskrit *kṛṣāṇa* person who ploughs). (In the Indian subcontinent) a peasant, an agricultural worker.

kishke /ˈkɪʃkə/ *noun* (also **kishka**, **kishkeh**) M20 Yiddish (from Polish *kiszka* or Ukrainian *kishka*: cf. Russian *kishka*). **1** Beef intestine casing stuffed with a savoury filling. **2** *singular* and in *plural* A person's guts. *United States slang.*

kismet /ˈkɪzmɛt/, /ˈkɪzmɪt/, /ˈkɪsmɛt/ *noun* E19 Turkish (*kısmet* from Arabic *ḳisma(t)* division, portion, lot, fate). Destiny, fate.

kissel /ˈkɪs(ə)l/, /kɪˈsjɛl/ *noun* E20 Russian (*kiselʹ*, from same base as *kislyĭ* sour). A Russian dessert dish made from fruit juice or purée boiled with sugar and water and thickened with potato or cornflour.

kist /kɪst/ *noun* ME Old Norse (*kista*; cf. Dutch *kist*). **1** (also **cist**) *Archaeology* A prehistoric coffin or burial chamber made from stone or a hollowed tree. **2** A chest used for storing clothes and linen. *South Africa.*

■ The early use of *kist*, mainly in the north of England and Scotland, derives from Old Norse, but its use in South African English in the sense of 'chest' is derived through Dutch and Afrikaans.

Kitab /kɪˈtɑːb/ *noun* L19 Arabic (*kitāb* piece of writing, record, book). The Koran. Also, among Muslims, the sacred book of any of certain other religions, such as Judaism or Christianity.

kitsch /kɪtʃ/ *noun & adjective* (also **Kitsch**) E20 German. **A** *noun* Art, objects, or design considered to be in poor taste because of excessive garishness or sentimentality, but sometimes appreciated in an ironic or knowing way; the qualities associated with such art, objects, or design. **B** *adjective* Of the nature of or relating to kitsch; garish, tasteless.

> **A 1995** *Country Life* I'm sorry, but at Christmas I want maximum kitsch, not ghastly good taste.

kiva /ˈkiːvə/ *noun* L19 Hopi (*kíva*). A chamber, built wholly or partly underground, used by male Pueblo Indians for religious rites. Cf. ESTUFA.

klatch /klatʃ/ *noun* (also **klatsch**) M20 German (*Klatsch* gossip). An informal social gathering at which coffee is served. Cf. KAFFEEKLATSCH.

kletterschuh /ˈklɛtəʃuː/ *noun* plural **kletterschuhe** /ˈklɛtəʃuːə/ E20 German (literally, 'climbing shoe'). A light boot with a cloth or felt sole, worn especially for rock climbing. Usually in *plural*.

klezmer /ˈklɛzmə/ *noun* plural same, **klezmorim** /ˈklɛzmərɪm/ M20 Yiddish (contraction of Hebrew *kēlēy zemer* musical instruments). Traditional eastern European Jewish music; a musician who plays this type of music.

kloof /kluːf/ *noun* M18 Dutch (= cleft). A steep-sided, wooded ravine or valley. *South African*.

klutz /klʌts/ *noun* (also **klotz**) M20 Yiddish (from German *Klotz* wooden block, from Middle High German *kloz*; cf. Old English *clot(t)*, whence modern English *clot* (in derogatory sense) stupid or awkward person). A clumsy awkward person, *especially* one considered socially inept; a fool.

> ■ North American slang.
> **1970** *Time* Basically I'm the klutz who makes a terrific entrance to the party and then trips and falls and walks around with food in her hair.

knaidel /ˈkneɪd(ə)l/ *noun* (also **kneidel**) plural **knaidlach** /ˈkneɪdlax/, **knaidels** M20 Yiddish (*kneydel* from Middle High German, German *knödel* dumpling). A type of dumpling eaten in Jewish households during Passover. Usually in *plural*.

kneidel variant of KNAIDEL.

knish /knɪʃ/ *noun* M20 Yiddish (from Russian (also *knysh*) kind of bun or dumpling). A baked or fried dumpling made of flaky dough filled with chopped liver, potato, or cheese.

knout /naʊt/, /nuːt/ *noun* M17 French (from Russian *knut* from Old Norse *knútr* related to 'knot'). *History* A scourge or whip used in imperial Russia, often causing death.

koan /ˈkəʊɑːn/ *noun* M20 Japanese (*kōan* matter for public thought, from Chinese *gōngàn* official business). *Zen Buddhism* A paradoxical anecdote or riddle without a solution, used to demonstrate the inadequacy of logical reasoning and provoke sudden enlightenment.

> **1972** *Times Literary Supplement* What he comes up with—his runes and enigmas and impromptu koans—builds gradually into a supplementary creation.

kobold /ˈkəʊbəld/ *noun* M19 German. (In Germanic mythology) a spirit who haunts houses or lives underground in caves or mines.

koeksister /ˈkʊksɪstə/ *noun* (also **koesister** /ˈkʊəsɪstə/) E20 Afrikaans (*koe(k)sister*, perhaps from *koek* cake + *sissen* sizzle). (In South Africa) a plaited doughnut dipped in syrup, a traditional South African confection.

kofta /ˈkɒftə/, /ˈkəʊftə/ *noun* L19 Urdu and Persian (*koftah* pounded meat). (In Middle Eastern and Indian cookery) a savoury ball made from mincemeat, paneer, or vegetables.

kohl /kəʊl/ *noun* L18 Arabic (*kuḥl*). A black powder, usually consisting of antimony sulphide or lead sulphide, used as eye make-up, especially in Eastern countries.

kohlrabi /kəʊlˈrɑːbi/ *noun* E19 German (*Kohlrabi* from (with assimilation to *Kohl* cole) Italian *cauli* or *cavoli rape*, plural of *cavolo rapa* (whence French *chou-rave*), representing medieval Latin *caulorapa*). A variety of cabbage with an edible turnip-shaped base to its stem.

koi /kɔɪ/ *noun* plural same E18 Japanese (= carp). A common carp of a large ornamental variety, originally bred in Japan. Also *koi carp*.

koine /ˈkɔɪniː/ *noun* L19 Greek (*koinē* feminine singular of *koinos* common, ordinary). **1** The common literary language of the Greeks from the close of the classical period to the Byzantine era.

2 *Linguistics* and *Philology* A language or dialect common to a wide area in which different languages or dialects are, or were, used locally; a lingua franca. **3** A set of cultural or other attributes common to various groups.

koinonia /kɔɪˈnəʊnɪə/ *noun* E20 Greek (*koinōnia* communion, fellowship). *Theology* Christian fellowship or communion, with God or, more commonly, with fellow Christians.

kolkhoz /ˈkɒlkɒz/, /kʌlkˈhɔːz/ *noun* plural same, **kolkhozes** /ˈkɒlkɒzɪz/, **kolkhozy** /kʌlkˈhɔːzi/ E20 Russian (from *kol(lektivnoe) khoz(yaistvo)* collective farm). A collective farm in the former USSR.

Kol Nidre /kɒl ˈniːdreɪ/ *noun* L19 Aramaic (*kol niḏrē* all the vows (the opening words of the prayer)). An Aramaic prayer annulling vows made before God, sung by Jews at the opening of the Day of Atonement service on the eve of Yom Kippur. Also, the service or the melody at or to which this prayer is sung.

kolo /ˈkəʊləʊ/ *noun* plural **kolos** L18 Serbo-Croat (= wheel). A Slavic dance performed in a circle.

kombu /ˈkɒmbuː/ *noun* L19 Japanese. A brown seaweed of the genus *Laminaria*, used in Japanese cooking, especially as a base for stock.

konfyt /kɒnˈfeɪt/ *noun* M19 Afrikaans (= Dutch *konfijt*, probably from French *confiture*). A preserve containing whole fruit or pieces of fruit. *South African.*

kop /kɒp/ *noun* M19 Afrikaans (from Dutch *kop* head). **1** A prominent hill or peak. Especially in place names. *South African.* **2** (*the Kop*) A high bank of terracing at certain soccer grounds where spectators formerly stood, originally and especially at the ground of Liverpool Football Club; the spectators massed on such terracing. *United Kingdom.*

■ In sense 2, also more fully *Spion Kop* /ˈspaɪən kɒp/, after a mountain in Natal which was the site of a Boer War battle in 1900, in which troops from Lancashire led the assault (Liverpool then being part of Lancashire).

koppie /ˈkɒpi/ *noun* (also **kopje**) M19 Afrikaans (from Dutch *kopje* diminutive of

kop head; cf. KOP). (In South Africa) a small hill, especially any of the flat-topped or pointed hillocks characteristic of the veld.

koradji /ˈkɒrədʒi/, /kəˈradʒi/ *noun* L18 Aboriginal. (In Australia) an Aboriginal who has recognized skills in traditional medicine and an important role in ceremonial life.

kore /ˈkɔːreɪ/ *noun* E20 Greek (*korē* = maiden). An ancient Greek statue of a young woman, standing and clothed in long loose robes. Cf. KOUROS.

korero /ˈkɔːrərəʊ/ *noun* plural **koreros** E19 Maori. (In New Zealand) a conversation, discussion, or meeting.

korma /ˈkɔːmə/ *noun* L19 Urdu (*ḳormā, ḳormah* from Turkish *kavurma*). A mildly spiced Indian curry dish of meat or fish marinaded in yogurt or curds.

kosher /ˈkəʊʃə/ *adjective & noun* M19 Hebrew (*kāšēr* fit, proper). **A** *adjective* **1** (Of food) prepared according to the Jewish law. **2** That sells or prepares such food; where such food is cooked or eaten. **3** (Of a person) observing Jewish food laws. **4** Genuine, legitimate. *Colloquial.* **B** *noun* **1** Kosher food; a kosher shop. **2** The Jewish law regarding food. Chiefly in *keep kosher.*

koto /ˈkəʊtəʊ/ *noun* plural **kotos** L18 Japanese. A long Japanese zither, now usually having thirteen silk strings, usually played on the floor.

kotow variant of KOWTOW.

koumiss /ˈkuːmɪs/ *noun* (also **kumis**, **kumiss**) L16 French (*koumis*, German *Kumiss*, Polish *kumys*, Russian *kumys* from Tartar *kumiz*). A fermented liquor prepared from mare's or other milk, used as a beverage and medicinally especially by central Asian nomadic tribes.

kouros /ˈkuːrɒs/ *noun* plural **kouroi** /ˈkuːrɔɪ/ E20 Greek (Ionic form of *koros* boy). An ancient Greek statue of a young man, standing and often naked. Cf. KORE.

kowtow /kaʊˈtaʊ/ *noun & verb* (also **kotow** /kaʊˈtaʊ/) E19 Chinese (*kētóu*, from *kē* knock, strike + *tóu* head). **A** *noun* **1** The action or practice, formerly customary in China, of kneeling and touching the ground with the forehead as a sign of extreme respect, submission, or worship. **2** An act of obsequious respect. **B** *intransitive verb* **1** Perform the kowtow. **2** Act in an obsequious manner: *she didn't have to kowtow to the boss.*

kraal /krɑːl/ *noun* M18 Afrikaans (from Portuguese *curral* from Nama). **1** (In southern Africa) a traditional village of huts enclosed by a fence or stockade, and often having a central space for cattle etc.; the community of such a village. **2** (In southern Africa) an enclosure for cattle or sheep, a stockade, a pen, a fold.

kraken /ˈkrɑːk(ə)n/ *noun* M18 Norwegian. A mythical sea monster of enormous size, said to appear off the coast of Norway.

krantz /krɑːns/ *noun* (also **krans**) L18 Afrikaans (from Dutch = coronet, chaplet from Old High German, Middle High German, German *Kranz* coronet, circle, encircling ring of mountains, from a base meaning 'ring'). (In South Africa) a wall of rock encircling a mountain or summit; a precipitous or overhanging cliff above a river or valley.

kraut /kraʊt/ *noun* M19 German (= vegetable, cabbage; cf. earlier SAUERKRAUT). **1** Sauerkraut. **2** (usually **Kraut**) A German, *especially* a German soldier. *Derogatory slang.*

kremlin /ˈkrɛmlɪn/ *noun* M17 French (from Russian *kreml'* citadel). A citadel or fortified enclosure within a Russian town or city, *especially* (*Kremlin*) that of Moscow; (*the Kremlin*) the Russian (or formerly) USSR government housed within the Kremlin.

kreplach /ˈkrɛplɑːx/ *noun plural* L19 Yiddish (*kreplech* plural of *krepel* from dialect German *Kräppel* fritter). (In Jewish cookery) triangular noodles filled with chopped meat or cheese and served with soup.

kriegspiel /ˈkriːgʃpiːl/ *noun* L19 German (from *Krieg* war + *Spiel* game). **1** A war game in which blocks representing armies or other military units are moved about on maps. **2** A form of chess with an umpire and two players,

in which each player plays at a separate board and has only limited information about the other's moves.

krill /krɪl/ *noun* (also **kril**) plural same E20 Norwegian (*kril* small fish fry). A small shrimp-like planktonic crustacean of the open seas, eaten by a number of larger animals, including some whales and seals.

■ Chiefly used as collective plural.

krimmer /ˈkrɪmə/ *noun* (also **crimmer**) M19 German (from *Krim* (Russian *Krym*) Crimea). The grey or black furry fleece of young lambs from the Crimean area; a cloth resembling this. Cf. KARAKUL.

kris /kriːs/ *noun* L16 Malay (*keris*, partly through Dutch *kris*, German *Kris*, Spanish, Portuguese *cris*, French *criss*, etc.). A Malay or Indonesian dagger with a wavy-edged blade.

krummholz /ˈkrʌmhɒlts/ *noun* E20 German (literally, 'crooked wood'). Stunted wind-blown trees growing near the treeline on mountains.

krummhorn /ˈkrʌmhɔːn/, /ˈkrʊmhɔːn/ *noun* (also **crumhorn**) L17 German (from *krumm* crooked, curved + *Horn* horn). A medieval and Renaissance wind instrument with an enclosed double reed and an upward-curving end, producing an even, nasal sound.

kuchen /ˈkuːxən/ *noun* plural **kuchens** M19 German (= cake). (In Germany or among German- or Yiddish-speaking people) a cake, especially one eaten with coffee.

kudos /ˈkjuːdɒs/ *noun* L18 Greek (= praise, renown). Praise and honour received for an achievement.

> **1996** *Times*... the video company ends up with the product, the TV company with first broadcast rights, the opera company with kudos and 'accessibility' brownie points.

kudzu /ˈkʊdzuː/ *noun* L19 Japanese (*kuzu*). A quick-growing East Asian climbing plant, *Pueraria lobata*, with reddish-purple flowers, used as a fodder crop and to prevent soil erosion. In full *kudzu vine.*

kuffiyeh variant of KEFFIYEH.

kugel /ˈkuːɡ(ə)l/ *noun* M19 Yiddish (= ball, from Middle High German *kugel(e)* ball, globe). (In Jewish cookery) a kind of savoury pudding, usually of potatoes or other vegetables, served as a separate course or as a side dish.

kukri /ˈkʊkri/ *noun* E19 Nepali (*khukuri*). A curved knife broadening towards the point and usually with the sharp edge on the concave side, used by Gurkhas.

kula /ˈkuːlə/ *noun* E20 Melanesian. (In some Pacific communities, especially in the Trobriand Islands) an inter-island system of ceremonial gift exchange as a prelude to or at the same time as regular trading.

kulak /ˈkuːlak/ *noun* L19 Russian (literally, 'fist, tight-fisted person' from Turkic *ḳol* hand). *History* A peasant in Russia wealthy enough to own a farm and hire labour.
▪ Emerging after the emancipation of serfs in the 19th century, the kulaks resisted Stalin's forced collectivization, but millions were arrested, exiled, or killed.
1996 *Times* To suggest that wealthier taxpayers should plan for the worst does not imply that Labour is studying Stalin's treatment of the kulaks as a post-election model.

Kultur /kʊlˈtuːr/ *noun* (also **kultur**) E20 German (*Kultur* from Latin *cultura* or French *culture* culture). German civilization and culture.
▪ Sometimes used in the aftermath of the Nazi era in a derogatory sense to suggest elements of racism, authoritarianism, or militarism.

Kulturkampf /kʊlˈtuːrˌkampf/ *noun* (also **kulturkampf**) L19 German (*Kultur* culture + *Kampf* struggle). The conflict in Germany between 1872 and 1887 between the government (headed by Bismarck) and the papacy for control of schools and ecclesiastical appointments; *transferred* a conflict of moral or social issues and ideas.
1996 *Spectator* The great North American *kulturkampf* between classes, between moral codes and between visions of the future has chosen as its latest battlefield a city that was once known, ironically, as Toronto the Good.

kumis(s) variant of KOUMISS.

kumkum /ˈkʊmkʊm/ *noun* M20 Sanskrit (*kuṅkuma* saffron). A red pigment used ceremonially, especially by Hindu women to make a small distinctive mark on the forehead; the mark so made.

kümmel /ˈkʊm(ə)l/ *noun* M19 German (representative of Middle High German, Old High German *kumil* variant of *kumîn* cumin). A sweet liqueur flavoured with caraway and cumin seeds.

kundalini /ˈkʊndəlmiː/ *noun* L19 Sanskrit (*kuṇḍalinī* literally 'snake'). *Yoga* **1** The latent female energy believed to lie coiled at the base of the spine. **2** A type of meditation which aims to direct and release this energy. In full *kundalini yoga*.

kung fu /kʊŋˈfuː/, /kʌŋˈfuː/ *noun* L19 Chinese (*gongfu* (Wade–Giles *kung fu*), from *gong* (*kung*) merit + *fu* master). A primarily unarmed Chinese martial art resembling karate.

kurgan /kʊəˈɡɑːn/ *noun* L19 Russian (of Turkic origin: cf. Turkish *kurgan* castle, fortress). *Archaeology* A prehistoric burial mound of a type found in southern Russia and Ukraine.

kuri /ˈkʊri/ *noun* M19 Maori (= dog). (In New Zealand) a dog, especially a mongrel; *slang* an unpleasant or disliked person.

kursaal /ˈkuːrsɑːl/ *noun* plural **kursile** /ˈkuːrsɛːlə/, **kursaals** /ˈkuːrsɑːlz/ M19 German (from as *Kur* cure + *Saal* hall, room). (Especially in Germany and German-speaking countries) a public building at a spa, in which entertainment is provided.

kurta /ˈkəːtə/ *noun* E20 Urdu and Persian (*kurtah*). A loose collarless shirt or tunic worn especially by Hindu men and women.

kurtosis /kəːˈtəʊsɪs/ *noun* E20 Greek (*kurtōsis* a bulging, convexity, from *kurtos* bulging, convex). *Statistics* The degree of sharpness of the peak of a frequency-distribution curve.

kuru /ˈkʊruː/ *noun* M20 New Guinea. *Medicine* A fatal viral brain disease found among certain peoples of New Guinea.

■ *Kuru* was formerly of mainly anthropological interest as a disease found amongst peoples of New Guinea who practised ritual cannibalism of human brain tissue. It became of interest to the wider medical establishment on account of its similarities to BSE (bovine spongiform encephalopathy) or *mad cow disease* which was identified in cattle in the UK in 1986. In 1990 it was discovered that cats could also contract the disease, maybe as the result of eating contaminated cattle brain or other tissue in pet foods, and the possibility that BSE could be transmitted to humans through cattle offal became the subject of urgent investigations.

kvass /kvɑːs/ *noun* (also **kvas**, **quass**) M16 Russian (*kvas*). (In Russia and some neighbouring countries) a fermented beverage, low in alcohol, made from rye flour or bread with malt; rye beer.

kvell /kvɛl/ *intransitive verb* M20 Yiddish (*kveln* from German *quellen* gush, well up). Boast; feel proud or happy; gloat.

■ United States slang.

kvetch /kvɛtʃ/ *noun & verb* M20 Yiddish (as noun from Yiddish *kvetsh*, as verb from Yiddish *kvetshn*, from German *Quetsche* crusher, presser, *quetschen*, crush, press). **A** *noun* A person who complains a great deal, a fault-finder; a complaint. **B** *intransitive verb* Complain persistently, whine. Chiefly as *kvetching* verbal noun.

■ North American slang.

kwashiorkor /ˌkwɒʃɪˈɔːkɔː/, /ˌkwaʃɪˈɔːkɔː/ *noun* M20 Ghanaian (local name). A form of malnutrition caused by severe protein and energy deficiency, chiefly affecting young (especially newly weaned) children in tropical Africa, and producing apathy, oedema, loss of pigmentation, diarrhoea, and other symptoms.

kwela /ˈkweɪlə/ *noun* M20 Afrikaans (perhaps from Zulu *khwela* climb, mount). A style of rhythmical, repetitive popular music of central and southern Africa, resembling jazz, in which the lead part is usually played on the penny whistle; a type of dance performed to kwela.

kylin /ˈkiːlɪn/ *noun* M19 Chinese (*qílín*, from *qí* male + *lín* female). A mythical animal of composite form figured on Chinese and Japanese pottery, a Chinese unicorn.

kylix /ˈkʌɪlɪks/, /ˈkɪlɪks/ *noun* (also **cylix**, plural **cylices** /ˈkʌɪlɪsiːz/) plural **kylikes** /ˈkʌɪlɪkiːz/ M19 Greek (*kulix*). An ancient Greek cup with a shallow bowl and a tall stem.

Kyrie eleison /ˌkɪriːeɪ ɪˈleɪɪzɒn/, /ˌkɪriːeɪ ɪˈleɪɪsɒn/ *noun phrase* ME Medieval Latin (from Greek *Kuriē eleēson* Lord, have mercy). The words ('Lord, have mercy') of a short repeated invocation or response used in the Roman Catholic, Greek Orthodox, and Anglican Churches, especially at the beginning of the Eucharist. Also, a musical setting of these words, especially as the first movement of a mass.

kyu /kjuː/ *noun* M20 Japanese (*kyū* class). A numbered grade of the less advanced level of proficiency in judo, karate, and other martial arts; a person who has achieved a kyu. Cf. DAN.

L l

La /lɑ/, /lɑ:/ *adjective* (*definite article*) (also **la**) M19 French (or Italian feminine definite article, from Latin *illa*, feminine of *ille* that). Used preceding the name of a prima donna, or (frequently *humorous* or *ironical*) the name of any woman. **1996** *Times* The doughty girl has a touch of the Katharine Hepburns about her. *La* Hepburn, 88, still goes swimming in the lake by her house, even if she has to break the ice...

laager /'lɑːgə/ *noun* M19 Afrikaans (= German *Lager*, Dutch *leger* camp). **1** *South African History* an encampment formed by a circle of wagons. **2** *figurative* An entrenched position or viewpoint that is defended against opponents.

■ In its figurative sense *laager* was often used attributively in the phrase *laager mentality* to denote the intransigent defensiveness of Afrikaners in their dealings with the outside world during the apartheid era. The noun gave rise (L19) to both transitive and intransitive verbal uses of *laager*, sometimes followed by *up*. *figurative* **1996** *Times* The stage appeared to be too big for his four-piece band, whose equipment was drawn up into a laager in the middle.

labarum /'labərəm/ *noun* E17 Late Latin (whence Byzantine Greek *labaron*). The imperial standard of Constantine the Great (306–337), which bore Christian symbolic imagery fused with the military symbols of the Roman Empire.

lac /lak/ *noun* (also (earlier) **lacca**) LME Medieval Latin (*lac, lac(c)a* from Portuguese *lac(c)a* from Hindi *lākh*, Persian *lāk*). A resinous substance secreted as a protective covering by the females of certain homopteran insects (especially *Laccifer lacca*) parasitic on South-East Asian trees, used (especially in the Indian subcontinent) to make shellac and dye.

■ Formerly (L16–E18) used also for the varnish made from lac or various other resinous wood varnishes (*lacquer*) and (L17–M18) for the crimson colour or pigment derived from lac (*lake*).

lacrimae rerum /ˌlakrɪmʌɪ 'reɪrəm/, /ˌlakrɪmiː 'rɪərəm/ *noun* (also **lachrymae rerum**) E20 Latin (literally, 'tears (for the nature) of things'). The sadness of life; tears for the sorrows of life.

■ A quotation from Virgil's *Aeneid* (i.462). The etymologically incorrect spelling *lachrymae* is also frequent. **1995** *Oldie* [Critics] wrote off Betjeman as a phoney and a doggerel rhymester. They had not sensed the *lachrymae rerum* in the poems.

lacuna /lə'kjuːnə/ *noun* plural **lacunae** /lə'kjuːniː/, **lacunas** M17 Latin (from *lacus* lake). **1** An unfilled space; a gap. **2** A missing portion in a manuscript or text. **3** *Anatomy* A cavity or depression, especially in a bone.

ladanum /'ladənəm/ *noun* M16 Latin (*ladanum, ledanum* from Greek *ladanon, lēdanon*, from *lēdon* mastic). A gum resin obtained from the twigs of a southern European rock rose, much used in perfumery and for fumigation.

ladino /lə'diːnəʊ/ *noun* E20 Italian. A large fast-growing variety of white clover (*Trifolium repens*), native to northern Italy and cultivated elsewhere, especially in the United States, as a fodder crop. In full *ladino clover*.

la dolce vita see DOLCE VITA.

l'affaire see AFFAIRE.

lager /'lɑːgə/ *noun* M19 German (*Lager-Bier* beer brewed for keeping, from *Lager* storehouse). A light kind of beer, originally German or Bohemian, which is stored to mature before use; a drink of this.

lahar /'lɑːhɑː/ *noun* E20 Javanese. *Geology* A destructive mudflow on the slopes of a volcano.

laissez-aller /ˌlɛseɪ'aleɪ/, *foreign* /lɛseale/ *noun* (also **laisser-aller**) E19 French (literally, 'allow to go'). Absence of restraint; unconstrained freedom.

laissez-faire /ˌlɛseɪˈfɛː/, *foreign* /lɛsefɛr/ *noun* (also **laisser-faire**) E19 French (literally, 'allow to do'). Government abstention from interference in the workings of the free market; (in general) the policy of leaving things to take their own course, without interfering.

■ The maxim *laissez faire et laissez passer* is associated particularly with the French free-trade economists of the 18th century. See also quotation at DIRIGISME.

1996 *Country Life* The professor's *laissez-faire* philosophy is quite clearly presiding over an impoverishment of English, which is losing not simply its richness but also its comprehensibility.

laissez-passer /ˌlɛseɪˈpɑːseɪ/, *foreign* /lɛsepɑse/ (*plural same*) *noun* (also **laisser-passer**) E20 French (literally, 'allow to pass'). A document allowing the holder to pass; a permit.

1955 *Times* He has been granted by the Greek Foreign Ministry a laisser-passer to the Greek military zone of the Greek–Bulgarian frontier.

lakh /lak/ *noun* (also **lac**) E17 Hindi (*lākh* from Sanskrit *lakṣa* mark, token, 100,000). (In the Indian subcontinent) one hundred thousand; occasionally, an indefinite large number.

lama /ˈlɑːmə/ *noun* M17 Tibetan (*bla-ma* (the *b* is silent), literally 'superior one'). **1** An honorific title applied to a spiritual leader in Tibetan Buddhism, whether a reincarnate lama or one who has earned the title in life. **2** A Tibetan or Mongolian Buddhist monk.

lambada /lamˈbɑːdə/ *noun* L20 Brazilian Portuguese (literally, 'beating, lashing'). A fast and erotic dance of Brazilian origin, in which couples dance with their stomachs touching each other; the music for this dance.

■ The *lambada*, danced in Brazil for many years, became a craze in the United States in the late 1980s, and media hype helped spread it to the United Kingdom and Australia. The speed and thoroughness with which this ethnic dance was marketed in the West gave rise to the coinage *lambadazation* for the whole process of taking up and marketing

elements of ethnic culture for Western consumers.

1990 *Sun* We danced the lambada face to face and sort of going up and down against each other.

lambda /ˈlamdə/ *noun* E17 Greek. **1** The eleventh letter (Λ, λ) of the Greek alphabet, transliterated as 'l'. **2** *Anatomy* The point at the back of the skull where the parietal bones and the occipital bone meet. **3** *Biology* A type of bacteriophage virus used in genetic research.

lamé /ˈlɑːmeɪ/ *noun* E20 French (from Old French *lame* from Latin *lamina*, *lamna* thin plate, especially of metal). Fabric with interwoven gold or silver threads.

lamia /ˈleɪmɪə/ *noun* plural **lamias**, **lamiae** /ˈleɪmiːˌiː/ LME Latin (from Greek = mythical monster, carnivorous fish). A mythical monster supposed to have the body of a woman, and to prey on human beings and suck the blood of children. Also, a witch, a she-demon.

lamina /ˈlamɪnə/ *noun* plural **laminae** /ˈlamɪˌniː/ M17 Latin (*la(m)mina*). (In technical use) a thin layer, plate, or scale of sedimentary rock, organic tissue, or other material.

lammergeier /ˈlaməɡʌɪə/ *noun* (also **lammergeyer**) E19 German (*Lämmergeier*, from *Lämmer* plural of *Lamm* lamb + *Geier* vulture). A long-winged, long-tailed vulture, *Gypaetus barbatus*, inhabiting lofty mountains in southern Europe, Asia, and Africa and noted for its habit of dropping bones from a height to break them. Also called *bearded vulture*.

lanai /ləˈnʌɪ/ *noun* (also (earlier) **ranai**) E19 Hawaiian. A porch or veranda, originally in Hawaii; a roofed structure with open sides near a house.

Land /lant/, /land/ *noun* plural **Länder** /ˈlɛndər/, **Lands** /landz/ E20 German (= land). A semi-autonomous unit of local government in Germany and Austria.

1996 *Bookseller* The location was chosen to attract booksellers in the reunified Germany's eastern *Länder*, although this did not deter those from Munich and Stuttgart.

landau /ˈlandɔː/, /ˈlandaʊ/ *noun* M18 German (from *Landau* name of town in Germany, where first made). Chiefly

History A four-wheeled horse-drawn carriage, with folding front and rear hoods enabling it to travel open, half-open, or closed. Also *landau carriage*.

Länder plural of LAND.

landrace /'landreɪs/ *noun* M20 Danish (= national breed). A breed of large white pig, originally developed in Denmark; an animal of this breed.

landsknecht see LANSQUENET.

langlauf /'laŋlaʊf/ *noun* (also **Langlauf**) E20 German (literally, 'long run'). Cross-country skiing; a cross-country skiing race.

langosta /laŋ'ɡɒstə/ *noun* L19 Spanish (from popular Latin alteration of Latin *locusta* locust). A LANGOUSTE.

■ Chiefly United States.

langouste /'lɒŋɡuːst/, *foreign* /lãɡust/ (*plural same*) *noun* M19 French (from Old Provençal *lagosta* from popular Latin alteration of Latin *locusta* locust, crustacean). A spiny lobster, *Palinurus vulgaris*, especially when prepared and cooked.

langoustine /'lɒŋɡʊstiːn/, *foreign* /lãɡustin/ (*plural same*) *noun* M20 French (from as preceding). The Norway lobster, especially when prepared and cooked.

langue /lãɡ/ *noun* plural pronounced same E20 French (from Latin *lingua* tongue, language). *Linguistics* A language viewed as an abstract system used by a speech community, in contrast to the actual linguistic behaviour of individuals. Opposed to PAROLE.

langue de chat /lãɡ də ʃa/, /ˌlɑːŋ də 'ʃaː/ *noun phrase* plural **langues de chat** (pronounced same) L19 French (literally, 'cat's tongue'). A long thin piece of chocolate; a long finger-shaped biscuit.

langue d'oc /lãɡ dɔk/ *noun phrase* E18 Old and Modern French (from as LANGUE + *de* of + *oc* yes (from Latin *hoc*)). The form of medieval French spoken south of the Loire, generally characterized by the use of *oc* to mean 'yes', and forming the basis of modern Provençal. Cf. LANGUE D'OÏL.

langue d'oïl /lãɡ dɔil/ *noun phrase* (also **langue d'oui** /lãɡ dwiʲ/) E18 Old and Modern French (from as LANGUE + *de* of + *oïl* (now *oui*) yes (from Latin *hoc ille*)). The form of medieval French spoken north of the Loire, generally characterized by the use of *oïl* to mean 'yes', and forming the basis of standard modern French. Cf. LANGUE D'OC.

langues de chat plural of LANGUE DE CHAT.

lansquenet /'lɑːnskənɛt/, /'lanskənɛt/ *noun* (also (in sense 1 now the usual form) **landsknecht** /'lan(d)sknɛkt/) E17 French (from German *Landsknecht*, from genitive of *Land* land + *Knecht* soldier). **1** *History* A member of a class of mercenary soldiers in the German and other continental armies in the 16th and 17th centuries. **2** A gambling card game of German origin.

lapillus /lə'pɪləs/ *noun* plural **lapilli** /lə'pɪlʌɪ/, /lə'pɪliː/ M18 Latin (diminutive of *lapis* stone; in plural also from Italian *lapilli*, plural of *lapillo*). *Geology* A fragment of rock or lava ejected from a volcano. Usually in *plural*.

■ Originally used in the general sense 'small stone or pebble'.

lapis /'lapɪs/ *noun* E19 Latin. LAPIS LAZULI.

lapis lazuli /ˌlapɪs 'lazjʊlʌɪ/, /ˌlapɪs 'lazjʊli/ *noun phrase* LME Latin (from Latin *lapis* stone + medieval Latin *lazuli* genitive of *lazulum*, varying with *lazur*, *lazurius*, from Persian *lāžward* lapis lazuli). **1** A bright blue metamorphic rock composed chiefly of a sulphur-containing silicate of sodium and aluminium, used for decoration and in jewellery. **2** A bright blue pigment formerly made by crushing lapis lazuli; a bright blue colour.

lapsus /'lapsəs/ *noun* plural same E17 Latin. A lapse, a slip, an error.

■ Chiefly in phrases below.

lapsus calami /ˌlapsəs 'kaləmʌɪ/ *noun phrase* L19 Latin. A slip of the pen.

lapsus linguae /ˌlapsəs 'lɪŋɡwiː/ *noun phrase* M17 Latin. A slip of the tongue.

lar /lɑː/ *noun* plural **lars**, **lares** /'lɑːriːz/ L16 Latin (= household god). **1** Singular of LARES. **2** The common or white-handed gibbon, *Hylobates lar*, of Thailand and Malaysia. More fully *lar gibbon*.

lardon /ˈlɑːdən/ *noun* (also **lardoon** /lɑːˈduːn/) LME French (from Old French *lard* bacon, from Latin *lar(i)dum* related to Greek *larinos* fat). *Cookery* A chunk or strip of bacon or pork inserted into other meat before cooking to give it flavour and keep it moist.

la recherche du temps perdu see RECHERCHE DU TEMPS PERDU.

lares /ˈlɑːriːz/ *noun plural* L16 Latin. **1** Gods of the household worshipped in ancient Rome; the protective gods of a house; also, the home. Cf. PENATES.
■ The phrase *lares et penates* (or *lares and penates*) is used figuratively of those components of a household that the owner holds dearest; thus in 1775 Horace Walpole wrote in a letter 'I am returned to my own Lares and Penates—to my dogs and cats'.

largesse /lɑːˈʒɛs/, /lɑːˈdʒɛs/ *noun* (also **largess**) ME Old and Modern French (from Proto-Romance, from Latin *largus* copious, liberal in giving). **1** Generosity in bestowing money or gifts upon others. **2** Money or gifts given generously.
2 1995 D. Lodge *Therapy* The youth came back soon afterwards, hoping for more *largesse*.

larghetto /lɑːˈgɛtəʊ/ *adverb, adjective, & noun* E18 Italian (diminutive of LARGO). *Music* **A** *adverb & adjective* (Especially as a direction) in a fairly slow tempo. **B** *noun plural* **larghettos** A movement or passage marked to be performed in this way.

largo /ˈlɑːgəʊ/ *adverb, adjective, & noun* L17 Italian (= broad). *Music* **A** *adverb & adjective* (Especially as a direction) in a slow tempo and dignified in style. **B** *noun plural* **largos** A passage, movement, or composition marked to be performed in this way.

larva /ˈlɑːvə/ *noun plural* **larvae** /ˈlɑːviː/ M17 Latin (= ghost, mask). An insect in a state of development (displaying little or no similarity to the adult) lasting from the time of its leaving the egg until its transformation into a pupa; a grub, a caterpillar. Also, an immature form in other animals that undergo some sort of metamorphosis, e.g. amphibians, tapeworms, etc.
■ In early use denoted a disembodied spirit or ghost.

lasagne /ləˈzanjə/, /ləˈsanjə/, /ləˈsɑːnjə/, /ləˈzɑːnjə/ *noun* (also **lasagna**) M19 Italian (plural of *lasagna*, ultimately from Latin *lasanum* chamber pot, perhaps also cooking pot). Pasta in the form of sheets or wide strips; an Italian dish consisting of this, baked with meat or vegetables and a cheese sauce.

lassi /ˈlʌsi/, /ˈlasi/ *noun* L19 Hindi (*lassī*). (In the Indian subcontinent) a sweet or savoury drink made from a buttermilk or yogurt base with water.

lasya /ˈlɑːsjə/ *noun* M20 Sanskrit (*lāsya*). A graceful Indian style of female dancing.

lathi /ˈlɑːtiː/ *noun* (also **lathee**) M19 Hindi (*lāṭhī*). (In the Indian subcontinent) a long heavy iron-bound bamboo stick, used as a weapon, especially by police.

latifundium /latɪˈfʌndɪəm/, /lɑːtɪˈfʌndɪəm/, /leɪtɪˈfʌndɪəm/ *noun plural* **latifundia** /lɑːtɪˈfʌndɪə/ M17 Latin (from *latus* broad + *fundus* landed estate; partly from Spanish *latifundio* from Latin). A large landed estate or ranch, frequently worked by peasants or slaves; *especially* one in Spain or Latin America or in ancient Rome.
■ Now usually occurring in the plural, *latifundium* was originally anglicized as *latifund*. Its opposite is a MINIFUNDIUM.

Latino /ləˈtiːnəʊ/ *noun & adjective* M20 Latin American Spanish. **A** *noun plural* **Latinos** A Latin American inhabitant of the United States. Chiefly *United States*. **B** *adjective* Relating to Latinos.

latke /ˈlʌtkə/ *noun* E20 Yiddish (from Russian *latka* earthenware cooking vessel, (dialect) dish cooked in such a vessel). (In Jewish cookery) a pancake, especially one made with grated potato.

latria /ləˈtrʌɪə/ *noun* E16 Late Latin (from Greek *latreia*, from *latreuein* to wait on, serve with prayer). *Roman Catholic Church* The highest form of worship, due to God alone; the veneration properly given to God. Cf. DULIA.

Latin

The influence of Latin on the English language is huge, with a vast number of common English words being ultimately of Latin origin. In addition, English-speakers make use of a great number of phrases that retain their original Latin form. Many legal phrases, in particular, are taken from Latin. Among those that appear as entries in this dictionary are *ad litem, amicus curiae, caveat emptor, doli incapax, ex parte, habeas corpus, in absentia, in camera, in re, lex loci, locus standi, mens rea, nolo contendere, non compos mentis, obiter dictum, pro bono publico, res gestae, sub judice, sui juris,* and *ultra vires.* Another area rich in Latin expressions is that of argument, debate, and reasoning. Examples include *a fortiori, a posteriori, a priori, ipso facto, non sequitur, prima facie, quod erat demonstrandum,* and *reductio ad absurdum.* Other Latin phrases that are part of everyday English include *ad hoc, ad nauseam, bona fide, ex gratia, in extremis, in situ, magnum opus, mea culpa, per se, pro rata, quid pro quo, sine qua non,* and *terra firma.*

Latin sayings and mottoes in use in modern English include *carpe diem; de gustibus non est disputandum; e pluribus unum; Et tu, Brute; in vino veritas; mens sana in corpore sano; multum in parvo; nil desperandum; o tempora, o mores!; quot homines, tot sententiae; sic transit gloria mundi; tempus fugit;* and *veni, vidi, vici.*

latte /ˈlɑːteɪ/, /ˈlateɪ/ *noun* (also **caffè latte**) L20 Italian (= milk (coffee)). A drink made by adding a shot of espresso coffee to a glass or cup of frothy steamed milk.

latticinio /lattiˈtʃiːnjo/, /latɪˈtʃiːnjəʊ/ *noun* Also written **latticino** /lattiˈtʃiːno/, /latɪˈtʃiːnəʊ/ M19 Italian (literally, 'dairy produce', from medieval Latin *lacticinium*). An opaque white glass used in threads to decorate clear Venetian glass.

laudator temporis acti /lɔːˌdeɪtə ˌtemp(ə)rɪs ˈaktʌɪ/ *noun phrase* plural **laudatores temporis acti** /lɔːdəˌtɔːriːz/ M18 Latin (= a praiser of times past). A person who holds up the past as a golden age.

■ *Laudator temporis acti se puero* 'a praiser of former times when he himself was a boy' is a quotation from a passage in Horace's *Ars Poetica* (173–4) on the tiresome traits that tend to accompany old age.

lavabo /ləˈveɪbəʊ/, *in sense 2* /ˈlavəbəʊ/ *noun* plural **lavabo(e)s** M18 Latin (= I will wash). **1** *Roman Catholic Church* A towel or basin used for the ritual washing of the celebrant's hands at the offertory of the Mass; ritual washing of this type.

2 A washing trough used in some medieval monasteries. **b** A washbasin or toilet.

lavage /ˈlavɪdʒ/, /laˈvɑːʒ/ *noun* L18 French (from *laver* to wash). *Medicine* Washing out of a body cavity, such as the colon or stomach, with water or a medicated solution.

■ Originally used in the general sense 'washing, a wash'.

layette /leɪˈjɛt/ *noun* M19 French (diminutive of Old French *laie* drawer, box, from Middle Dutch *laege*). A set of clothing, bedclothes, and sometimes toiletries for a newborn child.

lazaretto /lazəˈrɛtəʊ/ *noun* plural **lazarettos** M16 Italian (diminutive of *lazzaro* beggar). **1** *History* An isolation hospital for diseased people, especially those with leprosy or plague. **2** A military or prison hospital.

lebensraum /ˈleːbənsraʊm/, /ˈleɪbənzraʊm/ *noun* Also written **Lebensraum** E20 German (= living space). Space for living, room to exist and function freely; *specifically* territory which many German nationalists in the mid 20th century claimed was needed for the survival and healthy development of the nation.

■ Originally the biological concept of a space inhabited, or habitable, by a particular organism, *Lebensraum* was developed by the 19th-century German geographer Friedrich Ratzel to mean the space sufficient both for a people's material needs and for the evolution of its particular social and cultural identity. The concept was subsequently hijacked by the Nazis to justify the racist and expansionist policies of the Third Reich. **1995** *Spectator* The sub-text is that if the united Germany... can be closely bound into the Community she will never again be tempted to fight for *lebensraum*.

transferred **1996** *Spectator* My liver obviously needed *lebensraum* and was heavily leaning on its neighbours.

lechayim /lə'xajim/ *interjection* (also **lechaim** /lə'xʌɪm/ and other variants) M20 Hebrew (*lĕ-ḥayyīm*). (A drinking toast) to life!

lector /'lɛktɔ:/ *noun* LME Latin (from *lect-* past participial stem of *legere* to read). **1** A reader, especially someone who reads lessons in a church service. **2** A lecturer, especially one employed in a foreign university to teach in their native language.

lectrice /lɛk'tri:s/, /'lɛktri:s/ *noun* L19 French (from Latin *lectrix* feminine of Latin LECTOR). **1** A woman engaged as an attendant or companion to read aloud. **2** A female lector in a university.

lecythus /'lɛsɪθəs/ *noun* plural **lecythi** /'lɛsɪθʌɪ/ M19 Late Latin (from Greek *lēkuthos*). A thin narrow-necked vase or flask from ancient Greece.

lederhosen /'leɪdəhəʊz(ə)n/ *noun plural* M20 German (from *Leder* leather + *Hosen* plural of *Hose* trouser). Leather shorts with H-shaped braces, traditionally worn by men in Alpine regions such as Bavaria.

legato /lɪ'gɑ:təʊ/ *adjective, adverb, & noun* M18 Italian (past participle of *legare* to bind, from Latin *ligare*). *Music* **A** *adjective & adverb* (Especially as a direction) in a smooth flowing manner, without breaks between notes. **B** *noun* A legato style of performance; a piece

or passage marked to be performed legato.

legerdemain /ˌlɛdʒədə'meɪn/ *noun* LME French (*léger de main*, from *léger* light + *de* of + *main* hand). **1** Skilful use of one's hands when performing conjuring tricks; sleight of hand. **2** Trickery, deception.

legionnaire /ˌli:dʒə'nɛ:/ *noun* E19 French (*légionnaire*, from *légion* legion). A member of a legion, in particular an ancient Roman legion or the French Foreign Legion.

legume /'lɛgju:m/ *noun* M17 French (*légume* from Latin *legumen*, from *legere* to gather: so called because the fruit may be gathered by hand). **1** A leguminous plant, especially one grown as a crop. **2** A seed, pod, or other edible part of a leguminous plant, used as food. **3** *Botany* The long seed pod of a leguminous plant.

■ Originally used in English to denote the edible portion of the plant.

lei /leɪ/ *noun* M19 Hawaiian. A Polynesian garland made of flowers, feathers, shells, etc., often given as a symbol of affection. **1996** *Times* The lure of the lei, that garland of welcome traditionally bestowed on visitors by bare-bosomed young hula dancers, is considerable.

leitmotiv /'lʌɪtməʊti:f/ *noun* (also **leitmotif**) L19 German (from *leit-* leading + *Motiv* motive). **1** *Music* A theme associated throughout a work with a particular person, situation, or sentiment. **2** A recurrent idea or image in a literary work etc. **1995** *Spectator* Gray finds in Berlin's 'value pluralism' the *leitmotif* of all his writings.

lekker /'lɛkə/ *adjective* E20 Afrikaans (from Dutch (cf. German *lecker*) related to Dutch *likken* to lick). Pleasant, sweet, nice; good, excellent.

■ South African colloquial, used as a general term of approval.

lemma /'lɛmə/ *noun* plural **lemmas, lemmata** /'lɛmətə/ L16 Latin (from Greek *lēmma*, plural *lēmmata*, something taken for granted or assumed, theme, argument, title, from base also of *lambanein* to take). **1** A subsidiary or intermediate theorem in an argument or proof. **2** A heading indicating the subject or argument of a literary composition or annotation. **3** A word or phrase defined in a dictionary, glossed in a glossary, or entered in a word list.

lento /ˈlɛntəʊ/ *adverb, adjective, & noun* E18 Italian. **A** *adverb & adjective Music* (Especially as a direction) in slow time, slower than adagio. **B** *noun plural* **lentos** A passage or movement marked to be performed slowly.

leprechaun /ˈlɛprəkɔːn/ *noun* E17 Irish (*leipreachán* alteration of Middle Irish *luchrupán* alteration of Old Irish *luchorpán*, from *lu* small + *corp* body). (In Irish folklore) a small, mischievous sprite, often associated with shoemaking or buried treasure.

lèse-majesté /lɛzmaʒɛste/ *noun* (also **lese-majesty** /liːzˈmadʒɪsti/) LME French (from Latin *laesa majestas* injured sovereignty, from *laesa* feminine past participle of *laedere* to injure, hurt, *majestas* majesty). **1** The insulting of a monarch or other ruler. Also, treason. **2** Presumptuous or disrespectful behaviour.

▪ *Lese-* or *lèse-* is also used with other French or English words in humorous imitation of *lese-majesty* or *lèse-majesté*.
1 1995 *Times* [Wei Jingsheng] was brazen enough to write to Mr Deng and denounce him as a man 'who will be laughed at and condemned by history'. Such lèse-majesté is deeply wounding.
2 1995 *Spectator* To suppress or control such emotions is to be guilty of absurd and psychologically unhealthy stiff-upper-lippism; it is to commit the terrible crime of *lese-psychotherapie*.

le tout /lə tu/ *adjective phrase* E20 French. The whole of, everyone in, all (a place).

▪ Used before the name of a city to refer to its high society or people of importance, often in a context of making fun of social pretensions. The word(s) defined by *le tout* may be French, on the analogy of *le tout Paris* all Paris (meaning 'Parisian society'), or, in humorous use, more often English (see quotations). Cf. TOUT.
1995 *Spectator* I look forward to the day when *le tout Londres* goes to a lecture once a week as a matter of course ...
1996 *Oldie* When *Cav* and *Pag* were given by the Moldavian State Opera, *le tout* gentrified Hackney and Islington attended.

lettre de cachet /lɛtr də kaʃe/ *noun phrase* plural **lettres de cachet** (pronounced same) E18 French (literally, 'letter of seal'). **1** *History* (In France under the *ancien régime*) a warrant for the imprisonment of a person without trial at the pleasure of the monarch. **2** An (arbitrary) official order for imprisonment, exile, etc.

levade /lə'vɑːd/ *noun* M20 French (from *lever* to raise). A movement performed in classical riding, in which the horse lifts its forelegs from the ground and balances on its hind legs which are placed well forward under the body and deeply bent.

levee /ˈlɛvi/, /ˈlɛveɪ/ *noun* 1 L17 French (*levé* variant of *lever* rising, use as noun of *lever* to rise). *History* A reception of visitors on rising from bed; a morning assembly held by a person of distinction. **b** *History* An afternoon assembly for men only held by the British monarch or their representative. **c** A reception or assembly at any time of day. Now *archaic* except in *North America*.

levee /ˈlɛvi/, /lɪˈviː/ *noun* 2 E18 French (*levée* feminine of *levé* past participle of *lever* to raise). **1** An embankment built to prevent the overflow of a river. **b** *Geography* A low broad ridge of sediment deposited naturally alongside a river by overflowing water. **2** A landing place, a pier, a quay.

lex fori /lɛks ˈfɔːrʌɪ/ *noun phrase* E19 Latin (= law of the court). *Law* The law of the country in which an action is brought, as regulating procedure, evidence, execution of judgments, etc.

lexis /ˈlɛksɪs/ *noun* M20 Greek (= a word, phrase, from *legein* to speak). **1** The total stock of words in a language. **2** The level of language consisting of vocabulary, as opposed to grammar or syntax.

lex loci /lɛks ˈləʊsʌɪ/ *noun phrase* L18 Latin (= law of the place). *Law* The law of the country in which a transaction is performed, a tort is committed, or a property is situated.

▪ Frequently followed by a defining word or phrase, as in *lex loci contractus* the law of the country in which a contract was made or *lex loci delicti* the law of the country in which an offence was committed.

lex talionis /ˌlɛks talɪˈəʊnɪs/ *noun phrase* M17 Latin (from *lex* law + *talionis* genitive of *talio(n)* recompense). The law of retaliation, whereby a punishment resembles the offence committed in kind and degree, as in the Mosaic principle 'an eye for an eye, a tooth for a tooth'.

liaison /lɪˈeɪz(ə)n/, /lɪˈeɪzɒn/, /lɪˈeɪzɒ̃/ *noun* M17 French (from *lier* to bind, from Latin *ligare*). **1** Communication or co-operation which facilitates a close working relationship between people or organizations. **2** A person who acts as a link to assist communication or cooperation between people. **3** A sexual relationship, especially one that is secret or illicit. **4** *Cookery* A binding or thickening agent for sauces, consisting chiefly of the yolks of eggs. Formerly, the process of binding or thickening. **5** *Phonetics* The pronunciation of a normally silent final consonant before a vowel (or mute *h*) beginning the following word, especially in French. **b** Introduction of a consonant between a word that ends in a vowel and another that begins with a vowel, as in English *law and order*.

■ Originally used in English in sense 4. In sense 3 the word is sometimes found in the phrase *liaison dangereuse* (literally, 'dangerous acquaintance'), an allusion to the brilliant and scandalous epistolary novel *Les Liaisons dangereuses* (1782) by Pierre Laclos.

1996 *Times* The Auld Alliance is the Sunday name for the long flirtation between France and Scotland which, like all *liaisons dangereuses*, has provided the spice to keep the main marriage successful.

libero /ˈliːbero/ *noun* plural **liberi** /ˈliːberi/ M20 Italian (abbreviation of *battitore libero* free defender (literally, 'free beater')). *Soccer* A player stationed behind the other defenders, free to defend at any point across the field and sometimes initiating and supporting attacks; a sweeper.

libido /lɪˈbiːdəʊ/, /lɪˈbʌɪdəʊ/ *noun* E20 Latin (= desire, lust). **1** Sexual desire. **2** *Psychoanalysis* The energy of the sexual drive as a component of the life instinct.

1 **1996** *Times* Loss of libido is only one cause of failing potency. More often the spirit is willing but the mechanism has failed naturally.

libretto /lɪˈbrɛtəʊ/ *noun* plural **librettos**, **libretti** /lɪˈbrɛti/ M18 Italian (diminutive of *libro* book). The text of an opera or other long vocal composition.

lido /ˈliːdəʊ/, /ˈlʌɪdəʊ/ *noun* plural **lidos** L17 Italian (= shore, beach, from Latin *litus*). A public open-air swimming pool or bathing beach.

■ Originally specifically *the Lido*, a bathing beach near Venice.

liebchen /ˈliːpçən/, /ˈliːbtʃ(ə)n/ *noun* (also **Liebchen**) L19 German. A person who is very dear to another; a sweetheart, a darling.

■ Frequently used as a term of endearment.

lied /liːd/, /liːt/ *noun* plural **lieder** /ˈliːdə/ (also **Lied**) M19 German. A type of German song, especially one characteristic of the Romantic period, usually for solo voice with piano accompaniment.

lien /liːn/, /ˈliːən/, /ˈlʌɪən/ *noun* M16 French (from Old French *loien* from Latin *ligamen* bond, from *ligare* to tie). *Law* A right to retain possession of property belonging to another person until a debt owed by that person is discharged.

■ Often in the expression *have a lien on* (*something*), used both literally and figuratively.

lierne /lɪˈəːn/ *noun* LME French (perhaps transferred use of *lierne* clematis, dialectal variant of *liane*). *Architecture* A short rib connecting the bosses and intersections of the principal vaulting-ribs.

lieu /ljuː/, /luː/ *noun* ME French (from Latin *locus* place). Place, stead.

■ Only in *in lieu* 'in the place, instead': *the company issued additional shares to shareholders in lieu of a cash dividend*.

lignum vitae /ˌlɪgnəm ˈvʌɪtiː/, /ˈviːtʌɪ/ *noun* L16 Latin (= wood of life). GUAIACUM (senses 1–3).

limbo /ˈlɪmbəʊ/ *noun* plural **limbos** LME Latin (ablative singular of *limbus* edge, border (in medieval Latin, border of Hell),

in phrases like *in limbo, e* (= out of) *limbo*).
1 *Christian Church* The region supposed
in some beliefs to exist on the border of
Hell as the abode of the just who died
before Christ's coming and of unbap-
tized infants. **2** An uncertain period if
awaiting a decision or resolution; an
intermediate state or condition. **3** A
state of neglect or oblivion.

lingam /'lɪŋgam/ *noun* (also **linga** /'lɪŋgə/)
E18 Sanskrit (*liṅga* sign, (sexual) characteristic; variant influenced by Tamil *iliṅkam*).
Hinduism A symbol of divine generative
energy, especially a phallus or phallic
object as a symbol of the god Shiva.
Cf. YONI.

lingerie /lãʒ(ə)ri/, *foreign* /lɛ̃ʒri/ *noun*
M19 French (from *linge* linen). Originally,
linen articles collectively; all the articles of linen, lace, etc., in a woman's
wardrobe or trousseau. Now, women's
underwear and nightclothes.

lingua franca /ˌlɪŋgwə 'fraŋkə/ *noun*
phrase plural **lingua francas, lingue
franche** /ˌlɪŋgwɪ 'fraŋki/ L17 Italian (=
Frankish tongue). A mixture of Italian
with French, Greek, Arabic, Turkish,
and Spanish, formerly used in the
eastern Mediterranean (now *historical*).
Also, any language adopted as a common language between speakers
whose native languages are different;
a system of communication providing
mutual understanding.

■ 'Frank', in many local variants, was the
word generally used by the inhabitants of
the eastern Mediterranean region for a
person of western or northern European
origin—not only a Frenchman.

lingue franche plural of LINGUA
FRANCA.

linguine /lɪŋ'gwiːni/ *noun plural* M20
Italian (plural of *linguina* diminutive of
lingua tongue, from Latin). Pasta in the
form of narrow ribbons; an Italian dish
consisting largely of this and usually a
sauce.

liqueur /lɪ'kjʊə/ *noun* M18 French (= liquor). **1** A strong, sweet flavoured
alcoholic spirit, usually drunk after a
meal. Also, a glass of such a drink. **2** A
chocolate with a liqueur filling.

literae humaniores /ˌlɪtərʌɪ hjuː
ˌmanɪˈɔːriːz/ *noun phrase* M18 Latin (= the
more humane studies). The humanities,
secular learning as opposed to divinity;
especially at Oxford University, the honours course in classics, philosophy, and
ancient history.

■ Abbreviated as *lit. hum.*

literati /lɪtəˈrɑːtiː/ *noun plural* E17 Latin
(*lit(t)erati* plural of *lit(t)eratus* literate).
Well-educated people who are inter-
ested in literature; the learned class as a
whole.

1996 *Spectator*... much of his [sc. Larbaud's]
best writing is taken up with the subject of
getting away from France, a variant on the
theme currently much canvassed by American
campus literati under the label 'otherness'.

literatim /lɪtəˈreɪtɪm/, /lɪtəˈrɑːtɪm/ *adverb* M17 Medieval Latin (*lit(t)eratim*, from
lit(t)era letter, after *gradatim* step by step;
cf. VERBATIM). (Of the copying of a text)
letter by letter.

literato /lɪtəˈrɑːtəʊ/ *noun singular* (corresponding plural LITERATI) E18 Italian
(*litterato* (now usually *letterati*) from as
Latin *lit(t)eratus* literate). A member of
the literati; a man of letters.

litotes /lʌɪˈtəʊtiːz/ *noun* L16 Late Latin
(from Greek *litotēs*, from *litos* single,
simple, meagre). Ironical understate-
ment, in which an affirmative is expressed by the negative of the contrary.

■ Examples of this figure of speech are
'no small amount' and 'no mean feat'. It
is also called, less commonly, MEIOSIS.

littérateur /ˌlɪtəraˈtəː/, *foreign* /litera-
tœr/ (*plural same*) *noun* E19 French (from
Latin *litterator*). A person who is interested in and knowledgeable about
literature.

llanero /(l)jaˈneroʊ/, /ljɑːˈnɛːrəʊ/ *noun*
plural **llaneros** E19 South American Spanish (from next). An inhabitant of a llano,
in particular one who works as a cowboy.

llano /'(l)jano/, /'ljɑːnəʊ/ *noun* plural
llanos E17 Spanish (from Latin *planum*
level ground). A level treeless plain in
the south-western United States and
the northern parts of South America.

loa /'ləʊə/ *noun* plural same, **loas** M20
Haitian (creole *lwa*, from Yoruba *oluwa*

lord, owner). A god in the voodoo cult of Haiti.

lobo /ˈləʊbəʊ/ noun plural **lobos** M19 Spanish (from Latin lupus wolf). A large grey wolf of the south-western United States and Mexico.

lobola /ləˈbəʊlə/ noun (also **lobolo** /ləˈbəʊləʊ/) M19 Zulu and Xhosa. (Among southern African peoples) a bride price, traditionally one paid in cattle; the practice of paying a bride price.

locale /ləʊˈkɑːl/ noun L18 French (local (noun), respelt to indicate stress; cf. MORALE). A place where something happens or is set, or that has particular events associated with it.

loc. cit. /ˌlɒk ˈsɪt/ adverb phrase M19 Latin (abbreviation of Latin loco citato or locus citatus (in) the place cited). In the passage already cited.

loch /lɒk/, /lɒx/ noun LME Gaelic. (In Scotland) a lake; (more fully *sea loch*) an arm of the sea, especially when narrow or partially landlocked.

loci classici, loci standi plurals of LOCUS CLASSICUS, LOCUS STANDI.

loco /ˈləʊkəʊ/ adjective L19 Spanish (= insane). Crazy. Colloquial.

loco citato see LOC. CIT.

locum /ˈləʊkəm/ noun E20 Latin (abbreviation of medieval Latin locum tenens (= one holding a place)). **1** A person who stands in temporarily for someone else of the same profession, especially a cleric or doctor. **2** The situation of a locum; a post as a locum.

■ *Locum tenens*, now entirely superseded in everyday English usage, antedated *locum* in both sense 1 (from M17) and sense 2 (from L19).

locus /ˈləʊkəs/, /ˈlɒkəs/ noun plural **loci** /ˈləʊsʌɪ/, /ˈlɒkiː/ E18 Latin (= place). **1** A particular position or place where something occurs or is situated. **b** The effective or perceived location of something abstract. **c** *Genetics* A position on a chromosome at which a particular gene or mutation is located. **2** *Mathematics* A curve or other figure formed by all the points which satisfy a particular equation or are generated by a point,

line, or surface moving in accordance with mathematically defined conditions. **3** LOCUS STANDI.

locus citatus see LOC. CIT.

locus classicus /ˌləʊkəs ˈklasɪkəs/, /ˌlɒkəs/ noun phrase plural **loci classici** /ˌləʊsʌɪ ˈklasɪsʌɪ/, /ˌlɒkiː ˈklasɪkiː/ M19 Latin (= classical place). A passage considered to be the best known or most authoritative on a particular subject; the best-known occurrence of an idea or theme.

1996 *Times* You would certainly not suspect from this . . . production . . . that Strindberg's preface to *Miss Julie* is a *locus classicus* of naturalist theory.

locus poenitentiae /ˌləʊkəs piːnɪˈtɛnʃiːiː/, /ˌlɒkəs piːnɪˈtɛnʃɪʌɪ/ noun phrase plural **loci poenitentiae** /ˌləʊsʌɪ piːnɪˈtɛnʃiːiː/, /ˌlɒkiː piːnɪˈtɛnʃɪʌɪ/ M18 Latin (= place of penitence). A place of repentance; *Law* an opportunity allowed by law to a person to withdraw from a commitment or contract, especially an illegal one, so long as some particular step has not been taken.

■ The allusion is originally biblical, to Hebrews 12:17, where it is said of Esau that, trying to reverse the agreement whereby he sold his birthright, 'he found no place of repentance'.

locus standi /ˌləʊkəs ˈstandʌɪ/, /ˌlɒkəs ˈstandiː/ noun phrase plural **loci standi** /ˌləʊsʌɪ ˈstandʌɪ/, /ˌlɒkiː ˈstandiː/ E19 Latin (= place of standing). *Law* The right or capacity to bring an action or to appear in a court of law.

loden /ˈləʊd(ə)n/ noun & adjective (also **Loden**) E20 German. **A** noun **1** A heavy waterproof woollen cloth; a coat or cloak made of this. **2** A dark green colour in which the cloth is often made. **B** adjective Made of this cloth.

loess /ˈləʊɪs/, /ləːs/ noun M19 German (Löss from Swiss German lösch loose, from lisen to loosen). *Geology* A loosely compacted yellowish-grey deposit of wind-blown sediment of which extensive deposits occur in eastern China, the American Midwest, and elsewhere.

loge /lɔʒ/ (plural same), /ləʊʒ/ noun M18 French. A private box or enclosure in a theatre, opera house, etc.

loggia /ˈləʊʤə/, /ˈlɒʤə/, /ˈləʊʤɪə/ noun M18 Italian (= lodge). A gallery or room with one or more open sides, especially one that forms part of a house and has one side open to the garden.

Logos /ˈlɒɡɒs/ noun L16 Greek (= account, relation, ratio, reason(ing), argument, discourse, saying, speech, word, related to *legein* to choose, collect, gather, say). **1** *Theology* The Word of God, or principle of divine reason and creative order, identified in the Gospel of John with the second person of the Trinity incarnate in Jesus Christ. **2** (In Jungian psychology) the principle of reason and judgement, associated with the animus. Often contrasted with EROS.

■ Used in a mystic sense by Hellenistic and Neoplatonist philosophers, *Logos* entered Christian discourse primarily through its use in the opening passage of St John's Gospel.

longeron /ˈlɒnʤərɒn/ noun E20 French (= girder). *Aeronautics* A frame member running lengthways along a fuselage.

longueur /lɔ̃ɡœr/ (plural same), /lɔ̃(ŋ)ˈɡə:/ noun L18 French (= length). A lengthy or tedious passage of writing, music, etc.; a tedious stretch of time.

> **1995** *Spectator* Looking back, *The Name of the Rose* bears up pretty well, although the longueurs seem much more like inexperience in pacing a novel than an engaging, wacky academic wanting to share an odd bit of information with the reader.

loofah /ˈluːfə/ noun (also **luffa** /ˈlʌfə/) L19 Arabic (*lūfa* the plant, *lūf* the species). **1** The fibrous matter of the fluid-transport system of a marrow-like fruit, which is dried and used as a bath sponge. **2** The tropical climbing plant of the gourd family, *Luffa cylindrica*, which produces loofahs, which are also edible.

loquitur /ˈlɒkwɪtə/ intransitive verb M19 Latin (3rd person singular present of *loquor* to speak). Speaks.

■ Used with the speaker's name added, as a stage direction or to inform a reader. Abbreviated as *loq.*

lorgnette /lɔːˈnjɛt/, *foreign* /lɔrɲɛt/ (plural same) noun E19 French (from *lorgner* to squint, ogle). *singular* and in *plural* A pair of glasses or opera glasses held in front of a person's eyes by a long handle at one side.

louche /luʃ/, /luːʃ/ adjective E19 French (= cross-eyed, squinting). Disreputable or sordid in a rakish or appealing way.

> **1996** *Times* Enter that figure so beloved of late-Victorian dramatists, the siren with the louche past.

lox /lɒks/ noun M20 Yiddish (*laks*). Smoked salmon.

luau /ˈluːaʊ/ noun M19 Hawaiian (*lū'au*). A Hawaiian party or feast usually accompanied by some form of entertainment.

lucus a non lucendo /ˌluːkʊs ɑː nɒn luːˈkɛndəʊ/, /ˌl(j)uːkʊs eɪ nɒnl(j)uːˈsɛndəʊ/ noun phrase E18 Latin (literally, 'a grove from its not shining', i.e. *lucus* (a grove) is derived from *lucere* (to shine) because there is no light there). A paradoxical or otherwise absurd derivation; something of which the qualities are the opposite of what its name suggests.

■ Also abbreviated *lucus a non.* The phrase is discussed by the Roman rhetorician Quintilian in his *Institutio Oratoria* (i.6.34).

> **1958** R. Liddell *Morea* Was its name Hydraea (watery), a *lucus a non lucendo*—it is singularly waterless today.

ludo /ˈluːdəʊ/, /ˈljuːdəʊ/ noun L19 Latin (= I play). A simple board game played with dice and counters.

lues /ˈluːiːz/, /ˈljuːiːz/ noun M17 Latin (= plague). A serious infectious disease, particularly syphilis (also more fully *lues venerea* /vəˈnɪərɪə/).

■ *Lues* also appears in a modern Latin phrase apparently coined by Macaulay who in 1834 wrote in the *Edinburgh Review* of the *Lues Boswellianae* or 'disease of admiration' that tends to afflict biographers writing uncritically about their subjects—as James Boswell did in his life of Dr Johnson.

luffa variant of LOOFAH.

luge /luːʒ/ noun & verb L19 Swiss French. **A** noun A light toboggan for one or two people, ridden in a sitting or supine position; the sport in which competitors make a timed descent of a course riding luges. **B** intransitive verb Ride or race on a luge.

lumbago /lʌm'beɪgəʊ/ *noun* L17 Latin (*lumbago*, *lumbagino*, from *lumbus* loin). Rheumatic pain in the lower muscles of the back.

lumpenproletariat /ˌlʌmpənprəʊlɪ'tɛːrɪət/ *noun derogatory* E20 German (from *Lumpen* rag + PROLETARIAT). (Especially in Marxist terminology) the unorganized and unpolitical lower orders of society who are not interested in revolutionary advancement and make no contribution to the workers' cause.

■ Originally used by Karl Marx in *Die Klassenkämpfe in Frankreich* (1850).

1995 *Times* Which is preferable, to patronise 'ordinary people' with string quartets, or exploit them, treat them as a lumpenproletariat and ensure that they remain lumpen by depriving them of anything better?

lunette /luː'nɛt/, /ljuː'nɛt/ *noun* L16 French (diminutive of *lune* moon, from Latin *luna*). **1** *Architecture* **a** An arched aperture or window, especially one in a domed ceiling. **b** A crescent-shaped or semicircular alcove in a ceiling, dome, etc., decorated with paintings or sculptures; a piece of decoration filling such a space. **2** A fortification with two faces forming a projecting angle, and two flanks. **3** *Christian Church* A circular case, fitting into an aperture in a monstrance, for holding the consecrated host. **4** *Geography* A broad shallow mound of wind-blown material along the leeward side of a lake or dry lake basin, especially in arid parts of Australia, and typically crescent-shaped with the concave edge along the lake shore. **5** A ring or forked plate to or by which a field-gun carriage or other vehicle for towing is attached.

■ Originally a farriers' term, denoting a semicircular horseshoe for the front of the hoof only.

lunula /'luːnjʊlə/ *noun* plural **lunulae** /'luːnjʊliː/ L16 Latin (diminutive of *luna* moon). **1** A crescent-shaped mark or spot, *specifically* the pale area at the base of a fingernail. **2** *Archaeology* A gold crescent-shaped neck ornament of the early Bronze Age.

■ Originally a term used in geometry (since replaced by *lune*), denoting a crescent-shaped figure formed on a plane by arcs of two circles intersecting at two points.

lupara /luˈpɑːrɑ/, /luːˈpɑːrə/ *noun* M20 Italian ((slang), from *lupa* she-wolf). A sawn-off shotgun as used by the Mafia.

lustrum /'lʌstrəm/ *noun* plural **lustra** /'lʌstrə/, **lustrums** L16 Latin (originally, a purificatory sacrifice after a quinquennial census, later also, a period of five years: ultimate origin unknown). A period of five years.

lusus naturae /'luːsəs nəˈtjʊəriː/, /nəˈtjʊərʌɪ/ *noun* plural same /'luːsuːs/, **lususes** E17 Latin (*lusus naturae* a sport of nature). A freak of nature, an abnormal formation, a natural curiosity. This phrase denotes a supposed sportive action of Nature to which the origin of marked variations from the normal type of an animal or plant was formerly ascribed.

luthier /'luːtɪə/, /'ljuːtɪə/ *noun* L19 French (from *luth* lute). A maker of stringed instruments, such as violins or guitars.

luxe /lʌks/, /lʊks/ *noun* M16 French (from Latin *luxus* luxury, abundance). Luxury. Cf. DE LUXE.

lycée /lise/ (*plural same*), /'liːseɪ/ *noun* M19 French (from Latin LYCEUM). A secondary school in France that is funded by the state.

Lyceum /lʌɪ'siːəm/ *noun* L16 Latin (from Greek *Lukeion* (sc. *gumnasion* gymnasium) neuter of *Lukeios* epithet of Apollo (from whose neighbouring temple the Lyceum was named)). **1** The garden at Athens in which Aristotle taught his philosophy; Aristotelian philosophy and its adherents. **2** *United States History* (**lyceum**) An institution in which popular lectures were delivered on literary and scientific subjects.

Lyonnais /liːəˈneɪ/, *foreign* /ljɔnɛ/ *adjective* (feminine **Lyonnaise** /liːəˈneɪz/, *foreign* /ljɔnɛz/) E19 French (= characteristic of Lyons, a city in south-east France). (Of food, especially sliced potatoes) cooked with onions or with white wine and onion sauce.

Mm

maar /mɑː/ *noun* plural **maars, maare** /ˈmɑːrə/ E19 German (dialect). *Geology* A broad low-rimmed crater, typically filled by a lake, formed by a volcanic eruption with little lava.

■ Originally denoted a kind of crater lake in the Eifel district of Germany.

maas /mɑːs/ *noun* (also in Zulu form **amasi** /əˈmɑːsi/) E19 Afrikaans (from Zulu (plural) *amasi* curdled milk). (In South Africa) thick, naturally soured milk.

mabela /məˈbiːlə/ *noun* (also **mabele** /məˈbiːli/) E19 Bantu (cf. Zulu, Xhosa *ibele*, plural *amabele*). (In South Africa) sorghum of a variety grown in southern Africa, used for making porridge and beer; meal or porridge made from this.

macabre /məˈkɑːbr(ə)/, *foreign* /ma kabr/ *adjective* M19 French (Old French *macabré* adjective (modern *macabre*), perhaps alteration of *Macabé* Maccabaeus, Maccabee, with reference to a miracle play containing the slaughter of the Maccabees). Disturbing because concerned with or causing fear of death; grim, gruesome.

■ In early use perhaps regarded as a proper name and introduced into English as a noun; the earliest (LME) instance of the phrase *daunce of Machabree* is in the title of one of Lydgate's works, but this usage has long been obsolete. The modern adjectival sense likewise originated in the phrase *dance macabre*, an anglicized version of the French DANSE MACABRE. The deaths of seven Jewish brothers and their mother, tortured to death for their religion under Hellenistic rule in the second century BC, are narrated in the Apocrypha (2 Macca-

bees 7); the Western Christian Church honoured them as martyrs, with a feast day celebrated on 1 August.

macaroni /makəˈrəʊni/ *noun* plural **macaronies** L16 Italian (*mac(c)aroni*, later *maccheroni*, plural of *mac(c)arone*, *maccherone* from late Greek *makaria* barley food). **1** Pasta in the form of narrow tubes. **2** An 18th-century British fop or a dandy who imitated continental fashions.

■ Sense 2 seems to have developed from the name of the Macaroni Club, a name which in turn was probably adopted to indicate the preference of the members for foreign food, macaroni being at that time little eaten in England.

macchiato /makɪˈɑːtəʊ/ *noun* (also **caffè macchiato**) plural **macchiatos** L20 Italian (= stained, marked (coffee)). A serving of espresso coffee with a dash of frothy steamed milk.

macédoine /ˈmasɪdwɑːn/ *noun* E19 French (from *Macédoine* Macedonia, with reference to the diversity of peoples in the empire of Alexander the Great, King of Macedon). A mixture of fruit or vegetables cut up into small pieces; *figurative* a medley, a mixture.

machair /ˈmakə/, /ˈmaxə/ *noun* L17 Gaelic. (In Scotland) a flat or low-lying coastal strip of arable or grassland; land of this nature.

1996 *Country Life* Stand with your back to the sea on South Uist, where the most spectacular machair is to be found, and look inland across the vast, fenceless expanses...

mâche /mɑːʃ/ *noun* L17 French. Lamb's lettuce, corn salad.

■ Originally anglicized (only in plural) in the now obsolete form of *maches*.

macher /ˈmaxə/ *noun* M20 Yiddish (from German = maker, doer). A person who gets things done. *United States colloquial*. Also, an overbearing person, a braggart. *United States derogatory*.

machete /məˈtʃɛti/, /məˈʃɛti/ *noun* (also **matchet** /ˈmatʃɪt/) L16 Spanish (from *macho* hammer, from Latin *marcus*). A broad, heavy knife used as an implement or weapon, originating in Central America and the Caribbean.

machismo /məˈtʃɪzməʊ/, /məˈkɪzməʊ/ *noun* M20 Mexican Spanish (from as MACHO). The quality of being macho; strong or aggressive masculine pride.

1996 *Times* Spanish Man seems to have changed as well, at a pace remarkable for a society which was once so steeped in *machismo*.

macho /ˈmatʃəʊ/ *adjective & noun* E20 Mexican Spanish (= male animal or plant, (as adjective) masculine, vigorous). **A** *adjective* Masculine in an overly assertive or aggressive way. **B** *noun* plural **machos 1** A man who is aggressively proud of his masculinity. **2** MACHISMO.

■ Originally United States.

A 1996 *Times* There is no merit in adopting a macho attitude regardless of its efficacy.

Machtpolitik /ˈmaxtpɔlɪˌtiːk/ *noun* E20 German (from *Macht* power, strength + *Politik* policy, politics). Power politics; strength as a potential factor to use in gaining a desired result.

macramé /məˈkrɑːmi/ *noun & adjective* M19 Turkish (*makrama* handkerchief, tablecloth, towel from Arabic *mikrama* bedspread). **A** *noun* The art of knotting string in patterns to make decorative articles. **B** *attributive* or as *adjective* Made of or by macramé.

macro /ˈmakrəʊ/ *noun & adjective* M20 Greek (*makro-* combining form of *makros* large, long). **A** *noun* plural **macros**. **1** *Computing* A single instruction that expands into a set of instructions to perform a particular task. In full *macro instruction*. **2** *Photography* A lens suitable for taking photographs unusually close to the subject. In full *macro lens*. **B** *adjective* Large-scale; overall: *the analysis of social events at the macro level*; *Photography* relating to macrophotography.

■ An independent use of the combining form found in numerous English words derived from Greek, particularly in scientific terminology; cf. MEGA. *Macro* is frequently contrasted, either explicitly or implicitly, with *micro*.

macron /ˈmakrɒn/ *noun* M19 Greek (*makron* neuter of *makros* long). A straight horizontal line (ˉ) written or printed over a vowel to indicate length or stress.

macula /ˈmakjʊlə/ *noun* plural **maculae** /ˈmakjʊliː/, **maculas** LME Latin (= spot). **1** *Science* A spot, a stain; *Medicine* an area of skin discoloration. **2** (also **macula lutea** /ˈluːtɪə/) *Anatomy* An oval yellowish area surrounding the fovea near the centre of the retina in the eye, which is the region of keenest vision.

■ The French word *macule* deriving from *macula* was also found in English in sense 1 (from L15).

Madame /madam/, /məˈdɑːm/, /ˈmadəm/ *noun* (also **madame**, **madam**) plural **Mesdames** /medam/, /mɛˈdam/, /meɪˈdam/ ME Old French. A title or form of address used of or to a French-speaking woman, corresponding to English *Mrs*, *Lady*, etc.: *Madame Bovary*.

■ As a title, usually abbreviated to *Mme*. The plural *Mesdames* (abbreviation *Mmes*) is also used as the plural of *Mrs*. The usual anglicized version *madam* has also been current since the Middle Ages and is most generally used as a respectful form of address to a woman, although it has also evolved some derogatory associations (e.g. 'a spoilt or affected woman' (L16), 'a female brothel-keeper' (L19)).

madeleine /ˈmadleɪn/ *noun* M19 French (probably from *Madeleine* Paulmier, 19th-century French pastry cook). A small rich sponge cake, baked in a fluted tin or mould and decorated with coconut and jam.

■ Allusions to madeleines in English are often in the context of memory. In his masterpiece *À la recherche du temps perdu*, the French novelist Marcel Proust (1871–1922) repeatedly describes how a sensory stimulus in the present, such as the taste of a madeleine dipped in tea, can act as the unconscious trigger for a flood of memories from the past, especially from childhood.

Mademoiselle /madmwazɛl/, /ˌmadəmwəˈzɛl/ *noun* (also **mademoiselle**) plural **Mesdemoiselles** /medmwazɛl/, /ˌmɛdmwaˈzɛl/, /ˌmeɪdəmwəˈzɛl/, **Mademoiselles** /madmwazɛl/, /ˌmadəmwəˈzɛlz/ LME Old French. **1** A title or form of address used of or to an unmarried French-speaking woman, corresponding to English *Miss*. Also used as a respectful form of address to a female French teacher in an English-speaking school. **2** A young Frenchwoman; a female French teacher in an English-speaking school.

■ As a title, usually abbreviated to *Mlle*.

Madonna /mə'dɒnə/ *noun* (also **madonna**) L16 Italian (from *ma* old unstressed form of *mia* my (from Latin *mea*) + *donna* lady (from Latin *domina*)). **1** The Virgin Mary; a picture or statue of the Virgin Mary. **2** An idealized virtuous and beautiful woman.

■ Originally used as a respectful form of address to an Italian woman.

madrasa /mə'drasə/ *noun* (also **madrasah**, **medrese** /mɛ'drɛseɪ/) M17 Arabian (*madrasa*, noun of place from *darasa* to study). A college for Islamic instruction.

madrilene /madrɪ'liːn/, /madrɪ'lɛn/ *noun* E20 French ((*consommé à la*) *madrilène*, (soup in the style of) Madrid). A clear soup flavoured with tomato and served cold.

maelstrom /'meɪlstrəm/ *noun* L17 Early Modern Dutch ((now *maalstroom*), from *maalen* to grind, whirl round + *stroom* stream whence the Scandinavian forms (e.g. Swedish *malström*, Danish *malstrøm*). **1** A powerful whirlpool, originally one in the Arctic Ocean off the west coast of Norway, formerly supposed to suck in and destroy all vessels that ventured near it. **2** *figurative* A state of confused movement or violent turmoil.

maestoso /mʌɪ'stəʊsəʊ/ *adverb, adjective, & noun* E18 Italian (= majestic, from *maestà* from Latin *majestas, majestatis* majesty). *Music* **A** *adverb & adjective* (Especially as a direction) in a majestic manner. **B** *noun* plural **maestosos** A movement or passage marked to be performed this way.

maestro /'mʌɪstrəʊ/, *foreign* /ma'ɛstro/ *noun* plural **maestri** /'mʌɪstri:/, *foreign* /ma'ɛstri/, **maestros** E18 Italian (from Latin *magister* master). **1** A distinguished conductor or performer of classical music. **2** A distinguished figure in any art, profession, etc.

1 1996 *Spectator* I had some reservations about Bernard Haitink's conducting—unusually

for him (normally the most cushioning of maestros) he seemed at times to be pushing too hard...

Mafia /'mafɪə/ *noun* (also **mafia**, **maffia**) M19 Italian ((Sicilian) = bragging, specifically hostility towards the law and its upholders, frequently as manifested in vindictive crimes). **1** *the Mafia*, an organized international body of criminals, operating originally in Sicily and now especially in Italy and the US and having a complex and ruthless behavioural code; any organized group of criminals resembling the Mafia in its way of operating. **2** Any group regarded as exerting a hidden sinister influence.

2 1995 *Private Eye* Crofton himself is now in trouble with the council's race relations mafia having accused a black colleague... of failing to deal with these allegations.

Mafioso /mafɪ'əʊsəʊ/ *noun* plural **Mafiosi** /mafɪ'əʊsi/, **Mafiosos** feminine **Mafiosa** /mafɪ'əʊsə/ (also **mafioso**, **maffioso**) L19 Italian (from as MAFIA). A member or supporter of the Mafia or a similar criminal organization.

1996 *Times: Weekend* Adams's new thriller... is heavily laced with all the paraphernalia of the genre in the new world order, including post-Soviet Russian female mafiosi, a few mad generals...

Magen David /mɑː'gɛn dɑː'viːd/ *noun phrase* E20 Hebrew (literally, 'shield of David' (king of Israel from *c*.1000 BC)). The Star of David, a six-pointed figure consisting of two interlaced equilateral triangles, used as a symbol of Judaism.

magi plural of MAGUS.

magma /'magmə/ *noun* LME Latin (from Greek, from base of *massein* to knead). *Geology* A hot fluid or semi-fluid material beneath the crust of the earth or other planet, from which igneous rocks are formed by cooling and which erupts as lava.

■ Early use was in the sense 'residue of dregs after evaporation or pressing of a semi-liquid substance'.

Magna Carta /ˌmagnə 'kɑːtə/ *noun phrase* (also **Magna Charta**) L15 Medieval Latin (literally, 'great charter'). The charter of liberty and political rights obtained from King John of England in

1215, which came to be seen as the seminal document of English constitutional practice; *transferred* any similar document establishing rights.

magna cum laude /ˌmagnə kʌm 'lɔː diː/, /ˌmagnɑː kʊm 'laʊdeɪ/ *adverb & adjective phrase* L19 Latin (literally, 'with great praise'). With great distinction; of a higher standard than the average (with reference to university degrees and diplomas).
■ Chiefly North American; cf. CUM LAUDE, SUMMA CUM LAUDE.

magna opera see MAGNUM OPUS.

magnificat /mag'nɪfɪkat/ *noun* ME Latin (= magnifies, 2nd person singular present indicative of *magnificare* to magnify. **1** (the *Magnificat*) The hymn of the Virgin Mary in Luke 1:46–55, used as a canticle forming part of the Christian liturgy at evensong and vespers. Also, the music to which this is set. **2** *transferred* A song of praise.
■ The opening words of the hymn are *Magnificat anima mea Dominum* ('My soul magnifies the Lord').

magnifico /mag'nɪfɪkəʊ/ *noun* plural **magnifico(e)s** L16 Italian ((adjective) = magnificent). A very powerful, important, or eminent person; a grandee.
■ Originally used as a title for a Venetian magnate.

magnum opus /ˌmagnəm 'əʊpəs/, /'ɒpəs/ *noun phrase* (also **opus magnum**) plural **magnum opuses**, **magna opera** /ˌmagnə 'əʊpərə/, /ˌmagnə 'ɒpərə/ L18 Latin (= great work). A work of art, music, or literature that is regarded as the most important or best work that an artist, composer, or writer has produced.

magus /'meɪgəs/ *noun* (also **Magus**) plural **magi** /'meɪdʒʌɪ/ ME Latin (from Greek *magos* from Old Persian *maguš*). **1** *History* A member of an ancient Persian priestly caste; *transferred* a magician, a sorcerer. **2** the *Magi*, the three 'wise men' from the East who brought gifts to the infant Jesus (Matthew 2:1); a representation of these.

maharaja /ˌmɑː(h)ə'rɑːdʒə/, /ˌməhɑː 'rɑːdʒə/ *noun* (also **maharajah, maharaj**

/ˌmɑː(h)ə'rɑːdʒ/, **Maharaja**) L17 Sanskrit (*mahārājā*, from *mahā* great + *rājan* RAJA). (The title of) an Indian prince of high rank.

maharani /ˌmɑː(h)ə'rɑːni/, /ˌməhɑː'rɑː ni/ *noun* (also **maharanee, Maharani**) M19 Hindi (*mahārānī*, from Sanskrit *mahā* great + *rājñī* RANI). (The title of) the wife or widow of a maharaja.

maharishi /ˌmɑː(h)ə'rɪʃi/ *noun* (also **Maharishi**) L18 Sanskrit (alteration of Sanskrit *maharṣi*, from *mahā* great + *ṛṣi* holy man). (The title of) a great Hindu sage or spiritual leader. Cf. GURU.

mahatma /mə'hatmə/, /mə'hɑːtmə/ *noun* L19 Sanskrit (*mahātman*, from *mahā* great + *ātman* soul). **1** (*Mahatma*) (In the Indian subcontinent) (the title of) a revered person regarded with love and respect; a holy person or sage. **2** (In some forms of theosophy) a person in India or Tibet said to have preternatural powers.

Mahdi /'mɑːdi/ *noun* E19 Arabic ((al-)*mahdī*, literally, 'he who is rightly guided', from passive participle of *hadā* to lead on the right way, guide aright). (In popular Muslim belief) the restorer of religion and justice who will rule before the end of the world; a claimant of this title.
■ The *Mahdi* best known to history was Muhammad Ahmad of Dongola in Sudan who proclaimed himself such in 1881 and launched a political and revolutionary movement which overthrew the Turco-Egyptian regime.

mah-jong /mɑː'dʒɒŋ/ *noun* (also **mah-jongg**) E20 Chinese (dialect *ma jiang* sparrows). A Chinese game for four, played with 136 or 144 pieces called tiles, divided into five or six suits.

maillot /majo/ *noun* plural pronounced same L19 French. **1** A pair of tights, especially worn by ballet dancers and circus artistes. **2** A woman's swimsuit. **3** A jersey or top worn in cycle racing.

maiolica variant of MAJOLICA.

maisonette /meɪzə'nɛt/ *noun* L18 French (*maisonnette* diminutive of *maison* house). A part of a residential building which is occupied separately, usually on more than one floor.

maître d' /mɛtr(ə) də/; /ˌmeɪtrə 'də/, /'diː/ *noun phrase* (also **maître de** /'də/) plural **maîtres d'**, **maîtres de** (pronounced same) L19 French (colloquial abbreviation of MAÎTRE D'HÔTEL). The head waiter of a restaurant; the manager of a hotel dining room or restaurant.

> **1996** *Times* [Flowers] conducted with small, effete waves of his baton, like the maître d' of an upmarket restaurant waving his clients towards their table.

maître de ballet /mɛtr(ə) də balɛ/ *noun phrase* E19 French. *Ballet* Originally, the composer of a ballet who superintended its production and performance; now, a trainer of ballet dancers.

maître d'hôtel /mɛtr(ə) dotɛl/, /ˌmeɪtrə dəʊ'tɛl/ *noun phrase* plural **maîtres d'hôtel** (pronounced same) M16 French (literally, 'master of (the) house'). The head waiter of a restaurant; the manager of a hotel dining room or restaurant; a hotel manager.

> ■ Originally, a major-domo, a steward, a butler.

maîtres d', **maîtres d'hôtel** plurals of MAÎTRE D', MAÎTRE D'HÔTEL.

maîtresse en titre /mɛtrɛs ɑ̃ titr/ *noun phrase* (also **maîtresse-en-titre**, **maitresse en titre**) plural **maîtresses en titre** (pronounced same) M19 French (literally, 'mistress in name'). An official or acknowledged mistress.

> **1973** D. Chandler *Marlborough* Arabella [Churchill] was . . . combining the roles of maid-of-honour to the Duchess and *maîtresse-en-titre* to the Duke, to whom she bore several children.

maja /'maxa/ *noun* M19 Spanish. (In Spain and Spanish-speaking countries) a woman who dresses gaily.

> ■ Best known in English in the titles of two of Goya's paintings, the *Naked Maja* and the *Clothed Maja*.

majlis /maʤ'lɪs/ *noun* E19 Arabic (= assembly, place of session, from *jalasa* to be seated). The parliament of various North African and Middle Eastern countries, especially Iran.

majolica /mə'jɒlɪkə/, /mə'ʤɒlɪkə/ *noun* (also **maiolica** /mə'jɒlɪkə/) M16 Italian (from the former name of the island of Majorca). A fine kind of Renaissance Italian earthenware with coloured decoration on an opaque white glaze; any of various other kinds of glazed Italian ware. Also, a modern imitation of this.

majuscule /'maʤəskjuːl/ *noun* E18 French (from Latin *majuscula* (*littera*) diminutive of *major* major). Large lettering, either capital or uncial, in which all the letters are the same height; a large letter.

maladroit /'malədrɔɪt/ *adjective* L17 French (from *mal-* bad(ly) + *adroit* skilful). Lacking in adroitness or dexterity; awkward, bungling, clumsy.

> **1996** *Spectator* He has tried to introduce a sense of fun, though sometimes the tone is childishly maladroit . . .

mala fide /ˌmeɪlə 'fʌɪdiː/, /ˌmalə 'fiːdeɪ/ *adverb & adjective phrase* E17 Latin (= with bad faith (ablative of next)). *Law* In bad faith; with intent to deceive.

mala fides /ˌmeɪlə 'fʌɪdiːz/, /ˌmalə 'fiːdeɪz/ *noun phrase* L17 Latin (= bad faith). *Law* Bad faith, intent to deceive.

malaise /ma'leɪz/ *noun* M18 French (from Old French *mal* bad, ill (from Latin *malus*) + *aise* ease). A general feeling of discomfort, illness, or unease whose exact cause is difficult to identify: *a general air of malaise; a society afflicted by a deep cultural malaise.*

malapropos /ˌmalaprə'pəʊ/ *adverb & adjective* (also **mal-à-propos** and other variants) M17 French (*mal à propos*, from *mal* ill + *à* to + *propos* purpose). **A** *adverb* In an inopportune or awkward manner; at an inopportune or awkward time; inappropriately. **B** *adjective* Inopportune, inappropriate.

malaria /mə'lɛːrɪə/ *noun* M18 Italian (*mal' aria* = *mala aria* bad air). Originally, an unwholesome condition of the atmosphere in hot countries due to the exhalations of marshes, to which fevers were ascribed. Now (also *malaria fever*), any of a class of intermittent and remittent febrile diseases formerly supposed to result from this cause, but now known to be due to infection with parasitic protozoans of the genus *Plasmodium*, transmitted by the bite of a mosquito of the genus *Anopheles* in many tropical and subtropical regions.

mal de mer /mal də mɛr/ *noun phrase* L18 French. Seasickness.

mal du siècle /mal dy sjɛkl/ *noun phrase* E20 French (= sickness of the century). World-weariness, weariness of life, deep melancholy because of the condition of the world.

malebolge /malɪˈbɒldʒeɪ/, *foreign* /male ˈbɒldʒe/ *noun* M19 Italian (*Malebolge*, from *male* feminine plural of *malo* evil + *bolge* plural of *bolgia* literally 'sack, bag'). A pool of filth; a hellish place or condition.

■ In literary use only. Malebolge was the name given in Dante's *Inferno* to the eighth circle of Hell, consisting of ten rock-bound concentric circular trenches (see especially Canto xviii).

mallee /ˈmali:/ *noun* M19 Aboriginal. Any of various low-growing eucalypts which have many slender stems rising from a large underground stock; scrub or thicket formed by such trees, typical of some arid parts of Australia.

mambo /ˈmambəʊ/ *noun* plural **mambos** M20 American Spanish (probably from Haitian creole, from Yoruba, literally, 'to talk'). **1** A Latin American dance similar in rhythm to the rumba; a piece of music for this dance. **2** A voodoo priestess.

mana /ˈmɑːnə/ *noun* M19 Maori. (In Polynesian, Melanesian, and Maori belief) an impersonal supernatural power which can be associated with people or with objects and which can be transmitted or inherited.

mañana /maˈɲana/, /manˈjɑːnə/ *adverb & noun* M19 Spanish (= morning, tomorrow (in this sense from Old Spanish *cras mañana*, literally, 'tomorrow early') ultimately from Latin *mane* in the morning). Tomorrow, (on) the day after today; (in) the indefinite future (from the supposed easy-going procrastination of Spain and Spanish-speaking countries).

1995 *Oldie* And . . . of course the damage would be paid for . . . *mañana*.

mandala /ˈmandələ/, /ˈmʌndələ/ *noun* M19 Sanskrit (*máṇḍala* disc, circle). A circular figure, usually with symmetrical divisions and figures of deities, etc., in the centre, used in Hindu and Buddhist symbolism as a representation of the universe.

mandorla /manˈdɔːlə/ *noun* L19 Italian (= almond). An almond-shaped panel or decorative space in religious art, a VESICA PISCIS.

manège /maˈneɪʒ/ *noun* (also **manege**) M17 French (from Italian *maneggio* from *maneggiare* from Proto-Romance from Latin *manus* hand). **1** An enclosed area in which horses and riders are trained. **2** The movements in which a horse is trained in a riding school; the art or practice of training and managing horses; horsemanship.

manes /ˈmɑːneɪz/, /ˈmeɪmiːz/ *noun plural* LME Latin. (In Roman mythology) the souls of dead ancestors, worshipped as beneficent spirits.

manga /ˈmaŋɡə/ *noun* L20 Japanese (from *man* indiscriminate + *ga* picture). A Japanese genre of cartoons, comic books, and animated films, having a science-fiction or fantasy theme and sometimes including violent or sexually explicit material.

mangetout /ˈmɑ̃ʒtuː/, /mɑ̃ʒˈtuː/ *noun* plural same, **mangetouts** (pronounced same) E19 French (literally, 'eat-all'). A pea of a variety with an edible pod, eaten when the pod is young and flat. Also called *sugar pea* or *sugar snap*.

manicotti /manɪˈkɒti/ *noun plural* M20 Italian (plural of *manicotto* sleeve, muff). Large tubular pasta shapes; an Italian dish consisting largely of these and usually a sauce.

manifesto /manɪˈfɛstəʊ/ *noun* plural **manifestos, manifestoes** M17 Italian (from *manifestare* to show, display, from Latin *manifestus* from *manus* hand + *-festus* struck). A public declaration of policy and aims, especially one issued before an election by a political party or candidate.

manna /ˈmanə/ noun OE Late Latin (from Hellenistic Greek from Aramaic *mannā* from Hebrew *mān* corresponding to Arabic *mann* exudation of the tamarisk *Tamarix mannifera*). **1** (In the Bible) the edible substance described as miraculously supplied to the Israelites in the wilderness (Exodus 16). **2** (In Christian contexts) spiritual nourishment, especially the Eucharist. **3** Something beneficial that appears or is provided unexpectedly or opportunely (frequently *manna from heaven*). **4** A sweet gum obtained from the manna ash or a similar plant, used as a mild laxative.

mannequin /ˈmanɪkɪn/, /ˈmanɪkwɪn/ noun M18 French (from Dutch *manneken* diminutive of *man* man). **1** A dummy used to display clothes in a shop window; an artist's lay figure. **2** A woman (or occasionally a man) employed by a designer, costumier, etc., to display clothes by wearing them; a model.

mano a mano /ˌmɑːnəʊ ə ˈmɑːnəʊ/ foreign /ˌmano a ˈmano/ adjective, adverb, & noun phrase (also **mano-a-mano**) L20 Spanish (= hand to hand). **A** adjective & adverb phrase Head to head; one to one; face to face. **B** noun phrase An intense confrontation, contest, or fight between two adversaries.

manoir /manwɑr/ noun plural pronounced same M19 French. A large country house or manor house in France.

ma non troppo /ma nɒn ˈtrɒpəʊ/ adverb phrase E20 Italian. Music (In directions) but not too much: *allegro ma non troppo*.

manqué /mãke/, /ˈmɒŋkeɪ/ adjective (feminine **manquée**) L18 French (past participial adjective of *manquer* to lack). postpositive Having failed to become what one might have been.
> **1996** *Times Magazine* The subway genius is probably... a writer manqué, since many of his chosen citations deal with creating literature.

manta /ˈmantə/ noun L17 Latin American Spanish (= large blanket). A very large tropical ray of the genus *Manta* or the family Mobulidae. More fully *manta ray*.

mantelletta /mantɪˈlɛtə/ noun plural **mantellettas**, **mantellette** /mantɪˈlɛti/ M19 Italian (probably from medieval Latin *mantelletum* from Latin *mantellum* mantle). A sleeveless vestment reaching to the knees, worn by cardinals, bishops, and other high-ranking Catholic ecclesiastics.

mantilla /manˈtɪlə/ noun E18 Spanish (diminutive of *manta* mantle). A light scarf, frequently of black lace, worn over the head and shoulders, especially by Spanish women.

mantra /ˈmantrə/ noun (also (rare) **mantram** /ˈmantrəm/) L18 Sanskrit (literally, 'instrument of thought', from *man* to think). **1** A sacred Hindu text or passage, *especially* one from the Vedas used as a prayer or incantation; in Hinduism and Buddhism, a holy name or word, for inward meditation. **2** A frequently repeated phrase, statement, or slogan.
> **1995** *Spectator* The Princess 'just wants to be happy'. She wants everyone to be happy. We know this because she has said it time and time again, like a mantra.

manyatta /manˈjatə/ noun E20 Masai. (Among certain African peoples, especially the Masai) a group of huts forming a unit within a common fence.

manzanilla /manzəˈnɪlə/, /manzəˈniːljə/; foreign /manθaˈni(l)ja/, /mansaˈni(l)ja/ noun M19 Spanish (literally, 'chamomile' (because the flavour is reminiscent of that of chamomile tea)). A kind of pale, very dry Spanish sherry; a drink or glass of this.

maquette /maˈkɛt/ noun E20 French (from Italian *macchietta* speck, diminutive of *macchia* spot, from *macchiare* to spot, from Latin *maculare* to stain). A sculptor's small preliminary model or sketch.

maquiladora /ˌmakilaˈdora/ noun L20 Mexican Spanish (from *maquilar* to assemble). A factory in Mexico run by a foreign company and exporting its products to that company's country of origin.

maquillage /makijaʒ/ noun L19 French (from *maquiller* to make up one's face, from Old French *masquiller* to stain, alteration of *mascurer* to darken). Make-up, cosmetics; the application of this.

1959 R. Graves *Collected Poems* Confirming hazardous relationships By kindly maquillage of Truth's pale lips.

maquis /'mɑːkiː/ *noun* plural same M19 French (= brushwood, from Corsican Italian *macchia*, from Latin *macula* spot). **1** The dense scrub vegetation characteristic of certain Mediterranean coastal regions, especially in Corsica. **2** *History* (usually **Maquis**) the French resistance movement during the German occupation (1940–5); a member of the Maquis.

■ The maquis scrub was the traditional hiding place for fugitives, hence the connection between senses 1 and 2.

maquisard /ˌmɑːkiːˈsɑː/ *noun* M20 French. A member of the Maquis.

marabou /'marəbuː/ *noun* E19 French (from Arabic *murābiṭ* holy man (see next), the stork being regarded as holy). **1** A large African stork, *Leptoptilus crumeniferus*, with a massive bill and large neck pouch, which feeds mainly by scavenging. Also *marabou stork*. **2** A tuft of soft white down from the wings or tail of this stork, used for trimming hats or clothing; trimming made of this down.

marabout /'marəbuːt/ *noun* E17 French (from Portuguese *marabuto* from Arabic *murābiṭ*, from *ribāṭ* frontier station, where merit could be acquired by combat against the infidel). **1** A Muslim holy man or hermit, especially in North Africa. **2** A shrine marking the burial place of a marabout.

maraca /məˈrakə/ *noun* (also **maracca**) E17 Portuguese (*maracá* from Tupi *maráka*). A Latin American percussion instrument made from a hollow gourd or gourd-shaped container filled with beans, pebbles, or similar objects, and usually shaken in pairs. Usually in *plural*.

maraschino /marəˈskiːnəʊ/, /marəˈʃiːnəʊ/ *noun* plural **maraschinos** L18 Italian. A strong, sweet red liqueur made from small black Dalmatian cherries.

■ A *maraschino cherry* is a cherry preserved in maraschino or maraschino-flavoured syrup.

marc /mɑːk/ *noun* E17 French (from *marcher* to walk (originally, to tread, trample, ultimately from late Latin *marcus* hammer)). **1** The refuse of grapes or other fruit that have been pressed for wine-making. **2** An alcoholic spirit distilled from marc. Also *marc brandy*.

marcato /mɑːˈkɑːtəʊ/ *adverb & adjective* M19 Italian (past participle of *marcare* to mark, accent, of Germanic origin). *Music* (Especially as a direction) played with emphasis.

Mardi Gras /ˌmɑːdɪ ˈɡrɑː/ *noun phrase* L17 French (literally, 'fat Tuesday', alluding to the last day of feasting before the fast of Lent). A carnival held in some countries on Shrove Tuesday, most famously in New Orleans; a carnival or fair at any time.

mare clausum /ˌmɑːreɪ ˈklaʊsʊm/, /ˌmɛːrɪ ˈklɔːzəm/ *noun phrase* plural **maria clausa** /ˌmɑːrɪə ˈklaʊsə/, /ˌmɛːrɪə ˈklɔːzə/ M17 Latin (= closed sea). *Law* The sea that is under the jurisdiction of a particular country.

■ The title of a work published in 1635 by the English jurist John Selden (1584–1654), in answer to Grotius (see MARE LIBERUM). The terms *mare clausum* and *mare liberum* both originated in the struggle between the Dutch and English maritime empires in the 17th century.

mare liberum /ˌmɑːreɪ ˈliːbərʊm/, /ˌmɛːrɪ ˈlʌɪbərəm/ *noun phrase* plural **maria libera** /ˌmɑːrɪə ˈliːbərə/, /ˌmɛːrɪə ˈlʌɪbərə/ M17 Latin (= free sea). *Law* The sea that is open to all nations. Cf. MARE CLAUSUM.

■ The title of a treatise (1609) by Hugo Grotius (1583–1645), Dutch jurist.

maremma /məˈrɛmə/ *noun* plural **maremme** /məˈrɛmi/ M19 Italian (from Latin *maritima* feminine of *maritimus* maritime). (In Italy) an area of low, marshy land by the seashore.

marginalia /ˌmɑːdʒɪˈneɪlɪə/ *noun* plural M19 Latin. Notes written in the margins of a text.

mariachi /marɪˈɑːtʃi/ *noun* M20 Mexican Spanish (*mariache*, *mariachi* street singer). An itinerant Mexican folk band (also *mariachi band*); a member of such a band.

maria clausa plural of MARE CLAU-SUM.

mariage blanc /marjaʒ blɑ̃/ *noun phrase* plural **mariages blancs** (pronounced same) E20 French (literally, 'white marriage'). An unconsummated marriage.

> 1975 *Listener* Opal … suggested a *mariage blanc* between Natalie and Bosie that would enable Opal and Bosie to have a lasting liaison.

mariage de convenance /marjaʒ də kɔ̃vnɑs/ *noun phrase* plural **mariages de convenance** (pronounced same) M19 French. A marriage of convenience.

> 1995 *Country Life* The following year, she [sc. Sonia Delaunay] entered a brief *mariage de convenance* with the homosexual art dealer Wilhelm Uhde …

maria libera plural of MARE LIBERUM.

marijuana /marɪˈhwɑːnə/, /ˌmarjʊˈɑːnə/ *noun* (also **marihuana**) L19 American Spanish. **1** Cannabis, especially in a form for smoking. **2** Indian hemp, cannabis plant.

marimba /məˈrɪmbə/ *noun* E18 Kimbundu. A kind of deep-toned xylophone, originating in Africa and consisting of wooden keys on a frame with a tuned resonator beneath each key.

marina /məˈriːnə/ *noun* E19 Italian and Spanish (feminine of *marino* from Latin *marinus* marine). A harbour, usually specially designed or located, with moorings for pleasure yachts and other small craft.

marinade /marɪˈneɪd/ *noun* E18 French (from Spanish *marinada*, from *marinar* to pickle in brine (= Italian *marinare*, French *mariner*), from *marino*, from Latin *marinus* marine). A mixture of wine, vinegar, or other acidic liquid, with oil, herbs, spices, etc., in which meat, fish, or other food is soaked before cooking in order to flavour or soften it.

marinara /mɑːrɪˈnɑːrə/, /marɪˈnɑːrə/ *adjective* M20 Italian (*alla marinara* sailor-style, from feminine of *marinero* seafaring). (In Italian cooking) designating a sauce made from tomatoes, onions, and herbs, usually served with pasta.

marionette /ˌmarɪəˈnɛt/ *noun* E17 French (*marionnette*, from *Marion* diminutive of *Marie* Mary). **1** A puppet with jointed limbs operated by strings. **2** A person who is easily manipulated or controlled.

marmite /ˈmɑːmʌɪt/, *in sense 1 also foreign* /marmit/ (*plural same*) *noun* E19 French (from Old French *marmite* hypocritical (with reference to the hidden contents of the lidded pot)). **1** An earthenware cooking container. **2** (**Marmite**) (Proprietary name for) a dark savoury spread made from yeast extract and vegetable extract.

marocain /marəˈkeɪn/ *noun* E20 French (= Moroccan, from *Maroc* Morocco). A dress fabric of ribbed crêpe, made of silk or wool or both.

marque /mɑːk/ *noun* E20 French (back-formation from *marquer* to mark or brand, alteration of Old French *merchier*, from *merc* limit, of Scandinavian origin (cf. Old High German *marc(h)a* mark)). A make or brand of something, especially a car, as distinct from a specific model.

> 1996 *Country Life* All this might give the impression that Rafael Gonzalez is an ancient and noble marque …

marquise /mɑːˈkiːz/, *foreign* /markiz/ (*plural same*) *noun* E17 French (feminine of *marquis* marquess, from Old French *marchis* (later altered to *marquis* after Provençal *marques*, Spanish *marqués*) from Proto-Romance base of *march* border). **1** The wife or widow of a marquis; a woman holding the rank of marquis in her own right. **2** A finger ring set with a pointed oval gem or cluster of gems. Also more fully *marquise ring*.

marquisette /mɑːkɪˈzɛt/ *noun* E20 French (diminutive of MARQUISE). A fine light cotton, rayon, or silk gauze fabric, now used for net curtains.

marron glacé /ˌmarɒn ˈglaseɪ/, *foreign* /marɔ̃ glase/ *noun phrase* plural **marrons glacés** (pronounced same) L19 French (= iced chestnut). A chestnut preserved in and coated with sugar.

masa /ˈmasa/ *noun* E20 Spanish. (In Central and South American cuisine) a type of dough made from maize flour and used to make tortillas, tamales, etc.

masala /mə'sɑːlə/ *noun* L18 Urdu (*maṣālaḥ* from Persian and Urdu *masālīḥ* from Arabic *maṣāliḥ*). **1** Any of various spice mixtures ground into a paste or powder for use in Indian cookery; a dish flavoured with this. Cf. GARAM MASALA. **2** *figurative* Someone or something that comprises a varied mixture of elements: *an Indian who grew up with a masala of influences in England, Jamaica, and Italy.*

mascara /ma'skɑːrə/ *noun & verb* L19 Italian (*mascara*, *maschera* mask). **A** *noun* A cosmetic for darkening and colouring the eyelashes. **B** *transitive verb* Put mascara on.

mascarpone /ˌmaskar'poːne/ *noun* M20 Italian. A soft, mild Italian cream cheese.

masjid /'mʌsdʒɪd/, /'masdʒɪd/ *noun* M19 Arabic. A mosque.

Masorah /masə'rɑː/, /mə'sɔːrə/ *noun* (also **Massorah**, **Masora**) E17 Hebrew (variant of *māsōreṯ* bond (Ezekiel 20:37), from *'āsar* to bind (later interpreted as 'tradition' as if from *māsar* to hand down)). The body of traditional information and comment relating to the text of the Hebrew Scriptures, compiled by Jewish scholars in the tenth century and earlier; the collection of critical notes in which this information is preserved.

massage /'masɑːʒ/, /ma'sɑːʒ/, /'masɑːdʒ/ *noun & verb* L19 French (from *masser* to apply massage to, perhaps from Portuguese *amassar* to knead). **A** *noun* **1** The application (usually with the hands) of pressure and strain on the muscles and joints of the body by rubbing, kneading, etc., in order to stimulate their action and increase their suppleness; an instance or spell of such manipulation. **2** *euphemistic* The services of prostitutes. Chiefly in *massage parlour.* **B** *transitive verb* **1** Apply massage to; treat by means of massage. **b** Rub (lotion etc.) into the skin or hair. **2** Manipulate (data, figures, etc.), especially in order to give a more acceptable result.

massé /'maseɪ/ *adjective & noun* L19 French (past participle of *masser* to play a massé stroke, from *masse* mace). *Billiards and Snooker* (Designating) a stroke made with the cue more or less vertical, so as to impart extra swerve to the cue ball.

masseur /ma'səː/ *noun* (feminine **masseuse** /ma'səːz/) L19 French (from *masser* to apply massage to). A person who provides massage professionally.

massif /'masɪf/, /ma'siːf/, *foreign* /masif/ (*plural same*) *noun* E16 French (use as noun of *massif* massive). A large mountain mass; a compact group of mountains.
■ Originally used in the sense 'a large building'.

Massorah variant of MASORAH.

mastaba /'mastəbə/ *noun* E17 Arabic (*misṭaba*, *maṣ-*). **1** (In Islamic countries) a stone or brick bench or seat built into the wall of a house. **2** *Archaeology* An ancient Egyptian flat-topped tomb consisting of an underground burial chamber with rooms above it (at ground level) to store offerings. Also *mastaba tomb.*

matador /'matədɔː/ *noun* (also especially senses 2, 3) **matadore**) L17 Spanish (= killer, from *matar* to kill). **1** A bullfighter whose task is to kill the bull. **2** (In some card games, such as quadrille, ombre, and solo) any of the highest trumps so designated by the rules of the game. **3** A domino game in which halves are matched so as to make a total of seven; any of the dominoes which have seven spots altogether, together with the double blank.
■ The senses relating to games are extended uses, expressing a notion of 'dominance'.

matchet variant of MACHETE.

maté /'mateɪ/ *noun* E18 Spanish (*mate* from Quechua *mati*). A bitter infusion of the leaves of a South American shrub, which is high in caffeine; the leaves of the maté shrub; the shrub itself, *Ilex paraguariensis*. Also more fully *yerba maté.*

matelassé /mat(ə)'laseɪ/, *foreign* /mat lase/ (*plural same*) *noun & adjective* (also **matelasse**) L19 French (past participle of *matelasser* to quilt, from *matelas* mattress).

A *noun* A silk or wool fabric woven so as to have a raised surface with a quilted appearance. **B** *adjective* Having a raised design like quilting.

matelot /'matləʊ/ *noun* E20 French (= sailor). A sailor. *British colloquial*.
■ Originally nautical slang. The French word ultimately derives from Middle Dutch *mattenoot* 'bed companion', because sailors had to share hammocks in twos.
1995 *Spectator* When Floyd cooks for, say, a crew of matelots, you never know whether they really enjoyed his bouillabaisse or whether they are just doing it to please him.

matelote /'mat(ə)ləʊt/, *foreign* /matlɔt/ (*plural same*) *noun* E18 French (from as preceding). A dish of fish served in a sauce of wine and onions.

mater /'meɪtə/ *noun* L16 Latin (= mother). Mother. *British colloquial, dated.* Cf. PATER.

mater dolorosa /ˌmeɪtə dɒlə'rəʊsə/ *noun phrase* plural **matres dolorosae** /ˌmeɪtriːz dɒlə'rəʊsiː/ E19 Medieval Latin (literally, 'sorrowful mother'). The Virgin Mary sorrowing for the death of Christ, especially as a representation in art; *transferred* a woman resembling the sorrowful Virgin in appearance, manner, etc.

materfamilias /ˌmeɪtəfə'mɪlɪəs/ *noun* M18 Latin (from MATER + *familias* old genitive of *familia* family). The female head of a family or household.

materia medica /məˌtɪərɪə 'medɪkə/ *noun phrase plural* L17 Modern Latin (translation of Greek *hulē iatrikē* healing material). The remedial substances used in the practice of medicine; the branch of medicine that deals with the origins and properties of substances used in the practice of medicine.

matériel /materjɛl/, /məˌtɪərɪ'ɛl/ *noun* E19 French (use as noun of adjective). The equipment, supplies, etc., used in an army, navy, or business. Opposed to *personnel*.

matinée /'matɪneɪ/, *foreign* /matine/ (*plural same*) *noun* (also **matinee**) M19 French (= morning, what occupies a morning, from *matin* morning (because performances were formerly also in the morning)). An afternoon performance in a theatre or cinema.

matres dolorosae plural of MATER DOLOROSA.

matzo /'mʌtsə/, /'matsəʊ/ *noun* (also **matzah** /'mʌtsə/) plural **matzos, matzoth** /'mʌtsəʊt/ M19 Yiddish (*matse* from Hebrew *maṣṣāh*). A crisp biscuit of unleavened bread, traditionally eaten by Jews during Passover.

maulana /maʊ'lɑːnə/ *noun* M19 Arabic (*mawlānā* our master). (A title given to) a Muslim man revered for his religious learning or piety.

maulvi variant of MOULVI.

mau-mau /'maʊmaʊ/ *transitive verb* L20 Kikuyu (*Mau Mau*, a secret society dedicated to the expulsion of British settlers from Kenya in the 1950s). Terrorize, threaten.
■ United States slang.

mauvais pas /mɔvɛ pa/ *noun phrase* plural same E19 French (literally, 'bad step'). *Mountaineering* A place that is difficult or dangerous to negotiate.
■ Also known as a *bad step*.
1940 F. S. Chapman *Helvellyn to Himalaya* We decided to return once more to the couloir…thus short-circuiting the *mauvais pas* we had seen in our reconnaisance.

mauvais quart d'heure /mɔvɛ kar dœr/ *noun phrase* plural **mauvais quarts d'heure** (pronounced same) M19 French (literally, 'bad quarter of an hour'). An unpleasant but brief period of time; an unnerving experience.
1965 *Economist* John Kennedy had his *mauvais quart d'heure* between April and June, 1961.

maven /'meɪv(ə)n/ *noun* M20 Yiddish (*mēḇīn* understanding). An expert, a connoisseur. *North American*.
1975 *New York Times* Mama, who had managed to support herself by becoming a local real estate *maven*, negotiated the purchase.

maxixe /mak'siːks/, *foreign* /mə'ʃiʃə/ *noun* E20 Portuguese. A dance for couples, of Brazilian origin, resembling the polka and the local tango.

1995 *Spectator* From Brazil in the 20s there came a dance called the maxixe—a challenge to those not confident of their Portuguese pronunciation—followed by the samba and the more primitive baiao.

maya /'mɑːjə/ *noun* L18 Sanskrit (*māyā*, from *mā* create). *Hinduism* The supernatural power wielded by gods and demons; *Hinduism and Buddhism* the power by which the universe becomes manifest, the illusion or appearance of the phenomenal world.

mayonnaise /meɪə'neɪz/ *noun* E19 French (also *magnonaise*, *mahonnaise*, perhaps feminine of *mahonnais* adjective, from *Mahon* capital of Minorca). A thick creamy dressing consisting of egg yolks beaten up with oil and vinegar and seasoned; a dish having this sauce as a dressing.

mazel tov /'maz(ə)l toːv/, /tɒf/ *interjection* M19 Modern Hebrew (*mazzāl ṭôḇ*, literally, 'good star', from Hebrew *mazzāl* star). (Among Jewish people) good luck, congratulations.

mazuma /mə'zuːmə/ *noun* E20 Yiddish (from Hebrew *mĕzummān*, from *zimmēn* to prepare). Money, cash; *especially* betting money. *United States and Australian slang.*

mazurka /mə'zəːkə/, /mə'zʊəkə/ *noun* E19 French (or from German *masurka* from Polish *mazurka* woman of the province Mazovia). **1** A lively Polish dance in triple time, usually with a slide and hop. **2** A piece of music for this dance or composed in its rhythm, usually with accentuation of the second or third beat.

mbira /(ə)m'bɪərə/ *noun* L19 Shona (probably an alteration of *rimba* note). A musical instrument of southern Africa consisting of a set of keys or tongues attached to a resonator, which are plucked with the thumb and forefingers; a thumb piano. Also called *sansa*.

mea culpa /ˌmeɪə 'kʊlpə/, /ˌmiːə 'kʌlpə/ *interjection & noun phrase* LME Latin (literally, 'through my own fault'). **A** *interjection* Used as an acknowledgement of one's guilt or responsibility for an error. **B** *noun phrase* An utterance of '*mea culpa*'; an acknowledgement of

one's guilt or responsibility for an error.

■ Taken from the prayer of confession in the Latin liturgy of the Church. Also sometimes *mea maxima culpa* 'through my own great fault'. As an interjection, now often humorous.

B 1996 *Times* In fact, Mr de Klerk's statement was far from the *mea culpa* many had hoped for and was a masterfully bland performance.

mealie /'miːli/ *noun* (also **mielie**) E19 Afrikaans (*mielie* from Portuguese *milho* maize, millet, from Latin *milium*). (In South Africa) maize; a corncob (usually in *plural*).

mebos /'miːbɒs/, *foreign* /'meːbɔs/ *noun* L18 Afrikaans (probably from Japanese *umeboshi* dried and salted plums). A South African preserve made from dried apricots and other fruit, pulped or flattened.

médaillon /medajɔ̃/ *noun* plural pronounced same E20 French (from Italian *medaglione*, from *medaglia* medal). A small, flat, round or oval cut of meat or fish.

■ The cognate *medallion*, in the sense of 'large medal', was established in English much earlier (M17).

medina /mɪ'diːnə/ *noun* (also **Medina**) E20 Arabic (literally, 'town'). The old walled part of a North African town.

medrese variant of MADRASA.

meerschaum /'mɪəʃɔːm/, /'mɪəʃəm/ *noun* L18 German (from *Meer* sea + *Schaum* foam, translation of Persian *kef-i-daryā* foam of sea, with reference to its frothiness). **1** A soft white clay-like material consisting of hydrated magnesium silicate, found chiefly in Turkey. **2** A tobacco pipe with a bowl made from meerschaum. Also called a *meerschaum pipe*.

mega /'mɛgə/ *adjective* L20 Greek (*mega-* combining form of *megas* great) Very large, huge. Also, brilliant, excellent.

■ Originating in the United States, this is an independent colloquial use of a combining form, similar to that of MACRO.

megaron /ˈmɛgər(ə)n/ *noun* L19 Greek. *Archaeology* The great central hall of a type of house characteristic especially of the Mycenaean period.

Megillah /məˈɡɪlə/ *noun* (also **megillah**) M17 Hebrew (*mĕgillāh*, literally, 'roll, scroll'). **1** Each of five books of the Hebrew Scriptures (the Song of Solomon, Ruth, Lamentations, Ecclesiastes, and Esther) appointed to be read on certain Jewish notable days; *especially* the Book of Esther, read at the festival of Purim. Also, a copy of all, or any, of these books. **2** A long-winded story or complicated set of arrangements. Frequently in *a* or *the whole megillah*. *Slang*.

> **1970** S. Sheldon *Naked Face* 'Do you know the most peculiar thing about this whole megillah?' queried Moody thoughtfully.

meiosis /mʌɪˈəʊsɪs/ *noun* plural **meioses** /mʌɪˈəʊsiːz/ M16 Modern Latin (from Greek *meiōsis*, from *meioun* to lessen, from *meiōn* less). **1** LITOTES. **2** *Biology* A particular kind of cell division.

mélange /melɑ̃ʒ/ (*plural same*), /meɪˈlɒ̃ʒ/ *noun* M17 French (from *mêler* to mix). A varied mixture, a medley.

> **1995** *Times* Davenport-Hines denounces the usual biographical *mélange* of gossip, scandal and 'sexual tale-telling'.

mêlée /ˈmɛleɪ/ *noun* (also **melée, melee**) M17 French (from Old French *mellée* past participial adjective of *meller* variant of *mesler* to meddle; sense 2 probably a different word). **1** A battle at close quarters, a hand-to-hand fight; a confused fight or scuffle, especially involving many people; a confused crowd of people. **2** *collectively* Small diamonds less than about a carat in weight.

> **1 1996** *Times* He continued to kick and punch at officers as he was led away after the two-minute mêlée.

melisma /mɪˈlɪzmə/ *noun* plural **melismata**, /mɪˈlɪzmətə/, **melismas** L19 Greek (literally, 'song, melody'). *Music* Originally, a melodic tune, melodic music. Now, in singing, the prolongation of one syllable over a number of notes.

> **1996** *Times* Ray Charles is the name that invariably comes to mind in any discussion of Feliciano—not simply for the trite reason that they are both blind and fond of gospel melismata...

meltemi /mɛlˈtɛmi/ *noun* E20 Modern Greek (*meltémi*, Turkish *meltem*). A dry north-westerly wind blowing over the eastern Mediterranean region in summer; an Etesian wind.

membrum virile /ˌmɛmbrəm vɪˈriːli/ *noun phrase* M19 Latin (= male member). The penis. *Archaic* or *euphemistic*.

memento mori /mɪˌmɛntəʊ ˈmɔːrʌɪ/, /mɪˌmɛntəʊ ˈmɔːri/ *noun phrase* Latin (= remember that you have to die). An object kept as a reminder of the inevitability of death, such as a skull.

> **1996** *Country Life*...it explores the theme of life among the ruins...a powerful memento mori of departed grandeur.

memorabilia /ˌmɛm(ə)rəˈbɪlɪə/ *noun* plural L18 Latin (use as noun of neuter plural of *memorabilis* from *memorare* to bring to mind). **1** Objects kept or collected because of their association with memorable people or events. **2** Memorable or noteworthy observations or writings. *Archaic*.

> **1 1996** D. Chambers *Stonyground* As the museum of the house, this parlour of my childhood was filled with memorabilia: a loon, now stuffed, that my grandmother had rescued from a ditch and nursed to tameness; my great-uncle Hugh's bayonet from the First World War...

memorandum /mɛməˈrandəm/ *noun* plural **memoranda** /mɛməˈrandə/, **memorandums** L15 Latin (literally 'something to be brought to mind', gerundive of *memorare* to bring to mind, from *memor* mindful). **1** A written message in business or diplomacy. **2** A note to help the memory, a record of events or of observations on a particular subject, especially for future consideration or use. **3** *Law* A document recording the terms of a contract or other legal details.

■ *Memorandum* was first introduced (LME) as an adjective meaning 'to be remembered' and placed at the beginning of a note of something to be remembered or a record (for future reference) of something done, but this usage is now confined to legal contexts.

memsahib /ˈmɛmsɑːb/ *noun* M19 Anglo-Indian (from *mem* representing a pronunciation of 'ma'am' + SAHIB). A married

white woman (often used as a respectful form of address). *Indian, dated.*

ménage /meɪˈnɑːʒ/, *foreign* /menaʒ/ (*plural same*) *noun* (also **menage** ME French
(Old French *menaige, manaige* (modern
ménage) from Proto-Romance, from Latin
mansio station, abiding-place, from *mans-*
past participial stem of *manere* to stay,
remain). **1** A domestic establishment, a
household. Formerly also, the members of a household. **2** A sexual relationship; an affair; a MÉNAGE À TROIS. **3** The
management of a household, house-
keeping.

■ In sense 1 also occasionally found in
the phrases *ménage à deux* 'household of
two' and *ménage à quatre* 'household of
four', but by far the most frequent is
MÉNAGE À TROIS. The related French
word *menagerie* (introduced L17) meaning
'a collection of wild animals kept in
cages' is now completely anglicized in
pronunciation (/məˈnadʒ(ə)ri/).

ménage à trois /menaʒ a trwɑ/,
/meɪˈnɑːʒ a trwɑː/ (*plural same*) *noun
phrase* (also **ménage-à-trois**) L19 French
(= household of three). An arrangement
or relationship in which three people
live together, usually consisting of a
husband and wife and the lover of one
of them.
> **1996** *Spectator* He seemed saddened by
> some people's view that 'I might be having my
> cake and eating it', referring to his *ménage-
> à-trois* with wife Rosie and mistress Morrigan.

menhaden /mɛnˈheɪd(ə)n/ *noun* L18 Algonquian (perhaps from a base meaning
'fertilize'). A fish of the herring family,
Brevoortia tyrannus, of the Atlantic coast
of North America, an important source
of fish guano and oil.

menhir /ˈmɛnhɪə/ *noun* M19 Breton (*maen-
hir* (*maen* stone, *hir* long) = Welsh *maen hir*,
Cornish *mênhere*). *Archaeology* A single
tall upright monumental stone, especially of prehistoric times.

meniscus /mɪˈnɪskəs/ *noun* plural **me-
nisci** /mɪˈnɪskʌɪ/ L17 Modern Latin (from
Greek *mēniskos* crescent, diminutive of
mēnē moon). **1** The convex or concave
upper surface of a column of liquid in a
tube, caused by surface tension or
capillarity. **2** A lens convex on one side
and concave on the other; *especially* a

convexo-concave lens (i.e. one thickest
in the middle, with a crescent-shaped
section). **3** *Anatomy* A thin fibrous
cartilage situated between the surfaces
of certain joints, as those of the wrist
and knee.

meno /ˈmɛnəʊ/, /ˈmeɪnəʊ/ *adverb* L19
Italian. *Music* Less.

■ Used in directions, as *meno mosso* 'less
rapidly'.

menologium /ˌmɛnə(ʊ)ˈləʊdʒɪəm/ *noun*
(also **menology** /mɪˈnɒlədʒi/) plural
menologia /ˌmɛnə(ʊ)ˈləʊdʒɪə/, **meno-
logiums** E18 Modern Latin (from ecclesiastical Greek *mēnologion*, from *mēn* month +
logos account). An ecclesiastical calendar of the months.

■ The English form *menology* was introduced earlier (E17), but the form *menologium* is used in parallel with it, in
particular with reference to the Old
English metrical church calendar first
published in 1705. The Greek form
menologion is also used specifically to
mean a calendar of the Orthodox Church
containing biographies of the saints in
the order of the dates on which they are
commemorated.

menorah /mɪˈnɔːrə/ *noun* L19 Hebrew
(*mĕnōrāh* candlestick). A sacred candelabrum with seven branches that was
used in the ancient temple in Jerusalem; a candelabrum having any number of branches, but usually eight, used
in Jewish worship, especially during
Hanukkah; a representation of either
as a symbol of Judaism.

mensch /mɛnʃ/ *noun* M20 Yiddish (from
German = person). A person of integrity
and honour. *United States colloquial.*
> **1972** *New Yorker* What is a *mensch?* . . . It
> means you're a substantial human being.

menses /ˈmɛnsiːz/ *noun plural* L16 Latin
(plural of *mensis* month). The menstrual
discharge. Also, the time of menstrua-
tion.

mens rea /ˌmɛnz ˈriːə/ *noun phrase* M19
Latin (= guilty mind). *Law* The intention
or knowledge of wrongdoing that con-
stitutes part of a crime, as opposed
to the action or conduct of the accused.
Cf. ACTUS REUS.

1992 P. Manning *Erving Goffman and Modern Sociology* The law encourages this defense strategy by requiring prosecution lawyers to demonstrate *mens rea* on the part of the accused; that is, it requires proof that the accused intended to commit the crime.

mens sana in corpore sano /mɛns ˌsɑːnə ɪn ˌkɔːpəreɪ 'sɑːnəʊ/ *noun phrase* E17 Latin. A sound mind in a sound body, especially regarded as the ideal of education.

■ Also elliptical as *mens sana* (see quotation 1967). The quotation is from the *Satires* (x.356) of the Roman poet Juvenal.
1967 S. Johnson *Gold Drain* 'They' accused him of suffering from the effects of a public-school education, from the *mens sana* approach.

mentor /'mɛntɔː/ *noun* M18 French (from Latin *Mentor* from Greek *Mentōr* the guide and adviser of Odysseus' son Telemachus (probably chosen as a name as from base meaning 'remember, think, counsel')). An experienced and trusted adviser or guide; a teacher, a tutor.

menudo /mɪ'n(j)uːdəʊ/ *noun* M20 Mexican Spanish (use as noun of adjective = small from Latin *minutus* very small). A spicy Mexican soup made from tripe.

mercado /məˈkɑːdəʊ/, *foreign* /merˈkado/ *noun* plural **mercados** /məˈkɑːdəʊz/, *foreign* /merˈkados/ M19 Spanish (from Latin *mercatus* market). (In Spain and Spanish-speaking countries) a market.

merde /mɛrd/ *interjection* M20 French (from Latin *merda* excrement, dung). Used as a mild, generally humorous substitute for 'shit', expressing annoyance, exasperation, surprise, etc. Cf. MOT DE CAMBRONNE.

mère /mɛr/, /mɛː/ *noun* M19 French (= mother). The mother, elder.

■ *Mère* is appended to a name especially to distinguish between a mother and daughter of the same name (see quotation).
1968 J. Haythorne *None of Us Cared for Kate* Prentice *mère* has been bombarding the Secretary of State with letters.

merengue /məˈrɛŋgeɪ/ *noun* (also **meringue** /məˈraŋ/) L19 American Spanish. A dance of Dominican and Haitian origin, with alternating long and short stiff-legged steps; a piece of music for this dance, usually in duple and triple time.

meringue /məˈraŋ/, *foreign* /mərɛ̃g/ (*plural same*) *noun* E18 French (of unknown origin). A confection made chiefly of sugar and whites of eggs whipped together and baked crisp; a small cake or shell of this, usually decorated or filled with cream.

merino /məˈriːnəʊ/ *noun* plural **merinos** L18 Spanish (of unknown origin). **1** A sheep of a breed prized for the fineness of its wool, originating in Spain. **2** A soft fine material resembling cashmere, made of wool (originally merino wool) or wool and cotton; a fine woollen yarn used in the manufacture of hosiery and knitwear. **3** A garment, especially a dress or shawl, made of this; *West Indies* an undershirt, originally one made of merino wool.

mesa /'meɪsə/ *noun* M18 Spanish (= table, from Latin *mensa*). An isolated flat-topped hill with steep sides, found in landscapes with horizontal strata.

■ The earliest occurrences are in the names of particular plateaux or hills in the United States.

mésalliance /mezaljɑ̃s/ (*plural same*), /mɛˈzalɪəns/ *noun* L18 French (from *més-* mis- + *alliance* alliance). A marriage with a person thought to be unsuitable or of inferior social position.

■ The English form *misalliance* (M18) is also current for an inappropriate marital or sexual union, but it is also used more generally.

mes ami(e)s plural of MON AMI(E).

mescal /'mɛskal/, /mɛˈskal/ *noun* E18 Spanish (*mezcal* from Nahuatl *mexcalli*). **1** Any of several plants of the genus *Agave* found in Mexico and the southwestern United States, used as sources of fermented liquor, food, or fibre. **2** A strong intoxicating spirit distilled from the fermented sap of the American aloe or allied species. Cf. TEQUILA. **3** A small desert cactus, *Lophophora williamsii*, of Mexico and Texas; a preparation of this used as a hallucinogenic drug. Cf. PEYOTE.

Mesdames plural of MADAME.

Mesdemoiselles plural of MADEMOI-
SELLE.

meshuga /mɪˈʃʊɡə/ *adjective* (also **me-
shugga(h)**) L19 Yiddish (*meshuge* from
Hebrew *měshuggā'*; cf. German *meschugge*
crazy). Mad, crazy; stupid. *United States
colloquial.*

meshugaas /mɪˈʃʊɡɑːs/ *noun* (also
mishugas and other variants) E20 Yiddish (from Hebrew *měshuggā'*: see ME-
SHUGA). Madness, craziness; nonsense,
foolishness. *United States colloquial.*

meshugener variant of MESHUGGEN-
ER.

meshugga variant of MESHUGA.

meshuggener /mɪˈʃʊɡənə/ *noun* (also
meshugener) E20 Yiddish (from Hebrew
měshuggā': see MESHUGA). A person who
is mad, crazy, or stupid. *United States
colloquial.*

mestizo /mɛˈstiːzəʊ/ *noun* plural **mes-
tizos** (feminine **mestiza** /mɛˈstiːzə/) L16
Spanish (= mixed, from Proto-Romance
from Latin *mixtus* past participle of *miscere*
to mix). (In Latin America) a person of
mixed race, especially one having
Spanish and American Indian parentage.

metanoia /mɛtəˈnɔɪə/ *noun* L19 Greek
(from *metanoein* to change one's mind,
repent). Change in one's way of life
resulting from penitence or spiritual
conversion.

metastasis /mɪˈtastəsɪs/ *noun* plural
metastases /mɪˈtastəsiːz/ L16 Late Latin
(from Greek = removal, change, from
methistanai to remove, change). *Medicine*
The development of secondary malignant growths at a distance from one
point to another; a growth of this kind.

▪ Originally a rhetorical term, referring
to a rapid transition from one point to
another.

metate /məˈtɑːteɪ/ *noun* E17 American
Spanish (from Nahuatl *métatl*). (In Central
America) a flat or somewhat hollowed
oblong stone on which grain, cocoa,
etc., are ground by means of a smaller
stone. Also *metate stone.*

metathesis /mɛˈtaθɪsɪs/, /mɪˈtaθɪsɪs/
noun plural **metatheses** /mɛˈtaθɪsiːz/
L16 Late Latin (from Greek, from *metatithe-
nai* transpose, change). **1** *Grammar* The
transposition of sounds or letters in a
word; the result of such a transposition.
Formerly also, the transposition of
words. **2** *Chemistry* An interchange of
an atom or atoms between two different molecules; *especially* double decomposition.

méthode champenoise /metɔd ʃɑ̃
pənwaz/ *noun phrase* E20 French (literally,
'champagne method'). A method of
making sparkling wine by allowing
the last stage of fermentation to take
place in the bottle; a sparkling wine
made in this way.

> **1995** *Country Life* And, thanks to Napoleon's
> sister and the introduction of the *méthode
> champenoise*, bottles of the modest, local,
> sparkling brew, Malvasia.

métier /metje/, /ˈmeɪtɪeɪ/ *noun* L18 French
(from Proto-Romance alteration of Latin
ministerium service, ministry, probably
influenced by *mysterium* mystery). One's
occupation or department of activity.
Now usually, a field in which one has
special skill or ability; one's forte.

> **1995** *Spectator* Louisa Alcott was to find her
> true métier as a chronicler of family life ....

Metis /merˈtiːs/   *Canadian*   /merˈti/,
/ˈmeɪti/ *noun* plural same /merˈtiː(s)/,
/ˈmeɪti/, /ˈmeɪtɪz/ (feminine **Métisse**
/merˈtiːs/, /ˈmeɪtiːs/, plural **Métisses**)
E19 French (*métis* from Old French *mestis*
from Proto-Romance, from Latin *mixtus*
past participle of *miscere* to mix).
(In Canada) a person of mixed race,
especially one having white and American Indian parentage.

metope /ˈmɛtəʊp/, /ˈmɛtəpi/ *noun* M16
Latin (*metopa* from Greek *metopē*, from
meta between + *opē* hole in a frieze for a
beam end). *Architecture* A square space
between triglyphs in a Doric frieze.

metro /ˈmɛtrəʊ/, /ˈmeɪtrəʊ/ *noun* collo-
quial (also **Metro**) plural **metros** E20
French (*métro* abbreviation of (*Chemin de
Fer*) *Métropolitain* Metropolitan (Railway)).
An underground railway system in a
city, especially Paris.

meunière /məˈnjɛː/, *foreign* /mønjɛr/ *adjective* M19 French ((*à la*) *meunière*, literally,

'(in the manner of) a miller's wife').
Cookery (Especially of fish) cooked or
served in lightly browned butter with
lemon juice and parsley.

■ Usually postpositive, as in *trout meunière*.

meze /ˈmeɪzeɪ/ *noun* plural same,
mezes E20 Turkish (= snack, appetizer,
from Persian *maza* to taste, relish). (In
Turkish, Greek, and Middle Eastern
cookery) a selection of hot and cold
dishes, typically served as an hors
d'oeuvre.

mezuza /məˈzuːzə/ *noun* (also **mezu-
zah**) plural **mezuzoth** /məˈzuːzəʊt/ M17
Hebrew (*mĕzūzāh*, literally 'doorpost').
A piece of parchment inscribed with
religious texts enclosed in a case and
attached to the doorpost of a Jewish
house as a sign of faith.

■ The practice is based upon the injunction in Deuteronomy 6:9.

mezzani /mɛtˈsaːni/ *noun* L19 Italian
(plural of *mezzano*: see next). Pasta in
the form of medium-sized tubes; an
Italian dish consisting largely of this
and usually a sauce.

mezzanine /ˈmɛzəniːn/ *noun & adjective*
E18 French (from Italian *mezzanino* diminutive of *mezzano* middle, medium, from
Latin *medianus* median). **A** *noun* **1** A low
storey between two others in a build-
ing, usually between the ground floor
and the floor above. **2** The lowest
balcony of a theatre or cinema; a dress
circle. *North American.* **B** *adjective* **1** Designating an intermediate floor, storey,
etc. **2** *Commerce* Relating to or denoting
unsecured, higher-yielding loans that
are subordinate to bank loans and
secured loans but rank above equity.
B 1 1996 *Times Magazine* Even when the
overall area is divided into smaller units,
the tall ceilings provide an opportunity for
horizontal divisions such as mezzanine floors.

mezza voce /ˌmɛtsə ˈvɒtʃi/ *adverb, adjective, & noun phrase* L18 Italian (*mezza*
feminine of *mezzo* middle, half, *voce*
voice). *Music* **A** *adverb & adjective phrase*
Using about half the singer's vocal
power; restrained. **B** *noun phrase* Singing performed in this way.

mezzo /ˈmɛtsəʊ/ *adverb* M18 Italian (=
middle, half, from Latin *medius* medium).
Music (Qualifying a direction) half,
moderately, fairly: *mezzo forte*; *mezzo
piano*.

mezzo *noun* abbreviation of MEZZO-
SOPRANO.

mezzo-relievo /ˌmɛtsəʊrɪˈliːvəʊ/ *noun*
plural **mezzo-relievos** L16 Italian (*mezzo*
half + *relievo* relief). Half relief; a sculpture, moulding, carving, etc., in half
relief.

mezzo-soprano /ˌmɛtsəʊsəˈprɑːnəʊ/
noun plural **mezzo-sopranos** M18 Italian
(*mezzo* middle + SOPRANO). *Music* A
female singer with a voice pitched
between soprano and contralto; a singing voice of the mezzo-soprano type, or
a part written for one.

■ In informal contexts often abbreviated
to *mezzo*.

miasma /mɪˈazmə/, /mʌɪˈazmə/ *noun*
plural **miasmas**, **miasmata** /mɪˈazmətə/
M17 Greek (*miasma(t-)* defilement, pollution, related to *miainein* to pollute). **1** An
unpleasant or unhealthy smell or va-
pour. **2** *figurative* A polluting, oppressive, or foreboding atmosphere which
surrounds or emanates from something.

midinette /mɪdɪˈnɛt/, *foreign* /midinɛt/
(*plural same*) *noun* E20 French (from *midi*
midday + *dînette* light dinner). A seam-
stress or assistant in a Parisian fashion
house.

■ The word was originally a term for any
Parisian shop girl, only allowed to take a
short break at lunchtime.

mielie variant of MEALIE.

mignonette /mɪnjəˈnɛt/ *noun* E18 French
(*mignonnette* diminutive of *mignon* small
and sweet). Any of several plants of the
genus *Reseda*, with small greenish or
whitish flowers; specifically *R. odorata*,
cultivated for its fragrant flowers. **b** A
colour resembling that of the flowers of
the mignonette; greyish green or greenish white. **c** A perfume derived from or
resembling that of the flowers of the
mignonette.

migraine /ˈmiːɡreɪn/, /ˈmʌɪɡreɪn/ *noun*
LME Old and Modern French (from late

Latin *hemicrania* from Greek *hēmíkrania*, from *hēmi-* half + *kranion* skull). A recurrent throbbing headache, usually affecting one side of the head, often accompanied by nausea or disturbed vision; the illness or condition characterized by such headaches.

mihrab /ˈmiːrɑːb/ *noun* E19 Arabic (*miḥrāb* place for prayer). **1** A niche in the wall of a mosque, at the point nearest to Mecca, towards which the congregation faces to pray. **2** A niche motif on an oriental prayer rug, resembling the shape of a mihrab in a mosque.

mikva /ˈmɪkvə/ *noun* (also **mikvah**, **mikveh**) M19 Yiddish (*mikve* from Hebrew *miqweh*, literally, 'collection, mass, especially of water'). A bath in which certain Jewish ritual purifications are performed; the action of taking such a bath.

miles gloriosus /ˌmiːleɪz ɡlɔːrɪˈəʊsəs/, /ˌmʌɪliːz/ *noun* plural **milites gloriosi** /ˌmiːlɪteɪz ɡlɔːrɪˈəʊsiː/, /ˌmʌɪlɪtiːz ɡlɔːrɪˈəʊsʌɪ/ E20 Latin (= boastful soldier). A vainglorious soldier who boasts about his military exploits.

■ *Miles gloriosus* is the title of a comedy by the Roman playwright Plautus (*c*.250–184 BC). The *miles gloriosus* became a stock character of Renaissance comedy—Shakespeare's Parolles in *All's Well That Ends Well* is an example—and the phrase generally occurs in literary contexts.

milieu /ˈmiːljəː/, /mɪˈljəː/, *foreign* /miljø/ *noun* plural **milieus** /ˈmiːljəːz/, **milieux** /ˈmiːljəːz/, *foreign* /miljø/ M19 French (from *mi* (from Latin *medius* mid) + *lieu* place). **1** A person's social environment. **2** *transferred* A group of people with a shared (cultural) outlook; a social class or set.

milites gloriosi plural of MILES GLORIOSUS.

millefeuille /milfœj/, /ˈmiːlfəːj/ *noun* plural pronounced same L19 French (literally, 'a thousand leaves'). A rich cake consisting of thin layers of puff pastry and a filling of jam, cream, etc.

millefiori /ˌmiːlɪfɪˈɔːri/ *noun* M19 Italian (*millefiore*, from *mille* thousand + *fiore*

flowers). A kind of ornamental glass made by fusing together a number of glass rods of different sizes and colours and cutting the mass into sections which form various patterns.

millefleurs /ˈmiːlflə/ *noun* M19 French (literally, 'a thousand flowers'). A pattern of flowers and leaves used in tapestry, on porcelain, or in other decorative items.

millennium /mɪˈlɛnɪəm/ *noun* plural **millenniums**, **millennia** /mɪˈlɛnɪə/ M17 Modern Latin (from Latin *mille* thousand, after BIENNIUM). **1** A period of one thousand years, especially when calculated from the traditional date of the birth of Christ. **2** *Christian Theology* The period of one thousand years during which (according to one interpretation of Revelation 20:1–5) Christ will reign in person on earth. **3** A utopian period of peace, happiness, prosperity, and ideal government. **4** An anniversary of a thousand years. **5** The point at which one period of a thousand years ends and another begins.

mimbar variant of MINBAR.

mimesis /mɪˈmiːsɪs/, /mɪˈmʌɪsɪs/ *noun* M16 Greek (*mimēsis*, from *mimeisthai* to imitate, from *mimos* mime). **1** Imitative representation of the real world in art and literature. **2** *Sociology* The deliberate imitation of the behaviour of one group of people by another as a factor in social change. **3** *Zoology* The close external resemblance of an animal or plant to another animal, plant, or inanimate object.

minaret /ˈmɪnərɛt/, /mɪnəˈrɛt/ *noun* L17 French (or Spanish *minarete*, Italian *minaretto*, from Turkish *mināre* from Arabic *manāra* lighthouse, minaret, from *nāra* to shine). A slender tower or turret connected with a mosque and surrounded by one or more projecting balconies from which a muezzin calls Muslims to prayer.

minaudière /minodjɛr/ *noun* plural pronounced same E18 French (literally 'coquettish woman', from *minauder* to simper, flirt, from *mine* mien). A small decorative handbag without a handle or strap, a clutch bag.

minbar /'mɪnbɑ:/ *noun* (also **mimbar** /'mɪmbɑ:/) M19 Arabic (*minbar*, from *nabara* to raise). A short flight of steps used as a platform by a preacher in a mosque.

minestrone /mɪnɪ'strəʊni/ *noun* L19 Italian. A thick soup containing vegetables, beans, and pasta.

minifundium /mɪnɪ'fʌndɪəm/ *noun* plural **minifundia** /mɪnɪ'fʌndɪə/ (also **minifundio** /mɪnɪ'fʌndɪəʊ/, plural **minifundios**) M20 Modern Latin (or Spanish *minifundio* smallholding: cf. LATIFUNDIUM). (In Latin America) a small farm or property, especially one that is too small to support a single family. Usually in *plural*.

minimus /'mɪnɪməs/ *adjective* L16 Latin. Designating the youngest of several pupils with the same surname or the last to enter a school.

■ As an adjective appended to a surname, the usage is found especially in public schools; thus the eldest and middle brothers of the three of which Smith *minimus* was the youngest would be known respectively as Smith *major* and Smith *minor*. Cf. PRIMUS.

Minnesinger /'mɪnəsɪŋə/ *noun* (also **minnesinger**) E19 German (from *Minne* love + *Singer* (modern *Sänger*) singer). A German lyric poet and singer of the twelfth to fourteenth centuries, who performed songs of courtly love.

minutiae /mɪ'nju:ʃii:/, /mɪ'nju:ʃɪʌɪ/ *noun* plural (also **minutia** /mɪ'nju:ʃɪə/, /mʌɪ'nju:ʃɪə/) M18 Latin (= trifles, *minutia* smallness, from *minutus* small). The small, precise, or trivial details of something: *the minutiae of everyday life*.

minyan /'mɪnjan/ *noun* plural **minyanim** /'mɪnjanɪm/ M18 Hebrew (*minyān*, literally, 'count, reckoning'). The quorum of ten males over thirteen years of age required for traditional Jewish public worship.

mirabelle /'mɪrəbɛl/ *noun* E18 French. **1** A sweet yellow plum-like fruit that is a variety of the greengage; the tree that bears mirabelles. **2** A liqueur distilled from mirabelles, especially those grown in Alsace, France.

mirabile dictu /mɪˌrɑ:bɪleɪ 'dɪktu:/ *interjection* M19 Latin (*mirabile* neuter of *mirabilis* wonderful + *dictu* supine of *dicere* to say). Wonderful to relate.

■ Generally used sarcastically (see quotation).

1996 *New Scientist* '*Mirabile dictu!*' one might exclaim, though few people did. Most used an Anglo-Saxon term: hogwash.

mirador /mira'dor/ *noun* L17 Spanish (from *mirar* to look, observe). A turret or tower attached to a building and providing an extensive view.

mirage /'mɪrɑ:ʒ/, /mɪ'rɑ:ʒ/ *noun* E19 French (from *se mirer* to be reflected or mirrored, from Latin *mirare* look at). **1** An optical illusion caused by atmospheric conditions, especially the false appearance of a distant sheet of water in a desert or on a hot road caused by the refraction of light from the sky by heated air. Also, the appearance in the sky of a reflected image of a distant object, a wavelike appearance of warmed air just above the ground. **2** *figuratively* An unrealistic hope or wish that cannot be achieved; an illusion, a fantasy.

mirepoix /mirpwa/ *noun* plural same L19 French (from the Duc de *Mirepoix* (1699–1757), French diplomat and general). *Cookery* A mixture of sautéed diced vegetables used in sauces etc. or served as a separate dish.

mirliton /'mə:lɪtɒn/ *noun* E19 French (= reed pipe, of imitative origin). **1** A musical instrument resembling a kazoo, with a nasal tone produced by a vibrating membrane. **2** A CHAYOTE. *United States*.

miscellanea /mɪsə'leɪnɪə/ *noun* plural L16 Latin (neuter plural of Latin *miscellaneus* from *miscellus* mixed). Miscellaneous items, especially literary compositions, that have been collected together.

mise en place /miz ɑ̃ plas/ *noun* plural **mises en place** (pronounced same) M20 French (literally 'putting in place'). (In a professional kitchen) the preparation of dishes and ingredients before the beginning of service.

mise en scène /miz ɑ̃ sɛn/ *noun phrase* (also **mise-en-scène**) plural **mises en**

scène (pronounced same) M19 French (literally 'putting on stage'). **1** The arrangement of scenery and stage properties in a play. **2** The setting or surroundings of an event.

> **1 1996** *Spectator* Covent Garden has really done it proud, ... with a stupendously gorgeous staging by that genius of *mise-en-scène* Philip Prowse ...

> **2 1995** *Observer Review* ... the way the book imports real-life VIPs ... and restaurants ... into its narrative suggests the *mise en scène* isn't to be taken as entirely fantastical.

misère /mɪ'zɛ:/, *foreign* /mizɛr/ (*plural same*) *noun* E19 French (= poverty, misery). (In solo whist) a bid by which the caller undertakes not to win any tricks.

miserere /mɪzə'rɪəri/, /mɪzə'rɛ:ri/ *noun* ME Latin (imperative singular of *misereri* to have pity, have mercy, from *miser* wretched). **1** A psalm in which mercy is sought, especially Psalm 51 (50 in the Vulgate), beginning *Miserere mei Deus* 'Have mercy upon me, O God'; a musical setting of this psalm. **2** *transferred* A cry for mercy; a prayer in which mercy is sought. **3** A misericord seat.

mises en place, mises en scène plurals of MISE EN PLACE, MISE EN SCÈNE.

miso /'mi:səʊ/ *noun* E18 Japanese. Paste made from fermented soya beans and barley or rice malt, used in Japanese cookery.

mistral /'mɪstr(ə)l/, /mɪ'strɑ:l/ *noun* E17 French (from Provençal from Latin *magistralis (ventus)* master (wind)). A strong cold north-westerly wind which blows through the Rhône valley and southern France into the Mediterranean, mainly in winter.

> **1996** *Times Magazine* Overtones of Africa must be cheering in mid-winter when the *mistral* sweeps down the Rhône Valley from Siberia.

mit /mɪt/ *preposition & adverb* L19 German (= with). With (me, us, etc.). *Humorous* and *colloquial*.

mittimus /'mɪtɪməs/ *noun* LME Latin (literally, 'we send', the first word of the writ in Latin). **1** A warrant committing a person to prison. **2** A dismissal from office; a notice to quit.

■ First used as the opening word of the writ which transferred records from one court to another (late Middle English to the early 18th century). Sense 2 is chiefly used colloquially and in dialect in *get one's mittimus*, that is, 'be dismissed'.

mitzvah /'mɪtsvə/ *noun* plural **mitzvoth** /'mɪtsvəʊt/ M17 Hebrew (*miṣwāh* commandment). *Judaism* A precept or commandment. Also, a good deed done from religious duty. Cf. BAR MITZVAH, BAT MITZVAH.

moccasin /'mɒkəsɪn/ *noun* E17 Virginia Algonquian (*mockasin*, and in other North American Indian languages). **1** A soft leather slipper or shoe, strictly one without a separate heel, having the sole turned up on all sides and sewn to the upper in a single gathered seam, in a style originating among North American Indians. **2** A venomous North American snake.

moderato /mɒdə'rɑ:təʊ/ *adverb, adjective, & noun* E18 Italian (= moderate). *Music* **A** *adverb & adjective* (Especially as a direction) at a moderate pace or tempo: *allegro moderato*. **B** *noun* plural **moderatos** A passage marked to be performed at a moderate pace.

moderne /mə'dɛ:n/, *foreign* /mɔdɛrn/ *adjective* M20 French (= modern). Relating to a popularization of the art deco style marked by bright colours and austere geometric shapes, or (frequently *derogatory*) any ultra-modern style.

modiste /mɒ'di:st/, *foreign* /mɔdist/ (*plural same*) *noun* M19 French (from *mode* fashion, mode). A fashionable milliner or dressmaker.

> **1996** *Spectator* The result can be seen in the glorious 'Milliner's Shop' ... in which the *modiste* can be seen nestling behind her stock as if sheltering beneath brilliantly coloured tropical flowers.

modus /'məʊdəs/ *noun* plural **modi** /'məʊdʌɪ/, **moduses** L16 Latin. A mode; *especially* the way in which something is done; a mode or manner of operation.

■ Now chiefly in Latin phrases (see following entries) or used elliptically for MODUS OPERANDI.

modus operandi /ˌməʊdəs ɒpəˈrandiː/, /ˌməʊdəs ɒpəˈrandʌɪ/ *noun phrase* M17 Modern Latin (= way of operating). **1** A particular way or method of doing something. **2** The way in which something operates or works.

1 1995 *Spectator* Certainly, as the last *NoW* editor to benefit from the narks, Mr Morgan would be familiar with their *modus operandi*.

modus vivendi /ˌməʊdəs vɪˈvɛndiː/, /ˌməʊdəs vɪˈvɛndʌɪ/ *noun phrase* L19 Modern Latin (= way of living). A way of living or coping, especially an arrangement or agreement allowing conflicting parties to coexist peacefully, either indefinitely or until a final settlement is reached.

1996 *Times* It is the *modus vivendi* of Christianity which underpins European thought.

mohel /ˈməʊ(h)(ə)l/ *noun* M17 Hebrew (*mōhēl*). A Jew who performs the rite of circumcision.

moi /mwa/ *personal pronoun* L20 French (= me). Me; I, myself.

■ Since the late 1970s in humorous use as a pretentious reference to oneself. Chief popularizer of the expression was the character Miss Piggy in the television series *The Muppets*, the children's puppet show created by Jim Henson, and it was then also taken up by adult shows.

1996 *Times: Weekend* But naturally. Why do anything by halves? Cynical, moi? Not at all.

moire /mwa:/ *noun* M17 French (later form of *mouaire* mohair (the original fabric)). Silk fabric that has been subjected to heat and pressure rollers after weaving to give it a rippled appearance.

moiré /ˈmwa:reɪ/ *adjective* E19 French (past participle of *moirer* to give a watered appearance to, from as preceding). (Of silk) having a rippled, lustrous finish; having a pattern of irregular wavy lines like that of moire.

moksha /ˈmɒkʃə/ *noun* L18 Sanskrit (*mokṣa*, from *muc* to set free, release). *Hinduism* and *Jainism* The final release of the soul from the cycle of rebirth impelled by the law of karma; the transcendent state so attained. Also called *mukti*.

mole /ˈmoli/, /ˈməʊli/ *noun* M20 Mexican Spanish (from Nahuatl *molli* sauce, stew).

A highly spiced Mexican sauce made chiefly from chilli peppers and chocolate, served with meat.

molto /ˈmɒltəʊ/ *adverb* E19 Italian (from Latin *multus* much). *Music* Very.

■ Usually in directions modifying adjectives or adverbs from Italian: *molto maestoso*; *allegro molto*.

monad /ˈmɒnad/, /ˈməʊnad/ *noun* plural **monades** /ˈmɒnədiːz/ M16 French (*monade* or its source late Latin *monas, monad-* from Greek, from *monos* alone). **1** A single unit; the number one, unity. Now chiefly *Historical*, with reference to ancient Greek philosophy, in which the numbers were regarded as being generated from the unitary one. **2** *Philosophy* (Especially in the philosophy of Leibniz) an indivisible and hence ultimately simple entity, such as an atom or person. **3** *Biology* A single-celled organism, especially a flagellate protozoan, or a single cell. *Dated*.

mon ami /mɔn ami/ *noun phrase* (also (feminine) **mon amie**) plural **mes amis** (feminine **mes amies**) /mez ami/ L18 French. (As a form of address) my friend.

mon cher /mɔ̃ ʃɛr/ *noun phrase* L17 French. (As a form of address to a male) my dear, my dear fellow.

mondaine /mɔ̃dɛn/ *adjective & noun* L19 French (feminine of *mondain*). **A** *adjective* Belonging to fashionable society; worldly. **B** *noun* plural pronounced same. A fashionable woman. *Dated*. Cf. DEMI-MONDAINE.

mondo /ˈmɒndəʊ/ *adverb & adjective* M20 Italian (= world). Used in reference to something very striking or remarkable of its kind (often in conjunction with a pseudo-Italian noun or adjective): *I think it's going to be mondo weirdo this year, Andy*. Colloquial, chiefly United States.

■ This use of *mondo* derives ultimately from *Mondo Cane* (literally 'Dog's World'), the title of an Italian film (1961) showing bizarre behaviour (released in 1963 in the English-speaking world as *A Dog's Life*). The film became a cult and was imitated in similar titles such as *Mondo Bizarro* (1966). The use of the word in

223   **monocoque | morale**

English arose through the interpretation of, for instance, *mondo bizarro* as 'very bizarre'. In the 1980s *mondo* became simply an intensifier in American slang. It was taken up in this way by the children's comic-book characters the Teenage Mutant Ninja Turtles (in Britain, the Teenage Mutant Hero Turtles) in phrases such as *mondo cool* to express approval, and the usage spread to Britain during the Turtlemania of 1989–90.

monocoque /ˈmɒnə(ʊ)kɒk/ *noun* E20 French (from *mono-* single + *coque* shell). An aircraft or vehicle structure in which the chassis is integral with the body.

monsoon /mɒnˈsuːn/ *noun* L16 Early Modern Dutch (*monssoen* (modern *moesson*, influenced by French forms) from Portuguese *monção* (cf. Old Spanish *monzon*) from Arabic *mawsim* season, fixed period, from *wasama* to brand, mark). A seasonal prevailing wind in the region of the Indian subcontinent and south-east Asia, blowing from the south-west between May and September and bringing rain (the *wet monsoon*), or from the north-east between October and April (the *dry monsoon*). **b** The rainfall which accompanies the wet monsoon; the rainy season.

mons pubis /mɒnz ˈpjuːbɪs/ *noun phrase* L19 Latin (= mount of the pubes). *Anatomy* The rounded mass of fatty tissue lying over the joint of the pubic bones, in women typically more prominent and also called the MONS VENERIS.

monstre sacré /mɔ̃str sakre/ *noun phrase* plural **monstres sacrés** (pronounced same) M20 French (literally, 'sacred monster'). A striking, eccentric, or controversial public figure.

   1995 *Spectator* Since Scruton was demolishing the claims of much of the painting and sculpture featured in the Tate, its director, Nicholas Serota, the *monstre sacré* of London's modern art establishment, found it convenient to be in New York.

mons Veneris /mɒnz ˈvɛnərɪs/ *noun phrase* E17 Latin (= mount of Venus). *Anatomy* The rounded mass of fatty tissue on a female's lower abdomen, above the vulva. Cf. MONS PUBIS.

montage /mɒnˈtɑːʒ/, /ˈmɒntɑːʒ/ *noun* E20 French (from *monter* to mount). **1** The technique of selecting, editing, and piecing together separate sections of film to form a continuous whole; a sequence of film made using the technique of montage. **2** The process or technique of producing a new composite whole by combining several different pictures, pieces of music, or other elements, so that they blend with or into one another; the result of such a process.

monte /ˈmɒnti/ *noun* E19 Spanish (= mountain, pile of cards left after dealing). A Spanish and Spanish-American gambling game usually played with a pack of forty cards. Also (in full *three-card monte*), a form of three-card trick.

montuno /mɒnˈtuːnəʊ/ *noun* plural **montunos** M20 American Spanish (= native to mountains, wild, untamed). **1** A traditional costume worn by men from Panama, consisting of white cotton short trousers and an embroidered shirt. **2** An improvised passage in a rumba.

moquette /mɒˈkɛt/ *noun* M19 French (perhaps from obsolete Italian *mocaiardo* mohair). A thick pile fabric used for carpets and upholstery.

   1996 *Times The Virgin in the Garden* supplies the interior decor of a Fifties lower middle-class home in such evocative detail that you can feel the texture of the uncut moquette.

mor /mɔː/ *noun* M20 Danish (= humus). *Soil Science* Humus formed under acid conditions.

moraine /məˈreɪn/ *noun* L18 French (from Savoyard Italian *morena*, from southern French *mor(re)* muzzle, snout, from Proto-Romance word). *Geology* A mass or rocks and sediment carried down and deposited by a glacier, typically as ridges at its edges or extremity.

morale /məˈrɑːl/ *noun* M18 French (*moral*, respelt to indicate stress; cf. LOCALE). The mental and emotional attitude of a group or individual with regard to confidence, willingness, hope, etc.; degree of contentment with one's lot or situation.

moratorium /mɒrə'tɔ:rɪəm/ *noun* plural **moratoriums**, **moratoria** /mɒrə'tɔ:rɪə/ L19 Modern Latin (use as noun of neuter singular of late Latin *moratorius* delaying, from *morat-* past participial stem of *morari* to delay). **1** A deliberate temporary suspension or prohibition of some activity. **2** *Law* A legal authorization to a debtor to postpone payment for a certain time; the period of such a postponement.

1 *1995 New Scientist* ... there are plenty of grey whales migrating past Vancouver Island these days, after a decade-long moratorium on commercial whaling.

morbilli /mɔ:'bɪlʌɪ/ *noun plural* M16 Medieval Latin (plural of *morbillus* pustule, spot characteristic of measles, diminutive of Latin *morbus* disease). *Medicine* (The spots characteristic of) measles.

morceau /mɔ:'səʊ/, *foreign* /mɔrso/ *noun* plural **morceaux** /mɔ:'səʊz/, *foreign* /mɔrso/ M18 French (Old French *morsel*, *morcel* diminutive of *mors* from Latin *morsus* bite, from *mors-* past participial stem of *mordere* to bite). A short literary or musical composition.

mordent /'mɔ:d(ə)nt/ *noun* E19 German (from Italian *mordente* use as noun of verbal adjective from *mordere* to bite, from Proto-Romance alteration of Latin *mordere*). *Music* An ornament consisting of one rapid alternation of a written note with the note immediately below or above it in the scale. Cf. PRALLTRILLER.

mores /'mɔ:reɪz/, /'mɔ:ri:z/ *noun plural* L19 Latin (plural of *mos* manner, custom). **1** The essential or characteristic customs, assumptions, and conventions of a society or community. Cf. O TEMPORA, O MORES. **2** *Zoology* The habits, behaviour, etc., of a group of animals of the same kind.

1 *1996 Times* By posthumously according his official and unofficial families equal status, the former President held up a strange mirror to French *mores*.

morgue /mɔ:g/ *noun* M19 French (proper name of a Paris mortuary). **1** A mortuary. **2** A place that is quiet, gloomy, or cold. **3** In a newspaper office, the collection of miscellaneous information for use in future obituaries. *Colloquial.*

Morisco /mə'rɪskəʊ/ *noun* plural **Morisco(e)s** M16 Spanish (from *Moro* Moor). A Moor in Spain, especially one who had accepted Christian baptism.

morituri te salutamus /mɒrɪ,tʊri teɪ salʊ'ta:məs/ *interjection* (also **morituri te salutant** and other variants) E18 Latin (= we who are about to die salute you). *Roman History* The words addressed by gladiators to the Roman emperor as they entered the arena.

■ Quoted from Suetonius *Life of Claudius* xxi.6. Used allusively in English in many variant forms by people facing danger or difficulty.

mortadella /mɔ:tə'dɛlə/ *noun* plural **mortadellas**, **mortadelle** /mɔ:tə'dɛli/ E17 Italian (irregular from Latin *murtatum* (sausage) seasoned with myrtle berries). A type of light pink, smooth-textured Italian sausage containing pieces of fat, typically served in slices.

moscato /mə'ska:təʊ/ *noun* plural **moscatos** E20 Italian. A sweet Italian dessert wine.

moshav /'məʊʃɑ:v/ *noun* plural **moshavim** /'məʊʃɑ:vɪm/ M20 Modern Hebrew (*mōšāḇ* dwelling, colony). (In Israel) a group of agricultural smallholdings worked partly on a cooperative and partly on an individual basis.

mosso /'mɒsəʊ/ *adverb* L19 Italian (past participle of *muovere* to move). *Music* (Especially as a direction) rapidly, with animation.

mot /mo/, /məʊ/ (*plural same*) *noun* L16 French (= word, saying, from Proto-Gallo-Romance alteration of popular Latin *muttum* related to Latin *muttire* to murmur). A witty saying; a BON MOT.

1996 Country Life If I should leave my notebook open on the kitchen seat, I may find that some priceless thought, some *mot*, or maybe merely some item on a shopping list, has been eaten off the page.

mot de Cambronne /mo də kambrɔn/, /ˌməʊ də kam'brɒn/, *noun phrase* French (literally, 'Cambronne's word'). The French expletive *merde!*

■ The reputed reply of General Pierre Cambronne (1770–1842) when called upon to surrender at the Battle of Waterloo. The official version of what he said—*La garde meurt mais ne se rend pas* 'The Guard dies, but does not surrender'—seems to have been a happy journalistic invention, since the general himself denied saying it.

motif /məʊ'tiːf/ *noun* M19 French. **1** A decorative image or design, especially a repeated one forming a pattern; a decorative device applied to a garment or textile. **2** A dominant or recurring idea in an artistic work; *Music* a leitmotif or figure. **3** *Biochemistry* A distinctive sequence on a protein or DNA, having a three-dimensional structure that allows binding interactions to occur.

mot juste /mo ʒyst/, /məʊ 'ʒuːst/ *noun phrase* plural **mots justes** *(pronounced same)* E20 French (= exact word). The precisely appropriate word or expression.

moto /'məʊtəʊ/ *noun* M18 Italian. *Music* Movement, pace.
■ In various musical directions; cf. CON MOTO.

moto perpetuo /ˌməʊtəʊ pə'pɛtjʊəʊ/ *noun phrase* plural **moti perpetui** /ˌməʊtiː pə'pɛtjʊiː/ L19 Italian (= perpetual motion). A rapid instrumental composition consisting mainly of notes of equal length.

motte /mɒt/ *noun* L19 French (= mound). *History* A large man-made earthen mound with a flattened top, forming the site of a castle or camp.

motto /'mɒtəʊ/ *noun* plural **mottos, mottoes** L16 Italian (from Proto-Gallo-Romance word whence also MOT). **1** A short sentence or phrase chosen as encapsulating the beliefs or ideals of an individual, family, or institution; a maxim adopted as a rule of conduct. **2** *Music* A recurrent phrase having some symbolical significance.

motu proprio /ˌməʊtuː 'prəʊprɪəʊ/, /ˌməʊtuː 'prɒprɪəʊ/ *noun phrase* plural **motu proprios** E17 Latin (= of one's own volition). An edict issued by the Pope personally to the Roman Catholic Church, or to a part of it.

moue /muː/ *noun* M19 French (earlier having the sense 'lip'). A pouting expression used to convey annoyance or distaste.

moujik variant of MUZHIK.

moule /mul/ *noun* plural pronounced same L19 French. *Cookery* A mussel.
■ Usually in plural in names of dishes, as in *moules marinières* (mussels served in their shells and cooked in a wine and onion sauce).

moulin /'muːlɪn/, *foreign* /mulɛ̃/ *(plural same) noun* M19 French (literally, 'mill'). A vertical or nearly vertical shaft in a glacier, formed by surface water percolating through a crack in the ice.

moulvi /'muːlvi/ *noun* (also **maulvi** /'maʊlvi/, **molvi**) E17 Urdu (*maulvī* from Arabic *mawlawī* judicial (used as noun), from *mawlā* mullah). (Especially in the Indian subcontinent) a Muslim doctor of the law, an imam.

mousaka variant of MOUSSAKA.

moussaka /muːˈsɑːkə/, /muːsəˈkɑː/ *noun* (also **mousaka**) M20 Turkish (*musakka*, ultimately from Arabic *musakkā*; cf. modern Greek *mousakas*, Romanian *musaca*, Albanian, Bulgarian *musaka*, etc.). A Greek dish made of minced lamb, aubergines, and tomatoes, with a cheese sauce.

mousse /muːs/ *noun* M19 French (= moss, froth). **1** A sweet or savoury dish made as a smooth, light mass in which the main ingredient is whipped with cream and egg white. Frequently with specifying word: *chocolate mousse, salmon mousse*. **2** A soft, light, aerated gel such as a soap preparation: *shower mousse*; a frothy preparation that is applied to hair, enabling it to be styled more easily. **3** A frothy brown emulsion of seawater and oil produced by the weathering of oil spills and resistant to dispersal. More fully *chocolate mousse*.

mousseline /'muːsliːn/ *noun* L17 French. **1** A very fine, semi-opaque fabric similar to muslin. **2** A soft, light sweet or savoury mousse. **3** Hollandaise sauce that has been made frothy with whipped cream or egg white, served mainly with fish or asparagus. Also *sauce mousseline*.

mousseux /musø/, /mu:ˈsəː/ *adjective & noun* E19 French (from as *mousse* froth). **A** *adjective* (Of wine) sparkling: *vin mousseux.* **B** *noun* plural same. A sparkling wine.

moustache /məˈstɑːʃ/ *noun* (also **mustache**) L16 French (from Italian *mostaccio, mostacchio* from medieval Latin *mustacia*, ultimately from Greek *mustax, mustak-* upper lip, moustache). A strip of hair left to grow above the upper lip. **b** (*moustaches*) A long moustache. **c** A growth similar to a moustache, or a marking that resembles one, round the mouth of some animals.

moyen sensuel /mwajɛ̃ sɑ̃sɥɛl/ *adjective phrase* (also **moyen-sensuel**) E20 French. Of an average sensual and materialistic character.

■ Generally in the phrase HOMME MOYEN SENSUEL.

1996 *Spectator* He is told to 'go and sell that thou hast, and give to the poor', but with the proviso: 'If thou wilt be perfect...and...have treasure in heaven'—to which the *moyen sensuel* capitalist could reply: 'who is talking about perfection, and surely any place in Heaven is treasure?'

mozetta variant of MOZZETTA.

mozzarella /mɒtsəˈrɛlə/ *noun* E20 Italian (diminutive of *mozza* a kind of cheese, from *mozzare* to cut off). A firm white Italian cheese made from buffalo or cow's milk, used especially in pizzas and salads.

mozzetta /məʊˈzɛtə/, /məʊˈtsɛtə/ *noun* (also **mozetta**) L18 Italian (shortened form of *almozzetta*, from medieval Latin *almucia* amice). *Roman Catholic Church* A short cape with a hood, worn by the Pope, cardinals, and some other ecclesiastics.

mu /mjuː/ *noun* ME Greek. **1** The twelfth letter (M, μ) of the Greek alphabet, transliterated as 'm'. **2** Plural same. One micrometre (micron). Usually denoted by μ. **3** *Physics modifier* Relating to muons.

muchacha /mʊˈtʃɑːtʃə/ *noun* L19 Spanish (feminine of next). (In Spain and Spanish-speaking countries) a young woman; a female servant.

muchacho /mʊˈtʃɑːtʃəʊ/ *noun* plural **muchachos** L16 Spanish. (In Spain and Spanish-speaking countries) a young man; a male servant.

mudra /ˈmʌdrə/, /ˈmuːdrə/ *noun* E19 Sanskrit (*mudrā* seal, sign, token). A symbolic hand gesture used in Hindu religious ceremonies and statuary, and in Indian dance. Also, a movement or pose in yoga.

muesli /ˈmuːzli/, /ˈmjuːzli/ *noun* Swiss German. A mixture of oats and other cereals, dried fruit, and nuts, eaten with milk at breakfast. *Chiefly British.*

muezzin /muːˈɛzɪn/ *noun* L16 Arabic (dialectal variant of Arabic *muˈaddin* active participle of *ˈaddana* to call to prayer, from *ˈudn* ear). A man who calls Muslims to prayer from the minaret of a mosque.

mufti /ˈmʌfti/ *noun* L16 Arabic (*muftī* active participle of *aftā* to decide a point of law (related to FATWA)). A Muslim cleric or legal expert empowered to give rulings on religious matters; in the Ottoman Empire, a chief legal authority, especially of a large city (also *Grand Mufti*).

■ *Mufti* in the sense of 'plain or informal clothes worn by a person who wears a uniform for their job' (E19) may be a facetious use of this word, but its origins are uncertain.

mujahedin /ˌmʊdʒɑːhɪˈdiːn/ *plural noun* (also **mujahidin, mujaheddin,** or **mujahideen**) M20 Persian and Arabic (*mujāhidīn*, colloquial plural of *mujāhid*, denoting a person who fights a jihad). Guerrilla fighters in Islamic countries, especially those who are fighting against non-Muslim forces.

mukhtar /ˈmʊktɑː/ *noun* E20 Turkish (*muhtar* from Arabic *muḳtār* passive participle of *iḳtāra* to choose, elect). (In Turkey and some Arab countries) the head of the local government of a town or village; a minor provincial official.

mukti /ˈmʌkti/, /ˈmʊkti/ *noun* L18 Sanskrit (= release, from *muc* to set free, release). *Hinduism* and *Jainism* MOKSHA.

mulatto /mjuːˈlatəʊ/ *noun* plural **mulatto(e)s** L16 Spanish and Portuguese (*mulato* young mule, mulatto, irregularly from *mulo* mule). A person having one white and one black parent. *Dated, offensive.*

muleta /məˈleɪtə/ *noun* M19 Spanish. A red cloth fixed to a stick, brandished by a matador during a bullfight.

> **1996** *Spectator* Because some of the bulls tired quickly, opportunities for assessing performances with the *muleta* were limited.

mulga /ˈmʌlgə/ *noun* M19 Aboriginal. **1** Any of several small acacia, forming dense scrub in dry inland areas of Australia and sometimes used for fodder (also *mulga tree*); the land covered with such vegetation, (*colloquial*) the outback. **2** A thing made of the wood of a mulga tree, especially a club or shield. **3** A rumour, a message, a (false) report; the grapevine. In full *mulga wire*. *Australian slang.*

mullah /ˈmʌlə/, /ˈmʊlə/ *noun* E17 Persian (Urdu *mullā*, Turkish *molla* from Arabic *mawlā*). A Muslim learned in Islamic theology and sacred law.

multum in parvo /ˌmʌltəm ɪn ˈpɑːvəʊ/ *noun phrase* M18 Latin (= much in little). A great deal in a small space.

mumpsimus /ˈmʌmpsɪməs/ *noun* M16 pseudo-Latin (erroneously for Latin *sumpsimus* in the passage in the Eucharistic service that runs *quod in ore sumpsimus* 'which we have taken into the mouth'). **1** A traditional custom or idea obstinately adhered to although shown to be unreasonable. **2** A person who obstinately adheres to old customs or ideas, in spite of clear evidence that they are wrong or unreasonable.

■ The origin is Richard Pace's anecdote in *De Fructu* (1517) of an illiterate English priest who garbled the passage in the Mass quoted above by substituting the nonsense word *mumpsimus*. When corrected, he replied, 'I will not change my old mumpsimus for your new sumpsimus'. Now only in literary use. Cf. SUMPSIMUS.

mung /mʌŋ/, /muːŋ/ *noun* E19 Hindi (*mūng*). **1** A small round green bean. **2** The tropical Old World plant that yields mung beans, commonly grown as a source of bean sprouts.

munshi /ˈmuːnʃiː/ *noun* (also **moonshee**) L18 Persian and Urdu (*munšī* from Arabic *munši'* writer, author, active participle of *'anša'a* to write (a book)). (In the Indian subcontinent) a secretary or language teacher.

murex /ˈmjʊərɛks/ *noun* plural **murices** /ˈmjʊərɪsiːz/, **murexes** L16 Latin (perhaps related to Greek *muax* sea mussel). Any of various spiny-shelled predatory gastropod molluscs of the genus *Murex* and related genera, of tropical and temperate seas, from some of which the dye Tyrian purple was formerly obtained.

muscadel variant of MUSCATEL.

muscae volitantes /ˌmʌsiː ˌvɒlɪˈtantiːz / *noun plural* M18 Latin (= flying flies). *Medicine* Dark specks which appear to float before the eyes, frequently due to particles in the vitreous humour of the eye.

muscat /ˈmʌskat/ *noun* M16 Old and Modern French (from Provençal (= Italian MOSCATO), from *musc* musk). A variety of white, red, or black grape with a musky scent, grown in warm climates for wine or raisins or as table grapes; a wine made from muscat grapes, especially a sweet or fortified white wine.

muscatel /mʌskəˈtɛl/ *noun* (also **muscadel** /mʌskəˈdɛl/) LME Old French (*muscadel, muscatel* (= Italian *moscatello*) from Provençal diminutive of MUSCAT). **1** A muscat grape, especially as grown for drying to make raisins. In full *muscatel grape*. **2** A raisin made from the muscatel grape; a wine made from muscatel grapes.

musée /myze/ (*plural same*), /ˈmjuːzeɪ/ *noun* M17 French (from Latin *mus(a)eum* library, study, from Greek *mouseion* seat of the Muses). (In France and French-speaking countries) a museum.

musette /mjuːˈzɛt/ *noun* LME Old and Modern French (diminutive of *muse* bagpipe). **1** A kind of small bagpipe played with bellows, common in the French court in the 17th–18th centuries and in later folk music. **2** A soft pastoral air imitating the sound of the musette; a dance performed to such music. **3** A small and simple variety of oboe, used chiefly in 19th-century France. **4** A small knapsack. Also *musette bag*.

musica ficta /ˌmjuːzɪkə ˈfɪktə/ *noun phrase* E19 Latin (literally, 'feigned music'). *Music* (In early contrapuntal music) the introduction by a performer of sharps, flats, and other accidentals to avoid unacceptable intervals.

musicale /mjuːzɪˈkɑːl/ *noun* L19 French ((*soirée*) *musicale* musical evening). A musical gathering or concert, especially at a private address. *United States*.

musique concrète /myzik kɔ̃krɛt/, /mjuːˌziːk kɒnˈkrɛt/ *noun phrase* M20 French (= concrete music). Music constructed by mixing recorded sounds, first developed by experimental composers in the 1940s.

mustache variant of MOUSTACHE.

mutatis mutandis /mjuːˌtɑːtɪs mjuːˈtandɪs/, /muːˌtɑːtɪs/, /mjuːˈtandiːs/ *adverb phrase* L15 Latin (literally, 'things being changed that have to be changed'). (Used when comparing two or more cases or situations) making necessary alterations while not affecting the main point at issue.

> **1962** S. E. Finer *Man on Horseback* What is said of the army here is to be taken also to apply, *mutatis mutandis*, to the air force and the navy.

mutuel /ˈmjuːtʃʊəl/, /ˈmjuːtjʊəl/, *foreign* /mytɥɛl/ (*plural same*) *noun* E20 French (abbreviation of PARI-MUTUEL). (In betting) a totalizator, a PARI-MUTUEL. Chiefly *North American*.

muumuu /ˈmuːmuː/ *noun* E20 Hawaiian (*muʻu muʻu*, literally, 'cut off', from the original absence of a yoke). A woman's loose, brightly coloured dress, especially one worn in Hawaii.

muzhik /muːˈʒɪk/ *noun* (also **moujik**) M16 Russian. *History* A Russian peasant.

mystagogue /ˈmɪstəgɒg/ *noun* M16 French (Latin *mystagogus* from Greek *mustagōgos*, from *mustēs* initiated person + *agōgos* leading, from *agein* to lead). A person who introduces others to religious mysteries; a teacher or propounder of mystical doctrines.

mystique /mɪˈstiːk/ *noun* L19 French. A quality of mystery, glamour, or power associated with someone or something; an air of secrecy surrounding a particular activity or subject that makes it impressive or baffling to those without specialized knowledge.

mythoi plural of MYTHOS.

mythopoeia /ˌmɪθə(ʊ)ˈpiːə/ *noun* M20 Greek (*muthopoiia*). The creation of a myth or myths.

mythos /ˈmʌɪθɒs/ *noun* plural **mythoi** /ˈmʌɪθɔɪ/ M18 Greek (*muthos* myth). **1** A myth or body of myths: *the Arthurian mythos*. **2** A traditional or recurrent narrative theme or pattern; a standard plot in literature.

■ *Mythos* and its Latin derivative *mythus* (E19), both now used solely in literary contexts, were current before the anglicized *myth* (M19), which is now the form used in all general contexts for sense 1.

naan variant of NAN.

naartjie /ˈnɑːtʃi/, /ˈnɑːki/ noun (also **naartje**) L18 Afrikaans (from Tamil *nārattai* citrus). (In South Africa) a soft loose-skinned tangerine or mandarin orange.

nabi /ˈnɑːbiː/ noun plural (in sense 1) **nebiʻim** /nɛˈbɪɪm/, (in sense 2) **nabis** (also **Nabi**) L19 Hebrew (*nābī* prophet). **1** *Theology* A person inspired to speak the word of God; a prophet; *specifically* a prophetical writer of the Old Testament and Hebrew Scriptures. **2** A member of a group of late 19th-century French post-Impressionists following the artistic theories of the French painter Paul Gauguin (1848–1903).

nabob /ˈneɪbɒb/ noun E17 Portuguese (*nababo* or Spanish *nabab* from Urdu *nawwāb*, *nawāb* deputy governor: cf. NAWAB). **1** *History* (The title of) any of certain Muslim officials acting as deputy governors of provinces or districts in the Mogul Empire; a governor of an Indian town or district. **2** A person of conspicuous wealth or high status; *specifically* a European returning from India with a large fortune acquired there.

nacarat /ˈnakərat/ noun M18 French (perhaps from Spanish and Portuguese *nacarado*, from *nacar* nacre). A bright orange-red colour.

nacelle /nəˈsɛl/ noun E20 French (from late Latin *navicella*, diminutive of Latin *navis* ship). **1** A streamlined casing on the outside of an aircraft or motor vehicle, especially one housing an aircraft engine. **2** The passenger compartment of an airship.
■ Originally used in sense 2. In the core sense of 'a small boat', *nacelle* appears in Caxton's *Golden Legend* (1483), but it never achieved much currency in this sense, and seems not to have been used in English between the late 15th century and its modern reintroduction.

naches /ˈnʌxəs/ noun (also **nachas**) E20 Yiddish (*nakhes* from Hebrew *naḵaṯ* contentment). A sense of pleasure or pride, especially at the achievements of one's children; joy, gratification. *United States*.

nacho /ˈnatʃəʊ/ noun plural **nachos** M20 (Mexican) Spanish (origin uncertain: perhaps from Mexican Spanish *Nacho* pet form of male forename *Ignacio*, but cf. Spanish *nacho* flat-nosed). A small piece of tortilla, typically topped with melted cheese and spices.
■ Perhaps the invention of a Mexican chef, Ignacio Anaya, who worked in the Piedras Niegras area in the 1940s, the dish was originally found only in the northern Mexico–Texas area and did not spread much beyond there until the 1970s. Taken up by the fast-food chains in the 1980s, it is now a popular food item in Europe too. *Nacho* is always used in the plural except when attributive (see quotation).
1983 *Fortune* The chain of Mexican fast-food restaurants is busily expanding its product line to include…a nacho side dish, and a salad.

Nacht und Nebel /ˌnaxt ʊnt ˈneːb(ə)l/ noun phrase M20 German (literally, 'night and fog'). A situation characterized by mystery or obscurity, especially as associated with Nazi Germany between 1941 and 1945.
■ Under a German decree issued in December 1941, offending nationals in occupied countries disappeared suddenly and without trace, frequently during the night.

nacre /ˈneɪkə/ noun L16 French (probably ultimately of oriental origin). Mother-of-pearl.

nada /ˈnada/, /ˈnadə/ noun M20 Spanish (= nothing, from Latin (*res*) *nata* thing born, insignificant thing). Nothing.
■ Used especially in informal American English.

nadir /ˈneɪdɪə/ noun LME Old and Modern French ((also Spanish, Italian) from Arabic *naẓīr* (*as-samt*) opposite (the zenith)). **1** The lowest or most unsuccessful point in a situation. **2** *Astronomy* The point on the celestial sphere diametrically opposite to the zenith; the point directly below an observer.

naevus /ˈniːvəs/ noun (also **nevus**) plural **naevi** /ˈniːvʌɪ/ M19 Latin. A birthmark or mole on the skin, especially a birthmark in the form of a raised red patch.

naga /ˈnɑːɡə/ noun L18 Sanskrit (*nāga* serpent, snake). *Indian Mythology* A member of a race of semi-divine creatures, half-snake and half-human, associated with water and sometimes with mystical initiation.

nagana /nəˈɡɑːnə/ noun L19 Zulu (*nakane*). A disease of cattle, antelope, and other livestock in southern Africa, characterized by fever, lethargy, and oedema caused by trypanosome parasites transmitted by tsetse-flies.

naïf /nʌɪˈiːf/, /nɑːˈiːf/ adjective & noun plural of noun pronounced same L16 French (see NAIVE). **A** adjective NAIVE sense 1. **b** NAIVE sense 3. **B** noun A naive or ingenuous person.

naive /nʌɪˈiːv/, /nɑːˈiːv/ adjective (also **naïve**) M17 Old and Modern French (*naïve*, feminine of *naïf* from Latin *nativus* native, natural; cf. NAÏF). **1** (Of a person or action) showing a lack of experience, wisdom, or judgement. **2** (Of a person) natural and unaffected; innocent. **3** Of or denoting art produced in a style which deliberately rejects sophisticated artistic techniques and has a bold directness resembling a child's work, typically in bright colours with little or no perspective.

naïveté /naivte/, /nʌɪˈiːvteɪ/ noun plural pronounced same L17 French (from as preceding). **1** A naive action, remark, etc. **2** The state or quality of being naive.

namaskar /ˌnʌməsˈkɑː/ noun M20 Hindi (from Sanskrit *namaskāra*, from *namas* bowing + *kāra* action). A traditional Indian greeting or gesture of respect, made by bringing the palms together before the face or chest and bowing. ■ In Thailand a similar gesture is called *wai*.

namaste /ˈnʌməsteɪ/ noun & interjection M20 Hindi (from Sanskrit *namas* bowing, obeisance + *te* dative of *tvam* you (singular)). **A** noun A NAMASKAR. **B** interjection Expressing respectful greeting (said when giving a namaskar).

nan /nɑːn/ noun (also **naan**) E20 Persian and Urdu (*nān*). (In Indian cookery) a type of leavened bread, typically of teardrop shape and traditionally cooked in a clay oven.

naos /ˈneɪɒs/ noun L18 Greek (= temple). The inner chamber or sanctuary of a Greek or other ancient temple; also *Christian Church*, the main body or knave of a Byzantine church.

nappe /nap/ noun L19 French (literally, 'tablecloth'). *Geology* A sheet of rock which has moved sideways over neighbouring strata, as a result of an overthrust or folding.

narcosis /nɑːˈkəʊsɪs/ noun plural **narcoses** /nɑːˈkəʊsiːz/ L17 Greek (*narkōsis*, from *narkoun* to make numb). *Medicine* A state of stupor, drowsiness, or unconsciousness produced by drugs; the production of this state.

narghile /ˈnɑːɡɪleɪ/ noun (also **narghileh**) M18 Persian (*nārgīl* coconut, hookah, from Sanskrit *nārikela* coconut; partly through French *nargíleh*, *narguilé* from Turkish *nargile* from Persian *nārgīl*). An oriental tobacco pipe with a long tube that draws smoke through water; a hookah.

narthex /ˈnɑːθɛks/ noun L17 Latin (from Greek *narthēx* giant fennel, stick, casket, narthex). An antechamber, porch, or distinct area at the western entrance of some early Christian churches, separated by a railing; an antechamber or large porch in a modern church.

natatorium /ˌneɪtəˈtɔːrɪəm/ noun L19 Late Latin (use as noun of *natatorius* of a swimmer). A swimming pool, especially one that is indoors. *North American*.

natura naturans /naˌtjʊərə 'natjʊranz/ *noun phrase* E19 Latin (Latin *natura* nature + medieval Latin *naturans* (present participle) creating, from *naturare*). *Philosophy* Nature as creative; the essential creative power or act. Cf. next.

■ This Latin phrase is found from the 12th century in translators of the Islamic philosopher Averroës, and from the mid 13th century in a British source.

natura naturata /naˌtjʊərə natjʊ'rɑːtə/ *noun phrase* E19 Latin (Latin *natura* nature + medieval Latin *naturata* (past participle) created, from *naturare*). *Philosophy* Nature as created; the natural phenomena and forces in which creation is manifested. Cf. preceding.

nature morte /natyr mɔrt/ *noun phrase* plural **natures mortes** (pronounced same) E20 French. A still life.

■ Used as a descriptive term in French art since the 18th century.

navarin /'nav(ə)rɪn/, *foreign* /navarɛ̃/ (*plural same*) *noun* L19 French. A casserole of lamb or mutton with vegetables.

nawab /nə'wɑːb/, /nə'wɔːb/ *noun* (also (as a title) **Nawab**) M18 Urdu (*nawāb* from Urdu, Persian *nawwāb* variant of *nuwwāb* plural (used as singular) of (Arabic) *nā'ib* deputy; cf. NABOB). (In the Indian subcontinent) a native governor during the time of the Mogul empire (*historical*); a Muslim nobleman or person of high status.

NB abbreviation of NOTA BENE.

né /neɪ/, *foreign* /ne/ *adjective* M20 French (= born, masculine past participle of *naître* to be born). Born with the name, originally called: placed before the name by which a man was originally known.

■ Much more usual in the feminine NÉE.

nebbish /'nɛbɪʃ/ *noun & adjective* (also **nebbich**) L19 Yiddish (*nebech* poor thing). **A** *noun* A nobody, a nonentity, a submissive timid person. Also as *interjection*, expressing commiseration, dismay, etc. **B** *adjective* (Of a person) innocuous, ineffectual; timid, submissive. *Colloquial*.

nebulé /'nɛbjʊleɪ/ *adjective* (also **nebuly** /'nɛbjʊli/) M16 French (*nébulé* from medieval Latin *nebulatus* clouded (the curves being thought of as representing clouds), from *nebula* mist). *Heraldry* Divided or edged with a line formed of deeply interlocking curves.

nécessaire /nesɛsɛr/ *noun* plural pronounced same E19 French (= necessary (thing)). A small ornamental case for pencils, scissors, tweezers, and other small items.

necrosis /nɛ'krəʊsɪs/ *noun* plural **necroses** /nɛ'krəʊsiːz/ M17 Modern Latin (from Greek *nekrōsis* state of death, from *nekroun* to kill, mortify). *Medicine* and *Biology* The death of most or all of the cells in an organ or tissue due to disease, injury, or failure of the blood supply.

née /neɪ/, *foreign* /ne/ *adjective* (also **nee**) M18 French (= born, feminine past participle of *naître* be born; cf. NÉ). Born with the name, originally called.

■ Normally follows a woman's married name to indicate her family name before she married, as in 'Julia Smith *née* Jones'.

negligée /'nɛglɪʒeɪ/ *noun* (also **negligee**, **négligé** *also foreign* /neɡliʒe/ (*plural same*)) M18 French (*négligé*, literally 'given little thought or attention', past participle of *négliger* neglect). A woman's light dressing gown, especially one made of a filmy fabric.

■ First used in English to denote a kind of loose gown worn by women in the 18th century.

Negritude /'nɛɡrɪtjuːd/ *noun* (also **Négritude** /negrityd/, **negritude**) M20 French (*négritude* blackness, from Latin *nigritudo*, from *niger*, *nigr-* black). The quality or fact of being of black African origin; affirmation or consciousness of the value of black or African culture and identity.

nem. con. /nɛm 'kɒn/ *adverb phrase* L16 Latin (abbreviation of *nemine contradicente*). With no one contradicting; unanimously: *the motions were carried nem. con.*

■ The full form *nemine contradicente* (M17) is very seldom found in English.

nemine contradicente see NEM. CON.

nemo dat /ˌniːməʊ 'dat/, /ˌnɛməʊ dat/ *noun phrase* M17 Latin (abbreviation of *nemo dat quod non habet* no one gives what he or she does not have). *Law* The basic principle that a person who does not own property, especially a thief, cannot confer it on another except with the true owner's authority.

nepenthes /nɪ'pɛnθiːz/ *noun* L16 Latin (from Greek *nēpenthes* neuter of *nēpenthēs* banishing pain (qualifying *pharmakon* drug), from *nē-* not + *penthos* grief). **1** A drug mentioned in Homer's *Odyssey* (iv.221) as banishing grief or trouble from a person's mind; any drug or potion bringing welcome forgetfulness. Also, a plant yielding such a drug. **2** Any of various frequently climbing pitcher plants of the genus *Nepenthes*, chiefly of South-East Asia.

ne plus ultra /ˌniː plʌs 'ʌltrə/, /ˌneɪ plʊs 'ʊltrɑː/ *noun phrase* M17 Latin (= not further beyond). The furthest limit reached or attainable, in particular the perfect or most extreme example of something; the ultimate.

■ This was the inscription imagined by the inhabitants of the ancient Mediterranean world to be on the Pillars of Hercules (Strait of Gibraltar), prohibiting further westward passage by ships.

1996 *Country Life* ... in the United States, where Cuban cigars are not available, Davidoff cigars are regarded as the *ne plus ultra*.

neroli /'nɪərəli/ *noun* L17 French (*néroli*, from Italian *neroli*, said to be from the name of an Italian princess to whom the oil's discovery is attributed). An essential oil distilled from the flowers of the Seville orange and used in perfumery. Also *neroli oil*, *oil of neroli*.

netsuke /'nɛtski/, /'nɛtsʊki/ *noun* plural **netsukes**, same. L19 Japanese. A carved button-like ornament, especially of ivory or wood, formerly worn in Japan to suspend articles from the sash of a kimono.

Neue Sachlichkeit /ˌnɔyə 'zaxlɪçkaɪt/ *noun phrase* E20 German (literally, 'new objectivity'). A movement in the fine arts, music, and literature, which developed in Germany during the 1920s and was characterized by realism and a deliberate rejection of romantic attitudes.

névé /neve/ *noun* plural pronounced same M19 Swiss French (from Latin *nix*, *niv-* snow). Crystalline or granular snow, especially on the upper part of a glacier, where it has not yet been compressed into ice. Also, a field or bed of this. Also called FIRN.

nevus variant of NAEVUS.

ngoma /(ə)ŋ'gəʊmə/ *noun* E20 Kiswahili ((also *goma*) drum, dance, music). (In East Africa) a dance; a night of dancing and music.

nibbana /nɪ'bɑːnə/ *noun* E20 Pali (*nibbāna*, Sanskrit *nirvāṇa* nirvana). *Buddhism* NIRVANA.

niche /nɪtʃ/, /niːʃ/ *noun* E17 Old and Modern French (from Old French *nichier* (modern *nicher*) to make a nest, nestle, from Proto-Romance from Latin *nidus* nest). **1** A shallow recess, especially one in a wall to display a statue or other ornament. **2** A place or position suited to or intended for a person's capabilities, occupation, or status. **b** *Ecology* A position or role taken by a kind of organism within its community. **3** *Commerce* A specialized but profitable segment of the market.

Niçois /niswa/, /niː'swɑː/ *adjective* (feminine **Niçoise** /niswaz/, /niː'swɑːz/) L19 French (= of Nice, a city in southern France). Relating to Nice or its inhabitants; *specifically* in *Cookery*, designating food, especially garnished with tomatoes, capers, anchovies, etc., characteristic of Nice or the surrounding region.

■ Generally postpositive, as in *salade Niçoise*.

niello /nɪ'ɛləʊ/ *noun* plural **nielli** /nɪ'ɛli/, **niellos** E19 Italian (from Latin *nigellus* diminutive of *niger* black). **1** A black compound of sulphur with silver, lead, or copper, for filling in engraved designs in silver or other metals. **2** Objects decorated with niello.

niente /ni'ɛnte/, /nɪ'enti/ *noun*, *adverb*, & *adjective* E19 Italian. **A** *noun* Nothing. **B** *adverb* & *adjective Music* (Especially as a direction) with the sound or tone gradually fading away to nothing.

■ In 19th-century use the noun apparently existed in English only in the phrase DOLCE FAR NIENTE.

niet /'njɛt/ *adverb & noun* (also **nyet**) E20 Russian (*net* no). **A** *adverb* (In Russian) no, *especially* expressing a blunt refusal. **B** *noun* An utterance of 'niet'.

nihil obstat /ˌnʌɪhɪl 'ɒbstat/, /ˌnɪhɪl/ *noun phrase* M20 Latin (literally, 'nothing hinders' (the censor's formula of approval)). A certificate or statement recording that a work has been approved by the Roman Catholic Church as free of doctrinal or moral error; a statement of official approval, authorization.

nil admirari /ˌnɪl admɪ'rɑːri/ *noun* M18 Latin (= to wonder at nothing). An attitude of imperturbability or indifference to the distractions of the outside world.

■ A stance advocated by the Roman poet Horace in the opening lines of one of his *Epistles* (I.vi.1): *nil admirari prope res est una...solaque quae possit facere et servare beatum* 'to wonder at nothing is just about the only way a man can become contented and remain so.'

nil carborundum illegitimi /nɪl kɑːbəˌrʌndəm ɪlɪ'dʒɪtɪmʌɪ/ *interjection* M20 Latin. Don't let the bastards grind you down.

■ This cod Latin phrase was in circulation during the Second World War, though it may possibly be of earlier origin. It is also quoted in the forms *nil carborundum* and *illegitimi non carborundum*.

nil desperandum /ˌnɪl dɛspə'randəm/ *interjection* E17 Latin (= no need to despair). Do not despair, never despair.

■ From Horace *Odes* I.vii.27: *nil desperandum Teucro duce et auspice Teucro* 'no need to despair with Teucer as your leader and Teucer to protect you'.

ninja /'nɪndʒə/ *noun* plural same M20 Japanese (= spy). A person, especially a Japanese samurai, expert in NINJUTSU.

■ The word was little known in the West until the rise of interest in oriental martial arts in the 1970s. Ninjas then began to play a role in fantasy and computer games but it was the huge

popular and commercial success of the children's comic-book characters the Teenage Mutant Ninja Turtles in the United States at the end of the 1980s that brought the word into a wider circulation.

ninjutsu /nɪn'dʒʌtsuː/ *noun* M20 Japanese (from *nin* stealth, invisibility + *jutsu* art, science). The traditional Japanese technique of espionage, characterized by stealthy movement and camouflage, and developed in feudal times for military purposes and subsequently used in the training of samurai.

Niño, El see EL NIÑO.

ninon /'niːnɒn/, *foreign* /ninɔ̃/ *noun* E20 French. A lightweight dress fabric of silk, nylon, etc.

niqab /nɪ'kɑːb/ *noun* L20 Arabic. A veil worn by some Muslim women, covering all of the face and having two holes for the eyes.

nirvana /nɪə'vɑːnə/ *noun* M19 Sanskrit (*nirvāṇa* use as noun of past participle of *nirvā-* to be extinguished, from *nis-* out + *vā-* to blow). **1** In *Buddhism*, a transcendent state in which there is neither suffering, desire, nor sense of self, and the subject is released from the effects of KARMA and the cycle of death and rebirth. It represents the final goal of Buddhism. In *Hinduism* and *Jainism*, liberation of the soul from the effects of karma and from bodily existence. **2** A state of bliss, an ideal or idyllic state or place.

2 1996 *New Scientist* Without patents on extracted human material,... investment in biotechnology will drain out of Europe and into the patent nirvanas of the US and Japan...

nisei /'niːseɪ/ *noun* plural same M20 Japanese (from *ni-* second + *sei* generation). An American or Canadian whose parents were immigrants from Japan. Cf. ISSEI, SANSEI.

nisi /'nʌɪsʌɪ/ *postpositive adjective* M19 Latin (= unless). *Law* (Of a decree, order, or rule) that takes effect or is valid only after certain conditions are met, not final.

■ Generally in the phrase *decree nisi* 'a provisional order for divorce that will be made absolute unless cause to the contrary can be shown within a fixed period'.

noblesse /nəʊ'blɛs/, *foreign* /nɔblɛs/ *noun* ME Old and Modern French (from Latin *nobilis*). **1** Noble birth or rank; nobility, nobleness. **2** The nobility of a foreign country.

noblesse oblige /nɔblɛs ɔbliʒ/, /nəʊ ˌblɛs ɒ'bliːʒ/ *noun phrase* M19 French (= nobility obligates). Privilege entails responsibility.

1995 *Spectator* But then I decided they were victims of *noblesse oblige*, considering it incumbent upon themselves as dukes to supply any reasonable favour requested of them.

nocturne /'nɒktəːn/ *noun* M19 French (from Latin *nocturnus* of the night). **1** A short musical composition of a dreamy character, typically for the piano. **2** A painting of a night scene, a night piece.

Noel /nəʊ'ɛl/ *noun* (also **Noël**) E19 French (*Noël*). Christmas, especially as refrain in carols and on Christmas cards.

Noh /nəʊ/ *noun* (also **No**) L19 Japanese (*nō* (also = talent, accomplishment)). The traditional Japanese masked drama with dance and song, evolved from Shinto rites.

noir /nwɑː/ *noun* L20 French (from FILM NOIR). A genre of crime film or fiction characterized by cynicism, fatalism, and moral ambiguity; a film or novel of this genre.

1996 *Times Magazine* More noir than knock-about, thriller than caper, it is an effort to transport the [Dr Who] series in time and imbue it with the values of a new television era.

1996 *Bookseller* Higson . . . says that he is more conscious of the influence of the American *noir* writer Jim Thompson.

noisette /nwɑː'zɛt/ *noun* L19 French (diminutive of *noix* nut). **1** A small round piece of meat, especially lamb. **2** A chocolate made with hazelnuts.

nolens volens /ˌnəʊlɛnz 'vəʊlɛnz/ *adverb phrase* L16 Latin, from *nolens* not willing + *volens* willing). Whether a person wants or likes something or not, whether willing or not.

noli me tangere /ˌnəʊlʌɪ miː 'tan (d)ʒəri/, /ˌnəʊlɪ meɪ 'taŋ(ə)ri/ *noun* LME Latin (= do not touch me). **1** A warning or prohibition against meddling or interference. **2** A painting representing the appearance of Jesus to Mary Magdalen at the sepulchre after the Resurrection (John 20:17). **3** *Botany Impatiens noli-tangere*, touch-me-not, a plant of the balsam family, whose ripe seed capsules burst open explosively when touched.

■ The original injunction is the Vulgate version of the risen Christ's warning to Mary Magdalen when he appears to her outside the sepulchre (John 20:17).

nolle prosequi /ˌnɒli 'prɒsɪkwʌɪ/ *noun* L17 Latin (= be unwilling to pursue). *Law* A formal notice of abandonment by a plaintiff or prosecutor of all or part of a suit or prosecution; (in the United Kingdom) the dismissal or termination of legal proceedings by the Attorney General.

■ Also abbreviated to *nolle* in the United States.

nolo contendere /ˌnəʊləʊ kɒn'tɛndəri/ *noun* L19 Latin (= I do not wish to contend). *United States Law* A plea by which a defendant in a criminal prosecution accepts conviction but does not plead or admit guilt.

nom de guerre /nɔ̃ də gɛr/, /ˌnɒm də 'gɛː/ *noun phrase* plural **noms de guerre** (pronounced same) L17 French (= war-name). An assumed name under which a person fights or engages in some other action or enterprise.

1995 *Spectator* . . . Avraham Stern of the eponymous gang took the *nom de guerre* 'Yair' after the commander of the Sicarii garrison at Masada.

nom de plume /ˌnɒm də 'pluːm/, *foreign* /nɔ̃ də plym/ *noun phrase* plural **noms de plume** (pronounced same) E19 pseudo-French (formed from *nom* name, *de* of, *plume* pen, after *nom de guerre*). An assumed name used by a writer instead of their real name, a pen-name.

■ The phrase is not used in French. It was formed in English in the early 19th century from French words, to render the sense 'pen-name', on the pattern of *nom de guerre*.

1996 *Times*...Elytis was the *nom de plume* he chose to use in place of his family name...

nomenklatura /naˌmjɛnklaˈtura/, /nɒˌmɛnkləˈtjʊərə/ *noun* M20 Russian (from Latin *nomenclatura* list of names). (In the former Soviet Union) the system whereby influential posts in government and industry were filled by Party appointees; the holders of these posts collectively, the Soviet élite; also *transferred*.

1995 *Spectator* Naturally, the BBC's higher *nomenklatura*—all those Controllers and Heads of This and That—will reply that the two [sc. high ratings and public service broadcasting] are not incompatible.

nominis umbra /ˈnɒmɪnɪs ˈʌmbrə/ *noun phrase* M19 Latin (literally, 'the shadow or appearance of a name'). A name without substance; a thing which is not what the name implies.

■ The phrase comes from the Roman poet Lucan's reference to Pompey in *Pharsalia* (i. 135): *Stat magni nominis umbra* 'There stands the mere shadow of a mighty name'.

noms de guerre, noms de plume plurals of NOM DE GUERRE, NOM DE PLUME.

non /nɔ̃/ *noun* plural pronounced same L20 French (= no). (In France and French-speaking countries) an utterance of 'non', an absolute refusal or veto.

nonchalance /ˈnɒnʃ(ə)l(ə)ns/ *noun* L17 Old and Modern French (see next). The state of being nonchalant; lack of enthusiasm or interest; casual indifference, unconcern.

nonchalant /ˈnɒnʃ(ə)l(ə)nt/ *adjective* M18 Old and Modern French (from *non* + *chalant* present participle of *chaloir* to be concerned). Casually calm and relaxed; lacking or showing no enthusiasm, interest, or anxiety.

non compos mentis /nɒn ˌkɒmpɒs ˈmɛntɪs/ *adjective phrase* E17 Latin (= not having control of one's mind). Not sane or in one's right mind. Cf. COMPOS MENTIS.

■ Almost always predicative and often shortened to *non compos* (also E17).

non est factum /nɒn ɛst ˈfaktəm/ *noun phrase* E17 Latin (= it was not done). *Law* A plea that a written agreement is invalid because the defendant was mistaken about its character when signing it.

nonpareil /ˌnɒnpəˈreɪl/ *adjective & noun* LME French (from *non-* + *pareil* like, equal, from popular Latin *pariculus* diminutive of Latin *par*). **A** *adjective* Having no match or equal; unrivalled, unique. **B** *noun* A person or thing having no equal; an unrivalled or unique person or thing.

■ Formerly also a size of type roughly equivalent to modern 6 point (L17).

B 1996 *Spectator* She's a genius, an inspirational revolutionary, a great designer, a nonpareil...

non placet /nɒn ˈpleɪsɛt/ *noun & verb phrase* (as verb also **non-placet**) L16 Latin (= it does not please). **A** *noun phrase* Originally, an expression of dissent or disapproval. Later, a negative vote in a university or Church assembly. **B** *transitive verb phrase* Give a negative vote on (a proposition); reject (a measure).

■ A formula used especially in university and Church assemblies in giving a negative vote on a proposition.

nonplus /nɒnˈplʌs/ *noun & verb* L16 Latin (from *non plus* not more, no further). **A** *noun* A state of being very surprised and confused. **B** *transitive verb* (inflected -ss-) Bring (a person) to a nonplus; surprise and confuse (a person) so much that they are uncertain how to react. Frequently as *nonplussed* participial adjective.

■ The noun originally meant 'a state in which no more can be said or done'.

non sequitur /nɒn ˈsɛkwɪtə/ *noun phrase* M16 Latin (literally, 'it does not follow'). A conclusion or statement that does not logically follow from the previous argument or statement.

■ Earliest in a rare and obsolete use (only LME) for part of the collar of a shirt etc.; an unfastened collar.

1996 *Spectator* There are one or two odd slips and non sequiturs in the book, which may be attributed to inexpert editing...

nori /ˈnɔːri/ *noun* L19 Japanese. An edible seaweed of the genus *Porphyra*, eaten either fresh or dried in sheets, especially by the Japanese.

noria /ˈnɔːrɪə/ *noun* L18 Spanish (from Arabic *nāyʿūra*). (Especially in Spain and the East) a device for raising water from a stream or river, consisting of a chain of pots or buckets, revolving round a wheel driven by the water current.

nosh /nɒʃ/ *noun & verb* E20 Yiddish (cf. German *naschen* to nibble). **A** *noun* **1** Food, a meal. **2** A snack eaten between meals, a titbit. Chiefly *North American*. **B** *transitive and intransitive verb* **1** Eat food enthusiastically or greedily. **2** Nibble or eat a snack; eat between meals. Chiefly *North American*.

■ First used to denote a snack bar.

nostalgie de la boue /nɔstalʒi də la bu/ *noun phrase* L19 French (literally, 'yearning for mud'). A desire for degradation and depravity.

1995 *Spectator* Feinstein allows Mellors' inherent misogyny, fascism and *nostalgie de la boue* to overwhelm him, and permits Connie to be reclaimed by her own well-heeled bohemian class.

nostrum /ˈnɒstrəm/ *noun* plural **nostrums**, **nostra** /ˈnɒstrə/ E17 Latin (neuter singular of *noster* our). **1** A quack remedy; a medicine prepared by an unqualified person, especially one that is not considered effective. **2** A pet scheme, a favourite remedy, especially for bringing about some social or political reform or improvement.

2 1995 *Times* Every age has its prevailing fallacies, and most of them from a similar origin: the insensitive overuse of an apparently commonsense nostrum.

nota bene /ˌnəʊtə ˈbɛneɪ/ *verb phrase transitive & intransitive* (*imperative*) E18 Latin (from *nota* note + *bene* well). Observe carefully or take special notice (usually drawing attention to what follows).

■ In general use in the abbreviated form *NB*.

notes inégales /nɔts inegal/ *noun phrase plural* E20 French (literally, 'unequal notes'). *Music* (In baroque music) notes performed by convention in an uneven rhythm though notated as equal in the score.

notitia /nəʊˈtɪʃɪə/, /nəʊˈtɪʃə/ *noun* E18 Latin (= knowledge, (in late Latin) list, account, from *notus* known). A register or list of ecclesiastical sees or districts.

nougat /ˈnuːgɑː/, /ˈnʌgət/ *noun* (also (earlier) **nogat**) E19 French (from Provençal *nogat*, from *noga* nut, from Latin *nux*). A sweet made from egg white sweetened with sugar or honey and mixed with nuts and sometimes pieces of fruit.

noumenon /ˈnaʊmənɒn/, /ˈnuːmənɒn/ *noun* plural **noumena** /ˈnaʊmənə/ L18 German (from Greek, literally '(something) conceived', from *noien* to apprehend, conceive). *Philosophy* A thing as it is in itself, as distinct from a thing as it is knowable by the senses through phenomenal attributes.

■ Chiefly in the philosophy of Immanuel Kant (1724–1804); cf. DING AN SICH.

nous /naʊs/ *noun* (also **nouse**) L17 Greek. **1** *Greek Philosophy* Intuitive apprehension, intelligence; mind, intellect. **2** Common sense, practical intelligence, gumption. *Colloquial*.

2 1996 *Times* Taxpayers who follow them blindly, without using their nous, are fools.

nouveau /ˈnuːvəʊ/, /nuːˈvəʊ/, *foreign* /nuvo/ *adjective & noun* E20 French (= new). **A** *adjective* **1** NOUVEAU RICHE. **2** Modern, up to date. **B** *noun* plural **nouveaus**, **nouveaux** /ˈnuːvəʊ/, /ˈnuːvəʊz/, *foreign* /nuvo/. **1** A nouveau riche. Usually in *plural*. **2** BEAUJOLAIS NOUVEAU. *Colloquial*.

■ *Nouveau* seldom occurs independently in English, but is used elliptically and colloquially for such phrases as *Beaujolais nouveau* etc., the context making plain the meaning intended.

nouveau pauvre /nuvo povr/, /ˌnuːvəʊ ˈpɔːvrə/ *adjective & noun phrase* plural **nouveaux pauvres** (pronounced same) M20 French (literally, 'new poor', after NOUVEAU RICHE). **A** *adjective phrase* (Of a person) newly impoverished. **B** *noun phrase* A person who has recently become poor.

A 1995 *Times* Far better, for a *nouveau pauvre* hostess, to take advantage of the national mood of exhaustion among thirty-to-forty somethings...and issue instead a more casual invitation.

nouveau riche /nuvo riʃ/, /ˌnuːˈvəʊ ˈriːʃ/ *noun & adjective phrase* plural **nouveaux riches** (pronounced same) E19 French (literally, 'new rich'). **A** *noun phrase* People who have recently acquired wealth, typically those perceived as displaying their wealth ostentatiously or lacking in good taste. **B** *adjective phrase* Relating to or characteristic of such people.

> **B 1995** *Spectator* Throughout last week I had to endure the roar of *nouveaux riches* engines as their hideous-looking children gunned them to impress.

nouveau roman /nuvo rɔmɑ̃/ *noun phrase* M20 French (literally, 'new novel'). A style of avant-garde French novel which rejected traditional novelistic conventions in an attempt to reflect the sometimes random nature of experience.

> **1974** *Times Literary Supplement* The sources of Mr Gordon's off-the-peg technique are fairly clear: some Kafka; the Burroughs scissors; but mostly the *nouveau roman*. The novel, so this modish dogma asserts, is a 'vision of things', and the universe no more than the sum of the author's sensations.

nouveaux plural of NOUVEAU.

nouveaux pauvres, nouveaux riches plurals of NOUVEAU PAUVRE, NOUVEAU RICHE.

nouvelle /nuːˈvɛl/, *foreign* /nuvɛl/ *adjective* L20 French (feminine of NOUVEAU). Relating to or specializing in *nouvelle cuisine*.

nouvelle cuisine /nuvɛl kɥizin/, /ˌnuːvɛl kwɪˈziːn/ *noun phrase* L20 French (literally, 'new cookery'). A style of (especially French) cooking that avoids traditional rich sauces and emphasizes the freshness of the ingredients and attractive presentation.

> ■ The fashion for *nouvelle cuisine* spread beyond France in the 1970s and early 1980s, and its characteristics of lightness, short cooking times, and small helpings continued to endear it to the healthy eating lobby. In the hands of pretentious practitioners, however, the fashionable extremes of artistic presentation and meagreness of quantity have incurred considerable ridicule (see quotation).

> **1990** *Country Living* One establishment we visited served every dish flanked by the same ludicrously inappropriate clutter: a frilly lettuce leaf pinned down by a couple of hefty spring onions, a pallid slice of kiwi fruit and a strawberry. Oh nouvelle cuisine, what have you spawned!

nouvelle vague /nuvɛl vag/ *noun phrase* M20 French (literally, 'new wave'). A grouping of French film directors in the late 1950s and 1960s who reacted against established French cinema and sought to make more individualistic and stylistically innovative films.

> ■ Exponents included Claude Chabrol, Jean-Luc Godard, Alain Resnais, and François Truffaut.

nova /ˈnəʊvə/ *noun* plural **novae** /ˈnəʊviː/, **novas** L19 Latin (feminine singular of *novus* new). *Astronomy* Originally, a new star or nebula. Now *specifically* a star whose brightness suddenly increases by several magnitudes, with violent ejection of gaseous material, and then gradually returns to its original state.

> ■ The present astronomical term is a reintroduction, as *nova* was originally (L17) used in the rare and obsolete sense of 'a thick ring or roll of tobacco'.

novella /nəˈvɛlə/ *noun* E20 Italian (= novel). A short fictitious prose narrative, a short novel, a long short story.

> ■ The word was particularly applied to the tales in Boccaccio's *Decameron* and its Italian imitators before being transferred to a work in any language midway in length between a full-scale novel and a short story.

novena /nəˈ(ʊ)viːnə/ *noun* plural **novenae** /nəˈ(ʊ)viːniː/, **novenas** M19 Medieval Latin (from *novem* nine, after Latin *novenarius* of nine days). *Roman Catholic Church* A form of worship consisting of special prayers or services on nine successive days.

noyade /nwɑːˈjɑːd/, *foreign* /nwajad/ *noun* plural **noyades** /nwɑːˈjɑːdz/, *foreign* /nwajad/ E19 French (from *noyer* to drown, from Latin *necare* kill without a weapon, (later) drown, from *nex, nec-* slaughter). *History* An execution carried out by drowning, especially a mass execution in this way, as carried out in France in 1794.

noyau /nwɑːˈjəʊ/, foreign /nwajo/ noun plural **noyaux** /nwɑːˈjəʊz/, foreign /nwajo/ L18 French (earlier noiel kernel, based on Latin nux, nuc- nut). A liqueur made of brandy flavoured with the kernels of certain fruits.

nuance /ˈnjuːɑːns/ noun & verb L18 French (from nuer to show cloudlike variations in colour, from nue cloud, from popular Latin variant of Latin nubes). **A** noun A subtle variation in or shade of meaning, expression, or sound. **B** transitive verb Give a nuance or nuances to.

nudnik /ˈnʊdnɪk/ noun (also **nudnick**) M20 Yiddish (from Russian nudnyĭ tedious, boring + noun suffix -nik person connected with (something)). A pestering, nagging, or irritating person; a bore. United States slang.
> attributive **1972** New York Too many of our nudnik moviegoers . . . dread the prospect of sharing their pleasures with the plain folks.

nuée ardente /nɥe ardɑ̃t/ noun phrase plural **nuées ardentes** (pronounced same) E20 French (literally, 'burning cloud'). Geology A hot dense cloud of gas, ash, and lava fragments ejected from a volcano and flowing downhill like an avalanche.
> ■ The phrase was introduced into formal vulcanology in 1903 by A. Lacroix, who subsequently observed (in La Montagne Pelée et ses éruptions (1904)) that the expression had earlier been in use amongst the inhabitants of San Jorge in the Azores. While Lacroix said that by nuée ardente he meant brulant 'burning' rather than incandescent 'glowing', the phrase is nonetheless usually rendered in English as 'glowing cloud'.

nuit blanche /nɥi blɑ̃ʃ/ noun phrase plural **nuits blanches** (pronounced same) M19 French (literally, 'white night'). A sleepless night.

numdah /ˈnʌmdə/ noun E19 Urdu (namdā from Persian namad felt, carpet, rug). (In the Indian subcontinent and the Middle East) an embroidered rug or carpet made of felt or coarse woollen cloth; cloth of this type.

numen /ˈnjuːmən/ noun plural **numina** /ˈnjuːmɪnə/ E17 Latin (related to nuere to nod, Greek neuein to incline the head). The spirit or divine power presiding over a thing or place.

numero uno /ˌnjuːmərəʊ ˈuːnəʊ/ noun phrase plural **numero unos** L20 Italian and Spanish (= number one). The best or most important person.
> **1996** Spectator Then there is Enrique Ponce, acclaimed as numero uno and already being spoken of as the matador of the century.

numerus clausus /ˌnjuːmərəs ˈklaʊsəs/ noun phrase E20 Latin (literally, 'closed number'). A fixed maximum number of entrants admissible to an academic institution.

numina plural of NUMEN.

numnah /ˈnʌmnə/ noun M19 Urdu (namdā from Persian namad felt, carpet, rug). A pad, typically made of sheepskin or foam, placed under a saddle to prevent soreness.

nunatak /ˈnʌnətak/ noun L19 Eskimo ((Greenlandic) nunataq). An isolated peak of rock projecting above a surface of inland ice or snow in Greenland, Norway, etc.

Nunc Dimittis /ˌnʌŋk dɪˈmɪtɪs/ noun phrase M16 Latin (= now you let (your servant) depart). **1** The Song of Simeon in Luke 2:29–32 (in the Vulgate beginning Nunc dimittis, Domine), used as a canticle forming part of the Christian liturgy at evensong and compline. **2** (**nunc dimittis**) Permission to depart; dismissal.

nunchaku /nʌnˈtʃaku/ noun L20 Japanese (from Okinawa dialect). A Japanese martial arts weapon consisting of two hardwood sticks joined together by a chain, rope, or thong. Usually in plural.

nuncio /ˈnʌnsɪəʊ/, /ˈnʌnʃɪəʊ/ noun plural **nuncios** E16 Italian (nuncio, nuntio (now nunzio) from Latin nuncius, nuntius messenger). Roman Catholic Church A papal ambassador to a foreign court or government.

nuoc mam /nwɒk ˈmɑːm/ noun phrase E20 Vietnamese. A spicy Vietnamese fish sauce.

nuragh /'nʊərag/ *noun* plural **nuraghi** /'nʊəragi/ E19 Sardinian. *Archaeology* A type of massive tower-shaped stone structure found in Sardinia, dating from the Bronze and Iron Ages.

nux vomica /ˌnʌks 'vɒmɪkə/ *noun phrase* LME Medieval Latin (literally, 'emetic nut', from Latin *nux* nut + adjective from *vomere* to vomit). A spiny southern Asian tree, *Strychnos nux-vomica*, with berry-like fruit and toxic seeds that are a commercial source of strychnine; a homeopathic preparation of this plant used especially for the treatment of symptoms of overeating and overdrinking.

nyet variant of NIET.

nymphaeum /nɪm'fiːəm/ *noun archaic* plural **nymphaea** /nɪm'fiːə/ (also **nympheum**, plural **nymphea**) L18 Latin (from Greek *numphaion, -eion* temple or shrine of the nymphs, neuter of *numphaios, -eios* sacred to the nymphs, from *numphē* nymph). A grotto or shrine dedicated to a nymph or nymphs.

Oo

ob. abbreviation of OBIIT.

obbligato /ɒblɪˈɡɑːtəʊ/ *adjective and noun* (also **obligato**) L18 Italian (= obliged, obligatory). *Music* **A** *adjective* Indispensable; that cannot be omitted: designating a part or accompaniment forming an integral part of a composition, and the instrument on which it is played. **B** *noun* plural **obbligatos**, **obbligati** /ɒblɪˈɡɑːtiː/ An instrumental part, typically distinctive in effect, which is integral to a piece of music and should not be omitted in performance.

obelus /ˈɒb(ə)ləs/ *noun* plural **obeli** /ˈɒb(ə)lʌɪ/, /ˈɒb(ə)liː/ LME Latin (= spit, obelus, from Greek *obelos* pointed pillar, critical mark). A straight horizontal stroke (-), sometimes with a dot above and below (÷), used in ancient manuscripts to mark a word or passage as spurious, corrupt, or doubtful. Also, a dagger-shaped symbol (†) used in printed matter as a reference to a footnote etc., and in some dictionaries to denote obsoleteness. Also called *obelisk*.

obi /ˈəʊbi/ *noun* E19 Japanese (= belt). A broad sash worn round the waist of a Japanese kimono.

obiit /ˈɒbɪɪt/ *verb* Latin. He, she, or it died.

▪ Frequently on epitaphs, followed by the date of death; also abbreviated to *ob*.

obiit sine prole /ˌɒbɪɪt ˌsɪneɪ ˈprəʊleɪ/ *phrase* L19 Latin. He, she, or it died without offspring.

▪ Frequently in genealogies, usually abbreviated to *ob.s.p.* or *o.s.p.*

obiter /ˈɒbɪtə/ *adverb, adjective, & noun* L16 Latin (originally two words, *ob itur* by the way). **A** *adverb & adjective* (Chiefly in legal contexts) made or said in passing. **B** *noun* An OBITER DICTUM.

obiter dictum /ˌɒbɪtə ˈdɪktəm/ *noun phrase* plural **obiter dicta** /ˌɒbɪtə ˈdɪktə/ E19 Latin (= something that is said in passing). A judge's expression of opinion uttered in discussing a point of law or in giving judgment, but not essential to the decision and so not legally binding as a precedent; *generally* an incidental remark.

1996 *Spectator* The *obiter dicta* of earlier scientific materialists, all of them in their own day at least as eminent and confident as Dawkins, make hilarious reading today.

objet /ɒbʒɛ/, /ˈɒbʒeɪ/ *noun* plural pronounced same M19 French (= object). An object displayed or intended for display as an ornament.

1996 *Country Life* Occasionally, a composition is enriched by other *objets* such as shells, a jewel, even a skull.

objet d'art /ɒbʒɛ dar/, /ˌɒbʒeɪ ˈdɑː/ *noun phrase* plural **objets d'art** (pronounced same) M19 French (literally, 'object of art'). A small decorative or artistic object, typically when regarded as a collectable item.

objet trouvé /ˌɒbʒeɪ ˈtruːveɪ/ *noun phrase* plural **objets trouvés** (pronounced same) M19 French (literally, 'found object'). An object found by an artist and displayed with no, or minimal, alteration as a work of art.

obligato variant of OBBLIGATO.

oboe d'amore /ˌəʊbəʊ daˈmɔːreɪ/ *noun phrase* plural **oboes d'amore**, **oboi d'amore** /ˈəʊbɔɪ/ L19 Italian (literally, 'oboe of love'). A type of alto oboe with a pear-shaped bell and a pitch a minor third below that of the ordinary oboe, now used especially in baroque music.

obscurum per obscurius /əbˌskjʊər əm pər əbˈskjʊərɪəs/ *noun phrase* L19 Late Latin (literally, 'the obscure by the still more obscure'). An explanation which is harder to understand than what it is meant to explain. Cf. IGNOTUM PER IGNOTIUS.

ob.s.p. abbreviation of OBIIT SINE PROLE.

ocarina /ˌɒkəˈriːnə/ *noun* L19 Italian (from *oca* goose (with reference to its shape)). A simple wind instrument in the form of a hollow egg-shaped body with finger-holes and a hole to blow at.

octli /ˈəʊktli/ *noun* M19 Mexican Spanish. PULQUE.

oculus /ˈɒkjʊləs/ *noun* plural **oculi** /ˈɒkjʊlʌɪ/, /ˈɒkjʊliː/ M19 Latin (= eye). *Architecture* A round or eyelike opening or design; *specifically* a circular window (especially in a church); the central boss of a volute; an opening at the apex of a dome.

odalisque /ˈəʊd(ə)lɪsk/ *noun* L17 French (from Turkish *ōdalık*, from *ōda* chamber + lık suffix expressing function). A female slave or concubine in an Eastern harem, especially in the seraglio of the Sultan of Turkey (now *historical*); *transferred* an exotic sexually attractive woman.

oedema /ɪˈdiːmə/ *noun* plural **oedemata** /ɪˈdiːmətə/, **oedemas** LME Late Latin (from Greek *oidēma*, from *oidein* to swell). *Medicine* A condition characterized by an excess of watery fluid collecting in the cavities or tissues of the body; dropsy.

oeil-de-boeuf /œjdəbœf/ *noun* plural **oeils-de-boeuf** (pronounced same) M18 French (literally, 'ox-eye'). A small round window.

oesophagus /ɪˈsɒfəgəs/ *noun* (also **esophagus**) LME Medieval Latin (*ysophagus, iso-* from Greek *oisophagos*, from obscure first element + (apparently) *-phagos* eating, eater; current spelling after modern Latin). *Anatomy* and *Zoology* The part of the alimentary canal which connects the throat to the stomach; the gullet.

oestrus /ˈiːstrəs/, /ˈɛstrəs/ *noun* (also **estrus**) L17 Latin (from Greek *oistros* gadfly, breeze, sting, frenzy). *Zoology* and *Physiology* A recurring period of sexual receptivity and fertility in many female mammals; heat.

œuvre /œvr/, /ˈəːvrə/ *noun* (also **oeuvre**) plural pronounced same L19 French (= work). The whole body of work produced by an artist, composer, author, etc.; a work of art, music, literature, etc. Cf. CHEF-D'ŒUVRE.

> 1996 *Oldie* ... that he has been able to keep both aspects of his oeuvre alive and developing with such élan is in itself remarkable.

ogham /ˈɒgəm/ *noun* (also **ogam, Ogham**) E18 Old Irish (*ogam, ogum* (genitive *oguim*), modern Irish *ogham*, plural **oghaim**, Gaelic *oghum*, connected with its mythical inventor *Ogma*). An ancient British and Irish system of writing using an alphabet of twenty characters; any of these characters, consisting of a line or stroke, or a group of two to five parallel strokes, arranged alongside or across a continuous line or the edge of a stone (usually in *plural*). Also, an inscription in this alphabet.

olé /oˈle/, /əʊˈleɪ/ *interjection* & *noun* E20 Spanish. **A** *interjection* Bravo! **B** *noun* A cry of 'olé!'

olla podrida /ˌɒlə pə(ʊ)ˈdriːdə/ *noun phrase* L16 Spanish (literally 'rotten pot', from Latin *olla* pot, jar + *putridus* rotten, putrid). **1** A highly spiced stew of various meats and vegetables, of Spanish and Portuguese origin; *generally* any dish containing a great variety of ingredients. **2** *figurative* Any miscellaneous collection of things or elements; a hotchpotch, a medley; a variety act or show.

■ *Olio* (M17), an alteration of Spanish *olla* stew, is also used in all these senses.

> 2 1996 *Spectator* ... the RSC, so careful of Shakespeare on our behalf, long ago decided to commit this *olla podrida* of Bardic tricks [sc. *Cymbeline*] to the scrapheap for scholars to pick over ...

oloroso /ˌɒləˈrəʊsəʊ/ *noun* plural **olorosos** L19 Spanish (= fragrant). A heavy, dark, medium-sweet sherry; sherry which does not have a covering of flor (yeast) during production, used to make oloroso and cream sherries.

om /əʊm/ *interjection* & *noun* L18 Sanskrit (*oṃ, om*, sometimes regarded as composed of three sounds, *a-u-m*, symbolizing the three major Hindu deities). *Hinduism* and *Tibetan Buddhism* **A** *interjection* Used as a sacred mantra or auspicious formula at the beginning and end of most Sanskrit recitations, prayers, and texts. **B** *noun* An utterance of 'om'.

ombré /ɔbre/ *adjective* L19 French (past participle of *ombrer* to shade). (Of a fabric) having a dyed, printed, or woven design in which the colour is graduated from light to dark.

ombudsman /ˈɒmbʊdzmən/ *noun* plural **ombudsmen** M20 Swedish (= legal representative, from *ombud* commissioner, agent). An official appointed to investigate complaints by individuals against a company or organization, especially a public authority; a British official of this kind (officially called the Parliamentary Commissioner for Administration), first appointed in 1967.

omega /ˈəʊmɪɡə/ *noun* E16 Greek (ō *mega*, literally, 'great O', opposed to *o mikron* omicron). The last letter (Ω, ω) of the Greek alphabet, transliterated as 'o' or 'ō', having originally the value of a long open *o*; *figurative* the last of a series; the last word, the final development.

■ In the figurative use, often in the phrase 'the alpha and the omega' (see under ALPHA).

omertà /omerˈtaː/ *noun* L19 Italian (dialectal variant of *umiltà* humility). A code of silence observed by members or associates of the Mafia about criminal activity and a refusal to give evidence to the police; any similar code of silence observed by others engaged in clandestine activities.

■ The Italian sense of 'humility' originally referred to the Mafia code which enjoins submission of the group to its leader.

1996 *Times* Pressed time and again on quarantine by baffled Members of Parliament, she preserved the ministry *omertà* towards the kennel owners and referred only to her 'veterinary advisers'.

omnium gatherum /ˌɒmnɪəm ˈɡaðər əm/ *noun phrase* plural **omnium gatherums**, (*rare*) **omnium gathera** /ˌɒmnɪəm ˈɡaðərə/ M16 pseudo-Latin (from Latin *omnium* of all + English *gather*). A gathering or collection of all sorts of people or things; a confused medley. *Colloquial*.

omphalos /ˈɒmfəlɒs/ *noun* M19 Greek (literally, 'navel'). **1** (In ancient Greece) a conical stone, in the temple of Apollo at Delphi, reputed to mark the central point of the earth; a boss on an ancient Greek shield. **2** *figurative* The centre or hub of something.

on dit /ɔ̃ di/ *noun phrase* plural **on dits** (pronounced same) E19 French (= they say). A piece of gossip; something reported on hearsay.

onomatopoeia /ˌɒnə(ʊ)matəˈpiːə/ *noun* L16 Late Latin (from Greek *onomatopoiia* making of words, from *onomatopoios*, from *onomato-* combining form of *onoma* name + -*poios* making, from *poiein* to make, create). **1** The formation of a word by an imitation of the sound associated with what is named. **2** The use of onomatopoeia for literary effect.

oom /ʊəm/ *noun* E19 Afrikaans (= uncle, from Dutch *oom*). A man, especially an older one.

■ Frequently used by children or young people in South Africa as a respectful and affectionate form of address to an older or elderly man.

op. cit. /ɒp ˈsɪt/ *adverb phrase* L19 Latin (abbreviation of *opus citatum* the work quoted, or *opere citato* in the work cited). In the work already cited.

opéra bouffe /ɒpera buf/, /ˌɒp(ə)rə ˈbuːf/ *noun phrase* plural **opéras bouffe (s)** (pronounced same) L19 French (from as next). OPERA BUFFA; a French comic opera with dialogue in recitative and characters drawn from everyday life.

figurative **1995** *Times* Eventually their relationship turned into an *opera bouffe* of the most debilitating, if diverting, kind.

opera buffa /ˌɒp(ə)rə ˈbuːfə/, *foreign* /ˌopera ˈbuffa/ *noun phrase* plural **operas buffa**, **opere buffe** /ˌopere ˈbuffe/ E19 Italian (= comic opera). A comic opera (usually in Italian), especially one with characters drawn from everyday life.

1995 *Spectator* Yet much of this power is dissipated by the preceding *opera buffa* with the disguises. Those who wear Armani suits must behave like Armani suit-wearers.

opéra comique /ɔpera kɔmik/, /ˌɒp(ə)rə kɒˈmiːk/ *noun phrase* plural

opéras comiques (pronounced same) M18 French (= comic opera). An opera (usually in French) on a light-hearted theme, with spoken dialogue.

opéras bouffe(s), operas buffa, etc. plurals of OPÉRA BOUFFE, OPERA BUFFA, etc.

opera seria /ˌɒp(ə)rə ˈsɪərɪə/, foreign /ˌopera ˈsɛːrja/ noun phrase plural **operas seria, opere serie** /ˌopere ˈsɛːrje/ L19 Italian (= serious opera). An opera (especially one of the 18th century in Italian) on a serious, usually classical or mythological, theme.

opere buffe, opere serie plurals of OPERA BUFFA, OPERA SERIA.

operetta /ɒpəˈrɛtə/ noun L18 Italian (diminutive of opera). A short, originally one-act, opera on a light or humorous theme, and typically having spoken dialogue.

opus citatum see OP. CIT.

opus Dei /ˌɒpəs ˈdeɪiː/ noun phrase L19 Medieval Latin (= work of God). **1** Christian Church The work of God; specifically liturgical worship regarded as humankind's primary duty to God. **2** (Opus Dei) A Roman Catholic organization of priests and lay people founded in Spain in 1928 with the aim of re-establishing Christian ideals in society.

or /ɔː/ noun LME Old and Modern French (ultimately from Latin aurum gold). Originally, gold. Later, in heraldry, the tincture gold or yellow.

oratorio /ɒrəˈtɔːrɪəʊ/ noun plural **oratorios** E18 Italian (from ecclesiastical Latin oratorium oratory). A large-scale, usually narrative musical work for orchestra and voices, typically on a sacred theme, performed without costume, scenery, or action.

■ Originally (M17) in English in its more literal sense of 'a pulpit', but this is rare and became obsolete before its reintroduction in its modern sense, which derives from the musical services held in the church of the Oratory of St Philip Neri in Rome.

ordonnance /ˈɔːdənəns/, foreign /ɔrdɔnɑ̃s/ (plural same) noun M17 French (alteration of Old French ordenance after Old and Modern French ordonner to arrange). The systematic or orderly arrangement of parts, especially in art and architecture.

oregano /ɒrɪˈɡɑːnəʊ/, /əˈrɛɡənəʊ/ noun L18 Spanish and American Spanish (variant of ORIGANUM). An aromatic Eurasian plant related to marjoram, with small purple flowers and leaves used as a culinary herb.

organon /ˈɔːɡ(ə)nɒn/ noun L16 Greek (= instrument, organ). An instrument of thought, especially a means of reasoning or a system of logic.

■ In early use denoted a bodily organ. The Organon is the collective title of the logical treatises of Aristotle.

orgeat /ˈɔːdʒɪət/ foreign /ɔrʒa/ (plural same) noun LME French (from Provençal orjat, from ordi barley from Latin hordeum). A cooling drink made from orange flower water and either barley or almonds.

orientalia /ˌɔːrɪɛnˈteɪlɪə/, /ˌɒrɪɛnˈteɪlɪə/ noun plural E20 Latin (neuter plural of orientalis oriental). Things, especially books, relating to or characteristic of the Orient.

oriflamme /ˈɒrɪflam/ noun LME Old and Modern French (oriflambe, oriflamme, in medieval Latin auriflamma, from aurum gold + flamma flame). **1** History The sacred red or orange-red silk banner of St Denis, given to early kings of France by the abbot of St Denis on setting out for war. **2** A bright, conspicuous object.

origami /ɒrɪˈɡɑːmɪ/ noun M20 Japanese (from oru, -ori fold + kami paper). The Japanese art of folding paper into decorative shapes and figures. Also figurative.

figurative **1996** Spectator... any information about the songs has been left to rot in the unfathomable origami of CD booklets.

origanum /ɒˈrɪɡ(ə)nəm/ noun ME Latin (from Greek origanon, perhaps from oros mountain + ganos brightness, joy; cf. OREGANO). An aromatic plant of a genus (Origanum) that includes marjoram and oregano.

orthosis /ɔ:ˈθəʊsɪs/ *noun* plural **orthoses** /ɔ:ˈθəʊsiːz/ M20 Greek (*orthōsis* making straight, from *orthoun* to set straight). *Medicine* A brace, splint, or other artificial external device serving to prevent or assist relative movement in the limbs or the spine.

ortolan /ˈɔːt(ə)lən/ *noun* M17 French (from Provençal = gardener, from Latin *hortulanus*, from *hortulus* diminutive of *hortus* garden). A small Eurasian songbird, *Emberiza hortulana*, formerly eaten as a delicacy (also *ortolan bunting*).

■ Earlier (but only E16) in its original sense of 'gardener'.

orzo /ˈɔːdzo/ *noun* L20 Italian (= barley). Pasta in the shape of grains of rice.

o.s.p. abbreviation of OBIIT SINE PROLE.

osso bucco /ˌɒsəʊ ˈbuːkəʊ/ *noun phrase* M20 Italian (= marrowbone). An Italian dish made of shin of veal containing marrowbone, stewed in wine with vegetables.

ostinato /ɒstɪˈnɑːtəʊ/ *noun* plural **ostinati** /ɒstɪˈnɑːti/, **ostinatos** L19 Italian (= obstinate, persistent). *Music* A continually repeated musical phrase or rhythm.

1996 *Country Life* Matthew Richardson's short film, which told of the beginning of Lulu's downfall, was perfectly tailored to the catastrophic progress of the central orchestral *ostinato*.

Ostpolitik /ˈɒstpɒlɪˌtiːk/ *noun* M20 German (from *Ost* east + *Politik* policy). *History* The foreign policy of Western European countries with reference to the former communist bloc, especially the opening of relations with the Eastern bloc by the Federal Republic of Germany (West Germany) in the 1960s. Cf. WESTPOLITIK.

ostracon /ˈɒstrəkɒn/ *noun* plural **ostraca** /ˈɒstrəkə/ (also **ostrakon**, plural **ostraka**) L19 Greek (*ostrakon* hard shell, potsherd). *Archaeology* A potsherd used as a writing surface. Usually in *plural*.

o tempora, o mores! /əʊ ˈtɛmpərə əʊ ˌmɔːreɪz/ *interjection* M16 Latin (= o the times, o the manners!). What times, what ways!

■ Originally quoted from the Roman orator Cicero's impeachment of the conspirator Catiline (*In Catilinam* I.1) in 63 BC; now a general expression of alarm, contempt, amusement, etc., about behaviour in contemporary society.

1996 *Times* 'Even in the age of Aids, ... self-styled vampires drink blood—but from monogamous donors.' Sexually responsible vampires? *O tempora! O mores!*

ottava rima /ɒtˌtaːva ˈriːmaː/, /ɒˌtɑːvə ˈriːmə/ *noun* L18 Italian (= eighth rhyme). A form of poetry consisting of stanzas of eight lines, 11-syllabled in Italian, 10-syllabled in English, rhyming as *ababbacc*.

ottocento /ɒtəʊˈtʃɛntəʊ/ *adjective* E20 Italian (= eight hundred). Relating to the 19th century in Italy.

ou /əʊ/ *noun* plural **ouens** /ˈəʊənz/, **ous** M19 Afrikaans (from Dutch *oud* old). A man, a fellow. Cf. OUTJIE.

■ In South African colloquial speech, frequently used in terms of affection or casual reference.

oubliette /uːblɪˈɛt/ *noun* L18 French (from *oublier* to forget). A secret dungeon accessible only through a trapdoor in its ceiling.

oued see under WADI.

ouens plural of OU.

ouma /ˈəʊmə/ *noun* E20 Afrikaans (= grandmother, from OU old + *ma* mother). A grandmother; an elderly woman.

■ In South Africa, chiefly as a respectful or affectionate form of address or reference.

oupa /ˈəʊpə/ *noun* E20 Afrikaans (= grandfather, from OU old + *pa* father). A grandfather; an elderly man.

■ In South Africa, chiefly as a respectful or affectionate form of address or reference.

outjie /ˈəʊki/, /ˈəʊtʃi/ *noun* M20 Afrikaans (from as OU + diminutive suffix -*tjie*). A child, a little fellow.

■ In South African colloquial speech can also be used humorously or derogatively of an adult.

outré /utre/, /ˈuːtreɪ/ *adjective* E18 French (literally, 'exceeded'). Unusual and typically rather shocking; beyond the bounds of what is usual or proper; eccentric.

1996 *Country Life* Peter York celebrates some of the artefacts which still shine forth as emblems of the British soul, be they as conservative as the Bath Oliver biscuit or as outré as a Vivienne Westwood frock.

ouzo /ˈuːzəʊ/ *noun* plural **ouzos** L19 Modern Greek. A Greek aniseed-flavoured spirit.

ova plural of OVUM.

ovolo /ˈəʊvələʊ/ *noun* plural **ovoli** /ˈəʊvəli/ M17 Italian (diminutive of *uovo, ovo* from Latin *ovum* egg). *Architecture* A rounded convex moulding.

ovum /ˈəʊvəm/ *noun* plural **ova** /ˈəʊvə/ E18 Latin (= egg). *Biology* A mature female reproductive cell, especially of a human or other animal, which can divide to give rise to an embryo usually only after fertilization by a male cell.

oy /ɔɪ/ *interjection* L19 Yiddish. Used by Yiddish-speakers as an exclamation of dismay or grief.

■ Also in *oy vey, oy veh* /ɔɪ veɪ/ (Yiddish *vey* = woe).

oyer /ˈɔɪə/ *noun* LME Anglo-Norman (= Old French *oïr*: see next). *Law* The hearing of a case.

■ Exists only in the phrase *oyer and terminer* (formerly also *oyer (and) determiner*) 'a commission issued to judges on a circuit to hold courts'.

oyez /əʊˈjɛs/, /əʊˈjɛz/, /əʊˈjeɪ/ *verb & noun* (also **oyes** /əʊˈjɛs/) LME Anglo-Norman (Old French (also *oiez*) imperative plural of *oïr* (modern *ouïr*) from Latin *audire* to hear). **A** *intransitive verb* (*imperative*) Listen! **B** *noun* plural same, **oyesses**. A call or cry of 'oyez!'.

■ Uttered (usually three times) by a public crier or a court officer to command silence and attention before an announcement.

Pp

p.a. abbreviation of PER ANNUM.

paan /pɑːn/ *noun* (also **pan**) E17 Hindi (*pān* betel leaf, from Sanskrit *parṇa* feather, leaf). (In the Indian subcontinent) betel leaves prepared and used as a stimulant.

pabulum /'pabjələm/ *noun* M17 Latin (from stem of *pascere* to feed). Bland or insipid intellectual fare, entertainment, etc.

■ Originally used in the sense 'food, nutriment'.

1996 *Spectator* The dons who supply these masses with pabulum are not allowed to feel job-secure unless they are also engaged upon their own 'work'.

pace /'pɑːtʃeɪ/, /'peɪsɪ/ *preposition* L18 Latin (ablative singular of *pax* peace, as in *pace tua* by your leave). With due respect to (someone or their opinion).

■ Used especially as a courteous or ironical apology for a contradiction or difference of opinion (see quotation). Normally italicized to distinguish it from the English verb or noun 'pace'.

1996 *Spectator* Had he read the magnificent Turing biography by Andrew Hodges, which remains the best work on Bletchley Park to date (*pace* Robert Harris and his marvellous book), the hapless Volkman could have provided us with the theologically resonant denouement.

pacha variant of PASHA.

pachinko /pə'tʃɪŋkəʊ/ *noun* M20 Japanese. A variety of pinball popular in Japan.

pachisi /pə'tʃiːzi/ *noun* (also **parcheesi** /pɑː'tʃiːzi/, **Pachisi**) E19 Hindi (*pac(c)īsī* (throw of) twenty-five (the highest in the game), ultimately from Sanskrit *pañcaviṃśati* twenty-five). A four-handed Indian board game in which six cowries are used like dice.

pachuco /pə'tʃʊkəʊ/, *foreign* /pa'tʃuko/ *noun* plural **pachucos** /pə'tʃʊkəʊz/, *foreign* /pa'tʃukos/ M20 Mexican Spanish (literally, 'flashily dressed'). A member of a gang of young Mexican-Americans. Chiefly *North American*, *dated*.

1972 J. Wambaugh *Blue Knight* 'Órale, panzón,' he said, like a pachuco, which he put on for me. He spoke beautiful Spanish . . . but the barrios of El Paso Texas died hard.

padre /'pɑːdri/, /'pɑːdreɪ/ *noun* L16 Italian ((also Spanish, Portuguese) = father, priest, from Latin *pater*, *patr-* father). (In Italy, Spain, Portugal, Latin America, and other areas of Spanish influence) a title of a Christian clergyman, especially a Roman Catholic priest. Now chiefly (*colloquial*), a chaplain in the armed services.

padrone /pa'drəʊni/, *foreign* /pa'drone/ *noun* plural **padrones** /pa'drəʊnɪz/, **padroni** /pa'drəʊni/ (feminine (especially in sense (c)) **padrona** /pa'drəʊnə/, *foreign* /pa'drona/, plural **padronas** /pa'drəʊnəz/, **padrone** /pa'drone/) L17 Italian. A patron, a master; *specifically* (a) a Mafia boss; (b) (now chiefly *United States colloquial*) an employer, especially an exploitative employer of unskilled immigrant workers; (c) the proprietor of an inn or hotel in Italy.

paella /pʌɪ'ɛlə/, /pa'e(l)ja/ *noun* L19 Catalan (from Old French *paele* (modern *paêle*), from Latin *patella* pan, dish). A Spanish dish of rice, saffron, chicken, seafood, vegetables, etc., cooked and served in a large shallow pan.

figurative **1996** *Times* He is a full 20 seats short [of a parliamentary majority], compelling him to rely for survival . . . on a *paella* of regional parties.

pagoda /pə'gəʊdə/ *noun* L16 Portuguese (*pagode*, probably ultimately from Persian *butkada* idol temple, from *but* idol + *kada* habitation, alteration by association with Prakrit *bhagodī* divine, holy). **1** (In India and the Far East) a Hindu or Buddhist temple or sacred building, usually in the form of a many-tiered tower with storeys of diminishing size, each with an ornamented projecting roof. **2** An ornamental structure built in imitation of such a temple.

pagri /'pagri/ *noun* (also **puggaree** /'pʌg(ə)riː/) M17 Hindi (*pagrī* turban). (In the Indian subcontinent) a turban worn by employees of exclusive establishments or by people in the north of the region.

pahoehoe /pə'həʊɪhəʊi/ *noun* M19 Hawaiian. *Geology* Basaltic lava forming smooth, undulating or corded masses. Cf. AA.

paideia /pʌɪ'dʌɪə/ *noun* M20 Greek. (In ancient Greece) a system of broad cultural education; a society's culture.

paillette /pal'jɛt/, /pʌɪ'jɛt/ *noun* M19 French (diminutive of *paille* straw, chaff). **1** A small piece of glittering foil, shell, etc., used to decorate clothing; a spangle. **2** A decorative piece of coloured foil or bright metal used in enamel painting.

pain /pɛ̃/ *noun* LME Old and Modern French (from Latin *panis, pan-*). Bread, *specifically* in French bakery.
■ Formerly naturalized, it now occurs in English mainly in the names of French pastries such as *pain au chocolat* and *pain au raisin*.

paisano /pʌɪ'sɑːnəʊ/, *foreign* /pai'sano/ *noun* plural **paisanos** /pʌɪ'sɑːnəʊz/, *foreign* /pai'sanos/ M19 Spanish (= peasant, rustic). A peasant of Spanish or Italian ethnic origin. *North American.*

pak choi /pak 'tʃɔɪ/ *noun* M19 Chinese ((Cantonese) *paâk tsʼ oi* white vegetable: cf. PE TSAI). A Chinese cabbage of a variety with smooth-edged tapering leaves.

pakeha /'pɑːkɪhɑː/ *noun & adjective* E19 Maori. **A** *noun* A white New Zealander as opposed to a Maori. **B** *adjective* Relating to a pakeha. *New Zealand.*

pakora /pə'kɔːrə/ *noun* M20 Hindi (*pakoṛā* a dish of vegetables in gram flour). (In Indian cookery) a piece of vegetable or meat, coated in seasoned batter and deep-fried.

pa kua variant of BA GUA.

paladin /'palədɪn/ *noun* L16 French (from Italian *paladino*, from Latin *palatinus* officer of the palace). Each of the twelve bravest and most famous warriors of Charlemagne's court. Also, a knight renowned for heroism and bravery.

palaestra /pə'liːstrə/, /pə'lʌɪstrə/ *noun* (also **palestra** /pə'liːstrə/, /pə'lɛstrə/) LME Latin (from Greek *palaistra*, from *palaiein* wrestle). (In ancient Greece and Rome) a wrestling school or gymnasium.

palais /'paleɪ/ *noun* plural same /'paleɪz/ E20 French (literally, 'palace'). Abbreviation of PALAIS DE DANSE.
■ Often used in names, such as *Hammersmith Palais*.

palais de danse /ˌpaleɪ də 'dūs/ *noun phrase* plural same E20 French. A public hall for dancing.

palapa /pə'lapə/ *noun* L20 Mexican Spanish (= (the leaves and branches of) the palm *Orbignya cohune*). A traditional Mexican shelter roofed with palm leaves or branches. Also, any structure imitating this, especially on a beach. *United States.*

palazzo /pə'latsəʊ/ *noun & adjective* M17 Italian (from Latin *palatium* palace). **A** *noun* plural **palazzos**, (in sense 1) **palazzi** /pə'latsi/. **1** A palatial or imposing building, especially in Italy. **2** (in *plural*) Loose wide-legged trousers worn by women. **B** *adjective* Designating a loose wide-legged garment, outfit, etc.: *palazzo pants*.

1 1996 *Spectator* Of course, not everyone could afford imitation *palazzi* of their own.

palestra variant of PALAESTRA.

palette /'palɪt/ *noun* L18 French (diminutive of *pale* shovel). A thin (oval) board or slab, usually with a hole for the thumb, on which an artist lays and mixes colours. **b** The range of colours used by a particular artist or in a particular picture. **c** The range or variety of tonal or instrumental colour in a musical piece, composer's work, etc.; the verbal range of a writer etc. **d** *Computing* (In computer graphics) the range of colours or shapes available to the user. **e** The range or selection of available items.

pali /ˈpɑːli/ *noun* E19 Hawaiian. (In Hawaii) a steep cliff.

■ *The Pali* is a precipice on the island of Oahu.

palio /ˈpɑːlio/, /ˈpalɪəʊ/ *noun* L17 Italian (from Latin *pallium* covering, cover). A traditional horse race held in Italy, especially in Siena, every July and August. Also, the cloth or banner of velvet, silk, etc., given as the prize for winning this race.

palladium /pəˈleɪdɪəm/ *noun* plural **palladia** /pəˈleɪdɪə/ LME Latin (from Greek *palladion*, from *Pallas*, *Pallad-* epithet of the goddess Athene). **1** An image of the goddess Pallas (Athene), in the citadel of Troy, on which the safety of the city was supposed to depend, later reputed to have been taken to Rome. **2** A safeguard or source of protection.

2 1989 R. Milner-Gulland *Cultural Atlas of Russia* The icon of the 'Virgin of Vladimir,' the palladium of Vladimir and Moscow Grand Principalities, is of the iconographic type known as 'Tenderness' . . .

pallium /ˈpalɪəm/ *noun* plural **pallia** /ˈpalɪə/, **palliums** ME Latin (= covering, mantle). **1** A woollen vestment conferred by the Pope on an archbishop, consisting of a narrow circular band placed round the shoulders with a short lappet hanging from front and back. Also (*transferred*), the office or dignity of an archbishop. **2** *History* A man's large rectangular cloak, worn especially by Greek philosophical and religious teachers. **3** *Zoology* The mantle of a mollusc or brachiopod. **4** *Anatomy* and *Zoology* The outer wall of the cerebrum.

palmette /palˈmɛt/ *noun* M19 French (diminutive of *palme* palm leaf). *Archaeology* An ornament (in sculpture or painting) with radiating petals like a palm leaf.

palmier /palmje/ *noun* plural pronounced same E20 French (literally, 'palm tree'). A sweet crisp pastry shaped like a palm leaf.

palomino /paləˈmiːnəʊ/ *noun* plural **palominos** E20 American Spanish (from Spanish *palomino* young pigeon, from Latin *palumbinus* resembling a dove). **1** A horse with a light golden-brown coat and a white or pale mane and tail, originally bred in the southwestern United States. Also *palomino horse*. **2** A pale golden-brown colour.

pampas /ˈpampəs/, /ˈpampəz/ *noun* plural, also used as *singular* (also in singular form **pampa**) E18 Spanish (plural of *pampa* from Quechua = a plain). *plural* (treated as *singular* or *plural*). The extensive treeless plains of South America south of the Amazon. Also in *singular*, these plains considered collectively; any one of these plains.

pan variant of PAAN.

panacea /panəˈsiːə/ *noun* M16 Latin (from Greek *panakeia*, from *panakēs* all-healing, from *pan-* all + base of *akos* remedy). A remedy for all diseases; a thing for solving all difficulties or adopted in every case of difficulty.

panache /pəˈnaʃ/ *noun* M16 French (from Italian *pennacchio* from late Latin *pinnaculum* diminutive of *pinna* feather). **1** Originally, a tuft or plume of feathers, especially as a headdress or a decoration for a helmet. Also, a decoration like a plume of feathers, e.g. a tassel. **2** Flamboyant confidence of style or manner.

■ *Panache* (in sense 2) is represented as the key quality of the hero of Rostand's play *Cyrano de Bergerac* (1897).

2 1996 *Country Life* Lord Petersham drove his Cumberland cobs with considerable panache through the marathon obstacles in the horse pairs class . . .

panada /pəˈnɑːdə/ *noun* L16 Spanish ((also Portuguese) = Italian *panata*, represented a Proto-Romance derivation of Latin *panis* bread). Bread boiled in water to a pulp and flavoured. Also, a paste of flour, water, etc., used for thickening.

panatella /panəˈtɛlə/ *noun* M19 American Spanish (*panatela* long thin biscuit, sponge cake from Spanish from Italian *panatello* small loaf, diminutive of *panata* (as PANADA)). A long slender cigar, especially one tapering at the sealed end. Also more fully *panatella cigar*.

pancetta /panˈ(t)ʃɛtə/, *foreign* /panˈtʃetta/ *noun* M20 Italian (diminutive of *pancio* belly from Proto-Romance word (whence also 'paunch')). Italian cured belly of pork.

panem et circenses /ˌpanɛm ɛt sə:
'kɛnzi:z/, /kə:'kɛnseɪz/ *noun phrase* L18
Latin (= bread and circuses). State provision of popular entertainment and
distribution of food to win popularity
with the people.

■ Originally, the hand-outs and gladia-
torial games provided by Roman states-
men and emperors in the Circus of
ancient Rome to assuage the city's
notoriously volatile populace.
1961 D. L. Munby *God and Rich Society*
Leaders . . . win votes by offering *panem et
circenses* to those they despise.

panettone /panɪ'təʊni/, *foreign* /panet
'toni/ *noun* (also **panetone** /panɪ'təʊni/,
foreign /pane'tone/) plural **panettoni**
/panet'toni/ E20 Italian (from *panetto* cake,
bar, diminutive of *pane* bread, from Latin
panis). A rich Italian bread made with
eggs, fruit, and butter, and typically
eaten at Christmas.

panforte /pan'fɔ:ti/, *foreign* /pan'forte/
noun L19 Italian (from *pane* bread + *forte*
strong). A hard spicy Sienese cake containing nuts, candied peel, and honey.

panga /'paŋgə/ *noun* M20 Kiswahili. (In
East Africa) a bladed tool like a machete.

panino /pa'ni:no/ *noun* plural **panini**
/pa'ni:ni/ M20 Italian (= bread roll). A
sandwich made with a baguette or
with Italian bread, typically one that is
toasted.

panne /pan/ *noun* L18 French (of unknown origin). A soft silk or rayon
fabric with a flattened pile, resembling velvet. Also *panne velvet.*

panzanella /ˌpantsə'nɛlə/ *noun* L20
Italian (from *pane* bread + *zanella* small
basket). A type of Tuscan salad made
with anchovies, chopped salad vegetables, and bread soaked in dressing.

panzer /'panzə/, *foreign* /'pantsər/ *noun*
& *adjective* (also **Panzer**) M20 German (=
mail, coat of mail). A *noun* A German
armoured unit. Also, a German tank.
B *adjective* Relating to a panzer; *transferred* heavily armoured.
A *figurative* **1996** *Times Magazine* . . . the story
was also swiftly turned into a television
comedy, . . . the starring role being given to
'Wanda', a panzer among other cheerleader
moms.

B 1995 *Spectator* [The opposition's inform-
ants] were subsequently invited to leave
instantly, unless they wanted their departures
assisted by the steel-capped boot of a management which has proved over the past three
years that it can make a panzer division look
positively benign.

papabile /papa'bi:le/, /pə'pɑ:bɪli/ *adjective* (also **papabili** /papa'bi:li/) M20
Italian (from *papa* Pope). (Of a prelate)
worthy of being or eligible to be
elected Pope; *generally* suitable for
high office.
1964 *Spectator* He [sc. Harold Macmillan]
thought that three of the members of his
Cabinet who were in the House of Commons,
apart from Butler, were *papabile* and of
sufficient seniority to be considered: Maudling,
Heath and myself [sc. Iain Macleod].

paparazzo /papə'ratsəʊ/ *noun* plural
paparazzi /papə'ratsi/ M20 Italian. A freelance photographer who pursues celebrities in order to take their pictures.

■ From the surname of a character in
Federico Fellini's film *La Dolce Vita* (1960).
1995 *Times* Video paparazzi, who sell their
film to downmarket television shows, are
viewed as the vultures of the celebrity market,
sometimes seeking to pick fights with the
famous to secure pictures.

papier collé /papje kɔle/ *noun phrase*
plural **papiers collés** (*pronounced same*)
M20 French (= glued paper). A collage
made from paper; the technique of
using paper for collage.

papier mâché /ˌpapɪeɪ 'maʃeɪ/, *foreign*
/papje maʃe/ *noun* & *adjective phrase* M18
French (= chewed paper, from *papier*
paper + *mâché* past participle of *mâcher*
to chew, from Latin *masticare*). A *noun
phrase* A malleable mixture of paper
and glue, or paper, flour, and water,
that becomes hard when dry, used to
make boxes, trays, models, or ornaments. **B** *adjective phrase* Made of
papier mâché.
B 1996 *Times Magazine* A visit to the set of
Dr Who conjures up images of papier-mâché
monstrosities, nightmares in latex.

papillote see EN PAPILLOTE.

pappardelle /papɑ:'dɛli/ *noun* plural
L20 Italian (from *pappare* to eat hungrily).
Pasta in the form of broad flat ribbons,
usually served with a meat sauce.

paprika /ˈpaprɪkə/, /pəˈpriːkə/ *noun* L19 Hungarian. A powdered spice with a deep orange-red colour and a mildly pungent flavour, made from the dried and ground fruits of certain varieties of sweet pepper. **b** A deep orange-red colour.

papyrus /pəˈpʌɪrəs/ *noun* plural **papyri** /pəˈpʌɪrʌɪ/, /pəˈpʌɪriː/ LME Latin (from Greek *papuros* paper reed, of unknown origin). **1** An aquatic plant of the sedge family, formerly abundant in Egypt and the source of the writing material papyrus. **2** Material in the forms of fine strips of the stem of the papyrus plant, soaked in water, pressed together, and dried, to form a writing surface, used by the ancient Egyptians, Romans, etc. **3** A manuscript or document written on this.

parador /ˈparədɔː/ *noun* plural **paradores** /ˈparədɔːrez/, **paradors** M19 Spanish. A hotel in Spain owned and administered by the Spanish government. Formerly, any Spanish hotel or inn.
> **1995** D. Lodge *Therapy* It's now a five-star *parador*, one of the grandest hotels in Spain.

parados /ˈparədɒs/, *foreign* /parado/ *noun* plural **paradoses** /ˈparədɒsɪz/, same M19 French (from *para-* protection against + *dos* back). An elevation of earth behind a fortified place as a protection against attack from the rear; the mound along the back of a trench.

paramo /ˈparəməʊ/ *noun* plural **paramos** M18 Spanish ((also Portuguese) *páramo* from Spanish Latin *paramus* bare plain). A high plateau in the tropical parts of South America, bare of trees and exposed to wind and thick cold fogs.

parang /ˈpɑːraŋ/ *noun* M19 Malay. A large heavy knife used in Malaysia for clearing vegetation etc.

paratha /pəˈrɑːtə/ *noun* M20 Hindi (*parāṭhā*). (In Indian cookery) a flat piece of unleavened bread fried in butter, ghee, etc., on a griddle.

par avion /pɑː(r) aˈvjã/ *adverb phrase* M20 French (= by aeroplane). By airmail (written on a letter or parcel to indicate how it is to reach its destination).

parcheesi variant of PACHISI.

parens patriae /ˌparɛnz ˈpatriː/ *noun phrase* M18 Modern Latin (literally, 'parent of the country'). **1** *Law* The monarch, or any other authority, regarded as the legal protector of citizens unable to protect themselves. **2** The principle that political authority carries with it the responsibility for such protection.

parergon /pəˈrəːɡɒn/ *noun* plural **parerga** /pəˈrəːɡə/ E17 Latin (from Greek, from *para-* beyond, beside + *ergon* work). **1** A piece of work that is supplementary to or a by-product of a larger work. **2** Subsidiary work or business, apart from one's ordinary employment. *Archaic.*

par excellence /par ɛkslɑ̃s/, /pɑː(r) ˈɛks(ə)ləns/ *adverb phrase* L17 French (= by excellence). Better or more than all others of the same kind: *Nash is, to many, the Regency architect par excellence.*

parfait /ˈpɑːfeɪ/ *noun* L19 French (literally, 'perfect'). **1** A rich cold dessert made with whipped cream, eggs, and fruit. **2** A dessert consisting of layers of ice cream, meringue, and fruit, served in a tall glass.

parfleche /ˈpɑːflɛʃ/ *noun* E19 Canadian French (*parflèche*, from French *parer* ward off + *flèche* arrow). (In American Indian culture) a hide, especially a buffalo's hide, with the hair removed, dried by being stretched on a frame; an article, especially a bag, made from this.

parfumerie /parfymri/ *noun* plural pronounced same M19 French. A shop or department which sells perfume. Also, a perfume factory.

pariah /pəˈrʌɪə/ *noun* E17 Tamil (*paṟaiyar* plural of *paṟaiyan*, literally, 'hereditary drummer', from *paṟai* drum). **1** A member of a despised social class; an outcast. **2** A member of an indigenous people of southern India, originally functioning as ceremonial drummers but later having a low caste or no caste. *Absolete* except *historical.*
> **1** **1996** *Times* Nothing seems to boost a dictator so much as to be...ostracised. The

world's longest established rulers—Castro, Gaddafi, Assad, Saddam Hussein, the Ayatollahs—have all benefited from such pariah status.

pari-mutuel /parimytɥɛl/ (*plural same*); /ˌpɑːrɪˈmjuːtʃʊəl/ *noun* L19 French (= mutual stake or wager). A form of betting in which those backing the first three places divide the losers' stakes.

■ Often abbreviated to MUTUEL.

pari passu /ˌpɑːriː ˈpasuː/, /ˈpari/ *adverb phrase* M16 Latin (literally, 'with equal step'). With equal speed; side by side; simultaneously and equally. Also, on an equal footing, without preference.

> **1997** *Spectator* ... these blunders in public relations moved *pari passu* with the growth of the media ...

parka /ˈpɑːkə/ *noun* L18 Aleut (from Russian = skin jacket). A long hooded jacket made of animal skin, worn by Eskimos; a similar garment, usually of windproof fabric, designed to be worn in cold weather.

parlando /pɑːˈlandəʊ/ *adverb, adjective, & noun* L19 Italian (literally 'speaking'). *Music* **A** *adverb & adjective* (With reference to singing) expressive or declamatory in the manner of speech. **B** *noun* plural **parlandos, parlandi** /pɑːˈlandi/ Composition or performance in a parlando manner.

parmigiana /ˌpɑːmɪˈdʒɑːnə/ *adjective* L19 Italian (feminine of *parmigiano* of or pertaining to the city and province of Parma in northern Italy). (Of a dish) cooked or served with Parmesan cheese.

■ Chiefly used postpositively in names of dishes, as in *veal parmigiana*.

parole /pəˈrəʊl/, *in sense 3 usually foreign* /parɔl/ *noun & verb* L15 Old and Modern French (= word, formal promise, from ecclesiastical Latin *parabola* parable, from Greek *parabolē* comparison, analogy, proverb, from *paraballein* to put alongside, compare). **A** *noun* **1** The temporary or permanent release of a prisoner before the expiry of a sentence, on the promise of good behaviour. **2** *History* A promise or undertaking given by a prisoner of war to return to custody or act as a non-belligerent if released. **3** *Linguistics* The actual linguistic behaviour or performance of individuals, in contrast to the linguistic system of a community. Opposed to LANGUE. **B** *transitive verb* Release (a prisoner) on parole.

paronomasia /ˌparənəˈmeɪzɪə/ *noun* L16 Latin (from Greek, from *para-* beside, beyond + *onomasia* naming). A play on words, a pun; punning.

parquet /ˈpɑːki/, /ˈpɑːkeɪ/, *in sense 3 foreign* /parkɛ/ *noun* E19 Old and Modern French (= small marked-off area, diminutive of *parc* park). **1** Flooring composed of blocks of various woods arranged in a geometric pattern. Also *parquet flooring*. **2** The ground floor of a theatre or auditorium, especially the orchestra pit. Chiefly *United States*. **3** (In France and French-speaking countries) the branch of the administration of the law that deals with the prosecution of crime.

pars pro toto /ˌpɑːz prəʊ ˈtəʊtəʊ/ *noun phrase* E18 Latin (= part on behalf of the whole). A part or aspect of something taken as representative of the whole.

■ Frequently attributive.

parterre /pɑːˈtɛː/ *noun* E17 French (from *par terre* on or along the ground). **1** A level space in a garden occupied by an ornamental arrangement of flower beds. **2** The part of the ground floor of a theatre auditorium behind the orchestra pit, especially the part beneath the balconies. *United States*.

parti pris /parti pri/, /ˌpɑːtɪ ˈpriː/ *noun & adjective phrase* M19 French (literally, 'side taken'). **A** *noun phrase* plural **partis pris** (pronounced same). A preconceived view; a bias. **B** *adjective phrase* Prejudiced, biased; on the side of a particular party.

> **B 1995** *Spectator* He doesn't attempt to hide the fact that he is *parti pris*.

partita /pɑːˈtiːtə/ *noun* plural **partite** /pɑːˈtiːteɪ/, **partitas** L19 Italian (feminine past participle of *partire* to divide, from Latin *partiri* to part). *Music* A suite, typically one for a solo instrument or a chamber ensemble.

parure /pəˈrʊə/ *noun* E19 French (from *parer* to adorn, from Latin *parare* to prepare). A set of jewels or other ornaments intended to be worn together.

parvenu /'pɑːvənuː/, /'pɑːvənjuː/ *noun &*
adjective E19 French (use as noun of past
participle of *parvenir* to arrive from Latin
pervenire, from *per-* through + *venire* to
come). **A** *noun* (feminine **parvenue**) A
person of humble origin who has
gained wealth or position and risen
in society, *especially* one regarded as
unfitted for the position achieved in
this way, or as lacking the accomplish-
ments appropriate to it; an upstart.
B *adjective* That has recently risen to
wealth or position; resembling or
characteristic of a parvenu.

　A 1996 *Spectator* There are also several female
　whores ..., a witch, and the famous *parvenu*,
　Trimalchio, who gives a Lucullan banquet with
　perverse and ingenious cookery...
　B 1996 *Spectator* As a rule, though, the
　[Jockey] club has been happier cracking down
　on some flat-hatted trainer or parvenu owner
　who would never be allowed in.

pas /pɑ/, /pɑː/ *noun* plural same E18
French. A step in dancing, especially
in classical ballet.

■ Chiefly with qualifying word or phrase.

pas de basque /pɑ də bask/ *noun*
phrase E19 French (= step of a Basque). A
ballet step in three beats, with a
circular movement of the right leg
on the second beat; (especially in jigs
and reels) a step in three beats with
one long and two short movements,
transferring weight from one foot to
the other on the spot.

pas de bourrée /pɑ də bure/ *noun*
phrase E20 French. *Ballet* A sideways step
in which one foot crosses behind or in
front of the other; a BOURRÉE step.

pas de chat /pɑ də ʃɑ/ *noun phrase*
E20 French (literally, 'step of a cat'). *Ballet*
A jump in which each foot in turn is
raised to the opposite knee.

pas de deux /pɑ də dø/, /ˌpɑ də 'dəː/
noun phrase M18 French (= step of two). A
dance for two people (typically a man
and a woman), especially in classical
ballet.

　1995 *Times* Stuart Cassidy and Muriel Valtat,
　dressed in vaporous white, ... swirl and float
　through their romantic pas de deux.

pas de quatre /pɑ də katr/ *noun*
phrase L19 French (= step of four). A dance

for four people, especially in classical
ballet.

pas de trois /pɑ də trwɑ/ *noun phrase*
M18 French (= step of three). A dance for
three people, especially in classical
ballet.

pas devant /pɑ dəvɑ̃/ *interjection* M20
French (= not in front of). (Of a statement, action, etc.) not appropriate or
proper for the present company.

■ *Pas devant* is an elliptical version of the
warning expression *pas devant les enfants*
/lɛz ɑ̃fɑ̃/ 'not in front of the children'. The
assumption is that the children will not
understand a warning given in French.
Other nouns are substituted, as appropriate, for *les enfants*.

paseo /pɑ'seɪəʊ/, *foreign* /pɑ'seo/ *noun*
plural **paseos** /pɑ'seɪəʊz/, *foreign*
/pɑ'seos/ M19 Spanish (= step). (In Spain
or Spanish-speaking parts of the
south-western United States) a leisurely walk or stroll, especially one
taken in the evening in which young
people may socialize with each other.

pasha /'pɑːʃə/ *noun* (also **pacha**) M17
Turkish (*paşa*, from Persian *pād(i)šāh*,
Pahlavi *pati* lord + SHAH). *History* The
title of a Turkish officer of high rank,
as a military commander, provincial
governor, etc.

pashmina /pʌʃ'miːnə/ *noun* L20 Persian
(from *pašm* wool). A shawl made from
fine-quality goat's wool.

paskha /'pasxə/, /'paskə/ *noun* (also
paska) E20 Russian (= Easter). A rich
Russian dessert made with curd cheese,
dried fruit, nuts, and spices, set in a
mould and traditionally eaten at Easter.

paso doble /ˌpasə(ʊ) 'dəʊbleɪ/ *noun*
phrase plural **paso dobles** E20 Spanish
(= double step). A quick ballroom dance
based on a Latin American style of
marching; a piece of music for this
dance, usually in duple time.

pasquinade /ˌpaskwɪ'neɪd/ *noun* (originally **pasquinadata**) L16 Italian (*pas-
quinata*, French *pasquinade*, from *Pasquin*
the name of a statue in Rome on which
abusive Latin verses were annually
posted during the 16th century). A satire

or lampoon, originally one displayed or delivered in a public place.

passacaglia /pasə'kɑ:lɪə/ *noun* M17 Italian (from Spanish *pasacalle*, from *pasar* to pass + *calle* street (originally often played in the streets)). *Music* A slow musical composition usually with a ground bass and in triple time; an early kind of dance to this music.

passade /pə'seɪd/ *noun* M17 French (from Italian *passata* or Provençal *passada*, from medieval Latin *passare* to pass). A movement performed in advanced dressage and classical riding, in which the horse performs a forwards or backwards turn on the spot.

passata /pə'sɑ:tə/ *noun* L20 Italian. A thick paste made from sieved tomatoes and used especially in Italian cooking.

passé /'paseɪ/, *foreign* /pɑse/ *adjective* & *noun* L18 French (past participial adjective of *passer* to pass). **A** *adjective* **1** Past one's prime. *Archaic.* **2** No longer fashionable; out of date, behind the times. **B** *noun Ballet* The transitional movement of the leg from one position to the next.

> **A.2 1996** *Bookseller* European publishers who went to Milia last week to display their latest CD-ROM products with pride must have been more than a little put out to hear American visitors saying that CD-ROMs are passé.

passeggiata /ˌpassed'dʒiata/ *noun* plural **passeggiate** /ˌpassed'dʒiate/ M20 Italian. A leisurely walk or stroll, a promenade.

■ Usually referring to the evening stroll for relaxation and socializing habitually taken by citizens of Italy and other Mediterranean countries; the equivalent of the Greek *volta.*

> **1971** N. Fisher *Rise at Dawn* We drove into Viareggio one evening. It was the hour of the passeggiata ... The pavements thronged with strolling families.

passementerie /'pasm(ə)ntri/, *foreign* /pɑsmɑ̃tri/ *noun* E17 French (from *passement* gold lace, from *passer* to pass; the connection with Spanish and Italian *passamano* (apparently from *passare* to pass + *mano* hand) and the reason for this name are both obscure). Decorative

textile trimming consisting of gold or silver lace, gimp, or braid.

passepartout /ˌpaspɑ:'tu:/, /ˌpɑ:spɑ:'tu:/ *noun* L17 French (from *passer* to pass + *partout* everywhere). **1** A thing which goes or provides a means of going everywhere; *specifically* a master key. *Archaic.* **2** A simple picture frame consisting of two sheets of transparent material (or one sheet with a card backing) stuck together at the edges with adhesive tape. Also, adhesive tape used in making such a frame.

pas seul /pɑ sœl/ *noun phrase* plural **pas seuls** (*pronounced same*) E19 French (= single step). A dance for one person, especially in classical ballet.

passim /'pasɪm/ *adverb* & *adjective* E19 Latin (literally, 'scatteredly', from *passus* scattered, past participle of *pandere* to spread out). (Of an allusion or reference in a published work) to be found at various places throughout the text. Also *transferred* and *figurative*.

> **1996** *Country Life* ... a minister's life—see Tristan Garel-Jones *passim*—can and does include a certain salty lack of political correctness when it comes to dealing with foreigners.

passus /'pasəs/ *noun* plural same L16 Latin (= step, pace). A section, division, or canto of a story or poem, especially a medieval one.

pasta /'pastə/ *noun* L19 Italian (= paste, from late Latin *pasta* a small square piece of medicinal preparation, from Greek *pastē*). A type of dough made from durum wheat flour and water and extruded or stamped into particular shapes (and often dried if not for immediate use). Also, an Italian dish consisting largely of this and usually a sauce.

pasticcio /pa'stɪtʃɪəʊ/ *noun* plural **pasticcios** M18 Italian (= pie, pasty, from Proto-Romance, from late Latin *pasta* paste). A PASTICHE.

pastiche /pa'sti:ʃ/ *noun* & *verb* L19 French (from as PASTICCIO). **A** *noun* An artistic work in a style that imitates that of another work, artist, or period; an artistic work consisting of a medley of pieces imitating various sources.

B *transitive verb* Imitate the style of (an artist or work).
A *transferred* **1996** *Times Magazine* It's a pastiche of a fashionable London restaurant of the moment.

pasticheur /ˌpasti:'ʃəː/ *noun* E20 French (from PASTICHE). An artist who imitates the style of another artist.
1996 *Country Life* Miss Guest is an Edwards pasticheur..., creating wide-screen images of hounds in full cry and horses streaming across open country.

pastille /'past(ə)l/, /'pastɪl/ *noun* M17 French (from Latin *pastillus* little loaf or roll, lozenge, diminutive of *panis* loaf). **1** A small sweet or lozenge. **2** A small pellet of aromatic paste burnt as a perfume or deodorizer.

pastis /'pastɪs/, /pa'sti:s/ *noun* E20 French. An aniseed-flavoured aperitif.

pastorale /pastə'rɑ:l/, /pastə'rɑ:leɪ/ *noun* plural **pastorales, pastorali** /pastə'rɑ:li/ E18 Italian (use as noun of *pastorale* pastoral, from Latin *pastoralis* from *pastor* shepherd, from *past-* past participial stem of *pascere* to feed, graze). *Music* **1** A slow instrumental composition in compound time, often with drone notes in the bass suggestive of a shepherd's bagpipes. **2** A simple musical play with a rural subject.

pastourelle /pasturɛl/ (*plural same*), /pastu'rɛl/ *noun* L19 French (feminine of *pastoureau* shepherd). A medieval lyric whose theme is love for a shepherdess.
■ The Provençal or Portuguese word *pastorela* (L19) is also used.

pastrami /pa'strɑːmi/ *noun* M20 Yiddish (from Romanian *pastramă*, probably of Turkish origin). Highly seasoned smoked beef, typically served in thin slices.

pata-pata /ˌpɑːta'pɑːta/ *noun* M20 Xhosa and Zulu (*phathphatha* to feel with the hands). **1** (In South Africa) a sexually suggestive dance style in which pairs of dancers touch each other's bodies; kwela music arranged to suit this style of dance. **2** Sexual intercourse. *South African slang*.

patchouli /'patʃʊli/, /pə'tʃuːli/ *noun* (also **patchouly**) M19 Tamil (*paccuḷi*). **1** A strongly scented south-east Asian shrub of the mint family, *Pogostemon*

cablin, whose leaves yield an aromatic oil much used in perfumery. **2** The aromatic oil obtained from this plant.

pâte /pɑt/ *noun* M19 French. The paste of which porcelain is made.

pâté /'pateɪ/ *noun* E18 French (from Old French *pasté* pie of seasoned meat). A rich, savoury paste made from finely minced or mashed ingredients, typically seasoned meat or fish.

pâté de campagne /ˌpateɪ də kɒm'pɑːnjə/ *noun phrase* M20 French (= country pâté). A coarse pork and liver pâté.

pâté de foie gras /'pateɪ də fwɑː ˌgrɑː/ *noun phrase* E19 French. A smooth rich pâté of fatted goose liver.
■ Originally a pie filled with this paste, also known as a 'Strasbourg pie'; now applied just to the filling served as a separate dish.

patella /pə'tɛlə/ *noun* plural **patellae** /pə'tɛliː/ L16 Latin (diminutive of *patera* shallow dish). *Anatomy* The kneecap.

pâté maison /'pateɪ ˌmɛzɔ̃ː/ *noun phrase* M20 French (= house pâté). Pâté made to the recipe of a particular restaurant.

pater /'peɪtə/ *noun* ME Latin. **1** Father. *British colloquial, dated*. Cf. MATER. **2** *Anthropology* A person's legal as opposed to biological father. Cf. GENITOR.

patera /'pat(ə)rə/ *noun* plural **paterae** /'pat(ə)riː/ M17 Latin (from *patere* to be open). **1** A broad shallow dish used in ancient Rome especially for pouring libations. **2** *Architecture* A flat round ornament resembling a shallow dish. **3** A broad shallow bowl-shaped feature on the surface of a planet.

paterfamilias /ˌpeɪtəfə'mɪlɪas/, /ˌpatə fə'mɪlɪas/ *noun* plural **patresfamilias** /ˌpeɪtriːzfə'mɪlɪas/, /ˌpatriːzfə'mɪlɪas/ L15 Latin (from *pater* father + archaic genitive of *familia* family). **1** A male head of a family or household. **2** *Roman Law* The male head of a family or household having authority over its members. Also, any male legally independent and free from parental control.

paternoster /patə'nɒstə/, /ˌpɑːtə'nɒstə/ *noun* OE Latin (*paternoster* literally, 'our father', the first two words of the Lord's

Prayer in Latin). **1** (In the Roman Catholic Church) the Lord's Prayer, especially in the Latin version. **2** Any of several special beads occurring at regular intervals in a rosary to indicate that a paternoster is to be said. Also, the whole rosary. **3** A fishing line with hooks or weights attached at intervals. More fully *paternoster line*. **4** A lift consisting of a series of doorless compartments moving continuously on an endless belt. Also more fully *paternoster elevator, paternoster lift*.

pathos /'peɪθɒs/ *noun* L16 Greek (= suffering, feeling, related to *paskhein* to suffer, *penthos* grief). A quality in speech, writing, events, persons, etc., which evokes pity or sadness.

> **1996** *Country Life* ... the work's humour served deeply serious ends and was flecked with darker moments and a touchingly lyrical pathos.

patina /'patɪnə/ *noun* M18 Italian (from Latin = shallow dish or pan). A usually green film produced on the surface of bronze or similar metals by oxidation over a long period; a gloss or sheen on wooden furniture produced by age and polishing; the impression or appearance of something.

> **1996** *Country Life* In keeping with this patina of elder statesmanship, the tone is disconcertingly formal by today's standards ...

patio /'patɪəʊ/ *noun* plural **patios** E19 Spanish (= inner courtyard of a house). **1** A paved outdoor area adjoining a house. **2** A roofless inner courtyard in a Spanish or Spanish-American house.

patisserie /pə'tiːs(ə)ri/ *noun* (also **pâtisserie**) L16 French (*pâtisserie* from medieval Latin *pasticium*, from *pasta* paste). **1** A shop where pastries and cakes are sold. **2** Pastries and cakes collectively.

patissier /pə'tiːsɪə/, *foreign* /patisje/ *noun* (also **pâtissier**, feminine **patissiere**, **patissière** /pə'tiːsɪɛː/, *foreign* /patisjɛr/) E20 French. A pastry cook.

> **1995** *Times Magazine* If I were seriously rich and had a large kitchen, I sometimes think I would like to employ a pâtissier.

patois /'patwɑː/ *noun* plural same /'patwɑːz/ M17 Old and Modern French (= rough speech, perhaps from Old French *patoier* to handle roughly, trample, from

patte paw, of unknown origin). **1** The dialect of a particular region, especially one with low status in relation to the standard language of the country. **2** The jargon or informal speech used by a particular social group. **3** The creole of the English-speaking Caribbean, especially Jamaica.

> **1** **1995** G. Tindall *Celestine* In ... age he had become hard of hearing and had reverted in his own speech to the patois of long ago.

patresfamilias plural of PATERFAMILIAS.

patria /'patrɪə/, /'peɪtrɪə/ *noun* E20 Latin. One's native country or homeland.

patron /pa'trɒn/, *foreign* /patrɔ̃/, *foreign* /pa'tron/ *noun* L19 French (from Latin *patronus* protector of clients, advocate, defender, from *pater, patr-* father). The proprietor of an inn or restaurant, especially in France and Spain. Cf. Italian PADRONE.

> ■ *Patron*, with the pronunciation /'peɪtr(ə)n/, has also been fully anglicized since its introduction in Middle English, in senses derived from ecclesiastical and classical Latin.

patronne /patrɔn/ *noun* plural pronounced same L18 French (feminine of PATRON). (Especially in France) a woman who is the owner, or the wife of the owner, of a business, especially a café, hotel, or restaurant.

patte de velours /pat də vlur/ *noun phrase* M19 French (= paw of velvet). A cat's paw with the claws retracted, as a symbol of resolution or inflexibility hidden beneath apparent gentleness.

paupiette /pɔːp'jɛt/ *noun* (originally **poupiets**) E18 French (perhaps from Italian *polpetta*, from Latin *pulpa* pulp). A long thin slice of fish or meat, rolled and stuffed with a filling.

> ■ Usually in plural in names of dishes, as in *paupiettes de veau*. A dish of this sort is also sometimes called *alouettes sans tête* '(sky)larks without heads'. An alternative etymology perhaps connects with French *poupée 'doll'*; cf. the minced-meat dish called in modern Greek *koukla*, also meaning 'doll'.

pavane /pə'van/, /pə'vɑːn/ *noun* (also **pavan** /'pav(ə)n/) M16 French (probably from Italian dialect *pavana* feminine of *pavano* of Padua, from *Pavo* dialect name of Padua (Italian *Padova*)). **1** *History* A grave and stately dance in slow duple time, performed in elaborate clothing and popular in the 16th century. **2** A piece of music for this dance or in its rhythm.

pavé /'paveɪ/, *foreign* /pave/ (*plural same*) *noun* (also (earlier) anglicized as **pave** /peɪv/) LME French (= paved, past participle of *paver* to pave). **1** A paved street, road, or path. **2** A setting of precious stones placed so closely together that no metal is visible.

2 1996 *Country Life* The brooch... is a geometric platinum-set design of baguette and brilliant cut diamonds with *pavé*-set terminals...

pax /paks/ *noun & interjection* LME Latin (= peace). **A** *noun* (In the Christian Church) the kissing by all the participants at a mass of a tablet depicting the Crucifixion or other sacred object; the kiss of peace. **B** *interjection* A call for a truce, used especially by schoolchildren when playing. *British colloquial, dated.*

pax Romana /ˌpaks rəʊ'mɑːnə/ *noun phrase* L19 Latin (= Roman peace). The peace which existed between nationalities under the Roman Empire.

■ Originally from Pliny's *Natural History* (xxvii.3), *pax Romana* has been the model for other phrases with a Latin or modern Latin adjective referring to the dominant influence of a state, empire, etc. (see quotation 1996).

1993 G. Fowden *Empire to Commonwealth* They [sc. the Jews] benefited from the *pax Romana* to develop their communities, build impressive synagogues, and assert a claim to social esteem.

1996 *Times* They [sc. the Serbs] will fight, fight and fight again for this, long after the Americans lose interest in their *pax Americana*, as it becomes a desert...

paysage /peizaʒ/ *noun* plural pronounced same E17 French (from *pays* country). A rural scene or landscape, especially as depicted in art.

paysan /peizã/ *noun & adjective* E19 French (from Old French *païsant, païsent*, alteration of earlier *païsenc*, from *païs* (modern *pays*) country, from Proto-Ro-

mance alteration of Latin *pagus* rural district). **A** *noun* plural pronounced same. A peasant or countryman, especially in France. **B** *adjective* (Of a style of art, dress, etc.) resembling that of peasants.

paysanne /peizan/ *noun* plural pronounced same M18 French (feminine of PAYSAN). A peasant-woman or countrywoman, especially in France.

peau-de-soie /podəswa/, /ˌpəʊdə'swɑː/ *noun* M19 French (literally, 'skin of silk'). A smooth, finely ribbed fabric of silk or rayon.

peau d'orange /ˌpəʊ dɒ'rɒ̃z/ *noun* L19 French (literally, 'orange skin'). A pitted or dimpled appearance of the skin, especially as characteristic of some cases of breast cancer or due to cellulite.

peccadillo /pɛkə'dɪləʊ/ *noun* plural **peccadilloes, peccadillos** L16 Spanish (*pecadillo* diminutive of *pecado* sin). A relatively minor fault or sin; a trifling offence.

peccavi /pɛ'kɑːviː/ *interjection & noun* E16 Latin (= I have sinned). **A** *interjection* Acknowledging guilt. **B** *noun* An acknowledgement or confession of guilt.

■ As an interjection, now usually humorous; cf. MEA CULPA. The word features in the message supposedly sent by Charles Napier to Lord Ellenborough in 1843, announcing his conquest of the province of Sindh, '*Peccavi*—I have Sindh.' The 'message' appeared in *Punch*, 18 May 1844, and was in fact composed by Catherine Winkworth (1827–78).

pecorino /pɛkə'riːnəʊ/ *noun* M20 Italian (from *pecora* sheep). A hard Italian cheese made from ewe's milk.

peignoir /'peɪnwɑː/ *noun* M19 French (from *peigner* to comb (the garment was originally worn while combing the hair)). A woman's light dressing gown or negligee.

pelota /pɪ'lɒtə/, /pɪ'ləʊtə/ *noun* E19 Spanish (= ball, from *pella*, from Latin *pila* ball). **1** A Basque or Spanish game played in a walled court with a ball and basket-like wicker rackets attached to gloves. **2** The ball used in pelota.

peloton /ˈpɛlətɒn/ *noun* M20 French (= small ball (because of the concentrated grouping of the pack), from *pelote* from Proto-Romance diminutive of Latin *pila* ball). *Cycling* The main field, group, or pack of cyclists in a race.

■ The original senses in which *peloton* was introduced (both E18) are now rare or obsolete: 'a small ball or pellet' and (its modern French sense) 'a platoon'.
1996 *Times* Riis...has grown up in the peloton, the toughest school of all, and has no time for niceties.

pelta /ˈpɛltə/ *noun* plural **peltae** /ˈpɛltiː/ (also anglicized as **pelt**) E17 Latin (from Greek *peltē* a small light leather shield). **1** A small light shield, as used by the ancient Greeks and Romans. **2** An ornamental motif resembling a shield in architecture, metalwork, etc.

pemmican /ˈpɛmɪk(ə)n/ *noun* L18 Cree (*pimihkan*, from *pimiy* grease). A pressed cake of pounded dried meat mixed to a paste with melted fat and berries, originally made by North American Indians and later adapted by Arctic explorers.

penates /pɪˈnɑːtiːz/, /pɪˈneɪtiːz/ *noun plural* E16 Latin (*Penates* (plural), from *penus* provision of food, related to *penes* within). Household gods worshipped in conjunction with Vesta and the lares by the ancient Romans. Cf. LARES.
■ Often in English in the phrase *lares and penates*.

penchant /ˈpɒ̃ʃɒ̃/ *noun* L17 French (= leaning, inclining, present participle of *pencher* to lean, incline). A strong or habitual liking for something or tendency to do something.
1996 *Spectator* She had a *penchant* for younger men, on whom she squandered much of her money...

pendente lite /pɛnˌdɛntɪ ˈlʌɪtɪ/ *adverb phrase* E18 Latin (literally, 'with the lawsuit pending'). *Law* During litigation; depending on the outcome of litigation.

penetralia /pɛnɪˈtreɪlɪə/ *noun plural* M17 Latin (use as noun of *penetralia* neuter plural of *penetrālis* innermost). The innermost parts of a building; a secret or hidden place.

penne /ˈpɛneɪ/ *noun plural* L20 Italian (literally, 'quills, pens'). Pasta in the form of short wide tubes cut diagonally at both ends.

pensée /pɑ̃se/ *noun* plural pronounced same L19 French. A thought or reflection put into literary form; an aphorism.

pension /pɑ̃sjɔ̃/ (*plural same*) *noun* M17 French (Old French *pension* from Latin *pensio(n-)* payment, rent, from *pens-* past participial stem of *pendere* to weigh, pay). A small hotel or boarding house in France or another European country. Cf. EN PENSION.
■ *Pension* was first introduced in the LME period and, with the pronunciation /ˈpɛnʃ(ə)n/, is now wholly anglicized in its numerous senses deriving from Old French and Latin, almost all of which contain the idea of 'a fixed regular payment'. The sense above was also formerly anglicized.

pensione /pɛnsɪˈəʊneɪ/ *noun* plural **pensioni** /pɛnsɪˈəʊni/ M20 Italian. A small hotel or boarding house in Italy.

pentimento /pɛntɪˈmɛntəʊ/ *noun* plural **pentimenti** /pɛntɪˈmɛnti/ E20 Italian (literally, 'repentance'). A visible trace of earlier painting beneath a layer or layers of paint on a canvas; a painting revealed by such traces.

peon /ˈpiːən/, *in sense 1 also* /pjuːn/, *sense 2 also* /perˈɒn/, *foreign* /peˈon/ *noun* plural **peons** (*in sense 3 also* **peones** /ˈpiːənɪz/, *foreign* /peˈones/) E17 Portuguese and Spanish (in sense 1 from Portuguese *peão*; in senses 2 and 3 from Spanish *peón* peasant, from medieval Latin *pedo(n-)* foot-soldier). **1** (In the Indian subcontinent and South-East Asia) a low-ranking soldier or worker. **2** A Spanish-American day labourer or unskilled farm worker, *especially* one in poor circumstances; a person who does menial work. Also (*historical*), a debtor held in servitude by a creditor, especially in the southern United States and Mexico. **3** A BANDERILLERO.

peperoni variant of PEPPERONI.

peplos /ˈpɛplɒs/ *noun* L18 Greek. A rich outer robe or shawl worn by women in ancient Greece, hanging in loose folds and sometimes drawn over the head.

peplum /ˈpɛpləm/ *noun* L17 Latin (from Greek PEPLOS). **1** A short gathered or pleated strip of fabric attached to the waist of a woman's jacket, dress, or blouse to create a hanging frill or flounce. **2** (In ancient Greece) a woman's loose outer tunic or shawl.

pepperoni /pɛpəˈrəʊni/ *noun* (also **peperoni**) M20 Italian (*peperone* chilli, from *peper-*, *pepe* pepper, from Latin *piper* + augmentative suffix *-one*). Beef and pork sausage seasoned with pepper.

per /pə:/ *preposition* LME Latin (= through, by means of, whence Old French and Italian *per*, French *par* through). **1** For each, for every (used with units to express a rate). **2** By means of. *Archaic*. **3** *Heraldry* Divided by a line in the direction of. **4** In accordance with (usually *as per*).

per annum /pə(r) ˈanəm/ *adverb phrase* E17 Modern Latin (from as PER + accusative of Latin *annus* year). For or in each year (used in financial contexts).

■ Abbreviated to *p.a.*

percale /pəˈkeɪl/, *foreign* /pɛrkal/ *noun* E17 French (in modern use, but origin unknown (= Spanish *percal*, Italian *percalle*)). A closely woven fine cotton fabric.

per capita /pə ˈkapɪtə/ *adverb & adjective phrase* L17 Modern Latin (= by heads). For each person or head of population; in relation to people taken individually.

1996 *Times* Government expenditure in Scotland is nearly one-third higher *per capita* than that for England.

per centum /pə ˈsɛntəm/ *adverb phrase* M17 Modern Latin (Latinized form of *per cent*). Per cent.

■ Frequently in legal contexts.

per contra /pə: ˈkɒntrə/ *adverb & noun phrase* M16 Italian. **A** *adverb phrase* On the opposite side (of an account or assessment); on the other hand. **B** *noun phrase* The opposite side of an account or an assessment.

1996 *Times*…a mass exit by the City herd would make AIM shares even more volatile

than they are by nature. *Per contra*, AIM could become too respectable.

per diem /pə: ˈdiːɛm/, /ˈdʌɪɛm/ *adverb, adjective, & noun phrase* E16 Modern Latin (from as PER + accusative of Latin *dies* day). **A** *adverb phrase* For each day (used in financial contexts). **B** *adjective phrase* Daily (used in financial contexts). **C** *noun phrase* An allowance or payment made for each day.

C 1996 *Spectator*…Hollywood doesn't help at all and he goes crackers *con brio* with vanishing agents, certifiable producers, grotty hotels, stingy *per diems* and lurking rewrite men.

père /pɛr/, /pɛː/ *noun* E17 French (= father). The father, senior.

■ *Père* is appended to a name to distinguish between a father and son of the same name. Cf. FILS; also in phrase *père et fils* 'father and son'.

1995 *Spectator* And yet—another irony—Forte *père* remained, well beyond normal retirement age, a fiercely combative entrepreneur…

perestroika /pɛrɪˈstrɔɪkə/ *noun* L20 Russian (*perestroīka* restructuring). (In the former Soviet Union) the policy or practice of restructuring or reforming the economic and political system. First proposed by Leonid Brezhnev in 1979 and actively promoted under the leadership of Mikhail Gorbachev from 1985, perestroika originally referred to increased automation and labour efficiency, but came to entail greater awareness of economic markets and the ending of central planning; *transferred* any programme of fundamental reform. See also GLASNOST.

1996 *Spectator* Ostensibly, it's to pay for digital technology in radio and television,…but I don't accept that this is the main reason for such *perestroika*.

perfecta /pəˈfɛktə/ *noun* L20 American Spanish (shortened from *quiniela perfecta* perfect quinella). A bet in which the first and second finishers of a race must be predicted in the correct order. *North American*. Cf. QUINELLA.

perfecto /pəˈfɛktəʊ/ *noun* plural **perfectos** L19 Spanish (= perfect). A large thick cigar tapered at each end.

perfide Albion /pɛrfid albjɔ̃/ *noun phrase* M19 French (= perfidious Albion). England (with reference to its alleged habitual treachery towards other nations); an untrustworthy Englishman.

■ The French phrase *la perfide Albion* is said to have been first used by the Marquis de Ximenès (1727–1817).

pergola /'pə:gələ/ *noun* M17 Italian (from Latin *pergula* projecting roof, vine arbour, from *pergere* to come or go forward). An arched structure in a garden or park consisting of a framework covered with climbing or trailing plants.

peri /'pɪəri/ *noun* L18 Persian (*perī*). (In Persian mythology) a mythical superhuman being, originally represented as evil but subsequently as a good and graceful genie or fairy.

peridot /'pɛrɪdɒt/ *noun* E18 French (from Old French *peritot*, of unknown origin). A green semi-precious variety of forsterite (olivine).

peripeteia /ˌpɛrɪpɪ'tʌɪə/, /ˌpɛrɪpɪ'ti:ə/ *noun* (also **peripetia** /ˌpɛrɪpɪ'ti:ə/) L16 Greek (ultimately from *peri-* around + stem *pet-* of *piptein* to fall). A sudden reversal of fortune or change in circumstances, especially in reference to fictional narrative.

■ Used by Aristotle in his *Poetics* as a technical term for the sequence of events in the plot of a drama which, in the case of a tragic hero, takes the protagonist from happiness to misfortune.

1984 A.G. Lehmann *European Heritage* The insidious flatteries of the 'mirror' stage—the symmetrical throne-room scenes, the hero revolving great dilemmas, the god descending, the wonderful *peripeteia*—become lessons in style to haunt the prince's dream and shape his acts.

periphrasis /pə'rɪfrəsɪs/ *noun* plural **periphrases** /pə'rɪfrəsi:z/ M16 Latin (from Greek, from *periphrazein*, from *peri-* around + *phrazein* to declare). The figure of speech which consists in expressing a meaning by many or several words instead of by few or one; a roundabout way of speaking or writing; circumlocution.

peristyle /'pɛrɪstʌɪl/ *noun* E17 French (*péristyle* from Latin *peristylum* from Greek *peristulon* use as noun of neuter of *peristulos* having pillars all round, from *peri-* around + *stulos* column). *Architecture*

1 A row of columns surrounding a space within a building such as a court or internal garden, or edging a veranda or porch. 2 A space such as a court or porch that is surrounded or edged by a peristyle.

perpetuum mobile /pə:ˌpɛtjʊəm 'məʊ bɪli/, /pə:ˌpɛtjʊʊm/, /'məʊbɪleɪ/ *noun phrase* L17 Latin (from *perpetuus* perpetual + *mobilis* movable, mobile, after PRIMUM MOBILE). 1 Perpetual motion, motion that continues forever; *specifically* that of a hypothetical machine that runs forever; such a machine. 2 *Music* A MOTO PERPETUO.

per se /pə: seɪ/ *adverb phrase* L16 Latin. By or in itself or themselves; intrinsically.

1995 *Times* Knives—beyond a small variety such as flick-knives—are not 'offensive weapons' per se.

persiflage /'pə:sɪflɑːʒ/ *noun* M18 French (from *persifler* to banter, from as PER + *siffler* to whistle). Light and slightly contemptuous mockery or banter; frivolous talk.

persona /pə'səʊnə/ *noun* plural **personas**, **personae** /pə'səʊni:/ E20 Latin (originally = the mask worn by actors in ancient Greek and Roman drama). 1 A role or character adopted by an author, performer, etc., in their writing, work, etc. 2 The aspect of someone's character that is presented to or perceived by others. In psychology, often contrasted with ANIMA.

1 1996 *Times* She [sc. Aliki Vouyouklaki] combined two apparently contradictory types in her screen persona, the unspoiled girl-next-door and the sex bomb, wrapped up in one alluring package.

2 1996 *Times Magazine* He has finally moved into a new flat, which was decorated by someone else, and he has been totally sucked in by the persona imposed on him by the soft furnishings.

personae gratae, personae non gratae plurals of PERSONA GRATA, PERSONA NON GRATA.

persona grata /pəˌsəʊnə 'grɑːtə/ *noun phrase* plural **personae gratae** /pə ˌsəʊni: 'grɑːti:/ L19 Late Latin (from as PERSONA + Latin *grata* feminine of *gratus* pleasing). A person, especially a diplomat, acceptable to certain others.

persona non grata /pəˌsəʊnə nɒn ˈɡrɑːtə/, /nəʊn/ *noun phrase* plural **personae non gratae** /pəˌsəʊniː/, /ˈɡrɑːtiː/ E20 Late Latin (from as PERSONA GRATA + Latin *non* not). An unacceptable or unwelcome person.

1996 *Times* …in a tit-for-tat expulsion…, four Russian 'diplomats' had been expelled from London as four British 'spies' had been declared *personae non gratae*.

personnel /pəːsəˈnɛl/ *noun* E19 French (use as noun of adjective, as contrasted with MATÉRIEL). **1** The body of people employed in an organization or engaged in an organized undertaking such as military service. Opposed to *matériel*. **2** The department in an organization concerned with the appointment, training, and welfare of employees. Also more fully *personnel department*.

peshmerga /pɛʃˈməːɡə/ *noun* plural **peshmergas**, same M20 Kurdish (*pêshmerge* from *pêsh* before, in front of + *merg* death). A member of a Kurdish nationalist guerrilla organization.

pesto /ˈpɛstəʊ/ *noun* M20 Italian (contraction of *pestato* past participle of *pestare* to pound, crush). A sauce of crushed basil leaves, pine nuts, garlic, Parmesan cheese, and olive oil, typically served with pasta. Cf. PISTOU.

pétanque /petɑ̃k/, /pəˈtaŋk/ *noun* M20 French (from Provençal *pèd tanco*, literally 'foot fixed (to the ground)', describing the start position). A game similar to BOULE (noun 2) played chiefly in Provence.

pétillant /petijɑ̃/, /ˈpeɪtɪjɒ̃/ *adjective* L19 French. (Of wine) slightly sparkling.

petit /pəti/, /pəˈtiː/, /ˈpeti/; *same in plural collocations adjective* LME French (cf. feminine PETITE). Little, small; *Law* (of a crime) petty.

■ Occurs in various phrases used in English, and until the 17th century was in common use alongside the English form *petty*.

petit battement /pəti batmɑ̃/ *noun phrase* plural **petits battements** (*pronounced same*) E20 French. *Ballet* A BATTEMENT executed with the moving leg bent.

petit beurre /pəti bœr/ *noun phrase* plural **petits beurres** (*pronounced same*) E20 French (= little butter). A sweet butter biscuit.

petit bourgeois /ˌpɛti ˈbʊəʒwɑː/, /pəˌtiː/; *foreign* /pəti burʒwa/ *noun & adjective phrase* plural **petits bourgeois** (pronounced same); (feminine **petite bourgeoise** /pəˌtiːt ˈbʊəʒwɑːz/, *foreign* /pətit burʒwaz/, plural **petites bourgeoises** (pronounced same)) M19 French (literally, 'little citizen'). **A** *noun phrase* A member of the lower middle class, especially when perceived as conventional and conservative. **B** *adjective phrase* Of or characteristic of the lower middle class, especially with reference to a perceived conventionalism and conservatism.

■ Also partially anglicized (L19 onwards) as *petty bourgeois*.

B 1996 *Spectator* Mr Volkman rails about the CIA's petit bourgeois ignorance of foreign cultures in his account of a disastrous operation in Cuba…

petite /pəˈtiːt/, *foreign* /pətit/ *adjective* M16 French (feminine of PETIT). **1** (Of a woman) attractively small and dainty. **2** The French (feminine) for 'little, small', occurring in various phrases used in English.

1996 *Country Life* She is as bright and charming as she is petite and beautiful.

petite bourgeoise see PETIT BOURGEOIS.

petite bourgeoisie /pəˌtiːt bʊəʒwaˈziː/, *foreign* /pətit burʒwazi/ *noun phrase* E20 French (literally, 'little townsfolk'). The lower middle classes collectively.

■ Also partially anglicized (M19, but mainly 20) as *petty bourgeoisie*.

1995 *Spectator* Lack of a belief in the social explanation of crime is thought to be a failing of the petite bourgeoisie.

petite marmite /pətiːt maˈmiːt/ *noun phrase* plural **petites marmites** (*pronounced same*) E20 French (literally, 'little earthenware pot'). Soup served in an earthenware pot. See MARMITE.

petit four /ˌpɛti ˈfɔː/, *foreign* /pəti fur/ *noun phrase* plural **petits fours** /ˌpɛti ˈfɔːz/, *foreign* /pəti fur/ L19 French (literally, 'little oven'). A very small fancy cake, biscuit, or sweet, typically made with marzipan and traditionally served after a meal.

petitio principii /pɪˌtɪʃɪəʊ prɪnˈsɪpɪʌɪ/, /prɪŋˈkɪpɪʌɪ/ *noun phrase* M16 Latin (= assuming a principle, from *petitio* laying claim to + genitive of PRINCIPIUM). *Logic* A fallacy in which a conclusion is taken for granted in a premise; begging the question.

petit-maître /pətimɛtr/ *noun phrase* plural **petits-maîtres** (*pronounced same*) E18 French (literally, 'little master'). **1** A dandy, a fop. **2** An artist, writer, musician, etc., of minor importance.

■ In sense 2 sometimes translated as *little masters* with reference to practitioners of the minor arts, such as the engravers of late medieval Germany.

1996 *Spectator* These are the pictures that have earned him [sc. William Nicholson] the title of *petit maître*, a French expression for a rather English virtue of recognising one's limits and sticking within them.

petit mal /ˌpɛtɪ ˈmal/, /ˌpəti mal/ *noun phrase* L19 French (literally, 'little sickness'). A mild form of epilepsy characterized by brief spells of unconsciousness without loss of posture. Cf. GRAND MAL.

petit pain /pəti pɛ̃/ *noun phrase* plural **petits pains** (*pronounced same*) M18 French. A small bread roll.

petit point /pəti pwɛ̃/, /ˌpɛtɪ ˈpɔɪnt/ *noun phrase* L19 French (literally, 'little stitch'). A type of embroidery on canvas using small, diagonal, adjacent stitches.

petits battements, petits beurres, petits fours, etc. plurals of PETIT BATTEMENT, PETIT BEURRE, PETIT FOUR etc.

petits pois /ˌpɛtɪ ˈpwɑ:/, *foreign* /pəti pwa/ *noun phrase plural* E19 French (literally, 'small peas'). Young green peas that are picked before they are grown to full size.

petit suisse /pəti sɥis/, /ˌpɛtɪ ˈswi:s/ *noun phrase* E20 French. A small round cream cheese. Cf. FROMAGE FRAIS.

petit verre /pəti vɛr/ *noun phrase* plural **petits verres** (*pronounced same*) M19 French. A glass of liqueur.

1995 *Spectator* Instead of some monumental goddess at the dawn of time, . . . you see only a sagging model of the *quartier*, longing for a *petit verre* and the regained dignity of her corsets.

pétrissage /petrisaʒ/ *noun* L19 French (from *pétrir*, *pétriss-* to knead). A massage technique that involves kneading the body.

pe tsai /peɪ ˈtsʌɪ/ *noun* L18 Chinese ((Cantonese dialect) *báicài*, literally, 'white vegetable': cf. PAK CHOI). A kind of Chinese cabbage, *Brassica pekinensis*, with leaves in a loose head, grown as a winter vegetable.

peyote /peɪˈəʊti/ *noun* M19 American Spanish (from Nahuatl *peyotl*). A small blue-green spineless cactus, native to Mexico and the southern United States; a preparation of this used as a hallucinogenic drug. Also called MESCAL.

phaeton /ˈfeɪt(ə)n/ *noun* M18 French (*phaéton* from Latin *Phaethon* from Greek *Phaethōn* (*phaethōn* shining), in Greek mythology the son of Helios and Clymene, who was allowed to drive the sun's chariot for a day, with disastrous results). **1** Chiefly *History* A light four-wheeled open carriage, usually drawn by a pair of horses, and with one or two forward-facing seats. **2** A vintage touring car. *United States*.

phallus /ˈfaləs/ *noun* plural **phalli** /ˈfalʌɪ/, /ˈfali:/, **phalluses** E17 Late Latin (from Greek *phallos*). **1** The penis, especially when erect (typically used with reference to male potency or dominance). **2** An image or representation of an erect penis, typically symbolizing fertility or potency.

pharmacopoeia /ˌfɑ:məkəˈpi:ə/ *noun* (also **pharmacopeia**) E17 Modern Latin (from Greek *pharmakopoiia* art of preparing drugs, from *pharmakopoios* preparer of drugs, from *pharmaco-* combining form of *pharmakon* drug + *-poios* making, maker). **1** An official publication containing a list of medicinal drugs with their effects and directions for their use. **2** A collection or stock of medicinal drugs.

Phi Beta Kappa /ˌfʌɪ ˌbi:tə ˈkapə/ *noun phrase* M19 Greek (from the initial letters *phi, beta, kappa,* of *philosophia biou kuber-nētēs* philosophy the guide of life). (In the United States) an honorary society of undergraduates and some graduates to which members are elected on the basis of high academic achievement; a member of a Phi Beta Kappa society.

philosophia perennis /fɪləˌsɒfɪə pə'rɛnɪs/ *noun phrase* M19 Latin (= perennial philosophy). A core of philosophical truths which is hypothesized to exist independently of and unaffected by time or place, frequently taken to be exemplified in the writings of Aristotle and St Thomas Aquinas.

phobia /'fəʊbɪə/ *noun* L18 Latin (independent use of the Latin suffix *-phobia* from Greek *-phobos* fearing, from *phobos* fear). An extreme or irrational fear of or aversion to something.

■ *Phobia* as a suffix also appears in numerous abstract nouns, especially in modern coinages after the Greek denoting states in clinical psychology, such as *agoraphobia, arachnophobia,* etc., and in other (often humorous or nonce) formations such as *Anglophobia, Francophobia,* etc.

physique /fɪ'ziːk/ *noun* E19 French (use as noun of adjective = physical). The form, size, and development of a person's body.

pi /pʌɪ/ *noun* LME Greek (in sense 2 representative of initial letter of Greek *periphereia* circumference). **1** The sixteenth letter (Π, π) of the Greek alphabet, transliterated as 'p'. **2** *Mathematics* The numerical value of the ratio of the circumference of a circle to its diameter (approximately 3.14159). Usually written π. **3** (as *modifier*) *Chemistry* and *Physics* (Of an electron or orbital) with one unit of angular momentum about an internuclear axis.

piaffe /pɪaf/ *noun & verb* M18 French (*piaffer* to strut, make a show). **A** *noun* A movement performed in advanced dressage and classical riding, in which the horse executes a slow elevated trot without moving forward. **B** *intransitive verb* (Of a horse) perform a piaffe.

pianissimo /pɪə'nɪsɪməʊ/ *adverb, adjective, & noun* E18 Italian (superlative of *piano* (see PIANO adverb and adjective)). *Music* **A** *adverb & adjective* (Especially as a direction) very soft or softly. **B** *noun* plural **pianissimos, pianissimi** /pɪə'nɪsɪmi/ A passage performed or marked to be performed very softly.

■ As a musical direction abbreviated to *pp* or *ppp*.

B 1996 *Times* And on top is that 'brilliant technique',... and floating pianissimos to melt the sternest critical heart.

piano /'pjɑːnəʊ/ *noun* 1 plural **pianos, piani** /'pjɑːni/ M18 Italian (from Latin *planus* flat, (later of sound) soft, low). **1** *Music* A passage performed or marked to be performed softly. **2** A flat or storey in an Italian building. Cf. PIANO NOBILE.

piano /pɪ'anəʊ/ *noun* 2 plural **pianos** E19 Italian (abbreviation of PIANOFORTE or FORTE PIANO). **1** A large keyboard musical instrument with a wooden case enclosing a soundboard and metal strings, which are struck by hammers when the keys are depressed. The strings' vibration is stopped by dampers, with two or three pedals to regulate the volume or length of the notes. **2** The playing of this instrument.

piano /'pjɑːnəʊ/ *adverb & adjective* L17 Italian (from Latin *planus* flat, (later of sound) soft, low). **1** *adverb & adjective* *Music* (Especially as a direction) soft or softly. **2** *adjective* (Of a person) quiet, subdued.

■ As a musical direction usually abbreviated to *p*.

pianoforte /pɪˌanəʊ'fɔːti/ *noun* M18 Italian (earlier *pian(o) e forte,* literally, 'soft and loud' (expressing the gradation in tone); cf. FORTE PIANO). A PIANO noun 2 sense 1.

piano nobile /ˌpjɑːnəʊ 'nəʊbɪle/ *noun* L19 Italian (= noble floor, from *piano* floor, storey + *nobile* noble, great). *Architecture* The first floor of a large Palladian or Georgian house, containing the principal rooms.

1995 *Spectator* To let in Bishopsgate is the lavish modern mansion built for Standard Chartered, complete with *piano nobile.*

piazza /pɪˈatsə/ *noun* L16 Italian (= French *place* (town) square). **1** A public square or marketplace, especially one in an Italian town. **2** The veranda of a house. *United States*, now *archaic*.

pibroch /ˈpiːbrɒk/, /ˈpiːbrɒx/ *noun* E18 Gaelic (*pìobaireachd* the art of playing the bagpipe, from *pìobair* piper (from *pìob* pipe, from English *pipe*) + suffix of function *-achd*). A form of music for the Scottish bagpipes involving elaborate variations on a theme, usually of a martial or funerary character.

picador /ˈpɪkədɔː/ *noun* L18 Spanish (from *picar* to prick, pierce). (In bullfighting) a person mounted on horseback who goads the bull with a lance.

picaresque /pɪkəˈrɛsk/ *adjective* E19 French (from Spanish *picaresco*, from *pícaro* roguish, knavish, (noun) rogue; cf. next). **1** Relating to an episodic style of fiction dealing with the adventures of a rough and dishonest but appealing hero. **2** Drifting; wandering.

picaro /ˈpɪkərəʊ/ *noun* plural **picaros** E17 Spanish (see PICARESQUE). A rogue, a scoundrel.

picayune /pɪkəˈjuːn/ *noun & adjective* E19 French (*picaillon* old copper coin of Piedmont, halfpence, cash from Provençal *picaioun*, of unknown origin). **A** *noun* **1** Originally (in the southern United States), a Spanish half-real, worth 6¼ cents. Now, a five-cent piece or other coin of small value. **2** An insignificant person or thing. *North American colloquial*. **B** *adjective* Of little value or significance; petty. *North American colloquial*.

piccolo /ˈpɪkələʊ/ *noun* plural **piccolos** M19 Italian (= small). A small flute sounding an octave higher than the ordinary flute.

pickelhaube /ˈpɪk(ə)l(h)aʊbə/ *noun* plural **pickelhaubes**, **pickelhauben** /ˈpɪk(ə)l(h)aʊbən/ L19 German. *History* A spiked helmet worn by German soldiers, especially before and during the war of 1914–18.

picot /ˈpiːkəʊ/ *noun* E17 French (diminutive of *pic* peak, point, prick). A small loop or series of small loops of twisted thread in lace or embroidery, typically decorating the border of a fabric.

picotee /pɪkəˈtiː/ *noun & adjective* E18 French (*picoté(e)* past participle of *picoter* to mark with points, prick, from as PICOT). **A** *noun* A variety of carnation, having light petals marked or edged with a darker colour. **B** *adjective* (Of a colour, pattern, etc.) resembling that of the picotee.

> **B 1996** *Country Life* The last variant [of busy lizzie] was the picotee type... and the next will have speckled flowers.

pièce de résistance /pjɛs də re zistɑ̃s/, /pɪˌɛs də rɛˈzɪstɒ̃s/, /ˈrɛzɪstɒ̃s/ *noun phrase* plural **pièces de résistance** (pronounced same) L18 French (literally, 'piece (i.e. means) of resistance'). **1** (Especially with reference to creative work) the most important or outstanding item. **2** The main dish of a meal.

> **1 1996** *Country Life* The pièce de résistance was Thomas Cooper's enormous canvas, *The Monarch of the Meadows*...

pied-à-terre /ˌpjeɪdɑːˈtɛː/ *noun* plural **pieds-à-terre** (pronounced same) E19 French (literally, 'foot to earth'). A small flat, house, or room kept for occasional use.

> **1995** *Country Life* The ideal pied-à-terre should be compact, easy and economical to run, well placed for the City, the West End or escape routes to the country, and secure without being claustrophobic.

pied noir /pje nwar/ *noun phrase* plural **pieds noirs** (pronounced same) M20 French (literally, 'black foot'). A person of European origin who lived in Algeria during French rule, especially one who returned to Europe after Algeria was granted independence.

> ■ Competing explanations of the sobriquet are based either on the black leather shoes worn by Europeans but not by native Algerians or on the traditional employment of barefooted Algerians as stokers on French steamers.

pieds-à-terre, pieds noirs plurals of PIED-À-TERRE, PIED NOIR.

pierogi /pɪəˈrəʊgi/ *noun plural* (also **perogi, pirogi, pierogies**) E20 Polish (*pieróg*). Dough dumplings stuffed with a filling such as potato or cheese, typically served with onions or sour cream.

pierrot /'pɪərəʊ/, /'pjɛrəʊ/ noun (also **Pierrot**) M18 French (diminutive of the male given name *Pierre* Peter). A stock male character in French pantomime, with a sad white-painted face, a loose white costume, and a pointed hat.

Pietà /pɪeɪ'taː/, foreign /pje'ta:/ noun M17 Italian (from Latin *pietas* dutifulness). A painting or sculpture representing the Virgin Mary holding the dead body of Jesus on her lap or in her arms.

pietas /pi:'eɪtɑːs/ noun E20 Latin (= dutifulness). Respect due to an ancestor, country, institution, etc.

pietra dura /pi‚etra 'dura/ noun phrase plural **pietre dure** /pi‚etre 'dure/ E19 Italian (literally, 'hard stone'). Pictorial mosaic work using semi-precious stones, typically for table tops and other furniture.

piki /'pi:ki/ noun L19 Hopi (*pí:ki*). Maize-meal bread in the form of very thin sheets, made by the Hopi Indians of the south-western United States.

pilaf /pɪ'laf/ noun (also **pilaff**, **pilau** /pɪ'laʊ/, **pulao** /pə'laʊ/) E17 Turkish (*pilâv* cooked rice = Persian *pīlaw* boiled rice and meat). An Indian or Middle Eastern dish of rice (or occasionally other grain) cooked in stock with spices and often meat, fish, vegetables, etc.

pileus /'pʌɪlɪəs/ noun plural **pilei** /'pʌɪlɪʌɪ/ M18 Latin (= felt cap). *Botany* The cap of a mushroom or toadstool.

pimento /pɪ'mɛntəʊ/ noun plural **pimentos** L17 Spanish (PIMIENTO). **1** A red sweet pepper, a PIMIENTO. **2** The spice allspice; (more fully *pimento tree*) the West Indian tree, *Pimenta dioica*, of the myrtle family, from which allspice is obtained. Now *West Indies*.

pimiento /pɪmɪ'ɛntəʊ/, /pɪm'jɛntəʊ/ noun plural **pimientos** (also **pimento** pɪ'mɛntəʊ/) M17 Spanish (from Latin *pigmentum* paint, colour). A red sweet pepper.

pina colada /‚pi:nə kə'la:də/ noun (also **piña colada** /‚pi:njə kə'la:də/) E20 South American Spanish (literally, 'strained pine-

apple' from *piña* (Portuguese *pinha*) pine-apple (originally pine cone), from Latin *pinea* pine cone). A cocktail made with pineapple juice, rum, and coconut.

pince-nez /pans'neɪ/, foreign /pɛ̃sne/ noun (treated as *singular* or *plural*) L19 French (from *pincer* to pinch + *nez* nose). A pair of eyeglasses kept in position by a spring clipping the nose rather than by earpieces.

pinetum /pʌɪ'ni:təm/ noun plural **pineta** /pʌɪ'ni:tə/ M19 Latin (from *pinus* pine). A plantation or collection of pine trees or other conifers, for scientific or ornamental purposes.

pingo /'pɪŋgəʊ/ noun plural **pingo(e)s** M20 Inuit (*pinguq* NUNATAK). *Geology* A dome-shaped mound, often with a crater on top, consisting of a layer of soil over a large core of ice, occurring in permafrost areas.

pinole /pɪ'nəʊleɪ/ noun M19 American Spanish (from Aztec *pinolli*). Flour made from parched cornflour mixed with sweet flour made of mesquite beans, sugar, and spice. *United States*.

piñon /pɪ'njɒn/, /'pɪnjən/ noun plural **piñons**, **piñones** /pɪ'njəʊnɪz/ M19 Spanish. A small pine tree with edible seeds, native to Mexico and the south-western United States; a pine nut obtained from the piñon.

pinto /'pɪntəʊ/ adjective & noun plural **pintos** M19 Spanish (= painted, mottled, from Proto-Romance). **A** adjective **1** (Of a horse) piebald; skewbald. **2** *pinto bean*, a variety of kidney bean with mottled seeds, widely cultivated in Central America and the south-western United States; the seed of this. **B** noun A piebald horse.
■ With reference to horses, chiefly North American.

piolet /pjəʊ'leɪ/ noun M19 French ((Savoy dialect) diminutive of *piolo*, apparently cognate with *pioche*, *pic* pickaxe). A two-headed ice-axe used by mountaineers.

pipette /pɪ'pɛt/ noun & verb M19 French (diminutive of *pipe* pipe). **A** noun A slender tube attached to or incorporating a bulb, for transferring or measuring out small quantities of

liquid, especially in a laboratory.
B *transitive verb* Pour, convey, or draw
off using a pipette.

piquant /'piːk(ə)nt/, /'piːkɑːnt/ *adjective*
(also **piquante** /pɪ'kɑːnt/) E16 French
(present participial adjective of *piquer* to
prick, sting). **1** (Of food etc.) having a
pleasantly sharp taste or appetizing
flavour. **2** Pleasantly stimulating or
exciting to the mind.

■ This word was originally used in
English in the sense 'sharp or stinging
to the feelings; severe, bitter'.

pique /piːk/ *noun* M16 French (literally,
'pike', figuratively, 'cutting remark',
from *piquer* to prick, pierce, sting, irri-
tate, *se piquer* take offence, from Proto-
Romance, origin uncertain). **1** Originally, a quarrel or feeling of enmity
between two or more people; ill
feeling, animosity. **2** A feeling of
irritation or resentment resulting
from a slight or injury, especially to
one's pride; offence taken.

piqué /'piːkeɪ/ *noun* M19 French (= back-
stitched, past participle of *piquer* to
backstitch). Stiff fabric, typically cotton, woven in a strongly ribbed or
raised pattern (originally in imitation
of hand quilting); the raised pattern of
such a fabric.

piquet /pɪ'kɛt/ *noun* M17 French (of unknown origin). A trick-taking card-
game for two players with a pack of
32 cards, the cards from the two to the
six being excluded.

piri-piri /'pɪrɪpɪrɪ/ *noun* M20 Ronga (= pepper). A very hot sauce made with red
peppers. Also *piri-piri sauce*.

pirog /pɪ'rɒg/ *noun* plural **pirogi** /pɪ'rɒgɪ/,
pirogen /pɪ'rɒgən/ M19 Russian. A large
Russian pie. Cf. PIROSHKI.

pirogi variant of PIEROGI.

pirogue /pɪ'rəʊg/ *noun* E17 French (probably from Carib). A long narrow canoe
made from a single tree trunk, especially in Central America and the
Caribbean.

piroshki /pɪ'rɒʃkɪ/ *noun plural* (also **pirozhki** /pɪ'rɒzkɪ/) E20 Russian (*pirozhki*
plural of *pirozhok* diminutive of PIROG).

Small Russian savoury pastries or
patties filled with meat, fish, rice, etc.

pirouette /pɪrʊ'ɛt/ *noun & verb* M17
French (= spinning top, ultimate origin
unknown). **A** *noun* **1** *Ballet* An act of
spinning round on one foot, typically
with the raised foot touching the knee
of the supporting leg; *generally* a rapid
whirl of the body. **2** A movement
performed in advanced dressage and
classical riding, in which the horse
makes a circle by pivoting on a hind
leg, while cantering. **B** *intransitive verb*
Perform a pirouette.

pirozhki variant of PIROSHKI.

pis aller /pizale/ (*plural same*), /piːz 'aleɪ/
noun L17 French (from *pis* worse + *aller* to
go). The worst that can be or happen; a
last resort.

piscina /pɪ'siːnə/, /pɪ'sʌɪnə/ *noun* plural
piscinas, **piscinae** /pɪ'siːniː/ L16 Latin
(= fish pond, from *piscis* fish). **1** A stone
basin near the altar in Catholic and
pre-Reformation churches for draining water used in the Mass. **2** (In
ancient Roman architecture) a pool or
pond for bathing or swimming.

pisé /pize/, /'piːzeɪ/ *noun* L18 French (use
as noun of past participle of *piser* to beat,
pound, stamp (earth), from Latin *pinsere*).
A building material of stiff clay or
earth, sometimes mixed with gravel,
forced between boards which are
removed as it hardens; building with
this material. Also *pisé de terre* /də tɛr/,
/də tɛː/ (= of earth). Also called *terre
pisée*.

pissaladière /pisaladjɛr/ *noun* (also
pissaladiera /pisaladjera/) M20 French
(from Provençal *pissaladiero*, from *pissala*
salt fish). A Provençal open tart similar
to pizza, usually with onions, anchovies, and black olives.

pissoir /piswar/ (*plural same*), /piː'swɑː/,
/'pɪswɑː/ *noun* E20 French. A public
urinal, especially in France.

> **1996** *Bookseller* If I call this *pissoir* a great
> work of art and sign it, who are you to disprove
> that?

piste /piːst/ *noun* E18 French (= racetrack,
from Latin *pista* (sc. *via*) beaten track,
from feminine past participle of *pinsere*

to pound, stamp). A specially prepared or marked slope or trail of compacted snow used as a ski run.

pisteur /piːˈstəː/ *noun* M20 French. A person employed to prepare the snow on a piste.

pistou /piːstu/, /ˈpiːstuː/ *noun* M20 Provençal (= Italian PESTO). A sauce or paste made from crushed basil, garlic, and cheese, used especially in Provençal dishes; a thick vegetable soup made with this.

pita variant of PITTA.

pithos /ˈpɪθɒs/ *noun* plural **pithoi** /ˈpɪθɔɪ/ L19 Greek. *Archaeology* A large spherical wide-mouthed earthenware jar used for holding wine, oil, food, etc.

piton /ˈpiːtɒn/ *noun* L19 French (= eyebolt). **1** *Mountaineering* A metal peg or spike which is hammered into rock or ice and used to support a climber or a rope through an eye at one end. **2** A (steep-sided) volcanic peak, especially in the West Indies.

pitta /ˈpɪtə/ *noun* (also **pita**) M20 Modern Greek (*pêtta*, *pit(t)a* bread, cake, pie; cf. Turkish *pide*, Aramaic *pittā* in similar sense). A flat, hollow, slightly leavened bread of Mediterranean and Arab countries, which can be split open to receive a filling.

più /pjuː/ *adverb* E18 Italian. *Music* More.
■ Used in directions, as in *più mosso* more animatedly.

pizza /ˈpiːtsə/ *noun* L19 Italian (= pie). A dish of Italian origin, consisting of a flat round base of dough baked with a topping of tomatoes, cheese, meat, olives, etc.

pizzeria /ˌpiːtsəˈriːə/ *noun* M20 Italian. A place where pizzas are made or sold; a pizza restaurant.

pizzicato /ˌpɪtsɪˈkaːtəʊ/ *adverb, adjective, & noun* M19 Italian (= pinched, twitched, past participle of *pizzicare*, based on Old and Modern Italian *pizza* point, edge). *Music* **A** *adverb* (Often as a direction) plucking the strings of a violin or other stringed instrument with one's finger. **B** *adjective* Performed pizzicato. **C** *noun* plural **pizzicati**

/ˌpɪtsɪˈkaːti/, **pizzicatos** The technique of playing pizzicato; a note or passage played pizzicato.

placebo /pləˈsiːbəʊ/ *noun* plural **placebo(e)s** L18 Latin (= I shall be acceptable or pleasing (first word of Psalm 114:9), 1st person singular future indicative of *placere* to please). **1** A pill, medicine, procedure, etc., prescribed more for the psychological benefit to the patient of being given a prescription than for any physiological effect. Also, a substance with no therapeutic effect used as a control in testing new drugs etc. **2** A measure designed merely to humour or placate someone.

> **1** 1996 *New Scientist* However, the day when the placebo effect becomes a respectable medical tool is still some way off.

placet /ˈpleɪsɛt/, /ˈplakɛt/ *noun* L16 Latin (= it pleases, 3rd person singular present indicative of *placere* to please). An affirmative vote in a Church or university assembly.

plafond /plafɔ̃/ (*plural same*) *noun* M17 French (from *plat* flat + *fond* bottom). An ornately decorated ceiling, either flat or vaulted.

plage /plaʒ/, *in sense 2* /pleɪdʒ/ *noun* LME Old French (= region, (modern) beach (from Italian *piaggia*) from medieval Latin *plaga* open space). **1** A beach or promenade at a seaside resort, especially at a fashionable one; a seaside resort. **2** *Astronomy* A bright region of the sun's chromosphere, usually associated with sunspots. Also *plage region*.

planche /plɑːnʃ/ *noun* E20 French (literally, 'plank'). *Gymnastics* A position in which the body is held parallel to the ground by the arms, performed on the parallel bars, rings, or floor.

planchette /plɑːnˈʃɛt/ *noun* M19 French (diminutive of *planche* plank, (wooden) board). A small usually heart-shaped board, supported by two castors and a vertical pencil, which, when one or more people rest their fingers lightly on the board, supposedly writes automatic messages under spirit guidance.

plastique /plaˈstiːk/, *foreign* /plastik/ (*plural same*) *noun* M20 French (use as noun of adjective = plastic, from Latin *plasticus* from Greek *plastikos* from *plastos* past participle of *plassein* to mould, form). Plastic explosive; a plastic bomb.

plat /pla/ *noun* plural pronounced same M18 French. A dish of food.

plat du jour /pla dy ʒur/ *noun phrase* plural pronounced same E20 French (= dish of the day). A dish specially prepared by a restaurant on a particular day, in addition to the usual menu.

> **1996** *Spectator* Another *plat du jour* was breast of pheasant in a port wine sauce...

plateau /ˈplatəʊ/ *noun & verb* /ˈplatəʊz/, L18 French (Old French *platel*, from *plat* wide, flat, from popular Latin, from Greek *platus* broad, flat). **A** *noun* plural **plateaux plateaus 1** An elevated tract of comparatively flat or level land; a tableland. **2** A state of little or no change after a period of activity or progress. **B** *intransitive verb* Reach a state of little or no change after a period of activity or progress: *the industry's problems have plateaued out.*

platteland /ˈplatəland/ *noun* M20 Afrikaans (from Dutch *plat* flat + *land* country). The remote rural inland part of South Africa.

> ■ In South Africa often used attributively with derogatory connotations of backwardness and reaction, as in 'platteland mentality'.

playa /ˈplʌɪə/ *noun* M19 Spanish (= shore, beach, coast, from late Latin *plagia* open space). An area of flat, dried-up land, especially a desert basin from which water evaporates quickly.

plaza /ˈplɑːzə/ *noun* L17 Spanish (literally 'place'). **1** A public square, marketplace, or open public space in a built-up area. **2** A shopping centre.

plectrum /ˈplɛktrəm/ *noun* plural **plectrums, plectra** /ˈplɛktrə/ LME Latin (from Greek *plēktron* anything to strike with, from *plēssein* to strike). A thin flat piece of plastic, tortoiseshell, or other slightly flexible material held by or worn on the fingers and used to pluck the strings of a musical instrument such as a guitar. Also, the corresponding mechanical part of a harpsichord etc.

plein-air /plɛnɛr/ *adjective* L19 French (from EN PLEIN AIR (literally, 'in full air')). Denoting or in the manner of a 19th-century style of painting outdoors, which sought to represent the transient effects of atmosphere and light by direct observation from nature and which became a central feature of French Impressionism. Also, designating a work painted out of doors or representing an outdoor scene and painted with a spontaneous technique.

> ■ Also as a noun phrase *plein air*.
> **1995** *Spectator*... most of the Impressionist canvases on show smell of lamp-oil rather than *plein air*.

plenum /ˈpliːnəm/ *noun* L17 Latin (neuter of *plenus* full (sc. *spatium* space); in sense 2 later influenced by Russian *plenum* plenary session). **1** *Physics* A space completely filled with matter, or the whole of space regarded as being so filled. **2** An assembly of all the members of a group or committee.

pleroma /pləˈrəʊmə/ *noun* M18 Greek (*plērōma* that which fills, from *plēroun* to make full, from *plērēs* full). **1** (In Gnosticism) the spiritual universe as the abode of God and of the totality of the divine powers and emanations. **2** (In Christian theology) the totality of the Godhead which dwells in Christ; completeness, fullness (with allusion to Colossians 2:9).

plethora /ˈplɛθ(ə)rə/ *noun* M16 Late Latin (from Greek *plēthōrē* fullness, repletion, from *plēthein* to be full). **1** An excess of something; overfullness, oversupply; a glut. **2** *Medicine* An excess of bodily fluid, particularly blood.

> **1 1996** *Times Magazine*... I read the plethora of faxes detailing where and whither I am to be sent...

plié /plije/ *noun* plural pronounced same L19 French (past participle of *plier* to bend). A movement in which a dancer bends the knees and straightens them again, usually with the feet turned right out and heels firmly on the ground.

plissé /ˈpliːseɪ/, *foreign* /plise/ (*plural of noun same*) *noun & adjective* L19 French (past participle of *plisser* to pleat). **A** *noun*

Fabric with a puckered or crinkled finish produced by chemical treatment. **B** *adjective* (Of fabric) treated to give a permanent puckered or crinkled effect.

plongeur /plɔ̃ʒœr/ *noun* plural pronounced same M20 French (from *plonger* to plunge, immerse in liquid). A person employed to wash dishes and carry out other menial tasks in a restaurant or hotel.

■ The word entered English via George Orwell's account of menial labour in *Down and Out in Paris and London* (1933).

plus ça change /ply sa ʃɑ̃ʒ/ *interjection & noun phrase* E20 French (shortened form of *plus ça change, plus c'est la même chose* (= the more it changes, the more it stays the same)). Used to express resigned acknowledgement of the fact that certain things never change.

■ The observation was originally made by the French author and satirical journalist Alphonse Karr (1808–90) writing in *Les Guêpes* (January 1849).

1995 *Times* Both have printed reams of photographs through the decades. The pictures are shockingly similar—a serious case of *plus ça change*.

p.m. abbreviation of POST MERIDIEM.

pneuma /ˈnjuːmə/ *noun* L19 Greek (= wind, breath, spirit, that which is blown or breathed, from *pneein, pnein* to blow, breathe). The spirit of a person, as opposed to the soul; the breath of life.

■ In Stoic and Epicurean philosophy the *pneuma* was a person's vital force or energy, but modern usage takes its cue from the New Testament distinction between the spirit and the soul or PSYCHE (cf. 1 Thessalonians 5.23).

pochette /pɒˈʃɛt/ *noun* L19 French (= small pocket). A woman's handbag shaped like an envelope. Also *pochette bag*.

pocho /ˈpotʃo/ *noun & adjective* plural of noun **pochos** /ˈpotʃos/ M20 Mexican Spanish (= Spanish *pocho* discoloured, pale, faded). **A** *noun* A citizen of the United States of Mexican origin or a culturally Americanized Mexican. **B** *adjective* Relating to United States citizens of Mexican origin.

■ *Colloquial*, often *derogatory*.

podzol /ˈpɒdzɒl/ *noun* (also **podsol** /ˈpɒdsɒl/) E20 Russian (from *pod-* under + *zola* ash; variant altered after *-sol* from Latin *solum* soil). *Soil Science* An acidic, generally infertile soil characterized by a white or grey subsurface layer resembling ash, and occurring especially under coniferous woods or heaths in moist, usually temperate climates.

poète maudit /pɔɛt modi/ *noun phrase* plural **poètes maudits** (pronounced same) M20 French (literally, 'cursed poet'). A poet or other creative artist who is insufficiently appreciated by his or her contemporaries.

■ *Les Poètes maudits* (1884) was the title of a study of several such poets by the French Symbolist poet Paul Verlaine (1844–96).

1977 *Time* Once the ignored art, photography now stands robed in puffery, and . . . like painting, . . . has acquired its cast of heroes and *poètes maudits*.

pogrom /ˈpɒɡrəm/, /ˈpɒɡrɒm/, /pəˈɡrɒm/ *noun* E20 Russian (= devastation, from *gromit'* to destroy by violent means). An organized massacre of a particular ethnic group, in particular that of Jews in Russia or eastern Europe.

poi /pɔɪ/ *noun* E19 Polynesian. A Hawaiian dish made from the fermented root of the taro which has been baked and pounded to a paste.

poilu /ˈpwɑːluː/, *foreign* /pwaly/ (*plural same*) *noun* E20 French (= hairy, virile, from Latin *pilus* hair). *History* An infantry soldier in the French army, especially one who fought in the First World War. *Colloquial*.

point d'appui /pwɛ̃ dapɥi/ *noun phrase* E19 French (= point of support). A fulcrum; a strategic point; a support or prop.

pointe /pwɛ̃t/ *noun* plural pronounced same M19 French (= tip). *Ballet* The tips of the toes. Also, a dance movement executed on the tips of the toes. Cf. EN POINTE.

pointillisme /pwɛ̃tijism/ *noun* (also **pointillism** /ˈpwantɪlɪz(ə)m/) E20 French (*pointillisme*, from *pointiller* to mark with dots, from *pointille* from Italian *puntiglio* diminutive of *punto* point). **1** A technique of neo-Impressionist painting in which luminous effects are produced by tiny dots of various pure colours, which become blended in the viewer's eye. **2** *Music* The breaking up of musical texture into thematic, rhythmic, and tonal fragments.

polder /ˈpəʊldə/ *noun* E17 Dutch (from Middle Dutch *polre*). A piece of low-lying land reclaimed from the sea, a lake, etc., and protected by dykes, originally and especially in the Netherlands.

polenta /pə(ʊ)ˈlɛntə/, *foreign* /poˈlenta/ *noun* L16 Italian (from Latin = pearl barley). Maize flour as used in Italian cookery; a paste or dough made from this boiled and then often fried or baked.

policier /pɔlisje/ *noun* plural pronounced same L20 French (literally, 'detective novel'). A film based on a police novel, portraying crime and its detection by police.

> **1977** *Time* Not so in *Man on the Roof*, the Swedish-made *policier* based on one of the Martin Beck novels.

polis /ˈpɒlɪs/ *noun* plural **poleis** /ˈpɒleɪs/ L19 Greek (= city). A city state in ancient Greece, especially as considered in its ideal form for philosophical purposes.

> **1996** *Spectator* We are also political in that nearly everything that happens is looked at for the effect it is likely to have on the *polis*—or what politics graduates call 'the political process'.

Politbureau /ˈpɒlɪtˌbjʊərəʊ/ *noun* (also **politburo**, plural **politburos**) E20 Russian (*politbyuro*, from *polit*(*icheskii*) political + *byuro* bureau). The highest policy-making committee of a communist country or party, especially in the former USSR.

politesse /pɔlitɛs/ *noun* E18 French (from Italian *politezza*, *pulitezza*, from *pulito* from Latin *politus* past participle of *polire* to smooth, polish). Formal politeness or etiquette.

politico /pəˈlɪtɪkəʊ/ *noun* plural **politicos** M17 Spanish and Italian (= politic, or political person). A politician or person with strong political views.

> ■ *Colloquial*, often *derogatory*.

polka /ˈpɒlkə/ *noun* & *verb* M19 German (French from Czech *půlka* half-step). **A** *noun* **1** A lively dance of Bohemian origin in duple time. **2** A piece of music for this dance or in its rhythm. **B** *intransitive verb* Dance the polka.

> ■ The 19th-century craze for the *polka* led to the word's being attached to a variety of commercial articles; hence *polka dot* for a pattern of dots of uniform size and distribution.

pollo /ˈpɒləʊ/ *noun* plural **pollos** M19 Spanish (Italian = chicken). Chicken (as used in the names of Italian, Spanish, or Mexican dishes).

polonaise /pɒləˈneɪz/ *noun* & *adjective* M18 French (use as noun of feminine of *polonais* Polish, from medieval Latin *Polonia* Poland). **A** *noun* **1** A slow dance of Polish origin, consisting chiefly of an intricate march or procession, in triple time; a piece of music for this dance or in its time or rhythm. **2** A woman's dress with a tight bodice and a skirt open from the waist downwards, looped up to show a decorative underskirt, originally resembling a garment worn by Polish women. **B** *adjective* (Of a dish) garnished with chopped hardboiled egg yolk, breadcrumbs, and parsley.

poltergeist /ˈpɒltəɡʌɪst/ *noun* M19 German (from *poltern* to make a noise, create a disturbance + *Geist* ghost). A ghost or other supernatural being supposedly responsible for making noises and moving physical objects.

polynya /pəʊˈlɪnjə/ *noun* M19 Russian (from base of *pole*, *polyana* field). A stretch of open water surrounded by ice, especially in Arctic seas.

pomade /pəˈmeɪd/, /pəˈmɑːd/ *noun* & *verb* M16 French (*pommade*, based on Latin *pomum* apple (from which it was originally made)). **A** *noun* A scented ointment or oil for dressing the hair. **B** *transitive verb* Apply pomade to. Chiefly as *pomaded* participial adjective.

pomatum /pə(ʊ)'meɪtəm/ *noun & verb* M16 Modern Latin (from Latin *pomum* apple). **A** *noun* Hair ointment, pomade. **B** *transitive verb* Anoint with pomatum. Chiefly as *pomatumed* participial adjective.

pomme /pɔm/ *noun* plural pronounced same E20 French (short for POMME DE TERRE). A potato.

■ Chiefly plural and in phrases designating ways of cooking potatoes, as in *pommes allumettes* (matchstick-thin potato chips) and POMMES FRITES.

pomme de terre /pɔm də tɛr/ *noun phrase* plural **pommes de terre** (pronounced same) E19 French (literally, 'apple of the earth'). A potato.

pommes frites /pɔm friːt/ *noun phrase* plural E20 French (from *pommes de terre frites* fried potatoes). (Especially in recipes or on menus) fried potato chips.

pompadour /'pɒmpədʊə/ *noun & verb* L19 French (Jeanne-Antoinette Poisson, Marquise de *Pompadour* (1721–64), mistress of Louis XV of France). **A** *noun* **1** A man's hairstyle in which the hair is combed back from the forehead without a parting. *United States.* **2** A woman's hairstyle in which the hair is turned back off the forehead in a roll, sometimes over a pad. **B** *transitive verb* Arrange (hair) in a pompadour. Chiefly as *pompadoured* participial adjective.

pompier /pɔ̃pje/ (*plural same*), /'pɒmpɪə/ *noun* M19 French (= fireman, from *pompe* pump). An artist regarded as painting in an academic, imitative, vulgarly neoclassical style.

■ The designation of late 19th-century French academic artists as *pompiers* is probably based on their fondness for showing the Greek and Roman gods and heroes in their pictures wearing helmets that put the viewer in mind of the helmets worn by Parisian firefighters.

pompom /'pɒmpɒm/ *noun* (also **pompon** /'pɒmpɒn/) M18 French (*pompon*, of unknown origin). **1** A small woollen ball attached to a garment, especially a hat or slipper, for decoration. **2** A variety of chrysanthemum, dahlia, or aster, with small tightly clustered petals.

■ Originally denoting a bunch of ribbons, feathers, flowers, etc. formerly worn by women in the hair or on a dress.

poncho /'pɒntʃəʊ/ *noun* plural **ponchos** E18 South American Spanish (from Araucanian). A South American cloak made of a thick piece of cloth like a blanket with a slit in the middle for the head; any garment in this style.

pondok /'pɒndɒk/ *noun* (also **pondokkie** /pɒn'dɒki/) E19 Afrikaans (probably from Malay, ultimately from Arabic *funduq* hotel). A shack or shanty made of scraps of wood, cardboard, or corrugated iron; *transferred* a house etc. in a poor state of repair. *South African.*

pons asinorum /ˌpɒnz asɪ'nɔːrəm/ *noun phrase* M18 Latin (= bridge of asses). The point at which many learners fail, especially a theory or formula that is difficult to grasp.

■ The term is taken from the fifth proposition of the first book of Euclid, so called from the difficulty which beginners find in 'getting over' it.

pontifex /'pɒntɪfɛks/ *noun* plural **pontifices** /pɒn'tɪfɪsiːz/ L16 Latin (from *pons*, *pontis* bridge + *-fex* from *facere* to make). (In ancient Rome) a member of the principal college of priests.

pontil /'pɒntɪl/ *noun* M19 French (apparently from Italian *pontello*, *puntello* diminutive of *punto* point). *Glass-making* An iron rod used to hold or shape soft glass. Also called *punty*.

pooja variant of PUJA.

pooka /'puːkə/ *noun* E19 Irish (*púca*). (In Irish mythology) a hobgoblin or sprite able to take on the form of various animals.

■ The most famous use of the word is probably in Mary C. Chase's comic play *Harvey* (1944), subsequently made into a film starring James Stewart. In the play the main character Elwood P. Dowd claims to have been befriended by a pooka in the form of an invisible six-foot rabbit called Harvey.

poort /pʊət/ *noun* L18 Dutch (*poort* gate, port). (In South Africa) a narrow mountain pass, especially one cut by a stream or river.

popadom variant of POPPADOM.

poppadom /'pɒpədəm/ *noun* (also **popadom**, **poppadom**, and other variants) E19 Tamil (*pappaṭam*, perhaps from *paruppa aṭam* lentil cake). (In Indian cookery) a large circular piece of thin, spiced bread made from ground lentils and fried in oil.

portamento /pɔːtə'mɛntəʊ/ *noun* plural **portamenti** /pɔːtə'mɛnti/ L18 Italian (literally, 'a carrying'). *Music* A slide from one note to another, especially in singing or playing the violin. Also, piano playing in a manner intermediate between legato and staccato.

port de bras /pɔr də bra/ *noun phrase* plural **ports de bras** (pronounced same) E20 French (literally, 'bearing of the arms'). *Ballet* The action or manner of moving and posing the arms; any of a series of exercises designed to develop graceful movement and disposition of the arms.

porte cochère /ˌpɔːt kəʊ'ʃɛː/, *foreign* /pɔrt kɔʃɛr/ (*plural same*) *noun* (originally **port-cocher**; also **porte-cochère**) L17 French (= coach gateway, from *porte* gateway + *cochère* feminine adjective from *coche* coach). **1** A covered entrance large enough for vehicles to pass through, typically opening into a courtyard. **2** A porch where vehicles stop to set down passengers. Chiefly *United States*.

> **2 1996** *Times Magazine*... the view from the west corner is lost, as is something of the drama and excitement of being dropped off under the glittering lights of the porte cochère.

porteur /pɔrtœr/ *noun* plural pronounced same M20 French (literally, 'a person who carries'). *Ballet* A male dancer whose role is to lift and support a ballerina when she performs leaping or jumping movements.

portico /'pɔːtɪkəʊ/ *noun* plural **portico(e)s** E17 Italian (from Latin *porticus* porch). *Architecture* A structure consisting of a roof supported by columns at regular intervals, typically attached as a porch to a building.

portière /pɔrtjɛr/ *noun* plural pronounced same M19 French (from *porte* door). A curtain hung over a door or doorway, as a screen or for ornament, or to prevent draughts.

portmanteau /pɔːt'mantəʊ/ *noun & adjective* M16 French (*portemanteau* from *porte-* stem of *porter* to carry + *manteau* mantle). **A** *noun* plural **portmanteaus**, **portmanteaux** /pɔːt'mantəʊz/ A large travelling bag, typically made of stiff leather and hinged at the back so as to open into two equal parts. **B** *adjective* **1** (Of a word, expression, etc.) consisting of a blend, both in spelling and meaning, of two other words, for example *motel* or *brunch*. **2** Consisting of or combining two or more aspects or qualities: *a portmanteau movie composed of excerpts from his most famous films*.

ports de bras plural of PORT DE BRAS.

posada /pə'sɑːdə/, *foreign* /po'sada/ *noun* M18 Spanish (from *posar* to lodge). **1** (In Spain and Spanish-speaking countries) an inn or place of accommodation for travellers. **2** (In Mexico) each of a series of visits traditionally paid to different friends before Christmas, representing Mary's and Joseph's search for a lodging in Bethlehem.

poseur /pəʊ'zə:/ *noun* (feminine **poseuse** /pəʊ'zə:z/) L19 French (from *poser* to pose). A person who behaves affectedly in order to impress others; one who poses.

> **1996** *Times* His full, florid voice, face, wig and cravat all seem designed to evoke Wilde himself; but, as it turns out, less Wilde the poseur and paradoxist than Wilde the enemy of the rigid and frigid.

post-bellum /pəʊs(t)'bɛləm/ *adjective* L19 Latin (from *post* after + *bellum* war). Occurring or existing after a particular war, especially the American Civil War. Opposed to ANTE-BELLUM.

> **1996** *Spectator*... it was for the rural post-Bellum Virginia of her birth and her innate American roots she... yearned.

poste restante /pəʊst 'rɛstənt/, *foreign* /pɔst rɛstɑ̃t/ *noun phrase* M18 French (= mail remaining). A service offered by a post office whereby mail is kept for an agreed period until collected by the addressee.

post hoc /pəʊst 'hɒk/ *adjective & adverb phrase* M19 Latin (= after this). **A** *adjective phrase* Occurring or done after the event, especially with reference to the fallacious assumption that the occurrence in question has a logical relationship with the event it follows. **B** *adverb phrase* After the event.

postiche /pɒˈstiːʃ/ *noun* E18 French (= false, from Italian *posticcio* counterfeit, feigned). An imitation substituted for the real thing; *especially* a piece of false hair worn as an adornment. *Rare*.

post meridiem /pəʊs(t) məˈrɪdɪəm/ *adjective & adverb phrase* M17 Latin. After midday; between noon and midnight.

■ Abbreviated to *p.m.*

post-mortem /pəʊs(t)ˈmɔːtəm/ *noun, adjective, & adverb* M18 Latin (= after death). **A** *noun* **1** An examination of a body performed after death especially in order to determine the cause of death; an autopsy. **2** An analysis or discussion of an event held soon after it has occurred, especially in order to determine why it was a failure. **B** *adjective* **1** Relating to a post-mortem. **2** Happening after death. **C** *adverb* After death.

post-partum /pəʊs(t)ˈpɑːtəm/ *adjective & adverb* M19 Latin (*post partum* after childbirth). *Medicine* Following childbirth or the birth of young.

postscriptum /pəʊs(t)ˈskrɪptəm/ *noun* plural **postscripta** /pəʊs(t)ˈskrɪptə/ E16 Latin (use as noun of neuter past participle of *postscribere* to write after, from *post* after + *scribere* to write). Additional matter appended to any text, a postscript.

potage /pɒtaʒ/ (*plural same*), /pɒˈtɑːʒ/ *noun* ME Old and Modern French (literally, 'what is put in a pot', from *pot* pot). Thick soup.

■ Originally from Old French, the word was anglicized in the form *pottage*; it was later reintroduced from French first in Scotland and later (M17) in England with reference to dishes of French provenance.

potager /ˈpɒtədʒə/, *foreign* /pɔtaʒe/ (*plural same*) (also **potagère**) *noun* M17 French

(in *(jardin) potager* (garden) for the kitchen). A kitchen garden.

■ The original sense of *potager* as 'one who makes pot(t)ages' is long obsolete. The 17th-century garden writer John Evelyn introduced the word with its present sense in the form *potagere*.

1996 *Country Life* Chinese chives ... are worthy of a prominent place in a perennial border or potager.

pot-au-feu /pɒtofø/ *noun* plural **pot-au-feux** /pɒtofø/ L18 French (literally, 'pot on the fire'). A large cooking pot of a kind common in France; a French soup of meat, typically boiled beef, and vegetables cooked in such a pot.

pot-pourri /pəʊˈpʊəri/, /pəʊˈpʊəriː/, /pɒtˈpʊəri/ *noun* (also **potpourri**) E17 French (literally, 'rotten pot', from *pot* pot + *pourri* past participle of *pourrir* to rot (translating Spanish OLLA PODRIDA)). **1** A mixture of dried flower petals and spices placed in a bowl to perfume a room. Also, a container for holding this. **2** A mixture or medley of things, especially a musical or literary one.

■ Originally denoted a stew made of different kinds of meat.

potrero /pɒˈtrɛːrəʊ/ *noun* plural **potreros** M19 Spanish (from *potro* colt, pony). (In South America and the south-western United States) a paddock or pasture for horses or cattle.

pouf /puːf/ *noun* (in sense 3 usually **pouffe**) E19 French (ultimately imitative). **1** A part of a dress in which a large mass of material has been gathered so that it stands away from the body. **2** A bouffant hairstyle. **3** A cushioned footstool or low seat with no back.

poule de luxe /pul də lyks/ *noun phrase* plural **poules de luxe** (pronounced same) M20 French (= 'poule' (i.e. promiscuous woman) of luxury). A prostitute.

1976 *Times Literary Supplement* ... his wife has remarried and ... his daughter is in business as a *poule de luxe* and doing very well.

poulet /pulɛ/ (*plural same*), /ˈpuːleɪ/ *noun* M19 French. A chicken; a chicken dish.

■ Especially with reference to French cooking, usually with a qualifying adjective, as in *poulet Provençal* (Provençal chicken), *poulet rôti* (roast chicken), etc.

poult-de-soie /puːdə'swɑː/ *noun* (also **poult** /puːlt/, /pʊlt/) M19 French (alteration of *pou-de-soie* of unknown origin). A fine corded silk or taffeta, usually coloured.

pourboire /purbwar/ *noun* plural pronounced same E19 French (literally, 'for drinking'). A gratuity, a tip.

pour encourager les autres /pur ɑ̃kuraʒe lez otr/ *adverb phrase* E19 French (literally, 'to encourage the others'). As an example to others; to encourage others.

■ The source is a witticism of Voltaire's in *Candide* (1759) concerning the execution in 1757 of Admiral John Byng for failing to relieve Minorca when the island came under attack by the French in 1756: *Dans ce pays-ci il est bon de tuer de temps en temps un amiral pour encourager les autres* ('In this country [England] it is thought a good idea to kill an admiral from time to time to encourage the others').

1995 *Spectator* The only thing that could be said in its [the hospital's] favour was that it was better than Addenbrookes [Hospital], in Cambridge, with its giant crematorium chimney next to the entrance, *pour encourager les autres*, I suppose.

pousada /pəʊ'sɑːdə/ *noun* M20 Portuguese (literally, 'resting place', from *pausar* to rest). An inn or hotel in Portugal owned and administered by the government.

pousse-café /puskafe/ *noun* plural pronounced same L19 French (literally, 'push coffee'). A glass of various liqueurs or cordials poured in successive layers, taken immediately after coffee.

poussin /'puːsɑ̃/, *foreign* /pusɛ̃/ (*plural same*) *noun* M20 French. A young chicken for eating.

■ Earlier in *petit poussin*.

powwow /'paʊwaʊ/ *noun & verb* (also **pow-wow**) E17 Narragansett (*powah*, *powwaw* shaman (literally 'he dreams')). **A** *noun* **1** A North American Indian ceremony involving feasting and dancing. Also, a council or conference of or with Indians. **2** A conference or meeting for discussion, especially among friends or colleagues. Originally *United States*. **B** *intransitive verb* **1** (Of North American Indians) hold a powwow. **2** Confer, discuss, deliberate. Chiefly *North American*.

praenomen /priː'nəʊmɛn/ *noun* E17 Latin (= forename, from *prae* pre- + *nomen* name). An ancient Roman's first or personal name, for example *Marcus Tullius Cicero; generally* a first name, a forename.

praesidium variant of PRESIDIUM.

praline /'prɑːliːn/ *noun* E18 French (from Marshal de Plessis-*Praslin* (1598–1675), the French general whose cook invented the technique). A smooth, sweet substance made by boiling nuts in sugar and grinding the mixture, used especially as a filling for chocolates; a chocolate filled with praline.

1996 *Spectator* A real plantsman's border is as bitty as a chocolate praline.

pralltriller /'praltrɪlə/ *noun* plural same, **pralltrillers** M19 German (from *prallen* to bounce + *Triller* trill). *Music* An ornament consisting of one rapid alternation of the written note with the note immediately above it. Cf. MORDENT.

pratique /'pratiːk/, *foreign* /pratik/ *noun* E17 Old and Modern French (= practice, intercourse, corresponding to or from Italian *pratica* from medieval Latin *practica* use as noun (sc. *ars* art) of *practicus* from Greek *praktikos* from *prattein* to do). *History* Permission granted to a ship to use a port after quarantine or on showing a clean bill of health.

praxis /'praksɪs/ *noun* L16 Medieval Latin (from Greek, from *prattein* to do). **1** Practice, as distinguished from theory. **2** Accepted practice or custom.

1 **1996** *Oldie* He recalls that the lecturing, as opposed to praxis, was deficient and that most students went over to the Architectural Association for intellectual stimulus.

précis /'preɪsiː/ *noun & verb* (also **precis**) M18 French (use as noun of *précis*). **A** *noun* plural same /'preɪsiːz/. A summary or abstract, especially of a text or speech. **B** *transitive verb* Make a précis of; summarize.

B 1996 *Times* A glance at the subtitles which every few seconds précis the disorder in question...will testify to that...

predella /prɪ'dɛlə/ *noun* M19 Italian (= stool). **1** A step or platform on which an altar is placed, an altar-step. **2** A raised shelf above an altar; a painting or sculpture on the front of this, forming an appendage to an altarpiece above.

premier cru /prəmje kry/, /ˌprɛmɪə 'kruː/ *noun phrase* plural **premiers crus** (pronounced same) M19 French (literally, 'first growth'). A wine of a superior grade, or the vineyard that produces it.

première /'prɛmɪɛː/, *foreign* /prəmjɛr/ (*plural same*) *noun* & *verb* (also **premiere**) L19 French (feminine of *premier*; as *noun* short for *première représentation* first representation). **A** *noun* The first performance of a musical or theatrical work or the first showing of a film; a first night. **B** *verb* **1** *transitive verb* Give the first performance of. **2** *intransitive verb* (Of a musical or theatrical work or a film) have its first performance.

A 1996 *Spectator La Bohème* was not an instant success...at its Turin première on 1 February 1896...

premiers crus plural of PREMIER CRU.

presidio /prɪ'sɪdɪəʊ/, *foreign* /pre'sidjo/ *noun* plural **presidios** /prɪ'sɪdɪəʊz/, *foreign* /pre'sidjos/ M18 Spanish (from Latin *praesidium* garrison, fort). (In Spain and Spanish America) a fort, a fortified military settlement, a garrison town.

presidium /prɪ'sɪdɪʌm/, /prɪ'zɪdɪʌm/ *noun* (also **praesidium**) plural **presidia** /prɪ'sɪdɪə/, **presidiums** E20 Russian (*prezidium* from Latin *praesidium* protection, garrison). A standing executive committee in a communist country; **Presidium** (in the former USSR) the committee which functioned as the legislative authority when the Supreme Soviet was not sitting.

prestissimo /prɛ'stɪsɪməʊ/ *adverb*, *adjective*, & *noun* E18 Italian (superlative of PRESTO). *Music* **A** *adverb* & *adjective* (Especially as a direction) in a very

quick tempo. **B** *noun* plural **prestissimos, prestissimi** /prɛ'stɪsɪmi/ A movement or passage marked to be performed in a very quick tempo.

presto /'prɛstəʊ/ *adverb*, *adjective*, *noun*, & *interjection* L16 Italian (= quick, quickly, from late Latin *praestus* ready, for Latin *praesto* at hand). **A** *adverb* & *adjective Music* (Especially as a direction) in a quick tempo. **B** *noun* plural **prestos** *Music* A movement or passage marked to be performed in a quick tempo. **C** *interjection* Announcing the climax of a trick or a surprising dénouement. Frequently in *hey presto*.

C 1996 *Spectator* A ghetto upbringing, a broken home, an abusive parent and, presto, the criminal is 'emoting his feelings' as he maims, robs or even kills his victim.

prêt-à-porter /prɛtə'pɔːteɪ/, *foreign* /prɛtaporte/ *adjective* & *noun* M20 French (literally, 'ready to wear'). **A** *adjective* (Of clothes) sold ready to wear rather than made to measure. **B** *noun* Designer clothes sold ready to wear.

A 1996 *Times Magazine* No Anglo-Saxon squeamishness here—animals are either prêt-à-manger or prêt-à-porter.

B 1995 *Times* Paris, in October, goes *prêt à porter* mad.

pretzel /'prɛts(ə)l/ *noun* M19 German (South German dialect form of *Brezel* from Old High German *brizzila* (Italian *bracciello* usually taken as adaptation of medieval Latin *bracellus* bracelet)). A crisp biscuit baked in the form of a knot or stick and flavoured with salt, eaten originally in Germany.

Priapus /prʌɪ'eɪpəs/ *noun* (also **priapus**) plural **Priapi** /prʌɪ'eɪpʌɪ/, /prʌɪ'eɪpiː/, **Priapuses** LME Latin (from Greek *Priapos*, the Greek and Roman god of procreation whose symbol was the phallus, later adopted as a god of gardens). **1** A statue or image of the god Priapus, especially characterized by having large genitals. **2** A representation of the penis, especially when erect.

prie-dieu /priː'djəː/, *foreign* /pridjø/ *noun* plural **prie-dieux** (pronounced same), same M18 French (literally, 'pray God'). A piece of furniture for use during prayer, consisting of a kneeling surface and a narrow upright front with a rest for the elbows or for books.

Also, (more fully *prie-dieu chair*) a chair with a low seat and a tall sloping back, used especially as a prayer seat or stool and fashionable in the mid 19th century.

prima /'priːmə/ *noun* M18 Italian (feminine of PRIMO). A first or most important female; a prima donna, a prima ballerina.

prima ballerina /ˌpriːmə baləˈriːnə/ *noun phrase* L19 Italian (= first ballerina). The chief female dancer in a ballet or ballet company; a ballerina of the highest accomplishment or rank.

prima donna /ˌpriːmə ˈdɒnə/ *noun phrase* L18 Italian (literally, 'first lady'). **1** The principal female singer in an opera or opera company; a female opera singer of the highest accomplishment or rank. **2** A very temperamental person with an inflated view of their own talent or importance.

prima facie /ˌprʌɪmə ˈfeɪʃiː/ *adverb & adjective phrase* L15 Latin (= at first sight, from feminine ablative of *primus* first and of *facies* face). Based on the first impression; accepted as correct until proved otherwise.

> **1996** *Spectator* . . . the widespread acceptance of the phrase 'couch potato' is good *prima facie* evidence of the direction of that influence [of commercial television].

prima inter pares see PRIMUS INTER PARES.

primeur /priːmœr/ *noun* plural pronounced same L19 French (= newness, something quite new, from as *prime* first). A new or early thing; *specifically* (**a**) in *plural*, fruit or vegetables grown to be available very early in the season; (**b**) newly produced wines which have recently been made available. Cf. EN PRIMEUR.

primo /'priːməʊ/ *noun & adjective* plural (in senses A, B.1) **primi** /'priːmi/, (in sense A) **primos** M18 Italian (= first; cf. PRIMA). **A** *noun* Music The leading or upper part in a duet. **B** *adjective* **1** *Music* (Of a musician, performer, role, etc.) principal, chief; of highest quality or importance. **2** Of top quality or importance. *Slang* (chiefly *United States*).

primum mobile /ˌpriːməm ˈməʊbɪliː/, /ˌprʌɪməm ˈməʊbɪli/ *noun phrase* plural **primum mobiles** L15 Medieval Latin (literally, 'first moving thing', from Latin neuter of *primus* first + *mobilis* mobile). **1** (In the medieval version of the Ptolemaic system) an outermost sphere supposed to revolve round the earth in twenty-four hours, carrying with it the inner spheres. **2** The most important source of motion or action.

primus /'priːməs/, /'prʌɪməs/ *adjective* L16 Latin (= first). **1** First, original, principal. Originally and chiefly in Latin phrases. **2** Designating the first of several pupils with the same surname to enter a school. Cf. SECUNDUS, TERTIUS.

> ▪ Appended to a surname and used especially in public schools.

primus inter pares /ˌpriːməs ɪntə ˈpɑːriːz/, /ˌprʌɪməs/ *noun phrase* (feminine **prima inter pares** /ˌpriːmə/, /ˌprʌɪmə/) E19 Latin. A first among equals, the senior or representative member of a group.

> **1996** *Economist* A predecessor who made the mistake of behaving too much like an ordinary boss . . . and too little as *primus inter pares* did not last long.

princesse lointaine /prɛ̃sɛs lwɛ̃tɛn/ *noun phrase* plural **princesses lointaines** (pronounced same) E20 French (literally, 'distant princess'). An idealized unattainable woman.

> ▪ The title of a play (1895) by Edmond Rostand (1868–1918), based on the theme of the love of the twelfth-century troubadour poet Rudel for the Lady of Tripoli.

principium /prɪnˈkɪpɪəm/, /prɪnˈsɪpɪəm/ *noun* plural **principia** /prɪnˈkɪpɪə/ L16 Latin (from *princip-* first, chief). **1** *Roman History* In *plural* The general's quarters in an army camp. **2** A fundamental cause or basis of something; a principle.

> ▪ In scholastic philosophy the *principium individuationis* ('principle of individuation') was the criterion by which any individual was uniquely distinguished from any other. In sense 2 *Principia* occurs as the abbreviated title of either of two major works by English

philosophers: the *Philosophiae Naturalis Principia Mathematica* (1687) of Isaac Newton and the *Principia Mathematica* (1910–13) of Bertrand Russell and A. N. Whitehead.

prisiadka /prɪˈsjatkə/ *noun* M20 Russian (*prisyadka*). A dance step in which a squatting male dancer kicks out each leg alternately to the front; the dance which uses this step. Cf. KAZACHOC.

prix fixe /pri fiks/ *noun phrase* L19 French (literally, 'fixed price'). A meal consisting of several courses served at a total fixed price. Cf. À LA CARTE.

1996 *Spectator* Thus, taramasalata is there, and moussaka on the lunchtime *prix fixe* . . .

pro /prəʊ/ *preposition, adverb, noun & adjective* LME Latin (= before, in front of, for, on behalf of, in return for). **A** *preposition* **1** For. In Latin phrases (cf. PRO BONO PUBLICO, PRO FORMA). **2** In favour of. **B** *adverb* In favour (of a proposition etc.). **C** *noun* plural **pros** An advantage or argument in favour of something. **D** *adjective* Favouring, supportive.

■ As an adverb, chiefly in the phrase *pro and contra* or *pro and con* ('for and against'), and as a noun chiefly in the phrase *pros and cons* ('(the points) for and against').

pro bono publico /prəʊ ˌbɒnəʊ ˈpʊblɪkəʊ/, /prəʊ ˌbəʊnəʊ ˈpʌblɪkəʊ/ *adverb & adjective phrase* E18 Latin. For the public good.

■ In colloquial use often shortened to *pro bono*. This has given rise, originally in United States usage, to the adjective *pro bono* (or *pro bono*), designating legal work undertaken without charge, especially for a client on low income.

1995 *Times* Mr Goldsmith made his promise as he launched a Bar Council *pro bono publico* scheme . . . to co-ordinate the provision of free services by barristers.

1995 *Times* It is hoped that it may prompt lawyers to dig into their pockets or do more *pro bono* work.

procès-verbal /prɔsɛˈvɛrbal/, /ˌprʊseɪvəːˈbaːl/ *noun* plural **procès-verbaux** /prɔsɛvɛrbo/, /ˌprʊseɪvəːˈbəʊ/ M17 French. A detailed written report of proceedings; minutes; an authenticated written statement of facts in support of a charge.

proferens /prəˈfɛrɛnz/ *noun* plural **proferentes** /prɒfəˈrɛntiːz/ M20 Latin (present participle of *proferre* to bring forth, utter). *Law* The party which proposes or adduces a contract or a condition in a contract.

profiterole /prəˈfɪtərəʊl/ *noun* L19 French (diminutive of *profit* profit). A small hollow case of choux pastry usually filled with cream and covered with chocolate sauce, served as a dessert.

■ Earlier (E16–E18) evidence exists in English for the word in the sense of some kind of cooked food; the literal etymological sense of 'small gains', meaning the gratuities or tips that a servant can pick up, is attested in Cotgrave's French–English dictionary of 1611.

pro forma /prəʊ ˈfɔːmə/ *adverb, adjective, & noun phrase* E16 Latin. **A** *adverb phrase* As a matter of form or politeness. **B** *adjective phrase* **1** Done or produced as a matter of form. **2** Denoting a model or standard document or form, especially an invoice sent in advance of goods supplied or with goods sent on approval. **3** (Of a financial statement) showing potential or expected income, costs, assets, or liabilities, especially in relation to some planned act or situation. **C** *noun phrase* plural **pro formas** A pro forma invoice, document, or form.

B.3 1996 *Times* Somerfield is now being sold on a multiple of only 6.5 times its pro forma earnings to the end of April.

prolegomenon /prəʊlɪˈgɒmɪnən/ *noun* plural **prolegomena** /prəʊlɪˈgɒmɪnə/ M17 Latin (from Greek, use as noun of neuter present participle of *prolegein* to say beforehand). A critical or discursive introduction prefaced to a literary work.

proletariat /ˌprəʊlɪˈtɛːrɪət/ *noun* M19 French (*prolétariat*, from Latin *proletarius* a Roman citizen of the lowest class, from *proles* offspring (since such citizens were considered capable of serving the State only by producing offspring)). **1** The lowest class of any community, especially when regarded as uncultured. **2** Working-class people regarded collectively (often used with reference to Marxism).

prominenti /prɒmɪ'nɛnti/ *noun plural* M20 Italian (plural of noun from adjective *prominente* prominent, from Latin *prominent-* present participial stem of *prominere* to jut out). Distinguished or eminent people.

pronaos /prəʊ'neɪɒs/ *noun plural* **pronaoi** /prəʊ'neɪɔɪ/ E17 Latin (from Greek, from *pro-* before + *naos* temple). A vestibule at the front of a classical temple, enclosed by a portico and projecting side walls. Also, a narthex.

pronto /'prɒntəʊ/ *adverb* 1 & *adjective* M18 Italian (from Latin *promptus* prompt; cf. next). *Music* (Especially as a direction) quickly, promptly; quick, prompt.

pronto /'prɒntəʊ/ *adverb* 2 E20 Spanish (from Latin *promptus* prompt; cf. preceding). Quickly; promptly, at once.

■ Colloquial, originally United States.
1976 P. Cave *High Flying Birds* You tell that bastard to come and see me... Pronto.

pronunciamento /prə,nʌnsɪə'mɛntəʊ/ *noun* plural **pronunciamentos** M19 Spanish (*pronunciamiento*, from *pronunciar* (from Latin *pronuntiare* to pronounce)). (Especially in Spain and Spanish-speaking countries) a political manifesto or proclamation.
1995 *Oldie* The book keeps trumpeting such pseudo-omniscient *pronunciamentos* as that 'there is no reciprocity in love, harmony is not the human condition, and the thing sung will always be the unenjoyed ideal'.

pro-nuncio /prəʊ'nʌnsɪəʊ/, /prəʊ'nʌnʃɪəʊ/ *noun* M20 Italian (*pro-nunzio*, from *pro-* before + *nunzio* nuncio). A papal ambassador to a country which does not accord the Pope's ambassador automatic precedence over other ambassadors.

propaganda /prɒpə'gandə/ *noun* E18 Italian (from modern Latin *congregatio de propaganda fide* congregation for propagation of the faith). 1 (**Propaganda**) A committee of cardinals of the Roman Catholic Church responsible for foreign missions, founded in 1622 by Pope Gregory XV. Also more fully *Congregation* or *College of the Propaganda*.

2 Information, especially of a biased or misleading nature, used to promote a political cause or point of view; the dissemination of such information as a political strategy.

■ Sense 2 dates from the early 20th century.

propylaeum /prɒpɪ'liːəm/ *noun* plural **propylaea** /prɒpɪ'liːə/ E18 Latin (from Greek *propulaion* use as noun of neuter of adjective *propulaios* before the gate, from *pro-* before + *pulē* gate). *Architecture* The structure forming the entrance to a temple; *specifically* (**Propylaeum**) the entrance to the Acropolis at Athens.

■ The Greek word is represented in English in the form *propylon* (M19); both are current, although the Latin word is perhaps more common.

pro rata /prəʊ 'rɑːtə/, /'reɪtə/ *adverb* & *adjective phrase* L16 Latin (= according to the rate). **A** *adverb phrase* In proportion, proportionally. **B** *adjective phrase* Proportional.

proscenium /prə'siːnɪəm/, /prəʊ'siːnɪəm/ *noun* plural **prosceniums**, **proscenia** /prə'siːnɪə/ E17 Latin (from Greek *proskēnion*, from *pro-* before + *skēnē* scene, stage). 1 The part of a theatre stage in front of the curtain. **b** The stage of an ancient theatre. 2 An arch framing the opening between the stage and the auditorium in some theatres. In full *proscenium arch*.

prosciutto /prɒ'ʃuːtəʊ/ *noun* M20 Italian (= ham). Italian cured ham, usually served raw and thinly sliced as an hors d'oeuvre.

prosit /'proːzɪt/ *interjection* & *noun* (also **prost** /proːst/, (as noun) **Prosit**) M19 German (from Latin = may it benefit). An expression used in drinking a person's health.

prospectus /prə'spɛktəs/ *noun* M18 Latin (= view, prospect, use as noun of past participle of *prospicere* to look forward). A printed booklet advertising a school or university to potential parents or students or giving details of a share offer for the benefit of investors.

prosthesis /'prɒsθɪsɪs/, *in sense* 1 *usually* /prɒs'θiːsɪs/ *noun* plural **prostheses**

/ˈprɒsθɪsiːz/, *in sense 1 usually* /prɒsˈθiː
siːz/ M16 Late Latin (from Greek, from
prostithenai to add, from *pros* in addition +
tithenai to place). **1** An artificial body
part, such as a limb, a heart, or a
breast implant. **2** *Linguistics* The addition of a letter or syllable at the
beginning of a word, as in Spanish
escuela derived from Latin *scola*.

protégé /ˈprɒtɪʒeɪ/, /ˈprɒtɛʒeɪ/, /ˈprəʊtɪ-
ʒeɪ/ *noun* (feminine **protégée**) L18
French (past participial adjective of *proté-
ger* from Latin *protegere* to protect). A
person under the protection, care, or
patronage of another, especially of a
person of superior position or influence.

> **1996** *Spectator* I do so with [sc. doff my cap to]
> Mr Preston, even though he was rather rude
> about me ... after I had elsewhere written some
> disobliging comments about his newly
> appointed protégé, Mr Jaspan.

pro tem abbreviation of PRO TEMPORE.

pro tempore /prəʊ ˈtɛmpəri/ *adverb &*
adjective phrase LME Latin (= for the time).
A *adverb phrase* For the time being,
temporarily. **B** *adjective phrase* Temporary.
■ Also colloquially in abbreviated form
pro tem (E19).

proviso /prəˈvaɪzəʊ/ *noun* plural **provi-
so(e)s** LME Latin (neuter ablative singular
of past participle of *providere* to provide,
as in medieval Latin *proviso quod* (or *ut*) it
being provided that). A condition or
qualification attached to an agreement or statement.

provocateur /prɒvɒkatœr/ *noun* plural
pronounced same E20 French (= provoker).
A person who provokes a disturbance;
an agitator. Cf. AGENT PROVOCATEUR.

provolone /prɒvəˈləʊni/ *noun* M20
Italian (from *provola* buffalo's milk
cheese). An Italian soft smoked cheese,
often made in a variety of shapes. Also
provolone cheese.

prox. abbreviation of PROXIMO.

proxime accessit /ˌprɒksɪmeɪ akˈsɛsɪt/ *noun phrase* L19 Latin (literally,
'came very near'). Used to name the
person who comes second in an examination or is runner-up for an award.

> **1995** *Spectator* As Herbert Morrison found
> out, to be *proxime accessit* in Labour's class
> list is not much fun.

proximo /ˈprɒksɪməʊ/ *adjective* M19
Latin (from *proximo mense* in the next
month). Chiefly *Commerce* Of next
month. Now *dated*.
■ Often abbreviated to *prox.*, it is used
following the ordinal number denoting
the day, as in *1st proximo*.

pruritus /prʊəˈraɪtəs/ *noun* M17 Latin
(from *prurire* to itch). *Medicine* Severe
itching of the skin, as a symptom of
various ailments.
■ Frequently with modern Latin specifying word.

pseudepigrapha /ˌsjuːdɪˈpɪgrəfə/ *noun*
plural L17 Greek (use as noun of neuter
plural of *pseudepigraphos* with false title,
from *pseudo-* false + *epigraphein* to in-
scribe). Spurious or pseudonymous
writings, especially Jewish writings
ascribed to various biblical patriarchs
and prophets but composed *c.*200
BC–AD 200.

pseudo /ˈsjuːdəʊ/ *adjective & noun* LME
Greek (independent use of *pseudo-* false).
A *adjective* **1** Not genuine; sham.
2 Intellectually or socially pretentious;
insincere. **B** *noun* plural **pseudos**.
A pretentious or insincere person.
Abbreviated to *pseud* (*slang*).

psi /psʌɪ/, /sʌɪ/ *noun* LME Greek (*psei*).
1 The twenty-third letter (Ψ, ψ) of the
Greek alphabet, transliterated as 'ps'.
2 Supposed parapsychological or psy-
chic faculties or phenomena. Frequently *attributive*, as *psi powers* etc.

psyche /ˈsʌɪki/ *noun* M17 Latin (from
Greek *psukhē* breath, life, soul, mind,
related to *psukhein* to breathe). **1** The
soul, the spirit. Now chiefly *historical*.
2 The mind, especially in its spiritual,
emotional, and motivational aspects;
the collective mental or psychological
characteristics of a nation, people, etc.

psychopompos /ˌsʌɪkə(ʊ)ˈpɒmpɒs/
noun (also in English form **psycho-
pomp** /ˈsʌɪkə(ʊ)pɒmp/) M19 Greek (*psu-
khopompos*, from *psukhē* soul + *pompos*
conductor). (In Greek mythology) a
guide of souls to the place of the dead.

Also, the spiritual guide of a living person's soul.

pubes /'pju:bi:z/ *noun* plural same L16 Latin (= the pubic hair, the groin, the genitals). The lower part of the abdomen at the front of the pelvis, which becomes covered with hair from the time of puberty.

pudendum /pjʊ'dɛndəm/ *noun* plural **pudenda** /pjʊ'dɛndə/ M17 Latin (from *pudenda (membra)* (parts) to be ashamed of, from *pudere* to be ashamed). In *plural* and (occasionally) *singular*. A person's external genitals, especially a woman's.

pudeur /pydœr/ *noun* M20 French (from Latin PUDOR). A sense of shame or embarrassment, especially with regard to matters of a sexual or personal nature; modesty.

1995 D. Lodge *Therapy* A kind of *pudeur* restrained me.

Pseudo-foreign words

A number of words that look like foreign imports are not all that they seem. Some have been formed on the model of an existing foreign word and, while they have the appearance of a loanword, in fact have no equivalent in the supposed source language. *Nom de plume* is a good example. This term for 'an assumed name used by a writer instead of their real name, a pen-name' certainly looks French enough. But it was formed in English from French words in the early 19th century, based on the pattern of the genuinely French *nom de guerre*, 'an assumed name under which a person engages in combat or some other activity or enterprise'. Similarly, *bon viveur* is a pseudo-French coinage, formed from the French words for 'good' and 'living person' to match the earlier imported phrase *bon vivant*. The Italian-sounding *braggadocio*, denoting boastful or arrogant behaviour, was originally the name Edmund Spenser gave to a boastful character in his poem *The Faerie Queene*. The ending is based on the authentically Italian suffix *-occio* (suggesting something large of its kind); the first part comes from the English *brag* or *braggart*.

Sometimes a foreign word can act as a template for other, often humorous, coinages. *Literati*, from Latin, dates from the 17th century and refers to well-educated people who are interested in literature. Their modern descendants include the *glitterati* (fashionable people or celebrities), the *chatterati* (another term for the chattering classes, intellectual or artistic people who express liberal opinions), and the *digerati* (computing experts regarded as a class). *Sitzkrieg*, formed on the analogy of *blitzkrieg* (literally 'a lightning war'), was used in English in the 1940s to convey the idea of 'a sit-down war', a war, or a phase of a war, in which there is little or no active warfare. The Russian and Yiddish suffix *-nik* (as in words like *Sputnik* and *kibbutznik*) has been used, particularly since the 1950s, to form English words denoting a person associated with a specified thing or quality, such as *refusenik*, *peacenik*, *beatnik*, and *no-goodnik*.

El is the Spanish definite article, the equivalent of English *the*, as in *El Dorado* and *El Greco*. In the 20th century it has been used in English not only in titles such as *El Supremo*, but also in such colloquial expressions as *el cheapo*. First recorded in the 1960s, this means 'very cheap, of poor quality', the English adjective *cheap* made to resemble a Spanish word by the addition of an *o*. The *Costa Brava* and *Costa del Sol* have inspired other pseudo-Spanish names of resort areas such as the *Costa Geriatrica*, describing one largely frequented or inhabited by elderly people.

pudor /'pjuːdɔː/ *noun* E17 Latin (= shame, modesty, from *pudere* to be ashamed). Due sense of shame; bashfulness, modesty.

pueblo /'pwɛbləʊ/ *noun & adjective* plural **pueblos** E19 Spanish (literally 'people', from Latin *populus* people). **A** *noun* **1** A town or village in Spain, Latin America, or the south-western United States, especially an American Indian settlement. **2** (**Pueblo**) A member of any of various American Indian peoples, including the Hopi, occupying pueblo settlements chiefly in New Mexico and Arizona. **B** *adjective* (usually **Pueblo**) Relating to or denoting the Pueblo or their culture.

puggaree /'pʌg(ə)riː/ *noun* (also **pagri** /'pagriː/) M17 Hindi (*pagrī* turban). **1** A PAGRI. **2** A thin muslin scarf wound round the crown of a sun helmet or hat so that the ends of the scarf hang down over the wearer's neck and shield it from the sun.

⸱**2 1996** *Spectator* We are shown, above a wood engraving...of the two explorers doffing their headgear to one another at Ujiji, Stanley's helmet with its red check pagri and Livingstone's cap.

puisne /'pjuːni/ *adjective* L16 Old French ((modern *puîne*), from *puis* (from Latin *postea* afterwards) + *né* (from Latin *natus* born)). **1** *Law* (In the United Kingdom and some other countries) designating a judge of a superior court inferior in rank to chief justices. **2** Later, more recent, of subsequent date. Now chiefly in *puisne mortgage*.

■ First introduced (L16) as a noun, denoting a junior or inferior person.

puissance /'pjuːɪs(ə)ns/, /'pwiːs(ə)ns/, /'pwɪs(ə)ns/, *(especially in sense 2)* /'pwiːs̃s/ *noun* LME Old and Modern French (= power, from Proto-Gallo-Romance from Latin *posse* to be able). **1** Power, strength, force, might; influence. Chiefly *archaic* and *poetical*. **2** A competitive test of a horse's ability to jump large obstacles in showjumping.

puja /'puːdʒə/ *noun* (also **pooja**, **pujah**) L17 Sanskrit (*pūjā* worship). A Hindu ceremonial offering.

pukka /'pʌkə/ *adjective* (also **pukkah**, **pucka**) L17 Hindi (*pakkā* cooked, ripe, substantial). **1** Of full weight, full; genuine. **2** Certain, reliable; authentic, true; proper, socially acceptable. **3** Permanent; (of a building) solidly built. **4** Excellent. *British colloquial*.

■ Originally Anglo-Indian, often in phrases such as *pukka sahib*, a true gentleman; now colloquial. The word (in its 'excellent' sense) became associated with the British celebrity chef Jamie Oliver in the late 1990s when he used it in his television cookery programme *The Naked Chef*. The spelling *pucka* was the one in most frequent use prior to the 20th century.

2 1996 *Times Magazine* ...foreign literature, nevertheless, dominates—the study of indigenous Indian-language writers is not regarded as pukka by renowned institutions of learning.

pulao variant of PILAF.

pulque /'pʊlkeɪ/, /'pʊlki/ *noun* L17 American Spanish (from Nahuatl *puliúhki* decomposed). A Mexican alcoholic drink made by fermenting sap from the maguey plant.

pumpernickel /'pʊmpəˌnɪk(ə)l/, /'pʌmpəˌnɪk(ə)l/ *noun* M18 German (transferred use of earlier sense 'lout, bumpkin', ultimate origin unknown). Dark dense German bread made from coarsely ground wholemeal rye.

puna /'puːnə/ *noun* E17 American Spanish (from Quechua). **1** A high treeless plateau in the Peruvian Andes. **2** Difficulty of breathing, nausea, etc., caused by climbing to high altitudes; altitude sickness.

punctilio /pʌŋ(k)'tɪlɪəʊ/ *noun* plural **punctilios** L16 Italian and Spanish (from Italian *puntiglio(n-)* and Spanish *puntillo*, diminutive of Latin *punto* point). A fine or petty point of conduct or procedure.

punctum /'pʌŋ(k)təm/ *noun* plural **puncta** /'pʌŋ(k)tə/ L16 Latin (= a point, originally neuter of *punctus* past participle of *pungere* to prick). **1** *Technical* A small, distinct point; *Zoology*, *Botany*, *Medicine*, etc. a minute rounded speck, dot, or spot of colour, or a small elevation or depression on a surface. **2** *Anatomy* The opening of a tear duct. More fully *punctum lachrymale*.

punkah /'pʌŋkə/, /'pʌŋkaː/ *noun* (also **punka**) L17 Hindi (*paṅkhā* fan, from

Sanskrit *pakṣaka*, from *pakṣa* wing). (In the Indian subcontinent) a large cloth fan on a frame suspended from the ceiling, moved backwards and forwards by pulling on a cord. Chiefly *historical*. **b** An electric fan.

purdah /'pəːdə/ *noun* E19 Persian and Urdu (*parda* veil, curtain). **1** In the Indian subcontinent and South-East Asia, a curtain, a veil; *especially* one used to screen women from men or strangers. **2** The practice in certain Muslim and Hindu societies, especially in the Indian subcontinent, of screening women from men or strangers, especially by means of a veil or curtain. **b** *transferred* Seclusion; (medical) isolation or quarantine; secrecy. Chiefly in *in, into, out of, purdah*.

> **1977** D. Bagley *Enemy* When I came out of purdah, but before I was discharged, I went to see her.

purée /'pjʊəreɪ/, *as noun also foreign* /pyre/ (*plural same*) *noun & verb* E18 Old and Modern French (= purified, feminine past participle of *purer* from medieval Latin *purare* to refine (metal), from *purus* pure). **A** *noun* A smooth cream of liquidized or crushed fruit or vegetables. **B** *transitive verb* Make a purée of (fruit or vegetables).

puri /'puːri/ *noun* M20 Hindi (*pūrī* from Sanskrit *pūrikā*). (In Indian cookery) a small round piece of bread made of unleavened wheat flour, deep-fried and served with meat or vegetables.

puro /'puro/ *noun plural* **puros** /'puros/ M19 Spanish (literally, 'pure'). (In Spain and Spanish-speaking countries) a cigar.

puta /'puta/ *noun* M20 Spanish. (In Spanish-speaking countries or parts of America) a prostitute or promiscuous woman. *Slang*.

putonghua /puːˈtʊŋhwɑː/ *noun* M20 Chinese (*pǔtōnghuà*, from *pǔtōng* common + *huà* spoken language). The standard spoken form of modern Chinese, based on the dialect of Beijing.

putsch /pʊtʃ/ *noun* E20 Swiss German (= thrust, blow). **1** A violent attempt to overthrow a government; a coup. **2** A sudden vigorous effort or campaign. *Colloquial*.

> *transferred* **1 1996** *Times* [Chris Evans] boasts about how he is famous enough to leave for six weeks in Barbados while wimpier DJs clutch their headphones for fear of a putsch.

putto /'pʊtəʊ/, *foreign* /'putto/ *noun plural* **putti** /'pʊti/, *foreign* /'putti/ M17 Italian (from Latin *putus* boy). A representation of a naked child, especially a cherub or cupid in Renaissance and baroque art.

putz /pʊts/, /pʌts/ *noun* E20 German (= decoration, finery; in sense 2 from Yiddish). **1** In Pennsylvanian Dutch homes, a representation of the Nativity scene traditionally placed under a Christmas tree. *United States*. **2** The penis. *United States slang*. **b** A fool; a stupid or objectionable person. *North American slang*.

puy /pwiː/ *noun plural pronounced same* M19 French (= hill, from Latin *podium* elevated place). A small extinct volcanic cone; originally and *specifically* any of those in the Auvergne, France.

qadi variant of CADI.

qanat /kəˈnɑːt/ *noun* (also **kanat**) M19 Persian (from Arabic *ḳanāt* reed, lance, pipe, channel). (In the Middle East) a gently sloping underground channel or tunnel, especially one constructed to lead water from the interior of a hill to a village below.

qat variant of KHAT.

QED abbreviation of QUOD ERAT DEMONSTRANDUM.

QEF abbreviation of QUOD ERAT FACIENDUM.

qibla /ˈkɪblə/ *noun* (also **kiblah**) M17 Arabic (*ḳibla* that which is opposite). The direction of the Kaaba (the sacred building at Mecca), to which Muslims turn at prayer.

qq.v. see QUOD VIDE.

qua /kweɪ/, /kwɑː/ *adverb* M17 Latin (ablative singular feminine of *qui* who). In the capacity of; as being.
> **1996** *Spectator* So can the historian *qua* historian give any sort of credence to *any* of this?

quadrennium /kwɒˈdrɛnɪəm/ *noun* (also (earlier) **quadriennium** /kwɒdrɪˈɛnɪəm/) plural **quadrenniums**, **quadrennia** /kwɒˈdrɛnɪə/ E19 Latin (*quadriennium*, from *quadri-* combining form of *quottuor* four + *annus* year). A period of four years.

quadrille /kwəˈdrɪl/ *noun 1* M18 French (from Spanish *cuadrilla*, Italian *quadriglia* troop, company, from *cuadro*, *quadro* square). A square dance usually performed by four couples and containing five figures, each of which is a complete dance in itself; a piece of music for such a dance.

quadrille /kwəˈdrɪl/ *noun 2* (also **quadrillé** /kwɒˈdrɪleɪ/) L19 French (*quadrillé*, from *quadrille* small square from Spanish *cuadrillo* square block). A ruled grid of small squares, especially on paper.

quadrivium /kwɒˈdrɪʌɪəm/ *noun* E19 Latin (= place where four roads meet, from *quadri-* combining form of *quottuor* four + *via* way, road). A medieval university course involving the 'mathematical arts' of arithmetic, geometry, astronomy, and music. Cf. TRIVIUM.

quae vide plural of QUOD VIDE.

quai /keɪ/, *foreign* /ke/ (*plural same*) *noun* L19 French. **1** A public street or path along the embankment of a stretch of navigable water, usually having buildings on the land side; *specifically* such a street on either bank of the Seine in Paris. **2** The French Foreign Office. In full *Quai d'Orsay* /ˈdɔːseɪ/, *foreign* /dɔrsɛ/ (the quai on the south bank of the Seine where the French Foreign Office is situated).

quaich /kweɪk/, /kweɪx/ *noun* (also **quaigh**) M16 Gaelic (*cuach* cup, perhaps from *cua* hollow; cf. Latin *caucus* (Greek *kauka*), Welsh *caurg* bowl). (In Scotland) a shallow drinking cup, usually made of wooden staves hooped together and having two handles, but sometimes made of silver or fitted with a silver rim.

quantum meruit /ˌkwɒntəm ˈmɛrʊɪt/ *noun phrase* M17 Latin (= as much as he has deserved). *Law* A reasonable sum of money to be paid for services rendered or work done, when the amount due is not stipulated in a legally enforceable contract.

quartier /kartje/ *noun* plural pronounced same E19 French (from Latin *quartarius* fourth part of a measure, from *quartus* fourth). A district or area, originally of a French city; *elliptical* for *Quartier Latin* the Latin Quarter of Paris on the left bank of the Seine, where students and artists live.
> **1995** *Spectator* Twenty years ago, Covent Garden was a deserted no-man's-land at weekends. On Saturday night, a quarter of a

million people must have been carousing
through this now gilded *quartier*.

quasi- /ˈkweɪzʌɪ/, /ˈkweɪsʌɪ/ *combining
form* M17 Latin (from *quasi* as if, almost).
1 Apparently but not really; seemingly:
quasi-scientific. **2** Being partly or almost:
quasi-crystalline.

quatorze /kəˈtɔːz/ *noun* E18 French (= fourteen, from Latin *quattuordecim*). **1** (In
piquet) a set of four aces, kings, queens,
or jacks held by one player, scoring
fourteen. **2** In full *Quatorze Juillet* /ˈʒwiː-
jeɪ/. (In France) Bastille Day, 14 July.

quattrocento /ˌkwatrə(ʊ)ˈtʃɛntəʊ/
noun L19 Italian (= four hundred). The
15th century as a period of Italian art
or architecture.

■ Shortened from *milquattrocento* '1400',
used with reference to the years
1400–99.

quel /kɛl/ *adjective* plural **quels** (feminine **quelle**, plural **quelles**) L19 French.
What (a) (with following noun).

■ Only in French phrases and in English
phrases imitating them.
1996 *Spectator* 'Arnie! *Quelle surprise!* What
are you doing here?'

quenelle /kəˈnɛl/ *noun* M19 French (of
unknown origin). A seasoned ball or
roll of meat or fish ground to a paste.

querencia /keˈrenθjaˌ/, /keˈrensia/ *noun*
M20 Spanish (= lair, haunt, home ground,
from *querer* to desire, love). **1** (In
bullfighting) the part of a bullring where
the bull takes its stand. **2** *figurative* A
person's home ground, a refuge.
2 1952 R. Campbell *Lorca* Andalusia is
Lorca's *querencia*.

quesadilla /kesaˈdi(l)ja/, /ˌkeɪsəˈdiːljə/
noun plural **quesadillas** /kesaˈdi(l)jas/,
/ˌkeɪsəˈdiːljəz/ M20 Spanish. A tortilla
filled with cheese (or occasionally
other filling) and heated.

que sera sera /ˈkeɪ sərɑː sərɑː/ *interjection* L16 Spanish (*qué será será* what will
be, will be). Used to convey a fatalistic
recognition that future events are out
of the speaker's control.

■ Popularized by the 1956 song 'Que
Sera, Sera'.

questionnaire /ˌkwɛstʃəˈnɛː/, /ˌkɛstjəˈnɛː/
noun L19 French (from *questionner* to ques-

tion). A set of printed or written questions
with a choice of answers, devised for the
purposes of a survey or statistical study.

quiche /kiːʃ/ *noun* M20 French (from
Alsatian dialect *Küchen* (German *Kuchen*
cake)). A baked flan or tart with a
savoury filling thickened with eggs,
usually eaten cold.

quid pro quo /ˌkwɪd prəʊ ˈkwəʊ/ *noun
phrase* M16 Latin (= something for something). A favour or advantage granted
in return for something.

■ The term was first used in English
to denote a medicine substituted for
another.
1996 *Spectator* Mr Major's error was to let
the Chancellor pocket a concession without
extracting a quid pro quo.

quieta non movere /kwiːˌeɪtə nəʊn
məʊˈvɛːriː/ *verb phrase* L18 Latin (literally,
'not to move settled things'). Let sleeping dogs lie.
1960 *Encounter Quieta non movere* is the
motto of many once aggressive...radicals.

quietus /kwʌɪˈiːtəs/ *noun* LME Latin (abbreviation of medieval Latin *quietus est*,
literally, 'he is quit'). **1** Death regarded
as a release from life; something
which causes death. *Literary*. **2** Something that has a calming or soothing
effect.

■ *Quietus est* was originally used as a form
of receipt or discharge of payment of a
debt.

quinella /kwɪˈnɛlə/ *noun* (also (earlier)
quiniela /kwɪnɪˈɛlə/) E20 American Spanish (*quiniela*). A bet in which the first
two places in a race must be predicted,
but not necessarily in the correct
order. Originally *United States*. Cf.
PERFECTA.

quinquennium /kwɪŋˈkwɛnɪəm/ *noun*
plural **quinquenniums**, **quinquennia**
/kwɪŋˈkwɛnɪə/ E17 Latin (from *quinque*
five + *annus* year). **1** A fifth anniversary.
2 A period of five years.

quinta /ˈkintа/, /ˈkwɪntə/ *noun* M18 Spanish and Portuguese (from *quinta parte* fifth
part, originally the amount of a farm's
produce paid as rent). (In Spain, Portugal, and Latin America) a large house
or villa in the country or on the
outskirts of a town; a country estate,

in particular a wine-growing estate in Portugal.

quipu /ˈkiːpuː/, /ˈkwɪpuː/ *noun* (also **quipo**) E18 Quechua (*khípu* knot). An ancient Inca device for recording information, events, etc., consisting of variously coloured cords arranged and knotted in different ways.

qui vive /kiː ˈviːv/, *foreign* /ki viv/ *noun phrase* L16 French (literally, '(long) live who?'). An alert or watchful state or condition. Chiefly in *on the qui vive*, on the alert or lookout.

■ Originating in a sentry's challenge to a person approaching his post in order to ascertain to whom that person is loyal.
1996 *Spectator* Ever on the *qui vive* for the bore of the party, when sheep replace cows in the fields nearby he comments approvingly: 'Sheep have a more active, at least more interesting, social life than cows.'

quod erat demonstrandum /kwɒd əˌrat dɛmənˈstrandəm/ *interjection* M17 Latin (translating Greek *hoti edei deixai*). Which was to be demonstrated.

■ Generally abbreviated to QED and used to emphasize the clinching point in an argument or to mark the conclusion of a mathematical proof. Like the less widely used QUOD ERAT FACIENDUM, the phrase and its use are derived from the Greek mathematician Euclid (early 3rd century BC).

quod erat faciendum /kwɒd əˌrat faʃɪˈɛndəm/, /kwɒd əˌrat fakɪˈɛndəm/ *interjection* L17 Latin (translating *hoti edei poiein*). Which was to be constructed.

■ Abbreviated to QEF and appended to a geometrical proof.

quodlibet /ˈkwɒdlɪbɛt/ *noun* LME Medieval Latin (*quodlibet(um)* from Latin *quodlibet*, from *quod* what + *libet* it pleases). **1** A topic for or exercise in philosophical or theological discussion. *Archaic*. **2** *Music* A light-hearted combination of several tunes; a medley.

quod vide /kwɒd ˈviːdeɪ/ *noun phrase* plural **quae vide** /kwaɪ ˈviːdeɪ/ M18 Latin

(*quod* which + imperative singular of *videre* to see). Which see.

■ Abbreviated to *q.v.* (plural *qq.v.*) and used to direct a reader to further information under the reference cited.

quondam /ˈkwɒndəm/, /ˈkwɒndam/ *adverb, noun, & adjective* M16 Latin (= formerly). That once was or existed; former.

quorum /ˈkwɔːrəm/ *noun* LME Latin (literally, 'of whom (we wish that you be one, two, etc.)' (see note below)). The minimum number of members of an assembly or society that must be present at any of its meetings to make the proceedings of that meeting valid.

■ The word comes from the text of commissions for committee members designated by the Latin words *quorum vos... unum (duos, etc.) esse volumus* 'of whom we wish that you... be one (two, etc.)'.

quot homines, tot sententiae /kwɒt ˌhɒmɪneɪz tɒt sɛnˈtɛntɪʌɪ/ *interjection* M16 Latin. There are as many opinions as there are people.

■ Latin proverbial saying from the comedy *Phormio* (line 454) by the Roman playwright Plautus (died 184 BC).
1996 *Oldie* As then, so now: *quot homines, tot sententiae*, there are as many opinions as there are people.

quo vadis /kwəʊ ˈvaːdɪs/ *interjection* L16 Latin. Where are you going?

■ According to a legend first found in the apocryphal Acts of St Peter, the apostle Peter, fleeing the persecutions in Rome, met Christ on the Appian Way and asked him *Domine, quo vadis?* ('Lord, where are you going?'). Receiving the reply that Christ was going to be crucified again, Peter understood that this would be in his place; he accordingly turned back, and was martyred. The story features in Henryk Sienkiewicz's historical novel *Quo Vadis* (1896).

q.v. abbreviation of QUOD VIDE.

rabbi /ˈrabʌɪ/ *noun* OE ecclesiastical Latin and Greek (from Hebrew *rabbī* my master, from *raḇ* master). **1** A Jewish scholar or teacher, especially one who studies or teaches Jewish law. **2** A person appointed as a Jewish religious leader.

raclette /raˈklɛt/, *foreign* /raklɛt/ (*plural same*) *noun* M20 French (= small scraper (referring to the practice of holding the cheese over the heat and scraping it on to a plate as it melts)). A Swiss dish of melted cheese, typically eaten with potatoes.

raconteur /ˌrakɒnˈtəː/ *noun* E19 French (from *raconter* to relate). A person who tells anecdotes in a skilful and amusing way.

raconteuse /ˌrakɒnˈtəːz/ *noun* M19 French (feminine of RACONTEUR). A female teller of anecdotes.

> **1995** *Spectator* Freely is not an incisive polemicist, but she's an excellent raconteuse, and one who has knocked around enough to have a good fund of stories.

radicchio /raˈdiːkɪəʊ/ *noun* plural **radicchios** L20 Italian (= chicory). A variety of chicory from Italy, with reddish-purple white-veined leaves.

radix /ˈradɪks/, /ˈreɪdɪks/ *noun* plural **radices** /ˈradɪsiːz/, **radixes** E17 Latin (*radix, radic-* root of a plant). **1** *Mathematics* The base of a system of numeration. **2** A source or origin of something.

> ■ Sometimes in the phrase *radix malorum* 'the root of evil', with allusion to 1 Timothy 6:10 (Vulgate version). In the Bible it is 'love of money' (*cupiditas*) which is 'the root of all evil', while in popular use it is frequently just 'money'.

raffia /ˈrafɪə/ *noun* E18 Malagasy. **1** A palm tree native to tropical Africa and Madagascar. **2** The soft fibre from the leaves of such a palm, used for making items such as hats and baskets.

raga /ˈrɑːgə/ *noun* (also **rag** /rɑːg/) L18 Sanskrit (*rāga* colour, passion, melody). (In Indian classical music) a pattern of notes used as a basis for melodies and improvisations; a piece of music based on a particular raga.

Rr

Ragnarok /ˈragnarɒk/ *noun* (also **Ragnarök**) L18 Old Norse (*ragnarǫk, ragna-røkkr* (Icelandic *Ragnarök*), from *ragna* genitive of *regin* the gods + *rǫk* destined end or (later) *røkr, røkkr* twilight). *Scandinavian Mythology* The destruction or twilight of the gods; *specifically* the defeat of gods and men by monsters in a final battle. Cf. GÖTTERDÄMMERUNG.

ragout /raˈguː/ *noun* M17 French (*ragoût*, from *ragoûter* to revive the taste of). A highly seasoned dish of meat cut into small pieces and stewed with vegetables.

raison d'état /rɛzɔ̃ deta/ *noun phrase* plural **raisons d'état** (pronounced same) M19 French (= reason of state). A purely political reason for action on the part of a ruler or government, especially where a departure from openness, justice, or honesty is involved.

> **1996** *Spectator* This must be conducted on the basis of *raison d'état*, which includes secrecy.

raison d'être /rɛzɔ̃ dɛtr/, /ˈreɪzɔ̃ ˌdɛtrə/ *noun* plural **raisons d'être** (pronounced same) M19 French (= reason for being). The most important reason or purpose for someone or something's existence.

> **1996** *Spectator* . . . it had the bad luck to be the first big British company to become caught up in a lurching shift in society's perceptions of the rights, responsibilities and *raison d'être* of business.

raisons d'état, raisons d'être plurals of RAISON D'ÉTAT, RAISON D'ÊTRE.

raita /rɑːˈiːtə/ *noun* M20 Hindi (*rāytā*). An Indian side dish of yogurt, containing chopped cucumber or other vegetables, and spices.

raj /rɑː(d)ʒ/ *noun* E19 Hindi (*rāj* from Sanskrit *rājya*; cf. RAJA). **1** Sovereignty, rule; kingdom. *Indian*. **2** *History* (*the Raj*) The period of British rule in the Indian subcontinent before 1947. In full *British Raj*.

raja /ˈrɑːdʒə/ *noun* (also **rajah,** (as a title) **Raja**) M16 Sanskrit (*rājan* king, from *rāj* to reign or rule; probably through Portuguese and related to Latin *rex, regis,* Old Irish *rí, ríg* king). *History* Originally, an Indian king or prince. Later also, a title extended to minor dignitaries and nobles in India during the British Raj; a title extended by the British to a Malay or Javanese ruler or chief.

raja yoga /ˌrɑːdʒə ˈjəʊɡə/ *noun phrase* L19 Sanskrit (from *rājan* king + YOGA). A form of yoga aimed at gaining control over the mind and emotions.

raki /rəˈkiː/, /ˈraki/ *noun* L17 Turkish (*rāqī* (now *rakı* whence also modern Greek *rhakē, rhaki*) brandy, spirits). A strong alcoholic spirit made in eastern Europe or the Middle East.

raku /ˈrɑːkuː/ *noun* L19 Japanese (literally 'ease, relaxed state, enjoyment'). A kind of usually lead-glazed Japanese pottery, used especially for the tea ceremony.

rallentando /ˌralənˈtandəʊ/ *adverb, adjective, & noun* E19 Italian (present participle of *rallentare* to slow down). *Music* **A** *adverb & adjective* (Especially as a direction) with gradual decrease of speed. **B** *noun* plural **rallentandos, rallentandi** /ˌralənˈtandi/. A gradual decrease of speed; a passage marked to be played with a gradual decrease of speed.

ramada /rəˈmɑːdə/ *noun* M19 Spanish. An arbour, a porch. *United States*.

rambutan /ramˈbuːt(ə)n/ *noun* (also **rambootan**) E18 Malay (from *rambut* hair, in reference to the covering of the fruit). A Malaysian tree, *Nephelium lappaceum* (family Sapindaceae); the fruit of this tree, resembling a lychee and covered with soft bright red spines or prickles.

ramen /ˈrɑːmɛn/ *noun* (treated as *singular* or *plural*) L20 Japanese (from Chinese *lā* to pull + *miàn* noodles). (In oriental cuisine) quick-cooking noodles, usually served in a broth with meat and vegetables.

rancheria /ˌrɑːn(t)ʃəˈriːə/ *noun* E17 Spanish (*ranchería,* from as RANCHO). (In Spanish America and the western United States) a small Indian settlement.

ranchero /rɑːnˈtʃɛːrəʊ/ *noun* plural **rancheros** E19 Spanish (from as RANCHO). A person who farms or works on a ranch, especially in the south-western United States and Mexico.

rancho /ˈrɑːn(t)ʃəʊ/ *noun* plural **ranchos** E19 Spanish (= a group of people who eat together). **1** (In Latin America) a hut, a hovel, a very simple building; a group of these, a small village; *especially* one put up to accommodate travellers. Later also, a roadhouse, an inn; a meal at such a place. **2** (In the western United States) a cattle farm, a ranch.

rand /rand/, /rant/ *noun* plural **rands,** (in sense 2 also) same M19 Afrikaans (from Dutch *rand* edge). **1** (In South Africa) a rocky ridge or area of high sloping ground, especially overlooking a river valley; *specifically* (*the Rand*), the Witwatersrand, the chief gold-mining area of the Transvaal. **2** The basic monetary unit of South Africa since 1961.

ranee variant of RANI.

rangé /rɑ̃ʒe/ *adjective* (feminine **rangée**) L19 French (past participial adjective of *ranger* to range). (Of a person or their lifestyle) orderly, regular, settled.

▪ Earlier (L18) in dictionaries in a heraldic sense describing charges 'placed in a row' or 'set within a band', but this sense seems never to have gained wider circulation.

rangoli /raŋˈɡəʊli/ *noun* M20 Marathi (*rãgoḷī*). Traditional Indian decoration and patterns made with ground rice, particularly during festivals.

rani /ˈrɑːniː/ *noun* (also **ranee,** (as a title) **Rani**) L17 Hindi (*rānī* from Prakrit from Sanskrit *rājñī* feminine of *rājan* RAJA). *History* A Hindu queen; a raja's wife or widow.

rapide /rapid/, /ra'piːd/ *noun* plural pronounced same E20 French. (In France) an express train.

rapido /'rapɪdəʊ/, *foreign* /'rapido/ *adverb, adjective, & noun* L19 Italian. **A** *adverb and adjective* L19 *Music* (Especially as a direction) in rapid time. **B** *noun* plural **rapidi** /'rapɪdi/, **rapidos** /'rapɪdəʊz/. (In Italy) an express train.

rappel /ra'pɛl/ *noun* M20 French (from *rappeler* to recall). *Mountaineering.* An abseil.

rapport /ra'pɔː/ *noun* M17 French (from *rapporter* to bring back). A close and harmonious relationship in which the people or groups concerned understand each other's feelings or ideas and communicate well.

■ Originally (M16) introduced in the sense of 'report' or 'talk', but this was never widely current and has been totally ousted by the current sense. Cf. EN RAPPORT.

1996 *Times* The 'jungle fighter' boss, who rules by fear and manipulation, gets less out of the workforce than the manager who sets out to establish a close rapport with the employees.

rapporteur /ˌrapɔː'tə:/ *noun* L18 French (from *rapporter* to bring back). A person who is appointed by an organization to make a report of the proceedings of its meetings.

■ Introduced earlier (but used only L15) from Old French in the general sense of 'a reporter, a recounter', *rapporteur* is now used in English only in the very specific sense above.

rapprochement /rapɔ'ʃmā/, /ra'prɒʃmā/ *noun* E19 French (from *rapprocher* to bring closer together, from *re-* + *approcher* to approach). (Especially in international affairs) an establishment or resumption of harmonious relations.

1996 *Country Life* . . . the shooting down of two light planes by the Cuban airforce has reversed the rapprochement with the United States . . .

rara avis /ˌrɛːrə 'eɪvɪs/, /ˌrɑːrə 'avɪs/ *noun phrase* plural **rarae aves** /ˌrɛːriː 'eɪviːz/, /ˌrɑːriː/, /ˌrɑːreɪ 'aviːz/ E17 Latin (= rare bird). **1** A kind of person rarely encountered; an unusual or exceptional person. **2** A rarity; an unusual or exceptional occurrence or thing.

■ The expression comes from the Roman satirist Juvenal: *Rara avis in terries nigroque simillima cynco* ('a rare bird on this earth, like nothing so much as a black swan).'

rasa /'rʌsə/ *noun* (also **ras** /rʌs/) L18 Sanskrit (literally, 'juice, essence, flavour'). The agreeable quality of something, especially the emotional or aesthetic impression of a work of art.

ratafia /ratə'fɪə/ *noun* L17 French. **1** A liqueur flavoured with almonds or the kernels of peaches, apricots, or cherries. **2** An almond-flavoured biscuit resembling a small macaroon.

rataplan /ratə'plan/ *noun* M19 French (of imitative origin). A drumming or beating noise; a tattoo.

ratatouille /ratə'tuːi/, /ratə'twiː/ *noun* L19 French ((dialect) cf. French *touiller* to stir up). A vegetable dish of aubergines, courgettes, tomatoes, onions, and peppers fried and stewed in oil.

ravelin /'ravlɪn/ *noun* L16 French (from Italian *ravellina* (now *rivellino*), of unknown origin). *History* An outwork of fortifications, consisting of two faces forming a salient angle, constructed beyond the main ditch and in front of the curtain.

ravigote /ravigɔt/ *noun* M19 French (from *ravigoter* to invigorate). A mixture of chopped chervil, chives, tarragon, and shallots, used in cookery to give piquancy to a sauce or as a base for a herb butter.

ravioli /ravɪ'əʊli/ *noun* M19 Italian (plural of *raviolo*). Pasta in the form of small square cases filled with minced meat, vegetables, etc., usually served with a sauce.

ravissant /ravisã/ *adjective* (also (feminine) **ravissante** /ravisãt/) M17 French (present participial adjective of *ravir* (formerly) to seize, carry off, (now) to enchant). Ravishing, delightful.

■ Originally (ME–M16) used in English of an animal and reflecting the older French sense of *ravir*, hence 'ravening'; it also had a specific heraldic sense (E18) meaning 'in the half-raised posture of a wolf beginning to spring on its prey'.

razzia /ˈraːzɪə/ *noun* M19 French (from Algerian Arabic *ğāziya* raid, from Arabic *ğazā* to go forth to fight, make a raid). *History* A hostile raid for purposes of conquest, plunder, and capture of slaves, especially one carried out by Moors in North Africa.

re /reɪ/, /riː/ *preposition* E18 Latin (ablative of *res* thing). In the matter of, concerning, about.

realia /reɪˈɑːlɪə/, /rɪˈeɪlɪə/ *noun plural* M20 Late Latin (use as noun of neuter plural of *realis* real). **1** Objects and material from everyday life used as teaching aids. **2** Real things, actual facts, especially as distinct from theories about them.

realpolitik /reˌɑːlpɒliˈtiːk/, /reɪˈɑːl pɒliːtiːk/ *noun* E20 German (*real* real + *Politik* politics). Politics based on practical, rather than moral or ideological, considerations; practical politics.
    1995 *Spectator* The Defence Secretary, Michael Portillo, was at last moved by the spectacle of the Balkan tragedy to go beyond considerations of *realpolitik* to true moral indignation.

realpolitiker /reˌɑːlpɒˈliːtikə/, /reɪˈɑːl pɒˌliːtikə/ *noun* M20 German. A person who believes in, advocates, or practises REALPOLITIK.
    1995 *Spectator* Machiavelli . . . is not a mere *realpolitiker* writing a handbook counselling princes how to achieve and maintain themselves in power.

rebab /rɪˈbab/ *noun* M18 Arabic (*rabāb*). A bowed or plucked stringed instrument of Arab origin, used especially in North Africa, the Middle East, and the Indian subcontinent.

rebbe /ˈrɛbə/ *noun* L19 Yiddish (from Hebrew *rabbī* rabbi). A rabbi, especially a religious leader of the Hasidic sect.

rebbetzin /ˈrɛbɪtsɪn/ *noun* (also **rebbit-zin**) L19 Yiddish (feminine of REBBE). The wife of a rabbi; a female Jewish religious leader.

rebec /ˈriːbɛk/ *noun* (also **rebeck**) LME French (alteration of Old French *rebebe*, *rubebe*). Chiefly *History* A medieval musical instrument with usually three strings and played with a bow.

reblochon /rəblɔˈʃɔ̃/ *noun* E20 French. A soft French cheese made originally and chiefly in Savoy.

rebozo /rɪˈbəʊzəʊ/, /rɪˈbəʊsəʊ/ *noun* plural **rebozos** E19 Spanish. A long scarf covering the head and shoulders, traditionally worn by Spanish-American women.

rebus /ˈriːbəs/ *noun* E17 French (*rébus* from Latin *rebus* ablative plural of *res* thing). **1** A puzzle in which words are represented by combinations of pictures and individual letters. **2** *History* An ornamental device associated with a person to whose name it punningly alludes.

■ This usage originated in *De rebus quae geruntur* (literally, 'concerning the things that are taking place'), the title given in 16th-century Picardy to satirical pieces containing riddles in picture form.

réchauffé /reˈʃofe/, /reɪˈʃəʊfeɪ/ *noun &* *adjective* E19 French (past participle of *réchauffer* to reheat, from *re-* again + *échauffer* to warm (up), from Proto-Romance variation of Latin *cal(e)facere* to make warm, from *calere* to be warm + *facere* to make). **A** *noun* A dish of warmed-up food left over from a previous meal; *figurative* a rehash. **B** *adjective* (Of food) reheated; *figurative* rehashed.

recherché /rəˈʃɛːʃeɪ/ *adjective* L17 French literally, 'carefully sought out'. Rare, exotic, or obscure.
    1995 *Observer Review* Now there's nothing wrong with using *recherché* words—Nabokov did it all the time—and the inquisitive need only consult a dictionary.

recherche du temps perdu /rəʃɛrʃ dy tɑ̃ pɛrdy/ *noun phrase* M20 French (*à la recherche du temps perdu*, literally, 'in search of the lost time', title of novel by Marcel Proust (1871–1922)). A narration or evocation of one's early life.
    1996 *Spectator* Marcel Proust was never one of the great rugby players, but the entire impetus of the French rugby union team springs from *la recherche du temps perdu*.

recitativo /ˌretʃitaˈtiːvo/, /ˌrɛsɪtəˈtiːvəʊ/ *noun* plural **recitativi** /ˌretʃitaˈtiːvi/, **recitativos** /ˌrɛsɪtəˈtiːvəʊz/ M17 Italian (from Latin *recitat-* past participial stem of *recitare* to recite). *Music* A style of musical declamation of the kind usual in the narrative and dialogue parts of opera and oratorio, sung in the rhythm of ordinary speech with many words on the same note; recitative.

■ *Recitativo* may be accompanied either by the full orchestra (*recitativo accompagnato* or *recitativo stromentato* (literally, 'instrumented')) or by continuo instruments only (*recitativo secco*).

réclame /reklam/ *noun* plural pronounced same L19 French (from *réclamer* to ask for). Self-publicity, self-advertisement; public acclaim or notoriety.

1996 *Spectator* It is difficult for people today to realise the extraordinary *réclame* that T. E. Lawrence . . . had in those years between the wars.

recte /ˈrɛkteɪ/ *adverb* M19 Latin (literally, 'in a straight line, rightly'). Correctly.

■ Used when introducing a word or phrase as a correct version of that just given, as in 'Jane Blundell *recte* Blunden'.

recti plural of RECTUS.

rectius /ˈrɛktɪəs/ *adverb* M20 Latin (comparative of RECTE). More correctly (introducing a word or phrase as a more correct version of that just given).

recto /ˈrɛktəʊ/ *noun* plural **rectos** E19 Latin ((sc. *folio*) ablative of *rectus* right). The right-hand page of an open book; the front of a loose document, as opposed to the back or VERSO.

rectus /ˈrɛktəs/ *noun* plural **recti** /ˈrɛktʌɪ/ E18 Latin (= straight). *Anatomy* Any of several straight muscles, especially of the abdomen, thigh, neck, and eye. Frequently with modern Latin specifying word. Also *rectus muscle*.

reculer pour mieux sauter /rəkyle pur mjø sote/ *noun phrase* E19 French (literally, 'to draw back in order to leap better'). The use of a withdrawal or setback as a basis for further advance or success.

1996 *Country Life* Hostility towards mobiles runs high in the world of commuters for the train has traditionally provided a brief capsule of immunity from the real world, an opportunity to *reculer pour mieux sauter.*

redingote /ˈrɛdɪŋɡəʊt/ *noun* L18 French (from English *riding coat*). A woman's long coat with a cutaway front or a contrasting piece on the front.

redivivus /rɛdɪˈviːvəs/ *postpositive adjective* (feminine **rediviva** /rɛdɪˈviːvə/) L16 Latin (from *re-* again + *vivus* living, alive). Come back to life; reborn, renewed.

■ Always postpositive. Cf. REDUX.

1975 *Times* Some still believe in Stormont Redivivus.

reductio ad absurdum /rɪˌdʌktɪəʊ ad əbˈsəːdəm/ *noun phrase* M18 Latin (literally, 'reduction to the absurd'). *Logic* A method of proving the falsity of a premise by showing that its logical consequence is absurd or contradictory.

1995 *Times* Making criminal the carrying of all knives in public places could—and this is the *reductio ad absurdum*—lead to the prosecution of people going on a picnic.

reductio ad impossibile /rɪˌdʌktɪəʊ ad ɪmpɒˈsɪbɪliː/ *noun phrase* M16 Latin (literally, 'reduction to the impossible'). A method of proving a proposition by drawing an absurd or impossible conclusion from its contradictory.

redux /ˈriːdʌks/ *adjective* L19 Latin (from *reducere* to bring back). Brought back, revived, restored.

■ Usually postpositive and often in titles, from John Dryden's poem on the restoration of King Charles II *Astraea Redux* (1662) to John Updike's novel *Rabbit Redux* (1971) and Francis Ford Coppola's film *Apocalypse Now Redux* (a reissue in 2001 of his 1979 Vietnam film *Apocalypse Now*); cf. REDIVIVUS.

reflet /rəflɛ/ *noun* plural pronounced same M19 French (= reflection). Lustre or iridescence, especially on ceramics.

refugium /rɪˈfjuːdʒɪəm/ *noun* plural **refugia** /rɪˈfjuːdʒɪə/ M20 Latin (= place of refuge). *Biology* An area in which a population of organisms can survive through a period of unfavourable conditions, especially glaciation.

1996 *New Scientist* . . . during the last ice ages . . . less rain fell over Amazonia. As a result, the rainforest shrunk into isolated pockets, or refugia, in the wettest parts of the region.

regalia /rɪˈɡeɪlɪə/ *noun plural and collective singular* M16 Medieval Latin (= royal residence, royal rights, use as noun of neuter plural of *regalis* regal). **1** The emblems or insignia of royalty, especially the crown, sceptre, and other ornaments used at a coronation. **2** The distinctive clothing worn and ornaments carried at formal occasions as an indication of status.

■ Originally used in the sense 'royal powers'.

1 1996 *Times Magazine* Just as no one who lives in London has ever been…to see the crown jewels, so I had never been to Edinburgh Castle to see the Scottish regalia.

regardant /rɪˈɡɑːd(ə)nt/ *adjective* LME Old and Modern French ((also Anglo-Norman) present participle of *regarder* to look at). *Heraldry* (Usually of a lion) looking backwards over the shoulder. Usually *postpositive*.

regatta /rɪˈɡatə/ *noun* E17 Italian (Venetian dialect *regatta, rigatta, regata* a fight, a struggle, a contest). A sporting event consisting of a series of boat or yacht races.

regime /reɪˈʒiːm/ *noun* (also **régime**) L15 French (*régime* from Latin *regimen*). **1** A government, especially an authoritarian one. **2** A system or ordered way of doing things. **3** A coordinated programme for the promotion or restoration of health; a regimen. **4** The conditions under which a scientific or industrial process occurs.

regimen /ˈrɛdʒɪmən/ *noun* LME Latin (from *regere* to rule). **1** A prescribed course of medical treatment, diet, or exercise for the promotion or restoration of one's health. **2** A system of government. *Archaic*.

■ First used to denote the action of governing.

Regina /rɪˈdʒʌɪnə/ *noun* E18 Latin (= queen). The reigning queen (used following a name or in the titles of lawsuits, e.g. *Regina v. Jones*, the Crown versus Jones).

régisseur /reʒisœr/ *noun* plural pronounced same E19 French. A person who stages a theatrical production, especially a ballet.

Regius /ˈriːdʒɪəs/ *adjective* E17 Latin (= royal, from *rex, reg-* king). Designating (a professor holding) a university chair founded by a monarch or filled by Crown appointment.

Reich /rʌɪk/, /rʌɪx/ *noun* plural **Reiche** /ˈrʌɪkə/ E20 German (= kingdom, empire, state). Chiefly *History* The former German state or commonwealth, *especially* the Third Reich (the Nazi regime 1933–45).

reiki /ˈreɪki/ *noun* L20 Japanese (= universal life energy). A healing technique based on the principle that the therapist can channel energy into the patient by means of touch, to activate the natural healing processes of the patient's body and restore physical and emotional well-being.

reine /rɛn/ *noun* M19 French (= queen). *Cookery* Chiefly in *à la reine* (literally, 'in the fashion of a queen'), designating a dish prepared in some special way.

relevé /rələˈveɪ/ *noun* E19 French (= raised up). **1** *Ballet* A movement in which the dancer rises on the tips of the toes. **2** *Ecology* Each of a number of small plots of vegetation, analysed as a sample of a wider area.

relievo /rɪˈliːvəʊ/ *noun* plural **relievos** (also **rilievo** /rɪˈljeɪvəʊ/) E17 Italian (*rilievo* from *rilevare* to raise, ultimately from Latin *relevare* to raise again). **1** A method of moulding, carving, or stamping in which the design stands out from the plane surface; relief. Cf. ALTO-RELIEVO, BASSO-RELIEVO, MEZZO-RELIEVO. **2** The appearance of solidity given to a composition on a plane surface; *figurative* vividness or distinctness due to artistic presentation.

reliquiae /rɪˈlɪkwɪiː/ *noun plural* M17 Latin (use as noun of feminine plural of *reliquus* remaining, from as *re + liq-* stem of *linquere* to leave). Remains; *specifically* (a) *Geology* fossilized remains of animals or plants; (b) literary remains, unpublished or uncollected writings.

relleno abbreviation of CHILE RELLENO.

remora /ˈrɛmərə/ *noun* M16 Latin (= delay, hindrance, from *re-* + *mora* delay). A slender marine fish of the family Echeneidae, which attaches itself to a large fish by means of a sucker on top of the head, and which was formerly believed to hinder the progress of any sailing ship to which it attached itself.

rémoulade /ˈrɛmʊlɑːd/, *foreign* /remu lad/ (*plural same*) *noun* (also **remoulade**) M19 French (from Italian *remolata*, of unknown origin). A salad or seafood dressing made with hard-boiled egg yolks, oil, vinegar, herbs, etc.

remuage /rəmɥaʒ/, /ˌrɛmjʊˈɑːʒ/ *noun* E20 French (literally, 'moving about'). The periodic turning or shaking of bottled wine, especially champagne, to move sediment towards the cork.

remuda /rəˈmuːdə/ *noun* L19 American Spanish (from Spanish = exchange, replacement). A herd of horses that have been saddle-broken, from which ranch hands choose their mounts for the day. *North American*.

Renaissance /rɪˈneɪs(ə)ns/, *foreign* /rənɛsɑ̃s/ *noun* (also (especially in sense 2) **renaissance**) M19 French ((in specific use short for *renaissance des arts*, *renaissance des lettres*), from *re-* back, again + *naissance* birth from Latin *nascentia*, from *nasci* be born, or from French *naiss-* present stem of *naître* from Proto-Romance). **1** The revival of European art and literature under the influence of classical models between the 14th and 16th centuries, begun in Italy; the culture and style of art and architecture developed during this era. **2** A revival of or renewed interest in something.

rendezvous /ˈrɒndɪvuː/, /ˈrɒndeɪvuː/ *noun & verb* (also **rendez-vous**) *plural same* /ˈrɒndɪvuːz/ L16 French (use as noun of imperative *rendez-vous* 'present yourselves', from *rendre* from Proto-Romance alteration of Latin *reddere* to give back). **A** *noun* **1** A meeting at an agreed time and place. **2** A meeting place. **3** A bar, restaurant, or similar establishment that is used as a popular meeting place. **B** *intransitive verb* Meet at an agreed time and place.

rendzina /rɛndˈziːnə/ *noun* E20 Russian (from Polish *rędzina*). *Soil Science* A fertile lime-rich soil with dark humus above a pale soft calcareous layer, typical of grassland on chalk or limestone.

renga /ˈrɛŋɡə/ *noun* plural same, **rengas** L19 Japanese (from *ren* linking + *ga* from *ka* poetry). A Japanese poem in the form of a tanka (or series of tanka), with the first three lines composed by one person and the second two by another.

rente /rɑ̃t/ *noun* plural pronounced same L19 French. Stock, *especially* French government stock; the interest or income accruing from such stock.

rentier /rɑ̃tje/, /ˈrɒntɪeɪ/ *noun* plural pronounced same M19 French (from RENTE). A person living on income from property or investment.

> **1995** G. Tindall *Celestine* [The] composition seems redolent of the self-conscious world just being born: that of the *rentier* and the white-collar workers,...of trains and newspapers and morning coffee...

renvers /rɑ̃vɛrs/, /ˈrɛnvəs/ *noun* plural same L19 French (from *renverser*, from *re-* + *enverser* to overturn). A movement performed in dressage, in which the horse moves parallel to the side of the arena, with its head and neck facing forward and its hindquarters curved towards the wall.

repêchage /ˈrɛpəʃɑːʒ/ *noun* E20 French (from *repêcher*, literally, 'to fish out, rescue'). (In rowing and other sports) a contest in which the runners-up in the eliminating heats compete for a place in the final.

> **1996** *Times*...an unsettlingly sportless lull between the recorded highlights of, as I recall, the men's synchronised triple frisbee and the repechage of the women's 80m coxless egg-and spoon...

répétiteur /repetitœr/ (*plural same*), /rɛ ˌpɛtrˈtəː/ *noun* M20 French (= tutor, coach). **1** A person who teaches musicians and singers, especially opera singers, their parts. **2** A person who supervises ballet rehearsals etc.

> **1 1996** *Times* Maybe Savonlinna should beef up its team of répétiteurs; the raw material is marvellous, and could be further refined.

répondez s'il vous plaît /repɔ̃dei sil vu 'plɛ/ *interjection* M19 French. Please reply (used at the end of invitations to request a response).

■ Usually abbreviated to RSVP.

repoussé /rə'puːseɪ/ *adjective & noun* M19 French (= pushed back, past participle of *repousser*, from *re-* + *pousser* to push). **A** *adjective* (Of metalwork) hammered into relief from the reverse side. **B** *noun* Ornamental metalwork fashioned by the repoussé method; the process of hammering into relief.

reprise /rɪ'prʌɪz/, /rɪ'priːz/ *noun & verb* LME Old and Modern French (literally 'taken up again', feminine past participle of *reprendre*). **A** *noun* A repeated passage in music; a repetition or further performance of something. **B** *transitive verb* Repeat (a piece of music or a performance).

requiem /'rɛkwɪəm/, /'rɛkwɪɛm/ *noun* ME Latin (accusative of *requies* rest, first word of the introit in the Mass for the dead, *Requiem aeternam dona eis, Domine* Give them eternal rest, O Lord). **1** *Roman Catholic Church* A special Mass said or sung for the repose of the soul of a dead person. Also *requiem Mass.* **b** A musical composition setting parts of a requiem Mass, or of a similar character. **2** An act or token of remembrance.

requiescat /rɛkwɪ'ɛskat/ *noun* E19 Latin (from *requiescat in pace* may he or she rest in peace). A wish or prayer for the repose of a dead person.

■ The abbreviation RIP, used in memorial notices and inscriptions on gravestones, strictly speaking stands for the Latin phrase *requiescat in pace*, though it can also be taken as an abbreviation of the corresponding English phrase 'rest in peace'.

res /reɪz/ *noun* plural same E17 Latin (= thing). A thing, a matter.

■ Originally in legal terminology and still chiefly in Latin legal phrases, e.g. *res communis* 'common property', *res integra* 'a matter that has not been covered', *res judicata* 'a matter that has been adjudicated', *res nullius* 'no one's property'. Used alone, *res* can now also have the more general senses of 'the condition of something; the matter in hand, the point at issue, the crux' (see quotation).

1966 P. G. Wodehouse *Plum Pie* I saw that I had better come to the *res* without delay.

réseau /'reɪzəʊ/, foreign /rezo/ *noun* plural **réseaux** /'reɪzəʊ/, foreign /rezo/ L16 French (= net, web) **1** A plain net ground used in lacemaking. **2** A network or grid, especially one superimposed as a reference marking on a photograph in astronomy, surveying, etc. **3** A spy or intelligence network, especially in the French resistance movement during the German occupation (1940–5).

res gestae /reɪz 'gɛstʌɪ/, /reɪz 'dʒɛstiː/ *noun phrase plural* E17 Latin (= things done). *Law* The events, circumstances, remarks, etc. which relate to a particular case, especially as constituting admissible evidence in a court of law.

residuum /rɪ'zɪdjʊəm/ *noun* plural **residua** /rɪ'zɪdjʊə/ L17 Latin (use as noun of neuter of *residuus* remaining, from *residere* to reside). **1** That which remains; a residue. **b** *Chemistry* etc. A substance left after combustion, evaporation, etc., a residue. **2** *Sociology* A class of society that is unemployed and without privileges or opportunities.

res ipsa loquitur /reɪz ɪpsə 'lɒkwɪtə/ *noun phrase* M17 Latin (= the matter speaks for itself). *Law* The principle that the mere occurrence of some types of accident is sufficient to imply negligence.

res judicata /reɪz dʒuːdɪ'kɑːtə/ *noun phrase* plural **res judicatae** /reɪz dʒuː dɪ'kɑːtʌɪ/, /dʒuːdɪ'kɑːtiː/ L17 Latin (= judged matter). *Law* A matter that has been adjudicated by a competent court and therefore may not be pursued by the same parties.

responsum /rɪ'spɒnsəm/ *noun* plural **responsa** /rɪ'spɒnsə/ L19 Latin (= reply). A written reply by a rabbi or Talmudic scholar to an inquiry on some matter of Jewish law.

ressentiment /rəsɑ̃timɑ̃/ *noun* M20 German (*Ressentiment* from French *ressentiment*, from *ressentir* to resent). A psychological state resulting from suppressed feelings of envy and hatred which cannot be satisfied.

■ The term is particularly associated with the philosophy of Friedrich Nietzsche (1844–1900).

restaurant /'rɛst(ə)rɒnt/, /'rɛst(ə)r(ə)nt/, /'rɛst(ə)rɔː/, /'rɛst(ə)rō/, /'rɛst(ə)rɑː/ *noun* E19 French (use as noun of present participle of *restaurer* to provide food for, (literally) to restore to a former state). A place where people pay to sit and eat meals that are cooked and served on the premises.

restaurateur /rɛst(ə)rə'təː/, /ˌrɛstɒrə'təː/ *noun* L18 French (from *restaurer* to restore). A person who owns and manages a restaurant.

restitutio in integrum /rɛstɪˌtjuːtɪəʊ ɪn ɪn'tɛɡrəm/ *noun phrase* E18 Latin (= restoration to the whole (i.e. uninjured) state). *Law* Restoration of an injured party to the situation which would have prevailed had no injury been sustained; restoration to the original or pre-contractual position.

résumé /'rɛzjʊmeɪ/ *noun* (also **resumé**, in sense 2 **resume**) E19 French (past participle of *résumer* to resume). **1** A summary. **2** A CURRICULUM VITAE. Chiefly North American.

> **1** 1996 *Times* His 'quest' is in reality a literary convention: what Johnson has written is an excellent résumé of a traditional Catholic's faith.
> **2** 1996 *Spectator* Only incidentals on the résumé are different—Stanton missed Vietnam because of a crocked knee.

retable /rɪ'teɪb(ə)l/ *noun* E19 French (*rétable*, *retable* from Spanish *retablo* from medieval Latin *retrotabulum*, from Latin *retro-* behind + *tabula* table). A frame enclosing painted or decorated panels or a shelf or ledge for ornaments, raised above the back of an altar.

retablo /rɪ'tɑːbləʊ/ *noun* plural **retablos** M19 Spanish (see preceding). A RETABLE. Also, a votive picture displayed in a church.

retardataire /rətardatɛr/ *adjective* E20 French. (Of a work of art or architecture) executed in an earlier or outdated style.

> 1977 *Times Literary Supplement* The *retardataire* appearance of much colonial architecture is derived from the poor, often secondhand knowledge of contemporary architectectual practice as well as from a conservatism in patrons' tastes.

retiarius /rɛtɪ'ɑːrɪəs/, /rɛtɪ'ɛːrɪəs/ *noun* plural **retiarii** /rɛtɪ'ɑːrɪʌɪ/, /rɛtɪ'ɛːriː/ M17 Latin (from *rete* net). An ancient Roman gladiator who fought using a net with which to entangle his adversary.

reticule /'rɛtɪkjuːl/ *noun* E18 French (*réticule* from Latin *reticulum* diminutive of *rete* net). **1** A woman's small handbag, typically having a drawstring and decorated with embroidery or beading. **2** A grid of fine lines or threads set in the focal plane or eyepiece of an optical instrument, a reticle.

retiré /rətire/ *noun* plural pronounced same M20 French (= drawn back, past participle of *retirer*). *Ballet* A movement in which one leg is raised at right angles to the body until the toe is in line with the knee of the supporting leg.

retroussé /rə'truːseɪ/, *foreign* /rətruse/ *adjective* E19 French (past participle of *retrousser* to turn up, from *re-* + *trousser* from Old French *trusser*, medieval Latin *trossare*, probably from late Latin *torspast participial stem of *torquere* to twist). (Of a person's nose) turned up at the tip in an attractive way.

retsina /rɛt'siːnə/ *noun* E20 Modern Greek (from *retsini* from Greek *rētinē* pine resin). A Greek white or rosé wine flavoured with resin.

revanche /rəvɑ̃ʃ/ *noun* M19 French (earlier *revenche*, from Old French *revencher* from late Latin *revindicare* to avenge, claim). Revenge; retaliation; *specifically* a nation's policy of seeking the return of lost territory.

■ The policy of *revanchisme* was particularly associated with France's determination to recover Alsace-Lorraine after losing the territory to Germany in the Franco-Prussian War of 1870, but in other contexts the word is now generally anglicized as *revanchism*.

reveille /rɪ'vali/ *noun* (also (now *rare*)
reveillé /rɪ'valeɪ/) M17 French (*réveillez*
imperative plural of *réveiller* to awaken,
from *ré-* + *veiller* from Latin *vigilare* to
keep watch). A signal sounded especially on a bugle or drum to wake
personnel in the armed forces and
indicate that it is time to rise; (the
time of) the sounding of this signal.

réveillon /revɛjɔ̃/ *noun* plural pronounced same E19 French (from *réveiller*
to awaken). (In France and French-
speaking countries) a night-time feast
or celebration, originally one after
midnight on Christmas morning.

revenant /'rɛv(ə)nənt/, *foreign* /rəvənɑ̃/
(*plural of noun same*) *noun & adjective* E19
French (present participle of *revenir* to
return). **A** *noun* A person who has
returned, especially supposedly from
the dead; a ghost. **B** *adjective* Returned,
especially supposedly from the dead.
> **A** 1996 *Spectator* Evidently a revenant, a
> returning spirit, . . . really wants only to be
> allowed to die and stay dead.

revenons à nos moutons /rəvənɔ̃ a
no 'mutɔ̃/ *interjection* E19 French (literally,
'let us return to our sheep'). Let us
return to the matter in hand.
> ■ The phrase alludes to a confused court
> scene in the Old French *Farce de Maistre
> Pierre Pathelin* (*c.*1470). The judge, in order
> to bring the litigants back to the matter
> of the stolen sheep, exclaims *revenons à
> ces moutons!* ('let us return to these
> sheep!').

reverie /'rɛv(ə)ri/ *noun* (also **revery**) ME
French (from obsolete French *resverie*,
from Old French *reverie* rejoicing, revelry,
from *rever* to be delirious, of unknown
origin). **1** A state of being pleasantly
lost in one's thoughts; a daydream.
2 *Music* An instrumental composition
suggestive of a dreamy or musing
state. **3** A fanciful or impractical idea
or theory. *Archaic.*

revers /rɪ'vɪə/ *noun* plural same /rɪ'vɪəz/
M19 French (= reverse). The turned-back
edge of a garment revealing the undersurface, especially at the lapel. Usually
plural.

revue /rɪ'vju:/ *noun* L19 French (= review).
A light theatrical entertainment consisting of a series of short sketches,
comic turns, songs, etc., typically dealing satirically with topical issues. Also,
the genre comprising such entertainments.

Rex /rɛks/ *noun* E17 Latin (= king). The
reigning king (used following a name
or in the titles of lawsuits, e.g. *Rex v.
Jones*, the Crown versus Jones).

rho /rəʊ/ *noun* LME Greek (*rhō*). **1** The
seventeenth letter (Ρ, ρ) of the Greek
alphabet, transliterated as 'r' or (when
written with a rough breathing) 'rh'.
2 *Statistics* A correlation coefficient.

rhumba variant of RUMBA.

rhyton /'rʌɪtɒn/, /'rɪtɒn/ *noun* plural
rhytons, **rhyta** /'rʌɪtə/ M19 Greek (*rhuton*
neuter of *rhutos* flowing, related to *rhein*
to flow). A type of drinking vessel used
in ancient Greece, often in the form of
an animal's head, with one or more
holes at the bottom through which
liquid can flow.

ria /'riːə/ *noun* L19 Spanish (*ría* estuary).
Geography A long narrow inlet of the
sea formed by the partial submer-
gence of a river valley.

Rialto /rɪ'altəʊ/ *noun* (also **rialto**) M16
Italian (name of district of Venice in
which the Exchange was situated). A
market, an exchange.

richesse /riː'ʃɛs/, /'rɪtʃɛs/ *noun* ME Old
French (*richeise*, *richesce* (modern *richesse*),
from *riche* rich). *singular* and in *plural*
Wealth; richness; riches.
> ■ Long archaic, but cf. EMBARRAS DE
> RICHESSE.

ricochet /'rɪkəʃeɪ/, /'rɪkəʃɛt/ *noun* M18
French (= the skipping of a shot or of a flat
stone on water, of unknown origin).
Originally *Military* The action of a
projectile, especially a bullet or shell,
in rebounding at an angle off a surface
or surfaces after being fired; a shot or
hit that rebounds off a surface.
> 1996 *New Scientist* The fax messages are
> sent by someone living in 2024. Because of
> some ricochet of the arrow of time they are
> received by a present-day and startled
> Brazilian.

ricotta /rɪ'kɒtə/ *noun* L19 Italian (= re-
cooked, cooked twice, from Latin *recocta*

feminine past participle of *recoquere*, from *re-* again + *coquere* cook). A kind of soft white unsalted Italian cheese. Also *ricotta cheese*.

rictus /ˈrɪktəs/ *noun* M18 Latin (literally, 'open mouth', from *rict-* past participial stem of *ringi* to gape). A fixed grin or grimace.

riem /rɪm/, /riːm/ *noun* E19 Dutch (from Middle Dutch *rieme*). A strip of rawhide or worked leather, used as a rope or in making chairs and other furniture. *South African*.

riempie /ˈrɪmpi/, /ˈriːmpi/ *noun* & *adjective* (also **riempje**) M19 Dutch (*riempje*, from as RIEM + Afrikaans diminutive suffix *-ie*). **A** *noun* A fine narrow *riem* or leather thong. **B** *adjective* (Of furniture) having a seat or bottom of crisscrossed fine narrow leather thongs, as a *riempie chair* (Afrikaans *riempiestoel*). *South African*.

rigadoon /rɪɡəˈduːn/ *noun* (also **rigaudon** /ˈrɪɡədõ/ (*plural same*)) L17 French (*rigodon, rigaudon* said to be from *Rigaud* a dancing master who devised it). **1** A lively dance for couples, in duple or quadruple time, of Provençal origin. **2** A piece of music for this dance.

rigatoni /rɪɡəˈtəʊni/ *noun* M20 Italian (from *rigato* past participle of *rigare* to draw a line, make fluting, from *riga* a line). Pasta in the form of short hollow fluted tubes; an Italian dish consisting largely of this and usually a sauce.

rigor mortis /rɪɡə ˈmɔːtɪs/ *noun* M19 Latin (= stiffness of death). *Medicine* stiffening of the joints and muscles of a body a few hours after death, usually lasting from one to four days.

rijsttafel /ˈrʌɪsˌtɑːf(ə)l/ *noun* L19 Dutch (from *rijst* rice + *tafel* table). A South-East Asian meal consisting of a selection of different foods (such as eggs, meat, fish, fruit, curry, etc.) mixed with rice and served in separate dishes.

rillettes /ˈriːjɛt/ *noun* (treated as *singular* or *plural*) L19 French. Pâté made of minced pork, chicken, etc., seasoned and combined with fat.

rinderpest /ˈrɪndəpɛst/ *noun* M19 German (from *Rinder* cattle (plural of *Rind*) + *Pest* plague). An infectious disease of ruminants, especially oxen; cattle plague.

■ In South Africa, the phrase *before* (or *since*) *the rinderpest* means 'a long time ago' or 'for a very long time'. This refers to the 1896 epidemic, treated as a landmark.

ripieno /rɪpɪˈeɪnəʊ/ *noun* plural **ripienos, ripieni** /rɪpɪˈeɪni/ E18 Italian (from *ri-* again + *pieno* full). *Music* The body of instruments accompanying the concertino in baroque concerto music.

■ Originally used (in the early 18th century) in the sense 'supplementary'.

riposte /rɪˈpɒst/ *noun* E18 French ((earlier *risposte*) from Italian *risposta* use as noun of feminine past participle of *rispondere*, from Latin *respondere* from *re-* + *spondere* to pledge). **1** A quick, clever reply to an insult or criticism; a retaliatory action. **2** *Fencing* A quick thrust given after parrying a lunge; a return thrust.

1 1996 *Spectator* Unfortunately, a witty riposte invariably escaped me.

Risorgimento /rɪˌsɔːdʒɪˈmɛntəʊ/ *noun* plural **Risorgimenti** /rɪˌsɔːdʒɪˈmɛnti/, **Risorgimentos** L19 Italian (= renewal, renaissance). **1** *History* The movement which led to the unification of Italy as an independent state in 1870. **2** A revitalization or renewal of activity in any sphere.

risotto /rɪˈzɒtəʊ/ *noun* plural **risottos** M19 Italian (from *riso* rice). An Italian dish of rice cooked in stock with various other ingredients, such as meat, seafood, onions, etc.

risqué /ˈriːskeɪ/ /ˈrɪskeɪ/, /rɪˈskeɪ/ *adjective* (feminine **risquée**) M19 French (past participle of *risquer* to risk). Slightly indecent and liable to shock, especially by being sexually suggestive.

1996 *Spectator* The erotic poetry of the 17th and 18th centuries and the libertinism of Restoration drama, however risqué, lead you down a garden path with carefully laid out grassy borders.
1996 *Times* Nowadays, Vivienne [Westwood] is still considered *risquée*.

rissole /ˈrɪsəʊl/ *noun* E18 French (later form of Old French *ruissole* dialectal variant of *roisole*, *roussole* from Proto-Romance use as noun of feminine of late Latin *russeolus* reddish, from Latin *russus* red). A compressed mixture of meat and spices, coated in breadcrumbs and fried.

ristorante /rɪstɒ'rranteɪ/, /ˌrɪstɒ'rranti/ *noun* plural **ristoranti** /rɪstɒ'ranti/ E20 Italian. An Italian restaurant.

ritardando /rɪta:'dandəʊ/ *adverb, adjective, & noun* plural of noun **ritardandos**, **ritardandi** /rɪta:'dandi/ E19 Italian (present participle of *ritardare* to slow down). *Music* RALLENTANDO.

rite de passage /rit də pasaʒ/, /ˌri:t də pa'sɑːʒ/ *noun phrase* plural **rites de passage** (pronounced same) E20 French. *Anthropology* A ceremony or event marking the beginning of a new defined stage in a person's life, a rite of passage.

■ The phrase was coined by Arnold van Gennep in the title of his book *Les Rites de passage* (1909). In English use, the translation *rite of passage* appeared in the same year as van Gennep's book; the 1960 translators of *Les Rites de passage* suggested that *rites of transition* would have been a better rendering, but acknowledged that *rites of passage* had become too firmly established in general usage to dislodge. Although less frequent than the English version, *rite de passage* is still found.
1977 *Times* The [Newfoundland] seal hunt is... a necessary *rite de passage* for all young men.

ritenuto /rɪtə'nuːtəʊ/ *adverb, adjective, & noun* E19 Italian (= retained, restrained, past participle of *ritenere* from Latin *retinere* to hold back). *Music* **A** *adverb & adjective* (Especially as a direction) with immediate reduction of speed, restrained, held back in tempo. **B** *noun* plural **ritenuti** /rɪtə'nuːti/, **ritenutos** An immediate reduction of speed.

rites de passage plural of RITE DE PASSAGE.

ritornello /rɪtɔː'nɛləʊ/ *noun* plural **ritornellos**, **ritornelli** /rɪtɔː'nɛli/ L17 Italian (diminutive of *ritorno* return). *Music* A short instrumental refrain or interlude in a vocal work.

riviera /rɪvɪ'ɛːrə/ *noun* M18 Italian (= seashore, coast). **1** A coastal region with a warm climate and popularity as a holiday resort. **2** (**the Riviera**) Part of the Mediterranean coastal region of southern France and Northern Italy, extending from Cannes to La Spezia, famous for its beauty, mild climate, and fashionable resorts.

rivière /rivjɛr/ (*plural same*), /ˌrɪvɪ'ɛː/ *noun* L19 French (= river). A necklace of gems that increase in size towards a large central stone, typically consisting of more than one string.

rocaille /rə(ʊ)'kʌɪ/, *foreign* /rɔkaj/ *noun* M19 French (from *roc* rock). An 18th-century artistic or architectural style of decoration characterized by ornate rock- and shell-work, typical of grottos and fountains; a rococo style.

roche moutonnée /rɒʃ mutɔne/, /ˌrɒʃ mu:tɒ'neɪ/ *noun phrase* plural **roches moutonnées** (pronounced same) M19 French (literally, 'fleecy rock', from *roche* rock (from medieval Latin *rocca*, *rocha* of unknown origin) + *moutonnée* (from *mouton* sheep, from medieval Latin *multo(n-)*, probably of Gaulish origin). *Geology* A bare rock outcrop which has been shaped by glacial erosion, with one side smooth and gently sloping and the other steep, rough, and irregular.
1977 A. Hallam *Planet Earth* Many valleys are very deeply incised, with U-shaped cross-profiles and floors composed of smoothed, striated and streamlined rock hummocks (called roches moutonées).

rococo /rə'kəʊkəʊ/ *adjective & noun* M19 French (fanciful alteration of *rocaille* pebble- or shell-work from *roc* rock). **A** *adjective* **1** (Of furniture or architecture) characterized by an elaborately ornamental late baroque style of decoration prevalent in 18th-century continental Europe, with asymmetrical patterns involving motifs, scrollwork, etc. **2** (Of music, literature, etc.) extravagantly or excessively ornate. **B** *noun* The rococo style of art, decoration, or architecture.

rodeo /'rəʊdɪəʊ/, /rə'deɪəʊ/ *noun* plural **rodeos** M19 Spanish (from *rodear* to go round, based on Latin *rotare* to rotate). **1** A round-up of cattle for counting, inspecting, branding, etc.; a place where cattle are rounded up. **2** A display or competition exhibiting the skills of riding broncos, roping calves, wrestling steers, etc. **b** A similar (usually competitive) exhibition of other skills, as motorcycle riding, canoeing, etc.

■ Originally United States.

rodomontade /ˌrɒdə(ʊ)mɒnˈteɪd/ *noun, verb, & adjective* E17 French (from Italian *rodomontada, rodomontata,* from *Rodomonte* the name of a boastful character in the Renaissance *Orlando* epics). **A** *noun* **1** A brag, a boast; an extravagantly boastful or arrogant remark or speech. **2** Boastful or inflated language or behaviour; extravagant bragging. **B** *intransitive verb* Boast, brag; rant. **C** *adjective* Bragging, boastful; ranting.

roesti variant of RÖSTI.

rogan josh /ˌrəʊɡə(ə)n ˈdʒəʊʃ/ *noun phrase* (also **roghan josh**) M20 Urdu (*roġan još, rauġan-još* (preparation of mutton) stewed in ghee, from Urdu *roġan, rauġan* from Persian *rauġan* oil, ghee + Urdu, Persian *roġan još* act of braising or stewing). An Indian dish of curried meat (usually lamb) cooked in a rich tomato-based sauce.

roi fainéant /rwa fɛneɑ̃/ *noun phrase* plural **rois fainéants** (pronounced same) M19 French (literally, 'sluggard king'; cf. FAINÉANT). Any person with merely nominal power.

■ Originally applied to any of the later Merovingian kings of France, whose power was merely nominal.
1966 *Economist* The launching of the Sputnik in 1957, in the reign of the *roi fainéant,* President Eisenhower, seemed to justify Khrushchevian boasts that America's days of...supremacy were numbered.

roi soleil /rwa sɔlɛj/ *noun phrase* plural **rois soleils** (pronounced same) L19 French (literally, 'sun king', (the heraldic device of) Louis XIV of France). A pre-eminent person or thing.

romaine /rə(ʊ)ˈmeɪn/ *noun* E20 French (feminine of *romain* Roman). A cos lettuce. Also more fully *romaine lettuce.* Chiefly North American.

roman-à-clef /rɔmɑ̃ a kle/, /rəʊˌmɑːn ɑːˈkleɪ/ *noun phrase* (also **roman à clef**) plural **romans-à-clef** (pronounced same) L19 French (literally, 'novel with a key'). A novel in which real people or events appear with invented names.

1996 *Times: Weekend* Anonymous's novel is more than a political *roman à clef*...

roman-fleuve /rɔmɑ̃ flœv/ *noun phrase* plural **romans-fleuves** (pronounced same) M20 French (literally, 'river novel'). A novel featuring the leisurely description of the lives of closely related people; a sequence of related, self-contained novels.

rondavel /rɒnˈdɑːv(ə)l/ *noun* L19 Afrikaans (*rondawel*). A traditional circular African dwelling with a conical thatched roof. South African.

ronde /rɒnd/ *noun* M20 French (feminine of *rond* round). **1** A dance in which the participants move in a circle or ring. **2** A round or course of talk, activity, etc.; *figurative* a treadmill.

2 1977 *Times Literary Supplement* Heinz already represented the first step away from what was ultimately unbearable about the homosexual *ronde.*

rondeau /ˈrɒndəʊ/ *noun* plural **rondeaux** /ˈrɒndəʊ/, /ˈrɒndəʊz/ E16 Old and Modern French (later form of *rondel* from *rond* round). **1** A poem of ten or thirteen lines with only two rhymes throughout and with the opening words used twice as a refrain. **2** *Music* A RONDO.

rondo /ˈrɒndəʊ/ *noun* plural **rondos** L18 Italian (from French RONDEAU). A musical form with a recurring leading theme, often found in the final movement of a sonata or concerto.

ronin /ˈrəʊnɪn/ *noun* plural same, **ronins** L19 Japanese. (In feudal Japan) a wandering samurai who had no lord or master; an outlaw.

rooibos /ˈrɔɪbɒs/ *noun* E20 Afrikaans (= red bush, from *rooi* red + *bos* bush). An evergreen South African shrub of the pea family, the leaves of which are used to make tea.

rooinek /ˈrɔɪnɛk/ *noun* L19 Afrikaans (from *rooi* red + *nek* neck). A British or English-speaking South African.

■ In derogatory or humorous use in South African slang, the term was especially associated with the British troops in South Africa during the Boer War (1899–1902).

roquette /rɒˈkɛt/ *noun* E20 French. An edible Mediterranean plant of the cabbage family, whose leaves are eaten in salads; rocket.

rosbif /rɔzbif/ *noun* M19 French (from English *roast beef*). A French term for an English or British person. *Colloquial*, often *derogatory*.

rosé /ˈrəʊzeɪ/, *foreign* /roze/ *noun* L19 French (= pink). Any light pink wine, coloured by brief contact with red grape skins.

rosemaling /ˈrəʊsəˌmɑːlɪŋ/, /ˈrəʊsəˌmɔːlɪŋ/ *noun* M20 Norwegian (= rose-painting). The art, originating in Norway, of painting wooden furniture and objects with flower motifs; flower motifs, especially painted on wood.

rosolio /rəʊˈzəʊlɪəʊ/ *noun* (also **rosoglio**) plural **rosolios** E19 Italian (variant of *rosoli*, from Latin *ros solis* dew of the sun). A sweet cordial made especially in Italy from alcohol, raisins, sugar, rose petals, cloves, and cinnamon.

rösti /ˈrøsti/ *noun plural* (treated as *singular* or *plural*) (also **roesti**) M20 Swiss German. A Swiss dish of grated potatoes, formed into a small flat cake and fried; a flat cake of grated potato.

roti /ˈrəʊtiː/ *noun* E20 Hindi (*roṭī*). Bread, especially a flat round bread cooked on a griddle. *Indian*.

rotisserie /rə(ʊ)ˈtɪs(ə)ri/ *noun* M19 French (*rôtisserie*, from *rôtir* to roast). **1** A restaurant specializing in roasted or barbecued meat. **2** A cooking appliance with a rotating spit for roasting and barbecuing meat. Also *rotisserie oven*.

> **2 1996** *Times: Weekend* A few weeks ago I wrote that the demise of the spit (or rotisserie, if you prefer) had robbed us of roast meat...

roué /ˈruːeɪ/ *noun* E19 French (use as noun of past participle of *rouer* to break on the wheel (the punishment said to be deserved by such a person)). A debauched man, especially an elderly one; a rake.

> **1996** *Times*... I got hopelessly lost in the Casanova papers themselves, mainly because they assumed some knowledge of the old roué's life.

rouge /ruːʒ/ *noun & adjective* LME Old and Modern French (from Latin *rubeus* red). **A** *noun* **1** A red powder or cream used as a cosmetic to add colour to the lips or especially the cheeks. **2** Any of various metallic oxides etc. used as polishing powders; *especially* (in full *jeweller's rouge*) a fine preparation of ferric oxide used as a polish for metal and optical glass. Usually with specifying word. **3** Red as one of the two colours of divisions in rouge et noir and roulette. Earliest in ROUGE ET NOIR. **B** *adjective* (Of wine) red.

■ First used in English to denote the colour red, a meaning that is now obsolete, except in certain heraldic contexts. The cosmetic term dates from the mid 18th century.

rouge et noir /ˌruːʒ eɪ ˈnwɑː/ *noun phrase* L18 French (= red and black). A gambling game in which stakes are placed on a table marked with red and black diamonds.

rouille /ruj/ *noun* M20 French (literally, 'rust', with reference to the colour). A Provençal sauce made from pounded red chillies, garlic, breadcrumbs, and other ingredients, blended with stock, frequently added to bouillabaisse.

roulade /ruˈlɑːd/ *noun* E18 French (from *rouler* to roll). **1** *Music* A florid passage of runs in classical music for a solo virtuoso, especially one sung to one syllable. **2** A dish cooked or served in the form of a roll, typically made from a flat piece of meat, fish, or sponge, spread with a soft filling and rolled up into a spiral.

rouleau /ruˈləʊ/ *noun* plural **rouleaux** /ruˈləʊ/, **rouleaus** L17 French (from obsolete *roule*, originally, a roll or paper containing an actor's part). **1** A cylindrical packet of coins. **2** A coil or roll of ribbon, knotted wool, or other material, especially used as trimming.

roulement /rulmɑ̃/ *noun* plural pronounced same E20 French (literally, 'rolling'). *Military* Movement of troops or equipment, especially from a reserve force to provide relief.

roulette /ru'lɛt/ *noun* M18 French (diminutive of *rouelle* wheel, from late Latin *rotella* diminutive of *rota* wheel). **1** A gambling game in which a ball is dropped on to a revolving wheel with numbered compartments in the centre of a table, players betting on the number at which the ball comes to rest. **2** A tool or machine with a revolving toothed wheel; *specifically* (**a**) one for making dotted lines in etching and engraving; (**b**) one for perforating a sheet of paper.

■ A transferred use of sense 1 is in the phrase 'Russian roulette' (the act of bravado involving spinning the cylinder of a revolver, one chamber of which is loaded, and then pulling the trigger while pointing it at one's head); hence figuratively, *playing Russian roulette* means taking dangerous risks.

routier /rutje/ *noun* plural pronounced same M19 French (from *route* road). **1** *History* A member of any of numerous bands of mercenaries active in France during the later Middle Ages. **2** (In France) a long-distance lorry driver.

roux /ru:/ *noun* E19 French (from (*buerre*) *roux* browned (butter)). *Cookery* A blend of melted fat (especially butter) and flour used as a thickener in making sauces.

rubato /ru'bɑ:təʊ/ *noun & adjective* L18 Italian (literally, 'robbed'). *Music* **A** *noun* plural **rubatos**, **rubati** /ru'bɑ:ti/ also **tempo rubato** The temporary disregarding of strict tempo to allow an expressive quickening or slackening, usually without altering the overall pace. **B** *adjective* Performed with rubato.

rubella /ru'bɛlə/ *noun* L19 Latin (use as noun of neuter plural of Latin *rubellus* reddish, from *rubeus* red). German measles.

ruche /ru:ʃ/ *noun* E19 Old and Modern French (from medieval Latin *rusca* tree bark, of Celtic origin). A frill or pleat of fabric as decoration on a garment or soft furnishing.

rucola /'rʊkəʊlə/ *noun* L20 Italian. The rocket plant, used in cookery.

rumba /'rʌmbə/ *noun* (also **rhumba**) E20 American Spanish. A rhythmic dance with Spanish and African elements, originating in Cuba; a ballroom dance imitative of this, danced on the spot with a pronounced movement of the hips; the dance rhythm of this, usually in 2/4 time; a piece of music with this rhythm.

ruse de guerre /ryz də gɛr/ *noun phrase* plural **ruses de guerre** (pronounced same) E19 French (literally, 'ruse of war'). A stratagem intended to deceive an enemy in war; *transferred* a justifiable trick.

rus in urbe /ˌru:s ɪn 'ə:beɪ/ *noun phrase* M18 Latin (literally, 'country in city'). An illusion of countryside created by a building, garden, etc., within a city; an urban building etc which has this effect.

> **1976** *Times* Two foxes ... live in a corner of the allotments—which seems to be taking *rus in urbe* too far.

ryu /rɪ'u:/ *noun*) plural same L19 Japanese (*-ryū* school, style, system). Any Japanese school or style of art.

Ss

sabayon /ˈsabʌɪjɒn/ *noun* E20 French (from Italian *zabaione* variant of ZABA-GLIONE). Zabaglione.

sabha /səˈbɑː/ *noun* E20 Sanskrit (*sabhā*). (In the Indian subcontinent) an assembly; a council; a society.

■ Hence the *Lok Sabha* and the *Rajya Sabha* are respectively the lower and the upper houses of the Indian parliament.

sabkha /ˈsabkə/, /ˈsabxə/ *noun* L19 Arabic (*sabḵa* a salt flat). *Geography* An area of coastal flats subject to periodic flooding and evaporation, found especially in North Africa and Arabia.

sabot /ˈsabəʊ/ *noun* E17 French (from Old French *çabot* blend of *çavate* (modern SAVATE) and *bote* (modern *botte*) boot). **1** A kind of simple shoe made of a single piece of wood shaped and hollowed out to fit the foot, traditionally worn by French and Breton peasants. **2** A device which ensures the correct positioning of a bullet or shell in the barrel of a gun, attached either to the projectile or inside the barrel and falling away as it leaves the muzzle. **3** In baccarat and chemin de fer, a box for dealing the cards, a shoe.

sabotage /ˈsabətɑːʒ/ *noun & verb* E20 French (from *saboter* to kick with sabots, wilfully destroy, from as preceding). **A** *noun* Deliberate damage to or destruction of property, especially in order to disrupt the production of goods or as a political or military act. **B** *transitive verb* Commit sabotage on; deliberately destroy, damage, or obstruct something.

saboteur /ˌsabəˈtəː/ *noun* E20 French (from *saboter* (see SABOTAGE)). A person who engages in sabotage.

sabra /ˈsabrə/ *noun* (also **Sabra**) M20 Modern Hebrew (*ṣabbār* or its source Arabic *ṣabr* prickly pear). A Jew born in Israel (or before 1948 in Palestine).
    attributive 1995 *Times* Yitzhak Rabin was... the first *sabra*, or native-born, leader of his country.

sabreur /saˈbrəː/ *noun* M19 French (from *sabrer* to strike with a sabre). **1** A person, especially a cavalry soldier, who fights with a sabre. **2** A person who fences using a sabre.

saccade /səˈkɑːd/ *noun* E18 French (literally 'violent pull'). A brief rapid movement of the eye from one position of rest to another, whether voluntary or involuntary.

■ Originally used in the sense 'jerking movement'.

Sachertorte /ˈzaxərˌtɔrtə/ *noun* plural **Sachertorten** /ˈzaxərˌtɔrt(ə)n/ E20 German (from Franz *Sacher* Viennese pastry chef, its creator + *Torte* tart, pastry, cake). A chocolate gateau with apricot jam filling and chocolate icing.

sachet /ˈsaʃeɪ/ *noun* L15 Old and Modern French (diminutive of *sac* bag). **1** A small sealed bag or packet containing a small portion of a substance, e.g. sugar or shampoo. **2** A small bag containing dried scented material such as lavender, used to scent clothes. **3** Dried, scented material for use in scenting clothes.

sacrum /ˈseɪkrəm/ *noun* plural **sacrums, sacra** /ˈseɪkrə/ M18 Latin (short for late Latin *os sacrum*, translation of Greek *hieron osteon* sacred bone (from the belief that the soul resides in it)). *Anatomy* A triangular bone which is wedged between the two hip bones, forming the back of the pelvis and resulting from the fusing of (usually five) vertebrae.

sadhu /ˈsɑːdhuː/ *noun* (also **Sadhu**) M19 Sanskrit (*sādhu* adjective, good, (as noun) good man, holy man). *Hinduism* A holy man, a sage.

safari /sə'fɑːri/ *noun* L19 Kiswahili (from Arabic *safar* journey, trip, tour). An expedition to observe or hunt animals in their natural habitat, especially in East Africa. Frequently in *on safari*.

saga /'sɑːɡə/ *noun* E18 Old Norse (literally 'narrative'). **1** An Old Norse prose narrative of Iceland or Norway, *especially* one which recounts the traditional history of Icelandic families or of the kings of Norway. **b** *transferred* A narrative regarded as having the traditional characteristics of the Icelandic sagas; a story of heroic achievement. Also, a novel or series of novels recounting the history of a family through several generations. **2** A long and complicated account of a series of events.

saganaki /saɡə'nɑːki/ *noun* M20 Modern Greek (= small two-handled frying pan (traditionally used to prepare the dish)). A Greek dish consisting of breaded or floured cheese fried in butter, often with lemon juice, served as an appetizer.

sahib /'sɑː(h)ɪb/, /sɑːb/ *noun* (also **saab** /sɑːb/) L17 Urdu (through Persian from Arabic ṣāḥib friend, lord, master). A polite title or form of address for a man.

■ Anglo-Indian. Often affixed to a person's name or office, as in *Malarao Sahib, the inspector sahib*.

sainfoin /'seɪnfɔɪn/, /'sanfɔɪn/ *noun* (also **sanfoin**) M17 French (*saintfoin* (modern *sainfoin*), originally 'lucerne', from modern Latin *sanctum foenum*, literally, 'holy hay', alteration of *sanum foenum* wholesome hay, which was based on Latin *herba medica* erroneous alteration of *herba Medica*, literally, 'Median grass', translation of Greek *Mēdikē poa*). A pink-flowered plant of the pea family, *Onobrychis viciifolia*, which is native to Asia and grown widely for fodder.

sake /'sɑːki/, /'sakeɪ/ *noun* (also **saké**, **saki**) L17 Japanese. A Japanese alcoholic drink made from fermented rice.

salaam /sə'lɑːm/ *interjection & noun* E17 Arabic (*salām* peace). **A** *interjection* A common greeting in many Arabic-speaking and Muslim countries. **B** *noun* **1** A gesture of greeting or respect typically consisting of a low bow of the head and body with the hand or fingers touching the forehead. **2** In *plural* Respectful compliments.

salade niçoise /salad niswaz/ *noun phrase* plural **salades niçoises** (pronounced same) E20 French (= salad from Nice (in southern France)). A salad usually made from hard-boiled eggs, tuna, black olives, tomatoes, etc.

salami /sə'lɑːmi/ *noun* M19 Italian (plural of *salame*, representing popular Latin word from verb meaning 'to salt'). A type of highly seasoned sausage, originally from Italy, usually eaten cold in slices.

salariat /sə'lɛːrɪət/ *noun* E20 French (from *salaire* salary, after *prolétariat* PROLETARIAT). Salaried white-collar workers; the salaried class.

salep /'saləp/ *noun* M18 French (from Turkish *sālep* from Arabic *taʿlab* fox, shortening of *kuṣā 'ṯ-ṯaʿlab* orchid (literally, 'fox's testicles')). A starchy preparation of the dried tubers of various orchids, used in cookery and formerly as a tonic.

salina /sə'lʌɪnə/ *noun* L16 Spanish (from medieval Latin = salt pit; in Latin only as plural *salinae* salt pans). (Chiefly in the Caribbean or South America) a salt pan, salt lake, or salt marsh.

salmi /'salmi/ *noun* (also **salmis**) plural pronounced same M18 French (abbreviation of French *salmigondis* salmagundi). A ragout or casserole of game stewed in a rich sauce.

salon /'salɒn/, *foreign* /salɔ̃/ (*plural same*) *noun* L17 French (from Italian *salone* augmentative of *sala* hall). **1** A reception room in a palace or large house, especially in France or another continental country; a drawing room. **2** A regular social gathering, especially of writers and artists, at the house of a woman prominent in high society. **b** A meeting of intellectuals or other eminent people at the invitation of a celebrity or socialite. *North American*. **3** An establishment where a hairdresser, beautician, or couturier conducts trade.

salon des refusés /salɔ̃ de rəfyze/ *noun phrase* L19 French (= exhibition of rejected works). An exhibition ordered by Napoleon III in 1863 to display pictures rejected by the Salon. The artists represented included Manet, Cézanne, Pissarro, and Whistler. Also *transferred*.

▪ The Salon, the annual exhibition in Paris of painting, sculpture, etc., by living artists, was notoriously hostile to the works of Impressionist artists.

salopettes /salə'pɛts/ *noun plural* L20 French (*salopette*). Trousers with a high waist and shoulder straps, typically made of a padded fabric and worn for skiing.

salpicon /'salpɪkɒn/ *noun* E18 French (from Spanish, from *salpicar* to sprinkle (with salt)). A mixture of finely chopped ingredients bound in a thick sauce and used as a filling or stuffing.

salsa /'salsə/ *noun* M19 Spanish (= sauce; in sense 2 American Spanish). **1** (Especially in Latin American cookery) a spicy tomato sauce. **2** A type of Latin American dance music incorporating elements of jazz and rock; a dance performed to salsa music.

2 1996 *Country Life* Over the road, a salsa band blared out in raunchy competition.

saltarello /saltə'rɛləʊ/ *noun* plural **saltarellos, saltarelli** /saltə'rɛli/ L16 Italian (*salterello*, Spanish *salterelo* related to Italian *saltare*, Spanish *saltar* to leap, dance, from Latin *saltare*). *History* An energetic Italian and Spanish dance for a couple involving numerous sudden skips or jumps; a piece of music for this dance or in its rhythm.

saltimbocca /ˌsaltɪm'bɒkə/ *noun* M20 Italian (from *saltare* to leap + *in* in, into + *bocca* mouth). A dish consisting of rolled pieces of veal or poultry cooked with herbs, bacon, and other flavourings.

salut /sa'lu:/ *interjection* M20 French. Used to express friendly feelings towards one's companions before drinking.

salve /'salveɪ, 'salvi:/ *noun* LME Latin (= hail, greetings, imperative of *salvere* be well; in sense 1 from the opening words of the antiphon *salve regina* hail (holy) queen). **1** (usually **Salve**) More fully *Salve Regina* /rə'dʒi:nə/. A Roman Catholic hymn or prayer said or sung after compline. Also, a musical setting for this. **2** An utterance of 'salve'; a greeting or salutation on meeting. Now *rare* or *obsolete*.

sal volatile /ˌsal və'latɪli/ *noun phrase* M17 Modern Latin (= volatile salt). Ammonium carbonate, especially in the form of an aromatic solution in alcohol to be sniffed as a restorative in faintness etc.; smelling salts.

salwar /'ʃʌlvɑ:/ *noun* (also **shalwar**) E19 Persian and Urdu (*šalwār*). *singular* and in *plural* Loose, pleated trousers, usually tapering to a tight fit around the ankles, worn by women from the Indian subcontinent, typically with a KAMEEZ.

▪ Often in the combination *salwar kameez*, describing a woman's matching outfit.

1996 *Times* Shalwar kameez tunics were layered over tiered bloomers.

samadhi /sə'mɑ:di/ *noun* L18 Sanskrit (*samādhi* contemplation, literally, 'a putting together, joining'). *Hinduism* and *Buddhism* **1** A state of intense concentration induced by meditation, in which union with the divine is attained; the last stage of yoga. **2** A tomb. *Indian*.

samba /'sambə/ *noun* L19 Portuguese (of African origin). A Brazilian dance of African origin; a Latin American and ballroom dance imitative of this; a piece of music for this dance, usually in 2/4 or 4/4 time.

sambal /'sambal/ *noun* E19 Malay. (In Malayan and Indonesian cookery) a hot relish consisting of raw vegetables or fruit prepared with spices and vinegar.

sambhar /'sɑ:mbɑ:/ *noun* M20 Tamil (*cāmpār* from Marathi *sāb(h)ar* from Sanskrit *sambhāra* collection, materials). A spicy south Indian dish consisting of lentils and vegetables.

sambuca /sam'bʊkə/ *noun* L20 Italian (from Latin *sambucus* elder tree). An Italian aniseed-flavoured liqueur.

samfu /'samfuː/ *noun* M20 Chinese ((Cantonese) *shaam foò*, from *shaam* coat + *foò* trousers). A light suit consisting of a plain high-necked jacket and loose trousers, worn by women from China.

samisen /'samɪsɛn/ *noun* (also **shamisen** /'ʃamɪsɛn/) E17 Japanese (from Chinese *sānxián* (Wade–Giles *sān-hsien*), from *sān* three + *xián* string). A traditional Japanese long-necked three-stringed lute, played with a large plectrum. Cf. SAN-HSIEN.

samizdat /'samɪzdat/, /ˌsamɪz'dat/ *noun* (also **Samizdat**) M20 Russian (from *sam*(*o*-self + *izdat* (*el'stvo* publishing house). The clandestine or illegal copying and distribution of literature banned by the state, especially formerly in the communist countries of eastern Europe; an underground press; a text or texts produced by this.

> **1980** *Times Literary Supplement* The strongest works to have come out since 1962 … have appeared, and could only appear, in *samizdat*.

samosa /sə'məʊsə/ *noun* M20 Persian and Urdu (*samosa(h)*). A triangular pastry fried in ghee or oil, containing spiced vegetables or meat.

samovar /'saməvɑː/, /samə'vɑː/ *noun* M19 Russian (= self-boiler, from *samo*- self + *varit'* to boil). A Russian tea urn, with an internal heating device to keep the water at boiling point.

sampan /'sampan/ *noun* E17 Chinese (*sānban* (Wade–Giles *san-pan*) boat, from *sān* three + *bǎn* board). A small boat used in the Far East, usually with an oar or oars at the stern.

samsara /sam'sɑːrə/ *noun* L19 Sanskrit (*saṃsāra* a wandering through). *Hinduism* and *Buddhism* The material world; the endless cycle of death and rebirth to which life in the material world is bound.

samskara /səm'skɑːrə/ *noun* E19 Sanskrit (*saṃskāra* preparation, a making perfect). *Hinduism* A purificatory ceremony or rite marking a stage or an event in one's life.

samurai /'samʊrʌɪ/, /'samjʊrʌɪ/ *noun* plural same E18 Japanese. In feudal Japan, a member of a military caste, *especially* a member of the class of military retainers of the daimyos. Now also more widely, a Japanese army officer.

san /san/ *suffix* L19 Japanese (contraction of more formal *sama*). (In Japan) an honorific title added to a personal or family name as a mark of politeness: *Yamagouchi-san*.

sanbenito /ˌsanbə'niːtəʊ/ *noun* plural **sanbenitos** M16 Spanish (*sambenito*, from *San Benito* St Benedict, so called ironically from its resemblance to the Benedictine scapular). In the Spanish Inquisition, a yellow scapular-shaped garment, with a red St Andrew's cross before and behind, worn by a confessed and penitent heretic. Also, a similar black garment ornamented with flames, devils, and other devices, worn by an impenitent confessed heretic at an auto-da-fé.

sancocho /san'kotʃo/ *noun* M20 American Spanish (from Spanish = half-cooked meal, from *sancochar* to parboil). (In South America and the Caribbean) a thick soup consisting of meat, fish, and vegetables.

sancta plural of SANCTUM.

sancta sanctorum plural of SANCTUM SANCTORUM.

sancta simplicitas /ˌsan(k)tə sɪm'plɪsɪtɑːs/ *interjection* M19 Latin (literally, 'holy simplicity'). Expressing astonishment at a person's naivety.

> ■ These are said to have been the last words of the Bohemian religious reformer John Huss, burnt at the stake in 1415, on seeing an aged peasant bringing a bundle of twigs to add to the fire.

sanctum /'san(k)təm/ *noun* plural **sanctums**, **sancta** /'san(k)tə/ L16 Latin (neuter of *sanctus* holy; cf. next). **1** A sacred place or shrine in a temple or church. **2** A place where a person can be alone and free from intrusion; a private room, study, etc.

sanctum sanctorum /ˌsan(k)təm san(k)'tɔːrəm/ *noun phrase* plural **sancta sanctorum** /ˌsan(k)tə/ LME Latin (neuter singular and neuter genitive plural of *sanctus* holy, translation of Hebrew *qōḏeš haq-qŏḏāšīm* holy of holies). **1** *Jewish Antiquities* The holy of holies in the Jewish Temple. **2** A SANCTUM sense 1. **3** A SANCTUM sense 2.

sanctus /'saŋ(k)təs/ *noun* LME Latin (= holy, the first word of the hymn). *Christian Church* (also **Sanctus**) The hymn beginning *Sanctus, sanctus, sanctus* 'Holy, holy, holy', which forms a set part of the Mass; a musical setting of this.

sanfoin variant of SAINFOIN.

sang-de-boeuf /sãdəb'f/ *noun* L19 French (literally, 'ox's blood'). A deep red colour found on old Chinese porcelain; (porcelain bearing) a ceramic glaze of this colour.

sangfroid /sɒŋ'frwɑ:/ *noun* M18 French (from *sang-froid*, literally, 'cold blood'). Composure or coolness shown in the face of danger or difficult circumstances.

sangha /'saŋgə/ *noun* M19 Sanskrit (*saṃgha* community, from *sam* together + *han* to come in contact). *Buddhism* The Buddhist monastic order, including monks, nuns, and novices.

sangoma /saŋ'gɔːma/ *noun* (also **isangoma** /ɪsaŋ'gɔːma/) L19 Nguni. (In southern Africa) a traditional healer or diviner; a witch doctor.

sangre azul /ˌsangre a'θul/, /a'sul/ *noun phrase* M19 Spanish (= blue blood). The purity of blood claimed by certain ancient Castilian families, which professed to be free from Moorish or Jewish ancestry.

sangria /saŋ'griːə/ *noun* (also **Sangria**) M20 Spanish (*sangría*, literally, 'bleeding'). A Spanish drink made of red wine mixed with lemonade, fruit, and spices.

san-hsien /san'ʃjɛn/ *noun* (also **sanxian**) M19 Chinese (*sānxián* (Wade-Giles *sān-hsien*), from *sān* three + *xián* string). *Music* A Chinese three-stringed lute. Cf. SAMISEN.

sannyasi /sən'jɑːsi/ *noun* (also **sanyasi**, **sannyasin** /sən'jɑːsɪn/) E17 Sanskrit (*saṃnyāsī* nominative singular of *saṃnyāsin*

laying aside, abandoning, ascetic, from *saṃ* together + *ni* down + *as* throw). A Hindu religious mendicant, especially a Brahmin in the fourth stage of his life.

sans /sã(z)/, /san(z)/ *preposition* ME Old French (*san, sanz* (modern *sans*), earlier *sen* (*s*) from Proto-Romance variation of Latin *sine* without, partly influenced by Latin *absentia* absence). Without.

■ Although formerly fully naturalized, *sans* is now, apart from use in heraldic terminology, mainly literary and often humorous—especially with reference to Shakespeare's line on second childhood: 'Sans teeth, sans eyes, sans taste, sans everything' (*As You Like It* II.vii).
1996 *Times* Ms Thompson is not allowed to leave her house in a track-suit *sans* make-up without being pilloried by the press.

sansculotte /ˌsanzkjuː'lɒt/, *foreign* /sãkylɔt/ (*plural same*) *noun* (also **sans culotte**) L18 French (from *sans* without + *culotte* knee-breeches). **1** *History* A lower-class Parisian republican in the French Revolution; *generally* an extreme republican or revolutionary. **2** *transferred* A shabbily dressed person, a ragamuffin.

1 **1996** *Times* After my election ... I warned my council colleagues that if I were seen to be obstructed, it would not be long before *sans culottes* to the left of me emerged.

sansei /'sanseɪ/ *noun* plural same M20 Japanese (from *san* three, third + *sei* generation). An American or Canadian whose grandparents were immigrants from Japan. Cf. ISSEI, NISEI.

sanserif variant of SANS SERIF.

sans peur /sã pr̩/ *adjective phrase* E19 Old French. Without fear, fearless.

■ Especially in the phrase *sans peur et sans reproche* ('fearless and above reproach'), which was applied to the Chevalier de Bayard (1476–1524), a renowned soldier in the Italian wars of Charles VIII of France.
1995 *Spectator* Whether for religious reasons or because it hasn't got a licence, there's no alcohol in the place, though you can bring your own with you *sans peur et sans reprôche* [*sic*].

sans phrase /sanz 'frɑːz/ *adjective phrase* E19 Old French. Without more words, without exceptions or qualifications.

■ After *La mort sans phrase* ('death, without more words'), the expression allegedly used by the French abbot and statesman Emmanuel Sieyès (1748–1836) in giving his vote in the French Convention for the execution of Louis XVI.

sans reproche /sanz rə'prɔʃ/ *adjective phrase* M19 Old French. Without reproach, blameless.

■ Earlier (E19), and especially, in *sans peur et sans reproche*; cf. SANS PEUR.

sans serif /san 'sɛrɪf/ *noun & adjective phrase* (also **sanserif**) M19 French (apparently from SANS + *serif* cross-stroke of a letter (origin uncertain, but possibly from Dutch *schreef* dash, line)). *Typography* **A** *noun phrase* A style of typeface without serifs. **B** *adjective phrase* Having no serifs.

santeria /ˌsante'ria/ *noun* M20 Spanish (*santería*, literally, 'holiness, sanctity'). A pantheistic Afro-Cuban religious cult developed from the beliefs of the Yoruba people and having some elements of Catholicism.

santero /san'tero/ *noun* plural **santeros** /san'teros/ M20 Spanish. **1** (In Mexico and Spanish-speaking areas of the southwestern United States) a maker of religious images. **2** A priest of a religious cult, especially of santeria.

santir variant of SANTOOR.

santo /'santəʊ/ *noun* plural **santos** M19 Spanish (or Italian). (In Mexico and Spanish-speaking areas of the southwestern United States) a wooden representation of a saint or other religious symbol.

santon /'santɒn/ *noun* E20 French (from Spanish, from *santo* saint). (Chiefly in Provence) a figurine adorning a representation of the manger in which Jesus was laid.

santoor /san'tʊə/ *noun* (also **santour**, **santir** /san'tɪə/) M19 Arabic (*santīr*, *sintīr*, *santūr* (Persian *santūr*, Turkish *santur*), alteration of Greek *psaltērion* psaltery). An Indian musical instrument like a dulcimer, played by striking with a

pair of small, spoon-shaped wooden hammers.

sanyasi variant of SANNYASI.

sarabande /sarə'bɑːnd/ *noun* (also **saraband** /'sarəband/) E17 French (from Spanish or Italian *zarabanda*). A slow and stately Spanish dance in triple time; a piece of music for this dance or in its rhythm.

sarang variant of SERANG.

sarangi /sə'raŋɡi/, /sɑː'rʌŋɡi/ *noun* M19 Sanskrit (*sāraṅgī*). An Indian bowed stringed instrument.

sarape variant of SERAPE.

sarcoma /sɑː'kəʊmə/ *noun* plural **sarcomas**, **sarcomata** /sɑː'kəʊmətə/ E19 Modern Latin (from Greek *sarkōma*, from *sarkoun* to become fleshy, from *sarx*, *sark-* flesh). *Medicine* A malignant tumour of connective or other non-epithelial tissue.

sarcophagus /sɑː'kɒfəɡəs/ *noun* plural **sarcophagi** /sɑː'kɒfəɡʌɪ/, /sɑː'kɒfədʒʌɪ/ LME Latin (from Greek *sarkophagos* flesh-consuming, from *sarx*, *sark-* flesh + *-phagos* eating). A stone coffin, typically one adorned with a sculpture or inscription and associated with the ancient civilizations of Egypt, Rome, and Greece.

■ The stone of which these coffins was made was originally believed to be able to consume the flesh of the dead bodies deposited in it.

sari /'sɑːri/ *noun* (also **saree**) L18 Hindi (*sāṛī* from Sanskrit *śāṭikā*). A garment consisting of a length of cotton or silk elaborately draped around the body, traditionally worn by women from the Indian subcontinent.

sarod /sə'rəʊd/ *noun* M19 Urdu (from Persian *surod* song, melody). A lute used in classical North Indian music, with four main strings.

sarong /sə'rɒŋ/ *noun* M19 Malay (literally, 'sheath, quiver'). A garment consisting of a long piece of cloth worn wrapped round the body and tucked at the waist or under the armpits, traditionally worn by both sexes in the Malay archipelago, Java, and some Pacific islands; a woman's garment resembling this, worn especially on the beach.

sarsaparilla /ˌsɑːs(ə)pəˈrɪlə/ *noun* L16 Spanish (*zarzaparilla*, from *zarza* bramble + diminutive of Spanish *parra* vine, twining plant). **1** Any of several tropical American kinds of smilax used medicinally; the dried root of such a plant, used to treat rheumatism, skin complaints, and formerly also syphilis. Also, a carbonated drink flavoured with this root. **2** Any of several plants of other genera which resemble sarsaparilla or have a root used similarly. Chiefly with specifying word.

sashimi /ˈsaʃimi/ *noun* L19 Japanese (from *sashi* pierce + *mi* flesh). A Japanese dish of bite-sized pieces of raw fish served with grated horseradish and soy sauce.

sassafras /ˈsasəfras/ *noun* L16 Spanish (*sasafrás*, perhaps ultimately from Latin *saxifraga* saxifrage). **1** A tree of the genus *Sassafras*, of the laurel family, especially *S. albidum* native to the eastern United States. Its aromatic leaves are infused to make tea or ground into FILÉ. **2** An oil extracted from the leaves or bark of the sassafras, used medicinally and in perfumery. In full *sassafras oil*, also *oil of sassafras*. **3** Any of various similarly aromatic and medicinal trees of other genera and families; also, the wood or bark of such a tree.

sastrugi /saˈstruːgi/ *noun plural* (also **zastrugi** /zaˈstruːgi/) M19 German (from Russian *zastrugi* small ridges, furrows in snow, from *zastrugat'* to plane or smooth, from *strug* plane (the tool)). Parallel wave-like ridges caused by winds on the surface of hard snow, especially in polar regions.

> **1975** E. Hillary *Nothing Venture, Nothing Win* The surface, which had appeared so smooth from above, was … liberally peppered with large sastrugi—some of them up to three feet in height.

satay /ˈsateɪ/ *noun* (also **satai**, **saté**) M20 Malay (*satai*, *sate*, Indonesian *sate*; cf. SOSATIE). An Indonesian and Malaysian dish consisting of small pieces of meat grilled on a skewer and usually served with a spiced peanut sauce.

sati variant of SUTTEE.

satori /səˈtɔːri/ *noun* E18 Japanese (= awakening). *Buddhism* A sudden inner experience of enlightenment: *the road that leads to satori.*

satsuma /satˈsuːmə/, in sense 1 also /ˈsatsjʊmə/ *noun* (also (especially in sense 2) **Satsuma**) L19 Japanese (name of a province in the island of Kiusiu, Japan). **1** A variety of tangerine, originally from Japan, with a sharper taste and frequently seedless or with undeveloped seeds; the tree bearing this fruit. **2** A kind of cream-coloured Japanese pottery. In full *Satsuma ware.*

Saturnalia /satəˈneɪlɪə/ *noun* (treated as *singular* or *plural*) (in sense 2 also **saturnalia**) L16 Latin (use as noun of neuter plural of *Saturnalis* relating to *Saturnus* Saturn, the Roman god of agriculture and ruler of the gods until deposed by his son Jupiter). **1** The ancient Roman festival of Saturn, held in mid December and characterized by general unrestrained merrymaking, the precursor of Christmas. **2** A period of wild revelry or indulgence; an orgy.

satyagraha /sʌˈtjɑːɡrəhɑː/ *noun* E20 Sanskrit (*satyāgraha* force born of truth, from *satya* truth + *āgraha* obstinacy). **1** A policy of passive political resistance to British rule in India formulated by Mahatma Gandhi. **2** Any policy of non-violent resistance.

saucier /sosje/ *noun plural* pronounced same M20 French. A chef who prepares sauces.

saucisson /sosisɔ̃/ *noun plural* pronounced same M17 French (= large sausage). A large thick French sausage, typically firm in texture and flavoured with herbs.

saudade /sauˈdɑːdə/ *noun* E20 Portuguese. A feeling of longing, melancholy, or nostalgia that is supposedly characteristic of the Portuguese or Brazilian temperament.

■ Especially used with reference to songs or poetry.

sauerbraten /ˈsaʊəbrɑːt(ə)n/ *noun* L19 German (from *sauer* sour + *Braten* roast meat). A dish of German origin consisting of beef marinaded in vinegar with peppercorns, onions, and other seasonings and then cooked. *North American*.

sauerkraut /'saʊəkraʊt/ *noun* M17 German ((whence French *choucroute*), from *sauer* sour + *Kraut* vegetable, cabbage). Finely chopped pickled cabbage, a typical German dish.

■ In United States slang *Sauerkraut* was in use earlier (M19) as a derogatory word for 'a German' than its British equivalent KRAUT.

sauna /'sɔːnə/ *noun* L19 Finnish. A small room used as a hot-air or steam bath for cleaning and refreshing the body; a session in a sauna.

sauté /'səʊteɪ/ *adjective, noun, & verb* E19 French (past participle of *sauter* to leap). *Cookery* **A** *adjective* (Of meat, vegetables, etc.) fried quickly in a little hot fat. **B** *noun* **1** A dish cooked by frying quickly in a little hot fat. **2** *Ballet* A jump off both feet, landing in the same position. **C** *transitive verb* (past tense and participle *sautéd*, *sautéed*) Fry (food) quickly in a little hot fat.

sautoir /'səʊtwɑː/ *noun* M20 French (Old French *saut(e)our*, *sau(l)toir* stirrup cord). A long necklace consisting of a fine gold chain usually set with jewels.

■ An extended use of the original word which denoted a harness loop used as a stirrup for 'jumping' into the saddle.

sauve qui peut /sovkipø/ *noun & verb phrase* E19 French (literally, 'save-who-can'). **A** *noun phrase* A general stampede, a complete rout; panic, disorder. **B** *verb phrase intransitive* Stampede or scatter in flight.

A 1980 *Guardian* It is in those hallowed halls of the UN...that I feel most keenly the theatre of anarchy, of sauve-qui-peut.

savannah /sə'vanə/ *noun* (also **savanna**) M16 Spanish (*zavana*, *çavana* (now *sabana*) from Taino *zavana*). A grassy plain with few or no trees in a tropical or subtropical region.

savant /'sav(ə)nt/, *foreign* /savɑ̃/ (*plural same*) *noun* E18 French (use as noun of adjective, originally present participle of *savoir* to know). A learned person, especially a distinguished scientist.

savante /'sav(ə)nt/, *foreign* /savɑ̃t/ (*plural same*) *noun* M18 French (feminine of preceding). A female SAVANT, a learned woman.

savarin /'savərɪn/, *foreign* /savarɛ̃/ (*plural same*) *noun* L19 French (Anthelme Brillat-Savarin (1755–1826), French gastronome). A light ring-shaped cake made with yeast and soaked in liqueur-flavoured syrup.

savate /sə'vɑːt/, *foreign* /savat/ (*plural same*) *noun* M19 French (originally, a kind of ill-fitting shoe (cf. SABOT)). A French method of boxing in which the feet and fists are used.

savoir faire /savwar fɛr/ *noun phrase* (also **savoir-faire**) E19 French (literally, 'to know how to do'). The instinctive ability to act appropriately in social situations.

1996 *Spectator* Others who had some political savoir-faire (such as Fitzroy Maclean, who had been a diplomat in Moscow before the war) had no special knowledge of the Balkans.

savoir vivre /savwar vivr/ *noun phrase* M18 French (literally, 'know how to live'). Knowledge of the world and the ways of society, ability to conduct oneself well; worldly wisdom, sophistication.

sayonara /sʌɪə'nɑːrə/ *interjection* L19 Japanese (literally, 'if it be so'). Goodbye. *Colloquial, chiefly United States*.

sayyid /'seɪjɪd/ *noun* (also **saiyid, syed**, and other variants, **Sayyid**) M17 Arabic (= lord, prince). A Muslim claiming descent from Muhammad, especially through Husayn, a grandson of the prophet.

■ In Muslim countries, also as a respectful form of address.

sc. abbreviation of SCILICET.

scagliola /skal'jəʊlə/ *noun* M18 Italian (*scagli(u)ola* diminutive of *scaglia* scale, chip of marble). Imitation marble or other stone, made of plaster mixed with glue and dyes which is then painted or polished.

scald variant of SKALD.

scaloppine /ˌskalə(ʊ)'piːneɪ/ noun (also anglicized as **scallopini** /ˌskalə(ʊ)'piːniː/) M20 Italian (plural of *scaloppina* diminutive of *scaloppa* escalope). (In Italian cooking) a dish consisting of thin, boneless slices of meat (especially veal) sautéed or fried.

scampi /'skampi/ noun plural (also treated as *singular*; in sense 1 singular **scampo** /'skampəʊ/) E19 Italian (plural of *scampo*). **1** Norway lobsters. **2** A dish of these lobsters, usually fried in breadcrumbs or in a sauce. Usually treated as *singular*.

scarabaeus /ˌskarə'biːəs/ noun plural **scarabaei** /ˌskarə'biːʌɪ/ L16 Latin (= beetle: cf. Greek *karabos* horned beetle). **1** *Entomology* A scarabaeid beetle. Now only as modern Latin genus name. **2** *Antiquities* An ancient Egyptian amulet or seal in the form of a beetle with symbols on its flat underside, a scarab.

scenario /sɪ'nɑːrɪəʊ/ noun plural **scenarios** L19 Italian (from Latin *scena* scene). **1** A written outline of a film, novel, or stage work giving details of the plot and individual scenes. **2** A postulated sequence or development of events. **3** A setting, in particular for a work of art or literature.

> **2** 1996 *New Scientist* Once the current crisis is over, the most important question for the government will be why it never planned for a worst-case scenario when the risks of BSE were first raised in 1986.

scène à faire /sɛn a fɛr/ noun phrase plural **scènes à faire** (pronounced same) L19 French (literally, 'scene for action'). *Theatrical* The most important scene in a play or opera.

Schadenfreude /'ʃɑːd(ə)nfrɔɪdə/ noun (also **schadenfreude**) L19 German (from *Schaden* harm + *Freude* joy). Pleasure derived by someone from another person's misfortune.

> 1995 *Times* In a lifelong personal effort not to become a sour old besom, I fight very hard against Schadenfreude and its complement, Saki's 'natural displeasure at the good fortune of a friend'.

schalet /'ʃalɪt/, /ʃa'lɛt/ noun M20 Yiddish (*shalent*, *shalet* variant of *tsholnt* cholent). **1** CHOLENT. **2** A Jewish baked fruit pudding.

schappe /ʃap/, /'ʃapə/ noun L19 German (= silk waste). A fabric or yarn made from waste silk.

schema /'skiːmə/ noun plural **schemata** /'skiːmətə/, **schemas** L18 German (from Greek *skhēma*, *skhēmat-* form, figure). **1** A representation of a plan or theory in the form of an outline or model. **2** *Logic* A syllogistic figure. **3** In Kantian philosophy, a conception of what is common to all members of a class; a general or essential type or form.

schemozzle variant of SHEMOZZLE.

scherzando /skɛːt'sandəʊ/ adverb, adjective, & noun E19 Italian (= joking, from *scherzare* to joke, from SCHERZO). *Music* **A** adverb & adjective (Especially as a direction) in a playful manner. **B** noun plural **scherzandos**, **scherzandi** /skɛːt'sandi/. A movement or passage marked to be played playfully.

scherzo /'skɛːtsəʊ/ noun plural **scherzos**, **scherzi** /'skɛːtsi/ M19 Italian (literally, 'sport, jest'). *Music* A vigorous, light, or playful composition, typically comprising a movement in a symphony or sonata.

> *attributive* 1996 *Times* This is not to say that Ozick doesn't go at all her subjects with anything less energetic than a scherzo tempo...

schlemiel, **Schlemihl** /ʃlə'miːl/ noun (also **schle-mihl**, **Schlemihl**) L19 German (*Schlemihl*). An awkward or clumsy person; a foolish or unlucky person. *Colloquial*.

> ■ The word may ultimately be connected with the biblical *Shelumiel*, head of the tribe of Simeon (Numbers 1:6), who, according to the Talmud, came to an unfortunate end. Modern use of *schlemiel* is influenced by Adelbert von Chamisso's famous tale *Peter Schlemihls wundersame Geschichte* (1814), the eponymous hero of which sells his shadow.

schlenter /'ʃlɛntə/ noun & adjective (also (*Australia and New Zealand*) **slanter** /'slantə/ and other variants) M19 Afrikaans (or Dutch possibly from Dutch *slenter* knavery, trick). **A** noun **1** A counterfeit diamond. *South African.* **2** An illegal or dishonest scheme; a confidence trickster. *Australian and*

New Zealand colloquial. **B** *adjective* Dishonest, crooked; counterfeit, fake. *Australian, New Zealand,* and *South African colloquial.*

■ The history of this word is obscure; the likelihood is that the Australian and New Zealand usages derive from South African English, but the route of the borrowing is uncertain. In Australia and New Zealand the most common spelling is now *slanter*, presumably under the influence of *slant* (i.e. crooked).

schlep /ʃlɛp/ *noun* 1 M20 Yiddish (abbreviation). A SCHLEPPER. *United States colloquial.*

schlep /ʃlɛp/ *noun* 2 M20 Yiddish (probably from German *schleppen* to drag). A tedious or difficult journey. *Chiefly United States colloquial.*

schlep /ʃlɛp/ *verb* (also **schlepp;** inflected *-pp-*) E20 Yiddish (*shlepn* from German *schleppen* to drag). **1** *transitive verb* Haul, carry, drag. **2** *intransitive verb* Go or move reluctantly or with effort. *Colloquial.*

schlepper /'ʃlɛpə/ *noun* M20 Yiddish (as preceding). A person of little worth; a fool; a hanger-on. *United States colloquial.*

schlimazel /ʃlɪ'mɒz(ə)l/ *noun* (also **shlimazel, schlimazl**) M20 Yiddish (from Middle High German *slim* crooked ⊦ Hebrew *mazzāl* luck). A consistently unlucky or accident-prone person. *Chiefly United States colloquial.*

schlock /ʃlɒk/ *noun & adjective* E20 Yiddish (apparently from *shlak* apoplectic stroke, *shlog* wretch, untidy person, apoplectic stroke, from *shlogn* to strike). **A** *noun* Cheap, shoddy, or defective goods; inferior material, trash. **B** *adjective* Cheap, inferior, trashy.

■ Colloquial and chiefly North American.

A 1996 *Times Silver Lake* is a fascinating hybrid: certainly not an opera, but . . . not quite a musical either, at least not the escapist schlock that the term 'musical' so often suggests nowadays.

schlong /ʃlɒŋ/ *noun* M20 Yiddish (*shlang,* from Middle High German *slange* (German *Schlange*) snake). The penis. Also, a

contemptible person. *United States slang.*

schloss /ʃlɒs/ *noun* E19 German. A castle, *especially,* one in Germany or Austria.

1995 *Spectator* On the way we had a glimpse of Glamis Castle . . . [a] charming *schloss,* turreted and stucco'd . . .

schlub /ʃlʌb/ *noun* (also **shlub**) M20 Yiddish (perhaps from Polish *żłób* blockhead). A talentless, unattractive, or boorish person, an oaf. *United States slang.*

schmaltz /ʃmɔːlts/, /ʃmalts/ *noun & verb* M20 Yiddish (from German *Schmalz* dripping, lard). **A** *noun* Sentimentality, emotionalism; excessively sentimental music, writing, drama, etc. *Colloquial.* **B** *transitive verb* Impart a sentimental atmosphere to; play (music) in a sentimental manner. Frequently followed by *up. Colloquial.*

A 1995 *Spectator* This orgy of smug schmalz starts with Doris's dad dropping dead in church, presumably having seen the rest of the show in rehearsal . . .

schmatte /'ʃmatə/ *noun* (also **shmatte**) L20 Yiddish (*schmatte,* from Poland *szmata* rag). A rag; a ragged or shabby garment. *United States colloquial.*

schmear /ʃmɪə/ *noun* (also **schmeer, shmeer,** or **shmear**) M20 Yiddish (*schmirn* to flatter, grease, smear: cf. German *schmieren* smear). Bribery, corruption, flattery.

■ North American colloquial. Often in the phrase *the whole schmear* meaning 'everything (possible)'.

1969 E. Stewart *Heads* Why couldn't you burrow around and ferret out the whole shmear yourself?

schmooze /ʃmuːz/, /ʃmuːs/ *noun & verb* M20 Yiddish (*schmues* chat, gossip from Hebrew *šĕmū'ōṯ* plural of *šĕmū'āh* rumour). **A** *noun* Chat; gossip; a long and intimate conversation. *Chiefly North American colloquial.* **B** **1** *intransitive verb* Talk intimately and cosily; gossip. **2** *transitive verb* Talk in an intimate and cosy manner to someone, typically in order to manipulate them. *Chiefly North American colloquial.*

schmuck /ʃmʌk/ *noun* L19 Yiddish (*shmok* penis). A foolish or contemptible person; an idiot.

■ North American slang. *Schmo* is a more recent (M20) alternative.

schnapps /ʃnaps/ *noun* (also **schnaps**) E19 German (*Schnaps* dram of drink, liquor (especially gin) from Low German, Dutch *snaps* gulp, mouthful, from *snappen* to seize, snatch, snap). A strong alcoholic drink resembling gin.

■ The Dutch, Danish, and Swedish word *snaps* (M19) is less common in English.

schnitzel /ˈʃnɪts(ə)l/ *noun* M19 German. A veal cutlet.

■ Especially in *Wiener* (or *Vienna*) *schnitzel*, a veal cutlet coated with egg and breadcrumbs and fried.

schnook /ʃnʊk/ *noun* M20 German or Yiddish (perhaps from German *Schnucke* a small sheep, or Yiddish *shnuk* snout). A dupe, a sucker; a fool. *North American colloquial*.

schnorrer /ˈʃnɒrə/ *noun* L19 Yiddish (variant of German *Schnurrer*, from *schnurren* (slang) go begging). A beggar, a layabout, a scrounger. Chiefly *United States*.

schnozz /ʃnɒz/ *noun* M20 Yiddish (*shnoytz* from German *Schnauze* snout). The nose; a nostril.

■ North American slang. The Yiddish diminutive form of *shnoytz*, *shnoytzl*, has given rise to *schnozzle* /ˈʃnɒz(ə)l/ (M20), also a slang word for 'nose'.

scholium /ˈskəʊlɪəm/ *noun* plural **scholia** /ˈskəʊlɪə/ M16 Modern Latin (from Greek *skholion* from *skholē* learned discussion). An explanatory note or comment, *especially* one made by an ancient commentator on a classical text.

■ Generally used in the plural, but in the singular the Greek ending *-ion* (L16) is also found.

schottische /ʃɒˈtiːʃ/, /ˈʃɒtɪʃ/ *noun* M19 German ((*der*) *Schottische(tanz)* (the) Scottish (dance)). **1** A dance resembling a slow polka; a piece of music for this dance. **2** (*Highland Schottische*) A lively dance resembling the Highland fling.

schtum variant of SHTUM.

schtup variant of SHTUP.

schuss /ʃʊs/ *noun & verb* M20 German (literally, 'a shot'). **A** *noun* A straight downhill run on skis; the slope on which such a run is executed. Also *transferred*, a rapid downward slide. **B** *verb* **1** *transitive verb* Ski straight down (a slope etc.); cover (a certain distance) by means of a schuss. **2** *intransitive verb* Ski straight down a slope. Also *transferred*, move rapidly (especially downwards).

schwa /ʃwɑː/ *noun* (also **shwa**) L19 German. *Phonetics* The neutral central vowel sound /ə/, typically occurring in unstressed syllables, as the final syllable of 'sofa' and the first syllable of 'along'. Also, the symbol '/ə/' representing this sound, as in the International Phonetic Alphabet.

scilicet /ˈsʌɪlɪsɛt/, /ˈskiːlɪkɛt/ *adverb* LME Latin (from *scire licet* one is permitted to know; cf. VIDELICET). That is to say; namely.

■ Used to introduce a word to be supplied or an explanation of an ambiguity and generally abbreviated to *scil.* or *sc.*

scintilla /sɪnˈtɪlə/ *noun* L17 Latin. A tiny trace or spark of a specified quality or feeling.

1996 *Times* ... serious thinkers in sharp suits ... convene around shiny rosewood tables, on both sides of the Atlantic, to thrash out the last scintilla of marketing policy.

scirocco variant of SIROCCO.

scordatura /ˌskɔrdaˈtura/ *noun* plural **scordature** /ˌskɔrdaˈture/ L19 Italian (from *scordare* to be out of tune). *Music* The technique of altering the normal tuning of a stringed instrument to produce particular effects for certain pieces or passages; an instance of this.

scoria /ˈskɔːrɪə/ *noun* plural **scoriae** /ˈskɔːrɪiː/, (*rare*) **scorias** LME Latin (from Greek *skōria* refuse, from *skōr* dung). **1** *Geology* Basaltic lava ejected as fragments from a volcano, typically with a frothy texture. **2** Slag separated from molten metal during smelting.

■ Originally used in sense 2. The geological term dates from the late 18th century.

scorzonera /ˌskɔːzə(ʊ)ˈnɪərə/ noun E17 Italian (from *scorzone* from Proto-Romance alteration of medieval Latin *curtio(n)*-poisonous snake, against whose venom the plant may have been regarded as an antidote). Any of various plants constituting the genus *Scorzonera*; especially *S. hispanica*, cultivated in Europe for its tapering purple-brown edible root. Also, the root of *S. hispanica*, eaten as a vegetable.

scotia /ˈskəʊʃə/ noun M16 Latin (from Greek *skotia* from *skotos* darkness (with reference to the dark shadow within the cavity)). *Architecture* A concave moulding, especially at the base of a column.

scriptorium /skrɪpˈtɔːrɪəm/ noun plural **scriptoria** /skrɪpˈtɔːrɪə/, **scriptoriums** L18 Medieval Latin (from *script-* past participial stem of *scribere* to write). A room set apart for writing, especially one in a monastery where manuscripts were copied.

scrutator /skruːˈteɪtə/ noun L16 Latin (from *scrutat-* past participial stem of *scrutari* to search or examine). **1** A person who examines or investigates something or someone. **2** A person whose official duty it is to examine or investigate something closely; *especially*, a scrutineer at an election.

scungille /skunˈdʒɪlle/ noun plural **scungilli** /skunˈdʒɪlli/ M20 Italian (dialect *scunciglio*, probably alteration of Italian *conchiglia* seashell, shellfish). A mollusc, a conch; *especially* the meat of a mollusc eaten as a delicacy.

sebum /ˈsiːbəm/ noun L19 Modern Latin (use of Latin *sebum* suet, grease, tallow). *Physiology* The oily secretion of the sebaceous glands which lubricates and protects the hair and skin.

sec /sɛk/ adjective ME French (from Latin *siccus*). (Of wine) dry.

secateur /sɛkəˈtəː, ˈsɛkətəː/ noun M19 French (*sécateur*, irregularly from Latin *secare* to cut + *-ateur*). *singular* and (usually) in *plural* A pair of pruning clippers with crossed blades, for use with one hand. Also *pair of secateurs*.

secco /ˈsɛko/ noun & adjective M19 Italian (from Latin *siccus* dry; in sense A.1 elliptical for *fresco secco*, literally, 'dry fresco'). **A** noun plural **seccos 1** The process or technique of painting on dry plaster with colours mixed with water. **2** *Music* (A) RECITATIVO secco. **B** adjective *Music* (Of recitative) plain, lacking or having only sparse instrumental accompaniment.

secretaire /ˌsɛkrɪˈtɛː/ noun L18 French (*secrétaire* from late Latin *secretarius* confidential officer, use as noun of adjective from Latin *secretum* secret). A small writing desk with drawers and pigeon-holes; a bureau.

secretariat /ˌsɛkrəˈtɛːrɪət/ noun (also **Secretariat**) E19 French (*secrétariat* from medieval Latin *secretariatus*, from as SECRETAIRE). The administrative and executive department of a government or similar organization; such a department's staff or premises.

secundus /sɪˈkʌndəs/ adjective E19 Latin (= second). Designating the second of two or more pupils of the same surname to enter a school. Cf. PRIMUS adjective 2, TERTIUS.
■ Appended to a surname and used especially in public schools.

sederunt /sɪˈdɪərənt/ noun E17 Latin (= there were sitting (the following persons), use as noun of 3rd person plural perfect indicative of *sedere* to sit). (In Scotland) a sitting of a deliberative or judicial body, especially an ecclesiastical assembly.

sedile /sɪˈdʌɪli/ noun plural **sedilia** /sɪˈdɪlɪə/ L18 Latin (= seat, from *sedere* to sit). *Ecclesiastical* Each of a series of usually canopied and decorated stone seats, usually three in number, placed on or recessed into the south side of the choir near the altar for use by the clergy. Usually in *plural*.

segue /ˈsɛgweɪ/ verb & noun M18 Italian (3rd person singular present indicative of *seguire* to follow). *Music* **A** intransitive verb (In music and film) move without interruption from one piece of music or scene to another. Frequently followed by *into*. **B** *noun* An uninterrupted transition from one piece of music or film scene to another.

Sehnsucht /ˈzeːnzʊxt/ *noun* M19 German. Yearning, wistful longing.

seicento /seɪˈtʃɛntəʊ/ *noun* (also **Seicento**) E20 Italian (= six hundred). The style of Italian art and literature of the 17th century.

■ Shortened from *mille seicento* '1600', used with reference to the years 1600–99.

seiche /seɪʃ/ *noun* M19 Swiss French (perhaps from German *Seiche* sinking (of water)). *Geography* A temporary disturbance or oscillation in the water level of a lake or partially enclosed body of water, resembling a tide, caused especially by abrupt changes in atmospheric conditions or by small earth tremors.

seif /siːf/, /seɪf/ *noun* (also **sif**) E20 Arabic (*sayf*, literally, 'sword' (because of the shape)). *Geography* A sand dune in the form of a long narrow ridge parallel to the direction of the prevailing wind. Also *seif dune*.

seigneur /seɪˈnjəː/, *foreign* /sɛɲr/ (*plural* same) *noun* (also **Seigneur**) L16 Old and Modern French (from Latin *senior* comparative of *senex* old). A feudal lord, the lord of a manor. Chiefly *historical*.

seiza /ˈseɪzə/ *noun* M20 Japanese (from *sei* correct + *za* sitting). An upright kneeling position which is the Japanese traditional formal way of sitting and is used in meditation and as part of the preparation in martial arts.

Sekt /zɛkt/ *noun* E20 German. A German sparkling white wine.

selva /ˈsɛlvə/ *noun* M19 Spanish or Portuguese (from Latin *silva* wood). A tract of land covered by dense equatorial forest, especially in the Amazon basin. Usually in *plural*.

sempervivum /ˌsɛmpəˈvʌɪvəm/ *noun* (formerly anglicized as **sempervive**) L16 Latin (neuter of *sempervivus* everliving). Any of various succulent plants constituting the genus *Sempervivum*,

of the stonecrop family; *especially* houseleek, *S. tectorum*.

semplice /ˈsɛmplɪtʃi/ *adverb & adjective* M18 Italian (= simple). *Music* (Especially as a direction) in a simple style of performance.

sempre /ˈsɛmpreɪ/ *adverb* E19 Italian. *Music* (Especially as a direction) always, still, throughout: *sempre forte*.

senex /ˈsɛnɛks/ *noun* plural **senes** /ˈsɛneɪs/ L19 Latin (= old man). (In literature, especially comedy) an old man as a stock figure.

senhor /sɛnˈjɔː/, *foreign* /seˈɲor/ *noun* L18 Portuguese (from Latin *senior* comparative of *senex* old). (In Portuguese-speaking countries) a man (often used as a title or polite form of address).

senhora /sɛnˈjɔːrə/, *foreign* /seˈɲora/ *noun* E19 Portuguese (feminine of SEN-HOR). (In Portuguese-speaking countries) a woman, especially a married woman (often used as a title or polite form of address).

senhorita /sɛnjəˈriːtə/, /seɲoˈrita/ *noun* L19 Portuguese (diminutive of preceding). (In Portuguese-speaking countries) a young woman, especially an unmarried one (often used as a title or polite form of address).

señor /sɛnˈjɔː/ *foreign* /seˈɲor/ *noun* plural **señores** /sɛnˈjɔːrɪz/, *foreign* /seˈɲores/ E17 Spanish (from Latin *senior* comparative of *senex* old). A title or form of address used of or to a Spanish-speaking man, corresponding to *Mr* or *Sir*.

señora /sɛnˈjɔːrə/, *foreign* /seˈɲora/ *noun* L16 Spanish (feminine of SEÑOR). A title or form of address used of or to a Spanish-speaking woman, corresponding to *Mrs* or *Madam*.

señorita /sɛnjəˈriːtə/, *foreign* /seɲoˈrita/ *noun* E19 Spanish (diminutive of preceding). A title or form of address used of or to a Spanish-speaking unmarried woman, corresponding to *Miss*.

sensei /sɛnˈseɪ/ *noun* L19 Japanese (from *sen* previous + *sei* birth). (In martial arts) a teacher, an instructor.

sensorium /sɛnˈsɔːrɪəm/ *noun* plural **sensoria** /sɛnˈsɔːrɪə/, **sensoriums** M17 Late Latin (from Latin *sens-* past participial stem of *sentire* to feel). The sensory apparatus or faculties considered as a whole.

sensu lato /ˌsɛnsuː ˈlɑːtəʊ/ *adverb phrase* M20 Latin. (Of a scientific etc. term) in the broad sense. Opposite of SENSU STRICTO.

sensu stricto /ˌsɛnsuː ˈstrɪktəʊ/ *adverb phrase* M19 Latin (= in the restricted sense). (Of a scientific etc. term) strictly speaking, in the narrow sense. Opposite of SENSU LATO.

■ Also latterly (M20) as STRICTO SENSU.

sephira /ˈsɛfɪrɑː/ *noun* plural **sephiroth** /ˈsɛfɪrəʊθ/ M16 Hebrew (*sĕp̄īrāh* (plural *sĕp̄īrōt*), from *sāp̄ar* to number). (In the philosophy of the Jewish Kabbalah) each of the ten attributes or emanations surrounding the infinite, by means of which the infinite relates to the finite. Usually in *plural*.

seppuku /sɛˈpuːkuː/ *noun* L19 Japanese (from *setsu* to cut + *fuku* abdomen). HARA-KIRI.

sepsis /ˈsɛpsɪs/ *noun* L19 Greek (*sēpsis*, from *sēpein* to make rotten). *Medicine* The state of being septic; blood-poisoning, especially through infection of a wound.

septennium /sɛpˈtɛnɪəm/ *noun* plural **septennia** /sɛpˈtɛnɪə/, **septenniums** M19 Late Latin for (classical Latin *septuennium*, from Latin *septem* seven + *annus* year). A period of seven years.

septum /ˈsɛptəm/ *noun* plural **septa** /ˈsɛptə/ M17 Latin ((also *saeptum*), from *sepire, saepire* to enclose, from *sepes, saepes* hedge). *Anatomy* and *Biology* A partition separating two chambers, such as that between the nostrils or the chambers of the heart.

sequela /sɪˈkwiːlə/ *noun* plural **sequelae** /sɪˈkwiːliː/ L18 Latin (*sequel(l)ae*, from *sequi* to follow). *Medicine* A condition occurring as the result of a previous disease or injury. Usually in *plural*.

sequitur /ˈsɛkwɪtə/ *noun* M19 Latin (= it follows). An inference or conclusion which follows logically from the premises; a logical deduction, a logical remark. Cf. NON SEQUITUR.

serac /ˈsɛrak/, /səˈrak/ *noun* M19 Swiss French (*sérac*, originally the name of a compact white cheese, probably from Latin *serum* whey). A pinnacle or ridge of ice on the surface of a glacier where crevasses intersect.

seraglio /sɛˈrɑːlɪəʊ/, /sɪˈreɪlɪəʊ/ *noun* plural **seraglios** L16 Italian (*serraglio*, from Turkish *saray* palace, mansion, from Persian, with assimilation to Italian *serraglio* cage (from medieval Latin *serraculum* diminutive of Latin *sera* bolt)). **1** The women's apartments (harem) in a Muslim palace. **b** The women of a harem. **2** *History* A Turkish palace, especially that of the Sultan in Constantinople.

serai /səˈrʌɪ/ *noun* E17 Turkish (*saray* palace, mansion, from Persian: cf. preceding). (In various south-west Asian countries) a building for the accommodation of travellers, a caravanserai.

serang /səˈraŋ/ *noun* L18 Anglo-Indian (Persian and Urdu *sar-hang* commander, from *sar* head + *hang* authority). An Asian head of a Lascar crew. *Indian.*

serape /sɛˈrɑːpeɪ/, *foreign* /seˈrape/ *noun* (also **sarape** /saˈrɑːpeɪ/) E19 Mexican Spanish. A shawl or blanket worn as a cloak by people from Latin America.

seriatim /ˌsɪərɪˈeɪtɪm/ *adverb* L15 Medieval Latin (from as Latin *series* chain, row, series (from *serere* to join, connect) + *-atim* after Latin *gradatim, literatim*). Taking one subject after another in regular order; point by point: *it is proposed to deal with these matters seriatim.*

serin /ˈsɛrɪn/ *noun* M16 French (= canary, of unknown origin). Originally, a canary. Now, any bird of the same genus, *especially* (more fully *serin finch*) *Serinus serinus*, a small yellow European finch.

sertão /ˈsɛːtɑːʊ/ *noun* plural **sertãos** /ˈsɛːtɑːʊʃ/ E19 Portuguese. *Geography* An arid barren region of scrub in Brazil; the remote interior of Brazil.

serum /'sɪərəm/ *noun* plural **sera** /'sɪərə/, **serums** L17 Latin (= whey, watery fluid). **1** An amber-coloured protein-rich liquid which separates out when blood coagulates. **2** *Medicine* The blood serum of an animal used to provide immunity to a pathogen or toxin by inoculation or as a diagnostic agent.

serviette /sə:vɪ'ɛt/ *noun* L15 Old and Modern French (= towel, napkin, from *servir* to serve). A table napkin.

sestina /sɛ'sti:nə/ *noun* M19 Italian (from *sesto* from Latin *sextus* sixth). A form of rhymed or unrhymed poem of six stanzas of six lines and a concluding triplet in which the same six words at the line ends occur in each stanza in six different sequences.

se-tenant /sətɒnɑ̃/ *adjective* E20 French (literally, 'holding together'). *Philately* (Of postage stamps, especially of different denominations or designs) joined together as when printed.

settecento /sɛtɪ'tʃɛntəʊ/ *noun* E20 Italian (= seven hundred). The 18th century in Italy; the style of Italian art, architecture, music, etc., of this period.
■ Shortened from *mil settecento* '1700', used with reference to the years 1700–99.

seviche variant of CEVICHE.

sevruga /sɛv'ru:gə/ *noun* L16 Russian (*sevryuga*). A sturgeon of the Caspian and Black Seas; caviar obtained from this fish.

Sezession /ze,tsɛ'sio:n/ *noun* plural **Sezessien** /ze'tsɛsiən/ E20 German (= secession). *Art* A radical art movement that started in Vienna and was contemporaneous with and related to ART NOUVEAU.

sf abbreviation of SFORZANDO (*musical direction*).

sforzando /sfɔ:'tsandəʊ/ *adjective, adverb, & noun* E19 Italian (present participle of *sforzare* to use force). *Music* **A** *adjective & adverb* E19 (Especially as a direction) with sudden emphasis or loudness. Abbreviated to *sf, sfz*. **B** *noun* plural

sforzandi /sfɔ:'tsandi/, **sforzandos** A sudden marked emphasis.

sforzato /sfɔ:'tsa:təʊ/ *adjective, adverb, & noun* plural of noun **sforzati** /sfɔ:'tsa:ti/, **sforzatos** E19 Italian (past participle of *sforzare* to use force). *Music* SFORZANDO.

sfumato /sfu'mato/, /sfʊ'ma:təʊ/ *noun* M19 Italian (past participle of *sfumare* to shade off, from s- ex- + *fumare* to smoke). *Painting* The technique of softening outlines and allowing tones and colours to shade gradually into one another; an indistinct outline or hazy form produced in this way.

sfz abbreviation of SFORZANDO (*musical direction*).

sgraffito /sgra'fi:təʊ/ *noun* plural **sgraffiti** /sgra'fi:ti/ M18 Italian (from *sgraffiare* to scratch away: s- representing Latin ex- ex- + (later) GRAFFITO). A form of decoration or design made by scratching through wet plaster on a wall or through slip on pottery to reveal a different colour below.

shabti /'ʃabti/ *noun* (also **ushabti** /u:'ʃabti/) plural **shabtiu** /'ʃabtɪu:/, **shabtis** M19 Egyptian (*šbty* answerer). *Egyptology* A figurine of a dead person, made of faience, stone, wood, etc., and placed with the body in the tomb to substitute for the dead person in any work required in the afterlife.

shabu-shabu /,ʃabu:'ʃabu:/ *noun* L20 Japanese. A Japanese dish of pieces of thinly sliced beef or pork cooked quickly with vegetables in boiling water and then dipped in sauce.

shadoof /ʃə'du:f/ *noun* (also **shaduf**) M19 Arabic ((Egyptian) *šādūf*). A device consisting of a pivoted rod or pole with a bucket at one end and a counterbalancing weight at the other, used especially in Egypt for raising water.

shah /ʃɑ:/ *noun* (also (as title) **Shah**) M16 Persian (*šāh* from Old Persian *xšāyaθiya* king). *History* A title of the former monarch of Iran (Persia).

shahada /ʃə'hɑ:də/ *noun* (also **shahadah**) L19 Arabic (*šahāda* testimony, evidence). The Muslim profession of faith.

■ The *shahada—Lā ilāha illā (A)llāh, Muḥammadun rasūl Allāh* 'there is no god but Allah, and Muhammad is the messenger of Allah'—forms part of the regular call to prayer.

shahid /ʃəˈhiːd/ *noun* (also **shaheed**) L19 Arabic (*šahīd* witness, martyr). A Muslim martyr.

shaikh variant of SHEIKH.

shako /ˈʃeɪkəʊ/, /ˈʃakəʊ/ *noun* plural **shakos** E19 French (*schako* from Hungarian *csákó* probably from German *Zacken* peak, point, spike). A cylindrical or conical military hat with a peak and a plume or pompom.

shakudo /ˈʃakudəʊ/ *noun* M19 Japanese (from *shaku* red + *dō* copper). A Japanese alloy of copper and gold, typically having a blue patina.

shakuhachi /ˌʃakuˈhɑːtʃi/ *noun* L19 Japanese. A Japanese bamboo flute, held vertically when played.

shalom /ʃəˈlɒm/, *foreign* /ʃaˈlɔm/ *interjection & noun* L19 Hebrew (*šālōm* peace). Used as a salutation by Jews at meeting or parting, meaning 'peace'; an utterance of 'shalom'.

shalwar variant of SALWAR.

shaman /ˈʃamən/ *noun* L17 German (*Schamane*, Russian *shaman* from Tungusian *šaman*). A person regarded as having access to, and influence in, the world of good and evil spirits, especially among some peoples of northern Asia and North America. Typically such people enter a trance state during a ritual, and practise divination and healing.

shamba /ˈʃambə/ *noun* L19 Kiswahili. (In East Africa) a cultivated plot of ground. Also, a farm, a plantation.

shamisen variant of SAMISEN.

shanti /ˈʃɑːnti/ *interjection & noun* L19 Sanskrit (*śānti* peace, tranquillity). *Hinduism* Peace; peace be with you.

■ Usually repeated three times at the end of an Upanishad for the peace of the soul.

sharif /ʃəˈriːf/ *noun* (also **shereef, sherif**) L16 Arabic (*šarīf* noble, high-born). **1** A descendant of Muhammad through his daughter Fatima. **2** A Muslim ruler, magistrate, or religious leader.

shashlik /ˈʃaʃlɪk/ *noun* E20 Russian (*shashlyk* from Crimean Turkish *şişlik* from *şiş* skewer; cf. SHISH KEBAB). (In Asia and eastern Europe) a kebab of mutton and garnishings, frequently served on a skewer.

shauri /ˈʃaʊriː/ *noun* plural **shauri(e)s** E20 Kiswahili (from Arabic *šūrā* consultation, deliberation, counsel). (In East Africa) a debate, argument, or problematic issue.

1970 *Kenya Farmer* Often he can solve a problem by calling a meeting of the staff and obtaining their views and suggestions, not only on their personal *shauris*, but also on improvements in sales and service.

shchi /ʃtʃi/ *noun* E19 Russian. A Russian cabbage soup.

shebeen /ʃɪˈbiːn/ *noun* L18 Irish ((Anglo-Irish form of) *síbín*, of unknown origin). **1** (Especially in Ireland, Scotland, and South Africa) an unlicensed establishment or private house selling alcohol and typically regarded as slightly disreputable. **2** (In South Africa) an informal licensed drinking place in a township.

sheikh /ʃeɪk/, /ʃiːk/ *noun* (also **shaikh, sheik**) L16 Arabic (ultimately from Arabic *šayḵ* sheikh, old man, elder, from *šāḵa* to be or grow old). **1** (also **Sheikh**) An Arab leader, in particular the chief or head of an Arab tribe, family, or village. Also, a title of respect. **2** A leader of a Muslim community or organization.

■ In the 1920s the word (chiefly with the spelling *sheik*) came to mean a strong, romantic lover. This derived from the novel *The Sheik* (1919) by E. M. Hull, filmed in 1921 as *The Sheikh*, starring Rudolph Valentino as the desert hero who kidnaps the English girl whose lover he becomes.

shekel /ˈʃɛk(ə)l/ *noun* M16 Hebrew (*šeqel*, from *šāqal* to weigh). **1** *History* A silver coin and unit of weight used in the ancient Israel and the Middle East. **2** In *plural* Money; wealth. *Colloquial.* **3** The basic unit of currency of modern Israel.

■ In sense 2 often in colloquial phrases such as *bringing* (or *raking*) *in the shekels* meaning 'making a lot of money quickly and easily' (see quotation).
2 1996 *Spectator* They [sc. oysters] are sold all year round for some reason, which I think is a mistake, but doubtless it brings in the shekels.

shemozzle /ʃɪ'mɒz(ə)l/ *noun slang* (also **schemozzle**) L19 Yiddish (probably from as SCHLIMAZEL). A state of chaos and confusion; a muddle.

shereef, sherif variant of SHARIF.

sherpa /'ʃə:pə/ *noun* plural **sherpas**, same M19 Tibetan (*sharpa* inhabitant of an Eastern country). **1** (*Sherpa*) A member of a Himalayan people living on the borders of Nepal and Tibet, renowned for their skill in mountaineering. **2** (*sherpa*) A mountain guide or porter; an official who undertakes preparatory work prior to a summit conference.

shiatsu /ʃɪ'atsu:/ *noun* M20 Japanese (literally, 'finger pressure'). A kind of therapy of Japanese origin based on the same principles as acupuncture, in which pressure is applied with the thumbs and palms to certain points of the body.

shibboleth /'ʃɪbəlɛθ/ *noun* M17 Hebrew (*šibbōlet* ear of corn, stream in flood, used as a test of nationality for the difficulty for foreigners of pronouncing /θ/ (see Judges 12:4–6)). **1** A word used as a test for detecting people from another district or country by their pronunciation; a word or sound very difficult for foreigners to pronounce correctly. **b** A peculiarity of pronunciation or accent indicative of a person's origin; the distinctive mode of speech of a profession, class, etc. **c** A custom, habit, style of dressing, etc., distinguishing a particular class or group of people. **2** A longstanding custom, principle, or belief held (especially unreflectingly) by or associated with a particular group or class of people. Also, a received wisdom; a truism, a platitude.

shidduch /'ʃɪdəx/ *noun* L19 Yiddish (from Hebrew *šiddūk* negotiation, especially of an arranged marriage). A Jewish arranged marriage.

shiitake /ʃɪ'ta:keɪ/, /'ʃɪɪta:keɪ/ *noun* L19 Japanese (from *shii* a kind of oak + *take* mushroom). An edible mushroom, *Lentinus edodes*, cultivated in Japan and China on logs of various oaks and allied trees. Also *shiitake mushroom*.

shikar /ʃɪ'ka:/ *noun & verb* E17 Persian and Urdu (*šikār*). **A** *noun* Hunting as a sport. **B** *verb* Inflected -rr-. **1** *intransitive verb* Hunt animals for sport. **2** *transitive verb* Hunt (animals).

■ Originating and used almost solely in the Indian subcontinent, the word often occurs in the phrase *on shikar* 'on a hunting expedition'.

shikari /ʃɪ'ka:ri:/ *noun* E19 Urdu (from Persian *šikārī*: see SHIKAR). (In the Indian subcontinent) a hunter (either European or Indian); an expert guide or tracker.

shikhara /'ʃɪkhərə/ *noun* (also **sikhara**) E19 Sanskrit (*śikhara* peak, spire). A pyramidal tower on a Hindu temple, sometimes having convexly curved sides.

shiksa /'ʃɪksə/ *noun & adjective* L19 Yiddish (*shikse* from Hebrew *šiqṣāh* from *šeqeṣ* detested thing + feminine suffix -āh). **A** *noun* (Used especially by Jews) a gentile girl or woman. **B** *attributive* or as *adjective* (Of a girl or woman) gentile. *Derogatory*.

shish kebab /ʃɪʃ kɪ'bab/ *noun* E20 Turkish (*şiş kebab*, from *şiş* skewer + *kebab* roast meat; cf. SHASHLIK). A dish consisting of pieces of marinated meat (usually lamb) and vegetables grilled and served on skewers.

shiva /'ʃɪvə/ *noun* (also **shivah**) L19 Hebrew (*šiḇʻāh* seven). *Judaism* A period of seven days' formal mourning for the dead, beginning immediately after the funeral. Frequently in *sit shiva*, observe this period.

shivaree variant of CHARIVARI.

shlub variant of SCHLUB.

shmatte variant of SCHMATTE.

shmear, shmeer variants of SCHMEAR.

shochet /ˈʃɒxɛt/ *noun* plural **shochetim** /ˈʃɒxɛtɪm/ L19 Hebrew (*šōḥēṭ* present participle of *šāḥaṭ* to slaughter). A person officially certified as competent to kill cattle and poultry in the manner prescribed by Jewish law.

shofar /ˈʃəʊfə/ *noun* plural **shofroth** /ˈʃəʊfrəʊt/ M19 Hebrew (*šōp̄ār*, plural *šōp̄ārōṯ*). A ram's-horn trumpet used in Jewish religious ceremonies and in biblical times as a war trumpet.

shogun /ˈʃəʊɡʊn/ *noun* E17 Japanese (*shōgun*, from Chinese *jiāng jūn* general). *History* Any of a succession of hereditary commanders-in-chief of the Japanese army, before 1868 the virtual rulers of Japan.

shoyu /ˈʃəʊjuː/ *noun* E18 Japanese (*shōyu* from Chinese *jiàngyóu* (Wade-Giles *chiangyu*) from *jiàng* bean paste + *yóu* oil). A type of Japanese soy sauce. Also *shoyu sauce*.

shtetl /ˈʃtɛt(ə)l/, /ˈʃteɪt(ə)l/ *noun* plural **shtetlach** /ˈʃtɛt(ə)lɑːx/, **shtetls** M20 Yiddish (= little town, from German *Stadt* town). *History* A small Jewish town or village in eastern Europe.
  1996 *Times* Wiesenthal was born in a *shtetl* in Buczacz in Galicia.

shtick /ʃtɪk/ *noun* (also **shtik**) M20 Yiddish (from German *Stück* piece, play). An attention-getting or theatrical routine, gimmick, or talent.
  1996 *Spectator* Yes, as critics have pointed out, a lot of Carrey's shtick dies even as he utters it . . .

shtum /ʃtʊm/ *adjective & verb* (also **schtum** /ʃtʌm/) M20 Yiddish (from German *stumm* silent). **A** *adjective* Silent, mute; non-communicative. Chiefly in *keep* (or *stay*) *shtum*, refrain from disclosing information etc. **B** *intransitive verb* Be or become quiet and non-communicative, shut *up*.

shtup /ʃtʊp/ *verb & noun* (also **schtup**) M20 Yiddish. **A** *transitive verb* Have sexual intercourse with (someone). **B** *noun* An act of sexual intercourse. *Vulgar slang.*

shufti /ˈʃʊfti/ *noun* (also **shufty**) M20 Arabic (from colloquial Arabic *šuftī* have you seen?, from *šāfa* to see). A look, glance, a reconnoitre, especially a quick one.
  ■ Especially in *take* (or *have*) *a shufti*. Originally military slang, but also more generally used in British colloquial speech.
  1980 R. Adams *Girl in a Swing* Good idea, old boy. I'm game. Let's 'ave a crafty shufti round with that in mind, shall we?

shul /ʃuːl/ *noun* L19 Yiddish (from German *Schule* school). A synagogue.

shura /ˈʃʊərə/ *noun* M20 Arabic (*šūrā* consultation). The Islamic principle of consultation, in particular as applied to government; an Islamic consultative council.

shuriken /ˈʃʊərɪkɛn/ *noun* L20 Japanese (*shuri-ken*, literally, 'dagger in the hand', from *shu* hand + *ri* inside + *ken* sword, blade). A weapon in the form of a star with projecting blades or points, used as a missile in some martial arts.

sic /sɪk/ *adverb* L19 Latin (= so, thus). Used or spelt as written.
  ■ *Sic* is used in brackets after a copied or quoted word that appears odd or erroneous to show that the word is quoted exactly as it stands in the original.

sic et non /ˈsɪk ɛt ˌnɒn/ *noun phrase* E20 Latin (literally, 'yes and no'). *Theology* A method of argument used by medieval theologians, in which contradictory passages of scripture are presented without commentary in order to stimulate readers to resolve the contradictions themselves. Frequently *attributive*.
  ■ *Sic et non* was the title of a work by the twelfth-century French theologian and philosopher Peter Abelard, in which he employed this method, later imitated by other Scholastic philosophers.

siciliana /sɪtʃiˈljana/, /sɪˌtʃɪlɪˈɑːnə/ *noun* plural **siciliane** /sɪtʃiˈljane/, /sɪˌtʃɪlɪˈɑːneɪ/ (also **siciliano** /sɪtʃiˈljano/, /sɪˌtʃɪlɪˈɑːnəʊ/, plural **sicilianos** /sɪˌtʃɪlɪˈɑːnəʊz/, **siciliani** /sɪtʃiˈljani/) E18 Italian (feminine of *Siciliano* Sicilian). *Music* A piece of music for a Sicilian peasant dance, resembling a slow jig; a dance, song, or instrumental piece in 6/8 or 12/8 time, typically in a minor key, and evoking a pastoral mood.

sic transit gloria mundi /sɪk transɪt
glɔːrɪə mʌndi/ *interjection* E17 Latin. Thus
passes the glory of the world.

> ■ This Latin sentence is spoken during
> the coronation of a new Pope, while flax
> is burned to represent the transitoriness
> of earthly glory. It may ultimately derive
> from *O quam cito transit gloria mundi* ('Oh
> how quickly the glory of the world passes
> away') in *De Imitatione Christi* (*c.*1415–24)
> by the Augustinian theologian Thomas à
> Kempis.

siddha /ˈsɪdhə/ *noun* M19 Sanskrit. *Hinduism* An ascetic who has achieved
enlightenment.

Sieg Heil /ziːk ˈhaɪl/ *interjection* M20
German (literally, 'Hail victory'). A victory salute used especially at a political rally originally during the Nazi
regime in Germany.

sierra /sɪˈɛrə/, /sɪˈɛːrə/ *noun plural* **sier-
ras** M16 Spanish (from Latin *serra* saw). A
long mountain range rising in jagged
peaks, especially in Spain and Latin
America.

siesta /sɪˈɛstə/ *noun & verb* M17 Spanish
(from Latin *sexta* (*hora*) sixth hour of the
day). **A** *noun* An afternoon rest or nap,
especially one taken during the hot-
test hours of the day in a hot country.
B *intransitive verb* Take a siesta.

siffleur /siːˈfləː/ *noun* E18 French (from
siffler to whistle). A person who enter-
tains professionally by whistling.

siglum /ˈsɪɡləm/ *noun plural* **sigla**
/ˈsɪɡlə/ E18 Late Latin (*sigla* plural, perhaps
for *singula* neuter plural of *singulus* single). A letter (especially an initial) or
other symbol used as an abbreviation
for a word, proper name, etc., in a
printed text; *Bibliography* such a letter
or symbol used to designate a particular version of a literary text.

sigma /ˈsɪɡmə/ *noun* LME Latin (from
Greek). **1** The eighteenth letter (*Σ*, *σ*,
or, when final, *s*), of the Greek
alphabet, transliterated as 's'. **2** *Physics*
and *Chemistry* Used *attributively* to designate an electron or orbital with zero
angular momentum about an internuclear axis. **3** *Statistics* A (unit of)
standard deviation.

signor /ˈsiːnjɔː/ *noun plural* **signori**
/siːnˈjɔːri/ L16 Italian (reduced form of
signore, from Latin *senior*). A title or form
of address used of or to an Italian-speaking man, corresponding to *Mr* or *sir*.

signora /siːnˈjɔːrə/ *noun* M17 Italian (feminine of SIGNOR). A title or form of
address used of or to an Italian-speaking married woman, corresponding to
Mrs or *madam*.

signorina /ˌsiːnjəˈriːnə/ *noun* E19 Italian
(diminutive of SIGNORA). A title or form
of address used of or to an Italian-
speaking unmarried woman, corresponding to *Miss*.

silenus /saɪˈliːnəs/ *noun* (also **Silenus**)
plural **sileni** /saɪˈliːnaɪ/ E17 Latin (*Silenus*
from Greek *Seilēnos* foster-father of Bacchus and leader of the satyrs). *Greek
Mythology* A woodland spirit, a satyr,
especially one represented as a
bearded old man with the tail and
legs of a horse.

> ■ Earlier (L16) in the anglicized form
> *silen.*

silhouette /ˌsɪluˈɛt/ *noun & verb* L18
French (from Étienne de *Silhouette*
(1709–67), French author and politician).
A *noun* **1** A portrait obtained by
tracing the outline of a profile, head,
or figure, especially by means of its
shadow, and filling in the whole with
black or cutting the shape out of black
paper; a figure or picture drawn or
printed in solid black. **2** The dark
shape and outline of someone or
something visible in restricted light
against a brighter background. **b** The
contour or outline of a garment or a
person's body. **B** *transitive verb* Represent in silhouette, throw up the outline of. Usually in *passive* (followed by
against, *on*).

silo /ˈsaɪləʊ/ *noun plural* **silos** M19 Spanish (from Latin *sirus* from Greek *siros* corn
pit). **1** A pit or underground chamber
used for storing grain, roots, etc.;
specifically one in which green crops
are compressed and preserved for
fodder as silage. Also, a cylindrical
tower or other structure built above
ground for the same purpose. **2** An
underground structure in which a

guided missile is stored and from which it may be fired.

simcha /'sɪmtʃə/, /'sɪmtʃxa/ *noun* M20 Hebrew (*śimḥāh* rejoicing). A Jewish private party or celebration.

simoom /sɪ'muːm/ *noun* (also **simoon** /sɪ'muːn/) L18 Arabic (*samūm*, from *samma* to poison). A hot dry dust-laden wind blowing at intervals in the African and Asian (especially Arabian) deserts.

simpatico /sim'patiko/, /sɪm'patɪkəʊ/ *adjective* (feminine **simpatica** /sim-'patika/, /sɪm'patɪkə/) M19 Spanish (*simpático*, from *simpatía*, or Italian *simpatico* from *simpatia*, both from Latin *sympathia* from Greek *sumpatheia* from *sumpathēs* having a fellow-feeling). **1** Pleasing; likeable; congenial. **2** Having or characterized by shared attributes or interests; compatible.

> **1** 1995 *Oldie* And Fangio was so charming and so *simpatico*, and of course the damage would be paid for...

simplex /'sɪmplɛks/ *adjective & noun* L16 Latin (= single, variant of *simplus* simple, with second element as in *duplex*, *multiplex*, etc.). **A** *adjective* **1** Composed of or characterized by a single part or structure. **2** (Of a communication system, computer circuit, etc.) only allowing transmission of signals in one direction at a time. **B** *noun* A word without an affix; a simple uncompounded word.

simulacrum /sɪmjʊ'leɪkrəm/ *noun* plural **simulacrums**, **simulacra** /sɪmjʊ'leɪkrə/ L16 Latin (from *simulare* to simulate). **1** An image or representation of a person or thing. **2** An unsatisfactory imitation or substitute.

> **2** 1996 *Times* The effort to turn the whole continent into the economic simulacrum of Germany... has instilled pessimism and depression into the peoples of all Europe.

simurg /sɪ'məːɡ/ *noun* L18 Persian (*sīmurḡ*, from Pahlavi *sēn* eagle + *murḡ* bird). *Iranian Mythology* A giant bird believed to have the power of speech and reasoning and to be of great age.

sine die /sɪnɪ 'dʌiːi/, /sɪneɪ 'diːeɪ/ *adverb phrase* E17 Latin (= without a day, from *sine* without + *die* ablative singular of *dies* day). (With reference to business

or proceedings that have been adjourned) with no appointed day for resumption; adjourned indefinitely.

sine qua non /sʌɪnɪ kweɪ 'nɒn/, /sɪneɪ kwaː 'nəʊn/ *noun phrase* (also in Latin plural form **sine quibus non** /sʌɪnɪ kwiːbəs 'nɒn/, /sɪneɪ kwiːbəs 'nəʊn/, (chiefly *Scottish Law*) Latin masculine form **sine quo non** /sʌɪnɪ kwəʊ 'nɒn/, /sɪneɪ kwəʊ 'nəʊn/) E17 Latin ((*causa*) *sine qua non* literally, '(cause) without which not', from *sine* without + *qua* ablative singular feminine of *qui* which + *non* not). An essential condition or element; a thing that is absolutely necessary.

> 1996 *Times* A merchant banker in London... told me that at one stage an Eton and Oxbridge education was almost a *sine qua non* in his organisation...

sinfonia /sɪnfə'niːə/, /sɪn'fəʊnɪə/ *noun* L18 Italian (from Latin *symphonia* instrumental harmony, voices in concert, from Greek *sumphōnia* from *sumphōnos* harmonious). *Music* **1** A symphony. **2** (In baroque music) an orchestral piece used as an introduction to an opera, cantata, or suite. **3** (*Sinfonia*) (The title of) a small symphony orchestra.

sinfonietta /sɪnfəʊnɪ'ɛtə/ *noun* E20 Italian (diminutive of SINFONIA). *Music* **1** A short or simple symphony. **2** (*Sinfonietta*) (The title of) a small symphony orchestra.

Singspiel /'zɪŋʃpiːl/ *noun* plural **Singspiele** /'zɪŋʃpiːlə/ L19 German (from *singen* to sing + *Spiel* play). *Music* A form of German light opera, typically with spoken dialogue, popular especially in the late 18th century.

sirocco /sɪ'rɒkəʊ/ *noun* (also **scirocco**) plural **siroccos** E17 Italian (*scirocco* ultimately from Spanish Arabic *šalūḳ*, *šulūḳ*, *šalūk* south-east wind, perhaps of Romance origin). A hot, oppressive, and often dusty or rainy wind which blows from the north coast of Africa over the Mediterranean and parts of southern Europe; *generally* any hot southerly wind.

sistrum /'sɪstrəm/ *noun* plural **sistra** /'sɪstrə/, **sistrums** LME Latin (from Greek *seistron*, from *seiein* to shake). A musical instrument of ancient Egyptian origin, consisting of a metal frame with transverse metal rods which rattled when the instrument was shaken.

sitar /'sɪtɑː/, /sɪ'tɑː/ *noun* M19 Persian and Urdu (*sitār* from *sih* three + *tār* string). A stringed Indian musical instrument, resembling a lute, with a long neck and (usually) seven principal strings which the player plucks.

situs /'sʌɪtəs/ *noun* E18 Latin. *Law* **a** The place to which for purposes of legal jurisdiction or taxation a property belongs. Chiefly *United States*. **b** A worksite, *especially* (in full *common situs*) one occupied by two or more employers. *United States*.

sitzfleisch /'zɪts,flaɪʃ/ *noun* E20 German (from *sitzen* to sit + *Fleisch* flesh). **1** The ability to persist in or endure an activity; stamina. **2** A person's buttocks. *Colloquial*, chiefly *United States*.

> **1** 1975 *Harpers & Queen* Lenny hadn't got the patience, the concentration, the sitzfleisch.

sitzkrieg /'sɪtskriːg/ *noun* M20 pseudo-German (after BLITZKRIEG, as if from German *sitzen* to sit + *krieg* war). A war, or a phase of a war, marked by few or no active hostilities.

sjambok /'ʃambɒk/ *noun* L18 Afrikaans (from Malay *sambuk*, *chambuk* from Persian and Urdu *chābuk* horsewhip). (In South Africa) a long, stiff whip, originally made of rhinoceros hide.

skald /skɔːld/, /skald/ *noun* (also **scald**) M18 Old Norse (*skáld*, of unknown origin). *History* (In ancient Scandinavia) a composer and reciter of poems honouring heroes and their deeds.

skat /skɑːt/ *noun* M19 German (from Italian *scarto* (= French *écart*) cards laid aside, from *scartare* to discard; cf. ÉCARTÉ). A three-handed trick-taking card game with bidding, originating in Germany.

skene /'skiːni/ *noun* L19 Greek (*skēnē* hut, tent). (In ancient Greek theatre) a three-dimensional structure forming part of the stage or set and able to be decorated according to the current play's theme.

skijoring /'skiːdʒɔːrɪŋ/, /ʃiː'jɔːrɪŋ/ *noun* (also **skikjøring**) E20 Norwegian (*skikjør-ing*, from *ski* ski + *kjøring* driving). The

sport or recreation of being pulled over snow or ice on skis by a horse or dog.

> **1996** *Country Life* Racing on ice has a long history in St Moritz, and skikjøring races started in 1906.

skof /skɒf/ *noun* L18 Afrikaans (from Dutch *schoft* quarter of the day, each of the four meals of a day). A stage of a journey; a period of travel between outspans. Also, a period of work, a shift. *South African colloquial*.

slainte /'slɑːntʃə/ *interjection* E19 Gaelic (*slàinte* (*mhór*) = '(good) health'). Used to express friendly feelings towards one's companions before drinking.

slalom /'slɑːləm/ *noun & verb* E20 Norwegian (*slalåm*, from *sla* sloping + *låm* track). **A** *noun* **1** A downhill ski race on a zigzag course marked by artificial obstacles, usually flags, and descended singly by each competitor in turn. **2** A similar obstacle race for canoeists, waterskiers, skateboarders, etc. **B** *intransitive verb* Move or race in a winding path, avoiding obstacles.

slivovitz /'slɪvəvɪts/ *noun* (also **slivovic**) L19 Serbo-Croat (*šljivovica* from *šljiva* plum). A plum brandy made chiefly in the former Yugoslavia and in Romania.

smetana /'smɛtənə/ *noun* E20 Russian (from *smetat'* to sweep together, collect). Sour cream. Frequently in *smetana sauce*.

smorgasbord /'smɔːɡəsbɔːd/ *noun* L19 Swedish (*smörgåsbord*, from *smörgås* (slice of) bread and butter (from *smör* butter, *gås* goose, lump of butter) + *bord* board, table). **1** A range of open sandwiches served with delicacies as hors d'oeuvres or a buffet, originally and especially in Scandinavia. **2** A medley, a miscellany, a variety.

> **2** 1996 *Times* This being Dead Can Dance, there was a whole smorgasbord of musical styles on show...

smorzando /smɔː'tsandəʊ/ *adverb, adjective, & noun* E19 Italian (present participle of *smorzare* to extinguish). *Music* **A** *adverb & adjective* (Especially as a direction) dying away. **B** *noun* plural **smorzandos**, **smorzandi** /smɔː'tsandi/. A smorzando passage.

snoek /snuːk/, /snʊk/ *noun* plural same L18 Dutch (= pike). A long slender food fish of southern oceans, a barracouta. Chiefly *South African*.

soba /ˈsəʊbə/ *noun* (treated as *singular* or *plural*) L19 Japanese. Japanese noodles made from buckwheat flour.

sobriquet /ˈsəʊbrɪkeɪ/ *noun* M17 French (originally in the sense 'tap under the chin', of unknown origin). An epithet, a nickname.

∎ The older French form SOUBRIQUET is also found in English.

socle /ˈsəʊk(ə)l/, /ˈsɒk(ə)l/ *noun* E18 French (from Italian *zoccolo* wooden shoe, socle, representing Latin *socculus* diminutive of *soccus* sock). *Architecture* A low plinth serving as a pedestal for a statue, column, vase, etc.

sogo shosha /ˌsəʊɡəʊ ˈʃəʊʃə/ *noun phrase* plural same, **sogo shoshas** M20 Japanese (*sōgō shōsha*, from *sōgō* comprehensive + *shōsha* business firm, mercantile society). A very large Japanese company that trades internationally in a wide range of goods and services.

soi-disant /swadizɑ̃/ *adjective* (also **soi disant**) M18 French (from *soi* oneself + *disant* saying). **1** (Of a person) self-styled, would-be. **2** (Of a thing) so-called, pretended.

1 1995 *Times* A French *soi-disant* sexual scientist claims that women who are worried about being pestered by men on the beach this summer should go topless.

soigné /swaɲe/, /ˈswɑːnjeɪ/ *adjective* (feminine **soignée**) E19 French (past participial adjective of *soigner* to care for, from *soin* care). Dressed very elegantly; well-groomed.

1996 *Times* What could be more classic than a soigné tuxedo suit or an understated little black dress...?

soigneur /swaɲr/ *noun* plural pronounced same L20 French (from *soigner* to care for). In cycling, a person who gives training, massage, and other assistance to a team, especially during a race.

soirée /ˈswɑːreɪ/, *foreign* /sware/ (*plural* same) *noun* L18 French (from *soir* evening). An evening party or gathering, especially in a private house, for conversation or music.

soixante-neuf /swasɑ̃t nœf/ *noun* L19 French (= sixty-nine, after the position of the couple involved). Sexual activity between two people involving mutual oral stimulation of each other's genitals; a position enabling this.

1973 M. Amis *Rachel Papers* The other couple were writhing about still, now seemingly poised for a session of fully robed soixante-neuf.

sokaiya /ˈsəʊkʌɪjə/ *noun* plural same L20 Japanese (from *sōkai* general meeting + *-ya* dealer). A holder of shares in a company who tries to extort money from it by threatening to cause trouble for executives at a general meeting of the shareholders.

sola /ˈsəʊlə/ *adjective* M18 Latin (feminine of *solus* alone, or Italian, feminine of *solo* alone). (Of a woman) alone or unaccompanied. Used especially as a stage direction.

solarium /səˈlɛːrɪəm/ *noun* plural **solaria** /səˈlɛːrɪə/, **solariums** M19 Latin (= sundial, place for sunning oneself, from *sol* sun). **1** A room equipped with sunlamps or sunbeds which can be used to acquire an artificial suntan. **2** A room fitted with large areas of glass to admit sunlight.

solatium /səˈleɪʃɪəm/ *noun* plural **solatia** /səˈleɪʃɪə/ E19 Latin (= solace). A sum of money or other compensation given to a person to make up for loss, inconvenience, injured feelings, etc.; *specifically* in *Law*, such an amount awarded to a litigant over and above the actual loss.

sola topi see under TOPI.

solera /səˈlɛːrə/, *foreign* /soˈlera/ *noun* M19 Spanish (literally, 'crossbeam, stone base' from *suelo* ground, floor, dregs, from Latin *solum* soil). **1** A Spanish method of producing wine, especially sherry and Madeira, whereby small amounts of younger wines stored in an upper tier of casks are systematically blended with the more mature wine in the casks below. Also *solera system*. **2** A blend of sherry or Malaga wine produced by the Spanish solera system. Also *solera wine*. **3** A wine cask, typically one with a capacity of four hogsheads, on the bottom tier of the solera system and containing the oldest wine.

solfatara /sɒlfə'tɑːrə/ *noun* (also earlier **solfaterra** /sɒlfə'tɛrə/) L18 Italian (originally, a sulphurous volcano near Naples, from Italian *solfo* sulphur). *Geology* A volcanic crater which emits sulphurous and other gases.

solfège /sɒlfɛʒ/ *noun* plural pronounced same E20 French. *Music* SOL-FEGGIO. Also (*generally*), rudimentary musical instruction, especially using textless exercises for the voice.

solfeggio /sɒl'fɛdʒɪəʊ/ *noun* plural **solfeggi** /sɒl'fɛdʒi/, **solfeggios** L18 Italian (from *sol-fa* sol-fa). *Music* An exercise in singing using the sol-fa syllables. Also, solmization.

solidus /'sɒlɪdəs/ *noun* plural **solidi** /'sɒlɪdʌɪ/ ME Latin (*solidus* solid, used as noun; sense 3 from Latin *solidus (nummus)* a gold coin). **1** An oblique stroke (/) in print or writing, used in writing fractions, to separate figures and letters, or to denote alternatives or ratios; a slash. **2** *Chemistry* A curve in a graph of the temperature and composition of a mixture, below which the substance is entirely solid and above which it consists of solid and liquid in equilibrium. Also *solidus curve*. **3** *History* A gold coin of the later Roman Empire, originally worth about 25 denarii. Formerly also, in medieval England, a shilling.

solitaire /'sɒlɪtɛː/, /sɒlɪ'tɛː/ *noun* E18 French (from Latin *solitarius* solitary). **1** A game for one player played by removing pegs one at a time from a board by jumping others over them from adjacent holes, the object being to be left with only one peg. **2** The card game patience. *North American*. **3** A diamond or other gem set in a piece of jewellery by itself; a ring set with such a gem. **3** Either of two extinct flightless birds related to the dodo.

solus /'səʊləs/ *adjective* L16 Latin (cf. SOLA). Alone or unaccompanied. Used especially as a stage direction.

soma /'səʊmə/ *noun* L18 Sanskrit. *Hinduism* An intoxicating drink prepared from a plant and used in Vedic ritual, believed to be the drink of the gods. Cf. HOM.

■ In his novel *Brave New World* (1932), Aldous Huxley gave the name *soma* to the narcotic drug distributed by the state to keep people happy and acquiescent.

sombrero /sɒm'brɛːrəʊ/ *noun* plural **sombreros** L16 Spanish (from *sombra* shade). A broad-brimmed hat of felt or straw, of a type common in Mexico and the south-western United States.

sommelier /'sɒm(ə)ljeɪ/, /sə'mɛljeɪ/; *foreign* /sɔməlje/ (*plural same*) *noun* E19 French. A wine waiter.

1996 *Times: Weekend* For fun, we asked for the wine list, and irritated the sommelier by pondering a Pétrus 1955 Pomerol at £1,307 before settling for a glass of house white.

sonata /sə'nɑːtə/ *noun* L17 Italian (feminine past participle of *sonare* to sound). A classical composition for an instrumental soloist, often with a piano accompaniment, usually in several movements.

■ Varieties of *sonata* popular in the 17th and 18th centuries were the *sonata da camera* (literally, 'chamber sonata'), for one or more solo instruments and continuo and usually consisting of a suite of dance movements, and the *sonata da chiesa* (literally, 'church sonata'), likewise for one or more solo instruments and continuo, but usually consisting of four alternately slow and fast movements. Both phrases were introduced into English somewhat later (E19).

sonatina /sɒnə'tiːnə/ *noun* M18 Italian (diminutive of SONATA). A short or simple sonata.

sonde /sɒnd/ *noun* E20 French (= sounding-line, sounding). An instrument probe for transmitting information about its surroundings underground, under water, in the atmosphere, etc.

son et lumière /ˌsɒn eɪ 'luːmjɛː/, *foreign* /sɔn e lymjɛr/ *noun phrase* plural **son et lumières** /'luːmjɛːz/, *foreign* /lymjɛr/ M20 French (literally, 'sound and light'). An entertainment using recorded sound and lighting effects, usually presented at night at a historic monument or building to give a dramatic narrative of its history.

sopaipilla /sopai'pilja/, /ˌsəʊpʌɪ'pi:ljə/ *noun* plural **sopaipillas** /sopai'piljas/, /ˌsəʊpʌɪ'pi:ljəz/ M20 American Spanish (diminutive of Spanish *sopaipa* a kind of sweet fritter). (Especially in New Mexico) a deep-fried usually square pastry eaten with honey or sugar or as a bread.

soprani see SOPRANO.

sopranino /sɒprə'ni:nəʊ/ *noun* plural **sopraninos** E20 Italian (diminutive of SOPRANO). An instrument, especially a recorder or saxophone, higher than soprano.

soprano /sə'prɑːnəʊ/ *noun & adjective* M18 Italian (from *sopra* above, from Latin *supra*). **A** *noun* plural **sopranos, soprani** /sə'prɑːni/. **1** The highest singing voice. **b** A part written for a soprano voice. **2** A female or boy singer having such a voice; a person singing a soprano part. **b** An instrument of a high pitch, specifically of the highest pitch in a family. **B** *attributive* or as *adjective* Of or designating the highest singing voice or instrumental pitch.

    A.1 1996 *Spectator* Musetta and Mimí are both written for lyric sopranos, the commonest voices...

sorbet /'sɔːbeɪ/, /'sɔːbɪt/ *noun* L16 French (from Italian *sorbetto*, from Turkish *şerbet*, based on Arabic *šariba* to drink). **1** A water ice. **2** An Arabian sherbet. *Archaic*.

sordino /sɔː'dɪnəʊ/ *noun* plural **sordini** /sɔː'di:ni/ (also **sordine** /sɔː'di:n/) L16 Italian (from *sordo*, from Latin *surdus* deaf, mute). *Music* A mute for a wind or bowed instrument; a damper for a piano. Cf. CON SORDINO.

sortes /'sɔːtiːz/, /'sɔːteɪz/ *noun plural* also treated as *singular* L16 Latin (plural of *sors* lot, chance). Divination, or the seeking of guidance, by chance selection of a passage in a text regarded as authoritative.

    ■ The authorities traditionally consulted in this way are Virgil (in full *sortes Virgilianae* /ˌvəːdʒɪlɪ'ɑːniː/), Homer (in full *sortes Homericae* /həʊ'mɛrɪkiː/), and the Bible (in full *sortes Biblicae* /'bɪblɪkiː/).

sosatie /sɒ'sɑːti/, /sə'sɑːti/ *noun* M19 Afrikaans (ultimately from Malay *sesate*; cf. SATAY). A South African dish of cubes of curried or spiced meat grilled on a skewer.

sostenuto /ˌsɒstə'n(j)uːtəʊ/ *adjective & noun* E18 Italian (past participle of *sostenere* to sustain). *Music* **A** *adjective* (Of a passage of music) to be played in a sustained or prolonged manner. **B** *noun* plural **sostenutos**. A passage to be played in a sustained or prolonged manner; performance in this manner.

sotto voce /ˌsotto 'votʃe/, /ˌsɒtəʊ 'vəʊtʃi/ *adverb & adjective phrase* M18 Italian (*sotto* under + *voce* voice). **A** *adverb phrase* In a quiet voice or aside. **B** *adjective phrase* Uttered in a quiet voice; muted, understated.

    B 1995 *Spectator* Sir Edward [Heath] is not so rude (at least to foreigners) as to suggest that he believes today's apologetic and democratic Germany is a potential threat to European peace, but that is the *sotto voce* message nonetheless.

sou /suː/ *noun* L15 French (singular form deduced from *sous, soux* plural of Old French *sout*, from Latin *solidus* (sc. *nummus* coin) use as noun of *solidus* solid). *History* A former French coin of low value.

    ■ In English mainly used in one or other form of the colloquial expression *haven't a sou*, i.e. 'have absolutely no money at all'.

soubise /subiz/ *noun* plural pronounced same L18 French (Charles de Rohan *Soubise* (1715–87), French general and courtier). A thick white sauce made with onion purée and often served with fish and eggs.

soubresaut /subrəso/ *noun* plural pronounced same M19 French. *Ballet* A straight-legged jump from both feet with the toes pointed and feet together, one behind the other.

soubrette /suː'brɛt/ *noun* M18 French (from modern Provençal *soubreto* feminine of *soubret* coy, from *soubra* (Provençal *sobrar*) from Latin *superare* to be above). A minor female role in a comic play or opera, typically that of a pert or coquettish maidservant; an actress or singer playing such a role.

1996 *Spectator* ...she...can toss her auburn curls with the wily femininity of a soubrette from Offenbach.

soubriquet /ˈsuːbrɪkeɪ/ *noun* E19 French (older variant of *sobriquet*). A nickname, a SOBRIQUET.

souchong /ˈsuːʃɒŋ/ *noun* M18 Chinese ((Cantonese) *siú chúng* small sort). A fine black variety of China tea.

soucouyant /ˌsuːkuːˈjɒ̃/ *noun West Indies* (also **soucriant** /ˌsuːkriˈjɒ̃/ and other variants) M20 West Indian creole (probably related to Fulah *sukunyadyo* sorcerer, witch). (In eastern Caribbean folklore) a malignant witch believed to shed her skin by night and suck the blood of her victims.

soufflé /ˈsuːfleɪ/, *foreign* /sufle/ (*plural same*) *noun* E19 French (= blown, past participle of *souffler* from Latin *sufflare*, from *sub* under + *flare* to blow). A light spongy dish made by mixing egg yolks and other ingredients with stiffly beaten egg whites, usually baked in an oven until puffy.

souk /suːk/ *noun* (also **suk, sukh, suq**) E19 Arabic (*sūḳ* market, probably through French *souk*). An Arab market or marketplace, a bazaar.

soukous /ˈsuːkuːs/ *noun* L20 African (from French *secouer* to shake). A style of African popular music characterized by syncopated rhythms and intricate contrasting guitar melodies, originating in the Democratic Republic of the Congo (Zaire).

soupçon /ˈsuːpsɒn/, *foreign* /supsɔ̃/ *noun* M18 French (from Old French *sous(s)peçon*, from medieval Latin *suspectio(n-)*). A suspicion, a suggestion; a very small quantity, a trace.

1996 *Spectator* The bomb had had little effect on the markets—except for a *soupçon* of trouble for leisure groups with Northern Ireland interests.

soupe /sup/ *noun* M18 French. Soup, especially in French cooking.

■ Chiefly in phrases designating particular kinds of soup, as *soupe à l'oignon* onion soup.

sous- /su/, /suz/ *prefix* ME Old and Modern French (*sous* under, from Latin *subtus* under). Under-, sub-; subordinate.

■ Used in words adopted from French such as *sous-chef*, *sous-lieutenant*, etc.

sous vide /su vid/, /suː ˈviːd/ *noun, adjective, & adverb* L20 French (from *sous* under + *vide* vacuum). **A** *noun* A method of treating food by partial cooking followed by vacuum-sealing and chilling. **B** *adjective & adverb* (Of food or cooking) involving such preparation.

soutache /suːˈtaʃ/ *noun* M19 French (from Hungarian *sujtás*). A narrow flat ornamental braid used for decorative trimming. More fully *soutache braid*.

soutane /suːˈtɑːn/ *noun* M19 French (from Italian *sottana*, from *sotto* from Latin *subtus* under). A type of cassock worn by Roman Catholic priests.

souteneur /sutənr̩/ *noun* plural pronounced same E20 French (= protector, from *soutenir* to sustain). A pimp.

souterrain /ˈsuːtəreɪn/ *noun* M18 French (from *sous* under + *terre* earth, after Latin *subterraneus*). Chiefly *Archaeology* An underground chamber or passage.

souvenir /ˌsuːvəˈnɪə/ *noun* L18 French (use as noun of verb = to remember, from Latin *subvenire* to come into the mind, from *sub-* + *venire* to come). A thing that is kept as a reminder of a person, place, or event.

souvlaki /suːˈvlɑːki/ *noun* plural **souvlakia** /suːˈvlɑːkɪə/ M20 Modern Greek (*soublaki* from *soubla* skewer). A Greek dish of small pieces of meat grilled on a skewer.

sovkhoz /ˈsɒvkɒz/, /sʌvˈkɔːz/ *noun* plural same, **sovkhozes** /ˈsɒvkɒzɪz/, **sovkhozy** /ˈsɒvkɒzi/ E20 Russian (from *sov (etskoe khoz(yaĭstvo* Soviet farm). A state-owned farm in countries of the former USSR.

soya /ˈsɔɪə/ *noun* L17 Dutch (*soja* from Japanese *shōyu*; cf. SHOYU). **1** Protein derived from the beans of an Asian plant, used as a replacement for animal proteins in certain foods. **2** Soy sauce. **3** The widely cultivated plant of the pea family which produces soya beans.

spaghetti /spəˈgɛti/ *noun* M19 Italian (plural of diminutive of *spago* string). Pasta in the form of long solid threads, between MACARONI and VERMICELLI in thickness.

■ The term *spaghetti junction* is used to describe a complex multi-level road junction, especially one on a motorway. It originally applied to a major interchange on the M6 near Birmingham in the UK. *Spaghetti western* is an informal term for a western film made cheaply in Europe by an Italian director.

spaghettini /ˌspagɛˈtiːni/ *noun* M20 Italian (diminutive of preceding). Pasta in the form of strings of thin spaghetti.

Spätlese /ˈʃpɛtleːzə/ *noun* plural **Spätlesen** /ˈʃpɛtleːzən/, **Spätleses** M20 German (from *spät* late + *Lese* picking, vintage). A white wine of German origin or style made from grapes picked later than the general harvest.

spätzle /ˈʃpɛtslə/, /ˈʃpɛts(ə)l/ *noun plural* (also **spaetzle**) L19 German ((dialect) literally, 'little sparrows'). Small dumplings of a type made in southern Germany

and Alsace, consisting of seasoned dough poached in boiling water.

spécialité /spesjalite/ *noun* (also **specialité**) M19 French (Old French *especialité* from late Latin *specialitas*, from Latin *specialis* special, particular). **1** An article or service specially characteristic of, dealt in, or produced by, a particular place, firm, etc. **2** An unusual or distinctive thing.

■ *Speciality* in the sense of 'the quality of being special, distinctive, or limited in some respect' was adopted from Old French in the late medieval period and quickly anglicized, and the anglicized version of *spécialité* (and of closely related *(e)specialté*) is used in most general senses. In sense 1, *spécialité* is often used in the phrase *spécialité de la maison* 'speciality of the house', to mean a dish on which a particular restaurant prides itself.

specie /ˈspiːʃiː/, /ˈspiːʃi/ *noun* E17 Latin (ablative singular of *species* kind, originally (M16) in phrase *in specie* in the real, precise, or actual form). Coin money as opposed to paper money. Frequently *attributive*.

■ The legal term *in specie* means 'in the real, precise, or actual form specified'.

Spanish

Perceived national stereotypes sometimes account for the words that English borrows from other languages: French, for example, has contributed many words and expressions relating to romance and sex. In the case of Spanish, a number of loanwords (many originally adopted into American English from Mexican and Latin American varieties of the language) suggest a swaggering and ostentatious masculinity popularly associated with men from Spain and Spanish-speaking countries. These include *cojones*, *hombre*, *machismo*, *macho*, and *mano a mano*.

Many of the Spanish words that have entered the English language relate to specifically Spanish and South American culture, food, and clothing. Here is a sample: *adios*, *amigo*, *barrio*, *bolero*, *burrito*, *chorizo*, *flamenco*, *hacienda*, *nacho*, *paella*, *pampas*, *poncho*, *pueblo*, *salsa*, *sangria*, *siesta*, *sombrero*, *taco*, *tapas*, and *tortilla*. The vocabulary of bullfighting includes such terms as *banderillero*, *corrida*, *cuadrilla*, *matador*, *picador*, and *toreador*, and an *aficionado* was originally a devotee of bullfighting. Also quintessentially Spanish is the relaxed procrastination summed up by the word *mañana*.

Some other everyday English words of Spanish origin are *armada*, *bonanza*, *embargo*, *flotilla*, *guerrilla*, *incommunicado*, *marijuana*, *patio*, *peccadillo*, *plaza*, and *vigilante*.

speculum /'spɛkjʊləm/ *noun* plural **specula** /'spɛkjʊlə/, **speculums** LME Latin (from base of *specere* to look, see). **1** *Medicine* An instrument, usually of metal, used to dilate an orifice or canal in the body to allow inspection. **2** *Ornithology* A bright patch of plumage on the wings of certain birds. **3** Chiefly *Science* A mirror or reflector of glass or metal. **4** An alloy of copper and tin in a ratio of around 2:1, formerly used to make mirrors for scientific instruments. Also more fully *speculum metal*.

spermaceti /ˌspəːməˈsiːti/, /ˌspəːməˈsɛti/ *noun* L15 Medieval Latin (from late Latin *sperma* (from Greek = sperm, seed, from base of *speirein* to sow) + *ceti* genitive of *cetus*, Greek *kētos* whale (from its appearance or the belief that it represents whale spawn)). A soft white waxy substance formerly used in the manufacture of candles and ointments, found in the sperm whale and some other cetaceans, chiefly in a rounded organ in the head which focuses acoustic signals and aids control of buoyancy.

sphinx /sfɪŋks/ *noun* plural **sphinxes**, **sphinges** /'sfɪndʒiːz/ LME Latin (from Greek *Sphigx*, *Sphigg-*, apparently from *sphiggein* to draw tight). **1** *Greek Mythology* (*Sphinx*) A hybrid monster, usually described as having a woman's head and a winged lion's body, which plagued the Greek city of Thebes until Oedipus solved its riddle. **b** *figurative* An inscrutable or enigmatic person or thing; a mystery. **2** Any of several ancient Greek or (especially) Egyptian stone figures of a creature with a human or animal head and a lion's body. **3** A moth of the genus *Sphinx*, or of the family Sphingidae, so called from the typical attitude of the caterpillar; a hawkmoth. Also *sphinx moth*. Chiefly *United States*.

spiccato /spɪˈkɑːtəʊ/ *noun, adjective, & adverb* E18 Italian (= detailed, distinct). *Music* **A** *noun* A style of staccato playing on stringed instruments involving bouncing the bow on the strings. **B** *adjective & adverb* Performed or to be performed in this style.

spiel /ʃpiːl/, /spiːl/ *noun & verb* L19 German (from *Spiel* game). **A** *noun* An elaborate or glib speech or story, typically one used by a salesperson. **B 1** *transitive verb* Reel off; recite: *he solemnly spieled all he knew.* **2** *intransitive verb* Speak glibly or at length.

spinto /'spɪntəʊ/ *noun* plural **spintos** M20 Italian (past participle of *spingere* to push). *Music* A lyric soprano or tenor voice of powerful dramatic quality; a singer with a spinto voice.

spiritus rector /ˌspɪrɪtʊs ˈrɛktɔː/ *noun phrase* E20 Latin. A ruling or guiding spirit.

> **1980** *Encounter* More than fifteen years ago he was the *spiritus rector* of the *European Journal of Sociology.*

sporran /'spɒr(ə)n/ *noun* M18 Gaelic (*sporan* = Irish *sparán* purse, Middle Irish *sboran* from Latin *bursa* purse). A small pouch worn around the waist so as to hang in front of the kilt as part of men's Scottish Highland dress.

sportif /spɔrtif/ *adjective* M20 French. **1** Interested in athletic sports. **2** (Of a garment or style of dress) suitable for sport or informal wear; casually stylish.

> **1** **1996** *Oldie* . . . her sneering references to his game attempts to take up water-skiing on their honeymoon when he was a mere sixty-two have proved equally irritating to more *sportif* oldies.

Sprechgesang /'ʃprɛçɡəˌzaŋ/ *noun* E20 German (literally, 'speech song'). *Music* A style of dramatic vocalization intermediate between speech and song.

Sprechstimme /'ʃprɛçˌʃtɪmə/ *noun* E20 German (literally, 'speech voice'). *Music* SPRECHGESANG.

sprezzatura /ˌsprettsaˈtura/ *noun* M20 Italian. Studied carelessness, nonchalance, especially in art or literature.

> **1973** *Times Literary Supplement* Literary fashion and his own aristocratic *sprezzatura* demanded that he affect an unconcern.

springbok /'sprɪŋbɒk/ *noun* (in sense 1 also anglicized as **springbuck** /'sprɪŋbʌk/) L18 Afrikaans (from Dutch *springen* to spring + *bok* goat, antelope). **1** A common and gregarious southern

Sport

Italian football has popularized the term *catenaccio* (literally 'door-bolt'), referring to a rigidly defensive system of play originally practised in the 1960s by Inter Milan. Another term for a defensive sweeper is *libero*, from the Italian *battitore libero* ('free beater'). The Spanish football club Real Madrid may have famously imported its star signings or *galacticos* in recent years, but it has exported the word to the English language.

Coverage of the Tour de France has familiarized British cycling fans with a number of colourful French expressions. The *peloton* is the main pack of cyclists in the race. *Lanterne rouge* (literally 'red lantern') refers to the rider who finishes in last place in a race: the term derives from the red light found at the back of the last carriage on French trains. *Domestiques* (literally 'servants') are the riders whose primary job is to support and work for the team leader or another designated teammate. The *voiture balai* is literally the 'broom wagon', the vehicle that follows each stage to pick up riders unable to continue because of injury or fatigue. The *autobus* is the group of cyclists, usually the sprinters as opposed to the specialist mountain-climbers, who ride together on the mountain stages to help one another finish within the time limit. The Italian word *gruppetto* is also sometimes used.

The language of cricket does not seem to include many foreign words, though one notable exception is *doosra*, a Hindi or Punjabi word meaning 'second' or 'other'. It denotes a type of delivery which turns 'the wrong way', breaking from the leg side (to a right-handed batsman), though bowled with an apparent off-break action in order to deceive the batsman.

Finally, one foreign word with which sports fans become reacquainted every four years during coverage of the Olympic Games (particularly the rowing events) is *repêchage*. Borrowed from French, this is the term for a contest in which the runners-up in the eliminating heats compete for a place in the final.

African gazelle, characterized by the habit of leaping (pronking) when excited or disturbed. **2 (the Springboks)** the South African international rugby union team.

spritzer /ˈsprɪtsə/ *noun* M20 German (= a splash). A mixture of (usually white) wine and soda water; a drink or glass of this.

spruit /spreɪt/, *foreign* /sprɨt/ *noun* M19 Dutch (= sprout). (In South Africa) a small watercourse that is usually dry except in the rainy season.

spumante /spuːˈmanti/ *noun* E20 Italian (= sparkling). An Italian sparkling white wine, especially from the province of Asti (in full *Asti spumante*).

spumoni /spuːˈməʊni/ *noun* E20 Italian (*spumone*, from *spuma* foam). A rich dessert consisting of layered ice cream with candied fruits, nuts, and sometimes brandy. *North American.*

sputnik /ˈspʊtnɪk/, /ˈspʌtnɪk/ *noun* (also **Sputnik**) M20 Russian (literally, 'travelling companion, fellow-traveller', from *s* with + *put'* way, journey + noun suffix *-nik* person connected with (something)). Each of a series of Soviet artificial satellites launched between 1957 and 1961.

staccato /stəˈkɑːtəʊ/ *adjective, adverb, & noun* E18 Italian (= detached, past participle of *staccare* aphetic from *distaccare* to detach). **A** *adjective & adverb* Chiefly *Music* With each note or sound sharply separated or detached from the next, with a clipped style. Opposed to LEGATO. **B** *noun* A series of short, sharp sounds or words; a piece or passage of music marked to be performed staccato.

staffage /stəˈfɑːʒ/ *noun* L19 German (pseudo-French form from *staffieren* to fit out, decorate, perhaps from Old French *estoffer*, from *estoffe* stuff). Accessory items in a painting, especially figures or animals in a landscape picture.

Stalag /ˈstalag, ˈʃtalag/ *noun* M20 German (contraction of *Stammlager*, from *Stamm* base, main stock + *Lager* camp). (In the Second World War) a German prison camp, especially for non-commissioned officers and privates.

stanza /ˈstanzə/ *noun* plural **stanzas** L16 Italian (= standing place, stanza, from Proto-Romance, from Latin *stant-* present participial stem of *stare* to stand). **1** A group of (usually between four and twelve) lines of verse occurring as the basic metrical unit of a poem consisting of a series of such groups; a verse. **2** A group of four lines in some Greek and Latin metres.

stasis /ˈsteɪsɪs/, /ˈstasɪs/ *noun* plural **stases** /ˈsteɪsiːz/, /ˈstasɪs/ M18 Modern Latin (from Greek, literally, 'standing, stoppage', from *sta-* base of *histanai* to stand). **1** A period or state of inactivity or equilibrium. **2** *Medicine* A stagnation or stoppage of flow of a bodily fluid.

status quo /ˌsteɪtəs ˈkwəʊ/ *noun phrase* M19 Latin (= the state in which). The existing state of affairs, especially regarding social or political issues.
> **1996** *Times* This was the status quo, and it was a brave Tory who dared to challenge it.

status quo ante /ˌsteɪtəs ˌkwəʊ ˈanti/ *noun phrase* L19 Latin (= the state in which before). The previously existing state of affairs.
> **1996** *Spectator* Those who framed the peace treaties had objectives far beyond restoring the status quo ante, which would in most cases have been impossible.

stela /ˈstiːlə/ *noun* plural **stelae** /ˈstiːliː/ L18 Latin (from as STELE). *Archaeology* An upright stone slab or pillar, usually bearing a commemorative inscription or sculptured design and often serving as a gravestone.

stele /stiːl/, /ˈstiːli/ *noun* plural **steles**, (especially in sense 1) **stelae** /ˈstiːliː/ E19 Greek (*stēlē* standing block; cf. STELA). **1** *Archaeology* A stela. **2** *Botany* The central core of the stem and root of a vascular plant.

stelline /stɛˈliːni/ *noun plural* (also **stellini**) M20 Italian (from *stellina* diminutive of *stella* star). Small star-shaped pieces of pasta.

stemma /ˈstɛmə/ *noun* plural **stemmata** /ˈstɛmətə/ M17 Latin (from Greek (= wreath, garland), from *stephein* to crown). **1** A recorded genealogy of a family, a family tree; a pedigree. **2** A diagram showing the relationship between a text and its various manuscript versions.

steppe /stɛp/ *noun* L17 Russian (*step'*). Any of the vast level grassy usually treeless plains of south east Europe and Siberia. Also, any similar plain elsewhere.

stet /stɛt/ *verb* M18 Latin (3rd person singular present subjunctive of *stare* = let it stand). **1** Let it stand (used as an instruction on a printed proof to indicate that a correction or deletion should be ignored and that the original matter is to be retained). **2** *transitive verb* (inflected *-tt-*) Write 'stet' against (an accidental deletion, miscorrection, etc.).

stifado /stɪˈfɑːdəʊ/ *noun* plural **stifados** M20 Modern Greek (*stiphado* probably from Italian *stufato*). A Greek dish of meat stewed with onions and sometimes tomatoes.

stigma /ˈstɪgmə/ *noun* plural **stigmas**, **stigmata** /ˈstɪgmətə/, /stɪgˈmɑːtə/ L16 Latin (from Greek *stigma* a mark made by a pointed instrument, a dot, from base of *stizein* to prick). **1** A mark or sign of disgrace associated with a particular circumstance, quality, or person. **2** (**stigmata**) (In Christian tradition) marks corresponding to those left on Christ's body by the Crucifixion, said to have been impressed by divine favour on the bodies of certain saints. **3** *Medicine* A visible sign or characteristic of a disease or condition. **4** A spot or mark on the skin. **5** *Botany* That part of the pistil in flowering plants which receives the pollen during pollination.

■ Originally used in English to denote a mark made on the skin by pricking or branding, as punishment for a criminal or a mark of subjection.

1 1996 *Country Life* But generally it can be said that divorce has lost most, if not all, of its social stigma.

stiletto /stɪˈlɛtəʊ/ *noun* plural **stilettos** E17 Italian (diminutive of *stilo* dagger, ultimately from Latin *stilus* stylus). **1** A very high tapering heel on a woman's shoe; a shoe with such a heel. In full *stiletto heel*. **2** A short dagger with a tapering blade. **3** A small pointed instrument for making eyelet holes.

stoa /ˈstəʊə/ *noun* plural **stoas, stoai** /ˈstəʊʌɪ/ E17 Greek. **1** (*the Stoa*) The great hall in ancient Athens in which the Greek philosopher Zeno lectured; the Stoic school of philosophy. **2** A classical portico or a roofed colonnade.

■ The followers of Zeno (335–263 BC) were accordingly called Stoics.

stoep /stuːp/ *noun* L18 Afrikaans (from Dutch, related to *step*, from West Germanic; cf. STOOP). (In South Africa) a raised platform or veranda running along the front and sometimes round the sides of a house.

stollen /ˈstɒlən/, /ˈʃtɒlən/ *noun* E20 German. A rich German fruit loaf, often with nuts added.

stoop /stuːp/ *noun* M18 Dutch (cf. STOEP). A small raised platform at the entrance door of a house; a set of steps approaching this; a small porch or veranda. *North American*.

strabismus /strəˈbɪzməs/ *noun* L17 Modern Latin (from Greek *strabismos*, from *strabizein* to squint, from *strabos* squinting). *Medicine* A disorder of the eye muscles resulting in an inability to direct the gaze of both eyes to the same object simultaneously; squinting, a squint.

stracciatella /ˌstratʃəˈtɛlə/ *noun* M20 Italian. An Italian soup made with stock, eggs, and cheese.

strath /straθ/ *noun* M16 Gaelic (*Scottish s(t)rath* = Old Irish *srath* (modern *sraith*)). A broad mountain valley.

stretto /ˈstrɛtəʊ/ *noun & adverb* M18 Italian (literally, 'narrow'). *Music* **A** *noun* **1** A passage, especially at the end of an aria or movement, to be performed in quicker time. **2** A section at the end of a fugue in which successive introductions of the theme follow at shorter intervals than before, increasing the sense of excitement. **B** *adverb* (As a direction) in quicker time (especially in a final passage).

streusel /ˈstrɔɪz(ə)l/, /ˈstruːz(ə)l/ *noun* E20 German (from *streuen* to sprinkle). A crumbly topping or filling made from fat, flour, cinnamon, and sugar; a cake or pastry with a streusel topping.

stria /ˈstrʌɪə/ *noun* plural **striae** /ˈstrʌɪiː/ L17 Latin (= furrow, grooving). Chiefly *Science* A small groove, channel, or ridge; a narrow streak, stripe, or band of distinctive colour, structure, or texture; *especially* one of a number of similar parallel features.

stricto sensu /ˌstrɪktəʊ ˈsɛnsuː/ *adverb & adjective phrase* M20 Latin (= in the restricted sense). SENSU STRICTO.

stringendo /strɪnˈdʒɛndəʊ/ *adverb, adjective, & noun* M19 Italian (present participle of *stringere* to press, squeeze, bind together, from Latin *stringere* to bind). *Music* **A** *adverb & adjective* (Especially as a direction) with increasing speed and excitement. **B** *noun* plural **stringendos, stringendi** /strɪnˈdʒɛndi/. A passage performed or marked to be performed with increasing speed.

strophe /ˈstrəʊfi/ *noun* plural **strophes** /ˈstrəʊfiz/, **strophae** /ˈstrəʊfiː/ E17 Greek (*strophē* (whence late Latin *stropha*), literally, 'turning', from *stroph-* ablaut variant of base of *strephein* to turn). **1** The first section of an ancient Greek choral ode or of one division of it. **2** A group of lines forming a section of a lyric poem.

■ The term originally denoted a movement from right to left made by a Greek chorus, or lines of choral song recited during this movement.

strudel /'stru:d(ə)l/, /'ʃtru:d(ə)l/ *noun* L19 German (literally, 'eddy, whirlpool'). A dessert of thin layers of flaky pastry rolled up round a usually fruit filling and baked.

stucco /'stʌkəʊ/ *noun* L16 Italian (ultimately from Germanic). A fine plaster, especially made from gypsum and pulverized marble, used for coating wall surfaces or moulding into architectural decorations.

stupa /'stu:pə/ *noun* L19 Sanskrit (*stūpa*). A round usually domed structure erected as a Buddhist shrine.

Sturm und Drang /,ʃtʊrm ʊnt 'draŋ/ *noun phrase* M19 German (literally, 'storm and stress'). A literary and artistic movement in Germany in the late 1770s characterized by the violent expression of emotional unrest and the rejection of neoclassical literary norms; *transferred* a period of emotion, stress, or turbulence.

■ *Sturm und Drang* was the title of a 1776 play by Friedrich Maximilian Klinger (1752–1831).

transferred **1996** *Times* There are effective supporting performances from Paul Jesson as an implacable Burleigh, Ben Miles as a *Sturm und Drang* hero who wants simultaneously to rape and rescue Mary...

sub judice /sʌb 'dʒu:dɪsi/, /sʊb 'ju:dɪkeɪ/ *adjective phrase* E17 Latin (literally, 'under a judge'). *Law* Under judicial consideration and therefore prohibited from public discussion elsewhere: *the cases were still sub judice.*

sub rosa /sʌb 'rəʊzə/ *adjective & adverb phrase* M17 Latin (literally, 'under the rose'). Happening or done in secret: *the committee operates sub rosa.*

■ The concept of the rose as a symbol of confidentiality or secrecy may have originated in Germany and is enshrined in the German phrase *unter der Rose* (cf. Early Modern Dutch *onder de roose*).

sub specie aeternitatis /sʌb 'spi:ʃi: ɪ,tə:nɪ'ta:tɪs/ *adverb phrase* L19 Latin (literally, 'under the aspect of eternity'). Viewed in relation to the eternal; in a universal perspective.

■ In Spinoza's *Ethices* (*Posthuma Opera* (1677) V.xxix.254). The opposite of SUB SPECIE TEMPORIS.

sub specie temporis /sʌb ,spi:ʃi: tɛm'pɔ:rɪs/ *adverb phrase* L19 Latin (literally 'under the aspect of time'). Viewed in relation to time rather than eternity.

1960 *Encounter Sub specie temporis* his Combination Rooms say more to us than Beckett's wet and windy plains.

sub verbo /sʌb 'və:bəʊ/ *adverb phrase* E20 Latin (= under the word). SUB VOCE.

sub voce /sʌb 'vəʊsi/, /'vəʊtʃi/ *adverb phrase* M19 Latin (= under the voice). (In textual references) under the word or heading given; SUB VERBO.

■ Abbreviated to *s.v.*

succah /'sʊkə/ *noun plural* **succoth** /'sʊkɒt/ L19 Hebrew (*sukkāh*, literally, 'hut'). Any of the booths in which a practising Jew spends part of the feast of Tabernacles (Succoth).

succedaneum /sʌksɪ'deɪnɪəm/ *noun plural* **succedanea** /sʌksɪ'deɪnɪə/, **succedaneums** E17 Modern Latin (neuter singular of Latin *succedaneus* from *succedere* to come close after). A thing which takes the place of another; a substitute; *specifically* a medicine or drug substituted for another.

succès de scandale /syksɛ də skãdal/ *noun phrase* L19 French (= success of scandal). A success due to notoriety or scandalous character.

1996 *Spectator* His book had achieved a notable *succès de scandale* in this town, particularly amongst the Society's older members who remembered many of the characters mentioned.

succès d'estime /syksɛ dɛstim/ *noun phrase* M19 French (= success of opinion or regard). A success in terms of critical appreciation, as opposed to popularity or commercial gain.

1996 *Spectator* Being a *succès d'estime* is not enough for a mid-market newspaper which must rely on a much wider constituency than the chattering classes.

succès fou /syksɛ fu/ *noun phrase* L19 French (= mad success). A success marked by wild enthusiasm.

succubus /'sʌkjʊbəs/ *noun* plural **succubi** /'sʌkjʊbʌɪ/ LME Medieval Latin (= prostitute, from *succubare* from *sub-* under + *cubare* to lie). A demon in female form supposed to have sexual intercourse with sleeping men.

sucrier /'suːkrɪeɪ/, *foreign* /sykrie/ (*plural same*) *noun* M19 French (from *sucre* sugar). A sugar bowl, usually made of porcelain and with a cover.

sudarium /suːˈdɛːrɪəm/, /sjuːˈdɛːrɪəm/ *noun* plural **sudaria** /suːˈdɛːrɪə/ E17 Latin (= napkin, from *sudor* sweat). (In the Roman Catholic Church) a cloth supposedly impressed with an image of Christ's face, a veronica.

sudd /sʌd/ *noun* L19 Arabic (= obstruction, dam, from *sadda* to obstruct, block, congest). An area of floating vegetation which impedes navigation on the White Nile.

sudoku /suːˈdəʊkuː/ *noun* E21 Japanese (from *sū-* (in *sūji* number) + *-doku* (in *dokushin* single status), after *Sūji wa dokushin ni kagiru* 'the numbers are restricted to single status', former name of the puzzle). A type of puzzle, the object of which is to fill a grid of nine squares by nine squares with the numbers one to nine, in such a way that every number appears only once in each horizontal line, vertical line, and three-by-three block.

suede /sweɪd/ *noun* M17 French (*Suède* Sweden). Leather, originally especially kidskin, with the flesh side rubbed to make a velvety nap.

■ The French phrase *gants de Suède* 'gloves of Sweden' was misunderstood as referring to the material rather than to the country of origin.

suggestio falsi /sə͵dʒɛstɪəʊ ˈfalsʌɪ/ *noun phrase* plural **suggestiones falsi** /sə͵dʒɛstɪ͵əʊniːz/ E19 Modern Latin (literally, 'suggestion of what is false'). A misrepresentation of the truth whereby something incorrect is implied to be true.

■ Often in contexts with the associated verbal stratagem of SUPPRESSIO VERI.

sui generis /suːˈʌɪ ˈdʒɛn(ə)rɪs/, /suːˈiː/; /sjuːˈiː ˈdʒɛn(ə)rɪs/ *adjective phrase* L18 Latin (literally, 'of its own kind'). Unique.

sui juris /suːˈʌɪ ˈdʒʊərɪs/, /suːˈiː ˈdʒʊərɪs/, /sjuːˈiː ˈdʒʊərɪs/ *adjective phrase* E17 Latin (literally, 'of one's own right'). *Law* Of age; independent: *the beneficiaries are all sui juris.*

suite /swiːt/ *noun* L17 French. **1** A set of rooms in a hotel etc. for use by one person or group of people or for a particular purpose. **2** A set of furniture, especially a sofa and armchairs, of the same design. **3** *Music* A set of instrumental compositions, in dance style, to be played in succession; a set of selected pieces from an opera, ballet, etc., arranged to be played as one instrumental work. **4** A group of people in attendance on a monarch or other person of high rank; a retinue. **5** *Computing* A set of programs with a uniform design and the ability to share data. **6** *Geology* A group of minerals, rocks, or fossils occurring together and characteristic of a location or period.

suk, sukh variants of SOUK.

sukiyaki /sʊkɪˈjaki/, /sʊkɪˈjɑːki/ *noun* E20 Japanese. A Japanese dish consisting of thin slices of beef fried with vegetables in sugar, stock, and soy sauce.

sultan /'sʌlt(ə)n/ *noun* M16 French (or medieval Latin *sultanus*, from Arabic *sulṭān* power, ruler). **1** A Muslim sovereign. **b** (**the Sultan**) *History* the sultan of Turkey. **2** A plant of the Near East grown for its sweet-scented purple, pink, white, or yellow flowers. Now usually *sweet sultan*. **3** A small white-crested variety of domestic fowl, originally brought from Turkey.

sultana /sʌlˈtɑːnə/, *in sense 2 also* /s(ə)lˈtɑːnə/ *noun* L16 Italian (feminine of *sultano* sultan). **1** A wife or concubine of a sultan; the queen mother or any other woman of a sultan's family. **2** A small, light brown, seedless raisin used in puddings and cakes.

sulu /'suːluː/ *noun* M19 Fijian. A length of cotton or other light fabric wrapped about the body as a sarong, worn from the waist by men and full-length by women from the Melanesian Islands.

sumi /'suːmi/ *noun* E20 Japanese (= ink, blacking). A type of black Japanese ink prepared in solid sticks and used for painting and writing.

summa /'sʊmə/, /'sʌmə/ *noun plural* **summae** /'sʊmiː/ E18 Latin (= sum total). A summary of a subject; a compendium of knowledge.

> Archaic **1996** *Country Life* Bach's artistic last will and testament, *The Art of Fugue*, is a musical *summa* which demonstrates the expressive power of his beloved counterpoint.

summa bona plural of SUMMUM BONUM.

summa cum laude /ˌsʌmə kʌm 'lɔːdiː/, /ˌsʊmə kʊm 'laʊdeɪ/ *adverb & adjective phrase* L19 Latin (literally, 'with the highest praise'). With the highest distinction; (of a degree, diploma, etc.) of the highest standard: *he graduated summa cum laude; three scientific degrees, all summa cum laude.*

> ■ Chiefly North American; cf. CUM LAUDE, MAGNA CUM LAUDE.

summae see SUMMA.

summum bonum /ˌsʊməm 'bʊnəm/, /ˌsʌməm 'bəʊnəm/ *noun phrase* plural **summa bona** /ˌsʊmə 'bʊnə, /ˌsʌmə 'bəʊnə/ M16 Latin (= highest good). The chief or highest good; *specifically* (*Ethics*) the highest good as the ultimate goal or determining principle in an ethical system.

sumo /'suːməʊ/ *noun plural* **sumos**, same L19 Japanese (*sūmo*). A Japanese form of heavyweight wrestling in which a wrestler wins a bout by forcing his opponent outside a marked circle or by making him touch the ground with any part of the body except the soles of the feet. Also, a sumo wrestler.

sumpsimus /'sʌm(p)sɪməs/ *noun* M16 Latin (1st person plural perfect indicative

of *sumere* to take). A correct expression taking the place of an incorrect but popular one.

> ■ Cf. MUMPSIMUS. The expressions usually occur together in contexts contrasting obtuse conservatism with a more enlightened attitude.

sunyata /'ʃuːnjətɑː/, /'suːnjətə/ *noun* E20 Sanskrit (*śūnyatā* emptiness, from *śū nya* empty, void). *Buddhism* The doctrine that phenomena are devoid of an immutable or determinate intrinsic nature, often regarded as a means of gaining an intuition of ultimate reality.

superficies /ˌsuːpə'fɪʃɪiːz/, /ˌsjuːpə'fɪʃɪiːz/ *noun plural* same M16 Latin (from *super-* above + *facies* face). **1** A surface; the outer surface of an object. *Archaic.* **2** An outward part or appearance. *Literary.*

suppressio veri /səˌprɛʃɪəʊ 'vɪərʌɪ/ *noun phrase* plural **suppressiones veri** /səˌprɛʃɪˌəʊniːz/ M18 Modern Latin (literally, 'suppression of what is true'). A misrepresentation of the truth by concealing facts which ought to be made known.

> ■ In use often linked with SUGGESTIO FALSI.

supra /'suːprə/, /'sjuːprə/ *adverb* E16 Latin (= above, beyond). Used in academic or legal texts to refer to someone or something mentioned above or earlier.

suprême /syprɛm/, /suː'prɛm/ *noun* E19 French. A rich cream sauce; a dish of especially chicken breasts cooked in this sauce.

> ■ Latterly (M20) often anglicized as *supreme*, as in *chicken supreme*.

supremo /suː'priːməʊ/, /suː'preɪməʊ/, /sjuː'priːməʊ/ *noun* plural **supremos** M20 Spanish ((*generalísimo*) *supremo* supreme general). **1** A person in overall charge of an organization or activity. **2** A person with great authority or skill in a certain area.

> ■ *Supremo* was the nickname given to Earl Mountbatten of Burma during his time as Supreme Allied Commander, South East Asia.

1 1983 *Private Eye* A short list of possible replacements...included...the ruthless supremo of the Royal Philharmonic Orchestra.

suq variant of SOUK.

sura /'suərə/ *noun* E17 Arabic (*sūra*, (with definite article) *as-sūra*, probably from Syriac *ṣūrṭā* scripture). A chapter or section of the Koran.

■ *Sura* (M17) supplanted the now obsolete form *assura* (incorporating the Arabic definite article), in which the word was first used in English.

surah /'suərə/, /'sjuərə/ *noun* L19 French (representing French pronunciation of *Surat* a port in India where it was originally made). A soft twilled silk fabric.

sushi /'suːʃi/, /'suʃi/ *noun* L19 Japanese. A Japanese dish consisting of small balls or rolls of cold boiled rice flavoured with vinegar and garnished with vegetables, egg, or raw seafood.
1996 *Times* From the earliest records, fish have had a fried deal from chippers and a raw deal from sushi-eaters.

susurrus /sjuːˈsʌrəs/, /suːˈsʌrəs/ *noun* LME Latin (= a whisper, humming, muttering, of imitative origin). A low soft whispering or rustling sound.

■ Only in literary use.

sutra /'suːtrə/ *noun* E19 Sanskrit (*sūtra* thread, string, rule). 1 A rule or aphorism in Sanskrit literature, or a set of these on grammar or Hindu law or philosophy, expressed with maximum brevity. 2 A Buddhist scripture, usually doctrinal in content. Also, the Jain scriptures.

suttee /sʌˈtiː/, /'sʌti/ *noun* (also **sati**) L18 Sanskrit (*satī* faithful wife, feminine of *sat* good). Chiefly *History* 1 The former Hindu practice of a widow throwing herself on to her husband's funeral pyre. 2 A widow who committed such an act.

s.v. abbreviation of SUB VOCE.

svelte /svɛlt/ *adjective* E19 French (from Italian *svelto*). (Of a person) slender and elegant.

swami /'swɑːmi/ *noun* L18 Sanskrit (*svāmin*, nominative *svāmī*, master, prince). A male Hindu religious teacher.

swart gevaar /ˌswart xəˈfɑːr/ *noun phrase* M20 Afrikaans (literally, 'black peril', from Dutch *zwart* black + *gevaar* danger). *History* (In South Africa under apartheid) a threat perceived as being posed by black people to whites.
1996 T. Alexander *Unravelling Global Apartheid Die swart gevaar*—the black danger—united the white minority after their savage conflict in the Boer War.

swastika /'swɒstɪkə/ *noun* L19 Sanskrit (*svastika* from *svasti* well-being, luck, from *su* good + *asti* being). 1 An ancient symbol in the form of a cross with equal arms with a limb of the same length projecting at right angles from the end of each arm, all in the same direction and (usually) clockwise. 2 This symbol (with clockwise projecting limbs) used as the emblem of the German Nazi party; a HAKENKREUZ. Also, a flag bearing this emblem.

syce /sʌɪs/ *noun* (also **sice**) M17 Persian and Urdu (*sā'is* from Arabic). (In parts of Africa and Asia, and especially in the Indian subcontinent) a person who takes care of horses, a groom.

sympathique /sɛ̃patik/ *adjective* M19 French. (Of a thing, a place, etc.) agreeable, to one's taste, suitable. (Of a person) likeable, in tune with or responsive to one's personality or moods.
1996 *Times Magazine* I answer sometimes indiscreetly, which I tend to do when I find the interviewer intelligent and *sympathique*.

syncope /'sɪŋkəpi/ *noun* LME Late Latin (from Greek *sugkopē*, from *sun-* with + *kop-* stem of *koptein* to strike, cut off). 1 *Medicine* Fainting; temporary loss of consciousness caused by an insufficient flow of blood to the brain, frequently due to blood loss, shock, long standing, overheating, etc. 2 *Grammar* Shortening of a word by omission of one or more syllables or letters in the middle; a word so shortened.

synecdoche /sɪˈnɛkdəki/ *noun* LME Latin (from Greek *sunekdokhē*, from *sunekdekhesthai*, literally, 'to take with something else', from *sun-* with + *ekdekhesthai* take, take up). A figure of speech in which a more inclusive term is used for a less inclusive one or vice versa, as a whole for a part or a part for a whole.

1996 *Country Life* It is a remarkable thing that, now that the very synecdoche of these islands—Land's End and John o'Groats—have come up for sale, no national body...appears to be formulating a plan to buy them on behalf of the nation.

tabac /taba/ *noun* plural pronounced same E20 French. (In French-speaking countries) a tobacconist's shop.

tabbouleh /tə'bu:leɪ/ *noun* M20 Arabic (*tabbūla*). A Syrian and Lebanese salad of cracked wheat mixed with finely chopped ingredients such as tomatoes, onions, and parsley.

tabi /'tɑ:bi/ *noun* plural same **tabis** E17 Japanese. A thick-soled Japanese ankle sock with a separate section for the big toe.

tabla /'tʌblə/, /'tʌblɑ:/ *noun* M19 Persian and Urdu (*tabla(h)*, Hindi *tablā* from Arabic *ṭabl*). A pair of small hand drums of unequal size used in Indian music; the smaller of these drums.

tableau /'tablə⋁/, *foreign* /tablo/ *noun* plural **tableaux** /'tablə⋁z/, *foreign* /tablo/ L17 French (from Old French *tablel* diminutive of *table* from Latin *tabula* plank, tablet, list). A group of models or motionless figures representing a scene from a story or from history. **b** A TABLEAU VIVANT. **c** *Theatre* A motionless representation of the action at some (especially critical) stage in a play; a stage direction for this. Also, the sudden creation of a striking or dramatic situation.

■ Originally used, in the late 17th century, in the sense 'picture' and, figuratively, 'picturesque description'.

tableau vivant /ˌtablə⋁ 'vi:vɒ̃/, *foreign* /tablo vivɑ̃/ *noun* plural **tableaux vivants** (pronounced same) E19 French (literally, 'living picture'). A silent and motionless representation of a character, scene, incident, etc., by a person or group of people; *transferred* a picturesque actual scene.

1996 *Spectator* But viewed as the sequence of one glittering plastic set after another,... and a series of fantastically elaborate, dizzying *tableaux vivants*, no one could resist its poisoned brilliant intensity.

table d'hôte /ˌtɑ:b(ə)l 'də⋁t/, *foreign* /tablə dot/ *noun phrase* E17 French (= host's table). A restaurant meal offered at a fixed price and with few if any choices.

■ The term originally denoted a table in a hotel or restaurant where all guests ate together, hence a meal served there at a stated time and for a fixed price.

tablier /'tabliei/, *foreign* /tablje/ (*plural same*) *noun* M19 French (ultimately from Latin *tabula* plank, tablet, list). *History* A part of a woman's dress resembling an apron; the front of a skirt having the form of an apron.

taboo /tə'bu:/ *adjective & noun* (also **tabu**, (chiefly *New Zealand*) **tapu** /'tɑ:pu:/) L18 Tongan (*tabu* set apart, forbidden). **A** *adjective* **1** Set apart for or consecrated to a special use or purpose; forbidden to general use or to a particular person or class of people; sacred; forbidden. **2** (Especially of a word, topic, or activity) prohibited or restricted, especially by social custom. **B** *noun* A social or religious custom prohibiting or restricting a particular practice or forbidding association with a particular person, place, or thing.

■ The word was introduced into English by Captain Cook (1728–79).

tabouret /'tabərɛt/, /'tabəreɪ/ *noun* M17 French (diminutive of Old French *tabour* (also *tanbor*, *tamb(o)ur*), apparently of oriental origin; cf. Persian *tabīra*, *tabūrāk* drum). **1** A low backless seat or stool for one person. **2** A small table, especially one used as a stand for house plants; a bedside table. *United States*.

tabula rasa /ˌtabjʊlə 'rɑ:zə/ *noun phrase* Latin (literally, 'scraped tablet', denoting a tablet from which the writing has been erased, ready to be written on again). **1** An absence of preconceived ideas or predetermined goals; a clean slate. **2** A mind having no innate ideas (as in some views of the human mind at birth).

2 1995 J. D. Barrow *Artful Universe* No mind was ever a *tabula rasa*. We enter the world with minds that possess an innate ability to learn.

tac-au-tac /'takəʊtak/ *noun* E20 French (literally, 'clash for clash', from *tac* (imitative)). *Fencing* A parry combined with a riposte.

tacet /'teɪsɛt/, /'tasɪt/ *adverb & noun* E18 Latin (= is silent, from *tacere* to be silent). *Music* **A** *adverb* (As a direction) indicating that a voice or instrument is silent for a time. **B** *noun* A pause.

taco /'tɑːkəʊ/, /'takəʊ/ *noun* plural **tacos** M20 Mexican Spanish. A Mexican dish comprising a tortilla or cornmeal pancake rolled or folded and filled with various mixtures, such as seasoned mince, chicken, beans, etc.

taedium vitae /ˌtʌɪdɪəm 'viːtʌɪ/, /ˌtiːdɪəm 'vʌɪtiː/ *noun phrase* M18 Latin (*taedium* weariness, disgust + *vitae* genitive of *vita* life). Weariness of life; extreme ennui or inertia, often as a pathological state with a tendency to suicide.

tae kwon do /ˌtʌɪ kwɒn 'dəʊ/ /ˌteɪ kwɒn 'dəʊ/ *noun phrase* M20 Korean (literally, 'art of hand and foot fighting'). A modern Korean system of unarmed combat developed chiefly in the mid 20th century, combining elements of KARATE, ancient Korean martial art, and KUNG FU, differing from karate in its wide range of kicking techniques and its emphasis on different methods of breaking objects.

taenia /'tiːnɪə/ *noun* (also **tenia**) plural **taeniae** /'tiːnɪː/, **taenias** M16 Latin (from Greek *tainia* band, fillet, ribbon). **1** *Anatomy* A flat ribbon-like structure in the body. Usually with specifying word. **2** *Architecture* A fillet or band between a Doric architrave and frieze. **3** (In ancient Greece) a band or ribbon worn round a person's head.

Tafelwein /'tɑːfəlvaɪn/ *noun* L20 German (literally, 'table wine'). Ordinary German wine of reasonable quality, suitable for drinking with a meal.

tafia /'tafɪə/ *noun* M18 French (from West Indian creole, alteration of RATAFIA). (In the West Indies) a drink similar to rum, distilled from molasses or waste from the production of brown sugar.

tagliarini /taljə'riːni/ *noun* M19 Italian (*taglierini* plural, from *tagliare* to cut). Pasta made in very narrow ribbons.

tagliatelle /taljə'tɛli/ *noun* L19 Italian (from *tagliare* to cut; cf. preceding). Pasta made in narrow ribbons.

tahini /tɑː'hiːni/ *noun* (also **tahina** /tɑː'hiːnə/) M20 Modern Greek (*takhini* from Arabic *ṭaḥīnā* from *ṭaḥana* to grind, crush, pulverize). A Middle Eastern paste or spread made from ground sesame seeds.

t'ai chi /tʌɪ 'tʃiː/ *noun* M18 Chinese (*tàijí* (Wade-Giles *t'ai chi*), from *tài* extreme + *jí* limit). **1** (In Chinese philosophy) the ultimate source and limit of reality, from which spring yin and yang and all of creation. **2** A Chinese martial art and system of callisthenics, consisting of sequences of very slow controlled movements, believed to have been devised by a Taoist priest in the Song dynasty (960–1279). In full *t'ai chi ch'uan* /'tʃwɑːn/ (Chinese *quán* fist, boxing).

taiga /'tʌɪɡə/ *noun* L19 Russian (*taïga* from Mongolian). The swampy coniferous forest of high northern latitudes, especially that between the tundra and steppes of Siberia.

taiko /'tʌɪkəʊ/ *noun* plural same, **taikos** L19 Japanese. A Japanese barrel-shaped drum.

taille /tɑːj/, /taj/ *noun* plural pronounced same M16 French (from Old French *taillier* (modern *tailler*) from Proto-Romance (medieval Latin *tailliare*) from Latin *talea* rod, twig, cutting). **1** (In France before 1789) a tax levied on the common people by the king or an overlord. **2** *Music* (now *historical*). The register of a tenor or similar voice; an instrument of this register. **3** The juice produced from a second pressing of the grapes during winemaking; low-quality wine made from the second pressing of the grapes.

tailleur /tajœr/ *noun* plural pronounced same E20 French (from TAILLE). A woman's tailor-made suit.

> **1982** T. Fitzgibbon *With Love* I pressed the black *tailleur*, bought a gay scarf…and went off to look for a job.

taipan /'tʌɪpan/ *noun* M19 Chinese ((Cantonese) *daaíhbāan*). A foreigner who is head of a business in China.

takht /tɑːkt/ *noun* L20 Persian (*taḵt*). (In Eastern countries) a sofa or long bench, or a bed.

talaq /təˈlɑːk/ *noun* (also **talak**) L18 Arabic (*ṭalaḵ*, from *ṭalaḵat*, *ṭaluḵat* be repudiated). (In Islamic law) divorce, especially by the husband's verbal repudiation of his wife in the presence of witnesses.

talaria /təˈlɛːrɪə/ *noun* plural L16 Latin (neuter plural of *talaris* from *talus* ankle). (In Roman Mythology) winged sandals or small wings attached to the ankles of some gods and goddesses, especially Mercury.

taleggio /taˈlɛdʒɪəʊ/ *noun* L20 Italian. A type of soft Italian cheese made from cow's milk.

talik /'talɪk/ *noun* M20 Russian (from *tayat'* to melt). *Geology* An area of unfrozen ground surrounded by permafrost.

tallith /'talɪθ/ *noun* E17 Hebrew (rabbinical Hebrew *ṭallīt*, from biblical Hebrew *ṭillel* to cover). A shawl with fringed corners traditionally worn by male Jews at prayer.

talus /'teɪləs/ *noun* plural **taluses** M17 French (of unknown origin). **1** A sloping mass of rock fragments at the foot of a cliff. **2** The sloping side of an earthwork, or of a wall that tapers to the top.

tamagotchi /ˌtaməˈɡɒtʃi/ *noun* (also **Tamagotchi**) L20 Japanese (= lovable egg). *trademark* A small, portable electronic device displaying a digital image of a creature, which has to be looked after and responded to by the 'owner' as if it were a pet.

tamale /təˈmɑːli/ *noun* L17 Mexican Spanish (*tamal*, plural *tamales*, from Nahuatl *tamalli*). A Mexican dish of seasoned meat and maize flour steamed or baked in maize husks.

tamari /təˈmɑːri/ *noun* L20 Japanese. A Japanese variety of rich wheat-free soy sauce. Also *tamari sauce*.

tamasha /təˈmɑːʃə/ *noun* E17 Persian and Urdu (*tamāšā* (for *tamāšī*) walking about for amusement, entertainment, from Arabic *tamāšā* walk about together, from *mašā* walk). **1** (In the Indian subcontinent) a grand show, performance, or celebration, especially one involving dance. **2** A fuss, a commotion. *Colloquial*.

> **2 1981** S. Rushdie *Midnight's Children* Enough of this tamasha! No more of this… tomfoolery!

tambour /'tambʊə/ *noun* L15 French (Old French *tabour* (also *tanbor*, *tamb(o)ur*), apparently of oriental origin (cf. Persian *tabīra*, *tabūrāk* drum), spelling perhaps influenced by Arabic *ṭunbūr* a kind of lute or lyre). **1** *History* A small drum. **2** *Architecture* **a** A wall of circular plan, such as one supporting a dome or surrounded by a colonnade. **b** Each of a sequence of cylindrical stones forming the shaft of a column. **3** A lobby with a ceiling and folding doors serving to prevent draughts, especially in a church porch. **4** A sliding flexible shutter or door on a desk, cabinet, etc., made of strips of wood attached to a canvas backing. **5** A circular frame formed of one hoop fitting inside another, in which fabric is held taut for embroidering. **6** A projecting part of the main wall of a real tennis or fives court, with a sloping end face.

tandoor /'tandʊə/, /'tan'dʊə/ *noun* M19 Urdu (*tandūr*, Persian *tanūr* ultimately from Arabic *tannūr*). A clay oven of a kind used originally in northern India and Pakistan.

tandoori /tan'dʊəri/ *adjective & noun* M20 Persian and Urdu (from *tandūr*: see preceding). **A** *adjective* Denoting or relating to a style of Indian cooking based on the use of a tandoor. **B** *noun* Tandoori cooking or food; a tandoori dish.

tanga /ˈtaŋgə/ *noun* E20 Portuguese (ultimately of Bantu origin). **1** *Anthropology* A triangular loincloth or pubic covering worn by indigenous peoples in tropical America. **2** A pair of briefs consisting of small panels connected by strings at the sides.

tango /ˈtaŋgəʊ/ *noun & verb* plural **tangos** L19 American Spanish (perhaps of African origin). **A** *noun* **1** A ballroom dance originating in Buenos Aires, characterized by slow gliding movements and abrupt pauses; a piece of music written for or in the style of the tango, typically in a slow, dotted duple rhythm. **B** *intransitive verb* Dance a tango.

tanka /ˈtaŋkə/ *noun* plural same, **tankas** L19 Japanese (from *tan* short + *ka* song). A Japanese poem consisting of thirty-one syllables in five lines, giving a complete picture of an event or mood.

tant mieux /tɑ̃ mjø/ *interjection* M18 French. So much the better. Cf. TANT PIS.
> **1972** M. Kaye *Lively Game of Death* If your boss can pin his death on somebody, *tant mieux*.

tanto /ˈtantəʊ/ *adverb* L19 Italian (from Latin *tantum* so much). *Music* (As a direction) too much, so much.
■ Used to modify adjectives or adverbs from Italian, as in *allegro non tanto*, meaning 'fast, but not too much so'.

tant pis /tɑ̃ pi/ *interjection* L18 French. So much the worse; too bad. Cf. TANT MIEUX.
> **1995** D. Lodge *Therapy* I hope that Laurence and I can go back to our chaste, companionable relationship, but if we can't, *tant pis*.

tantra /ˈtantrə/ *noun* (also **Tantra**) L18 Sanskrit (= loom, warp, groundwork, system, doctrine). **1** A Hindu or Buddhist mystical or magical text, dating from the seventh century or earlier. **2** Adherence to the doctrines or principles of the tantras, involving mantra, meditation, yoga, and ritual.

Taoiseach /ˈtiːʃəx/ *noun* M20 Irish (= chief, leader). The Prime Minister of the Irish Republic.

tapas /ˈtapəs/ *noun plural* M20 Spanish (*tapa*, literally, 'cover, lid' (because the dishes were given free with the drink, served on a dish balanced on, therefore 'covering', the glass)). Small Spanish savoury dishes, typically served with drinks at a bar.

tapenade /ˈtapənɑːd/ *noun* M20 French (from Provençal *tapeno*). A Provençal savoury paste or dip, made mainly from black olives, capers, and anchovies.

tapis /ˈtapi/ *noun* plural same L15 French (= carpet, tablecloth, from Old French *tapiz* (also modern *tapis*) from late Latin *tapetium* from Greek *tapētion* diminutive of *tapēs*, *tapēt-* tapestry). A tapestry or richly decorated cloth, used as a hanging or a covering. Now *archaic*.
■ The phrase *(up)on the tapis* (L17) meaning 'under discussion (*or* consideration)', is a partial translation of French *sur le tapis* (literally, 'on the tablecloth'), also occasionally used in English.

tapotement /təˈpəʊtm(ə)nt/ *noun* L19 French (from *tapoter* to tap). Rapid and repeated striking of the body as a technique in massage.

taqueria /ˌtɑːkəˈriːə/ *noun* L20 Mexican Spanish (from TACO). (In the United States) a Mexican restaurant specializing in tacos.

tarantella /ˌtar(ə)nˈtɛlə/ *noun* (also **tarantelle** /ˌtar(ə)nˈtɛl/) L18 Italian (diminutive of *Taranto* (Latin *Tarentum*), a town in southern Italy: popularly associated with *tarantola* tarantula). **1** A rapid whirling dance originating in southern Italy. **2** A piece of music for such a dance or composed in its triplet rhythm, with abrupt transitions from the major to the minor.
■ The dance was at one time thought to be a cure for tarantism (a psychological illness characterized by an extreme impulse to dance, believed in the 15th to 17th centuries to be caused by the bite of a tarantula), the victim dancing the tarantella until exhausted.

tarboosh /tɑːˈbuːʃ/ *noun* (also **tarbush**) E18 Arabic ((Egyptian) *ṭarbūš* from Ottoman Turkish *terpōš*, Turkish *tarbuş* from

Persian *sarpūš*, from *sar* head + *pūš* cover). A cap similar to a fez, usually of red felt with a tassel at the top, worn by Muslim men.

targa /ˈtɑːgə/ *adjective & noun* L20 Italian (= plate, shield; the name of a model of Porsche motor car (introduced in 1965) with a detachable hood, probably after the *Targa Florio* (= Florio Shield), a motor time trial held annually in Sicily). **A** *adjective trademark* Designating a type of convertible sports car with a detachable roof hood or panelling, which when removed leaves a central roll-bar for passenger safety. **B** *noun* A car having this feature.

tarot /ˈtarəʊ/ *noun* L16 French (from Italian *tarocchi* plural of *tarocco*, of unknown origin). **1** (**the Tarot**) playing cards, traditionally a pack of 78 with five suits, used for fortune-telling and (especially in Europe) in certain games. **2** A card game played with tarot cards. **3** A card from a pack of tarot cards. Also *tarot card*.

tastevin /tastəvɛ̃/ *noun* plural pronounced same M20 French (*tastevin*, *tâtevin* wine taster). A small shallow (especially silver) cup for tasting wines, of a type used in France. Also (**Tastevin**), a member of a French order or guild of wine tasters.

tatami /təˈtɑːmi/ *noun* E17 Japanese. A rush-covered straw mat forming a traditional floor covering in Japan. Also *tatami mat*.

tathata /tatəˈtɑː/, /taθəˈtɑː/ *noun* M20 Pali (*tathatā* true state of things, from *tathā* in that manner, so). *Buddhism* The ultimate nature of all things, as expressed in phenomena but inexpressible in language.

tau /tɔː/, /taʊ/ *noun* ME Greek (from Hebrew *tāw* final letter of Hebrew alphabet). **1** The nineteenth (originally the final) letter (T, τ) of the Greek alphabet, transliterated as 't'. **2** (More fully *tau cross*) a cross in which the transverse piece surmounts the upright piece (also called *St Anthony's cross*). **3** *Physics* An unstable subatomic particle of the lepton class. Also *tau lepton*, *tau particle*.

taupe /təʊp/ *noun* E20 French (from Latin *talpa* mole). Grey with a tinge of brown, resembling the colour of moleskin.

taverna /təˈvɜːnə/ *noun* E20 Modern Greek (from Latin *taberna* tavern). A small Greek restaurant or cafe.

tazza /ˈtatsə/ *noun* plural **tazze** /ˈtatseɪ/, **tazzas** E19 Italian (from Arabic *ṭasa* bowl). A shallow ornamental wine cup or vase, especially one mounted on a foot.

tchotchke /ˈtʃɒtʃkə/ *noun* (also **tsatske** /ˈtsɒtskə/) M20 Yiddish (from Slavonic: cf. Russian *tsatska*). **1** A small object that is decorative rather than strictly functional; a trinket. **2** A pretty girl or woman. *United States colloquial*.

1977 *New Yorker*… stocked with a careful selection of New York's best tchotchkes. These include thirteen-inch-long matchbooks.

Te Deum /tiː ˈdiːəm/, /teɪ ˈdeɪəm/ *noun phrase* OE Latin. **1** An ancient Latin hymn of praise beginning *Te deum laudamus* 'We praise you, O God', sung as an expression of thanksgiving on special occasions, and sung or recited regularly at Roman Catholic matins and (in translation) at Anglican matins. **2** An expression of thanksgiving or exultation.

teepee variant of TEPEE.

tefillin /tiːˈfɪliːn/ *noun* plural E17 Aramaic (*tĕpillīn* prayers). Jewish phylacteries; the texts inscribed on these.

tegula /ˈtɛɡjʊlə/ *noun* plural **tegulae** /ˈtɛɡjʊliː/ E19 Latin (= tile, from *tegere* to cover). *Entomology* A small scale-like sclerite covering the base of the forewing in many insects.

tekke /ˈtɛkeɪ/ *noun* M17 Turkish (*tekke*, Arabic *takiyya*, Persian *takya* place of repose, pillow, abode of a dervish or fakir, perhaps ultimately from Arabic *ittaka'a* to lean on). A monastery of dervishes, especially in Ottoman Turkey.

telamon /ˈtɛləmən/, /ˈtɛləməʊn/ *noun* plural **telamones** /tɛləˈməʊniːz/ E17 Latin (*telamones* (plural) from Greek *telamōnes* plural of *Telamōn* Telamon, a mythical hero). *Architecture* A male figure used as a pillar to support an entablature or other structure.

■ The female equivalent is a *caryatid*.

téléphérique /teleferik/ *noun* (also **teleferic** /tɛlɪˈfɛrɪk/, **téléférique** /tele ferik/ (*plural same*), **telepherique** /ˌtɛlɪfɛˈriːk/) plural pronounced same E20 French (Italian *teleferica*, from Greek *tēle-* far + *pherein* to carry). A cableway; a mountain cable car.

telos /ˈtɛlɒs/ *noun* plural **teloi** /ˈtɛlɔɪ/ M16 Greek (= end). An ultimate object or aim.

> **1995** *Spectator* The *telos* of society became increasing amounts of health, wealth and happiness.

temblor /tɛmˈblɔː/ *noun* L19 American Spanish. An earthquake. *South-western United States.*

temenos /ˈtɛmənɒs/ *noun* plural **temene** /ˈtɛməniː/ E19 Greek (from stem of *temnein* to cut off, sever). Chiefly *Archaeology* A piece of ground surrounding or adjacent to a temple; a sacred enclosure or precinct.

tempeh /ˈtɛmpeɪ/ *noun* M20 Indonesian (*tempe*). An Indonesian dish made by deep-frying fermented soya beans.

tempera /ˈtɛmp(ə)rə/ *noun* M19 Italian (in *pingere a tempera* paint in distemper). A method of painting using especially an emulsion e.g. of pigment with egg, especially as a fine art technique on canvas. Also, the emulsion etc. used in this method.

tempo /ˈtɛmpəʊ/ *noun* plural **tempi** /ˈtɛmpiː/, **tempos** M17 Italian (from Latin *tempus* time). **1** *Music* The speed at which a passage of music is or should be played. **2** The rate or speed of motion or activity; pace.

■ Originally used (in the mid 17th century) as a fencing term denoting the timing of an attack so that one's opponent is within reach.

tempo rubato /ˌtɛmpəʊ ruˈbɑːtəʊ/ *noun phrase* L18 Italian (literally, 'stolen time'). Cf. RUBATO.

temps levé /ˌtã ləˈveɪ/ *noun* plural same L19 French (literally, 'raised time'). *Ballet* A movement like a small hop in which there is no transfer of weight from one foot to the other.

temps perdu /tã pɛrdy/ *noun phrase* M20 French (literally, 'time lost'). The past, contemplated with nostalgia and a sense of irretrievability. Cf. RE-CHERCHE DU TEMPS PERDU.

tempura /ˈtɛmpʊrə/ *noun* E20 Japanese (probably from Portuguese *têmpêro* seasoning). A Japanese dish consisting of shellfish or whitefish and often vegetables, fried in batter.

tempus fugit /ˌtɛmpəs ˈfjuːdʒɪt/, /ˌtɛmpəs ˈfuːɡɪt/ *interjection* L18 Latin Time flies.

■ Originally from a line from Virgil's *Georgics, Sed fugit interea, fugit inreparabile tempus* ('But meanwhile it is flying, irretrievable time is flying').

tendresse /tãdrɛs/ *noun* plural pronounced same LME French (from *tendre* tender). A feeling of fondness or affection.

> **1996** *Bookseller*...he played a shy landowner, struggling with the *tendresse* he felt for Ted..., his estate manager.

tendu /tãdy/ *adjective* E20 French (past participle of *tendre* to stretch). *Ballet* Stretched out or held tautly.

tenet /ˈtɛnɪt/, /ˈtiːnɛt/ *noun* L16 Latin (literally, 'he holds', 3rd person present singular of *tenere* to hold). A principle or belief, especially one of the main principles of a religion or philosophy.

■ Since E18 has entirely superseded the earlier form *tenent* (M16).

tenorino /tɛnəˈriːnəʊ/ *noun* plural **tenorini** /tɛnəˈriːni/ M19 Italian (diminutive of *tenore* tenor). A high tenor.

tenuto /təˈnuːtəʊ/ *adverb, adjective & noun* M18 Italian (past participle of *tenere* to hold). *Music* **A** *adverb & adjective* (Of a note) held for its full time value or slightly more. Abbreviated to *ten*. **B** *noun* plural **tenutos**, **tenuti** /təˈnuːti/ A note or chord performed in this way.

teocalli /tiːəˈkali/ *noun* E17 American Spanish (from Nahuatl *teoːkalli*, from *teoːtl* god + *kalli* house). A temple of the Aztecs or other Mexican peoples, typically standing on a truncated pyramid.

tepache /teˈpatʃe/ *noun* E20 Mexican Spanish (from Nahuatl *tepiatl*). Any of several Mexican drinks of varying degrees of fermentation, typically made with pineapple, water, and brown sugar.

tepee /ˈtiːpiː/ *noun* (also **teepee**, **tipi**) M18 Sioux (*tʰípi* dwelling). A conical tent made of skins, cloth, or canvas stretched over a frame of poles fastened together at the top, used by American Indians of the Plains and Great Lakes regions. Now also, a structure imitating or resembling such a tent.

tephra /ˈtɛfrə/ *noun* M20 Greek (= ashes). *Geology* Dust and rock fragments that have been ejected into the air by a volcanic eruption.

tepidarium /tɛpɪˈdɛːrɪəm/ *noun* plural **tepidaria** /tɛpɪˈdɛːrɪə/ E19 Latin. In an ancient Roman bath, the warm room between the frigidarium and the caldarium.

teppanyaki /ˈtɛpanjaki/ *noun* L20 Japanese (from *teppan* steel plate + *yaki* fry). A Japanese dish of meat, fish, or both, fried with vegetables on a hot steel plate forming the centre of the table.

tequila /tɛˈkiːlə/ *noun* M19 Mexican Spanish (from the name of a town producing the drink). A Mexican alcoholic spirit made by distilling the fermented sap of an agave. Cf. MESCAL sense 2.

terai /təˈrʌɪ/ *noun* L19 Hindi (*tarāī* marshy lowlands). **1** A wide-brimmed felt hat with a double-layered crown and a vent, worn chiefly by travellers in subtropical regions. In full *terai hat*. **2** A belt of marshy jungle lying between the southern foothills of the Himalayas and the plains.

tercet /ˈtəːsɪt/ *noun* L16 French (from Italian *terzetto*, from *terzo* from Latin *tertius* third). *Prosody* A set or group of three lines of verse rhyming together or connected by rhyme with an adjacent triplet.

teriyaki /tɛrɪˈjɑːki/ *noun* M20 Japanese (from *teri* gloss, lustre + *yaki* grill). **1** A Japanese dish consisting of fish or meat marinated in soy sauce and grilled. **2** (also *teriyaki sauce*) A mixture of soy sauce, sake, ginger, and other flavourings, used in Japanese cookery as a marinade or glaze for fish or meat dishes.

terminus ad quem /ˌtəːmɪnəs ad ˈkwɛm/ *noun phrase* M16 Latin (= end to which; cf. TERMINUS A QUO). The finishing point of an argument, policy, period, etc.; an aim or goal.

terminus ante quem /ˌtəːmɪnəs antɪ ˈkwɛm/ *noun phrase* M20 Latin (= end before which). The finishing point of a period, the latest possible date for something.

▪ Also elliptically as *terminus ante*.

terminus a quo /ˌtəːmɪnəs ɑ ˈkwəʊ/ *noun phrase* M16 Latin (= end from which). The starting point of an argument, policy, period, etc.; the earliest possible date for something.

▪ Like TERMINUS AD QUEM, originally part of the technical vocabulary of the 13th-century scholastic philosophers (Albertus Magnus, Thomas Aquinas, etc.).

terminus post quem /ˌtəːmɪnəs pəʊst ˈkwɛm/ *noun phrase* M20 Latin (= end after which). The starting point of a period, the earliest possible date for something.

▪ Also elliptically as *terminus post*.

terra alba /ˌtɛrə ˈalbə/ *noun phrase* E20 Latin (= white earth). Any of various white earths, as pipeclay, kaolin, etc.; now *specifically* white pulverized gypsum used in the manufacture of paper, paint, etc.

terra cognita /ˌtɛrə kɒɡˈniːtə/ *noun phrase* M20 Latin (= known land). *figurative* Familiar territory. Opposite of TERRA INCOGNITA.

1962 E. Snow *Other Side of River* My last remark had put them back on terra cognita and it would have been an appropriate moment to leave.

terracotta /ˌtɛrəˈkɒtə/ *noun & adjective* E18 Italian (*terra cotta* baked earth from Latin *terra cocta*). **A** *noun* **1** A type of fired clay, typically of a brownish-red colour and unglazed, used as an ornamental building material and in modelling. **b** A statuette or figurine made of this substance. **2** A strong brownish-red or brownish-orange colour. **B** *adjective* Relating to or made of terracotta; of the typical colour of terracotta, brownish red.

terra firma /ˌtɛrə ˈfəːmə/ *noun phrase* M17 Latin (= firm land). The ground as distinguished from the sea or air; dry land.

■ Originally used in English as the name of the territories on the Italian mainland which were subject to the state of Venice. Then later used for the northern coastland of South America (Colombia), as distinguished from the West Indies.

terra incognita /ˌtɛrə ɪnˈkɒɡnɪtə/, /ɪnˈkɒɡˈniːtə/ *noun phrase* E17 Latin (= unknown land). **1** An unknown or unexplored territory, land, or region. **2** An unknown or unexplored area of study, knowledge, or experience.

■ Frequently without article.
2 1996 *New Scientist* . . . sequencing the yeast genome has revealed a vast *terra incognita*. Biologists have no clue as to the function of 40 per cent of the genes they have identified . . .

terra rossa /ˌtɛrə ˈrɒsə/ *noun phrase* L19 Italian (*terra* earth + feminine of *rosso* red). *Soil Science* A reddish soil occurring on limestone in Mediterranean climates.

terra sigillata /ˌtɛrə sɪdʒɪˈleɪtə/ *noun phrase* LME Medieval Latin (= sealed earth). **1** Astringent clay from Lemnos or Samos, formerly valued as a medicine and antidote. *Obsolete* except *historical*. **2** A type of fine, glossy, reddish-brown pottery widely made in the Roman Empire. Also called *Samian ware*.

terrasse /tɛras/ *noun* plural pronounced same L20 French. (Originally in France) a flat, paved area outside a building, especially a café, where people sit to take refreshments.

terrazzo /təˈratsəʊ/ *noun* plural **terrazzos** E20 Italian (= terrace, balcony). A flooring material made of chips of marble or granite set in concrete and polished to give a smooth surface.

terre-à-terre /tɛratɛr/ *adjective & adverb phrase* E18 French (from Italian *terra a terra* level with the ground). *Ballet* (Of a step or manner of dancing) in which the feet remain on or close to the ground. Also *transferred*, without elevation of style; down-to-earth, realistic; pedestrian, unimaginative.

terreplein /ˈtɛːpleɪn/, *foreign* /tɛrplɛ̃/ (*plural same*) *noun* L16 French (*terre-plein* from Italian *terrapieno*, from *terrapienare* to fill with earth, from *terra* earth + *pieno* (from Latin *plenus*) full). Chiefly *History* The level base (above, on, or below the natural surface of the ground) on which a battery of guns is mounted.

■ In early use denoted a sloping bank of earth behind a wall or rampart.

terre-verte /tɛːˈvɛːt/ *noun* M17 French (= green earth). A greyish-green pigment made from a kind of clay (glauconite) and used especially as a pigment for watercolours and tempera. Also called *green earth*.

terribilità /ˌtɛrribiliˈta/ *noun* L19 Italian. **1** *Art* Awesomeness or emotional intensity of conception and execution in an artist or work of art; originally a quality attributed to Michelangelo by his contemporaries. **2** *generally* Terrifying or awesome quality.
2 1975 *New Yorker* Fathers have voices, and each voice has a *terribilità* of its own.

terrine /təˈriːn/ *noun* E18 French (= large earthenware pot, feminine of Old French *terrin* earthen, from Latin *terra* earth). **1** Originally a tureen. Now, an earthenware or similar fireproof vessel, especially one in which a terrine or pâté is cooked or sold. **2** A meat, fish, or vegetable mixture that has been cooked or otherwise prepared in advance and allowed to cool or set in its container, typically served in slices.

terroir /tɛrwar/ *noun* L20 French (= soil). The complete natural environment in which a particular wine is produced, including factors such as the soil, topography, and climate; (also *goût de terroir* /ɡu də/) the characteristic taste and flavour imparted to a wine by the environment in which it is produced.
1995 *Country Life* The world of still wine continues to preach the 'small is beautiful'

message, the importance of the individual grower and winemaker, the influence of *terroir* (that elusive mix of soil and climate) and the effect of both on wines.

tertium quid /ˌtəːʃɪəm ˈkwɪd/, /ˌtəːtɪəm ˈkwɪd/ *noun phrase* E18 Late Latin (translation of Greek *triton ti* some third thing). A third thing that is indefinite or left undefined but is related in some way to two definite or known things.

tertius /ˈtəːʃɪəs/, /ˈtəːtɪəs/ *adjective* E19 Latin (= third). Designating the third of three or more pupils of the same surname to enter a school. Cf. PRIMUS adjective 2, SECUNDUS.
■ Appended to a surname and used especially in public schools.

terza rima /ˌtɛːtsə ˈriːmə/ *noun phrase* E19 Italian (= third rhyme). *Prosody* A form of iambic verse of Italian origin, consisting of triplets in which the middle line of each triplet rhymes with the first and third of the next.
■ Best known as the metre of Dante's *Divine Comedy*.

terzetto /tɛːtˈsɛtəʊ/, /təːtˈsɛtəʊ/ *noun* plural **terzettos**, **terzetti** /tɛːtˈsɛti/ E18 Italian. *Music* A vocal or (occasionally) instrumental trio.

tessera /ˈtɛs(ə)rə/ *noun* plural **tesserae** /ˈtɛs(ə)riː/ M17 Latin (from Greek, neuter of *tesseres* variant of *tessares* four). **1** A small block of stone, tile, glass, or other material used in the construction of a mosaic. **2** (In ancient Greece and Rome) a small tablet of wood or bone used as a token, tally, or ticket.

tessitura /tɛsɪˈtʊərə/ *noun* L19 Italian (= texture). *Music* The range within which most notes of a vocal part fall.
1978 *Early Music* He chose singers for whom the resulting tessituras did not mean any strain.

tête-à-tête /ˌteɪtɑːˈteɪt/, /ˌtɛtaˈtɛt/ *noun, adverb, & adjective* (also **tête à tête**) L17 French (literally, 'head to head'). **A** *noun* **1** A private conversation or interview, especially between two people. **2** An S-shaped sofa, enabling two people to sit face to face. **B** *adverb* Together in private; face to face. **C** *adjective* Private, confidential; involving or attended by only two people.

A.1 1995 D. Lodge *Therapy* I knew I was in for a long, harrowing *tête à tête*.

tête-bêche /tɛtbɛʃ/; /tɛtˈbɛʃ/, /teɪtˈbɛʃ/ *adjective* L19 French (from *tête* head + *bêche* (reduced from *béchevet*), literally, 'double bedhead'). *Philately* (Of a postage stamp) printed upside down or sideways relative to the next stamp in the same row or column.

tête de cuvée /tɛt də kyve/ *noun phrase* plural **têtes de cuvées** (pronounced same) E20 French (literally, 'head of the vatful'). A wine produced from the first pressing of the grapes, generally considered superior in quality; a vineyard producing the best wine in the locality of a village.

thali /ˈtɑːli/ *noun* M20 Hindi (*thālī* from Sanskrit *sthālī*). A metal platter on which Indian food is served; an Indian meal comprising a selection of assorted dishes, especially served on such a platter.

thalweg /ˈtɑːlvɛg/, /ˈθɑːlwɛg/ *noun* (also **talweg**) M19 German (from *thal* (now *Tal*) valley + *Weg* way). *Geology* The line of fastest descent from any point on land; *especially* one connecting the deepest points along a river channel or the lowest points along a valley floor.
1996 M. Anderson *Frontiers* According to the 1913 Protocol of Constantinople, part of the frontier was to follow the *Thalweg*, but the waters of the lower part of the river and the estuary remained Turkish.

thé dansant /te dɑ̃sɑ̃/ *noun phrase* plural **thés dansants** (pronounced same) E19 French (literally, 'dancing tea'). An afternoon entertainment at which there is dancing and tea is served, a tea dance.
1995 *Spectator* One afternoon I went to Hatchett's to observe a typical afternoon *thé dansant*. What a strange thing to have done.

thermae /ˈθəːmiː/ *noun* plural M16 Latin (from Greek *thermai* hot baths). (In ancient Greece and Rome) hot baths used for public bathing.

thesis /ˈθiːsɪs/; *in sense 3 also* /ˈθɛsɪs/ *noun* plural **theses** /ˈθiːsiːz/ LME Late Latin (from Greek = putting, placing; a proposition, an affirmation, from *the-* base of *tithenai* to put, place). **1** A proposition laid down or stated, especially one maintained or put forward as a premise in an argument, or to be proved. **2** A long essay or dissertation involving personal research, written by a candidate for a university degree. **3** *Prosody* An unstressed syllable or part of a metrical foot in Greek or Latin verse. Opposed to ARSIS.

theta /ˈθiːtə/ *noun* LME Greek (*thēta*). **1** The eighth letter (Θ, θ) of the Greek alphabet, transliterated as 'th'. Also, the phonetic symbol θ, used *specifically* in the International Phonetic Alphabet to represent a voiceless dental fricative. **2** *Chemistry* Used *attributively* to designate the temperature of a polymer solution at which it behaves ideally as regards its osmotic pressure (also θ, Θ *temperature*), and the conditions, solvent, etc., associated with such behaviour.

■ In a transferred use of sense 1, *theta* is a sign of doom or a death sentence, in allusion to the custom of using θ as standing for *thanatos* 'death' on the ballots used in voting on a sentence of life or death in ancient Greece.

tholos /ˈθɒlɒs/ *noun* plural **tholoi** /ˈθɒlɔɪ/ M17 Latin (*tholus*, Greek *tholos*). *Architecture* A dome-shaped tomb of ancient Greek origin, especially one dating from the Mycenaean period. Also *tholos tomb*.

Thule /ˈθjuːli/, *in sense 2* /θuːl/, /ˈθjuːl/ *noun* OE Latin (*Thule*, *Thyle* from Greek *Thoulē*, *Thulē*, of unknown origin; in sense 2, from *Thule* (now Dundas), a settlement in North West Greenland). **1** A land (variously conjectured to be the Shetland Islands, Iceland, and, most plausibly, Norway) to the north of Britain, believed by ancient Greek and Roman geographers to be the most northerly region in the world. Cf. ULTIMA THULE. **2** *Archaeology* A prehistoric Eskimo culture. Frequently *attributive*.

Thummim /ˈθʌmɪm/ *noun* M16 Hebrew (*tummīm* plural of *tōm* completeness). One of the two objects of a now unknown nature worn on the breastplate of a Jewish high priest (Exodus

28:30). Chiefly in *Urim and Thummim*. See URIM.

thyrsus /ˈθəːsəs/ *noun* plural **thyrsi** /ˈθəːsʌɪ/, /ˈθəːsiː/ L16 Latin (from Greek *thursos* stalk of a plant, Bacchic staff). (In ancient Greece and Rome) a staff or spear tipped with an ornament like a pine cone, carried by Bacchus and his followers.

tian /tjɑ̃/ *noun* plural pronounced same M20 Provençal (ultimately from Greek *tēganon* frying pan, saucepan). A large oval earthenware cooking pot traditionally used in Provence; a dish of sliced vegetables cooked in olive oil and then baked *au gratin*.

tic /tɪk/ *noun* E19 French (from Italian *ticchio*). **1** A habitual spasmodic contraction of the muscles, most often in the face. **2** A whim, an idiosyncrasy.

2 1978 C. P. Snow *Realists* He had the tic, common to many writers, of insisting that the table be kept pernicketily tidy.

tic douloureux /ˌtɪk duːləˈruː/, /ˌtɪk duːləˈrə/ *noun phrase* E19 French (= painful tic). Trigeminal neuralgia, in which spasms of pain are frequently accompanied by twitching of the facial muscles.

tiens /tjɛ̃/ *interjection* M20 French (imperative singular of *tenir* hold). Expressing surprise.

tignon /ˈtiːjɒn/ *noun* L19 Louisiana French (from French *tigne* dialectal variant of *teigne* moth). A piece of cloth worn as a turban headdress especially in Louisiana by Creole women.

tika /ˈtiːkɑː/, /ˈtɪkɑː/ *noun* L19 Hindi (*ṭīkā*, Punjabi *ṭikkā*). A TILAK.

tiki /ˈtɪki/ *noun* L18 Maori (= image). A large wooden or small ornamental greenstone image of an ancestor or any human figure. *New Zealand*.

tikka /ˈtɪkə/, /ˈtiːkə/ *noun* M20 Punjabi (*ṭikkā*). An Indian dish of small pieces of meat or vegetable marinated in spices and cooked on a skewer. Frequently with qualifying word, as *chicken tikka*, *lamb tikka*.

tilak /ˈtɪlək/ *noun* L19 Sanskrit (*tilaka*). A mark worn by a Hindu on the forehead to indicate caste, status, or sect, or as an ornament.

tilde /ˈtɪldə/ *noun* M19 Spanish (based on Latin *titulus* title). **1** The diacritic mark ~ placed in Spanish above *n* to indicate the palatalized sound /ɲ/, as in *señor*; a similar mark in Portuguese above *a* and *o* and in some phonetic transcriptions to indicate nasality. **2** This mark used as a symbol in mathematics and logic, chiefly to indicate negation or inversion.

tilleul /tɪˈjəːl/ *noun* M16 French (from Latin diminutive form from *tilia* linden). **1** A lime or linden tree. **2** A tea made from an infusion of the flowers of the lime or linden tree, originally used as a remedy for headache.

timbale /tamˈbɑːl/, /ˈtɛbal/ (*plural same*); *in sense 2* /tɪmˈbɑːli/ *noun* E19 French (= drum; in sense 2, perhaps from Spanish *timbal*, plural *timbales* of same origin). **1** A drum-shaped dish made of finely minced meat or fish cooked in a pastry crust or a mould. **2** In *plural* Two single-headed drums played as a pair with drumsticks in Latin American dance music.

tinnitus /tɪˈnʌɪtəs/, /ˈtɪnɪtəs/ *noun* M19 Latin (from *tinnire* to ring, tinkle, of imitative origin). *Medicine* A sensation of ringing or buzzing in the ears.

tinto /ˈtɪntəʊ/ *noun* L16 Spanish (= tinted, dark-coloured). Spanish or Portuguese red wine.

tipi variant of TEPEE.

tirade /tʌɪˈreɪd/, /tɪˈreɪd/ *noun* E19 French (from Italian *tirata* volley, from *tirare* Proto-Romance verb meaning 'draw'). A long, angry speech of criticism or accusation.

tirailleur /ˌtɪrʌɪˈjəː/ *noun* L18 French (from *tirailler* to shoot independently, from *tirer* to draw, shoot). *French History* Any of a body of skirmishers employed in the French Revolutionary War in 1792; a skirmisher, a sharpshooter.

tiramisu /ˌtiːrəmɪˈsuː/ *noun* L20 Italian (from phrase *tira mi sù* pick me up). An Italian dessert consisting of layers of sponge cake soaked in coffee and brandy or liqueur with powdered chocolate and mascarpone cheese.

tiro variant of TYRO.

tisane /tɪˈzan/ *noun* M20 French. A herbal tea.

titre /ˈtʌɪtə/, /ˈtiːtə/ *noun* (also (*United States*) **titer**) M19 French. **1** (*Chemistry*) The concentration of a solution as determined by titration. **2** *Medicine* The concentration of an antibody, as measured by the extent to which it can be diluted before ceasing to give a positive reaction with antigen.

tjurunga variant of CHURINGA.

tmesis /ˈtmiːsɪs/ *noun* plural **tmeses** /ˈtmiːsiːz/ M16 Greek (*tmēsis* cutting, from *temnein* to cut). *Grammar* The separation of the elements of a compound word by an intervening word or words (e.g. *abso-bloody-lutely*).

toccata /təˈkɑːtə/ *noun* E18 Italian (use as noun of feminine past participle of *toccare* to touch). *Music* A musical composition for a keyboard instrument designed to exhibit the performer's touch and technique. Also, a fanfare for brass instruments.

tochus /ˈtəʊkəs/ *noun* (also **tokus**) E20 Yiddish (*tokhes* from Hebrew *taḥaṯ* beneath). The buttocks; the anus. *North American slang.*

tofu /ˈtəʊfuː/ *noun* L18 Japanese (*tōfu* from Chinese *dòufu*, from *dòu* beans + *fǔ* rot, turn sour). A soft white substance made from mashed soya beans, used chiefly in Asian and vegetarian cookery.

toga /ˈtəʊɡə/ *noun* E17 Latin (related to *tegere* to cover). A loose flowing outer garment worn by the citizens of ancient Rome, made of a single piece of cloth and covering the whole body apart from the right arm.

togt /tɒxt/ *adjective* E20 Afrikaans (from Dutch *tocht* expedition, journey). (Of a labourer or their work) hired or paid for by the day; casual. *South African.*

tohubohu /ˌtəʊhuːˈbəʊhuː/ *noun* E17 Hebrew (*thōhū wa-bhōhū* emptiness and desolation (Genesis 1:2)). A state of chaos; utter confusion. *North American colloquial.*

toile /twɑːl/ *noun* LME French. **1** An early version of a finished garment made up in cheap material so that the design can be tested and perfected. **2** Any of various linen or cotton fabrics. Frequently with French specifying words, as in *toile de Jouy.*

■ Originally denoted cloth or canvas for painting on.
1 1982 *Times* I spent seven months of a two-year couture course *just* making toiles for skirts.

tokamak /ˈtəʊkəmak/ *noun* M20 Russian (from *toroidal'naya kamera s magnitnym polem*, toroidal chamber with magnetic field). *Physics* A toroidal (ring-shaped) apparatus for producing controlled fusion reactions in a hot plasma.

tokoloshe /tɒkəˈlɒʃi/ *noun* M19 Sesotho (*thokolosi, t(h)koloshi*, Xhosa *uThikoloshe*, Zulu *utokoloshe*). (In southern African folklore) a mischievous and lascivious hairy water sprite.

tokus variant of TOCHUS.

tole /təʊl/ *noun & adjective* (also **tôle** /toːl/) M20 French (*tôle* sheet iron, from dialect *taule* table, from Latin *tabula* a flat board). **A** *noun* Painted, enamelled, or lacquered tin plate used for making decorative metalwork. Also *tôle peinte.* **B** *adjective* Made of tole.
1996 *Country Life*... a decorative feature was the use of locally made *tôle peinte*, or japanned tinware, in imitation of porcelain ... a splendid pair of *tôle* vases on red lacquer, pagoda-shaped stands...

tomatillo /ˌtɒməˈtɪləʊ/ *noun* E20 Mexican Spanish (= small tomato). An edible purple or yellow fruit which is chiefly used in sauces and preserves; the Mexican plant which bears the tomatillo.

tombola /tɒmˈbəʊlə/ *noun* L19 French (or Italian, from Italian *tombolare* to turn a somersault, tumble). A kind of lottery with tickets usually drawn from a revolving drum-shaped container, especially at a fête or fair.

tombolo /ˈtɒmbələʊ/ *noun* plural **tombolos** L19 Italian (= sand dune). A bar of

shingle or sand joining an island to the mainland.

tomme /tɒm/ *noun* plural pronounced same M20 French. Any of various cheeses made in Savoy, a region of south-east France.

ton /tɔ̃/ *noun* M18 French (from Latin *tonus* tone). **1** Fashionable style or distinction. **2** Fashionable people collectively; fashionable society. Treated as *singular* or *plural.*
2 1969 H. Elsna *Abbot's House* A waste, when all the *ton* will flock here for this event.

tondo /ˈtɒndəʊ/ *noun* plural **tondi** /ˈtɒndi/, **tondos** L19 Italian (= a round, a circle, a compass, shortened from *rotondo* round). An easel painting of circular form; a carving in relief within a circular space.

tong /tɒŋ/ *noun* L19 Chinese ((Cantonese) *t'ŏng* (= Mandarin *táng*) hall, meeting place). A Chinese association or secret society, frequently associated with organized crime.

tonneau /ˈtɒnəʊ/ *noun* plural **tonneaus**, in sense 1 also **tonneaux** L18 French (= barrel, cask). **1** A unit of capacity for French (especially Bordeaux) wine, usually equal to 900 litres (198 gallons). **2** The part of a car, typically an open car, occupied by the back seats; a protective cover for the seats of an open car or cabin cruiser when they are not in use (in full *tonneau cover*).

tontine /tɒnˈtiːn/ *noun* M18 French (from Lorenzo Tonti (1630–95), Neapolitan banker, who started such a scheme to raise government loans in France around 1653). **1** A financial scheme by which subscribers to a loan or common fund each receive an annuity for life, the amount increasing as each dies, till the last survivor enjoys the whole income. Also, the share or right of each subscriber in such a scheme; the subscribers collectively; the fund so established. **2** A scheme for life assurance in which the beneficiaries are those who survive and maintain a policy to the end of a given period.

tonto /ˈtɒntəʊ/ *noun & adjective* L20 Spanish. **A** *noun* plural **tontos**. A foolish or stupid person. **B** *adjective* Foolish, crazy; mad.

■ Colloquial, originally United States.

topi /ˈtəʊpi/ *noun* (also **topee**) M19 Anglo-Indian (Hindi *ṭopī* hat). A hat; *specifically* a pith helmet, a sola topi.

■ *Sola topi* has no etymological connection with the sun or *solar*, but refers to the tropical Asian swamp plants (Bengali *solā*, Hindi *śolā*) from the lightweight pith of which the sun helmets were made.

topos /ˈtɒpɒs/ *noun plural* **topoi** /ˈtɒpɔɪ/ M20 Greek (= place). A traditional theme in a literary composition; a rhetorical or literary formula.

toque /təʊk/ *noun* E16 French (corresponding obscurely to Italian *tocca*, *tocco*, Spanish *toca*, Portuguese *touca* cap, woman's headdress, of unknown origin). **1** A woman's small hat, typically having a narrow, closely turned-up brim. **2** *History* A small cap or bonnet resembling a toque worn by a man or a woman. **3** A tall white hat with a full pouched crown, worn by chefs.

torc /tɔːk/ *noun* (also **torque**) M19 French (*torque*, from Latin *torques* necklace, wreath, from *torquere* to twist). *History* A neck ornament formed from a twisted band of (usually precious) metal, worn especially by the ancient Gauls and Britons.

torchère /tɔːˈʃɛː/, *foreign* /tɔrʃɛr/ *noun* plural pronounced same E20 French (from Old and Modern French *torche* torch, from Proto-Romance, from Latin *torqua* variant of *torques* necklace, wreath, from *torquere* to twist). A tall ornamental flat-topped stand for a candlestick.

1995 *Country Life* A detail of a painting of the interior...shows in the niches...gilt metal torchères in tripod form...

torchon /ˈtɔːʃ(ə)n/, *foreign* /tɔrʃɔ̃/ *noun* M19 French (= duster, dishcloth, from *torcher* to wipe). A coarse loose-textured kind of bobbin lace with geometrical designs. In full *torchon lace*.

toreador /ˈtɒrɪədɔː/, /ˌtɒrɪəˈdɔː/ *noun* plural **toreadors**, **toreadores** /ˈtɒrɪədɔːrɪz/ E17 Spanish (from *torear* to fight bulls, from *toro* bull). A bullfighter, especially one on horseback. Cf. TORERO.

torero /tɒˈrɛːrəʊ/, *foreign* /toˈrero/ *noun* plural **toreros** /tɒˈrɛːrəʊz/, *foreign* /toˈreros/ E18 Spanish (from *toro* bull). A bullfighter, especially one on foot. Cf. TOREADOR.

tori plural of TORUS.

torii /ˈtɔːriː/ *noun* plural same E18 Japanese (from *tori* bird + *i* sit, perch). A ceremonial gateway of a Japanese Shinto shrine, with two uprights and two crosspieces.

toro /ˈtɔːrəʊ/, *foreign* /ˈtoro/ *noun* plural **toros** /ˈtɔːrəʊz/, *foreign* /ˈtoros/ M17 Spanish (from Latin *taurus* bull). A bull used in bullfighting.

torque variant of TORC.

torsade /tɔːˈseɪd/ *noun* L19 French (from Latin *tors-* past participial stem of *torquere* to twist). A decorative twisted braid, ribbon, or other strand used as trimming; an artificial plait of hair.

Torschlusspanik /ˈtɔːrʃlʊsˌpaːnɪk/ *noun* M20 German (= last-minute panic (literally, 'shut door panic')). A sense of alarm or anxiety at the passing of life's opportunities, said to be experienced in middle age.

torso /ˈtɔːsəʊ/ *noun* plural **torsos** L18 Italian (= stalk, stump, trunk of a statue, from as THYRSUS). **1** The trunk of the human body; the trunk of a statue, without or considered independently of head and limbs. **2** *figurative* An incomplete or mutilated thing, especially a work of art or literature.

torte /ˈtɔːt/ *noun* plural **tortes**, **torten** /ˈtɔːt(ə)n/ M18 German (*Torte* tart, pastry, cake, from Italian *torta* from late Latin). A sweet cake or tart.

■ Originally (ME–M16) used in English in the sense of 'round loaf of bread', probably deriving directly from late Latin *torta* meaning 'round loaf or cake', but the sense derived from German is now the only one current.

tortellini /tɔːtɪˈliːni/ *noun plural* M20 Italian (plural of *tortellino* diminutive of *tortello* small cake, fritter). Small squares of pasta stuffed with meat, cheese, etc., rolled and shaped into rings; an

Italian dish consisting largely of this and usually a sauce.

torticollis /ˌtɔːtɪˈkɒlɪs/ *noun* E19 Modern Latin (from Latin *tortus* crooked, twisted + *collum* neck). *Medicine* A condition in which the head is persistently or intermittently turned or twisted to one side, often associated with painful muscle spasms.

tortilla /tɔːˈtiːjə/ *noun* L17 Spanish (diminutive of *torta* cake, from late Latin; see TORTE). **1** (In Mexican cookery) a thin flat maize pancake, eaten hot or cold, typically with a savoury filling. **2** (In Spanish cookery) a thick flat omelette frequently eaten cold in wedges.

torus /ˈtɔːrəs/ *noun* plural **tori** /ˈtɔːrʌɪ/, **toruses** M16 Latin (= swelling, bolster, round moulding). **1** *Geometry* A surface or solid formed by rotating a closed curve, especially a circle, about a line which lies in the same plane but does not intersect it (e.g. like a ring doughnut). **2** A ring-shaped object, especially a large ring-shaped chamber used in physical research. **3** *Architecture* A large convex moulding, especially at the base of a column. **4** *Botany* The receptacle of a flower. **5** *Anatomy* A ridge of bone or muscle.

tostada /tɒˈstaːdə/ *noun* (also **tostado** /tɒˈstaːdəʊ/, plural **tostados**) M20 Spanish (past participle of *tostar* to toast). A Mexican deep-fried maize pancake topped with a seasoned mixture of beans, mincemeat, and vegetables.

Totentanz /ˈtotəntants/ *noun* plural **Totentänze** /ˈtotəntɛntsə/ L18 German (literally, 'death dance'). A representation of Death leading people of all ranks in a dance towards the grave; the Dance of Death. Cf. DANSE MACABRE.

totsiens /tɒtˈsɪns/, /tɒtˈsiːns/ *interjection* M20 Afrikaans (*tot* (*weer*)*siens* until we meet again, from Dutch *tot* until + *zien* see). (In South Africa) until we meet again; goodbye.

touché /tuːˈʃeɪ/ *interjection* E20 French (past participle of *toucher* to touch). **1** *Fencing* Expressing acknowledgement of a hit by one's opponent. **2** Expressing good-humoured acknowl-edgement during a discussion of a valid or clever point or justified accusation made by another person.

2 1981 A. Price *Soldier no More* 'Touché...' he nodded, accepting the rebuke.

toupet /ˈtuːpeɪ/, /ˈtuːpɪt/, *foreign* /tupɛ/ (*plural same*) *noun* E18 French. A patch of artificial hair or a small wig to cover a bald spot.

■ The more common form *toupee* is an alteration of the French word. In early use, a *toupet* denoted a curl or artificial lock of hair worn on the top of the head, especially as part of a wig, or a wig or natural hair dressed to create such a topknot. Formerly also, a wearer of a toupee or topknot, hence a fashionable person.

tour de force /ˌtʊə də ˈfɔːs/, *foreign* /turdəfɔrs/ *noun phrase* plural **tours de force** (pronounced same) E19 French (literally, 'feat of strength'). An achievement or performance that has been accomplished with great skill.

1995 *New Scientist* The book is a *tour de force* by nearly 40 contributing authors...

tour d'horizon /tur dɔrizɔ̃/ *noun phrase* plural **tours d'horizon** (pronounced same) M20 French (literally, 'tour of the horizon'). An extensive tour. Chiefly *figurative*, a broad general survey or summary of an argument or event.

1995 *Times* His [sc. the Foreign Secretary's] aim, after a *tour d'horizon* of world affairs, was to press against the Opposition the charge of inconsistency and on Europe, abdication.

tour en l'air /tʊə ɑ̃ lɛː/ *noun phrase* plural **tours en l'air** (pronounced same) M19 French (literally, 'turn in the air'). *Ballet* A movement in which a dancer jumps straight upwards and completes at least one full revolution in the air before landing.

tournedos /ˈtʊənədəʊ/, *foreign* /turnədo/ *noun* plural same /ˈtʊənədəʊz/, *foreign* /turnədo/ L19 French (from *tourner* to turn + *dos* back). A small round thick cut from a fillet of beef, with a surrounding strip of fat.

tourniquet /ˈtʊənɪkeɪ/ *noun* L17 French (perhaps alteration of Old French *tournicle* variant of *tounicle*, *tunicle* coat of mail, by association with *tourner* to turn). A device for stopping or slowing the flow of blood through an artery, typically by compressing a limb with a cord or tight bandage.

tours de force, tours d'horizon plurals of TOUR DE FORCE, TOUR D'HORIZON.

tourtière /tʊətɪˈɛː/, *foreign* /turtjɛr/ (*plural same*) *noun* M20 French (from *tourte* pie, tart). **1** A kind of meat pie traditionally eaten at Christmas in Canada. **2** A tin or round baking sheet for tarts and pies.

tout /tu/ *adjective, noun, & adverb* E18 French. All, everything; quite entirely.
■ Mainly in following phrases, but see also LE TOUT, which may be shortened to *tout*, with similar high society connotations, as in *tout Paris* 'all Paris'.
1996 *Country Life Tout* Shropshire (and Hereford) were invited to drinks...

tout au contraire /tut o kɔ̃trɛr/ *adverb phrase* E18 French. Quite the contrary. Cf. AU CONTRAIRE.

tout compris /tu kɔ̃pri/ *adverb & adjective phrase* E18 French. All included, inclusive.

tout court /tu kur/ *adverb phrase* E18 French (literally, 'very short'). In short, simply, without qualification or addition.
1995 *Spectator* Unlike Selwyn Lloyd, who was sacked *tout court*, Mr Lamont was offered another job...

tout de suite /tu də sɥit/ *adverb phrase* E18 French (literally, 'quite in sequence'). At once, immediately.
■ The anglicized form *toot sweet* is sometimes used in colloquial English.
1995 D. Lodge *Therapy* I chipped in *tout de suite* to say that I quite understood.

tout ensemble /tut ɑ̃sɑ̃mbl/ *noun phrase* E18 French (from TOUT + ENSEMBLE *noun*). A thing, or its parts, viewed as a whole.
■ Independent use of *ensemble* in this sense is slightly later (M18).

tout le monde /tu lə mɔ̃d/ *noun phrase* E18 French. All the world, everyone.

tout Paris see under LE TOUT, TOUT.

tout seul /tu sœl/ *adverb phrase* E18 French. Quite alone, on one's own.

tout simple /tu sɛ̃pl/ *adverb phrase* M20 French. Quite simply, just that.

tovarish /tɒˈvɑːrɪʃ/ *noun* (also **tovarich**) E20 Russian (*tovarishch* from Turkic, perhaps Tatar). (In the former USSR) comrade.
■ Frequently as a form of address.

tracasserie /trəˈkas(ə)ri/ *noun* M17 French (from *tracasser* to bustle, worry oneself). A state of disturbance or annoyance; a fuss; a petty quarrel. *Archaic.*
■ Usually in plural.

tragédienne /trəˌdʒiːdɪˈɛn/ *noun* M19 French (feminine of *tragédien* tragedian). An actress who specializes in tragic roles.

trahison des clercs /traizɔ̃ de klɛr/ *noun phrase* M20 French (literally, 'the treachery of the scholars'). A compromise of intellectual integrity or betrayal of standards by writers, artists, and thinkers.
■ From *La Trahison des Clercs*, the title of a work by Julien Benda (1927).
1978 *Listener* Look, they say, terrorism is a phenomenon of our times. Let us... acknowledge that a diplomat... is fair game... I find this *trahison des clercs*.

traiteur /trɛtœr/ *noun* plural pronounced same M18 French (from *traiter* to treat). (In France or French-speaking countries) a delicatessen.

tramontana /ˌtramɒnˈtaːnə/ *noun* ME Italian (*tramontana* north wind, polestar, *tramontani* dwellers beyond the mountains, from Latin *transmontanus*, from *trans-* across + *mons, mont-* mount). **1** A cold north wind blowing in Italy or the adjoining regions of the Adriatic and Mediterranean. **2** A person living or originating from beyond the mountains, especially the Alps as seen from Italy; (especially from the Italian point of view) a foreigner. *Archaic.*

tranche /trɑːnʃ/, /trɑ̃ʃ/ *noun* plural pronounced same or /trɑːnʃɪz/ L15 Old and Modern French (= slice, from *trancher* to cut, ultimately from Latin *truncare*).

A portion of something, especially money.

1995 *Spectator* The initial tranche of applications has been remarkably evenly spread.

transire /tranˈzʌɪə/, /trɑːnˈzʌɪə/, /tranˈsʌɪə/, /tranˈzʌɪri/ *noun* L16 Latin (= to go across). *Law* (In the United Kingdom) a customs document on which the cargo loaded on to a ship is listed, issued to prove that the goods listed on it have come from a home port rather than an overseas one.

travers /travɛr/, /ˈtravəs/ *noun* plural same L19 French (*pied de travers* foot askew, from *travers* breadth, irregularity, from *traverser* to traverse). A movement performed in dressage, in which the horse moves parallel to the side of the arena, with its shoulders carried closer to the wall than its hindquarters and its body curved towards the centre.

travois /traˈvɔɪ/ *noun* plural same /traˈvɔɪz/ M19 North American French (alteration of French *travail*). A type of sledge formerly used by North American Indians to carry goods, consisting of two joined poles pulled by a horse.

trebuchet /ˈtrɛbjʊʃɛt/, /ˈtrɛbəʃɛt/, *foreign* /trebyʃɛ/ (*plural same*) *noun* ME Old and Modern French (*trébuchet* (medieval Latin *trebuchetum*, *trabuchetum*), from *trébucher* to overturn, overthrow, stumble, fall, ultimately from *tra-*, *tres-* (from Latin *trans-* expressing displacement) + *buc* trunk (of the body), bulk, from Frankish *bûk* belly). *History* A machine used in medieval siege warfare for hurling heavy stones and other missiles.

trecento /treɪˈtʃɛntəʊ/ *noun* M19 Italian (= three hundred). The fourteenth century as a period of Italian art, architecture, or literature.

■ Shortened from *milletrecento* '1300', used with reference to the years 1300–99.

trefa /ˈtreɪfə/ *adjective* (also **trifa** /ˈtrʌɪfə/, **tref** /treɪf/, and other variants) M19 Hebrew (*ṭĕrēpāh* flesh of an animal torn or mauled, from *ṭārap* to tear, rend). (Of food) not prepared according to Jewish law, forbidden to Jews, not kosher.

1966 H. Kemelman *Saturday the Rabbi went Hungry* When a utensil becomes tref, the way you cleanse it is to bury it in the earth.

trek /trɛk/ *noun* M19 Afrikaans (from Dutch *trekken* to pull). **1** A long and arduous journey or expedition, especially one made on foot or by inconvenient means. **2** A journey, especially an organized migration or expedition; a stage of such a journey. *South African*, chiefly *historical*.

tremolando /trɛməˈlandəʊ/ *noun, adverb, & adjective* M19 Italian (present participle of *tremolare* to tremble). *Music* **A** *noun* plural **tremolandos**, **tremolandi** /trɛməˈlandi/ A TREMOLO senses 1, 2a. **B** *adverb & adjective* (Especially as direction) with tremolo.

tremolo /ˈtrɛm(ə)ləʊ/ *noun, adjective, & adverb* M18 Italian (from Latin *tremulus* from *tremere* to tremble). *Music* **A** *noun* plural **tremolos 1** A wavering effect in a musical tone, produced either by rapid repeated slight variation in the pitch of a note, or by sounding two notes of slightly different pitches to produce prominent overtones. Cf. VIBRATO. **2a** A mechanism in an organ producing a tremolo effect; a tremulant. Also *tremolo stop*. **b** A lever on an electric guitar, used to produce a tremolo effect (also *tremolo arm*); an electrical device of similar effect in an amplifier etc. **B** *adjective & adverb* (As a musical direction) with tremolo.

trente et quarante /trɑ̃tɛkarɑ̃t/, /trɑ̃teɪkaˈrɑ̃t/ *noun* L17 French (literally, 'thirty-and-forty', these being winning and losing numbers respectively in the game). A gambling game in which cards are turned up on a table marked with red and black diamonds.

très /trɛ/, /treɪ/ *adverb* E19 French. Very.

■ Colloquial, usually with reference to a fashionable or modishly superior quality.

triage /ˈtriːɑːʒ/ *noun & verb* E18 Old and Modern French (from *trier* to sort out). **A** *noun* *Medicine* The assignment of degrees of urgency of need in order to decide the order of treatment of a large number of patients or casualties.

b *generally* The process of determining the most important people or things from amongst a large number that require attention; prioritization. **B** *transitive & intransitive verb* Assign a degree of urgency of need to (a patient or casualty); separate *out* by triage.

■ The noun was originally used, in the early 18th century, in the sense 'the action of sorting items according to quality'. The current sense dates from the 1930s, from the military system of assessing the wounded on the battlefield.

A.b 1995 *Times Magazine* With so many girls arriving every week, only the strongest are put up for adoption, and the orphanages are forced to practise a sort of triage.

tribade /ˈtrɪbəd/ *noun* E17 French (or its source Latin *tribas, tribad-* from Greek *tribas,* from *tribein* to rub). A lesbian.

triclinium /trʌɪˈklɪnɪəm/, /trʌɪˈklʌɪnɪəm/ *noun* plural **triclinia** /trʌɪˈklɪnɪə/ M17 Latin (from Greek *triklinion* diminutive of *triklinos* dining room with three couches, from *tri-* combining form of *treis* three + *klinē* couch, bed). A dining table with couches along three sides, used in ancient Rome. Also, a room containing such a table.

tricorne /ˈtrʌɪkɔːn/ *noun & adjective* (also **tricorn**) M18 French (*tricorne* or Latin *tricornis* three-horned, from *tri-* combining form of *tris* three + *cornu* horn). **A** *noun* A hat with the brim turned up on three sides. **B** *adjective* Having three horns; (of a hat) having the brim turned up on three sides.

tricot /ˈtrɪkəʊ/, /ˈtriːkəʊ/ *noun* L18 French (from *tricoter* to knit). A fine warp knitted fabric made of a natural or man-made fibre, produced in any of various designs.

tricoteuse /trikɔtøz/ *noun* plural pronounced same M19 French (from *tricoter* knit). **1** *History* One of a number of women who, during the French Revolution, sat and knitted while attending public executions by guillotine. **2** A small table with a gallery used for sewing.

2 1996 *Country Life* Until about that date [1848], the term *tricoteuse* would presumably not have been popular in France for a lady's tray-top worktable. Marie Antoinette had had one, but after that, the word would have been painful to Royalists.

tric-trac /ˈtriktrak/ *noun* L17 French (from the clicking sound made by the pieces in the playing of the game). *History* A form of backgammon.

triduum /ˈtrɪdjʊəm/, /ˈtrʌɪdjʊəm/ *noun* E18 Latin (use as noun of adjective (sc. *spatium* space), from *tri-* combining form of *tres* three + *dies* day). (Especially in the Roman Catholic Church) a period of three days' observance, specifically Maundy Thursday, Good Friday, and Holy Saturday.

triennium /trʌɪˈɛnɪəm/ *noun* plural **trienniums**, **triennia** /trʌɪˈɛnɪə/ M19 Latin (from *tri-* combining form of *tres* three + *annus* year). A period of three years.

trifa variant of TREFA.

triforium /trʌɪˈfɔːrɪəm/ *noun* plural **triforia** /trʌɪˈfɔːrɪə/ E18 Anglo-Latin (of unknown origin). *Architecture* A gallery or arcade above the arches at the sides of the nave, choir, and sometimes transepts of some large churches.

trio /ˈtriːəʊ/ *noun* E18 Italian (from Latin *tres, tria* three, after DUO). **1** *Music* **a** A composition written for three musicians. Also, a group or company of three musicians. **b** The central section of a minuet, scherzo, or march, frequently in a different key and style from the preceding and following main division. **2** A group or set of three things or people.

triquetra /trʌɪˈkwɛtrə/, /trʌɪˈkwiːtrə/ *noun* plural **triquetrae** /trʌɪˈkwɛtriː/, **triquetras** L16 Latin (feminine of *triquetrus* three-cornered). A symmetrical triangular ornament formed of three interlaced arcs or lobes.

■ In early use denoted a triangle.

triste /triːst/ *adjective* (originally anglicized as **trist**) LME Old and Modern French (from Latin *tristis* sad). **1** Feeling or expressing sorrow; sad, melancholy; causing sorrow, lamentable. **2** Not lively or cheerful; dull, dreary.

2 1996 *Country Life* When the photographs and descriptions are truly breath-taking ..., I get the particulars. As my purchasing power is nil, this may seem a triste activity.

tristesse /trɪˈstɛs/ *noun* LME Old French (*tristesce* (modern *tristesse*) from Latin *tristitia*, from *tristis* sad). A state of melancholy sadness.

triumvir /trʌɪˈʌmvə/ *noun* plural **triumvirs**, **triumviri** /trʌɪˈʌmvɪrʌɪ/ LME Latin (from *triumviri* plural, back-formation from *trium virorum* genitive plural of *tres viri* three men). **1** (In ancient Rome) each of three public officers jointly responsible for overseeing any of the administrative departments. Also *specifically*, each member of the first or second triumvirate. **2** *transferred* In *plural* Any group of three persons or things in a joint position of power or authority.

trivia /ˈtrɪvɪə/ *noun plural* E20 Modern Latin (plural of TRIVIUM, influenced in sense by *trivial*). Details, considerations, or pieces of information of little importance or value.

> **1996** *Times* But the message is surely universal: lift your eyes to the hills, to the greater questions, away from the trivia that clutter our frantic modern lives.

trivium /ˈtrɪvɪəm/ *noun* E19 Latin (= place where three ways meet, from *tri-* combining form of *tres* three + *via* way). *History* An introductory course at a medieval university involving the study of grammar, rhetoric, and logic. Cf. QUADRIVIUM.

Trockenbeerenauslese /ˈtrɔkən beːrənˌaʊsleːzə/ *noun* (also **trockenbeerenauslese**) plural **Trockenbeerenauslesen** /ˈtrɔkənbeːrənˌaʊsleːzən/, **Trockenbeerenausleses** M20 German (from *trocken* dry + as BEERENAUSLESE). A sweet German white wine made from selected individual grapes picked later than the general harvest and affected by noble rot.

troika /ˈtrɔɪkə/ *noun* M19 Russian (*troĭka*, from *troe* a set of three). **1** A Russian vehicle drawn by three horses abreast; the team of horses for such a vehicle. **2** A group of three people or things working together, especially in an administrative or managerial capacity.

> **2 1996** *Spectator* ... the terrible troika of Steven Spielberg, Jeffrey Katzenberg and David Geffen announced they were setting up a billion dollar entertainment company ...

trompe l'oeil /trɔ̃p lœj/ *noun phrase* plural **trompe l'oeils** (pronounced same) L19 French (literally, 'deceives the eye'). Visual illusion in art, especially as used to trick the eye into perceiving a painted detail as a three-dimensional object; a painting or design intended to create a visual illusion.

> **1995** *Times Magazine* Barnes's most recent favourite downstairs cloakroom was a trompe l'oeil potting shed: 'I painted three of the walls as glasshouse walls, with views to the garden beyond, and a brick wall on the fourth wall with shelves covered in garden equipment, such as gloves and watering cans.'

tronc /trɒŋk/ *noun* E20 French (= collecting box). (In a hotel or restaurant) a common fund into which tips and service charges are paid for distribution to the staff.

> *attributive* **1981** *Times* The money was massaged by managements and distributed on their behalf to staff ... or paid into an independent tronc fund.

troppo /ˈtrɒpəʊ/ *adverb* E20 Italian. *Music* (In directions) too much; excessively.

> ■ Especially in adverb phrase *ma non troppo* 'but not too much'.

troubadour /ˈtruːbədɔː/ *noun* E18 French (from Provençal *trobador* (= Old French *troveor*), from *trobar* (= Old French *trover*) to find, compose in verse, invent, ultimate origin unknown; cf. TROUVÈRE). **1** *History* Any of a class of French medieval lyric poets composing and singing in Provençal especially on the themes of chivalry and courtly love, living in southern France, eastern Spain, and northern Italy between the 11th and 13th centuries. **2** A person who writes verse to music.

> ■ The northern French equivalent of the *troubadour* was the TROUVÈRE.

trousseau /ˈtruːsəʊ/ *noun* plural **trousseaus**, **trousseaux** /ˈtruːsəʊz/ M19 French (from Old French *troussel* diminutive of *trousse* truss). The clothes, linen, and other belongings collected by a bride in preparation for her marriage.

> ■ Originally (ME) in the sense of 'a bundle or package', later 'a bunch', but long rare or obsolete with this meaning. Old French *troussel* in this sense was also represented in English as *trussell* (LME only).

trouvaille /truˈvɑj/ *noun* plural pronounced same M19 French (from *trouver* to find). A lucky find; a windfall.

> **1996** *Spectator* It is not only the curious *trouvailles* that make this travel book a special pleasure.

trouvère /truːˈvɛː/, *foreign* /truvɛr/ (*plural same*) *noun* (also **trouveur** /truːˈvəː/, *foreign* /truvœr/ (*plural same*)) L18 French (Old French (*trovere* (modern *trouvère*, *trouveur*) from *troveor*, from *trover* (modern *trouver* to find) to compose in verse, invent, find, ultimate origin unknown; cf. TROUBADOUR). *History* Any of a class of French medieval epic poets composing especially *chansons de geste* and fabliaux, living in northern France between the 11th and 14th centuries.

trumeau /truːˈməʊ/ *noun* plural **trumeaux** /truːˈməʊz/ L19 French (literally, 'calf of the leg'). *Architecture* A section of wall or a pillar between two openings, especially a pillar dividing a large doorway in a church.

tsaddik /ˈtsadɪk/ *noun* (also **tzaddik**) plural **tsaddikim** /ˈtsadɪkɪm/, **tsaddiks** L19 Hebrew (*ṣaddīq* just, righteous). *Judaism* A Hasidic spiritual leader or sage.

tsar /zɑː/, /tsɑː/ *noun* (also **czar**; also (especially in titles) with capital initial) M16 Russian (*tsar'* Old Church Slavonic *cěsarĭ* ultimately representing Latin *Caesar*, probably through Germanic; the spelling with *cz-* is not Slavonic).
1 *History* (The title of) an emperor of Russia before 1917; (the title of) certain other eastern European rulers.
2 *transferred* A person given great authority or power in a particular area: *America's new drug tsar*.

tsarevich /ˈzɑːrɪvɪtʃ/, /tsɑːˈrjeɪvɪtʃ/ *noun* (also **czarevich**; also (especially in titles) with capital initial) E18 Russian (from as TSAR + patronymic *-evich*). *History* The eldest son of an emperor of Russia; the (male) heir of a tsar.

tsarevna /zɑːˈrɛvnə/, /tsɑːˈrɛvnə/ *noun* (also **czarevna**; also (especially in titles) with capital initial) L19 Russian. *History* A daughter of a tsar.

tsarina /zɑːˈriːnə/, /tsɑːˈriːnə/ *noun* (also **czarina**; also (especially in titles) with capital initial) E18 Italian and Spanish (*tzarina*, *(c)zarina*, French *tsarine*, *czarine*, from German *Zarin*, *Czarin* feminine of *Zar*, *Czar*). The wife of a tsar; *History* (the title of) an empress of Russia before 1917.

tsatske variant of TCHOTCHKE.

tsimmes /ˈtsɪməs/ *noun* (also **tzimmes**, **tzimmis**) plural same L19 Yiddish (*tsimes*, of unknown origin). A Jewish stew of sweetened vegetables or vegetables and fruit, sometimes with meat; *figurative* a fuss, a muddle.

> **1974** R. L. Simon *Wild Turkey* Why are you making such a *tsimmis*? Hecht is dead.

tsores variant of TSURIS.

tsotsi /ˈtsɒtsi/ *noun* M20 Bantu. (In South Africa) a young black urban criminal; *History* a young black gangster belonging to a group prominent in the 1940s and 1950s, affecting a special language and flashy dress.

tsuba /ˈtsuːba/ *noun* plural same, **tsubas** L19 Japanese. A Japanese sword guard, typically elaborately decorated and made of iron or leather.

tsukemono /tsuːkɪˈmɔːnɔ/, /tsuːkɪˈməʊnəʊ/ *noun* L19 Japanese (from *tsukeru* pickle + *mono* thing). A Japanese side dish of pickled vegetables, usually served with rice.

tsunami /tsuːˈnɑːmi/ *noun* plural **tsunamis**, same L19 Japanese (from *tsu* harbour + *nami* wave). A long high sea wave caused by an earthquake or similar underwater disturbance, travelling at great speed and in shallow waters often building up enough height and force to flood the land.

> **1995** *New Scientist* A tsunami—a series of mountainous waves—is generated when a section of the ocean floor lurches upwards during an earthquake and lofts a vast body of water with it.

tsuris /ˈtsʊrɪs/ *noun* plural (also **tsores** /ˈtsɒrəs/) E20 Yiddish (plural of *tsore* trouble, woe, from Hebrew *ṣārāh*). Problems or difficulties; (treated as *singular*) trouble, worry. United States *colloquial*.

tsutsumu /tsʊˈtsuːmuː/ *noun* L20 Japanese (= wrap). The Japanese art of wrapping items in an attractive and appropriate way.

tufa /ˈtuːfə/, /ˈtjuːfə/ *noun* L18 Italian (obsolete local variant of *tufo*, from late Latin *tofus*). Geology A soft porous calcium carbonate rock formed by precipitation from water, e.g. around mineral springs. Also, a light, porous rock formed by consolidation of volcanic ash; tuff.

tuile /twiːl/ (*plural same*) *noun* M20 French (= tile). A thin curved biscuit, usually made with almonds.

tule /ˈtuːli/ *noun* M19 Spanish (from Nahuatl *tollin, tullin*). Either of two species of bulrush, *Scirpus validus* and *S. acutus*, abundant in flooded marshy areas in south-west North America, especially in California; an area of low-lying ground in the United States dominated by such a plant.

■ The plural, *tules*, has given rise to the Canadian word *toolies* (M20) meaning 'the backwoods'.

tulle /t(j)uːl/ *noun* E19 French (*Tulle*, a town in south-west France where originally made). A soft, fine silk, cotton, or nylon material like net, used for veils and dresses.

tumbaga /tʊmˈbɑːgə/ *noun* M20 Spanish (from Malay *tembaga* copper, brass). An alloy of gold and copper commonly used in pre-Columbian South and Central America.

tumulus /ˈtjuːmjʊləs/ *noun* plural **tumuli** /ˈtjuːmjʊlʌɪ/, /ˈtjuːmjʊliː/ LME Latin (related to *tumere* to swell). An ancient burial mound, a barrow.

tundra /ˈtʌndrə/ *noun* L16 Lappish. A vast, nearly level, treeless Arctic region of Europe, Asia, and North America in which the subsoil is permanently frozen.

tupik /ˈtuːpɪk/ *noun* M19 Inuit (*tupiq*). A hut or tent of skins used by Inuits in the Canadian Arctic as a summer dwelling.

tuque /tuːk/ *noun* L19 Canadian French (from French *toque*). (In Canada) a close-fitting knitted cap, especially a knitted stocking cap sealed at both ends, one end being tucked into the other to form a cap.

turlough /ˈtʊələʊx/ *noun* L17 Irish (*turloch*, from *tur* dry + *loch* lake). (In Ireland) a low-lying area on limestone which becomes flooded in wet weather through the welling up of ground-water from the rock.

turron /tʊˈrɒn/ *noun* plural **turrones** /tʊˈrɒneɪs/, **turrons** E20 Spanish (*turrón*). A kind of Spanish confectionery resembling nougat, made from almonds and honey; a piece of this.

tutoyer /tʊˈtwɑːjeɪ/ *transitive verb* inflected **tutoy-**, past tense also written **tutoyered** /tʊˈtwɑːjeɪd/ L17 French (from the singular pronoun *tu, toi, te*). In French, address with the singular and more familiar pronoun *tu, toi, te* rather than the plural and more formal *vous*; *generally* treat or address with familiarity.

tutti-frutti /tuːtɪˈfruːti/ *noun* M19 Italian (= all fruits). A type of ice cream containing or flavoured with mixed fruits and sometimes nuts.

tutu /ˈtuːtuː/ *noun* E20 French (childish alteration of *cucu* diminutive of *cul* buttocks). A female ballet dancer's costume consisting of a bodice and an attached skirt made up of layers of fabric, this being either short and stiff and projecting horizontally from the waist (the *classical tutu*) or long, soft, and bell-shaped (the *romantic tutu*).

tuyère /twiˈjɛː/, /tuːˈjɛː/ *noun* (also **tuyere**) L18 French (from *tuyau* pipe). A nozzle through which the air is forced into a forge or furnace.

tycoon /tʌɪˈkuːn/ *noun* M19 Japanese (*taikun* great lord or prince, from Chinese *dà* great + *jūn* prince). **1** A wealthy, powerful person in business or industry. **2** History A title applied by foreigners to the shogun of Japan in power between 1857 and 1868.

typhoon /tʌɪˈfuːn/ *noun* L16 Portuguese (partly from Portuguese *tufão* from Urdu *tūfān* hurricane, tornado, from Arabic, perhaps from Greek *tuphōn*; partly from Chinese dialect *tai fung* big wind, from Chinese *dà* big + *fēng* wind). A tropical storm occurring in the region of the Indian or western Pacific oceans.

tyro /ˈtʌɪrəʊ/ *noun* (also **tiro**) plural **tyros** LME Latin (= young soldier, recruit). A beginner, a learner, a novice.

     1996 *Spectator* . . . all the business people . . . , whether tyros or managing directors of major corporations, were unanimous about their value.

tzatziki /tsatˈsiːki/ *noun* M20 Modern Greek (from Turkish *cacık*). A Greek side dish made with yogurt, cucumber, garlic, and usually mint.

tzedakah /tseˈdɔka/ *noun* (also **tzeda-ka**) M20 Hebrew (*sĕḏāqāh* righteousness). (Among Jewish people) charitable giving, typically seen as a moral obligation.

tzigane /tsɪˈɡɑːn/ *noun* M18 French (from Hungarian *czigany*, *cigány*). A Hungarian Gypsy.

tzimmes variant of TSIMMES.

Uu

über may be attached to an English noun (see ÜBER-).

ubi sunt /ˌʊbɪ ˈsʊnt/ *adjective phrase* E20 Latin (= 'where are', the opening words or refrain of certain medieval Latin works). *Literary Criticism* Designating or characterizing a literary theme or passage lamenting the mutability of things.
> *attributive* **1996** *Spectator* The whole thing is in fact a subtle homage to all the classic '*ubi sunt*' poems ever written about deserted places where human life once reverberated ...

U-bahn /ˈuːbɑːn/, /ˈjuːbɑːn/ *noun* M20 German (from *U* (abbreviation of *Untergrund*) underground + *Bahn* railway). (In Germany and Austria) the underground railway in various major cities.

über- /ˈyːbə/ *prefix* (also **uber** /ˈuːbə/) L20 German (= over). Denoting an outstanding or supreme example of a particular kind of person or thing: *an uberbabe; the uberregulator*.
> **1996** *Times Magazine* ...the nadir came with whispers that *Baywatch*'s uber-babe Pamela Anderson was being lined up to star with Eric Idle's Doctor.

über alles /ˌyːbər ˈaləs/ *adjective & adverb phrase* M20 German (from *über* over + *alles* all). Above all else.
> ■ Generally used with implicit reference to the opening words of the German national anthem *Deutschland über alles*, misunderstood to mean 'Germany supreme'.

Übermensch /ˈyːbərmɛnʃ/ *noun* plural **Übermenschen** /ˈyːbərmɛnʃən/ L19 German (back-formation from *übermenschlich* superhuman, from *über* over + *menschlich* human, from *Mensch* person). The highest type of human being, superman.
> ■ The concept was important in the philosophy of Friedrich Nietzsche (1844–1900), from whom George Bernard Shaw borrowed it for his comedy *Man and Superman* (1903). It—and its opposite UNTERMENSCH—subsequently became part of the vocabulary of the Nazi ideology of the master race. In English translations of Nietzsche, Übermensch is often translated as 'Overman', thus sidestepping the cartoon associations of 'Superman'. In humorous use

udon /ˈuːdɒn/ *noun* E20 Japanese. (In Japanese cookery) wheat pasta made in thick strips.

uhlan /ˈuːlɑːn/, /ˈjuːlɑːn/, /ʊˈlɑːn/ *noun* M18 French (*uhlan*, German *U(h)lan* from Polish *ułan*, *hułan* from Turkish *oğlan* youth, servant). *History* A type of cavalryman or lancer in certain European armies, especially that of Poland or (later) Germany.

uhuru /ʊˈhuːruː/ *noun* (also **Uhuru**) M20 Kiswahili (= freedom). National independence of an African country, *specifically* Kenya.
> **1984** *Listener* An entire continent has seemed hell-bent on self-destruction, despite uhuru, despite the bright hopes of the many thousands who died seeking it.

uitlander /ˈeɪtlandə/, /ˈɔɪtlandə/, *foreign* /ˈœytlandər/ *noun* L19 Afrikaans (from Dutch *uit* out + *land* land). (In South Africa) a foreigner or outsider; *specifically* a British person who went to South Africa before the Boer War of 1899–1902.

ujamaa /ˌʊdʒaˈmɑː/ *noun* M20 Kiswahili (= brotherhood, from *jamaa* family, from Arabic *jamāʻa* group (of people), community). A kind of socialism introduced in Tanzania by President Nyerere in the 1960s, in which self-help village cooperatives were established.

ukase /juːˈkeɪz/ *noun* E18 Russian (*ukaz* ordinance, edict, from *ukazat* show, order, decree). **1** A decree or edict, having legal force, issued by the tsarist Russian government. **2** *generally* Any proclamation or decree; an arbitrary or peremptory command.

2 1995 *Times*... when I am made Emperor of the Universe, my first ukase will be to make it a capital offence to complain about anyone's dead relatives...

ukiyo-e /ˌukijoˈjeː/, /ˌuːkɪjəʊˈjeɪ/ *noun* L19 Japanese (from *ukiyo* fleeting world (from *uku* float, go by fleetingly + *yo* world) + *e* picture). A school of Japanese art depicting subjects from everyday life simply in woodblock prints or paintings.

ukulele /ˌjuːkəˈleɪli/ *noun* L19 Hawaiian (literally, 'jumping flea'). A small four-stringed guitar originating in Hawaii but developed from an earlier Portuguese instrument.

■ Colloquially abbreviated to *uke*.

ulema /ˈʊləmə/, /ˈuːlɪmə/, /uːləˈmɑː/ *noun* (also **ulama** /ˈʊləmə/, /uːləˈmɑː/) L17 Arabic (Turkish, Persian) ('ulamā', plural of 'ālim, 'alīm learned, from 'alima to have (religious) knowledge). **1** *collectively* or in *plural* A body of Muslim scholars who are recognized as having specialist knowledge of Islamic sacred law and theology. **2** A member of such a body.

ult. abbreviation of ULTIMO.

ultimata plural of ULTIMATUM.

ultima Thule /ˌʌltɪmə ˈtjuːli/ *noun phrase* (also **ultima thule**) L18 Latin (= furthest Thule). A distant unknown region; the extreme limit of travel and discovery. Cf. THULE.

ultimatum /ˌʌltɪˈmeɪtəm/ *noun* plural **ultimatums**, **ultimata** /ˌʌltɪˈmeɪtə/ M18 Latin (use as noun of neuter of late Latin *ultimatus* in the medieval Latin senses 'final, completed'). A final demand or statement of terms, the rejection of which will result in retaliation or a breakdown in relations.

ultimo /ˈʌltɪməʊ/ *adjective* L16 Latin (from *ultimo mense* in the last month). Of last month. Now *dated*.

■ Frequently written *ult.*, *ulto*, it is used following the ordinal number denoting the day, as in *3rd ultimo*.

ultra /ˈʌltrə/ *noun* E19 Latin (independent use of *ultra-* lying beyond). A person holding extreme views, an extremist. *Colloquial*.

■ Originally introduced as an abbreviation for French *ultra-royaliste*, referring to a political party in early 19th-century France.

1996 *Spectator* He hopes to encourage the Thatcherite ultras to continue undermining Mr Major...

ultra vires /ˌʌltrə ˈvʌɪriːz/, /ˌʊltrɑː ˈviːreɪz/ *adverb phrase* L18 Latin (= beyond the powers). Chiefly *Law*. Beyond the powers or legal authority of a corporation or person.

1996 *Times* The only possible challenge would be to claim Mr Lang's block for the... merger was *ultra vires*, that it was not in Mr Lang's power to make such a decision.

umbilicus /ʌmˈbɪlɪkəs/, /ˌʌmbɪˈlʌɪkəs/ *noun* plural **umbilici** /ʌmˈbɪlɪsʌɪ/, **umbilicuses** L17 Latin (from base of UMBO, related to Greek *omphalos* and Indo-European base of navel). **1** *Anatomy* The navel. **2** *Zoology* A depression or hole at the centre of the shell whorls of some gastropod molluscs and many ammonites; a hole at each end of the hollow shaft of a feather.

umbo /ˈʌmbəʊ/ *noun* plural **umbones** /ʌmˈbəʊniːz/, **umbos** E18 Latin (= shield boss, knob). **1** *History* The central boss of a shield. **2** A rounded or conical projection or knob, especially in the centre of a rounded natural structure.

umbra /ˈʌmbrə/ *noun* plural **umbras**, **umbrae** /ˈʌmbriː/ L16 Latin (= shade). **1** The fully shaded inner region of a shadow cast by an opaque object, especially the shadow cast by the moon or earth during an eclipse. **2** Shadow or darkness.

■ In early use denoted a phantom or ghost.

umfaan /ˈʊmfɑːn/ *noun* M19 Zulu and Xhosa (*umFana* small boy). (Among Xhosa-speaking people) a young man who has gone through initiation but is not yet married; (among Zulu-speaking people) a boy. *South African*.

umfundisi /ʊmˈfʊndɪsi/, /ˌʊmfʊnˈdiːzi/ *noun* E19 Xhosa and Zulu (*umFundisi*). (Among speakers of Xhosa and Zulu) a teacher, a minister, a missionary. Also used as a respectful form of address. *South African*.

umiak /'u:mɪak/ *noun* M18 Inuit (*umiaq*). An Eskimo open boat with a wooden frame covered in skins, traditionally rowed by women.

umlaut /'ʊmlaʊt/ *noun* M19 German (from *um-* about + *Laut* sound). **1** A mark (¨) placed over a vowel, especially in German, to indicate a different vowel quality. **2** *Philology* The process in Germanic languages by which the quality of a vowel was altered in certain phonetic contexts, resulting for example in the differences between modern German *Mann* and *Männer*.

umma /'ʊmə/ *noun* L19 Arabic (= people, community, nation). The Muslim community, originally founded by Muhammad at Medina, comprising individuals bound to one another predominantly by religious ties.

umrah /'ʊmrɑ:/ *noun* E19 Arabic ('*umra*). The non-mandatory lesser pilgrimage made by Muslims to Mecca independently of or at the same time as the ʜᴀᴊᴊ, and consisting of a number of devotional rituals performed within the city.

Umwelt /'ʊmvɛlt/ *noun* plural **Umwelten** /'ʊmvɛltən/ M20 German (= environment). The outer world as it affects and is perceived by the organisms inhabiting it; the environment.

una corda /ˌu:nə 'kɔːdə/ *adverb, adjective, & noun phrase* M19 Italian (= one string). *Music* **A** *adverb & adjective phrase* (Especially as a direction) using the soft pedal of the piano. **B** *noun phrase* A device in a piano that shifts the mechanism slightly to one side when the soft pedal is depressed, so that the hammers do not strike all of the strings when sounding each note and the tone is therefore quieter.

unheimlich /ʊn'haɪmlɪç/ *adjective* L19 German. Uncanny, weird.

unicum /'ju:nɪkəm/ *noun* plural **unica** /'ju:nɪkə/ L19 Latin (neuter singular of *unicus* unique). A unique example, specimen, or thing.

Untermensch /'ʊntərˌmɛnʃ/ *noun* plural **Untermenschen** /'ʊntərˌmɛnʃən/ M20 German (= underperson). (Especially in Nazi Germany) a person considered racially or socially inferior.

> **1996** *Country Life* Himmler believed that their [sc. the Austrians'] historical involvement with other races made them more suitable than pure Germans for dealing with the *Untermensch*.

upsilon /ʌp'sʌɪlən/, /'ʊpsɪlɒn/, /ju:p'sʌɪlən/ *noun* M17 Greek (*u psilon* simple or slender u, from *psilos* slender, with reference to the need to distinguish upsilon from the diphthong οɪ, with which upsilon shared a pronunciation in late Greek). **1** The twentieth letter (Υ, υ) of the Greek alphabet, transliterated as 'u' or (chiefly in English words derived through Latin) as 'y'. **2** *Physics* A meson thought to contain a *b* quark bound to its antiparticle, produced in particle accelerators. Also *upsilon particle*.

ur- /ʊə/ M19 German (combining form). **1** Forming words with the sense 'primitive, original, earliest': *urtext*. **2** Denoting someone or something regarded as embodying the basic or intrinsic qualities of a particular class or type: *ur-thespians Patrick Stewart and Ian McKellen*.

uraeus /jʊ'ri:əs/ *noun* plural **uraei** /jʊ'ri:ʌɪ/ M19 Modern Latin (from Greek *ouraios* (perhaps from *oura* tail), representing Egyptian word for 'cobra'). A representation of a sacred serpent as an emblem of supreme power, especially worn on the headdresses of ancient Egyptian deities and sovereigns.

urbi et orbi /ˌəːbɪ ɛt 'ɔːbɪ/ *adverb phrase* M19 Latin. (Of a papal proclamation etc.) to the city (of Rome) and to the world; for general information or acceptance, to everyone.

> **1973** M. Bence-Jones *Palaces of Raj* One of the nobles, whose bard would, every two hours of the night, proclaim *urbi et orbi*...his titles and honours.

urbs /əːbz/ *noun* M20 Latin (= city). The city, especially as a symbol of harsh or busy modern life.

Urim /'jʊərɪm/ *noun* M16 Hebrew ('*ūrīm* plural of '*ōr*). One of the two objects of a now unknown nature worn on the breastplate of a Jewish high priest. Chiefly in *Urim and Thummim*. Cf. THUMMIM.

> *figurative* **1996** *Oldie* Everybody has to have a say nowadays, and the practitioner who can hit the media headlines becomes a pundit, a Urim and Thummim.

urtext /'uːrtɛkst/ *noun* plural **urtexte** /'uːrtɛkstə/, **urtexts** M20 German (*Urtext*, from UR- + *Text* text (ultimately from Latin *textus*)). An original or the earliest version of a text, to which later versions can be compared.

> **1983** *London Review of Books* Elaborate versions often point back to the gospel of Mark as a kind of cryptic *Urtext*.

ushabti variant of SHABTI.

utopia /juːˈtəʊpɪə/ *noun* (also **Utopia**) M16 Modern Latin (= no-place, from Greek *ou* not + *topos* place). **1** An imaginary place or state of things considered to be perfect; a condition of (ideal) social perfection. **2** An impossibly ideal scheme, especially for social improvement.

■ The origin of the name and of all subsequent *utopias* was the political fable *Utopia* (1516) written in Latin by Sir Thomas More (1477–1535) and translated into English in 1551. The antithesis of a *utopia* is a *dystopia* (modern Latin from Greek *dys-* bad + *topos*), a nightmare society of the kind depicted in, for example, Aldous Huxley's *Brave New World* (1932). The word *dystopia* (M19) was coined originally by J. S. Mill but it has only gained currency since the mid 20th century, especially in sociological contexts.

> **1 1996** *Spectator* The narrator, the 'Black Widow', Brady and Chico hope to take the fast lane into that middle-class utopia by robbing a bank.

v. abbreviation of VERSUS.

vacherin /vaʃrɛ̃/ *noun* M20 French. A soft French or Swiss cheese made from cow's milk.

vade mecum /ˌvɑːdɪ ˈmeɪkəm/, /ˌveɪdɪ ˈmiːkəm/ *noun* E17 French (from modern Latin use as noun of Latin *vade mecum* go with me). **1** A small book or manual carried on one's person for ready reference; a handbook, a guidebook. **2** Anything useful commonly carried about or kept available for use by a person.

vae victis /ˌvʌɪ ˈvɪktɪs/ *interjection* E17 Latin (= woe to the conquered). Woe to the conquered (a cry noting or calling for the humiliation of the vanquished by their conquerors).

■ A Latin proverbial saying. It is said by Livy to have been uttered by the Gallic king, Brennus, on capturing Rome in 390 BC.

vale /ˈvɑːleɪ/ *interjection & noun* M16 Latin (imperative singular of *valere* to be well). **A** *interjection* Farewell. Cf. AVE ATQUE VALE. **B** *noun* A written or spoken farewell.

valet /ˈvalɪt/, /ˈvaleɪ/ *noun & verb* L15 Old and Modern French ((also *vaslet*, *varlet* varlet), ultimately related to *vassal* from medieval Latin *vassallus* manservant, retainer). **A** *noun* **1** A man's personal male attendant, responsible for his clothes and appearance. **2** A hotel employee who attends to the clothes of guests. **3** A person employed to clean or park cars. *North American.* **B** *verb* **1** *transitive & intransitive verb*

Act as a valet (to). **2** *transitive verb* Clean (a car), especially on the inside.

■ Originally denoting a footman acting as an attendant or servant to a horseman.

valeta variant of VELETA.

Valhalla /valˈhalə/ *noun* L17 Modern Latin (from Old Norse *Valhall-*, *Valhǫll*, from *valr* those slain in battle (= Old English *wæl*, Old Saxon, Old High German *wal*) + *hǫll* hall). **1** *Scandinavian Mythology* A hall in which heroes who died in battle were believed to feast with Odin for eternity. **2** A place or sphere assigned to a person or thing worthy of special honour. Also, paradise; a place or state of perfect bliss.

valise /vəˈliːz/ *noun* E17 French (from Italian *valigia* corresponding to medieval Latin *valesia*, of unknown origin). A small travelling bag or suitcase, now usually made of leather and of a size suitable for carrying by hand, formerly also for strapping to a horse's saddle. Now chiefly *United States*.

vallum /ˈvaləm/ *noun* E17 Latin (collectively from *vallus* stake, palisade). (In ancient Rome) a defensive wall, rampart, or stockade.

valse /vɑːls/, /vɔːls/ *noun* L18 French (from German *Walzer* waltz). A waltz (especially as used in the titles of pieces of music).

valuta /vəˈljuːtə/, /vəˈluːtə/ *noun* L19 Italian (= value). The value of one currency in respect of its exchange rate with another; a currency considered in this way.

Vanitas /ˈvanɪtɑːs/ *noun* (also **vanitas**) E20 Latin (= vanity). A still-life painting of a 17th-century Dutch genre incorporating symbols of death or change as a reminder of their inevitability.

vanitas vanitatum /ˌvanɪtɑːs vanɪˈtɑːtəm/ *noun phrase* M16 Late Latin (= vanity of vanities). Futility.

■ Quotation from the Vulgate version of Ecclesiastes 1:2, often as an exclamation of disillusionment or pessimism.

vaporetto /vapəˈrɛtəʊ/ *noun* plural **vaporetti** /vapəˈrɛti/, **vaporettos** E20 Italian (= small steamboat, diminutive of *vapore* from Latin *vapor* steam). (In Venice) a canal boat (originally a steamboat, now a motor boat) used for public transport.

vaquero /vəˈkɛːrəʊ/ *noun* plural **vaqueros** E19 Spanish (from *vaca* cow; cf. Portuguese *vaqueiro*). (In Spanish-speaking parts of America) a cowboy, a cowherd; a cattle driver.

■ *Buckaroo*, a now archaic term used (from E19) in the United States for 'a cowboy', was an alteration of *vaquero*.

vardo /ˈvɑːdəʊ/ *noun* plural **vardos** (also **varda** /ˈvɑːdə/) E19 Romany. A Gypsy caravan. Originally *slang*.

variorum /ˌvɛːrɪˈɔːrəm/ *adjective & noun* E18 Latin (literally, 'of various (people)', genitive plural of *varius* various, especially in phrase *editio cum notis variorum* edition with the notes of various (commentators)). **A** *adjective* **1** (Of an edition of an author's works) having notes by various editors or commentators. **2** (Of an edition of an author's works) including variant readings from manuscripts or earlier editions. **B** *noun* A variorum edition.

varna /ˈvɑːnə/, /ˈvʌrnə/ *noun* M19 Sanskrit (*varṇa*, literally, 'appearance, aspect, colour'). Each of the four Hindu castes, Brahman, Kshatriya, Vaisya, and Sudra.

varve /vɑːv/ *noun* E20 Swedish (= layer, turn). *Geology* A pair of thin layers of clay and silt of contrasting colour and texture which represent the deposit of a single year (summer and winter) in still water at some time in the past (especially in a lake formed by a retreating ice sheet).

vaudeville /ˈvɔːdəvɪl/, /ˈvəʊdəvɪl/ *noun* M18 French (earlier *vau* (plural *vaux*) *de ville*, *vau de ville*, said to be the name given originally to songs composed by Olivier Basselin, a 15th-century fuller born in *Vau de Vire* in Normandy, north-west France). **1** A type of entertainment popular chiefly in the United States in the early 20th century, featuring a mixture of speciality acts such as burlesque comedy and song and dance. **2** A light stage play or comedy with interspersed songs. **3** A satirical or topical song with a refrain. Now *rare*.

vedette /vɪˈdɛt/ *noun* L17 French (from Italian *vedetta*, alteration (after *vedere* to see) of southern Italian *veletta*, perhaps from Spanish *vela* watch, from *velar* to keep watch, from Latin *vigilare*). **1** *History* A mounted sentry positioned beyond an army's outposts to observe the movements of the enemy; a scout. **2** A leading star of stage, screen, or television.

veena /ˈviːnə/ *noun* (also **vina**) L18 Sanskrit and Hindi (*vīṇā*). An Indian stringed instrument with a gourd at one or either end of a fretted finger-board and seven strings.

vega /ˈveɪɡə/ *noun* M17 Spanish and Catalan (*vega* = Portuguese *veiga*). (In Spain and Spanish America) an extensive, usually fertile and grass-covered, plain or valley.

veld /vɛlt/ *noun* (also **veldt**) L18 Afrikaans (from Dutch = field). Open, uncultivated country or grassland in southern Africa.

■ Frequently with specifying word, as in *bushveld*, *sandveld*.

veldskoen /ˈfɛltskʊn/, /ˈfɛlskʊn/ *noun* E19 Afrikaans (= field shoe, ultimately by assimilation to VELD of earlier *velschoen*, from *fel* skin, + *schoen* shoe). A strong but usually soft leather or suede boot or shoe. *South African*.

■ The term is used in South Africa as a symbol of conservative or reactionary attitudes.

veldt variant of VELD.

veleta /vəˈliːtə/ *noun* (also **valeta**) E20 Spanish (= weathervane). A ballroom dance in triple time, faster than a waltz and with partners side by side.

velours /vəˈlʊə/ *noun* (also **velour**) E18 French (= velvet, from Old French *velour*, *velous* from Latin *villosus* hairy, from *villus* hair). **1** A plush woven fabric similar to velvet and chiefly used for hats and soft furnishings. **2** A hat made of velours. *Dated*.

■ The French phrase *velours croché* 'hooked velvet' has given rise to the proprietary name Velcro (M20) for a form of fastening widely used for fabrics, consisting of two strips of nylon with complementary meshed and hooked surfaces which adhere to each other when pressed together.

velouté /vəˈluːteɪ/ *noun* M19 French (= velvety). A rich white sauce made from a roux of butter and flour with chicken, veal, or pork stock. More fully *velouté sauce*.

vendange /vɑ̃dɑ̃ʒ/ *noun* plural pronounced same M18 Old and Modern French. (In France) the grape harvest; the vintage or grapes harvested; a particular vintage of wine.

vendetta /vɛnˈdɛtə/ *noun* M19 Italian (from Latin *vindicta* vengeance). **1** A blood feud in which the family of a murdered person seeks vengeance on the murderer or the murderer's family, especially as customary in Corsica and Sicily. **2** A similar blood feud, or prosecution of private revenge. Also, a prolonged bitter quarrel with or campaign against a person etc.

vendeuse /vɑ̃døz/ *noun* plural pronounced same E20 French (from *vendre* to sell). A saleswoman, especially one in a fashionable dress shop.

> **1996** *Times Magazine* Abandoning the stage, she worked as a *vendeuse* for the fashion house Worth.

vendue /vɛnˈdjuː/ *noun* L17 Dutch (*vendu, vendue* from Old and Modern French (now dialect) *vendue* sale, from *vendre* to sell). A public sale; an auction. *United States* and *West Indies*.

veni, vidi, vici /ˈveɪmi ˈviːdi ˈviːki/ *interjection* L16 Latin. I came, I saw, I conquered.

■ According to the ancient biographer Plutarch, the words in which Julius Caesar reported his victory at Zela over Pharnaces, king of Pontus in Asia Minor, in 47 BC. Used with reference to any swift and overwhelming success.

ventre à terre /vɑ̃tr a tɛr/ *adverb phrase* M19 French (literally, 'belly to the ground'). At full speed, with legs stretched out in line with the belly (used especially of a horse's movement or its representation in paintings).

> **1977** E. Crispin *Glimpses of Moon* Man and horse ... went on to gallop almost *ventre à terre* in the direction of the hedge.

venue /ˈvɛnjuː/ *noun* L16 Old and Modern French (use as noun of feminine past participle of *venir* to come, from Latin *venire*). **1** The place where something happens, especially an organized event such as a concert, conference, or sports competition. **2** *Law* The jurisdiction within which a criminal or civil case may or must be heard.

■ Originally used to denote a thrust or bout in fencing and a sally in order to attack someone.

vera causa /ˌvɛːrə ˈkaʊzə/ *noun phrase* M19 Latin (= real cause). (In Newtonian philosophy) the true cause of a natural phenomenon, by an agency whose existence is independently evidenced.

veranda /vəˈrandə/ *noun* (also **verandah**) E18 Hindi (*varaṇḍā* from Portuguese *varanda* railing, balustrade, balcony, of unknown origin). **1** A roofed platform along the outside of a house, level with the ground floor. **2** A roof or canopy extending over the pavement outside a shop or business establishment. *Australia* and *New Zealand*.

verbatim /vəˈbeɪtɪm/ *adverb & adjective* L15 Medieval Latin (from Latin *verbum* word; cf. LITERATIM). **A** *adverb* Word for word; in exactly the same words as were used originally. **B** *adjective* Corresponding with or following an original word for word.

verboten /fɛrˈboːtən/ *adjective* E20 German. Forbidden, especially by an authority.

verbum sapienti /ˌvəːbəm sapˈɪɛnti/ *interjection* E19 Latin (*verbum sapienti sat est* a word is sufficient for a wise person). A word to the wise (implying that any further explanation or comment is unnecessary or inadvisable).

■ Usually found in the abbreviated form *verb. sap.* /vəːb ˈsap/.

verd-antique /ˌvəːdanˈtiːk/ *noun* M18 French (*verd* (now *vert*) green + *antique* antique). **1** A green ornamental variety of marble, consisting chiefly of serpentine mixed with calcite and dolomite. **2** A greenish patina or incrustation on ancient bronze or copper; verdigris. **3** A green form of porphyry.

verglas /'vɛːglɑ:/ *noun* E19 French (from *verre* glass + *glas* (now *glace*) ice). A glassy coating of ice or frozen rain on the ground or an exposed surface.

verismo /vɛ'rɪzməʊ/ *noun* E20 Italian. Realism or naturalism in the arts, especially with reference to late 19th-century Italian opera.

> **1996** *Times Verismo* is a bogus and self-contradictory term—all theatre is illusion—but there is abundant, near-unbearable human truth in these episodes [of *La Bohème*].

vérité /verite/ *noun* M20 French (= truth). Realism or naturalism, especially in cinema, radio, and television; documentary method. Cf. CINÉMA-VÉRITÉ.

verkrampte /fer'krɑmptə/ *adjective & noun* (also (as predicative adjective) **verkramp** /fer'krɑmp/) M20 Afrikaans (= narrow, cramped). **A** *adjective* Politically or socially conservative or reactionary, especially as regards apartheid. **B** *noun* Such a conservative or reactionary person.

> ■ Originally used in South Africa of politicians on the conservative wing of the Nationalist Party, but now more generally of any die-hard reactionary, especially a hardline segregationist Afrikaner. The word often appears in contexts in which it is explicitly or implicitly contrasted with VERLIGTE.

verligte /fer'lɪxtə/ *adjective & noun* (also (as predicative adjective) **verlig** /fer'lɪx/) M20 Afrikaans (= enlightened). **A** *adjective* Progressive or enlightened, especially as regards apartheid. **B** *noun* Such a progressive or enlightened person.

> ■ In South Africa, the opposite of VERKRAMPTE (see quotation).
>
> **1981** *Observer* Like most black African Muslims, Edvis favours a liberal interpretation of the Koran, being *verligte* rather than *verkrampte* in that regard.

vermicelli /ˌvəːmɪ'(t)sɛli/ *noun* M17 Italian (plural of *vermicello* diminutive of *verme* worm, from Latin *vermis*). **1** Pasta in the form of long slender threads, often added to soups. **2** Shreds of chocolate used to decorate cakes or other sweet foods.

vernaccia /və'natʃə/ *noun* E19 Italian. A dry white wine produced in the San Gimignano area of Italy and in Sardinia; the grape from which this is made.

vernissage /vɛrnisaʒ/ *noun* plural pronounced same E20 French (literally, 'varnishing'). Originally, a day before an exhibition of paintings on which exhibitors could retouch and varnish pictures already hung. Now usually, a private view of paintings before public exhibition.

veronique /vɛrə'niːk/, *foreign* /verɔnik/ *postpositive adjective* also **Véronique** E20 French (*Véronique* Veronica). Denoting a dish, especially of fish or chicken, prepared or garnished with grapes.

verre églomisé /vɛr eglɔmize/ *noun phrase* E20 French (*verre* glass + *églomisé*, from *Glomy*, 18th-century Parisian picture-framer). Glass decorated on the back with engraved gold or silver leaf or paint.

> **1996** *Country Life* The pair of mirrors with red and gold *verre oglomisé* frames ... are in the arched alcoves above.

versant /'vəːs(ə)nt/ *noun* M19 French (use as noun of present participle of *verser* to tilt over, from Latin *versare*). A region of land sloping in one general direction.

vers de société /vɛr də sɔsjete/ *noun phrase* L18 French (literally, 'verse of society'). Verse treating topics provided by polite society in a light, often witty style.

vers libre /vɛr libr/ *noun phrase* plural **vers libres** (pronounced same) E20 French (literally, 'free verse'). Poetry that does not rhyme or have a regular rhythm. Also known as *free verse*.

verso /'vəːsəʊ/ *noun* plural **versos** M19 Latin (*verso* (sc. *folio*) = (the leaf) being turned, ablative singular neuter of *versus* past participle of *vertere* to turn). **1** The left-hand page of an open book; the back of a loose document, as opposed to the front or RECTO. **2** The reverse side, especially of a coin, medal, or painting.

Verstehen /fɛr'ʃteːən/ *noun* M20 German (= understanding, comprehension). *Sociology* Empathic understanding of human action and behaviour.

versus /'vəːsəs/ *preposition* LME Medieval Latin (use of Latin *versus* towards, in sense of *adversus* against). Against, in opposition to.

■ Used especially in legal or sporting contexts, where it is generally abbreviated *v.* or *vs*, as in *City v. United*.

vertigo /'vəːtɪgəʊ/ *noun* LME Latin ((stem *vertigin-*) = whirling about, giddiness, from *vertere* to turn). A sensation of whirling and loss of balance, associated particularly with looking down from a great height, or caused by disease affecting the inner ear or the vestibular nerve; giddiness.

vertu variant of VIRTU.

vesica /'vɛsɪkə/, /'viːsɪkə/ *noun* M17 Latin (= bladder, blister). **1** *Anatomy* A bladder. Usually with Latin specifying word. *Rare.* **2** Elliptical for VESICA PISCIS.

vesica piscis /ˌvɛsɪkə 'pɪskɪs/, /ˌviːsɪkə 'pɪskɪs/ *noun phrase* (also **vesica piscium** /ˌvɛsɪkə 'pɪskɪʌm/) E19 Latin (= fish's (or fishes') bladder). A pointed oval figure used as an architectural feature and as an aureole enclosing figures such as Christ or the Virgin Mary in medieval painting and sculpture.

■ The origin of the name is uncertain; one 19th-century writer objected that it was not a bladder belonging to a fish but a bladder which, when filled, would be in the shape of a fish. Another attributed the invention of the term to the German artist Albrecht Dürer (1471–1528).

veto /'viːtəʊ/ *noun & verb* E17 Latin (= I forbid, used by Roman tribunes of the people to oppose measures of the Senate or actions of the magistrates). **A** *noun* plural **vetoes** A constitutional right to reject a decision or proposal made by a law-making body; a rejection by right of veto; any ban or prohibition. Frequently in *apply*, *place*, or *put a veto on* or *to*. **B** *transitive verb* Exercise a veto against (a decision or proposal); refuse to accept or allow.

veuve /vəːv/, *foreign* /vœv/ *noun* L18 French. (In France) a widow.

■ Frequently as a title prefixed to a woman's surname and perhaps most familiar as part of a proprietary name of a brand of champagne: *Veuve Clicquot.*

vexillum /vɛk'sɪləm/ *noun* plural **vexilla** /vɛk'sɪlə/ E18 Latin (= flag, banner, from *vex-, vect-, vehere* to carry, convey). **1** (In ancient Rome) a military standard or banner; a body of soldiers grouped under this. **b** A small piece of linen or silk attached to the upper part of a bishop's crozier. **2** *Botany* The standard or large uppermost petal of a papilionaceous flower. **3** *Ornithology* The vane of a feather.

via /'vʌɪə/, /'viːə/ *preposition* L18 Latin (ablative singular of *via* way). **1** By way of; by a route passing through or over. **2** By means of; with the aid of; through.

via affirmativa /ˌviːə əfəːmə'tʌɪvə/ *noun phrase* M19 Modern Latin (= affirmative way). *Theology* The approach to God through positive statements about his nature. Cf. VIA NEGATIVA.

Via Crucis /ˌviːə 'kruːtʃɪs/ *noun phrase* M19 Latin (= way of the cross). **1** The route followed by Christ to Calvary; *Christian Church* the Way of the Cross as a series of devotions or, *especially* in the Roman Catholic Church, a series of 'stations' or shrines set around a church interior for devotion and meditation. **2** *figurative* An extremely painful or distressing experience requiring strength or courage to bear.

Via Dolorosa /ˌviːə dɒlə'rəʊzə/ *noun phrase* L19 Latin (literally, 'sorrowing way'). **1** The route believed to have been taken by Christ through Jerusalem to Calvary. **2** *figurative* A prolonged ordeal.

2 1996 C. Lis and H. Soly *Disordered Lives* Married life for him was a *via dolorosa*: his wife beat him till the blood flowed, killed their cat and dog, set the household furniture on fire and threw burning embers at passers-by...

via media /ˌviːə 'miːdɪə/ *noun phrase* M19 Latin A middle way; an intermediate course, a compromise.

1996 *Spectator* The Anglican *via media* was almost always Burke's way...

via negativa /ˌviːə nɛɡəˈtʌɪvə/ *noun phrase* M19 Modern Latin (= negative way). *Theology* The approach to God believing no positive statements can be made about his nature; *transferred* a way of denial.

viaticum /vʌɪˈatɪkəm/ *noun* plural **viatica** /vʌɪˈatɪkə/ M16 Latin (use as noun of neuter of *viaticus* pertaining to a road or journey, from *via* road). **1** *Christian Church* The Eucharist as administered to a person near or in danger of death. **2** A supply or official allowance of money for a journey; travelling expenses. **b** A supply of food for a journey.

vibrato /vɪˈbrɑːtəʊ/ *noun & adverb* M19 Italian (past participle of *vibrare* vibrate). *Music* **A** *noun* plural **vibratos** A rapid slight variation in pitch in singing or playing some musical instruments, producing a stronger or richer tone. Cf. TREMOLO. **B** *adverb* With a rapid slight variation in pitch.
 A 1996 *Times* The real weight lies in the middle of the voice, with the sweetest of vibratos...

vice anglais /vis ɑ̃glɛ/ *noun phrase* M20 French (literally, 'English vice'). A vice considered characteristic of the English; *especially* the use of corporal punishment for sexual stimulation.

vicereine /ˈvʌɪsreɪn/ *noun* E19 French (from *vice-* vice- + *reine* queen). The wife of a viceroy. Also, a female viceroy.

vice versa /ˌvʌɪsə ˈvəːsə/, /ˌvʌɪs/ *adverb phrase* E17 Latin (literally, 'the position being reversed', from as *vice* ablative of *vix* change, place, stead + *versa* ablative feminine singular of *versus* past participle of *vertere* to turn). With the main items in the preceding statement the other way round; contrariwise, conversely.
 1996 *Spectator* The medium seems to have chosen him rather than vice versa.

vichyssoise /ˌviːʃiːˈswɑːz/ *noun* M20 French (*crème vichyssoise glacée*, literally, 'iced cream soup of Vichy'). A soup made with potatoes, leeks, and cream, and usually served cold.

victor ludorum /ˌvɪktə luːˈdɔːrəm/ *noun phrase* E20 Latin (= victor of the games). The overall champion in a sports competition, especially at a school or college; the sports competition itself.
 figurative **1996** *Times* Though his former teacher Brunetto Latini is condemned to run forever on the burning marl among the sodomites, Dante treats him as a father figure, and as an intellectual *victor ludorum*.

vicuña /vɪˈkjuːnjə/, /vɪˈkuːnjə/ *noun* (also **vicuna** /vɪˈkjuːnjə/, /vɪˈkuːnə/) E17 Spanish (from Quechua *wikúña*). **1** A hoofed mammal of the high Andes, *Vicugna vicugna*, which is related to the llama and guanaco and has a fine silky coat used for textile fabrics. **2** A fine fabric made from the wool of the vicuña (also more fully *vicuña cloth*). Also, a garment made of this fabric.

vicus /ˈvʌɪkəs/, /ˈviːkəs/ *noun* plural **vici** /ˈvʌɪkiː/ M19 Latin (= village, group of dwellings). In the Roman Empire, a village, a settlement; *specifically* the smallest unit of ancient Roman municipal administration, consisting of a village or part of a town. Also, a medieval European township.

vide /ˈvʌɪdi/, /ˈvɪdeɪ/ *transitive verb* (*imperative*) M16 Latin (imperative singular of *videre* to see). See, refer to, consult.
 ■ Used as an instruction in a text referring the reader to a specified passage, work, etc., for fuller or further information. Also abbreviated to *vid.*
 1996 *Spectator* ...English intellectuals like to define themselves by their philistinism about sport. This is not true of intellectuals elsewhere: *vide* my prized collection of Renaissance goalkeepers, which includes Albert Camus, Vladimir Nabokov,...

videlicet /vɪˈdɛlɪsɛt/, /vʌɪˈdɛlɪsɛt/, /vɪˈdɛlɪkɛt/ *adverb & noun* LME Latin (from *vide-* stem of *videre* to see + *licet* it is permissible; cf. SCILICET). **A** *adverb* Usually introducing an amplification or explanation of a previous statement or word; that is to say, namely. **B** *noun* The word 'videlicet' introducing an explanation or amplification, especially in a legal document.
 ■ Frequently abbreviated to *viz(.)* (M16), the *z* representing the usual medieval Latin symbol of contraction for -*et*.

vie de Bohème /vi də bɔɛm/ *noun phrase* L19 French. An unconventional or informal way of life, especially as practised by an artist or writer; a Bohemian way of life.

vie en rose /vi ɑ̃ roz/ *noun phrase* M20 French. A life seen through rose-coloured spectacles.

▪ A phrase popularized by the French singer Edith Piaf (1915–63), one of whose songs was called 'La Vie en rose'.

1974 M. Cecil *Heroines in Love* So many hopes had tumbled that magazine writers were reluctant to present an unending *vie en rose*.

vi et armis /ˌviː ɛt ˈɑːmiːs/ *adverb phrase* E17 Latin (= with force and arms). Violently, forcibly, by compulsion; *specifically* in *Law* (now *historical*), with unlawful violence.

vieux jeu /vjø ʒø/ *adjective* plural of noun **vieux jeux** (pronounced same) L19 French (literally, 'old game'). Old-fashioned, hackneyed, passé.

viga /ˈviːgə/ *noun* M19 Spanish. (In the United States) a rough-hewn roof timber or rafter, especially in an adobe building.

vigilante /vɪdʒɪˈlanti/ *noun* M19 Spanish (from Latin *vigilant-* present participial stem of *vigilare* to keep awake). A member of a self-appointed group of citizens who undertake law enforcement in their community without legal authority, typically because the legal agencies are thought to be inadequate. Originally *United States*.

vigneron /ˈviːnjərɒn/, *foreign* /viɲərɔ̃/ (*plural same*) *noun* LME French (from *vigne* vine). A person who cultivates grapes for winemaking; a vine grower.

vignette /viːˈnjɛt/, /vɪˈnjɛt/ *noun & verb* LME Old and Modern French (diminutive of *vigne* vine). A *noun* 1 A brief evocative description, account, or episode. 2 A small illustration or portrait photograph which fades into its background without a definite border. 3 A small ornamental design filling a space in a book or carving, typically based on foliage. B *transitive verb* 1 Portray (someone) in the style of a vignette. 2 Produce (a photograph) in the style of a vignette by softening or shading away the edges of the subject.

▪ First used in English in sense 3 of the noun. Another early use was as an

architectural term denoting a carved representation of a vine.

A.1 1996 *Spectator* The minor characters seem alive; the incidental vignettes are as well told as the climaxes...

vihara /vɪˈhɑːrə/ *noun* L17 Sanskrit (*vihāra*). A Buddhist temple or monastery.

villa /ˈvɪlə/ *noun* E17 Italian and Latin (partly from Latin *villa* country house, farm, partly from Italian *villa* from Latin). 1 (Especially in continental Europe) a large and luxurious country house in its own grounds. 2 A detached or semi-detached house in a suburban or residential district; a rented holiday home abroad. 3 A large country house of Roman times, having an estate and consisting of a farm and residential buildings arranged around a courtyard.

villancico /ˌvi(l)janˈθiko/, /ˌvi(l)jan ˈsiko/ *noun* plural **villancicos** /ˌvi(l) janˈθikos/, /ˌvi(l)janˈsikos/ E19 Spanish (diminutive of *villano* peasant, rustic). *Music* A form of Spanish and Portuguese song consisting of short stanzas separated by a refrain, originally a kind of folk song but later used in sacred music, and now especially as a Christmas carol.

villanella /vɪləˈnɛlə/ *noun* plural **villanelle** /vɪləˈnɛleɪ/, **villanellas** L16 Italian (see next). *Music* A form of Italian part-song originating in Naples in the 16th century, in rustic style with a vigorous rhythm.

villanelle /vɪləˈnɛl/ *noun* L16 French (from Italian *villanella* feminine of *villa-nello* rural, rustic, from *villano* peasant, rustic). A pastoral or lyrical poem of nineteen lines, with only two rhymes throughout, and some lines repeated.

ville /vɪl/, /vʌɪl/ *noun* M19 French (= town). A town, a village.

▪ Colloquial, chiefly United States, where *-ville* occurs in the names of many towns (e.g. *Louisville*). Hence used humorously as a suffix to form the name of a fictitious place that epitomizes the quality concerned: *Dullsville*.

1972 *Publishers' Weekly* There are some who will simply not get the fun of it out there in mass-marketville.

1977 M. Herr *Dispatches* Once we fanned over a little ville that had just been airstruck.

vin /vɛ̃/ *noun* L17 French (= wine). French wine.

vina variant of VEENA.

vinaigrette /ˌvɪneɪ'grɛt/, /ˌvɪnɪ'grɛt/ *noun* LME French (from *vinaigre* vinegar). **1** A salad dressing of oil and wine vinegar with seasoning. Also more fully *vinaigrette dressing*. **2** *History* A small ornamental bottle or box for holding a sponge saturated with smelling-salts.

vin blanc /vɛ̃ blɑ̃/ *noun phrase* L18 French. White wine.

vinculum /'vɪŋkjʊləm/ *noun plural* **vincula** /'vɪŋkjʊlə/ M17 Latin (from *vincire* to bind). **1** *Anatomy* A connecting band or band-like structure; *especially* a narrow tendon. **2** *Mathematics* A horizontal line over two or more terms, denoting that they are to be treated as a unit in the following operation.

■ Originally used in the sense 'bond, tie'.

vindaloo /vɪndə'lu:/ *noun* L19 Portuguese (probably from Portuguese *vin d'alho* wine and garlic sauce, from *vinho* wine + *alho* garlic). A highly spiced hot Indian curry dish made with meat or fish. Also *vindaloo curry*.

vin de garde /vɛ̃ də gɑ:d/ *noun phrase* E20 French (= wine for keeping). Wine which will significantly improve in quality if left to mature.

vin de paille /vɛ̃ də pɑj/ *noun phrase* M19 French (= straw wine). A rich dessert wine made from grapes that have been dried in the sun on straw mats or wire frames before being pressed.

vin de pays /vɛ̃ də pə(j)i/ *noun phrase* (also **vin du pays** /vɛ̃ dy pə(j)i/) L18 French (literally, 'wine of the region'). French wine produced in a particular area and meeting certain standards of quality, superior to vin de table.

vin de table /vɛ̃ də tabl/ *noun phrase* M20 French. Wine of reasonable quality, suitable for drinking with a meal.

■ The English phrase *table wine* (L17) is also used, especially of non-French wines; the German equivalent is TAFELWEIN.

vin d'honneur /vɛ̃ dɔnœr/ *noun phrase* E20 French (= wine of honour). A wine formally offered in honour of a special guest; the reception at which the wine is offered.

vin du pays variant of VIN DE PAYS.

vingt-et-un /vɛ̃t e œ̃/ *noun* Also written **vingt-un** L18 French (= twenty-one). The card game pontoon or blackjack.

vinho /'viɲu/, /'vi:nəʊ/ *noun* M19 Portuguese. Portuguese wine.

vinho verde /ˌviɲu 'verdə/, /ˌviɲu 'və:di/ *noun phrase* M20 Portuguese (literally, 'green wine'). A young Portuguese wine, not allowed to mature.

vin jaune /vɛ̃ ʒon/ *noun phrase* M19 French (literally, 'yellow wine'). A strong yellowish wine from the Jura region of eastern France.

vino /'vinɒ/, *especially in sense 2* /ˌvi:nəʊ/ *noun* L17 Spanish and Italian (= wine). **1** Spanish or Italian wine. **2** Wine, especially of an inferior kind. *Colloquial*, often *humorous*.

2 1976 P. Cave *High Flying Birds* I was far too stoned to take much notice of Lloyd's vino-inspired ramblings.

vino da tavola /ˌvino da 'tɑ:vala/ *noun phrase* M20 Italian (= table wine). Italian wine of reasonable quality, suitable for drinking with a meal.

vin ordinaire /vɛ̃ ɔrdinɛr/ *noun phrase* E19 French (literally, 'ordinary wine'). Cheap table wine for everyday use.

■ Also referred to elliptically as *ordinaire* (M19).

vin rouge /vɛ̃ ruʒ/ E20 French. Red wine.

viola da braccio /vɪ'əʊlə da ˌbratʃə/ *noun phrase* M19 Italian (literally, 'viol for the arm'). An early musical instrument of the violin family (as distinct from a viol), specifically one corresponding to the modern viola.

viola da gamba /vɪˌəʊlə də 'gambə/ *noun phrase* (also (earlier) **viol da gamba** /ˌvʌɪəl də 'gambə/) L16 Italian (literally, 'viol for the leg'). **1** A viol, specifically a bass viol (corresponding to the modern cello). **2** An organ stop resembling this instrument in tone.

viola d'amore /vɪˈəʊlə daˌmɔːreɪ/ *noun phrase* E18 Italian (literally, 'viol of love'). A sweet-toned 18th-century musical instrument similar to a viola, but with six or seven strings, and additional sympathetic strings below the fingerboard.

violoncello /ˌvʌɪələnˈtʃɛləʊ/, /ˌviːələn ˈtʃɛləʊ/ *noun* E18 Italian (diminutive of *violone*). A cello.

violon d'Ingres /vjɔlɔ̃ dɛ̃gr/ *noun phrase* plural **violons d'Ingres** (pronounced same) M20 French (literally, 'Ingres' violin'). An interest or activity other than that for which a person is best known; an occasional pastime.

■ The allusion is to the French painter J.-A.-D. Ingres (1780–1867), who was a keen amateur violinist and said to have been more proud of his violin-playing than of his highly acclaimed pictures.

virago /vɪˈrɑːgəʊ/, /vɪˈreɪgəʊ/ *noun* plural **viragos** LME Latin (from *vir* man). **1** A woman of masculine strength or spirit; a female warrior, an amazon. *Archaic.* **2** A domineering woman; a fierce or abusive woman.

■ Earlier (OE–L16) meaning 'woman', but only in biblical allusions with reference to the name given by Adam to Eve.

virga /ˈvəːgə/ *noun* plural **virgae** /ˈvəːgiː/ E20 Latin (= rod). *Meteorology, singular* and in *plural* Streaks of precipitation that appear to hang from the undersurface of a cloud and usually evaporate before reaching the ground.

virgo intacta /ˌvəːgəʊ ɪnˈtaktə/ *noun phrase* E18 Latin (literally, 'untouched virgin'). Chiefly *Law* A girl or woman who has never had sexual intercourse, originally a virgin whose hymen is intact.

virgule /ˈvəːgjuːl/ *noun* M19 French (= comma, from Latin *virgula* diminutive of *virga* rod). **1** A slanting or upright line used especially in medieval manuscripts to mark a caesura, or as a punctuation mark equivalent to a comma. Now also a SOLIDUS sense 1. **2** *Watchmaking* A type of escapement

in which the teeth of the wheel have the shape of a comma. More fully *virgule escapement*.

virtu /vəːˈtuː/ *noun* (also **vertu**, **virtù**) E18 Italian (*virtù* virtue; the form *vertu* altered as if from French). **1** A love of or interest in works of art; a knowledge of or expertise in the fine arts; the fine arts as a subject of study or interest. **2** *collective* Objects of art; curios. **3** The strength or worth inherent in a person or thing; *especially* inherent moral worth or virtue.

virtuoso /vəːtjʊˈəʊsəʊ/, /vəːtjʊˈəʊzəʊ/ *noun & adjective* E17 Italian (= learned, skilful, from late Latin *virtuosus*). **A** *noun* plural **virtuosi** /vəːtjʊˈəʊsiː/, **virtuosos** **1** A person highly skilled in music or another artistic pursuit. **2** A person who has a special knowledge of or interest in the fine arts; a connoisseur. **B** *adjective* Relating to a virtuoso; displaying the skills of a virtuoso; characterized by virtuosity.

visa /ˈviːzə/ *noun* M19 French (from Latin = things seen, neuter plural of past participle of *videre* to see). An endorsement on a passport indicating that the holder is allowed to enter, leave, or stay for a specified period of time in a country.

visagiste /ˌviːzaːˈʒiːst/ *noun* M20 French. A make-up artist.

vis-à-vis /ˌviːzaːˈviː/ *preposition, adverb, & noun* M18 Old and Modern French (literally, 'face to face', from Old French *vis* visage + *à* to + *vis*). **A** *preposition* In relation to, with regard to; as compared with, as opposed to. **B** *adverb* Opposite; facing one another. *Archaic.* **C** *noun* plural same. **1** A person or thing facing or situated opposite to another, especially in certain dances. **b** A person or group occupying a corresponding position to that of another in a different sphere; a counterpart, an opposite number. **2** A face-to-face meeting. **3** A light horse-drawn carriage for two people sitting face to face. *Obsolete except historical.*

A 1996 *Times* But the Foreign Office must accept that its own obsessive secrecy...has ensured a climate of deep suspicion about anything involving its own role *vis-à-vis* the

Jews and their treatment at the hands of the Nazis.

vis medicatrix naturae /ˌvɪs mɛdɪˌkeɪtrɪks ˈnatʃərʌɪ/ *noun phrase* E19 Latin (= the healing power of nature). The body's natural ability to heal itself.

vista /ˈvɪstə/ *noun* M17 Italian (= view). **1** A pleasing view. **2** A long narrow view as between rows of trees or buildings, especially one closed by a building or other structure. **3** A mental view of a succession of re-membered or anticipated events.

vita /ˈviːtə/ *noun* M20 Latin (= life). **1** A biography, a life history, *especially* a short Latin biography of a saint. **2** A CURRICULUM VITAE. *United States.*

vita nuova /ˌviːtə ˈnwəʊvə/ *noun phrase* M20 Italian (= new life). A fresh start or new direction in life, especially after some powerful emotional experience.
■ With allusion to the title of a work by Dante describing his love for Beatrice.
1975 P. Organ *House on Cheyne Walk* Not a very good way to begin *la vita nuova*, with more lies.

vitello tonnato /viˈtɛllo tonˈnaːto/ *noun phrase* M20 Italian (from *vitello* veal + *tonno* tuna). An Italian dish consisting of roast or poached veal served cold in a tuna and anchovy mayonnaise.

viva /ˈviːvə/ *interjection & noun* 1 M17 Italian (= live!, 3rd person singular pre-sent subjunctive of *vivere* to live, from Latin). **A** *interjection* Long live! (used to express acclaim or support for a specified person or thing). **B** *noun* A cry of this as a salute or cheer. Cf. VIVAT, VIVE (interjection).

viva /ˈvʌɪvə/ *noun* 2 & *verb* L19 Latin (abbreviation of VIVA VOCE). **A** *noun* A VIVA VOCE examination. **B** *transitive verb* past tense *vivaed*, *viva'd* /ˈvʌɪvəd/. Subject to a viva voce examination, examine orally.
A 1996 *Spectator* The candidate in search of a doctorate was not alone in being taken aback by the honesty of Richard at their *viva* when he stated that he had not read all of the thesis.

vivarium /vʌɪˈvɛːrɪəm/, /vɪˈvɛːrɪəm/ *noun* plural **vivaria** /vʌɪˈvɛːrɪə/, **vivar-iums** E17 Latin (= warren, fish pond, use as noun of *vivarius* from *vivus* alive, from

vivere to live). An enclosure, container, or structure used for keeping animals under conditions approximating to the natural conditions, for observa-tion or study or as pets; an aquarium or terrarium.

vivat /ˈvʌɪvat/, /ˈviːvat/ *interjection & noun* L16 Latin (= may he or she live, 3rd person singular present subjunctive of *vivere* to live). **A** *interjection* Long live! (used to express acclaim or support for a specified person or thing). **B** *noun* A cry of this as a salute or cheer. Cf. VIVA, VIVE.

viva voce /ˌvʌɪvə ˈvəʊtʃɪ/ *adverb, adjec-tive, & noun phrase* M16 Medieval Latin (literally, 'by or with the living voice'). **A** *adverb phrase* Orally rather than in writing. **B** *adjective phrase* **1** Expressed in speech rather than writing, spo-ken. **2** (Of an examination) conducted orally. **C** *noun phrase* An oral examina-tion, typically for an academic qualifi-cation.
■ In the nominal sense frequently ab-breviated to VIVA (noun 2).

vive /viv/ *interjection* L16 French (= may he, she, or it live, from *vivre* from Latin *vivere* live). Long live! (used to express acclaim or support for a specified person or thing). Cf. VIVA (interjec-tion), VIVAT.

vive la différence /viv la diferɑ̃s/ *interjection* M20 French (= long live the difference). Expressing approval of difference, especially between the sexes.
■ In humorous use.
1995 *Times* Three compatriots argued that there was little scope for significant tax cuts . . . But—*vive la différence*—two others argued for *higher* public spending.

viz. abbreviation of VIDELICET.

vlei /fleɪ/, /vlʌɪ/ *noun* L18 Afrikaans (from Dutch *vallei* valley). (In South Africa) a shallow natural pool of water; a piece of low-lying marshy ground covered with water during the rainy season.

vobla /ˈvɒblə/ *noun* M20 Russian. Dried and smoked roach eaten in Russia as a delicacy.

vodka /ˈvɒdkə/ *noun* E19 Russian (diminutive of *voda* water). A colourless alcoholic spirit of Russian origin made by distillation of rye, wheat, or potatoes.

voetsak /ˈfʊtsak/ *interjection & verb* (also **voetsek** /ˈfʊtsɛk/) M19 Afrikaans (*voe(r)tsek*, from Dutch *voort zeg ik* be off I say). **A** *interjection* (Especially to a dog) go away!, off you go! **B** *verb transitive verb* Chase (a dog) away. **2** *intransitive verb* Leave, go away. *South African.*

voilà /vwala/, /vwɑːˈlɑ:/ *interjection* (also **voila**) M18 French (from imperative of *voir* see + *là* there). There it is; there you are.
1996 *New Scientist* Just as there is nothing north of the North Pole, so there was nothing before the Big Bang. Voilà! We are supposed to be convinced by that...

voile /vɔɪl/, /vwal/ *noun* L19 French (= veil). A thin, semi-transparent fabric of cotton, wool, or silk.

voir dire /ˈvwɑː ˌdɪə/ *noun* (also **voire dire**) L17 Law French (from Old French *voir* true, truth + *dire* to say). *Law* A preliminary examination of a witness or the jury pool by a judge or counsel. Also, an investigation into the truth or admissibility of evidence, held during a trial.

voix céleste /vwa səlɛst/, /ˌvwɑː sɪˈlɛst/ *noun phrase* plural **voix célestes** (pronounced same) L19 French (= heavenly voice). A soft stop on an organ or harmonium which is tuned slightly sharp to produce a tremolo effect, traditionally regarded as reminiscent of celestial voices. Also called *vox angelica.*

vol-au-vent /ˈvɒlə(ʊ)ˌvɒ̃/ *noun* E19 French (literally, 'flight in the wind'). A small round case of puff pastry filled with a savoury mixture, typically of meat or fish in a richly flavoured sauce.

volet /ˈvɒleɪ/, *foreign* /vɔlɛ/ (*plural same*) *noun* M19 Old and Modern French (literally, 'shutter', from *voler* from Latin *volare* to fly). Each of the panels or wings of a triptych (picture or carving on three panels).

volk /fɒlk/ *noun* (also (German) **Volk**) L19 Afrikaans (from Dutch or German = nation, people). **1** A nation or people, in particular the Afrikaner people. *South African.* **2** The German people (especially with reference to Nazi ideology).
1 1996 T. Alexander *Unravelling Global Apartheid* ... was access to global markets amd finance ultimately more important than self-determination and local supremacy for the Afrikaner *volk*?

Völkerwanderung /ˈføːlkərˌvandərʊŋ/, /ˈføːlkəˌvɑːndərʊŋ/ *noun* plural **Völkerwanderungen** /ˈføːlkərˌvandərʊŋən/ M20 German (from *Völker* nations + *Wanderung* migration). A migration of peoples; *specifically* that of Germanic and Slavic peoples into and across Europe from the 2nd to the 11th centuries.

völkisch /ˈføːlkɪʃ/ *adjective* M20 German. (Of a person or ideology) populist or nationalist, and typically racist.

volte /vɒlt/, /vəʊlt/ *noun* L17 French (from Italian *volta* turn, use as noun of feminine past participle of *volgere* to turn, from Latin *volvere* to roll). **1** *Fencing* (now *historical*) A sudden jump or other movement to avoid a thrust, especially a swinging round of the rear leg to turn the body sideways. **2** A movement performed in dressage and classical riding, in which a horse describes a circle of 6 yards diameter.

volte-face /vɒltˈfɑːs/, /vɒltˈfas/ *noun* E19 French (from Italian *voltafaccia*, from *voltare* to turn (ultimately from frequentative of Latin *volvere* to roll) + *faccia* (ultimately from Latin *facies*) face). **1** The act or an instance of turning round so as to face in the opposite direction. **2** An abrupt and complete reversal of attitude, opinion, or position in an argument.
2 1995 *Times* This volte-face confirms the suspicion that the earlier limits were set artificially low by the health education industry...

volupté /vɔlypte/ *noun* E18 French. Voluptuousness.

volute /vəˈl(j)uːt/ *noun & adjective* M16 French (Latin *voluta* use as noun of feminine of *volutus* past participle of *volvere* to roll, to wrap). **A** *noun* **1** *Architecture* A spiral scroll characteristic of Ionic capitals and also used in

Corinthian and composite capitals. **2** A deep-water marine mollusc with a thick colourful spiral shell. **B** *adjective* Forming a spiral curve or curves.

vomitorium /vɒmɪˈtɔːrɪəm/ *noun* plural **vomitoria** /vɒmɪˈtɔːrɪə/ M18 Late Latin (use as noun of neuter of Latin *vomitorius* vomitory). **1** A passage or opening in an ancient Roman amphitheatre or theatre, leading to or from the seats. Usually in *plural*. **2** A place in which, according to popular misconception, the ancient Romans are supposed to have vomited during feasts to make room for more food.

Voortrekker /ˈfʊətrɛkə/ *noun* L19 Afrikaans (from *voor-* before + *trekken* to trek). *South African History* A member of one of the groups of Dutch-speaking people who migrated by wagon from the Cape Colony into the interior from 1836 onwards, in order to live beyond the borders of British rule.

Vorsprung Durch Technik /ˈfɔːrʃprʊŋ dʊrx təknɪk/ *interjection* L20 German (literally 'advancement through technology'). Progress through technology.

■ An advertising slogan used by the German car manufacturer Audi. It is often quoted humorously in contexts relating to Germany's reputation for technical expertise and efficiency.

Vorstellung /ˈfɔːrʃtɛlʊŋ/ *noun* (also **vorstellung** plural **Vorstellungen** /ˈfɔːrʃtɛlʊŋ(ə)n/ E19 German. *Philosophy* and *Psychology* An idea, a mental picture.

voulu /vuly/ *adjective* L19 French (past participle of *vouloir* to wish). Lacking in spontaneity; contrived.

voussoir /ˈvuːswɑː/ *noun* ME Old French (*vausoir*, *vaussoir*, etc. (modern *voussoir*) from popular Latin *volsorium* ultimately from Latin *vols-* past participial stem of *volvere* to roll, to turn). Each of the wedge-shaped or tapered stones, bricks, etc., used to construct an arch or vaulting.

vox angelica /ˌvɒks anˈʤɛlɪkə/ *noun phrase* M19 Latin (= angelic voice). A VOIX CÉLESTE.

vox humana /ˌvɒks hjʊˈmɑːnə/ *noun phrase* E18 Latin (= human voice). An organ stop with a tone supposedly resembling the human voice.

vox populi /ˌvɒks ˈpʊpjʊlʌɪ/, /ˌvɒks ˈpʊpjʊliː/ *noun phrase* M19 Latin (= voice of the people). Popular opinion; the opinion or beliefs of the majority.

■ In modern colloquial use abbreviated to *vox pop*, usually referring to popular opinion as represented by informal comments from members of the public, especially when broadcast or published. The Latin tag from which the phrase derives, *vox populi, vox Dei* 'the voice of the people is the voice of God', has been cited or alluded to in English from the 15th century.

voyeur /vwɑːˈjəː/ *noun* E20 French (from *voir* to see). **1** A person who gains sexual pleasure from watching others when they are naked or engaged in sexual activity. **2** A person who enjoys seeing the pain or distress of others.

vrou /frəʊ/ *noun* (also **vrouw**) E17 Dutch (= German *Frau*). A woman or a wife; *especially* one of Dutch origin. Chiefly *South African*.

Ww

in forest trees and vegetation in central Europe as a result of atmospheric pollution.

■ The term has been current in English since about 1983, originally with reference to dieback through environmental causes affecting Germany's forest trees, but now applied to the same phenomenon elsewhere.

wallah /ˈwɒlə/ *noun* (also **walla**) L18 Hindi (*-vālā* suffix expressing relation, from Sanskrit *pālaka* keeper). **1** A person, formerly usually a servant, concerned with or in charge of a usually specified thing, task, etc. Chiefly as second element of combination. **2** An Indian Civil servant appointed by competitive examination. More fully *competition-wallah*. **3** Any functionary doing a routine administrative job; a civil servant, a bureaucrat.

■ The Hindi suffix was commonly apprehended by Europeans as a noun with the sense 'man, fellow'; in Anglo-Indian speech it was used chiefly as the second element in combinations such as *box-wallah* ('an itinerant Indian pedlar'). *Wallah* is now only used colloquially with a derogatory suggestion of 'an office-bound functionary' (see quotation 1974) and generally (harking back to the Anglo-Indian usage) with a defining word (see quotation 1996).

3 1974 *Courier-Mail* (Brisbane) Some wallahs in Canberra are sitting in air-conditioned offices telling us what has been flooded and what hasn't.
3 1996 *Times* As the heritage wallahs lord it in the media during the summer tourist season, they would do well to reflect upon how shallowly rooted and fragile is their present high status.

Walpurgisnacht /valˈpʊrgɪsˌnaxt/ *noun* E19 German (genitive of *Walpurga* (name) + *Nacht* night). Walpurgis night, the eve of May Day, marked (according to German folklore and especially Goethe's *Faust*) by a witches' sabbath or a feast of the powers of darkness; *transferred* an orgiastic celebration or party.

■ St Walpurga (or Walburga) was an eighth-century Anglo-Saxon nun who became abbess of Heidenheim in Germany. May Day marks the occasion of the translation of her bodily remains to Eichstätt, where her shrine became

wabi /ˈwabi/ *noun* M20 Japanese (literally, 'solitude'). (In Japanese art) a quality of simple and serene beauty of a slightly austere or melancholy kind expressing a mood of spiritual solitude recognized in Zen Buddhist philosophy.

wadi /ˈwɑːdi/, /ˈwɒdi/ *noun* (also **wady**) plural **wadis**, **wadies** E17 Arabic (*wādī* valley, river bed). (In certain Arabic-speaking countries) a rocky watercourse which is dry except during the rainy season; the stream running through such a watercourse.

■ French *oued*, a later (M19) introduction, represents the same Arabic word. *Oued* now mainly occurs in English with reference to place names in Francophone North African territories.

wagon-lit /vagɔ̃ˈliː/ *noun* plural **wagon-lits** /vagɔ̃ˈliːz/, **wagons-lits** /vagɔ̃ˈliː/ L19 French (from *wagon* railway coach + *lit* bed). A sleeping car on a train in continental Europe.

wahine /wɑːˈhiːni/, *foreign* /waˈhine/ *noun* L18 Maori. (In New Zealand) a Maori woman or wife.

wai see under NAMASKAR.

waka /ˈwaka/ *noun* E19 Maori. (In New Zealand) a traditional Maori canoe.

wakame /ˈwakameɪ/ *noun* L20 Japanese. An edible brown seaweed, used typically in dried form, in Chinese and Japanese cookery.

Waldsterben /ˈvaltˌʃtɛrbən/ *noun* L20 German (from *Wald* wood, forest + *Sterben* dying, death). *Ecology* Disease and death a pilgrimage centre. The connection with the powers of darkness is nothing to do with the saintly abbess but is a fortuitous association with pagan festivities formerly celebrated on that date.

1996 *Spectator* . . . the new freedom she finds is mirrored by the licentiousness of her lover's half-mad identical twin, who turns up at her house to burn her books and caper in a demonic spirit of *Walpurgisnacht*.

wampum /ˈwɒmpəm/ *noun* M17 Algonquian (*wampumpeag* (from *wap* white + *umpe* string + plural suffix *-ag*) abbreviated on the erroneous analysis of the word as *wampum* + *peag*). **1** Chiefly *History*. Small cylindrical beads made from the ends of shells rubbed down, polished, and threaded on strings, worn by North American Indians as decoration or (formerly) used as money. **2** Money. *Slang*.
▪ Chiefly North America.

Wanderjahr /ˈvandərjɑːr/ *noun plural* **Wanderjahre** /ˈvandərjɑːrə/ L19 German (*wander* wander + *Jahr* year). A year spent travelling abroad, typically immediately before or after a university or college course. Chiefly *North American*.
▪ Formerly a period of travel by an apprentice to improve his skill and broaden his experience.

wanderlust /ˈwɒndəlʌst/ *noun* E20 German. A strong desire to travel.

1996 *Times* But what America really seems to suit is her wanderlust, her sparkle.

Wandervogel /ˈvandəˌfəvɡəl/ *noun* plural **Wandervögel** /ˈvandəˌfəːɡəl/ E20 German (literally, 'bird of passage'). A member of a German youth organization founded at the end of the 19th century for the promotion of outdoor activities (especially hiking) and folk culture; *transferred* a rambler, a hiker.

waqf /wɑːkf/ *noun* M19 Arabic (= stoppage, immobilization (of ownership of property), from *waqafa* to stop, come to a standstill). (In Islamic countries) endowment or settlement of property under which the proceeds are to be devoted to a religious, educational, or charitable purpose; land or property endowed in this way.

wasabi /wəˈsɑːbi/ *noun* E20 Japanese. A Japanese plant, *Eutrema wasabi*, whose thick green root tastes like strong horseradish and is used in Japanese cookery, usually ground as an accompaniment to raw fish.

wat /wat/ *noun* M19 Thai (from Sanskrit *vāṭa* enclosure). (In Thailand, Cambodia, and Laos) a Buddhist monastery or temple.

wayang /ˈwɑːjaŋ/ *noun* E19 Javanese (*wajang*, *wayang*). (In Indonesia and Malaysia) a theatrical performance employing puppets or human dancers; *specifically* a Javanese and Balinese shadow puppet play (also *wayang kulit* /ˈkuːlɪt/ (Javanese = skin, leather)).

wazir /wəˈzɪə/ *noun* E18 Arabic (*wazīr* helper, counsellor). *History* A high official in some Muslim countries, especially in the Ottoman empire; a vizier.

Wehrmacht /ˈveːrmaxt/ *noun* M20 German (literally, 'defence force'). *History* The German armed forces, especially the army, between 1921 and 1945.

wei ch'i /weɪ ˈtʃiː/ *noun* L19 Chinese (*wéiqí* (Wade–Giles *wei-ch'i*), from *wei* to surround + *qí* (*ch'i*) chess). A traditional Chinese board game of territorial possession and capture. Cf. GO.

Weinstube /ˈvaɪnʃtuːbə/, /ˈvaɪnstuːbə/ *noun* plural **Weinstuben** /ˈvaɪnʃtuːbən/, **Weinstubes** L19 German (from *Wein*, wine + *Stube* room). A small German wine bar or tavern.

Wein, Weib, und Gesang /vaɪn ˈvaɪp ʊnt ɡəˈzaŋ/ *noun phrase* L19 German. Wine, woman, and song.
▪ Proverbially considered the essential ingredients for carefree entertainment and pleasure for men. The expression was popularized as the title of a Strauss waltz (1869).

Weisswurst /ˈvaɪsvəːst/, /ˈvaɪsvʊəst/ *noun* M20 German (from *weiss* white + *Wurst* sausage). Whitish German sausage made chiefly of veal.

Weltanschauung /ˌvɛltanˈʃaʊʊŋ/ *noun* plural **Weltanschauungen** /ˌvɛltanˈʃaʊʊŋən/, **Weltanschauungs** M19 German (from *Welt* world + *Anschauung* perception). A particular philosophy or view of life; the world view of an individual or group.

> 1996 *Spectator* In my case, of course, this shattering event would have to be something pleasant, since my *Weltanschauung* is one of nihilistic despair—that is to say, I am a realist.

Weltpolitik /ˈvɛltpoliˌtiːk/ *noun* E20 German (from *Welt* world + *Politik* politics). International politics; a particular country's policy towards the world at large.

Weltschmerz /ˈvɛltʃmɛrts/ *noun* L19 German (from *Welt* world + *Schmerz* pain). A weary or pessimistic feeling about life; an apathetic or vaguely yearning attitude.

> 1996 *Times* The music does not have to drip with emotion, but surely a love-song can be allowed to exude Weltschmerz as well as passion.

wendigo variant of WINDIGO.

Westpolitik /ˈvɛstpɒliˌtiːk/ *noun* L20 German (from *West* west + *Politik* policy: cf. OSTPOLITIK). *History* (In European politics) a policy of establishing or developing diplomatic and trading relations with Western European countries, especially on the part of the former communist bloc. Cf. OSTPOLITIK.

whare /ˈwɒri/ *noun* E19 Maori. (In New Zealand) a Maori house or hut; *generally* a hut, a shed, *specifically* one on a sheep station, where the hands sleep or eat.

wickiup /ˈwɪkɪʌp/ *noun* M19 Algonquian ((Menominee *wikiop*), perhaps a variant of *wikiwam* wigwam). An American Indian hut consisting of an oval frame covered with brushwood or grass; *colloquial* any small hut or shanty.

wiener /ˈviːnə/ *noun* E20 German (adjective from *Wien* Vienna). Abbreviation of WIENERWURST. *North American.*

Wiener schnitzel see under SCHNITZEL.

wienerwurst /ˈviːnəˌvəːst/, /ˈwiːnə ˌwəːst/ *noun* L19 German. Viennese sausage.

wiki /ˈwɪki/, /ˈwiːkiː/ *noun* L20 Hawaiian (*wiki wiki* very quick, emphatic form of *wiki* quick). A website or database developed collaboratively by a community of users, allowing any user to add and edit content.

> ■ Although its ultimate source is Hawaiian, the use of the term in English comes directly from *WikiWikiWeb* (1995), the name of the first website of this kind, coined by the US programmer Ward Cunningham.

wili /ˈviːli/ *noun* M20 German or French (from Serbo-Croat *víla* nymph, fairy). (In Slavic and eastern German legends) a spirit of a betrothed girl who has died from grief at being jilted by her lover (used especially with reference to the ballet *Giselle*).

willy-willy /ˈwɪlɪˌwɪli/ *noun* L19 Aboriginal. (In north-west Australia) a whirlwind or dust storm.

windigo /ˈwɪndɪɡəʊ/ *noun* (also **wendigo** /ˈwɛndɪɡəʊ/) plural **windigo(e)s** E18 Ojibwa (*wintiko*). (In the folklore of the northern Algonquian Indians) a cannibalistic giant; a person who has been transformed into a monster by the consumption of human flesh.

Wirtschaftswunder /ˈvɪrtʃaftsˌvʊndər/ *noun* (also **Wirtschaftwunder**) M20 German (*Wirtschaft* economy + *Wunder* miracle). The economic recovery of West Germany after the war of 1939–45. Also *transferred.*

> 1996 *Times* But this ominous comparison makes no impression on the self-confidence of German public and political opinion, still mesmerised by the myth of the Wirtschaftswunder of the 1950s.

Wissenschaft /ˈvɪsənʃaft/ *noun* M19 German (= knowledge). The systematic pursuit of knowledge, learning, and scholarship (especially as contrasted with its application).

witblits /ˈvɪtblɪts/ *noun* M20 Afrikaans (from *wit* white + *blits* lightning). (In South Africa) a type of raw spirits, often one that has been illicitly distilled.

witloof /ˈwɪtluːf/ *noun* L19 Dutch (literally, 'white leaf'). A variety of broad-leaved chicory grown for blanching.

wok /wɒk/ *noun* M20 Chinese (Cantonese). A large bowl-shaped frying pan used typically in Chinese cookery.

Winds

The names given to winds in different parts of the world form a colourfully multilingual set. The *sirocco* (Italian) is a hot, oppressive, and often dusty or rainy wind which blows from the north coast of Africa over the Mediterranean and parts of southern Europe. This hot dry wind is known by different local names in other parts of the world. In North Africa, for example, it is called the *ghibli* (Arabic). In Egypt it is the *khamsin* (Arabic), an oppressive hot southerly wind which blows at intervals for about fifty days (hence its name, from the Arabic word for 'fifty') in March, April, and May, filling the air with sand from the desert. The *simoom* (or *simoon*) is a hot dry dust-laden wind blowing at intervals in the African and Asian (especially Arabian) deserts. This suffocating wind, whose name derives from the Arabic word *samma*, meaning 'to poison', is known to cause heatstroke because the body is unable to perspire quickly enough.

The *mistral* (French) is a strong cold north-westerly wind which blows through the Rhône valley and southern France into the Mediterranean. Another cold wind is the *tramontana* (Italian), a north wind blowing in Italy or the adjoining regions of the Adriatic and Mediterranean. *Meltemi* is a Greek and Turkish name for a refreshing dry north-westerly wind blowing over the eastern Mediterranean region in summer, also known as an Etesian wind.

Föhn (a German word), originally referring to a hot southerly wind which blows in the European Alps, is now used as a generic term for any warm dry wind of this type developing on the lee side of a mountain range. The *harmattan* (Akan) is a dry and dusty easterly or north-easterly wind on the West African coast. The term *monsoon* (Early Modern Dutch) usually calls to mind torrential rain, but it properly refers to a seasonal prevailing wind in the region of the Indian subcontinent and south-east Asia, blowing from the south-west between May and September and bringing rain (the wet monsoon), or from the north-east between October and April (the dry monsoon). By extension, the term also refers to the rainfall which accompanies the wet monsoon.

Two other 'wind' words worth mentioning are *kamikaze* and *vol-au-vent*. The literal Japanese meaning of *kamikaze* is 'divine wind', alluding to the gale which in Japanese tradition destroyed the fleet of invading Mongols in 1281. The word was applied in the Second World War to Japanese aircraft which made a deliberate suicidal crash on an enemy target. And, in French, *vol-au-vent* is literally 'flight in the wind', suggesting the lightness of the puff pastry case.

wonton /wɒnˈtɒn/ *noun* (also **won ton**) M20 Chinese ((Cantonese) *wān t'ān*). (In Chinese cookery) a small round dumpling or roll with a savoury filling, usually eaten boiled in soup.

woonerf /ˈvuːnəːf/ *noun* plural **woonerfs**, **woonerven** /ˈvuːnəːv(ə)n/ L20 Dutch (from *woon-* residential (from *wonen* to live) + *erf* ground, premises). A road in a residential area, in which a number of devices are employed to create a safer environment by reducing and slowing the flow of traffic.

Wunderkammer /ˈvʊndərkamər/ *noun* L20 German (from *Wunder* wonder + *Kammer* chamber). A place where a collection of curiosities and rarities is exhibited.

wunderkind /ˈvʊndəkɪnt/ *noun* (also **Wunderkind**) plural **wunderkinds**,

wunderkinder /'vʊndəkɪndər/ L19 German (from *Wunder* wonder + *Kind* child). **1** A highly talented child; a child prodigy, especially in music. **2** A person who achieves remarkable success at an early age. *Colloquial.*

  2 1996 *Times* Marion's lyricist, the 20-year-old *wunderkind* Jaime Harding, wails hard and long...

wurst /və:st/, /wə:st/; *foreign* /vʊrst/ *noun* M19 German (*Wurst*). German or Austrian sausage.

wushu /wuːˈʃuː/ *noun* L20 Chinese (*wŭshù*, from *wŭ* military + *shù* technique, art). The Chinese martial arts.

xoanon /ˈzəʊənɒn/ *noun* plural **xoana** /ˈzəʊənə/ E18 Greek (related to *xein* to carve). (In ancient Greece) a primitive simply carved image of a deity, originally of wood, and often said to have fallen from heaven.

xystus /ˈzɪstəs/ *noun* plural **xysti** /ˈzɪstʌɪ/ M17 Latin (from Greek *xustos* smooth, from *xuein* to scrape). (In ancient Greece) a long covered portico or court used by athletes for exercise. Also, (in ancient Rome) a garden walk or terrace.

Y y

opposing forces of the universe, characterized as male and creative and associated with heaven, heat, and light. Cf. YIN. **B** *adjective* That represents yang; masculine.

yantra /'jantrə/ *noun* L19 Sanskrit (= device or mechanism for holding or fastening, from *yam* to hold, support). A geometrical diagram used as an aid to meditation in tantric worship; any object used similarly.

yaourt see under YOGURT.

yacker variant of YAKKA.

yagna variant of YAJNA.

yahrzeit /'jɑːtsʌɪt/ *noun* M19 Yiddish (from Middle High German *jarzît* anniversary, from Old High German *jar* (German *Jahr*) year + *zît* (German *Zeit*) time). *Judaism* The anniversary of the death of a person, especially a parent.

yajna /'jʌdʒnjə/ *noun* (also **yagna**) E19 Sanskrit (*yajña* worship, sacrifice). *Hinduism* A ritual sacrifice with a specific objective, often involving the burning of substantial offerings.

yakitori /jakɪˈtɔːri/ *noun* M20 Japanese (from *yaki* toasting, grilling + *tori* bird). A Japanese dish consisting of pieces of chicken grilled on a skewer.

yakka /'jakə/ *noun* (also **yacker**) L19 Aboriginal. Work, especially of a strenuous physical kind; toil.

■ Australian slang, especially in the phrase *hard yakka*.

yakuza /jəˈkuːzə/ *noun* plural same M20 Japanese (from *ya* eight + *ku* nine + *za* three, with reference to the worst kind of hand in a gambling game). **1** (**the Yakuza**) a powerful Japanese criminal organization. **2** A member of the Yakuza; a Japanese gangster or racketeer.

attributive **1995** *Spectator* Yakuza gangsters, with extreme right-wing connections, were instantly recognisable by their dress and demeanour...

yang /jaŋ/ *noun & adjective* L17 Chinese (*yáng* sun, positive, male genitals). **A** *noun* In Chinese philosophy, the male or active principle of the two

yarmulke /'jɑːmʊlkə/ *noun* (also **yarmulka**) E20 Yiddish (*yarmolke*, from Polish *jarmułka* cap, probably from Turkish *yağmurluk* raincoat, cape, from *yağmur* rain). A skullcap worn in public by orthodox Jewish men or during prayer by other Jewish men.

yashmak /'jaʃmak/ *noun* M19 Arabic (*yašmaḳ* from Turkish *yaşmak* use as noun of *yaşmak* to hide oneself). A veil concealing the face below the eyes, worn by some Muslim women in public.

yataghan /'jatəgan/ *noun* (also **ataghan** /'atəgan/) E19 Turkish (*yatağan*). Chiefly *History* A sword or long dagger having a handle without a guard and often a double-curved blade, used in Muslim countries.

yenta /'jɛntə/ *noun* (also **yente**) E20 Yiddish (originally a personal name; see quotation). A woman who is a gossip or busybody. *North American colloquial*.

1968 *Encounter* Yenta, I am told, was a perfectly acceptable name for a lady, derived from the Italian *gentile*—until some ungracious *yenta* gave it a bad name.

yerba /'jəːbə/ *noun* E19 Spanish (= herb). MATÉ. More fully *yerba maté*.

yeshiva /jəˈʃiːvə/ *noun* plural **yeshivas**, **yeshivot(h)** /jəˈʃiːvɒt/ M19 Hebrew (*yĕšîḇāh*, from *yāšhaḇ* to sit). An Orthodox Jewish college or seminary; a Talmudic academy.

yeti /'jɛti/ *noun* M20 Tibetan (*yeh-teh* little manlike animal). A large hairy creature resembling a human or bear, said to live in the highest part of the Himalayas. Also called *Abominable Snowman*.

Yiddish

The majority of the Yiddish words that are used in English originated in American English, particularly the variety spoken in New York. These words were brought by the nearly three million Yiddish-speaking Jews who emigrated to North America in the late 19th and early 20th centuries.

Nosh is a Yiddish word, as are such items of food as *bagel, gefilte fish, latke, lox, matzo,* and *pastrami.* Yiddish also boasts a colourful range of words with a disparaging or somewhat negative meaning. These include *kibitz, klutz, kvetch, nebbish, nudnik,* and a host of expressive words beginning with the letters *sch-,* such as *schlep, schlimazel, schlock, schlub, schmaltz, schmear, schmuck, schnook,* and *schnorrer.* More approving in meaning, though, is *chutzpah,* which, while it suggests shameless audacity or effrontery, also contains an element of admiration.

yin /jɪn/ *noun & adjective* L17 Chinese (*yīn* shade, feminine, the moon). **A** *noun* In Chinese philosophy, the female or passive principle of the two opposing forces of the universe, characterized as female and sustaining and associated with earth, dark, and cold. Cf. YANG. **B** *adjective* That represents yin; feminine.

ylang-ylang /iːlaŋˈiːlaŋ/ *noun* (also **ilang-ilang**) L19 Tagalog (*ilang-ílang*). A tree of tropical Asia, *Cananga odorata,* with fragrant greenish-yellow flowers from which an essential oil is obtained; the sweet-scented essential oil obtained from this tree, used in perfumery and aromatherapy.

yoga /ˈjəʊgə/ *noun* L18 Sanskrit (literally, 'union'). A Hindu spiritual and ascetic discipline, a part of which, including breath control, simple meditation, and the adoption of specific bodily postures, is widely practised for health and relaxation.

■ Frequently specifically HATHA YOGA.

yogi /ˈjəʊgi/ *noun* (also **yogin** /ˈjəʊgɪn/) E17 Sanskrit (*yogin,* nominative singular *yogī,* from YOGA). A person who is proficient in yoga.

yogini /ˈjəʊgɪniː/ *noun* M20 Sanskrit (*yoginī* feminine of *yogin* yogi). A woman who is proficient in yoga; a female yogi.

yogurt /ˈjɒgət/ *noun* (also **yoghurt**) E17 Turkish (*yoğurt*). A semi-solid, somewhat sour food, now often fruit-flavoured, made from milk fermented by the addition of certain bacteria.

■ The spelling *yaourt* /ˈjaʊət/ (E19) as a representation of the pronunciation of *yogurt* is now rare or obsolete.

yokozuna /ˌjəʊkəˈzuːnə/ *noun* M20 Japanese (from *yoko* crosswise + *tsuna* rope (originally a kind of belt presented to the champion)). A grand champion sumo wrestler.

yoni /ˈjəʊni/ *noun* L18 Sanskrit (= source, womb, female genitals). Chiefly Hinduism A figure or representation of the female genitals as a sacred symbol or object.

yuga /ˈjʊgə/ *noun* L18 Sanskrit (*yuga* yoke, an age of the world). (In Hindu cosmology) each of four periods, each shorter than and inferior to its predecessor, together totalling 4,320 million human years. Cf. KALPA.

yukata /jʊˈkata/ *noun* E19 Japanese (from *yu* hot water, bath + *kata(bira)* light kimono). A light cotton kimono, frequently with stencil designs, originally worn indoors after a bath.

yurt /jʊət/ *noun* L18 Russian (*yurta* (through French *yourte* or German *Jurte*) from Turkic *jurt*). A circular tent of felt or skins on a collapsible framework, used by nomads in Mongolia, Siberia, and Turkey. Also, a semi-subterranean hut, usually of timber covered with earth or turf.

Zz

zabaglione /zaba'ljəʊni/ *noun* L19 Italian (perhaps ultimately from late Latin *sabaia* an Illyrian drink). An Italian dessert consisting of egg yolks, sugar, and usually Marsala wine, whipped to a frothy texture over a gentle heat and served either hot or cold. Cf. SABAYON.

zaftig /'zaftɪg/ *adjective* (also **zoftig** /'zɒftɪg/) M20 Yiddish (from German *saftig* juicy). (Of a woman) plump, having a full rounded figure. *North American colloquial.*

zaibatsu /zʌɪ'batsu:/ *noun* plural same M20 Japanese (from *zai* wealth + *batsu* clique). *Commerce* Originally, a Japanese capitalist organization usually based on a single family having controlling interests in a variety of companies. Now, a large Japanese business conglomerate.

zakat /zə'kɑ:t/ *noun* E19 Persian and Urdu (*zakā(t)*, Turkish *zekât*, from Arabic *zakā(t)* almsgiving). An obligatory payment made annually under Islamic law on certain kinds of property and used for charitable and religious objects.

zakuska /zaˈkuska/ *noun* (also **zakouska**) plural **zakuskas**, **zakuski** /zaˈkuski/ L19 Russian (usually as plural *zakuski*). A substantial Russian hors d'oeuvre item such as caviar sandwiches or vegetables with sour cream, all served with vodka.

zapateado /za,patɪˈɑːdəʊ/, *foreign* /θa,pateˈado/, /sa,pateˈado/ *noun* plural **zapateados** /za,patɪˈɑːdəʊz/, /sa,patɪˈados/, /θa,pateˈados/, /sa,pateˈados/ M19 Spanish (from *zapato* shoe). **1** A flamenco dance involving complex syncopated stamping of the heels and toes in imitation of castanets. **2** Dancing or footwork of this kind.

zarda /'zɑːdə/ *noun* L19 Persian and Urdu (*zardah*, from Persian *zard* yellow). Indian chewing tobacco flavoured with spices.

zareba variant of ZARIBA.

zari /zari/ *noun* M20 Persian and Urdu (*zarī*, from Persian *zar* gold). A type of gold thread used decoratively on Indian clothing; *colloquial* a sari decorated with this.

zariba /zəˈriːbə/ *noun* (also **zareba**) M19 Arabic (*zarība* pen or enclosure for cattle). (In Sudan and neighbouring countries) a fence, usually made of thorn trees, fortifying a camp or village against enemies or wild animals.

zarzuela /θarˈθwela/, /sarˈswela/ *noun* L19 Spanish. **1** A traditional form of operetta in Spain, with spoken dialogue, songs, and dances. **2** A Spanish dish consisting of various kinds of seafood cooked in a rich sauce.

zastrugi variant of SASTRUGI.

zazen /zɑːˈzɛn/ *noun* E18 Japanese (from *za* sitting, a seat + *zen* Zen). Zen meditation, usually conducted in the lotus position.

zeitgeber /'tsaɪtgeːbər/, /'zʌɪtgeɪbə/ *noun* plural same, **zeitgebers** M20 German (from *Zeit* time + *Geber* giver). *Physiology* A rhythmically occurring natural phenomenon which acts as a cue in the regulation of certain biological rhythms in an organism.

Zeitgeist /'tsaɪtgaɪst/, /'zʌɪtgʌɪst/ *noun* M19 German (from *Zeit* time + *Geist* spirit). The spirit of the age; the defining spirit or mood of a particular period of history as shown by the ideas and beliefs of the time and as reflected in its literature, art, etc.

> **1995** *Times* Like the seasoned politician he [sc. M. Mitterand] is, he has once again identified the *zeitgeist* in France, where dying has become the subject of some debate.

Zen /zɛn/ *noun* E18 Japanese (from Chinese *chán* quietude, from Sanskrit *dhyāna* meditation). A school of Mahayana

Buddhism emphasizing meditation and intuition rather than ritual worship or study of scriptures.

■ Also more fully *Zen Buddhism.* Influential in Japanese life from the 13th century onwards, *Zen* became significantly fashionable in the West during the 1960s.

zenana /zə'nɑːnə/ *noun* M18 Persian and Urdu (*zanānah*, from *zan* woman). (In India and Iran) the part of a house for the seclusion of women.

zeugma /'zjuːgmə/ *noun* LME Latin (from Greek, literally, 'yoking', from *zeugnunai* to yoke, related to *zugon* a yoke). A figure of speech in which a single word is made to refer to two or more words in a sentence, especially when applying to them in different senses (e.g. *John and his driving licence expired last week*).

zita /'ziːtə/ *noun* plural **zite** /'ziːteɪ/, **ziti** /'ziːti/ M19 Italian. Pasta in the form of tubes resembling large macaroni.

zoftig variant of ZAFTIG.

zollverein /'tsɔlfəraɪn/ *noun* M19 German (from *Zoll* toll, customs + *Verein* union). *History* The customs union of German states in the 19th century.

zombie /'zɒmbi/ *noun* E19 Bantu (cf. JUMBIE). **1** A corpse said to be revived by witchcraft, especially in certain African and Caribbean religions. **2** A person who is or appears lifeless, apathetic, or completely unresponsive to their surroundings. *Colloquial.*

zori /'zɔːri/ *noun* plural **zoris**, same E19 Japanese (*zōri*, from *sō* grass, (rice) straw + *ri* footwear, sole). A traditional Japanese sandal, having a simple thong between the toes and a flat sole originally of straw but now often of rubber or felt.

Zouave /zuːˈɑːv/, /zwɑːv/ *noun* M19 French (from Kabyle *Zouaoua* name of a tribe). **1** A member of a body of light infantry in the French army, originally formed of Algerian Kabyles, and long retaining the original oriental uniform. **2** (**zouaves**) Women's trousers with wide tops, tapering to a narrow ankle.

zouk /zuːk/ *noun* L20 French (apparently from Antillean creole *zouk* to party, possibly influenced by United States slang *juke* (or *jook*) to have a good time). An exuberant style of popular music combining Caribbean and Western elements and having a fast heavy beat.

■ Developed in Paris as a style of Antillean popular music intended to hold its own against Western pop and disco music, *zouk* was popularized in France during the 1980s by the group called Kassav, and began to feature on the British and American music scene at the end of the decade (see quotation).
1987 *Guardian* Tonight, the first ever zouk on British soil kicks off this year's Camden Festival International arts programme... Zouk, especially Kassav, is the pulse of Paris streets and the soundtrack for her nightclubs.

zucchetto /tsʊˈkɛtəʊ/ *noun* plural **zucchettos** (also **zucchetta** /tsʊˈkɛtə/) M19 Italian (*zucchetta* diminutive of *zucca* gourd, head). The skullcap worn by Roman Catholic clerics, black for priests, purple for bishops, red for cardinals, and white for the Pope.

zucchini /zʊˈkiːni/ *noun* plural same, **zucchinis** E20 Italian (plural of *zucchino* small marrow, courgette, diminutive of *zucca* gourd). A courgette.

■ Chiefly in North America and Australia; in Britain *courgette* is the usual word.

zugzwang /'zʌɡzwaŋ/ *noun* E20 German (from *Zug* move + *Zwang* compulsion, obligation). *Chess* A position in which a player must move but cannot do so without disadvantage; the obligation to make a move even when disadvantageous.

■ Frequently in *in zugzwang.*

zuppa inglese /ˌtsuppa iŋˈɡlese/ *noun phrase* M20 Italian (= English soup). A rich Italian dessert resembling trifle.

zut /zyt/ *interjection* E20 French. Expressing irritation, contempt, impatience, etc.

■ Also *zut alors!*, in which *alors* acts as an intensifier.
1996 *Times: Weekend* So just what is it in the end that brings together the woman with the

hair lip, the dirty dancer, a quixotic French cameraman—zut alors!—and a group of troglodyte descendants of lost Vikings with a liking for high technology?

zwieback /ˈtsviːbak/ *noun* L19 German (= twice-bake). A rusk or biscuit made by baking a small loaf, and then toasting slices until they are dry and crisp.

zwischenzug /ˈtsvɪʃənˌtsuːk/ *noun* M20 German (from *zwischen* intermediate + *Zug* move). *Chess* A move interposed in a sequence of play in such a way as to alter the outcome.

Appendix

Aboriginal languages

EIGHTEENTH CENTURY
boomerang
cooee
corroboree
gibber
koradji

NINETEENTH CENTURY
alcheringa
billabong
bunyip
churinga
gilgai
gunyah
mallee
mulga
willy-willy
yakka

TWENTIETH CENTURY
bombora
didgeridoo

African languages

SEVENTEENTH CENTURY
harmattan
juju

EIGHTEENTH CENTURY
buckra
kierie
marimba

NINETEENTH CENTURY
accra
donga
impi
induna
inyanga
jumbie
lobola
mabela
mbira
nagana
sangoma
tokoloshe
umfaan

umfundisi
zombie

TWENTIETH CENTURY
alhaji
balafon
dashiki
kalimba
kente
kwashiorkor
manyatta
mau-mau
pata-pata
piri-piri
soukous
tsotsi

Afrikaans/ Dutch

SEVENTEENTH CENTURY
dagga
jong

EIGHTEENTH CENTURY
doek
hanepoot
kaross
kraal
krantz
mebos
naartjie
sjambok
skof
springbok
stoep
veld
vlei

NINETEENTH CENTURY
berg
biltong
dop
hamel
inspan
jukskei
konfyt
kop
koppie

laager
maas
mealie
oom
ou
pondok
rand
rondavel
rooinek
schlenter
sosatie
togt
trek
Uitlander
veldskoen
voetsak
volk
Voortrekker

TWENTIETH CENTURY
apartheid
boerewors
braai
braaivleis
dominee
koeksister
kwela
lekker
ouma
oupa
outjie
platteland
rooibos
swart gevaar
totsiens
verkrampte
verligte
witblits

American Indian languages

SEVENTEENTH CENTURY
moccasin
powwow
wampum

EIGHTEENTH CENTURY
menhaden
pemmican

quipu
tepee
windigo

NINETEENTH CENTURY
cassareep
cheechako
hogan
kachina
kiva
piki
wickiup

Anglo-Indian

SEVENTEENTH CENTURY
brinjal

EIGHTEENTH CENTURY
chhi-chhi
serang

NINETEENTH CENTURY
chota
memsahib
topi

Arabic

SIXTEENTH CENTURY
cadi
hashish
jibba
muezzin
mufti
sharif
sheikh

SEVENTEENTH CENTURY
arak
Eid
fakir
fatwa
hakim
haram
imam
kebab
khamsin
kiblah
madrasa
mastaba
salaam

sayyid
sura
ulema
wadi

EIGHTEENTH CENTURY
afreet
bismillah
dhow
fellah
ghazi
Hadith
hajj
kohl
rebab
simoom
talaq
tarboosh
wazir

NINETEENTH CENTURY
abaya
agal
askari
azan
bint
fedayeen
ghibli
halal
hamza
inshallah
jebel
jellaba
jihad
jinn
kameez
keffiyeh
khat
kif
Kitab
loofah
Mahdi
Majlis
masjid
Maulana
mihrab
mimbar
sabkha
santoor
shadoof
shahada
shahid
souk
sudd
umma
umrah
yashmak
zariba

TWENTIETH CENTURY
Bedu
burghul
falafel
hijab
hummus
imshi
intifada
medina
niqab
seif
shufti
shura
tabbouleh

Aramaic

SEVENTEENTH CENTURY
Kaddish
tefillin

NINETEENTH CENTURY
Kol Nidre

Bantu languages see under African languages

Bengali

TWENTIETH CENTURY
jalfrezi

Breton

NINETEENTH CENTURY
menhir

Catalan

NINETEENTH CENTURY
paella

Chinese

SEVENTEENTH CENTURY
ginseng
sampan
yang
yin

EIGHTEENTH CENTURY
feng-shui
pe tsai
souchong
T'ai Chi

NINETEENTH CENTURY
ba gua
chop suey
chow mein
kowtow
kung fu
kylin
pak choi
san-hsien
taipan
tong
wei ch'i

TWENTIETH CENTURY
cheongsam
dazibao
dim sum
erh hu
gung-ho
hoisin
lei
mah-jong
putonghua
samfu
tou ts'ai
wok
wonton
wushu

Czech

TWENTIETH CENTURY
háček

Danish

TWENTIETH CENTURY
landrace
mor

Dutch

SIXTEENTH CENTURY
kermis
monsoon

SEVENTEENTH CENTURY
maelstrom
polder
soya
vendue
vrou

EIGHTEENTH CENTURY
baas
kloof
poort
snoek
stoop

NINETEENTH CENTURY
Boer
riem
riempie
rijsttafel
spruit
witloof

TWENTIETH CENTURY
woonerf

Egyptian (Ancient)

NINETEENTH CENTURY
ankh
shabti

Eskimo languages

EIGHTEENTH CENTURY
kabloona
kayak
parka
umiak

NINETEENTH CENTURY
igloo
nunatak
tupik

TWENTIETH CENTURY
anorak
pingo

Fijian

NINETEENTH CENTURY
sulu

Finnish

NINETEENTH CENTURY
sauna

French

MIDDLE ENGLISH
accidie
amour
avoirdupois
bourdon
chemise
corvée
douce
flèche
fleur-de-lis
godet
hydria
langue
largesse

lieu
Madame
ménage
noblesse
parure
patron
peridot
potage
reverie
richesse
sans
sec
sous-
tablier
trebuchet
venue
voussoir

LATE MIDDLE ENGLISH

absinth
adieu
antipodes
avant-garde
ballade
Bedouin
blancmange
bruit
catechumen
cenacle
cham
chaperone
chevalier
chevron
cicatrice
cohabitation
commissar
confrère
congé
couchant
coup
crise
dariole
dauphin
distrait
douceur
droit
envoi
equivoque
fête
finesse
fleuron
gourmand
hélas
honi soit qui
    mal y pense
introit
jaune

jujube
lardon
legerdemain
lèse-majesté
lierne
Mademoiselle
migraine
muscatel
musette
nadir
noir
nonpareil
or
orgeat
oriflamme
oyer
oyez
pain
pavé
péage
pensée
petit
plage
puissance
rebec
regardant
reprise
rouge
tendresse
tisane
toile
triste
tristesse
tuile
vigneron
vignette
vinaigrette

FIFTEENTH CENTURY

blonde
brochette
chanson
cheval
convenance
entremets
faubourg
parole
regime
sachet
serviette
sou
tambour
tapis
tranche
valet

SIXTEENTH CENTURY

abbé

à la
à la mode
aliquot
armoire
auberge
banderole
bastide
baton
bayadère
bibliothèque
bocage
bon
bonjour
bonne
bonze
bourgeois
bourse
brunette
burnous
cabochon
cachou
cafard
canaille
canton
cap-à-pie
capriole
cartel
cestui
chamois
champignon
chancre
clientele
commis
concierge
confiture
corps
courante
croissant
démenti
demoiselle
doge
dolman
emir
escritoire
esplanade
esprit
faille
feme covert
feme sole
framboise
fricassée
fugue
fusee
gabion
gendarme
gendarmerie
gigot

girasol
gnomon
gonfalonier
guidon
haut-goût
hippodrome
jacquerie
kermes
kumis
lien
lunette
luxe
maître d'hôtel
massif
monad
mot
moustache
muscat
mystagogue
nacre
naïf
nebulé
paladin
panache
patisserie
pavane
petite
phaeton
piquant
pique
pomade
portmanteau
puisne
qui vive
ravelin
rendezvous
réseau
rondeau
santon
seigneur
serin
sorbet
sultan
taille
tarot
tercet
terreplein
tilleul
toque
villanelle
vive
volte
volute

SEVENTEENTH
CENTURY

aide-de-camp

allemande
amende
   honorable
ampoule
andouille
à outrance
apropos
arabesque
assegai
atelier
aubade
au revoir
baccalaureate
badinage
bagatelle
ballet
banquette
bascule
beau
beau monde
bel esprit
belle
belles-lettres
bidet
bijou
billet-doux
bisque
bizarre
bon vivant
bon voyage
bouilli
bouillon
bourrée
boutade
brusque
bureau
burin
burlesque
cabaret
cachet
cadet
caique
caisson
calumet
capot
caprice
caracole
carousel
carte blanche
cartouche
casque
catafalque
cervelat
chaconne
chagrin
chaise
chandelier

charivari
chassis
chef-d'œuvre
chevaux de frise
chicane
cirque
clairvoyant
coiffure
commissionaire
compote
contretemps
coquette
cortège
corvette
coup d'état
coup de grâce
coup de mâitre
courbette
court bouillon
couscous
creole
critique
croupade
curé
cuvette
dégagé
de haut en bas
démarche
déshabillé
double entendre
doyen
dragée
éclaircissement
éclat
embonpoint
enceinte
en passant
entre nous
environs
epode
ergot
espalier
etui
exergue
facade
faïence
fainéant
fanfaronade
farceur
faux pas
feu de joie
flageolet
flambeau
forte
fronton
gala
garçon

gavotte
genie
gigue
girandole
glacis
goitre
gondolier
grand seigneur
gratin
grillade
haricot
hauteur
honnête
   homme
impromptu
intendant
jalap
jargonelle
je ne sais quoi
knout
kremlin
lansquenet
legume
levee
liaison
mâche
maladroit
malapropos
manège
marabout
marc
Mardi gras
marionette
marquise
mélange
mêlée
minaret
mistral
moire
mon cher
mousseline
musée
naive
naïveté
neroli
niche
nom de guerre
nonchalance
odalisque
ordonnance
ortolan
par excellence
parterre
passade
passementerie
passepartout
pastille

patois
paysage
penchant
pension
percale
père
peristyle
picot
piquet
pirogue
pirouette
pis aller
plafond
porte cochère
potager
pot-pourri
pratique
procès-verbal
ragout
rapport
ratafia
ravissant
rebus
recherché
reveille
rigadoon
rodomontade
rouleau
routier
sabot
sainfoin
salon
sans façon
sarabande
saucisson
sobriquet
suede
suite
tableau
table d'hôte
tabouret
talus
terre-verte
tête-à-tête
tourniquet
tracasserie
trente et
   quarante
tribade
tric-trac
tutoyer
vade mecum
valise
vedette
vin
voir dire

abatis
accouchement
accoucheur
acharnement
aigrette
aiguille
allée
amateur
amour propre
ancien régime
aplomb
appliqué
aubergine
au contraire
au courant
au fait
au fond
avalanche
baguette
bain-marie
bal masqué
banco
bandeau
barbette
barcarole
bateau
batterie
batterie de cuisine
béchamel
bergère
bistre
bivouac
blanc
blanquette
bonbon
bonhomie
bon mot
bonne bouche
boudoir
bougie
boulevard
bouleversement
bouquet
bourgeoise
bourgeoisie
boutique
bravo
brisé
brochure
buffet
cabriole
cabriolet
cache
cadeau
café au lait
cannelure

cantaloupe
caoutchouc
carafe
carillon
carriole
casserole
catalogue
   raisonné
cause célèbre
celadon
centrifuge
chalumeau
chambranle
chanterelle
chapeau-bras
charade
chargé d'affaires
charlotte
chasse
chasseur
château
chatoyant
chenille
chez
chiffon
chiffonier
chignon
chou
ci-devant
cipolin
clique
colporteur
comme il faut
compère
connoisseur
conservatoire
cordon bleu
corps
   diplomatique
coterie
cotillion
coup d'œil
coup de foudre
coup de main
coup de théâtre
coupé
coureur
crèche
crêpe
critique
croquette
croupier
cuisine
cul-de-sac
curette
cyme

dame de
   compagnie
daube
debris
début
dehors
déjeuner
demi-caractère
demilune
denouement
derrière
detour
de trop
diablerie
Directoire
divertissement
douche
duchesse
duvet
eau de vie
echelon
égalité
élite
embarras de
   richesse
embouchure
embrasure
emigré
enceinte
encore
en face
en famille
enfilade
en masse
ennui
en papillote
en route
ensemble
en suite
entrechat
entrée
entrepôt
entresol
en ventre sa
   mère
epaulette
esprit de corps
etiquette
extrados
farce
farouche
faute de mieux
fauteuil
fête champêtre
fichu
figurant
fille de joie

fourchette
foyer
fracas
fricandeau
frisson
fronde
frondeur
galère
galette
galipot
gauche
gaucherie
gîte
grande dame
grippe
grisette
guillotine
ha-ha
hors d'oeuvre
hors de combat
houri
insouciance
intrados
intriguant
jalousie
jeu d'esprit
jongleur
julienne
kaolin
kasbah
langue d'oc
langue d'oïl
lavage
lettre de cachet
levee
liqueur
locale
loge
longueur
maisonette
majuscule
malaise
mal de mer
mannequin
manqué
marinade
matelote
mentor
meringue
mésalliance
métier
mezzanine
mignonette
minaudière
mirabelle
mon ami
moraine

morale
morceau
nacarat
née
negligée
nonchalant
nouvelle
noyau
nuance
oeil-de-boeuf
opéra comique
oubliette
outré
palette
panne
papier mâché
partie carrée
pas
pas de deux
pas de trois
passé
pâté
patronne
paupiette
paysanne
persiflage
petit-maître
petit pain
piaffe
picotee
pièce de
  résistance
pierrot
pisé
piste
plat
plateau
politesse
polonaise
pompadour
pompon
poste restante
postiche
pot-au-feu
poupée
praline
précis
prie-dieu
protégé
purée
quadrille
quatorze
rapporteur
redingote
restaurateur
reticule
ricochet

riposte
rissole
rouge et noir
roulade
roulette
saccade
salep
salmi
salpicon
sangfroid
sansculotte
savant
savante
savoir vivre
secretaire
siffleur
silhouette
socle
soi-disant
soirée
solitaire
Soubise
soubrette
soupçon
soupe
souterrain
souvenir
tafia
tant bien que
  mal
tant mieux
tant pis
terre-à-terre
terrine
tirailleur
ton
tonneau
tontine
toupet
tournure
tout
tout au contraire
tout compris
tout court
tout de suite
tout ensemble
tout le monde
tout seul
traiteur
triage
tricorne
tricot
troubadour
trouvère
tuyère
tzigane
uhlan

valse
vaudeville
velours
vendange
verd-antique
vers de société
veuve
vin blanc
vin de pays
vingt-et-un
vis-à-vis
voilà
volupté

NINETEENTH CENTURY
abattoir
à cheval
à deux
affaire
agent
  provocateur
aide-mémoire
à la carte
amour courtois
anonym
aperçu
aperitif
après nous le
  déluge
aquarelle
arête
argot
arrière-pensée
arrondissement
artiste
à trois
attaché
au gratin
au naturel
au pair
baba
baccarat
bagasse
ballon
barbotine
barège
barré
bassinet
batiste
battement
battue
béarnaise
beau ideal
beau sabreur
beauté du diable
beaux arts
beaux yeux

beignet
berceuse
beret
bête noire
bêtise
bibelot
bijouterie
blague
blagueur
blasé
bombe
bon appétit
bonbonnière
bonne femme
bouchée
bouclé
bouffant
bouillabaisse
boulevardier
bouquet garni
bouton
boutonnière
brandade
brasserie
bric-à-brac
brioche
briquette
broderie anglaise
brouhaha
brut
burette
butte
cabotage
cachepot
cadre
café
café noir
cafetière
camaraderie
camisole
canapé
canard
cancan
capote
carnet
carte-de-visite
cartonnage
cassis
causerie
celeste
cep
cerise
chacun à son
  goût
chaise longue
champlevé
changement

chanson de geste
chanteuse
charabanc
charcuterie
chargé
charlotte russe
chartreuse
chassé
Chateaubriand
chatelaine
chauffeur
chef
chef d'école
chef d'orchestre
chemin de fer
chemisette
cheval de bataille
chevet
chibouk
chic
chiffonade
chinoiserie
chipolata
chocolatier
choucroute
chypre
cire perdue
clair-de-lune
clairvoyance
claque
claqueur
cliché
cloche
cloisonné
clou
coco de mer
cocotte
coiffeur
col
colportage
comedienne
communard
communiqué
compte rendu
concessionaire
consommé
conte
contredanse
cor anglais
corbeille
cordon sanitaire
corniche
corps d'élite
corps de ballet
corsetière
coryphée
costumier

coudé
coulée
coulisse
couloir
coupe
couvade
crème
crème anglaise
crème brûlée
crème de la
 crème
crêpe de Chine
crépinette
crépon
cretonne
crevasse
crochet
croustade
croûton
cru
culottes
curettage
cuvée
danse macabre
danseur
danseuse
débâcle
débutant
débutante
déclassé
décolletage
décolleté
décor
dégringolade
de luxe
demi-mondaine
demi-monde
demitasse
démodé
de rigueur
dernier cri
détenu
diseuse
distingué
divorcee
doctrinaire
donnée
dos-à-dos
dot
doublure
doyenne
dramaturge
droit de seigneur
duxelles
eau
eau de Cologne
eau de Nil

écarté
éclair
écorché
écossaise
ecru
élan
embarras de
 choix
en bloc
en cabochon
enchaînement
en clair
enclave
en échelon
enfant gâté
enfant terrible
en fête
engagé
en grand
 seigneur
en pension
en plein air
en pointe
en prise
en rapport
ensilage
entente
entente cordiale
entourage
entr'acte
entrecôte
entrepreneur
épée
erg
escargot
espadrille
estaminet
etagere
étude
exalté
exposé
fabliau
fait accompli
famille jaune
famille noire
famille rose
famille verte
farandole
fer de lance
ferronnière
feu follet
feuilleton
fiancé
fiancée
filé
filet
filet de boeuf

fils
fin de siècle
fine champagne
fines herbes
flacon
flageolet
flambé
flâneur
flic
flicflac
foie gras
folie de grandeur
fondant
fondue
force majeure
fouetté
foulard
franc tireur
frappé
frotteur
frou-frou
fusain
fusillade
galop
gamin
gamine
gangue
gateau
genre
gilet
glacé
glissade
gouache
goujon
gourmet
grand battement
grande
 horizontale
grand mal
Grand Prix
grand siècle
graticule
grenadine
grimoire
griot
grisaille
grosgrain
gros point
guilloche
guimpe
guipure
habitué
hachure
haute
 bourgeoisie
haute école
haut monde

haut-relief
hollandaise
hors concours
houp-la
idée fixe
immortelle
impasse
inconnu
ingénue
insouciant
jabot
jacquard
jardinière
jaspé
j'adoube
jeté
jeunesse dorée
joie de vivre
jolie laide
juste milieu
kepi
La
laissez-aller
laissez-faire
langouste
langue de chat
layette
lectrice
legionnaire
lingerie
littérateur
lorgnette
louche
luthier
lycée
Lyonnais
macabre
macédoine
madeleine
maillot
maître d'
maître de ballet
maîtresse en titre
mangetout
manoir
maquillage
maquis
marabou
mariage de
   convenance
marmite
marron glacé
massage
massé
masseur
matelassé
matériel

matinée
mauvais pas
   d'heure
mayonnaise
mazurka
ménage à trois
mère
metis
meunière
milieu
millefeuille
millefleurs
mirage
mirepoix
mirliton
mise en scène
misère
modiste
moiré
mondaine
moquette
morgue
motif
motte
moue
moule
moulin
mousse
mousseux
musicale
mystique
nappe
navarin
nécessaire
Niçois
noblesse oblige
nocturne
noel
noisette
nostalgie de la
   boue
nougat
nouveau riche
noyade
nuit blanche
objet
objet d'art
objet trouvré
œuvre
ombré
on dit
opéra bouffe
paillette
palmette
parados
parfait

parfumerie
pari-mutuel
parquet
parti pris
parvenu
pas de basque
pas de quatre
pas seul
pastiche
pastourelle
pâte
pâté de foie gras
patte de velours
paysan
peau-de-soie
peau d'orange
peignoir
perfide Albion
personnel
pétillant
petit bourgeois
petit four
petit mal
petit point
petits pois
petit verre
pétrissage
pétroleur
physique
picaresque
picayune
pied-à-terre
pince-nez
piolet
pipette
piqué
piton
planchette
plastique
plein-air
plié
plissé
pochette
point d'appui
pointe
pomme de terre
pompier
pontil
portée
portière
poseur
pouf
poulet
poult-de-soie
pourboire
pour encourager
   les autres

pousse-café
premier cru
première
pré salé
primeur
prix fixe
procédé
profiterole
puy
quadrille
quai
quand même
quartier
quel
quenelle
questionnaire
raconteur
raconteuse
raison d'état
raison d'être
rangé
rappel
rapprochement
rataplan
ratatouille
ravigote
razzia
réchauffé
réclame
reculer pour
   mieux sauter
reflet
régisseur
reine
relevé
rémoulade
Renaissance
rente
rentier
renvers
répondez s'il
   vous plaît
repoussé
restaurant
résumé
retable
retroussé
revanche
réveillon
revenant
revenans à nos
   moutons
revers
revue
rillettes
risqué
rivière

rocaille
roche
  moutonnée
rococo
roi fainéant
roi soleil
roman-à-clef
ronde
rosbif
rosé
rotisserie
roué
roux
ruche
ruse de guerre
sabreur
salon des refusés
sang-de-boeuf
sans peur
sans phrase
sans recours
sans reproche
sans serif
sauté
sauve qui peut
savarin
savate
savoir faire
scène à faire
secateur
secretariat
secret de
  Polichinelle
shako
soigné
soixante-neuf
sommelier
soubresaut
soubriquet
soufflé
soutache
soutane
spécialité
succès d'estime
succès de
  scandale
succès fou
sucrier
suprême
surah
svelte
sympathique
tableau vivant
tapotement
temps levé
terrasse
tête-bêche

thé dansant
tic
tic douloureux
timbale
tirade
titre
tombola
torc
torchon
torsade
tour de force
tour en l'air
tournedos
tragédienne
travers
très
tricoteuse
trompe l'oeil
trousseau
trouvaille
trumeau
tulle
velouté
ventre à terre
verglas
versant
vicereine
vie de Bohème
vieux jeu
ville
vin de paille
vin jaune
vin ordinaire
virgule
visa
voile
voix céleste
vol-au-vent
volet
volte-face
voulu
wagon-lit
Zouave

TWENTIETH CENTURY

actualité
affairé
a gogo
aileron
aioli
amour fou
amuse-gueule
anomie
à point
appellation
  contrôlée
après

après-ski
arrivisme
arriviste
art nouveau
aubusson
auteur
autoroute
avant la lettre
bal musette
barre
barrette
bateau mouche
beau geste
Beaujolais
  nouveau
belle époque
beurre blanc
beurre manié
bidonville
bien pensant
bistro
bloc
blouson
bœuf
bœuf
  bourguignon
boîte
bombé
bondieuserie
boudin
boule
brassière
bricolage
bricoleur
bustier
cache-sexe
cagoule
calque
calvados
camouflage
cassoulet
c'est la guerre
c'est la vie
chaîné
chambré
charmeuse
chef d'équipe
cherchez la
  femme
cher maître
chèvre
chichi
cinéaste
cinematheque
cinéma-vérité
ciné-vérité
cinq-à-sept

ciré
clementine
clochard
cloqué
collage
comme ci,
  comme ça
commère
communautaire
conche
concours
  d'élégance
contre-jour
coq au vin
couchette
coulis
courgette
couture
couverture
craquelure
crème caramel
crème de cacao
crème de menthe
crème fraîche
crêpe Suzette
cri de cœur
crime passionnel
crise de
  conscience
crise de nerfs
croque-monsieur
crotale
croûte
crudités
danseur noble
dauphinois
debitage
découpage
déjà vu
demi-glace
demi-pension
demi-sec
de nos jours
dépaysé
déraciné
derailleur
détente
développé
diamanté
digestif
dirigisme
dirigiste
discothèque
domaine
douceur de vivre
dressage
du jour

eau de toilette
élan vital
embourgeoise-
    ment
éminence grise
en brosse
en croûte
en daube
en pantoufles
en poste
en primeur
épater
épater les
    bourgeois
équipe
escarole
esprit de
    l'escalier
etrier
événement
extraordinaire
faisandé
fauve
faux
faux amis
faux-naïf
femme
femme fatale
fête galante
filet mignon
film noir
fine
fléchette
florentine
folie à deux
franglais
frisée
froideur
fromage blanc
fromage frais
frottage
fruits de mer
fuselage
gaffe
gaga
garconnière
georgette
gigolo
glissé
grand cru
grand jeté
Grand Guignol
gratiné
haute couture
haute cuisine
homme moyen
    sensuel

hotelier
idée reçue
idiot savant
intimism
intimist
j'accuse
jetton
jus
kir
laissez-passer
lamé
langoustine
le tout
levade
longeron
madrilene
mal du siècle
maquette
maquisard
mariage blanc
marocain
marque
marquisette
matelot
médaillon
merde
méthode
    champenoise
metro
midinette
mise en place
moderne
moi
monocoque
monstre sacré
montage
mot de
    Cambronne
mot juste
moyen sensuel
musique
    concrète
mutuel
nacelle
nature morte
né
Negritude
ninon
non
notes inégales
nouveau
nouveau pauvre
nouveau roman
nouvelle cuisine
nouvelle vague
nuée ardente
numéro

palais
palais de danse
palmier
papier collé
par avion
pas de bourrée
pas de chat
pas devant
pasticheur
pastis
pâté de
    campagne
pâté maison
patissier
peloton
pétanque
petite battement
petit beurre
petite
    bourgeoisie
petite marmite
petit suisse
pied noir
pissaladière
pissoir
pisteur
planche
plat du jour
plongeur
plus ça change
poète maudit
poilu
pointillisme
policier
pomme
pommes frites
port de bras
porteur
poule de luxe
poussin
prêt-à-porter
princesse
    lointaine
provocateur
pudeur
quiche
raclette
rapide
reblochon
recherche du
    temps perdu
remuage
repêchage
répétiteur
retardataire
retiré
rite de passage

romaine
roman-fleuve
roquette
rouille
roulement
sabayon
sabotage
saboteur
salade niçoise
salariat
salopettes
salut
saucier
sautoir
se-tenant
soigneur
solfège
sonde
son et lumière
sous vide
souteneur
sportif
tabac
tac-au-tac
tailleur
tapenade
tastevin
taupe
téléphérique
temps perdu
tendu
terroir
tête de cuvée
tiens
tole
tomme
torchère
touché
tour d'horizon
tourtière
tout simple
trahison des clercs
tronc
tutu
vacherin
vendeuse
vérité
vernissage
veronique
verre églomisé
vers libre
vice anglais
vichyssoise
vie en rose
vin d'honneur
vin de garde
vin de table

vin doux (naturel)
vin rouge
violon d'Ingres
visagiste
visite de
  digestion
vive la différence
voyeur
zouk
zut

French (American)

EIGHTEENTH CENTURY
bayou

NINETEENTH CENTURY
jambalaya
tignon
travois

TWENTIETH CENTURY
beguine

French (Canadian)

NINETEENTH CENTURY
babiche
frazil
parfleche
tuque

TWENTIETH CENTURY
joual

French (and German)

NINETEENTH CENTURY
galant

French (and Italian)

SEVENTEENTH
CENTURY
bis

French (or Latin)

SEVENTEENTH
CENTURY
concordat

French (or Urdu)

SEVENTEENTH
CENTURY
tandoor

Gaelic

LATE MIDDLE ENGLISH
loch

SIXTEENTH CENTURY
quaich
strath

SEVENTEENTH
CENTURY
deoch an doris
machair

EIGHTEENTH CENTURY
pibroch
sporran

NINETEENTH CENTURY
slainte

Gaelic (and Irish)

LATE MIDDLE ENGLISH
clachan

German

MIDDLE ENGLISH
Hanse

SIXTEENTH CENTURY
junker

SEVENTEENTH
CENTURY
automat
Fräulein
Graf
krummhorn
sauerkraut
shaman

EIGHTEENTH CENTURY
gneiss
hausfrau
landau
meerschaum
noumenon
pumpernickel
schema
torte
Totentanz

NINETEENTH CENTURY
ablaut
alpenhorn
alpenstock
althorn
Auslese
barouche
bergschrund
buhl

conservatorium
Dasein
delicatessen
Ding an sich
docent
doppelgänger
dummkopf
durchkompon-
  iert
ersatz
euchre
Ewigkeit
fest
firn
flügelhorn
föhn
Fraktur
frankfurter
Frau
gasthaus
gasthof
gemütlich
Gemütlichkeit
giro
glockenspiel
glühwein
graupel
horst
Kaffeeklatsch
Kaiser
kapellmeister
kaput
Karren
Karrenfeld
karst
katzenjammer
kindergarten
kinder, kirche,
  küche
kirsch
kobold
kohlrabi
kraut
kriegspiel
krimmer
kuchen
kulturkampf
kümmel
kursaal
lager
lammergeier
leitmotiv
liebchen
lied
loess
maar
Minnesinger

mit
mordent
pickelhaube
polka
poltergeist
pralltriller
pretzel
prosit
rinderpest
sastrugi
sauerbraten
Schadenfreude
schappe
schlemiel
schloss
schnapps
schnitzel
schottische
schwa
Sehnsucht
singspiel
skat
Spätzle
spiel
stadthaus
staffage
strudel
Sturm und Drang
tendenzroman
thalweg
Übermensch
umlaut
unberufen
unheimlich
ur-
Vorstellung
Walpurgisnacht
Wanderjahr
Weinstube
Wein, Weib, und
  Gesang
Weltanschauung
Weltschmerz
wiener
wienerwurst
Wissenschaft
wunderkind
wurst
Zeitgeist
zollverein
zwieback

TWENTIETH CENTURY
Abitur
abseil
angst
Anschluss

autobahn
Bauhaus
Beerenauslese
bierhaus
Bildungsroman
blitzkrieg
bratwurst
buckling
diktat
dirndl
Drang nach
  Osten
echt
Einfühlung
Eiswein
Festschrift
führer
Gastarbeiter
Gemeinschaft
gestalt
Gestapo
gesundheit
Gleichschaltung
goldwasser
Götterdämmer-
  ung
Hakenkreuz
Heldentenor
Herrenvolk
Heuriger
inselberg
Judenrat
judenrein
Jugendstil
kamerad
karabiner
kitsch
klatch
kletterschuh
krummholz
kultur
Land
langlauf
lebensraum
lederhosen
loden
lumpenproletar-
  iat
Machtpolitik
Nacht und Nebel
Neue
  Sachlichkeit
Ostpolitik
panzer
putz
realpolitik
realpolitiker

Reich
ressentiment
Sachertorte
schlag
schnook
schuss
Sekt
Sezession
Sieg Heil
Sitzfleisch
Spätlese
Sprechgesang
Sprechstimme
spritzer
Stalag
stollen
streusel
Tafelwein
Torschlusspanik
Trockenbeeren-
  auslese
U-bahn
über-
über alles
Umwelt
Untermensch
Urfirnis
Urtext
verboten
Verstehen
Völkerwander-
  ung
völkisch
Vorsprung Durch
  Technik
Waldsterben
wanderlust
Wandervogel
Wehrmacht
Weisswurst
Weltpolitik
Westpolitik
wili
Wirtschafts-
  wunder
Wunderkammer
zeitgeber
zugzwang
zwischenzug

Greek

MIDDLE ENGLISH
cosmos
mu
tau

LATE MIDDLE
ENGLISH
eta
iota
kappa
pi
pseudo
psi
rho
theta

SIXTEENTH CENTURY
acme
agora
anamnesis
anastrophe
archon
cacodemon
gnosis
haltere
Logos
mimesis
omega
organon
pathos
peripeteia
telos
tmesis

SEVENTEENTH
CENTURY
acropolis
agape
agonistes
atlantes
bema
boustrophedon
eidolon
eureka
exegesis
glaucoma
hapax legomenon
Hebe
hexapla
hoi polloi
ichor
kinesis
lambda
miasma
narcosis
nous
octapla
pseudepigrapha
stoa
strophe
upsilon

EIGHTEENTH CENTURY
amnesia

anabasis
analgesia
anamorphosis
anti
bathos
demos
epsilon
hamartia
kudos
mythos
naos
peplos
pleroma
xoanon

NINETEENTH CENTURY
anthemion
aphasia
ascesis
ataraxia
benthos
boule
calliope
chi-rho
chiton
chroma
daimon
Diaspora
dromos
dysphoria
epyllion
halma
hetaera
hubris
ion
kenosis
koine
kylix
macron
megaron
melisma
metanoia
nabla
omphalos
ostracon
Phi Beta Kappa
pithos
pneuma
polis
psychopompos
rhyton
sepsis
skene
stele
temenos

TWENTIETH CENTURY
cathexis

esoterica
hegemon
kairos
koinonia
kore
kouros
kurtosis
lexis
macro
mega
mythopoeia
orthosis
paideia
tephra
topos

Greek (Modern)

SEVENTEENTH CENTURY
dolma

NINETEENTH CENTURY
iconostasis
ouzo

TWENTIETH CENTURY
bouzouki
enosis
feta
filo
gyro
katharevousa
keftedes
meltemi
pitta
retsina
saganaki
souvlaki
stifado
tahini
taverna
tzatziki

Haitian (creole)

TWENTIETH CENTURY
loa

Hawaiian

NINETEENTH CENTURY
aa
aloha
hula
kahuna
lanai
lei

luau
pahoehoe
pali
ukulele

TWENTIETH CENTURY
kapu
muumuu
wiki

Hebrew

MIDDLE ENGLISH
aleph

SIXTEENTH CENTURY
sephira
shekel
Thummim
Urim

SEVENTEENTH CENTURY
haham
hazzan
Masorah
Megillah
mezuza
mitzvah
mohel
shibboleth
tallith

EIGHTEENTH CENTURY
kiddush
minyan

NINETEENTH CENTURY
bar mitzvah
cheder
chuppah
genizah
goy
hasid
kosher
menorah
nabi
shalom
shiva
shochet
shofar
succah
trefa
tsaddik
yeshiva

TWENTIETH CENTURY
bat mitzvah
challah

eruv
Kashrut
lechayim
Magen David
maven
olim
simcha
tzedakah

Hebrew (Modern)

NINETEENTH CENTURY
mazel tov

TWENTIETH CENTURY
kibbutz
kippa
moshav
sabra

Hindi

SEVENTEENTH CENTURY
pagri
pukka

EIGHTEENTH CENTURY
sari
wallah

NINETEENTH CENTURY
apsara
ganja
jhil
mung

TWENTIETH CENTURY
bhaji
darshan
doosra
gherao
goonda
namaskar
namaste

Hindustani

SIXTEENTH CENTURY
achar

SEVENTEENTH CENTURY
dhal
dhoti
ghat
ghee
lakh
paan

pagri
punkah
rani

EIGHTEENTH CENTURY
babu
bania
dacoit
dak
veranda

NINETEENTH CENTURY
ankus
basmati
burra
chapatti
chappal
chela
dekko
dhobi
ekdam
haldi
jalebi
jati
lassi
lathi
maharani
pachisi
raj
terai
tika

TWENTIETH CENTURY
achkan
choli
gharana
hartal
kisan
pakora
paratha
puri
raita
roti
thali

Hungarian

NINETEENTH CENTURY
cimbalom
csardas
goulash
paprika

Indonesian

TWENTIETH CENTURY
tempeh

Irish

LATE MIDDLE
ENGLISH
 currach

FIFTEENTH CENTURY
 clarschach

SEVENTEENTH
CENTURY
 crannog
 curragh
 leprechaun
 turlough

EIGHTEENTH
CENTURY
 feis
 ogham
 shebeen

NINETEENTH CENTURY
 brogan
 ceilidh
 pooka

TWENTIETH
CENTURY
 craic
 fleadh
 Taoiseach

Italian

MIDDLE ENGLISH
 tramontana

SIXTEENTH CENTURY
 alto
 amoretto
 bagnio
 basta
 bazaar
 biretta
 bordello
 bravo
 canto
 canzone
 cupola
 duo
 duomo
 fresco
 gamba
 gesso
 gondola
 illuminati
 inamorato
 lazaretto
 macaroni
 Madonna
 magnifico

majolica
mezzo-relievo
motto
nuncio
pasquinade
per contra
piazza
presto
Rialto
saltarello
scagliola
seraglio
signor
sordino
stanza
stucco
sultana
villanella
viola da gamba

SEVENTEENTH
CENTURY
adagio
agio
allegro
alto-relievo
antipasto
baldachin
basso-relievo
campanile
capriccio
chiaroscuro
col legno
contadino
Corso
dado
ditto
felucca
furioso
generalissimo
ghetto
gusto
inamorata
incognito
intaglio
largo
lido
lingua franca
manifesto
mortadella
orlo
ovolo
padrone
palazzo
palio
passacaglia
pergola

piano
Pietà
portico
putto
recitativo
regatta
relievo
ritornello
scorzonera
signora
sirocco
sonata
stiletto
tarsia
tempo
vermicelli
virtuoso
vista
viva

EIGHTEENTH
CENTURY
alfresco
alla breve
alla cappella
allegretto
andante
appoggiatura
arco
aria
arioso
arpeggio
a tempo
ballerina
bambino
basso
basso continuo
bravura
breccia
brio
buffo
cadenza
cantabile
cantata
cantilena
capriccioso
caro sposo
casino
castrato
chitarrone
cicerone
cicisbeo
cinquecento
coda
cognoscente
coloratura
con amore

concertante
concertino
concerto
concerto grosso
condottiere
conservatorio
continuo
contralto
conversazione
cortile
crescendo
da capo
dilettante
diminuendo
divertimento
divisi
falsetto
fantasia
finale
finocchio
forte
forte piano
fortissimo
furore
imbroglio
impasto
impresario
influenza
intermezzo
larghetto
legato
lento
libretto
literato
loggia
maestoso
maestro
malaria
maraschino
mezza voce
mezzo
mezzo-soprano
moderato
moto
mozzetta
obbligato
operetta
oratorio
ottava rima
pasticcio
pastorale
patina
pianissimo
piano
pianoforte
più
portamento

prestissimo
prima
prima donna
primo
pronto
propaganda
ripieno
riviera
rondo
rubato
segue
semplice
sgraffito
siciliana
sinfonia
solfatara
solfeggio
sonatina
soprano
sostenuto
sotto voce
spiccato
staccato
stretto
tarantella
tempo rubato
tenuto
terracotta
terzetto
toccata
torso
tremolo
trio
tufa
viola d'amore
violoncello
virtu

NINETEENTH CENTURY
a cappella
accelerando
acciaccatura
agitato
allargando
andantino
basso profundo
bel canto
ben trovato
calando
Camorra
canzona
capo tasto
carabiniere
cassone
cavatina
cembalo

commedia
   dell'arte
commendatore
con brio
confetti
con moto
con sordino
contadina
contessa
cotta
credenza
dal segno
decrescendo
disinvoltura
diva
dolce far niente
espressivo
fata morgana
fermata
fianchetto
fiasco
fioritura
fresco secco
frottola
fugato
fustanella
galleria
glissando
gnocchi
graffito
granita
grappa
grissino
gruppetto
inferno
intarsia
karezza
lasagne
latticinio
Mafia
Mafioso
malebolge
mandorla
mantelletta
marcato
maremma
mascara
meno
mezzani
millefiori
minestrone
molto
mosso
moto perpetuo
niello
niente
oboe d'amore

ocarina
omertà
opera buffa
opera seria
ostinato
panforte
parlando
parmigiana
partita
pasta
piano
piano nobile
piccolo
pietra dura
pizza
pizzicato
predella
prima ballerina
quattrocento
rallentando
rapido
ravioli
ricotta
Risorgimento
risotto
ritardando
ritenuto
rosolio
salami
scampi
scenario
scherzando
scherzo
scordatura
secco
sempre
sestina
sforzando
sforzato
sfumato
signorina
smorzando
spaghetti
stringendo
tagliarini
tagliatelle
tanto
tazza
tempera
tenorino
terra rossa
terribilità
terza rima
tessitura
tombolo
tondo
trecento

tremolando
tutti-frutti
una corda
valuta
vendetta
vernaccia
vibrato
viola da braccio
zabaglione
zita
zucchetto

TWENTIETH CENTURY
agnolotti
al dente
autostrada
biennale
bimbo
bruschetta
calamari
calzone
cannelloni
capo
cappuccino
carpaccio
cassata
catenaccio
ciabatta
ciao
classico
consigliere
contrapposto
Cosa Nostra
crostini
diabolo
dolce vita
duce
espresso
farfalle
fettuccine
focaccia
frittata
fritto misto
fusilli
gelato
gonzo
graffiti
gran turismo
ladino
latte
libero
linguine
lupara
macchiato
manicotti
ma non troppo
marinara

mascarpone
moscato
mozzarella
novella
numero uno
orzo
osso bucco
ottocento
pancetta
panettone
panino
panzanella
papabile
paparazzo
pappardelle
passata
passeggiata
pecorino
penne
pensione
pentimento
pepperoni
pesto
pizzeria
prominenti
pro-nuncio
prosciutto
provolone
radicchio
rigatoni
ristorante
rucola
saltimbocca
sambuca
scaloppine
scungille
seicento
settecento
sinfonietta
sopranino
spaghettini
spinto
sprezzatura
spumante
spumoni
stelline
stracciatella
taleggio
targa
terra irredenta
terrazzo
tiramisu
tortellini
troppo
uomo universale
vaporetto
verismo

vino da tavola
vita nuova
vitello tonnato
zucchini
zuppa inglese

Italian (and Latin)

SEVENTEENTH CENTURY
villa

Italian (and Spanish)

SIXTEENTH CENTURY
punctilio

SEVENTEENTH CENTURY
politico

EIGHTEENTH CENTURY
tsarina

NINETEENTH CENTURY
marina

Italian, Spanish, Portuguese

SIXTEENTH CENTURY
padre

Japanese

SEVENTEENTH CENTURY
inro
kami
katana
kimono
sake
samisen
shogun
tabi
tatami

EIGHTEENTH CENTURY
adzuki
daimyo
kana
katakana
koi
koto
miso
samurai
satori
shoyu
tofu
torii

zazen
Zen

NINETEENTH CENTURY
banzai
bushido
futon
go
haiku
hakama
hara-kiri
hibachi
hiragana
hokku
jinricksha
judo
ju-jitsu
kabuki
kakemono
kamikaze
kombu
kudzu
netsuke
Noh
nori
obi
raku
renga
ronin
ryu
san
sashimi
satsuma
sayonara
sensei
seppuku
shakudo
shakuhachi
shiitake
soba
sumo
sushi
taiko
tanka
tsuba
tsukemono
tsunami
tycoon
ukiyo-e
yukata
zori

TWENTIETH CENTURY
aikido
anime
basho
bonsai

dan
dojo
fugu
gaijin
hibakusha
honcho
ikebana
ippon
issei
judoka
juku
kaizen
kanban
kanji
karaoke
karate
karoshi
kata
katsura
keiretsu
kendo
koan
kyu
manga
mondo
ninja
ninjutsu
nisei
nunchaku
origami
pachinko
ramen
reiki
sansei
seiza
shabu-shabu
shiatsu
shuriken
sogo shosha
sokaiya
sukiyaki
sumi
tamagotchi
tamari
tempura
teppanyaki
teriyaki
tsutsumu
udon
wabi
wakame
wasabi
yakitori
yakuza
yokozuna
zaibatsu

TWENTY-FIRST CENTURY
sudoku

Javanese
NINETEENTH CENTURY
batik
gamelan
wayang

TWENTIETH CENTURY
lahar

Kiswahili
NINETEENTH CENTURY
baraza
boma
bwana
safari
shamba

TWENTIETH CENTURY
kanzu
khanga
kikoi
ngoma
panga
shauri
uhuru
ujamaa

Korean
NINETEENTH CENTURY
kimchi

TWENTIETH CENTURY
chaebol
tae kwon do

Kurdish
TWENTIETH CENTURY
peshmerga

Lappish
SIXTEENTH CENTURY
tundra

Latin
OLD ENGLISH
paternoster
polenta
Te Deum
Thule

MIDDLE ENGLISH
alpha
amphora
ave
Ave Maria

benedicite
beta
credo
delta
et
et cetera
gloria
jubilate
magnificat
magus
miserere
origanum
pallium
pater
placebo
requiem
solidus

LATE MIDDLE ENGLISH
Agnus Dei
alias
amphisbaena
ampulla
aqua vitae
aurora
bubo
cave
chimera
cicada
clepsydra
colossus
contra
corpus
cortex
cum
custos
de profundis
echinus
ergo
fenestella
feria
fiat
finis
gamma
genitor
gratis
habeas corpus
herpes
hyperbole
idem
in excelsis
item
lamia
lapis
lapis lazuli
lector
limbo

macula
magma
manes
mea culpa
mittimus
noli me tangere
obelus
palaestra
palladium
papyrus
pax
per
plectrum
Priapus
pro
pro tempore
proviso
quietus
quorum
regimen
salve
sanctum
   sanctorum
sanctus
sarcophagus
scilicet
scoria
sedile
sigma
sistrum
speculum
sphinx
summa
susurrus
synecdoche
triumvir
tumulus
tyro
vertigo
videlicet
virago
zeugma

FIFTEENTH CENTURY
aqua fortis
aureola
exeunt
memorandum
mutatis mutan-
   dis
patella
paterfamilias
prima facie

SIXTEENTH CENTURY
ab origine
ab ovo
absit omen

acanthus
acumen
ad hominem
ad rem
albumen
alga
alter ego
ambrosia
anaphora
Anno Domini
annulus
ante meridiem
anthropophagi
antonomasia
a priori
arcanum
armiger
atrium
ballista
basilica
boletus
bona fide
cacoethes
caduceus
caesura
callus
cantor
cantus
caries
caveat
caveat emptor
cerebellum
cloaca
coccyx
codex
colloquium
colostrum
compendium
coram
coryza
daemon
de jure
Deo gratias
diaeresis
dictum
encomium
ephemeris
epiphora
epithalamium
epitome
errata
erratum
esse
Et tu, Brute
exit
ex nihilo
ex officio

exordium
facetiae
fasces
fascia
fidus Achates
flora
genus
helix
helot
hiatus
hippocampus
homo
hyperbaton
iambus
id est
ignoramus
indecorum
in esse
in extremis
in fine
innuendo
interim
interregnum
in vino veritas
invita Minerva
ipse dixit
ipso facto
jus gentium
ladanum
lar
lemma
lignum vitae
lunula
lustrum
Lyceum
mater
menses
metope
minimus
miscellanea
modus
murex
nepenthes
nolens volens
non placet
nonplus
non sequitur
nunc dimittis
obiter
o tempora, o
  mores!
panacea
pari passu
paronomasia
passus
peccavi
penates

periphrasis
per se
petitio principii
piscina
placet
pontifex
postscriptum
primus
principium
pro forma
pro rata
pubes
punctum
quid pro quo
quondam
quot homines,
  tot sententiae
quo vadis
radix
redivivus
reductio ad
  impossibile
remora
sanctum
Saturnalia
scarabaeus
scotia
scrutator
sempervivum
simplex
simulacrum
solus
sortes
stigma
stria
summum bonum
sumpsimus
superficies
supra
taenia
talaria
tenet
terminus ad
  quem
terminus a quo
thermae
thyrsus
torus
transire
triquetra
ultimo
umbra
vale
veni, vidi, vici
viaticum
vide
vivat

SEVENTEENTH
CENTURY
ab initio
ab urbe condita
addendum
ad hoc
ad infinitum
ad libitum
ad nauseam
ad valorem
adytum
aegis
afflatus
a fortiori
alibi
alluvium
Alma Mater
alumnus
amanuensis
angelus
apex
a posteriori
aqua regia
arbor vitae
argumentum ad
  hominem
calyx
cantoris
caput mortuum
caret
cella
census
cento
cerebrum
cestus
chorea
cognomen
collectanea
coma
compos mentis
consensus
continuum
copula
coran judice
crux
cui bono
culmen
cultus
cum grano salis
cumulus
curia
data
decennium
de facto
Dei gratia
de novo
desideratum

dies non
  juridicus
differentia
digamma
dithyramb
doli capax
doli incapax
dolus
dominie
donatio mortis
  causa
duodecimo
duumvir
dyspnoea
Ecce Homo
elenchus
embolus
eo ipso
Eros
ex cathedra
exempli gratia
exequatur
exit
ex parte
ex pede
  Herculem
ex post facto
exuviae
facies
farrago
felo de se
ferae naturae
festina lente
frustum
genius loci
hic jacet
homunculus
honorarium
honoris causa
horresco
  referens
hortus siccus
hypogeum
ibid
impedimenta
imperium
imprimatur
index librorum
  prohibitorum
indicia
in flagrante
in potentia
in propria
  persona
in re
insomnia
instanter

inter alia
inter alios
in vacuo
juvenilia
lacuna
lamina
lapsus
lapsus linguae
larva
lex talionis
liberum arbitrium
literati
lues
lumbago
lusus naturae
mala fide
mala fides
mare clausum
mare liberum
mens sana in
corpore sano
mons Veneris
motu proprio
narthex
nemine
contradicente
nemo dat
ne plus ultra
nil desperandum
nolle prosequi
non compos
mentis
non est factum
nostrum
numen
obiit
oestrus
olim
ovum
pabulum
parergon
patera
pelta
penetralia
peplum
perpetuum
mobile
plenum
post meridiem
praenomen
prolegomenon
pronaos
proscenium
pruritus
psyche
pudendum
pudor

qua
quantum meruit
quasi
quinquennium
quod erat demon-
strandum
quod erat
faciendum
rara avis
Regius
reliquiae
res
res gestae
residuum
res ipsa
loquitur
res judicata
retiarius
Rex
scintilla
sederunt
septum
serum
sic transit gloria
mundi
silenus
sine die
sine qua non
specie
stemma
sub judice
sub rosa
sudarium
sui juris
telamon
terra firma
terra incognita
tessera
tholos
toga
triclinium
umbilicus
vae victis
vallum
vesica
veto
via media
vice versa
vi et armis
vinculum
vivarium
xystus

EIGHTEENTH CENTURY
ad captandum
vulgus
ad interim

ad litem
aegrotat
angina pectoris
apologia
aurora australis
aurora borealis
bibliotheca
bona fides
caldarium
camera lucida
camera obscura
campus
carcinoma
cervix
cilium
cirrus
columbarium
conceptus
contra mundum
datum
decani
de gustibus non
est disputandum
Deo volente
discobolus
disjecta membra
dominium
dramatis
personae
dux
emeritus
e pluribus unum
excelsior
exeat
exedra
ex gratia
ex-voto
frigidarium
gradus
habitat
humus
ibidem
imago
in flagrante
delicto
ingesta
in medias res
in personam
in rem
in situ
in toto
in utero
lapillus
laudator
temporis acti
lavabo
lex loci

locus
locus
poenitentiae
lucus a non
lucendo
magnum opus
materfamilias
memorabilia
minutiae
morituri te
salutamus
multum in parvo
muscae
volitantes
nil admirari
nota bene
notitia
nymphaeum
pace
panem et
circenses
pars pro toto
pendente lite
phobia
pileus
pons asinorum
post-mortem
pro bono publico
propylaeum
prospectus
quieta non
movere
quod vide
re
rectus
reductio ad
absurdum
Regina
restitutio in
integrum
rictus
rus in urbe
sacrum
sequela
situs
sola
stela
stet
sui generis
tacet
taedium vitae
tempus fugit
triduum
triforium
ultima Thule
ultimatum
ultra vires

umbo
variorum
vexillum
via
virgo intacta
vox humana

NINETEENTH CENTURY

ad lib
aetatis
alumna
animus
ante
ante-bellum
ante-mortem
anthrax
arbiter
  elegantiae
arboretum
armamentarium
ave atque vale
candelabrum
carpe diem
casus belli
circa
cogito
coitus
coitus
  interruptus
collegium
consortium
conspectus
corpus delicti
corrigendum
culpa
cum laude
cunnilingus
curiosa
curriculum
damnosa heredi-
  tas
damnum
dies irae
dies non
ego
ejecta
et al.
et seq.
ex
excreta
excursus
exemplum
ex libris
exotica
famulus
filioque
flagellum

floreat
flore pleno
floruit
fons et origo
furor scribendi
gens
Homo sapiens
impluvium
in absentia
incipit
incunabulum
indumentum
in extenso
infra
infra dig
in loco parentis
in memoriam
in statu pupillari
inter vivos
in vitro
ipsissima verba
jus cogens
jus primae noctis
lapsus calami
latifundium
lex fori
loc. cit.
locus classicus
locus standi
loquitur
ludo
magna cum
  laude
marginalia
membrum virile
memento mori
mens rea
mirabile dictu
mons pubis
mores
musica ficta
naevus
natura naturans
natura naturata
nisi
nolo contendere
nominis umbra
nova
obiit sine prole
obiter dictum
oculus
op. cit.
passim
pax Romana
philosophia
  perennis
pinetum

post-bellum
post hoc
post-partum
primus inter pares
proxime accessit
proximo
quadrennium
quadrivium
recte
recto
redux
requiescat
responsum
rubella
sancta simplicitas
secundus
senex
sensu stricto
sequitur
sic
solarium
solatium
status quo
status quo ante
sub specie
  aeternitatis
sub specie
  temporis
sub voce
summa cum laude
tabula rasa
tegula
tepidarium
tertius
tinnitus
triennium
trivium
ultra
unicum
urbi et orbi
vera causa
verbum sapienti
verso
vesica piscis
Via Crucis
Via Dolorosa
vicus
vis medicatrix
  naturae
viva
vox angelica
vox populi

TWENTIETH CENTURY

academia
actus reus
ad personam

aloe vera
anima
biennium
colluvium
contra
  proferentem
curriculum vitae
deus absconditus
diabolus in
  musica
dissensus
eheu fugaces
ex silentio
felix culpa
figura
gravida
gravitas
id
in parvo
intacta
in vivo
lacrimae rerum
libido
locum
miles gloriosus
nihil obstat
nil carborundum
  illegitimi
numerus
  clausus
orientalia
patria
persona
pietas
proferens
rectius
refugium
rigor mortis
sensu lato
sic et non
spiritus rector
stricto sensu
sub verbo
terminus ante
  quem
terminus post q-
  uem
terra alba
terra cognita
tertium
  comparationis
ubi sunt
urbs
Vanitas
victor ludorum
virga
vita

Latin (ecclesiastical)

OLD ENGLISH
exodus
rabbi

LATE MIDDLE ENGLISH
Abba
Apocrypha

SIXTEENTH CENTURY
anathema
apotheosis

SEVENTEENTH
CENTURY
charisma

EIGHTEENTH CENTURY
catechesis

NINETEENTH CENTURY
albedo

Latin (Late)

OLD ENGLISH
manna

MIDDLE ENGLISH
incubus

LATE MIDDLE
ENGLISH
antithesis
arsis
enchiridion
ignotum per
    ignotius
oedema
syncope
thesis

SIXTEENTH CENTURY
antistrophe
aporia
bolus
cornucopia
hypothesis
hysteron
    proteron
intermedium
latria
litotes
metastasis
metathesis
onomatopoeia
plethora
prosthesis
vanitas
    vanitatum

SEVENTEENTH
CENTURY
acedia
anorexia
catheter
colophon
explicit
golgotha
gravamen
labarum
phallus
sensorium

EIGHTEENTH CENTURY
anacoluthon
siglum
tertium quid
vomitorium

NINETEENTH CENTURY
anorexia
    nervosa
in camera
natatorium
obscurum per
    obscurius
persona grata
septennium

TWENTIETH CENTURY
persona non
    grata
realia

Latin (Medieval)

MIDDLE ENGLISH
Kyrie eleison

LATE MIDDLE ENGLISH
dulia
lac
nux vomica
oesophagus
quodlibet
succubus
terra sigillata
versus

FIFTEENTH CENTURY
Magna Carta
primum mobile
seriatim
spermaceti
verbatim

SIXTEENTH CENTURY
affidavit
cabbala
ciborium

factotum
hegira
hendiadys
ignoratio
    elenchi
morbilli
praxis
regalia
viva voce

SEVENTEENTH
CENTURY
ambo
anglice
ephemera
literatim

EIGHTEENTH CENTURY
dulciana
scriptorium

NINETEENTH CENTURY
cantus firmus
Mater Dolorosa
novena
opus Dei

Latin (Modern)

SIXTEENTH CENTURY
guaiacum
ignis fatuus
meiosis
per diem
pomatum
scholium
utopia

SEVENTEENTH
CENTURY
abscissa
amicus curiae
annus mirabilis
catalysis
ceteris paribus
chiasmus
coma
deus ex
    machina
entasis
ex hypothesi
florilegium
materia medica
meniscus
millennium
modus operandi
necrosis
per annum
per capita
per centum

pharmacopoeia
sal volatile
sarcoma
strabismus
succedaneum
Valhalla

EIGHTEENTH CENTURY
ad referendum
anaesthesia
condominium
fauna
menologium
parens patriae
stasis
suppressio veri

NINETEENTH CENTURY
amoeba
anacrusis
apparatus
    criticus
asphyxia
catharsis
cyanosis
delirium tremens
editio princeps
feijoa
horribile dictu
horror vacui
modus vivendi
moratorium
sebum
suggestio falsi
torticollis
uraeus
via affirmativa
via negativa

TWENTIETH CENTURY
annus horribilis
candida
ex ante
ex post
minifundium
trivia

Malagasy

EIGHTEENTH CENTURY
raffia

Malay

SIXTEENTH CENTURY
kris

EIGHTEENTH CENTURY
rambutan

NINETEENTH CENTURY
agar-agar

gutta-percha
parang
sambal
sarong

TWENTIETH CENTURY
ikat
satay

Maori

EIGHTEENTH
CENTURY
tiki
wahine

NINETEENTH CENTURY
haka
hangi
kai
kapai
kia ora
korero
kuri
mana
pakeha
waka
whare

TWENTIETH
CENTURY
karanga

Maori (and Hawaiian)

NINETEENTH CENTURY
hui

Marathi

TWENTIETH CENTURY
rangoli

Melanesian

TWENTIETH CENTURY
kula

Nepali

NINETEENTH CENTURY
kukri

New Guinea

TWENTIETH CENTURY
kuru

Norwegian

SEVENTEENTH
CENTURY
fiord

EIGHTEENTH CENTURY
kraken

NINETEENTH CENTURY
aquavit

TWENTIETH CENTURY
gjetost
gravadlax
krill
rosemaling
skijoring
slalom

Old Norse

MIDDLE ENGLISH
kist

EIGHTEENTH CENTURY
Ragnarok
saga
skald

NINETEENTH CENTURY
jotun

Pali

NINETEENTH CENTURY
bhikkhu

TWENTIETH CENTURY
dhamma
nibbana
tathata

Panjabi

TWENTIETH CENTURY
bhangra
gurdwara
jatha
khadi
kirpan
tikka

Persian

LATE MIDDLE ENGLISH
khan

SIXTEENTH CENTURY
caravanserai
shah

SEVENTEENTH
CENTURY
attar
hafiz
hajji
mullah

EIGHTEENTH CENTURY
baksheesh

ghazal
narghile
peri
simurg

NINETEENTH CENTURY
hom
izzat
kenaf
qanat

TWENTIETH CENTURY
ayatollah
mujahedin
pashmina
takht

Persian (and Urdu)

SIXTEENTH CENTURY
amir
bhang

SEVENTEENTH
CENTURY
begum
chador
charpoy
chokidar
durbar
havildar
moulvi
sahib
shikar
syce
tamasha

EIGHTEENTH
CENTURY
bundobust
hookah
howdah
khalsa
masala
munshi
nawab
zenana

NINETEENTH
CENTURY
badmash
bibi
burka
chaprasi
chikan
khaki
kofta
korma
numdah
numnah

purdah
sarod
shalwar
shikari
sitar
tabla
tarkaski
zakat
zarda

TWENTIETH
CENTURY
balti
biryani
garam masala
jilbab
kurta
nan
rogan josh
samosa
tandoori
zari

Polish

EIGHTEENTH
CENTURY
hetman

TWENTIETH
CENTURY
kielbasa
pierogi

Polynesian

NINETEENTH CENTURY
poi

Portuguese

SIXTEENTH CENTURY
amok
banyan
betel
pagoda
typhoon

SEVENTEENTH
CENTURY
copaiba
ipecacuanha
maraca
nabob

EIGHTEENTH CENTURY
auto-da-fé
ayah
commando
cuspidor
senhor

NINETEENTH CENTURY
amah
carioca
fazenda
fazendeiro
garimpeiro
guarana
samba
senhora
senhorita
sertão
vindaloo
vinho

TWENTIETH CENTURY
bossa nova
churrasco
fado
favela
feijoada
maxixe
pousada
saudade
tanga
vinho verde

Portuguese (Brazilian)
TWENTIETH CENTURY
lambada

Portuguese (and Spanish)
SIXTEENTH CENTURY
copra

SEVENTEENTH CENTURY
peon

Provençal
TWENTIETH CENTURY
pistou
tian

pseudo-French
EIGHTEENTH CENTURY
bêche-de-mer

NINETEENTH CENTURY
bon viveur
nom de plume

TWENTIETH CENTURY
en travesti

pseudo-German
TWENTIETH CENTURY
sitzkrieg

pseudo-Italian
SIXTEENTH CENTURY
braggadocio

pseudo-Latin
SIXTEENTH CENTURY
mumpsimus
omnium
  gatherum

NINETEENTH CENTURY
celesta

Romany
NINETEENTH CENTURY
chal
vardo

Russian
SIXTEENTH CENTURY
boyar
kvass
muzhik
sevruga
tsar

SEVENTEENTH CENTURY
steppe

EIGHTEENTH CENTURY
balalaika
tsarevich
ukase
yurt

NINETEENTH CENTURY
artel
ataman
blin
borscht
chernozem
dacha
droshky
duma
feldsher
karakul
kasha
kulak
kurgan
pirog
polynya
samovar
shchi
taiga
troika
tsarevna

vodka
zakuska

TWENTIETH CENTURY
agitprop
apparat
apparatchik
babushka
Bolshevik
glasnost
Gulag
intelligentsia
kazachoc
kissel
kolkhoz
niet
nomenklatura
paskha
perestroika
piroshki
podzol
pogrom
Politbureau
Presidium
prisiadka
rendzina
samizdat
shashlik
smetana
sovkhoz
sputnik
talik
tokamak
tovarish
vobla

Sanskrit
SIXTEENTH CENTURY
raja

SEVENTEENTH CENTURY
guru
maharaja
puja
sannyasi
vihara
yogi

EIGHTEENTH CENTURY
atman
avatar
brahman
chakra
dharma
kalpa
lingam

maharishi
mantra
maya
moksha
mukti
naga
om
raga
samadhi
soma
suttee
swami
tantra
veena
yoga
yogini
yoni
yuga

NINETEENTH CENTURY
acharya
ahimsa
Arhat
bhakti
deva
devadasi
dharmsala
garuda
gopura
Jina
Kama Sutra
karma
kundalini
mahatma
mandala
mudra
nirvana
raja yoga
rasa
sadhu
samsara
samskara
sangha
sarangi
shanti
shikhara
siddha
stupa
sutra
swastika
tilak
varna
yajna
yantra

TWENTIETH CENTURY
ashram
ayurveda
bhajan

hatha yoga
hatha yogi
kumkum
lasya
sabha
satyagraha
sunyata

Sardinian

NINETEENTH CENTURY
nuragh

Serbo-Croat

EIGHTEENTH CENTURY
kolo

NINETEENTH CENTURY
slivovitz

TWENTIETH CENTURY
chetnik

Spanish

SIXTEENTH CENTURY
alcalde
alguacil
armada
bacalao
batata
bonito
cacique
cedilla
copal
cordovan
don
frijoles
hidalgo
infanta
machete
mestizo
Morisco
muchacho
olla podrida
panada
peccadillo
que sera sera
salina
sanbenito
sarsaparilla
sassafras
savannah
señora
sierra
sombrero
tinto

SEVENTEENTH
CENTURY
alcazar

balsa
caldera
chilli
chinchilla
dinero
duenna
embargo
estancia
llano
manta
matador
mirador
picaro
pimento
pimiento
plaza
rancheria
santo
señor
siesta
toreador
toro
tortilla
tumbaga
vega
vicuña

EIGHTEENTH
CENTURY
adobe
alameda
alpaca
banderilla
banderillero
bolero
cherimoya
cordillera
fandango
flotilla
garbanzo
hacienda
mantilla
maté
merino
mesa
mescal
noria
oregano
pampas
paramo
picador
posada
presidio
torero

NINETEENTH
CENTURY
adios
aficionado

aguardiente
alfalfa
alpargata
amigo
amontillado
arroyo
azulejo
bajada
barrio
bodega
bolas
bonanza
bronco
burro
caballero
cabana
cabildo
camarilla
canyon
carabinero
caramba
cascara sagrada
caudillo
chaparral
chilli con
  carne
chorizo
compadre
conquistador
cooncan
copita
coquina
coquito
corrida
criollo
cuadrilla
cuesta
descamisado
El Niño
espada
esparto
estufa
fiesta
fino
flamenco
gazpacho
gringo
guerrilla
guiro
habanera
hacendado
hombre
horchata
incommunicado
jaleo
jota
langosta
lobo

loco
maja
mañana
manzanilla
mercado
monte
muchacha
muleta
oloroso
paisano
parador
paseo
patio
pelota
perfecto
piñon
pinto
playa
pollo
potrero
pronunciamento
pueblo
puro
ramada
ranchero
rancho
rebozo
retablo
ria
rodeo
salsa
sangre azul
señorita
silo
simpatico
solera
tilde
tule
vaquero
viga
vigilante
villancico
yerba
zapateado
zarzuela

TWENTIETH
CENTURY
abrazo
altiplano
anchoveta
autogiro
autopista
campesino
canasta
chicano
chile relleno
cilantro

cogida
cojones
costa
curandero
cursillo
desaparecido
duende
empanada
farruca
finca
hasta la vista
jai alai
mano a mano
masa
Morisca
nada
olé
paso doble
pronto
puta
querencia
quesadilla
sangria
santeria
santero
supremo
tapas
tonto
tostada
turron
vargueño
veleta

TWENTY-FIRST
CENTURY
  galactico

Spanish
(American)
SEVENTEENTH
CENTURY
  chicha
  metate
  pulque
  puna
  teocalli

NINETEENTH CENTURY
  cafeteria
  campo
  chicharron
  chicle
  cholo
  enchilada
  gaucho
  marijuana
  panatella
  peyote

pinole
remuda
tango
temblor

TWENTIETH CENTURY
  bongo
  burrito
  cha-cha
  chino
  clave
  conga
  cueca
  exacta
  guacamole
  mambo
  merengue
  montuno
  palomino
  perfecta
  quinella
  rumba
  sancocho
  sopaipilla

Spanish
(Mexican)
SEVENTEENTH
CENTURY
  tamale

EIGHTEENTH
CENTURY
  Apache
  coyote

NINETEENTH
CENTURY
  cenote
  chaparejos
  ejido
  huarache
  jacal
  octli
  serape
  tequila

TWENTIETH CENTURY
  ayahuasca
  charro
  chipotle
  fajitas
  huevos
    rancheros
  jalapeño
  jojoba
  machismo
  macho
  maquiladora

mariachi
menudo
mole
nacho
pachuco
palapa
pocho
taco
taqueria
tepache
tomatillo

Spanish (South
American)
SEVENTEENTH
CENTURY
  guano

EIGHTEENTH
CENTURY
  poncho

NINETEENTH CENTURY
  llanero

TWENTIETH CENTURY
  basuco
  ceviche
  Latino
  pina colada

Spanish (West
Indian)
NINETEENTH CENTURY
  dengue

Spanish (and
Italian)
SEVENTEENTH
CENTURY
  amoroso
  vino

NINETEENTH CENTURY
  cantina

Spanish (and
Portuguese)
SIXTEENTH CENTURY
  corral
  infante
  mulatto

SEVENTEENTH
CENTURY
  junta

EIGHTEENTH
CENTURY
  albino

curare
quinta

NINETEENTH CENTURY
  selva

Swedish
EIGHTEENTH CENTURY
  isblink

NINETEENTH
CENTURY
  smorgasbord

TWENTIETH CENTURY
  fartlek
  glögg
  ombudsman
  varve

Swiss French
EIGHTEENTH
CENTURY
  chalet

NINETEENTH
CENTURY
  luge
  névé
  seiche
  serac

Swiss German
TWENTIETH
CENTURY
  muesli
  putsch
  rösti

Tagalog
NINETEENTH CENTURY
  ylang-ylang

TWENTIETH CENTURY
  boondocks

Tamil
SEVENTEENTH
CENTURY
  catamaran
  pariah

NINETEENTH
CENTURY
  patchouli
  poppadom

TWENTIETH CENTURY
  sambhar

Thai

NINETEENTH
CENTURY
  wat

Tibetan

SEVENTEENTH
CENTURY
  lama

NINETEENTH CENTURY
  sherpa

TWENTIETH CENTURY
  yeti

Tongan

EIGHTEENTH CENTURY
  kava
  taboo

Turkic

NINETEENTH CENTURY
  barchan

Turkish

SIXTEENTH CENTURY
  aga
  bey
  caftan
  dervish

SEVENTEENTH
CENTURY
  baklava
  effendi
  hammam
  harem
  khoja
  pasha
  pilaf
  raki
  serai
  tekke

yogurt

NINETEENTH
CENTURY
  fez
  kilim
  kismet
  macramé
  yataghan

TWENTIETH CENTURY
  bulgar
  dolmus
  doner kebab
  imam bayildi
  meze
  moussaka
  mukhtar
  shish kebab

Urdu (see Persian (and Urdu))

Vietnamese

TWENTIETH CENTURY
  nuoc mam

Welsh

SEVENTEENTH
CENTURY
  cromlech

EIGHTEENTH
CENTURY
  Gorsedd

NINETEENTH CENTURY
  bach
  cariad hwyl
  cwm

TWENTIETH CENTURY
  bara brith

West Indian creole

EIGHTEENTH CENTURY
  goombay

TWENTIETH CENTURY
  soucouyant

Yiddish

SEVENTEENTH
CENTURY
  halva

NINETEENTH CENTURY
  chutzpah
  gefilte fish
  golem
  kreplach
  kugel
  matzo
  meshuga
  mikva
  nebbish
  oy
  rebbe
  rebbetzin
  schmuck
  schnorrer
  shemozzle
  shidduch
  shiksa
  shul
  tsimmes
  yahrzeit

TWENTIETH CENTURY
  bagel
  blintze
  cholent
  dreck
  dreidel
  dybbuk
  kibbutznik
  kibitz

kishke
klezmer
klutz
knaidel
knish
kvell
kvetch
latke
lox
macher
mazuma
mensch
meshugaas
naches
nosh
nudnik
pastrami
schalet
schlep
schlepper
schlimazel
schlock
schlong
schlub
schmaltz
schmatte
schmear
schmooze
schnozz
shtetl
shtick
shtum
shtup
tchotchke
tochus
tsuris
yarmulke
yenta
zaftig

AskOxford.com
Oxford Dictionaries Passionate about language

For more information about the background to Oxford Quotations Dictionaries, and much more about Oxford's commitment to language exploration, why not visit the world's largest language learning site, www.AskOxford.com

Passionate about English?

What were the original 'brass monkeys'? **AskOxford.com**

How do new words enter the dictionary? **AskOxford.com**

How is 'whom' used? **AskOxford.com**

Who said, 'For also knowledge itself is power?' **AskOxford.com**

How can I improve my writing? **AskOxford.com**

If you have a query about the English language, want to look up a word, need some help with your writing skills, are curious about how dictionaries are made, or simply have some time to learn about the language, bypass the rest and ask the experts at AskOxford.com.

Passionate about language?

If you want to find out about writing in French, German, Spanish, or Italian, improve your listening and speaking skills, learn about other cultures, access resources for language students, or gain insider travel tips from those in the know, ask the experts at **AskOxford.com**

OXFORD

Oxford Paperback Reference

The Concise Oxford Dictionary of Quotations
FIFTH EDITION
Edited by Elizabeth Knowles

Now based on the highly acclaimed sixth edition of *The Oxford Dictionary of Quotations*, this new edition maintains its extensive coverage of literary and historical quotations, and contains completely up-to-date material. A fascinating read and an essential reference tool.

The Oxford Dictionary of Political Quotations
Edited by Antony Jay

This lively and illuminating dictionary from the writer of 'Yes Minister' presents a vintage crop of over 4,000 political quotations. Ranging from the pivotal and momentous to the rhetorical, the sincere, the bemused, the tongue-in-cheek, and the downright rude, examples include memorable words from the old hands as well as from contemporary politicians.

'funny, striking, thought-provoking and incisive…will appeal to those browsing through it at least as much as to those who wish to use it as a work of reference'
Observer

Oxford Dictionary of Modern Quotations
Edited by Elizabeth Knowles

The answers to all your quotation questions lie in this delightful collection of over 5,000 of the twentieth century's most famous quotations.

'Hard to sum up a book so useful, wayward and enjoyable'   *Spectator*

The Oxford Dictionary of Literary Quotations
Edited by Peter Kemp

Containing 4,000 of the most memorized and cited literary quotations, this dictionary is an excellent reference work as well as an enjoyable read.

The Oxford Dictionary of Humorous Quotations
Edited by Ned Sherrin

From the sharply witty to the downright hilarious, this sparkling collection will appeal to all senses of humour.

OXFORD

Oxford Paperback Reference

The Concise Oxford Dictionary of English Etymology
T. F. Hoad

A wealth of information about our language and its history, this reference source provides over 17,000 entries on word origins.

'A model of its kind'

Daily Telegraph

A Dictionary of Euphemisms
R. W. Holder

This hugely entertaining collection draws together euphemisms from all aspects of life: work, sexuality, age, money, and politics.

Review of the previous edition
'This ingenious collection is not only very funny but extremely instructive too'

Iris Murdoch

The Oxford Dictionary of Slang
John Ayto

Containing over 10,000 words and phrases, this is the ideal reference for those interested in the more quirky and unofficial words used in the English language.

'hours of happy browsing for language lovers'

Observer

OXFORD

Oxford Paperback Reference

The Oxford Dictionary of Art & Artists
Ian Chilvers

Based on the highly praised *Oxford Dictionary of Art*, over 2,500 up-to-date entries on painting, sculpture, and the graphic arts.

'the best and most inclusive single volume available, immensely useful and very well written'

Marina Vaizey, *Sunday Times*

The Concise Oxford Dictionary of Art Terms
Michael Clarke

Written by the Director of the National Gallery of Scotland, over 1,800 terms cover periods, styles, materials, techniques, and foreign terms.

A Dictionary of Architecture and Landscape Architecture
James Stevens Curl

Over 6,000 entries and 250 illustrations cover all periods of Western architectural history.

'splendid . . . you can't have a more concise, entertaining, and informative guide to the words of architecture.'

Architectural Review

'excellent, and amazing value for money . . . by far the best thing of its kind.'

Professor David Walker

OXFORD

Oxford Companions

'Opening such books is like sitting down with a knowledgeable friend. Not a bore or a know-all, but a genuinely well-informed chum ... So far so splendid.'

Sunday Times [of *The Oxford Companion to Shakespeare*]

For well over 60 years Oxford University Press has been publishing Companions that are of lasting value and interest, each one not only a comprehensive source of reference, but also a stimulating guide, mentor, and friend. There are between 40 and 60 Oxford Companions available at any one time, ranging from music, art, and literature to history, warfare, religion, and wine.

Titles include:

The Oxford Companion to English Literature
Edited by Dinah Birch
'No guide could come more classic.'

Malcolm Bradbury, *The Times*

The Oxford Companion to Music
Edited by Alison Latham
'probably the best one-volume music reference book going'
Times Educational Supplement

The Oxford Companion to the Garden
Edited by Patrick Taylor
'Focused, enlightening . . . This is a book anyone interested in horticulture must buy'

Gardens illustrated

The Oxford Companion to Food
Alan Davidson
'the best food reference work ever to appear in the English language'
New Statesman

The Oxford Companion to Wine
Edited by Jancis Robinson
'the greatest wine book ever published'

Washington Post

Great value ebooks from Oxford!

An ever-increasing number of Oxford subject reference dictionaries, English and bilingual dictionaries, and English language reference titles are available as ebooks.

All Oxford ebooks are available in the award-winning Mobipocket Reader format, compatible with most current handheld systems, including Palm, Pocket PC/Windows CE, Psion, Nokia, SymbianOS, Franklin eBookMan, and Windows. Some are also available in MS Reader and Palm Reader formats.

Priced on a par with the print editions, Oxford ebooks offer dictionary-specific search options making information retrieval quick and easy.

For further information and a full list of Oxford ebooks please visit: www.askoxford.com/shoponline/ebooks/

OXFORD

Oxford Paperback Reference

The Kings of Queens of Britain
John Cannon and Anne Hargreaves

A detailed, fully-illustrated history ranging from mythical and pre-conquest rulers to the present House of Windsor, featuring regional maps and genealogies.

A Dictionary of World History

Over 4,000 entries on everything from prehistory to recent changes in world affairs. An excellent overview of world history.

A Dictionary of British History
Edited by John Cannon

An invaluable source of information covering the history of Britain over the past two millennia. Over 3,000 entries written by more than 100 specialist contributors.

Review of the parent volume
'the range is impressive . . . truly (almost) all of human life is here'
Kenneth Morgan, *Observer*

OXFORD

Oxford Paperback Reference

The Concise Oxford Companion to English Literature
Margaret Drabble and Jenny Stringer

Based on the best-selling *Oxford Companion to English Literature*, this is an indispensable guide to all aspects of English literature.

Review of the parent volume
'a magisterial and monumental achievement'

Literary Review

The Concise Oxford Companion to Irish Literature
Robert Welch

From the ogam alphabet developed in the 4th century to Roddy Doyle, this is a comprehensive guide to writers, works, topics, folklore, and historical and cultural events.

Review of the parent volume
'Heroic volume ... It surpasses previous exercises of similar nature in the richness of its detail and the ecumenism of its approach.'

Times Literary Supplement

A Dictionary of Shakespeare
Stanley Wells

Compiled by one of the best-known international authorities on the playwright's works, this dictionary offers up-to-date information on all aspects of Shakespeare, both in his own time and in later ages.

OXFORD

Oxford Paperback Reference

The Concise Oxford Dictionary of World Religions
Edited by John Bowker

Over 8,200 entries containing unrivalled coverage of all the major world religions, past and present.

'covers a vast range of topics ... is both comprehensive and reliable'
The Times

The Oxford Dictionary of Saints
David Farmer

From the famous to the obscure, over 1,400 saints are covered in this acclaimed dictionary.

'an essential reference work'   *Daily Telegraph*

The Concise Oxford Dictionary of the Christian Church
E. A. Livingstone

This indispensable guide contains over 5,000 entries and provides full coverage of theology, denominations, the church calendar, and the Bible.

'opens up the whole of Christian history, now with a wider vision than ever'

Robert Runcie, former Archbishop of Canterbury

OXFORD